# MEME MEDIA AND
# MEME MARKET ARCHITECTURES

# MEME MEDIA AND MEME MARKET ARCHITECTURES

### Knowledge Media for Editing, Distributing, and Managing Intellectual Resources

**YUZURU TANAKA**
*Hokkaido University, Japan*

IEEE Computer Society, *Sponsor*

**IEEE PRESS**

**A JOHN WILEY & SONS, INC., PUBLICATION**

*Library of Congress Cataloging-in-Publication Data:*

Tanaka, Y. (Yuzuru)
    Meme media and meme market architectures: Knowledge media for editing, distributing, and managing intellectual resources / Yuzuru Tanaka.
        p. cm.
    Includes bibliographical references and index.
    ISBN 0-471-45378-1 (cloth)
    1. Multimedia systems.   2. Knowledge management.   3. Computer architecture.   4. Mass media.   I. Title.

QA76.575.T355 2003
006.7—dc21                                                          2003041112

# CONTENTS

## 5   Object Orientation and MVC   **92**

## 6   Component Integration   **106**

## 7   Meme Media Architecture   128

## 8   Utilities for Meme Media   152

# PREFACE

In retrospect, the last three decades of computer systems can be summarized as follows. In the 1970s, we focused on the integrated management of enterprise or organization information. The relational model of databases proposed in 1970 provided a mathematical foundation for the discussion of the logical structure and operation of a database independent of its physical implementation and applications. It works as a pivot with various different candidates of implementation, and with various different applications. Such independence encouraged studies on its physical organization without considering its applications, and also studies on its applications and semantic data models without considering its physical organization. The former studies led to the development of high-performance relational database management systems, and the latter studies to the development of natural language interfaces and graphical user interfaces to databases, which led to the extension of queries toward object-orientation and logical inference. Integrated management of information increased data consistency and data integrity of enterprise and organization information, which information management using file systems could not achieve.

In the 1980s, we focused on the integrated environment of personal information processing and office information processing. The rapid development of personal computers and workstations that began in the late 1970s provided personal tools for writing documents, calculating tables, drawing pictures, and making charts. Their developers became interested in embedding figures, tables, and charts in document pages for printing. This is what we call desktop publishing. Then they became interested in directly editing such printed image of documents on the display screen and developed so-called WYSIWYG (what you see is what you get) systems. At the same time, developers became interested in keeping chart representations of data consistent with a table representations of the same data, which required a functional linkage between chart tools and table tools. Such functional linkages were also applied to the data consistency between these tools and a database, which led to the development of so-called integrated personal environment and office environment systems. These systems had to deal with functional linkages between different tools and different servers. They had to embed graphical representations of these different tools in document pages and manage these graphical objects to respond to user operations. They required a uniform way of treating different tools, their graphical representations, user events, and database servers as entities that react to given messages issued either from users or from other entities. The object-orientation studies that began in the mid-1970s and bloomed in the 1980s provided a solution to these requirements. The object orientation, together with integrated personal environment and office environment systems, led to the development of compound-document architectures, object-oriented GUI systems, visual programming environments, multimedia authoring tools, object-oriented languages, and object-oriented databases.

The last decade in 1990s can be easily characterized by the World-Wide Web (WWW) and its browsers. Although preceded by related visions like Xanadu, proposed in the 1960s, both the WWW and its browsers were developed in the 1990s. In the 1990s, we focused on publication and browsing of intellectual assets. People became liberated in publishing their intellectual assets. The WWW and its browsers have brought an enormous change to our social life. However, many of you will agree to the claim that this is just a beginning of a bigger change.

What will characterize this new decade of 2000? This book will answer this question. "Meme market" is the answer. "Meme" is a term coined by Richard Dawkins. He pointed out a similarity between genetic evolution of biological species and cultural evolution of knowledge and art, and used "meme" to denote the cultural counterpart of a biological gene. As biological genes are replicated, recombined, mutated, and naturally selected, ideas are replicated, recombined, modified with new fragments, and selected by people. The acceleration of memetic cultural evolution requires media to externalize memes, and to distribute them among people. Such media should allow people to reedit their knowledge content and redistribute them. Such media may be called meme media. They work as knowledge media for the reediting and redistribution of intellectual assets.

Although the WWW and browsers enabled us to publish and browse intellectual assets, they could not liberate these assets from the servers that store them. This situation is similar to that before Johann Gutenberg's invention of printing technologies. Books in the library were secured by chains, and could not be taken out. After his invention, books became portable media that could be distributed among people, and became independent of the time and place of their publication, which significantly increased the chance of replication, recombination, mutation, and natural selection of memes published in books. The WWW and browsers do not enable people to reedit and redistribute memes published in meme media. When memes are liberated from their servers and distributed among people for their reediting and redistribution, they are accumulated by society to form a meme pool, which will work as a gene pool to bring a rapid evolution of intellectual assets shared by this society. This will cause an explosive increase of intellectual assets, similar to the flood of consumer products in our present consumer societies. The explosive increase of intellectual assets is not only inevitable, but also fundamental for their rapid evolution, since these increased intellectual assets form a sufficiently large meme pool and increase the chance and the variety of recombination. Meme media will bring us a consumer society and consumer culture of knowledge resources, which requires new services for distribution, management, and retrieval. The variety of consumer products was mainly brought about by business competition. Therefore, it is fundamental to introduce business activities into a meme pool, which will make it a meme market.

This book focuses on meme media: their potential for enabling technology, their software architecture, and their applications. It also focuses on meme pool and meme market architectures for the reediting and redistribution of memes without violating competitive business activities. The reader may download sample systems from the following Websites: *http://ca.meme.hokudai.ac.jp/index.html,* which is administered at Hokkaido University, and *http://www.pads.or.jp/english/,* which is administered by the IntelligentPad Consortium.

I started this research project in early 1987. My goal at that time was to develop a media toolkit architecture for the open integration of personal and office information processing environments. Then around 1992, I came across the concept of meme media. Since 1989 when my group finished the development of the first Smalltalk implementation of the system, our group has been living in the system and coevolving with it. We have learned a lot from the different versions of the system about in which direction to conduct the project. We are still opening new vistas for detailed study. This is one of the reasons why I have spent several years writing this book.

My collaborators and I established a consortium in 1993 for the promotion of system architectures. Since then, I have worked with many collaborators in industry and academia. They became fascinated by the system concept and/or system architecture, and dedicated themselves to work as system developers, application developers, evangelists, or managers. These people include Toshifumi Murata of Softfront, Jun-ichi Fujiwara of Sapporo Electronics Center, Tatezumi Furukawa, Nobuyuki Makimura, Taiji Okamoto of Fujitsu, Yasushi Miyaoka, Masafumi Shimoda, Kazuyuki Tanaka of Hitachi Software, Kazushige Oikawa of K-Plex Inc., Yuji Miyawaki of Fuji Xerox, Katsuhiko Sakaguchi of Canon (now with Softfront), Nobuya Kawachi of Khangrande, Takeshi Mori of NEC, John Cheuck of Metrowerks, Jiro Yamada of C's Lab, Seigo Matsuoka of Editorial Engineering Laboratory, Yoshimitsu Hirai of JIPDEC, Takafumi Noguchi of Kushiro Technical Collage, Takeshi Sunaga of Tama Art Collage, Shin Nitoguri of Tokyo Gakugei University, Yoshiaki Yanagisawa of National Language Research Institute, Kazuhiro Sato and Masaki Chiba of Sapporo Gakuin Collage, Mina Akaishi, Akihiro Yamamoto, Makoto Haraguchi, Kiyoshi Kato of Hokkaido University, and Yoshihiro Okada of Kyushu University. The people who contributed to the research and development of IntelligentPad/IntelligentBox and their applications are too numerous to list. Some of them influence the direction of my research. Kazushige Oikawa introduced me to Xerox PARC's views on object-oriented paradigms in early 1980s. Seigo Matsuoka enlarged my research vision toward media as cultural infrastructures. Ryoichi Mori, who proposed "superdistribution" in 1983, encouraged me to integrate meme media and meme pool architectures with the idea of superdistribution. I was also encouraged and supported by many other people. They include Setsuo Ohsuga of Waseda University, Makoto Nagao of Kyoto University, Yasushi Takeda of Hitachi, Tsutomu Sato of Hitachi Software, Iwao Toda of Fujitsu, Yukio Mizuno of NEC, and Tohru Takahashi of Canon. Marvin Minsky, Donald Knuth, Doug Engelbart, Ted Nelson, and Bill Atkinson privately encouraged me and supported my project.

With the support of these people, I have continuously obtained significant support from the Agency for Science and Technologies and Ministry of Education (Japan). From 1991 to 1995, I conducted a project under the support from Agencies for Science and Technologies. In 1995, I won a three-year Grant in Aid for Specially Promoted Research from the Ministry of Education. In the same year, the ministry set up the Meme Media Laboratory for my research. In 1999, the ministry selected me to conduct a new five-year project on "intuitive human interface for the organization and access of intellectual assets" based on meme media and meme pool architectures. This book will cover most of the research achievements of these projects. In the Meme Media Laboratory, I started collaborations with Klaus Jantke of the German Research Center for Artificial Intelligence (DFKI), and Nicolas Spyratos of the University of Paris South. They and their colleagues are now helping me to distribute the concept and architecture of meme media in Europe.

I would like to express my thanks to all these people. Without their help, I could not have written this book. The project is still in progress. I had to omit many new ideas in this book only because they are not implemented in any version. Furthermore, the systems are still opening new vistas for detailed study.

I also would like to thank my former students involved in IntelligentPad or IntelligentBox projects. Takamoto Imataki and Akira Nagasaki worked on the development of IntelligentPad, while Yoshihiro Okada worked on IntelligentBox. Akira Nagasaki also studied the FieldPad architecture for event sharing, while Mina Akaishi studied the StagePad architecture for scripting user operations. Mitsunori Nakagawa studied workflow applications, while Ryota Hirano studied the decomposability and composability of specifications based on the meme media architecture. My present students are also making significant contributions to meme media and meme pool architectures. They include Kimihito Ito working on the Web application linkage, Makato Ohigashi and Tsuyoshi Sugibuchi on database visualization, and Jun Fujima on Topica framework. In writing this book, Aran Lunzer and Bruce Darling of the Meme Media Laboratory helped improve the draft of the book.

I would like to thank Hokkaido University and the Graduate School of Engineering for providing me a comfortable research environment, and, especially, Ryozaburo Tagawa for the pleasure of conducting research projects in Sapporo.

Finally, I would like to thank my wife Tazune and daughter Shikiko; they have been patiently waiting for the completion of this writing project and encouraging me. I also would like to thank my parents.

YUZURU TANAKA

*Sapporo, Japan*
*April 2003*

# CHAPTER 1

# OVERVIEW AND INTRODUCTION

This book examines meme media architectures and their application frameworks developed by the author and his colleagues for allowing people to reedit and redistribute intellectual resources over the Internet just through direct manipulation. Intellectual resources denote not only multimedia documents, but also application tools and services provided by local or remote servers. They cannot be simply classified as information content since they also include tools and services.

Media used to externalize some of our knowledge as intellectual resources and to distribute them among people are generally defined as knowledge media. Some people may use the term "information media" to denote a similar type of media. Whereas information media denote those media that externalize information content, knowledge media are used to externalize not only information content but also tools and services, and, furthermore, to distribute them among people. Some knowledge media that provide direct manipulation operations for people to reedit and redistribute their content are called meme media. Chapters 2 and 3 discuss the details of these definitions. This chapter shows why we need meme media, and how meme media change the environment of publishing, reediting, and redistributing intellectual resources for their further reuse by other people.

## 1.1 WHY MEME MEDIA?

During the last decade, we observed the rapid accumulation of intellectual resources on the Web. These intellectual resources include not only multimedia documents, but also application tools running on the client side, and services provided by remote servers. Today, from the Web, you can almost obtain whatever information items, application tools, or services you may think of. You can just access some search engine and type in appropriate keywords that characterize the intellectual resource you want to access. Then the search engine returns an address list of candidate Web pages. In this list, you will probably find more than one appropriate Web page including the intellectual resource you want to get.

1

The publication and reuse of intellectual resources using Web technologies can be characterized by the schematic model in Figure 1.1. In order to publish your set of intellectual resources, you have to represent it in HTML (Hyper Text Markup Language), and to register it in an HTTP (Hyper Text Transfer Protocol) server on the Internet. The world-wide distribution of HTTP servers, together with the HTTP protocols on the Internet, forms a worldwide publication repository called the WWW (World-Wide Web), or simply the Web. Web publication uses a compound document representation of intellectual resources. Compound documents denote documents with embedded content such as multi-media content, visual application tools, and/or interactive services provided by servers. Such a compound document published on the Web is called a Web page. In order to access Web pages published by other people, you need to know their URL (Uniform Resource Locator) address. You may input a URL to a Web browser such as Internet Explorer or Netscape Navigator to view the corresponding Web page. Some Web pages may have a button to upload or to download a file to and from a remote server. Some others may have input forms for you to fill in. Such Web pages use your inputs to issue a query to the corresponding application server or database server, which then sends back a new Web page as its output.

In the model in Figure 1.1, we do not have any support for extracting any portion of published Web pages, combining them for their local reuse, or publishing the newly defined composite object as a new Web page. We need some support to reedit and redistribute Web content for their further reuse.

It is widely recognized that a large portion of our paperwork consists of taking some portions of already existing documents, and rearranging their copies in different formats on different forms. This tendency has been significantly growing since we began to perform our paperwork on personal computers. Since the reediting is so fundamental in our daily information processing, personal computers introduced the copy and paste operations as fundamental operations. Now these operations are undoubtedly the most frequently used operations on digital content.

Figure 1.2 shows a new model that the author proposes in this book for the worldwide publication, reediting, and redistribution of intellectual resources. As in the case of the Web, you can publish a set of your intellectual resources as a compound document into a worldwide publication repository. You can use a browser to view such documents pub-

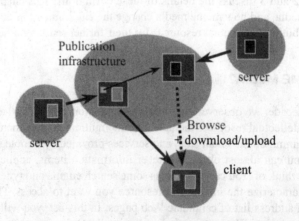

**Figure 1.1**   The publication and reuse of intellectual resources using Web technologies.

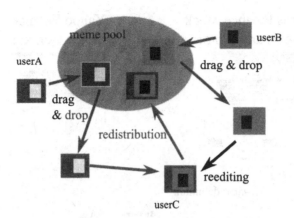

**Figure 1.2** A new model that the author proposes in this book for the worldwide publication, reediting, and redistribution of intellectual resources.

lished by other people. In addition to these operations, you can extract any portions of viewed documents as reusable components, combine them together to define a new compound document for your own use, and publish this new compound document in the repository for its reuse by other people. This new model of publishing, reediting, and redistributing intellectual resources assumes that all these operations can be performed only through direct manipulation. Meme media technologies that are discussed in detail in this book realize this new model. They provide the direct manipulation operations necessary for reediting and redistributing intellectual resources. Current Web technologies provide none of these direct manipulation operations.

## 1.2 HOW DO MEME MEDIA CHANGE THE REUSE OF WEB CONTENT?

Figures 1.3 to 1.5 show an example process of reediting and redistributing intellectual resources over the Web. The "meme media" technologies provide these operations as generic operations on intellectual resources represented as "meme media" objects. This example accesses two Web pages, i.e., Lycos Finance Stock Quotes and Charts, and Yahoo Finance Currency Conversion (Figure 1.3). The former allows you to specify an arbitrary company, and then shows its current stock quote together with its stock quote chart. The latter allows you to specify two currencies and the amount in one of them, and then outputs its conversion to the other currency. Browsers showing the two Web pages are wrapped by meme media wrappers, and work as meme media objects. These wrapped browsers allow us to specify any input forms and/or any displayed objects such as character strings and images to work as I/O ports for interoperation with other meme media objects. You can directly specify which portions will work as ports through mouse operations.

On the conversion Web page, you may fill in the source and target currency input forms with "U.S. dollar" and "Japanese Yen." Then you may specify the amount input form to work as an I/O port, and the character string representing the converted amount to work as

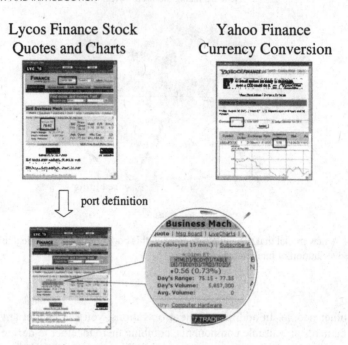

**Figure 1.3** Access of two Web pages, i.e., Lycos Finance Stock Quotes and Charts, and Yahoo Finance Currency Conversion, and specification of I/O ports on the former Web page.

an output port. You may connect a text I/O component to each of these ports, make the wrapped browser hide its display, and resize it (Figure 1.4). The result is a currency conversion tool from U.S. dollars to Japanese Yen. This tool wraps the Yahoo Finance Currency Conversion service, and works as an interoperable meme media object. Through mouse operations, you can also specify that the dollar input port will work as the primary port of this media object.

On the Stock Quote and Chart Web page, you may input some company in the input form, and specify the output portion representing the current stock quote to work as an output port (Figure 1.3). Now you can paste the wrapped currency conversion tool on this Stock Quote and Chart Web page, and connect the primary port of the conversion tool to the current stock quote port of the Stock Quote and Chart page (Figure 1.5). This defines a composite tool that combines two services provided by the two different servers. Now you may input a different company in the input form of the base Web page. Then the composite tool will return its current stock quote both in U.S. dollars and in Japanese yen.

Meme media technologies also allow us to republish this composite tool as a new Web page. Other people can access this Web page and reuse its composite function using a legacy Web browser.

Figure 1.6 shows another example of reediting Web content to define a new tool as a Web page. Here we access the Google search engine, and specify its keyword input form to work as an input port, and the first four search-result Web links to work as output ports. Then we make the background display of this page invisible, and paste one text I/O component and four browsers, all represented as meme media objects, on this page. The text I/O component is connected to the keyword input port, whereas the four browsers are con-

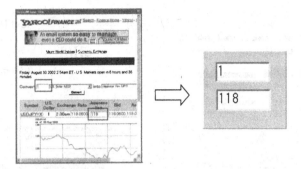

**Figure 1.4**   You can easily wrap the Yahoo Finance Currency Conversion page to create a new interoperable tool, simply by specifying the amount input form and the converted amount to work as an I/O port or as an output port, respectively.

nected to the four Web link ports. The result is a new tool that accesses Google to search for Web pages including input keywords, and shows the first four candidate Web pages. You may publish this tool as a new Web page on the Web.

If we apply meme media representation to all types of intellectual resources including those on the Web and local tools, we can combine extracted Web contents with local tools to compose a new tool. Figure 1.7 shows such an example. Here we access the Yahoo Finance Historical Prices Web page. You may input a company code to obtain the details of its stock quote changes as a table. Meme media technologies allow you to extract this table as a meme media object just through mouse operations. The extracted meme media object

wrapped currency
conversion tool

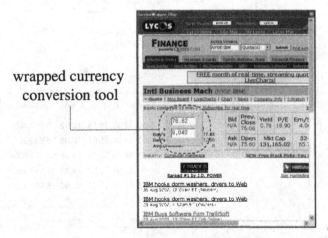

Lycos Finance Stock Quotes and Charts

**Figure 1.5**   You can paste the wrapped currency conversion tool on the Stock Quote and Chart Web page, and connect the primary port of the conversion tool to the current stock quote port of the Stock Quote and Chart page to define a new composite tool.

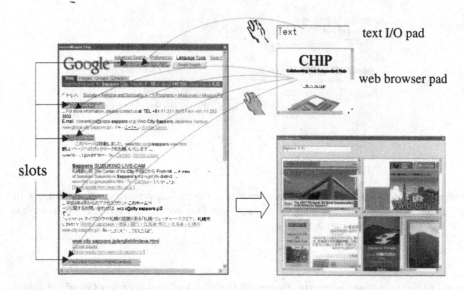

**Figure 1.6** You can easily wrap the Google Web page to define a portal that shows the first four candidate Web pages for arbitrarily given keywords.

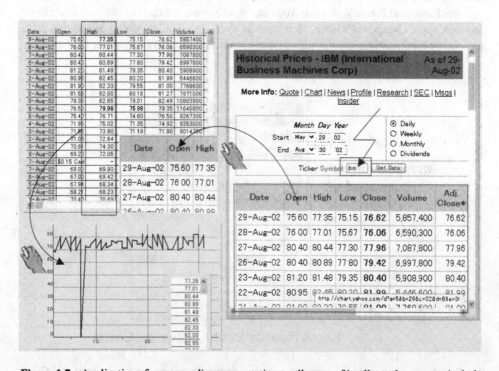

**Figure 1.7** Application of meme media representation to all types of intellectual resources including those on the Web and local tools allows us to easily combine extracted Web content with local tools for the composition of new tools.

has a polling function to periodically access the Yahoo Finance server for updating its table contents. In this figure, the extracted table is dropped on a table tool to transfer its contents to this tool. This table tool allows you to extract a column as another meme media object, which you may drag and drop on a chart tool to obtain its chart representation.

All the above examples tell us how fundamental the reediting and redistribution operations are to the creative reuse of a large accumulation of available contents, application tools, and services. These operations are especially fundamental in the evolution of knowledge in science and technology. Based on the knowledge of published research works, researchers make new assumptions, evaluate them, establish new knowledge, and publish it for others to reuse. People used to use books and journals to publish their knowledge. Because of this restriction, they had to type printed table data for analysis using computer programs. They had to develop a program to calculate a printed formula even if the author of this formula had already developed such a program. Publication with paper media did not allow authors to publish their new formulas together with the corresponding calculation programs. Web publishing has remarkably changed these situations. We can make a copy of Web content and paste it on a local document or on a table we are currently editing. We can publish a formula together with its calculation program. However, we cannot reedit Web contents including application tools and services through direct manipulation.

In bioinformatics, for example, more than 3000 different services are now available on the Web. They include data base services, data analysis services, simulation services, and related reference information services. Researchers in this field, however, have no tools to interoperate some of these services for their own use. There is no way on the client side to connect the output of one service to the input form of another service other than making a copy of the appropriate output text portion on the source page and pasting it in the input form of the target page. Meme media technologies that we will discuss in detail in this book will open a new vista in the advanced reuse and interoperation of such services.

## 1.3   HOW DO MEME MEDIA WORK?

Instead of directly dealing with component objects as in the case of object-oriented, component-based software systems, meme media wrap each object with a standard media wrapper and treat it as a meme media object. They can wrap not only Web content as shown in the previous sections, but also any objects including multimedia documents, multimedia components, application programs, and services provided by either local or remote servers. Each meme media object has both a standard user interface and a standard connection interface. The user interface of every meme media object has a card-like view on the screen and a standard set of operations such as "move," "resize," "copy," "paste," and "peel." As a connection interface, every meme media object provides a list of I/O ports called slots, a standard set of messsages—"set" and "gimme"—to access each of these slots, and another standard message, "update," to propagate a state change of one meme media object to another.

Since meme media objects have card-like appearances on the screen, they are called pads. This book will also introduce the three-dimensional version of meme media, called boxes. You may paste a pad on another pad through mouse operation on the screen. You may use paste operations in arbitrary ways; for example, to overlay multiple translucent component pads of the same size, or to arrange multiple component pads on the same base component pad. When a pad $P_2$ is pasted on another pad $P_1$, the pad $P_2$ becomes a child pad of $P_1$, and $P_1$ becomes the parent pad of $P_2$. Our meme media architecture allows you to connect each child pad to one of the slots provided by its parent pad. Each child pad interoperates with its parent pad by exchanging three standard messages through their slot connection. No pad may have more than one parent pad. Pads are decomposable persistent objects. You can easily decompose any composite pad by simply peeling off the primitive or composite pad from its parent pad.

## 1.4 FREQUENTLY ASKED QUESTIONS AND LIMITATIONS

Some readers of this book may think that Web service technologies can provide us with similar functions for the interoperation of Web contents. Web service technologies enable us to interoperate services published over the Web. However, they assume that the API (application program interface) library to access such a service is a priori provided by the server side. You need to write a program to interoperate more than one Web service. Meme media technologies, on the other hand, provide only the client-side direct manipulation operations for users to reedit intellectual resources embedded in Web pages, to define a new combination of them together with their interoperation, and to republish the result as a new Web page. Chapter 11 of this book will compare, in detail, the meme media technologies on the Web with Web service technologies. In addition, meme media technologies are applicable not only to the Web, but also to local objects. Meme media can wrap any documents and tools, and make each of them work as interoperable meme media objects. Their wrapping, however, cannot use the same generic wrapper as in the case of wrapping Web contents. Different types of tools may require different wrappers.

Some other readers of this book may become worried about the copyright problem. Copyright policies, however, have been reconsidered and modified every time people introduced new media technologies. Whenever a new media technology is introduced, the consensus on new copyright policies gradually coevolves with new copyright protection and/or license management technologies. We have been and are observing such coevolution of new policies with the Web technologies. Some have established closed services on the Web that are exclusive to their members, whereas others have established a closed network, such as the I-mode cellular phone network in Japan by NTT DoCoMo, to implement a micropayment scheme for charging each access to the registered information services. Many other types of license and account management are currently being tried on the Web. The same situation will occur for meme media technologies. Chapter 12 of this book provides a basis to solve the technological aspects of this problem.

Meme media may wrap any objects, whether they are texts, images, figures, charts, or program modules, to provide them with both their visual representations on the display screen and I/O ports to interoperate with each other. Between 1993 and 1997, major software industries in Japan mistook meme media technologies for CBSD (component-based software development) technologies. Around that time, Fujitsu tried to exploit meme media technologies as the basis of their middleware architecture. Since meme media objects work as interoperable components, and allow us to combine them together easily through direct manipulation, their technologies are applicable to the component-based development of client systems with visual man–machine interfaces. Chapter 16 of this book discusses software engineering with meme media technologies.

It should be noted, however, that there are significant differences in the granularity of reusable components between their applications to the reediting and redistribution of intellectual resources and their use as component-based software development environments. Whereas components in the former applications are reused by users who reedit content only through direct manipulation, those in the latter applications are reused by programmers for software development. Although users are usually not interested in modifying internal mechanisms of tools, programmers like to modify them. Therefore, the typical granularity of reusable components in the latter applications is generally much finer than that in the former applications.

It should be also pointed out that meme media technologies cannot be applied to the development of all types of software. Their application is limited to the development of client systems with compound-document interfaces. It is obvious that we cannot even define any visual components if we try to apply meme media technologies to the development of some language compilers.

Meme media objects are assumed to be manually combined by users to compose new ones. Meme media technologies themselves do not focus on how machine intelligence can perform such composition for given specifications; they provide only a basic framework on which you may study such machine intelligence.

In order to make some object work as a meme media object, you have to wrap it with a meme media wrapper. In general, this is not an easy task, and requires programming skill. However, for those objects with de facto standard object architectures such as the HTML document architecture and the Microsoft ActiveX control architecture, we can a priori provide generic meme media wrappers; users can easily wrap any of these objects, without writing any program, to make them work as meme media objects.

## 1.5   ORGANIZATION OF THIS BOOK

This book proposes meme media architectures and their application frameworks. Chapter 1 gives a brief description of why we need meme media, how meme media change the environment of publishing, reediting, and redistributing intellectual resources for their further reuse by other people, and what the limitations of meme media are. It also provides guidelines on how to read this book.

Chapter 2 gives a philosophical introduction to knowledge media and meme media. It clarifies the difference between information media, knowledge media, and meme media. Then it discusses the importance of meme media for all kinds of human interaction with information and knowledge through their life cycle. Meme media together with their worldwide publication repository form a meme pool, i.e., a worldwide pool of reeditable and reusable intellectual resources. Such a meme pool will evolve through people's reediting and redistributing meme media objects. Chapter 2 discusses the similarity between biological evolution and meme pool evolution, and clarifies what kind of technologies are required to accelerate meme pool evolution. We will review the history of books to see the importance of media architectures, and to understand the roles of knowledge media and meme media.

Chapter 3 gives a survey of past and current research and development efforts and technologies that are closely related to meme media and meme pool architectures and technologies. It gives a brief technological history of augmentation media and knowledge media on computers, and a brief survey on current Web technologies as knowledge media technologies. It also clarifies the difference between Web technologies and meme media technologies.

Chapter 4 gives an outline of two meme media systems—IntelligentPad and IntelligentBox. They externalize some of our knowledge respectively using 2D (two-dimensional) and 3D (three-dimensional) representations.

If you are interested in meme media concepts, but not in the technical details, you may read only Chapters 1, 2, 3, and 4. These first four chapters focus on concepts rather than technical details. They are intended to help readers understand the concept of meme media, their use in related technologies, and their capabilities as well as limitations. The remaining chapters, which constitute the main body of this book, clarify the technical details of meme media architectures, their utilities, and their application frameworks.

If your interest is in technical aspects of meme media architectures, you should proceed to Chapters 5, 6, and 7. These chapters focus on the basic architecture of the 2D meme media system, IntelligentPad. Chapters 5 and 6 provide basic knowledge on the MVC (model, view, controller) framework, and on component integration architectures, respectively. These two chapters are fundamental to understanding the component architecture and the interoperation architecture of meme media systems. Chapter 7 gives the technical details of 2D meme media architectures.

Chapters 8, 11, 12, and 19 focus on meme media utilities and their architectures. Chapter 8 provides basic utilities. These include a collaboration tool for more than one user, and a script programming tool to simulate user's manipulation of meme media objects. Chapter 11 gives the architectures for publishing meme media objects, and discuses their relationships to Web technologies. This chapter will propose several different versions of meme pool architectures. Chapter 11 is the highlight of this book. If you are interested in how meme media objects can be published, reedited, and redistributed to form a world-wide meme pool, you should read this chapter. Readers interested in Web services are also strongly recommended to read this chapter. Chapter 12 clarifies how the reediting and redistribution of meme media objects can be allowed without violating the rights of authors and distributors. Readers who are interested in copyrights and the billing should read this chapter. Chapter 19 deals with how to organize and access a huge accumulation of meme media objects, and proposes a new framework named Topica. In this chapter, readers interested in Semantic Web will find another approach to the semantic organization and access of intellectual resources.

Chapters 9, 10, 13, 14, and 17 focus on its application frameworks. Chapters 9 and 10 provide multimedia and database application frameworks, respectively. Readers who are involved in the development of database applications are strongly urged to read Chapter 10. Chapter 13 gives application frameworks for the spatiotemporal editing of meme media objects. Chapter 14 discusses the interoperability of meme media objects and workflow modeling to coordinate their interoperations. Chapter 17 gives a survey of other applications of meme media.

Chapters 15 and 16 discuss software engineering aspects of meme media technologies. Chapter 15 introduces concurrency among meme media objects, whereas Chapter 16 discusses CBSD with meme media technologies. If you are interested in software engineering aspects of meme media technologies, you should read Chapter 16.

Chapter 18 extends the preceding discussions to 3D representation in meme media. If you are interested in 3D computer animation, 3D information visualization, or 3D scientific visualization, you will learn in this chapter how 3D meme media technologies provide direct manipulation capabilities as well as the capabilities of reediting and redistributing their environments and component objects.

Chapter 20 gives some concluding remarks with information about available meme media software systems.

# CHAPTER 2

---

# KNOWLEDGE MEDIA AND MEME MEDIA

---

Media to externalize some of our knowledge as intellectual resources and to distribute them among people are generally defined as knowledge media. Knowledge media that provide direct manipulation operations for people to reedit and to redistribute their content are called meme media.

This chapter gives a philosophical introduction to knowledge media and meme media. It will answer the following questions:

1. What kind of media technologies will enable us to edit, distribute, and manage a large variety of knowledge in the age of personal computers connected to the Internet?
2. What distinguishes knowledge media and meme media from multimedia and hypermedia?
3. What are the potential of meme media? How will meme media change our society?
4. What are the limitations of meme media?

You may just read this chapter and Chapter 4 to obtain a rough sketch of meme media, their concept, technologies, and potential.

## 2.1  INTRODUCTION TO KNOWLEDGE MEDIA AND MEME MEDIA

In his inspiring book, *The Dragons of Eden,* Carl Sagan briefly described the coevolution of biological species and the mechanisms for information inheritance between individuals [1]. Primitive creatures can inherit information only through genes of their parents; they can inherit only genetic information. The development of brains, however, led to oral communication and, for human beings alone, unlike the other creatures, development of external ways to record and store information. The most typical one is a book. Such information is referred to as being "extrasomatic," in contrast to "somatic" information stored in a brain. The externalization of knowledge fragments out of brains and into books makes them continue to exist independently from their previous owners. Books carry knowledge across time and space, allowing us to share knowledge with people who died thousands of years ago, or with those in different countries. The development of extrasomatic ways of storing knowledge remarkably accelerated the evolution of human beings and their cultures.

Marshall McLuhan considered media to be not only communication mediators but also augmentors of our physical capabilities such as seeing, hearing, speaking, walking, grasping, understanding, and thinking [2]. In this sense, books serve as augmentators of our memory.

Computers were originally developed as computation tools; they augment our natural computation capabilities. Computers can store a large amount of information, so they can also serve as augmentors of our memory. People have been trying to externalize various human capabilities and to implement them in computers. In this sense, today's personal computers are augmentation media that provide us with various tools for entertainment and thought; they provide tools to augment our individual capabilities. Some researchers and developers have been further expanding the target of augmentation from individual people to groups of people; their goal is to provide group-augmentation media that support collaborative activities. Their systems are called groupware systems.

Media for the externalization of knowledge enable each of us to extrasomatically record and archive knowledge fragments, and to distribute them to other people in our community. This encourages people to reuse and to edit the archived knowledge to create new knowledge fragments, which are again added to the knowledge shared by society. This accumulation is what we call a culture. Books are typical examples of such media. Their main role is not the augmentation of individuals or groups, but the distribution and the accumulation of knowledge as common property of our society. Knowledge media are such media. The WWW (World-Wide Web) is an advanced example of knowledge media. The process of knowledge accumulation in a society consists of six activities to:

1. Externalize
2. Record and archive
3. Distribute
4. Share
5. Quote or to reuse
6. Edit fragments of knowledge

The current Web technologies support these six activities at the level of representation description languages such as HTML (Hyper Text Markup Language), XML (Extensible Markup Language), and XSL (Extensible Stylesheet Language). However, they do not provide users with direct manipulation operations for reediting and redistributing Web content. Therefore, Web content is not widely reused, except static content such as texts and images. There are no tools for us to directly extract some portion of Web pages, whether they are static or dynamic, to recombine them together through direct manipulation, and to publish the composed result as a new Web page. The augmentation of societies for the promotion of their cultural evolution requires a new type of knowledge media that provides direct manipulation operations for these six activities in an integrated way.

Biological evolutions are based on genes. We require media similar to genetic media for the augmentation of societies and to promote their cultural evolution. Such media should be able to replicate themselves, to recombine themselves, and to be naturally selected by their environment. They may be called "meme media" since they carry what Richard Dawkins called "memes" [3]. Their environment in this context means the society of their producers and consumers, namely, authors and users. Strictly speaking, meme media do not replicate nor recombine themselves. Their users replicate them and recombine them through direct manipulation. Mark Stefik also pointed out in 1986 the importance of understanding and building an interactive knowledge medium that embodies the characteristics of memes to distribute and to exchange knowledge fragments in a society [4].

The accumulation of memes in a society will form a meme pool, which will work as a gene pool to bring about a rapid evolution of knowledge resources shared by society. This will cause an explosive increase of knowledge resources, similar to the flood of consumer products in our present consumer societies. The explosive increase of knowledge resources is not only inevitable, but also fundamental for society's rapid evolution since such increase forms a sufficiently large meme pool and increases the chances for the variety of recombination. Meme media will bring us a consumer society and consumer culture of knowledge resources, which requires new services for distribution, management, and retrieval.

This book focuses on meme media: their potential as enabling technology, their software architecture, and their applications.

### 2.1.1  Information Life Cycle and Knowledge Media

People interact with information in various ways. We have a lot of verbs to express these interactions. Some examples are listed below:

1. Generation of new information—conceive, create, generate, acquire
2. Externalization of information—externalize, write, scribe, represent
3. Recording of information—record, archive, store, remember, accumulate
4. Protection of information—protect, hide, secure, control
5. Communication of information—communicate, tell, inform, exchange
6. Distribution of information—distribute, publish, open, leak, broadcast
7. Sharing of information—share
8. Reference to information—reference, cite, quote, reuse
9. Editing of information—edit, process, compose, arrange
10. Search of information—search, retrieve, look for, seek
11. Analysis of information—analyze, evaluate
12. Management of information—manage
13. Annihilation of information—annihilate, discard, forget, destroy, eliminate

Information can be thought of as having its own life cycle during which people interact with it through these actions. Information that is either created or acquired by a person is either just kept in his or her brain, or externalized through some medium outside of him- or herself. The externalization requires some medium. Here we consider only the case in which information is externalized. We are interested in the application of computer technologies to externalized information.

Once information is externalized, it is shared by different individuals across time and space. Externalization of media can be classified into four categories depending on whether they can hold information across different times or different locations (Figure 2.1). Each of them is further classified into three categories depending on the number of people who are involved (Figure 2.2). The human voice is a medium used by people sharing the same moment and the same location. Over the telephone, it becomes a medium used by people sharing the same moment at different locations. A media like memo boards or monuments are used by people at the same location at different times. A book falls in the upper right quadrant in Figure 2.1, where information can be shared across different times and different locations.

Externalization of information is not independent from its editing. The editing of information, on the other hand, requires that it be already externalized. Externalized fragments of information can be distributed or published. They can be quoted in another fragment of information, or can be recombined into a new fragment of information. When they lose their significance, they are discarded. In some cases, they continue to exist but the information necessary to access them is discarded. The accumulation of externalized information fragments sooner or later requires their management, which makes people create a new type of information, i.e., information to access existing information. This new type of information is called meta-information.

During its life cycle, a fragment of information may change its representation and medium. However, it cannot exist at any moment without some representation and some medium. People always interact with fragments of information through their media. The use of personal computers as augmentation media has led to the development of various tools to support these interactions. Among them are word processors, spreadsheets, chart tools, drawing tools, and database management systems. These tools are augmentation media. They are not only media in McLuhan's sense, but also media that carry fragments of knowledge. Word processors, for example, carry their procedural knowledge on how to perform word processing. Although such knowledge is not readable, it can be transported to other people so that they may apply the same knowledge to their own documents. In this view, information media and the tools applied to them are both considered to be knowledge media. Tools as media behave as information media. They are used to externalize procedural or rule-based knowledge. They can be distributed among people, provided this does not violate their copyrights. They can be combined to define new tools, al-

| Time | different | monumental media | transportable media |
|------|-----------|------------------|---------------------|
|      | same      | ephemeral media  | concurrent media    |
|      |           | same             | different           |
|      |           | Space            |                     |

**Figure 2.1**   Classification of externalization media in terms of time and space.

|  | Person | | |
|---|---|---|---|
|  | same | different | public |
| ephemeral media | idea generation | face-to-face communication | speech |
| monumental media | memo board | message board | bulletin board |
| concurrent media | n.a. | telecommunication | broadcasting |
| transportable media | portable memo | letter | publication |

**Figure 2.2**    Further classification of externalization media in terms of people.

though usually it is not easy to do so.

People interact with fragments of information through various tools and media during the life cycle of these information fragments. These tools and media have been independently developed, and cannot effectively interact with each other. Furthermore, tools have been considered different from media. "Media," in daily conversation, means only tools for communication among different people. From McLuhan's point of view, media are augmentation tools. The total support of our interaction with fragments of information and knowledge requires a universal set of media that may cover all kinds of human interaction with information and knowledge through their life cycle. These media must be able to cooperate with each other through functional linkage and data conversion. Otherwise, they cannot continuously support our activities at different stages of the information life cycle in a seamless way.

### 2.1.2 Artificial Intelligence Versus Knowledge Media

In his reflective and perspective paper published in 1986 [4], Mark Stefik of Xerox PARC said, "The most widely understood goal of artificial intelligence is to understand and build autonomous, intelligent, thinking machines. A perhaps larger opportunity and complementary goal is to understand and build an interactive knowledge medium."

He picked out three stories about the growth of knowledge and cultural change. They concern the spread of hunting culture, the spread of farming culture, and the rapid change in late 19th to early 20th century France that led peasants to recognize their identity as "Frenchmen." The first two stories illustrate how the complexity of a culture affects its diffusion rate. The last story shows that a technology can accelerate cultural change. It discusses the introduction of roads and railroads in France between the years 1870 and 1914, and the subsequent sweeping changes and modernization that took place.

Then he took up Richard Dawkins' concept of memes, and reinterpreted the above stories in terms of memes. In his book, *The Selfish Gene,* Dawkins suggested provocatively that ideas (he called them memes) are like genes and that societies have meme pools in just the same way as they have gene pools. Basic human capabilities for communication and imitation modulate the rate at which the memes spread. The spreading rate of memes, however, is not the only factor that determines the evolution rate of a culture. Roads did more than change France into a marketplace for goods. They also transformed it into a marketplace for memes. By bringing previously separate memes into competition, roads triggered a shift in equilibrium. Ideas from faraway places were continuously reinterpreted and reapplied. The very richness of this process accelerated the generation of recombinant memes.

Memes require carriers, each of which is an agent that can remember a meme and communicate it to another agent. People are such carriers and so are books. However, there is an important difference. People can apply knowledge, whereas books only store it. Programs running on computers can apply knowledge as well, which makes computer systems very important for creating an active knowledge medium.

Stefik then compares books with expert systems. Books can simply store fragments of knowledge. It is people who apply books, distribute them, and recombine them into new books. Expert systems can store and also apply fragments of knowledge. However, it is difficult for people to apply expert systems, to distribute them, or to recombine them into new expert systems. Books are passive knowledge media that we can edit, whereas expert systems are active knowledge media that we cannot presently edit. We need new active knowledge media that we can edit. Meme media defined in this book are such media.

He also pointed out that building a knowledge medium is a long-term goal, complementary to the goal of building artificially intelligent agents. He predicted that this goal would be reached through other work in the larger field of computer science, such as databases and network technology.

The evolution rate of a meme pool depends on several factors. Among them are

1. The number of people accessing this pool
2. How easy it is for them to recombine memes
3. How often they encounter interesting memes

There are three corresponding ways to accelerate the meme pool evolution:

1. To increase the number of people accessing the pool, we may establish a worldwide reservoir of memes and provide an easy way of accessing this reservoir.
2. To make meme recombination easier, we may develop a user-friendly editing system for end-users to compose, decompose, and recombine memes.
3. Finally, to increase the chance for people to encounter interesting memes, we may develop a good browser or a good reference service system for people to search the meme pool for what interests them.

In addition to these three ways of accelerating evolution of the meme pool, we should not forget the fourth way, which is based on a fundamental hypothesis of population genetics: when two groups become isolated from each other there is always genetic drift, a change in the relative distribution of genes, between the two gene pools. In general, larger populations have more stable distributions in their gene pools than smaller populations. Sometimes, however, new species appear and displace related species much more rapidly than would be predicted by the apparent change of environment or expected rate of genetic drift. This phenomenon of speciation and displacement is called a punctuated equilibrium [5]. The leading model for explaining this process comprises three stages: isolation, drift, and displacement. First, a group becomes geographically isolated from the main population. This group undergoes selection and genetic drift more rapidly than does the larger body. Finally, the geographic isolation is removed, and the slightly fitter group competes against and displaces the original population. This hypothesis can be read in the context of memes as follows: To accelerate meme pool evolution, it is not a good strategy to provide a single monolithic meme pool. Instead, it is better to provide a meme pool that enables people to dynamically develop smaller subpools for subcommunities, to cultivate a local culture in each of them, and to dynamically merge some of them.

Such a punctuated equilibrium in a meme pool can be observed in various situations. Interdisciplinary studies between two well-developed research fields may often yield new development. Researchers like to organize a small community for intensive and deep discussion whenever a new research field starts to develop. Lego Group, famous for its toy block systems, distributes more than 60 new kits with different stories and themes every year, which has stimulated the development of new meme subpools of Lego culture: a doll's house world, an airport world, a train station world, a zoo world, a pirates' world, and so on.

### 2.1.3 Meme Media for All Users

Media may restrict people who utilize their content. A language as a medium allows only those who can speak it to access its content. In the history of media, human beings have always been searching for more universal media than those already available. The aim is to distribute, exchange, share, edit, and reuse varieties of knowledge among people across time and space.

On the other hand, the total support of our interaction with fragments of information and knowledge requires a universal set of media that may cover all kinds of interaction through the life cycle of information and knowledge. These media must be able to cooperate with each other through functional linkage and data conversion. Otherwise, they cannot continuously support our activities at different stages of the information life cycle in a seamless way. As Alan Kay pointed out [6], current personal computers have effectively developed into meta-media. They provide a universal set of media to cover varieties of interaction with information and knowledge fragments throughout their life cycle. These media can be easily used by end-users. However, they cannot cooperate effectively with each other. Their cooperation requires definition by a program, which is too difficult or even impossible to write unless a standard application linkage protocol is defined a priori among these media.

Although steady progress has been made, many have observed that current personal computers are still relatively hard for a novice to use. A lot of tools are available for end-users, but it is hard either to connect them or to extract a specific portion of the function provided by one of them. These tools are not decomposable. For example, although sorting modules are used in lots of tools, none of them can be extracted as an independent module reusable for different applications. As things stand now, user-friendliness, higher-level languages, and most advanced features of end-user computing are typically determined by the perceptions and the imaginations of computer developers and software programmers. These language and user-interface designers determine what is best for the naive end-user through analyzing what is best for themselves. "User friendliness" and "naive end-users" are the most misleading words. User-friendly systems often denote foolproof systems. Naive end-users are often considered as those who can only use foolproof systems. These are typical misunderstandings of computer developers and software designers.

Professional photographers are not satisfied with foolproof cameras that allow them only to release the shutter. They have better or more specific knowledge than camera developers about the setting of aperture and shutter speed. They are nonetheless end-users, because they have no engineering knowledge of cameras. We often observe that some widely used professional tools are too sophisticated and complicated for nonprofessionals to use. They are still user-friendly systems for professionals. Foolproof tools, on the other hand, are likely to have limited capability in order to simplify their operations. This is, however, a lazy way of designing tools. Limitations on the capability of a tool also limit the capability of its users.

Foolproof tools, however, may popularize the process for which they are intended. Foolproof cameras have popularized the art of taking pictures. Such popularization enlarges the meme pool of the corresponding function, and increases the number of people who share this pool.

Foolproof tools and professional tools should be able to functionally interoperate with each other and with other tools. Otherwise, we may have two isolated, independent meme pools, one of amateurs and the other of professionals. Lego Group, for example, has been providing two types of toy blocks—Lego blocks and Dupro blocks. Dupro blocks were specially designed for younger children below four or five years old. Although Dupro blocks are much bigger in size than Lego blocks, these two types of blocks are designed to be connected with each other.

There are seven groups of meme media users:

1. Novice end-users: inexperienced or untrained users who have some difficulty in learning the art of utilizing the media functions. Children under the age of three or four are the typical examples. Their meme media should be robust against misuse. They do not learn from instructions but through trial and error. Such use should not result in any system errors. At the same time, most of the possible functions should interest the users. Otherwise, they will lose their interest and give up using the media. Meme media should provide point-and-click and drag-and-drop playgrounds of interoperable and interactive documents and tools. These documents and tools should be usable in combination with those for nonnovice users.

2. Nonprofessional end-users: the public at large—users who do not care about either the engineering needed to implement various media functions or the professional skill required to utilize these functions. They can learn from instruction manuals and from examples. It is especially important to provide them with various sample groups of application tools as well as online manuals. They can start with these samples, and decompose them or replace some part with another to compose new tools.

3. Professional end-users: users who do not care about the engineering to implement various media functions, but are eager to develop their professional skill to utilize these functions in their professional activities. Among them are engineers, physicists, chemists, medical doctors, mathematicians, biologists, lawyers, economists, accountants, designers, architects, and teachers. They have profound knowledge in their fields. Some of them may even develop their programming skill to program their tools by themselves. These people are classified in the next category, i.e., su-

perusers. Professional end-users form a community in each of their professional fields, and exchange both their knowledge resources on meme media and their know-how about how to utilize these media. Such a society often includes some superusers who develop professional tools for the society to share. Such a society also forms a niche market of tools, which fosters the tool development business. It is especially important to provide a networked infrastructure for these users to easily exchange their meme media objects. The reediting and the redistribution of meme media objects by these users are especially important to form a meme pool of knowledge in each of their professional societies.

4. Superusers: professional users who have developed their programming skill so they can develop useful tools by themselves to support their professional activities. Almost every professional field has such superusers. Some portion of the development tools for the meme media should be open to the public to encourage these superusers to utilize them to develop varieties of useful meme media objects. Their meme media objects, when published, will significantly increase the value of the meme pools for their professional field, which will encourage more people to share these pools, and more superusers to develop more tools. This positive feedback loop will accelerate the evolution of these meme pools, and hence the evolution of both the professional fields and their societies.

5. System Integrators: users' consultants who advise users on how to utilize meme media, or to integrate available meme media to compose new ones that fulfill users' requirements. They just combine tools available in the market. There is a large business opportunity for them.

6. Application developers: including database designers and administrators, various application system developers, custom software developers, and so on. Meme media promise to help application developers by the use of patterns and frameworks for varieties of typical applications. Patterns and frameworks are the concepts on which some object-oriented software development researchers have recently come to focus their attention [7, 8]. The use of patterns in design activities was first proposed by Christopher Alexander in the area of architecture [9]. A pattern in meme media means a common composition structure and hence a common editing structure of meme media shared by the composite tools for the same typical application. As detailed in later chapters, form interfaces of a database, for example, share the same composition structure when implemented by the composition of meme-media objects. A framework in meme media means a set of meme-media components and the composition rules that are typically used in the development of a specific kind of application. Patterns and frameworks allow users to develop their applications just by editing these patterns and frameworks. Patterns and frameworks are also provided for Lego blocks as varieties of kits that come with sample composition manuals. These have been playing an essential role in promoting sales. The patterns and frameworks are themselves developed by application developers. These are accumulated as application developers' know-how, and shared by developers. Application developers reuse their patterns and frameworks to develop new application systems. Patterns and frameworks themselves may also become commercial products.

7. System developers: including developers of platforms, application-independent servers, and general-purpose utility systems. Among these systems are spreadsheets, word processors, operating systems, and database servers. For these experts,

meme media help them to accumulate and to exchange their know-how. In the development of client systems, they can use patterns and frameworks of meme-media objects. However, system development by composition of meme-media objects is not relevant for the development of server systems.

Several different features of meme media will satisfy the varying needs of these different kinds of users.

### 2.1.4  Meme Media and Compound Documents

Meme media can be loosely described as media that can carry any kinds of knowledge resources, dynamically interrelate them to cooperate with each other, and allow people to distribute, exchange, share, and reuse these resources. Our knowledge resources include numerical data, multimedia documents, hardware tools, software tools, facts, rules, inference rules, inference tools, artifacts, design models, and the knowledge about how to access these resources. Current computer systems are already effective at handling these, apart from hardware tools and artifacts themselves. Indeed, they can even handle the design models of hardware tools and artifacts. Current computers can carry these kinds of knowledge resources. However, they cannot dynamically interrelate them so that they cooperate with each other, nor do they allow people to distribute, exchange, share, and reuse these resources.

Meme media should provide knowledge resources as generic components so that their users can easily combine them and edit composite documents and tools to dynamically interrelate them. Meme media should also allow us to distribute them as decomposable objects so that we can easily extract any component or any composed portion to reuse for different purposes.

One possible approach that would satisfy these requirements is the adoption of the compound-document model as the basic media architecture, and the extension of this document-media architecture to cope with other types of knowledge. The compound-document model was first adopted on computers by desktop publishing systems. They allowed us to embed images, drawings, tables, and charts into a single text page. Since then, the variety of embedded components available for compound documents has gradually increased to include animations, video clips, and script programs. Now, the compound-document model can treat any object in the object-orientation paradigm as an embedded component whenever this object is given an appropriate media component representation. Objects in the object-oriented paradigm are, in general, reactive; they exchange messages with each other. Some of them interact with their users. The model with this extension is called the reactive compound-document model.

Meme media provide any object with its reactive media-component representation, which allows us to embed this object, as a media component, into another reactive media component. Meme media components are different from GUI (graphical user interface) objects. They use GUI objects to implement their representation on the display screen. Every meme media component consists of two objects: a display object and a model object. Its display object defines its appearance and its reaction to user operations as a media component on the screen, whereas its model object defines its content. The display object changes the appearance depending on the content defined by the model object. The appearance is not uniquely determined by the content. The appearance also includes styles, formats, and decorations. Furthermore, the appearance may reflect only some part of the content. For example, some meme media components may appear as blank cards with some functions. These functions are the contents of these meme media components, but have nothing to do with their appearance.

Since meme media are reactive objects, their composition is not simply layout composition as in the case of nonreactive compound documents. The embedding of a component into another should also define a functional linkage between the two. Such a composite object is called a composite meme media object. When a component is peeled off from another component, their functional linkage should be broken. Our system-design problem is how to merge these two different composition operations—the physical layout-composition operation and the logical functional-composition operation—into a single simple operation. The functional linkage definition through layout composition is quite different from diagrammatic visual programming methods that visually define a program as a data-flow graph with visually represented functional component objects as its nodes. Visual programming methods represent both application objects and GUI objects as icons on the screen and allow users to set links between arbitrary pairs of icons. They may also allow users to embed some GUI object icons into other GUI object icons. However, their embedding operations have nothing to do with their functional linkage operations. Meme media, however, basically unify a layout-composition operation and a functional-composition operation into a single operation.

Meme media objects are persistent objects. They continue to exist unless explicitly deleted. For their future reediting, composite meme media objects should be kept decomposable. Ease of object composition is the common goal shared by current authoring tools, toolkit systems, and visual programming tools. However, these systems do not maintain composed objects as decomposable objects. Although these systems only focus on rapid prototyping, meme media also focus on the future reediting of composite objects and reuse of the results.

Meme media also require a distribution infrastructure to form a meme pool. In addition to offline distribution infrastructures such as the traditional book-publishing market, we need an online distribution infrastructure through the Internet to accelerate meme pool evolution. A peer-to-peer transportation facility is not sufficient to form a meme pool. We have to organize a marketplace wherein all people can publish their achievements, browse through the achievements published by others, and arrange selling and buying of these achievements between arbitrary pairs of people. Meme media thus require another medium that works as their marketplace.

Like genes, meme media objects should be capable of recombination, replication, and mutation. These media objects should be subject to natural selection. These operations are performed by people who access their meme pool. Mutation of meme media objects denotes the addition of a new component to an existing composite object. The natural selection is based on how often each meme media object is replicated for its reuse, and, as a consequence, on how many replicas exist in a meme pool for each meme media object.

### 2.1.5 Objects and Media

From the software engineering point of view, a meme media architecture constitutes a new object-oriented software architecture both for the graphical user interface and for object wiring and containment. It is also a new fine-grain component software architecture.

Meme media are different from GUI systems. Conventionally, the GUI was considered to be secondary. The primary consideration was always the application systems themselves. Their GUI was considered after the complete development of application programs. GUI toolkit systems based on this convention represent each application program that is to be provided with its GUI as a single icon on the screen, and allow users to graphically define links between this icon and various GUI widgets (Figure 2.3). These links define functional linkage between the application program and these GUI widgets. Meme media, however, are based on the media-based architecture in which every user-manipulable object is provided with a standard software wrapper that works as a medium to hold this object. This composite is called a primitive media object; its original object works as its content object. Users cannot directly manipulate any content objects; only primitive media objects are user-manipulable objects. Primitive media objects are atomic since they are not user-decomposable.

For each object, the wrapper defines its physical representation and logical structure. Its physical representation defines its appearance on the screen and direct manipulability, whereas its logical structure defines the functional linkage interface to other primitive media objects. The wrapper of a primitive media object provides its content object not only with its visual image but also with its direct manipulability. In object-oriented GUI terminology, this wrapper works as a display object for its content object. As shown in Figure 2.4, each primitive media object should be implemented as a pair consisting of a display object and a content object. The wrapper of each primitive media object also defines its functional linkage interface to other primitive media objects, which implies that the application linkage protocol of each primitive media object should be defined .

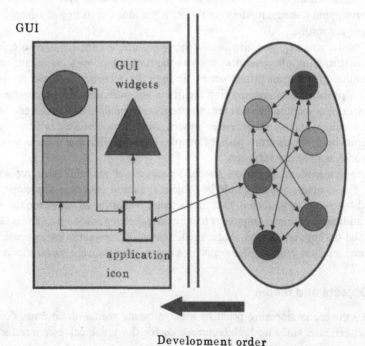

Development order

**Figure 2.3**  A human interface as the second matter to consider.

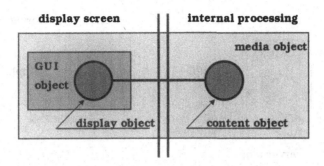

**Figure 2.4** A GUI object and a media object.

not by its content object but by its display object. This allows us to directly manipulate functional linkages. The standardization of primitive media objects results in the standardization of their wrappers, namely of their physical representation and their logical structure.

Primitive media objects require some interapplication communication mechanism to combine some of their functions and/or GUIs. They may use some of the four different graphical definitions of interapplication communication mechanisms, i.e., (1) cut-and-paste, (2) drag-and-drop, (3) object wiring, and (4) object containment. The first two probably require no explanation. Object wiring involves graphical definition of a link to interrelate two different application objects. Object containment involves a reactive compound document model in which a reactive compound document created by a client application may contain various component objects linked to different server applications. The object-containment mechanisms are further classified into two categories: (1) widget containment, and (2) media containment (Figure 2.5). In widget containment, the link between a component and a server application is not fixed. It needs to be defined by the object-wiring mechanism. A single server application can be differently linked to more than one component. GUI-toolkit systems are widget-containment systems; NeXT Interface-Builder [10] falls into this category. In media containment, the link between a component and a server application is fixed and never changes wherever this component is embedded; this fixed pair defines a primitive media object. The embedding of a primitive media object into another primitive media object defines an application linkage between these two primitive media objects. IntelligentPad, developed by my group, adopts the media-containment mechanism [11]. Suppose that you make a copy of an object with some embedded objects. With widget containment, this copy cannot inherit its original's links to the server applications; it loses the original function. With media containment, however, such a copy inherits its original function.

In OLE terminology [12], both "object linking" and "object embedding" mean what we call object containment in this section. With OLE's object linking, the containment of a component only holds a reference pointer to the original component, whereas with OLE's object embedding, the contained component is an independent copy of the original component.

Current computers handle various types of intellectual resources [Figure 2.6 (a)]. These include multimedia documents, system utilities, application systems, and user environments. Unless a system provides a dedicated functional linkage between any pair of

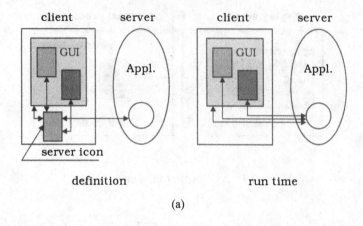

(a)

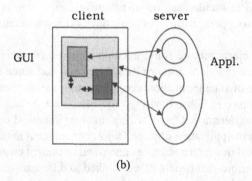

(b)

**Figure 2.5** Widget containment and media containment. (a) Widget containment. (b) Media containment.

these object types, it fails to integrate these objects [Figure 2.6 (b)]. By a functional linkage is meant not only a data-communication linkage but also an application linkage through message exchange. Different pairs require different types of linkages. If there are $n$ different types, we require $O(n^2)$ different types of linkages. This is the essential challenge of integration systems that are open to the future addition of new intellectual resource types.

Meme media architectures solve this problem by separating media from their contents and standardizing the logical structure and the interface of the primitive media objects. Media of a certain type in general play their most important role in providing a uniform access protocol for various types of intellectual resources. Books are the most typical example. They have a long history of development of their common structure starting with a front cover, followed by a table of contents, then a body with hundreds of pages, indices, and ending with a rear cover. Books are organized in this way to provide their readers with a uniform access protocol. Although media of the same kind share the same organization structure, their contents can contain different structures of information. The same idea is adopted by meme media architectures. Each primitive media object consists of its wrapper and its content [Figure 2.7 (a)]. Its wrapper defines its

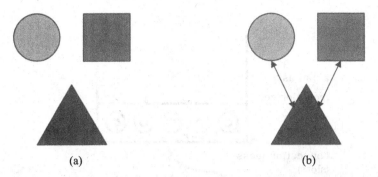

(a)                                    (b)

**Figure 2.6**  Objects and their linkages in object-oriented architectures. (a) Three independent objects. (b) Different functional linkages for different object pairs.

standard media structure and interface. It is up to the developer of each primitive media object to decide how its content object is implemented in the standard wrapper. Although meme media basically use an object-oriented architecture, their architectures are more restricted. Therefore, we call them media-based architectures to distinguish them from conventional object-oriented architectures.

In a media-based architecture, only one type of functional linkage is used to connect any pair of wrappers [Figure 2.7 (b)]. In IntelligentPad, developed by our group as a meme media system, each wrapper has an arbitrary number of connection jacks called slots, and a single pin-plug to connect itself to one of the slots of another wrapper (Figure 2.8). IntelligentPad calls its primitive media object a "pad." The wrapper architecture and the standard linkage facility are provided by the kernel of the IntelligentPad system. Neither users nor media object developers have to worry about them. Chapter 7 will give the architectural details of IntelligentPad, and Chapter 18 will show a 3D extension of IntelligentPad.

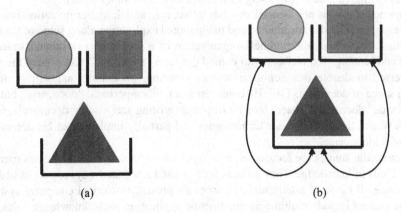

(a)                                    (b)

**Figure 2.7**  Objects and their linkages in media-based architectures. (a) Three independent media objects. (b) The same linkage mechanism for different media–object pairs.

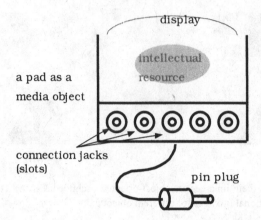

**Figure 2.8**   The logical structure of each pad that works as a generic media component.

### 2.1.6   Multimedia, Hypermedia, and Meme Media

Research studies on meme media share technological and application interest with multimedia and hypermedia studies.

Multimedia studies are focused on how to deal with various forms of information on computers. Multimedia researches have been extending their scope to deal with texts, charts, drawings, tables, images, movies, sounds, script programs, and environments. They have developed dedicated technologies to edit, distribute, and manage each of these different forms of information. Additionally, they have developed a compound document architecture that allows us to embed different forms of information on a single document page. A compound document looks like a printed text page with embedded images, charts, and tables. Its page may even contain embedded movies and/or sounds. Recent multimedia studies have also focused on how to edit, distribute, and manage compound documents. These include studies on multimedia-document editors with scripting languages [13], multimedia exchange formats based on various compression technologies [14], and multimedia databases using various retrieval technologies [15].

Hypermedia studies are focused on associative, referential, and/or quotation relationships among multimedia documents, and navigational exploration along some of these relationships. They focus on nonlinear organization of a multimedia-document space for writing and reading. Ted Nelson, who coined the term "hypertext," also coined the word "docuverse" to denote this nonlinear writing, reading, publishing, annotating, and/or quoting space of documents [16]. He considered not only a personal "docuverse" but also a worldwide "docuverse" shared by a lot of people writing and reading documents. Later, the WWW and the Web browser technologies had partially implemented his dream of a world-wide docuverse.

Meme media studies are focused on new types of media that work as memes carrying various kinds of knowledge. They address uniform and integrated ways to edit, distribute, and manage all kinds of intellectual resources on present networked computer systems. These resources include multimedia documents, application tools, knowledge rules, and design models. Meme media studies are aimed at forming an open set of primitive media components and a standard functional-composition mechanism allowing the easy composition/decomposition of multimedia documents and tools through direct manipulation.

Meme media studies are also focused on a worldwide marketplace architecture for the publication of various intellectual resources on meme media, their reuse, reediting, and the redistribution of reedited intellectual resources; it is assumed that all these operations are performed by end-users through direct manipulation.

When they are published, composite multimedia documents need not be decomposable. However, when they are published, composite meme media objects, must be kept decomposable for their further reediting by other people.

### 2.1.7 Meme Media and Meme Pools

As Mark Stefik pointed out, meme media should work as memes [4]. They should be able to be recombined, replicated, and naturally selected by people. Since they should be easily recombined, they should be easily composed from primitive components and be distributed as decomposable composites. The set of primitive components should be open for future extension. The replication of meme media objects is done by copy operations. Each copy of a meme media object, when created, has the same state as the original, and later changes its state independently from its original's state.

The natural selection of memes by people requires a marketplace wherein people can easily publish and sell the meme media objects they composed, browse what others have published, buy copies of what they want, and bring these copies into their own private space for their reuse. Such a marketplace cannot be formed by simply providing the meme media with peer-to-peer transportability through worldwide networks. In peer-to-peer transportation, people cannot publish what they have composed without specifying who will reuse them; they cannot browse the products of other people without asking each person to show what he or she has. We need a marketplace that works as a meme pool. Its formation requires a worldwide publication reservoir.

Meme media requires the development of three subsystems, namely, a meme media editing system, a meme media management system, and a meme pool system. A meme media editing system provides us with an open library of primitive meme media objects, and enables us to create composite meme media objects by easily and directly combining these components. A meme pool system provides a worldwide marketplace of meme media objects. We are especially interested in a meme pool system that works on the Internet. A meme media management system works as a database system for media objects. We have to consider two types of meme media management systems: one for the local management of meme media objects, and the other for the global clearing service. The latter manages and searches meme media objects in the worldwide meme pool system.

Chapter 11 will give the details of our meme media and meme pool architectures based on the IntelligentPad architecture that will be described in Chapter 7. Chapter 10 will discuss architectural details on meme-media management systems.

## 2.2 FROM INFORMATION TECHNOLOGIES TO MEDIA TECHNOLOGIES

Since their birth, computers have been tools for information processing. Computer science and software engineering have been focusing their studies on information structures and information operations. No one had ever paid much attention to media structures or media operations on computer systems before the architectural studies on hypermedia systems. This is quite an unusual situation in the history of human cultures. Human beings have spent a lot of years in developing each of the various types of media. Let us consider the history of books. After the invention of the "codex," the folded and sewn manuscript books, it took more than 1300 years for books to have page numbers. It took more than another century to develop indices. It really took an incredibly long time to establish their current structure. Now, it is time for us to focus on media structures and media operations on computer systems.

### 2.2.1 Information Architectures and Media Architectures

Today's advanced information society has three major problems. The first problem is the so-called "information explosion"; it arises from the fact that information production technologies have developed much more rapidly than the technologies for information management, retrieval, and filtering. Today's information explosion has resulted from the following two causes:

1. People's insufficient understanding of the ecology of information in the research and development of conventional information processing technologies
2. People's insufficient attention to the important roles of media in human societies

In designing information processing technologies, people have not focused on *how* and *why* varieties of information are communicated, classified, acquired, filtered, and discarded. Information system developers have not yet formed any mental models about the ecological systems of information. We need a new media architecture that may foster such mental models. In our long human history, whenever new media technologies were developed, they always brought with them new mental models on how to manipulate and to manage information.

The second problem is the so-called "software crisis." Although information productivity has remarkably improved in these decades, software productivity still remains the same as 10 or 20 years ago. The ever-increasing demand for new software systems is caused by seriously increasing backlogs. The remarkable improvement of information productivity during the past couple of decades can be attributed to the development of document editing, reproduction, and distribution technologies. These technologies are not yet well developed for software.

There have been many projects aimed at improving software productivity. Software developers tried to provide software components and to distribute them for their reuse. However, none has managed to achieve particular success. The main reason, I believe, lies in the fact that none of them considered the distribution of composed software products in a reeditable form. They only considered the distribution of components. They assumed that the composite products need not be decomposable. In fact, however, it is hard for us to completely understand the role of a component used in a specific situation only from its functional description. Some knowledge about its use in a certain context would greatly help us in understanding how to use it. Together with the publication of various components, we need to publish instances of their typical use within composed software products. In this respect, some researchers in object-oriented software development recently have begun to emphasize the use of patterns and/or frameworks [7, 8], which corresponds to the above discussion. The distribution of components is not sufficient to promote their reuse. We need to distribute a complete application product in its decomposable form so that other people can easily decompose this into subsystems, not only to reuse some of them for other purposes, but also to learn how to use each component with others. This requires a new type of medium that externalizes software modules as user-manipulable visible components and allows us to easily edit them through their direct composition and decomposition.

Recently, many people have discussed the importance of open system architectures in which varieties of application software systems in their open market are dynamically interoperable with each other across different platforms. Dynamic interoperability means that a user can dynamically define functional linkage among more than one application and make them interoperate with each other. However, we cannot have such systems without developing new media capable of supporting the editing and distribution of software modules as user-manipulable visual objects.

Chapter 5 will discuss the architectural details of software components, their integration, and their network distribution. Chapter 16 will discuss software engineering using the knowledge-media system architecture of IntelligentPad.

The third problem is the fact that current computer systems are still poor vehicles for our culture. As discussed in Section 2.1.1, we need the development of new knowledge media that totally support our interaction with information fragments through their life cycle.

All these three problems can be attributed to the lack of a new type of media that would allow us to edit, distribute, and manage all kinds of intellectual resources including multimedia documents and software modules in a uniform and integrated manner. Their editing must define not only their physical layout but also their functional linkages. It is time for us to shift our focus from information architectures to media architectures.

## 2.2.2   Roles of Media

From the engineers' point of view, media play the following three important roles:

1. A medium adds varieties of functions to an information fragment.
2. Media of the same type treat varieties of information in a uniform way, and provide them with a standard access and operation protocol.
3. A medium integrates varieties of information.

In the history of media, human beings developed various media to provide information fragments with various functions, including verbalization media, visualization media, recording media, archiving media, transportation media, and replication media.

Media provide varieties of information with the same standard access and operation protocol. Books are good examples. Although books may contain various types of information, their forms are standardized for easy use and management. Books share the same structure. They have a series of pages sewn together and contain a table of contents followed by the body and indices. This standard structure provides a uniform protocol for the access and the manipulation of different types of information. As mentioned above, it took a long time to develop this standard structure.

A medium allows people to editorially arrange various information fragments from different sources, and to integrate them to create a single new intellectual resource. Various articles are collected in a newspaper as a single new intellectual resource. A notebook is used to record fragments of ideas, quotations, and references, and it later works as a new source of knowledge.

The concept of media that play the above-mentioned roles, when successfully implemented on computers, will allow us to treat varieties of information and knowledge using a single type of media. Such media provide their content information and knowledge with various functions, and furthermore, standardize the protocol for accessing and managing varieties of information and knowledge. They can be used to integrate different information and knowledge fragments into a single intellectual resource.

### 2.2.3 History of Books

It is worthwhile to review how books, the most advanced conventional knowledge medium, developed into their present form.

The Egyptian book took the form of a scroll, usually composed of twenty papyrus sheets, each of the same dimensions, rolled round a wooden, bone, or ivory bar or cylinder. The writing used on papyri ran parallel to the horizontal fibers, and was usually only on one side, in narrow columns that were progressively numbered. The columns were termed "paginae." Each column was composed of a variable number of lines. The length of scrolls varied according to need.

Papyrus appeared in Greece around the seventh century BC. The Greeks called the unwritten sheet of papyrus "charters," which in Latin became "charta," hence "card." Greeks called the papyrus scroll "chilindros"; the Romans, "volumen" or "liber."

A text of long works was divided among several scrolls, keeping the length of each portion more or less the same, while respecting chapter breaks. Short texts, on the other hand, were joined together in a single scroll, indicating a tendency to adopt a uniform length. Long scrolls were naturally difficult to store. For this reason, the Romans put suitable works such as poetry on small scrolls, whereas historical works were on scrolls of a larger format. The nature of the scroll forced authors to publish their works in relatively short sections, hence the divisions into somewhat short books of the major works of Latin authors. One of the most important characteristics of media is that the form of media influences not only the style of its knowledge content but, furthermore, the way that both writers and readers think about that content.

A strip bearing the identification of the work was glued on to the outside of the scroll; it was called the "index" or "titulus." When, much later on, works came to be given titles, they were written at the inner end of the scroll, probably because placing them within the roll served to protect them.

The folded and sewn manuscript book is properly called a "codex." During the early first century AD, the scroll or "volumen" met competition from, and was then replaced by, the codex. The codex is a group of "quires" sewn together, each quire consisting of a number of folded sheets. Usually, a quire consisted of four sheets folded in half to make eight leaves or folios, i.e., 16 pages. Though it is not clear when the codex superseded the scroll, from the fourth century onward, the codex gradually took the place of the volumen as the normal form for books. The format, that is, the height and the width of the page, became known as "forma" or "volumen" during the Middle Ages. The oldest format was square. This was followed by a rectangular shape with the height greater than the width. In a special category are miniature volumes, or books of unusual shapes and sizes. Some were created for practical reasons, others merely as exercises of virtuosity.

Like their predecessors the papyrus scrolls, medieval manuscripts usually did not have title pages. Instead, a phrase from the beginning of the text was written at the head of the text. The name of the author was not stated. Attention was drawn to the opening phrase by the use of red ink and large capital letters. Information about the author and the work's title were placed at the end of the book.

Since the large number of quires needed to make a codex could easily be gathered in the wrong order when bound, copyists developed the custom of numbering the quires with marks on the last pages. In the thirteenth century, after the founding of the first universities had increased the demand for books, a system was needed that would also indicate the order of the pages within each quire, to permit the designer and illuminator to work in sequence on the same volume without any confusion. By the end of the thirteenth century, the folios were sometimes numbered throughout a volume.

The history of books is a good example of how long it takes to develop one type of media. Note that this long history was required to develop the structure of the medium, namely the presentation structure of information, but not the representation structure of information.

### 2.2.4  From Information Processing to Social Information Infrastructure

Current computers are capable of dealing with varieties of intellectual resources. Among them are multimedia documents, tools, procedures, rules, and design models. This list covers most of our descriptive knowledge. Although it is important to add new types of intellectual resources to this list, much more important and fundamental for us is how to provide these intellectual resources with functional linkage mechanisms, and how to make these resources exchangeable and reusable across different platforms through networks.

Computers are rapidly proliferating today, and not independent from one another; many of them are mutually connected by the Internet. Typically, more than one computer is used by a single user, who often needs to transport data and documents from one computer to another to perform his or her jobs. WWW on the Internet [17] and its browser systems such as NCSA Mosaic [18], Netscape Navigator [19], and Microsoft Internet Explorer allow people to publish, exchange, and reuse multimedia documents and data. Varieties of new browser technologies are rapidly expanding the types of intellectual resources that we can exchange through the Internet.

Human beings, as social creatures, communicate with others to exchange information and ideas, and share common knowledge and culture. Although computer systems in 1980s dramatically expanded the repertoire of what can be processed, they provided only personal and organizational information-processing and management environments. Computer systems in 1990s, together with their Internet connections, have opened a new vista toward worldwide publishing and reuse of intellectual resources. Computers and networks are coming to work together as a social information infrastructure for sharing intellectual resources. Our focus on information systems is shifting from information-processing technologies to social information infrastructures. Meme media will work as fundamental vehicles for social information infrastructures.

### 2.2.5  Editing, Distribution, and Management

Conventionally, engineers have focused on communication aspects of media. In addition to communication aspects, media have various other aspects. Especially for knowledge media, the most important aspects are the editing, distribution, and management of knowledge fragments. Currently available media on computers are too immature to evaluate from these three aspects. Books are well-matured conventional knowledge media.

They have coevolved with professionals, institutions, and systems for editing, distribution, and management.

Almost nothing is known of Egyptian libraries of the New Kingdom period (1500–1085 BC). In general, libraries were associated with temples or other religious centers. At Edfu, in southern Egypt, the wall of a Temple of Horus was decorated with a list of the works in the library. In the tomb of a father and son found near Thebes, inscriptions include the title "librarian." Ptolemy II Philadelphia (285–246 BC), a son of Ptolemy I Soter who made Alexandria the Egyptian capital, founded the famous Alexandrian Library, with the intention of bringing together all of Greek literature in the best copies, edited and assembled with the help of professionals.

The art of bookmaking was well organized in Greece, and books were exported. Initially, the copyist and the bookseller were one and the same person. Only around the fifth century BC did book dealers, called "bibliopoli," begin to form a separate profession and carry on their trade in shops open to the public. Besides being the places where books were sold, these shops were meeting places where the educated gathered to listen to readings of the newest works, to determine whether to buy them or hire the authors. Such readings offered the producers and sellers of books a chance to assess popular taste in order to meet the need for new works. The active book trade in the Greek world is confirmed by the existence of several celebrated public and private libraries. For example, Pisistratus, Tyrant of Athens, founded a public library in 550 BC, and Aristotle's private library was well known.

Around the first century BC, the "editor" appears. The first and most famous of these was Titus Pomponius Atticus, a friend of Cicero's. He was also a librarian. He gathered around him a large number of copyists who worked to create both works for his personal library and works to be sold. We know that Titus Pomponius paid for the publication of the works of Cicero and recovered his costs from the sale of the books. However, nothing like author's royalties then existed. Indeed, no law protected literary property and everyone was free to copy any text and sell the book at any price.

The invention of portable media to record varieties of knowledge was immediately followed by the development of editors, libraries, and markets. This is surprising when we notice that all this happened before the invention of printing technologies, during the time when their replication required lots of time, money, and skill.

Communication is not always the main function of media. Media that are portable and capable of recording knowledge would soon be extended to support their editors, and promote the development of meta-media for their management and distribution.

Due to the development of the open system concept and the popularization of the Internet, media on computers are becoming more portable across different platforms through the Internet. Media history clearly indicates that these portable media will soon extend their capability to support their editors, and develop their meta-media for their management and worldwide distribution. This change will happen very rapidly since, unlike the case of books before Johann Gutenberg, the replication of computer media does not require any time, money, or skill. The only serious obstacle might be the necessity to develop new royalty and security services. However people's desire to share varieties of knowledge with each other will surely overcome this drawback; researchers will develop new technologies such as "superdistribution" proposed by Ryoichi Mori [19]. Superdistribution does not restrict the replication or redistribution of media content. It charges a user for his or her every use of media content, instead of charging for getting each copy of them. The former charging scheme is called pay-per-use billing, whereas the latter is called pay-per-copy billing.

### 2.2.6 Superdistribution of Knowledge Media

Distribution of software products has a unique characteristic that distribution of physical products does not have. Replication of software products does not require any cost. Copy protection has been required in distribution of commercial software products. However, ease of replication is not always a demerit. It allows users to redistribute software products to other users without any cost, which accelerates the distribution and brings natural selection of products by users. Ease of replication plays an essential role in the distribution of knowledge media. If replication is prohibited, knowledge media cannot work as meme media. How can we allow replication in distribution of commercial software products? Ryoichi Mori addressed this question more than 20 years ago, and proposed the concept of "superdistribution" in 1983. It requires a shift from pay-per-copy to pay-per-use billing. Superdistribution realizes pay-per-use billing by keeping and collecting usage records that hold who has used how much of what. Varieties of simplification are possible. This book also discusses and extends these in Chapter 12 for the distribution, reediting, and redistribution of meme media objects.

## 2.3 SUMMARY

Media for the externalization of knowledge enable each of us to extrasomatically record and archive knowledge fragments, and to distribute them to other people in our community. This encourages people to reuse and to edit the archived knowledge to create new knowledge fragments, which are again added to the knowledge shared by society. This accumulation is what we call a culture. The augmentation of societies for the promotion of their cultural evolution requires a new type of media.

Biological evolution is based on genes. We require similar genetic media for the augmentation of societies to promote their cultural evolution. Such media should be able to replicate themselves, recombine themselves, and be naturally selected by their environment. They may be called meme media. The accumulation of memes in a society will form a meme pool, which will work as a gene pool to bring about rapid evolution of knowledge resources shared by this society. This will cause an explosive increase of knowledge resources, similar to the flood of consumer products. Meme media will bring us a consumer society and consumer culture of knowledge resources, which requires new services for distribution, management, and retrieval.

People interact with fragments of information through various tools and media during the life cycle of these information fragments. These tools and media have been independently developed, and cannot effectively interact with each other. The total support of our interaction with fragments of information and knowledge requires a sufficiently large set of different media that may collaboratively cover all kinds of human interaction with information and knowledge through their life cycle. These media must be able to cooperate with each other through functional linkage and data conversion.

Meme media can be loosely described as media that can carry any kinds of knowledge resources, dynamically interrelate them to cooperate with each other, and allow people to distribute, exchange, share, and reuse these resources. Our knowledge resources include numerical data, multimedia documents, hardware tools, software tools, facts, rules, inference rules, inference tools, artifacts, design models, and the knowledge about how to access these resources. Current computer systems are already effective at handling these.

However, they cannot dynamically interrelate them so that they cooperate with each other, nor do they allow people to distribute, exchange, share, and reuse these resources.

Meme media should provide knowledge resources as generic components so that their users can easily combine them and edit composite documents and tools to dynamically interrelate them. Meme media should also allow us to distribute them as decomposable objects so that we can easily extract any component or any composed portion to reuse for different purposes.

## REFERENCES

1. C. Sagan. *The Dragons of Eden: Speculations on the Evolution of Human Intelligence.* Ballantine Books, New York, 1989

2. M. McLuhan. *Understanding Media, The Extensions of Man.* McGraw-Hill, New York, 1964.

3. R. Dawkins. *The Selfish Gene.* Oxford University Press, Oxford, 1976.

4. M. Stefik. The Next Knowledge Medium. *AI Magazine, 7*(1): 34–46, 1986.

5. N. Eldredge and S. J. Gould. Punctuated equilibrium: An alternative to phyletic gradualism. In *Models in Paleobiology* (J. M. Schopf, ed.), Freeman Cooper, San Francisco, 82–115, 1972.

6. A. C. Kay. *The Reactive Engine.* Ph.D. thesis, University of Utah, 1969.

7. E. Gamma, R. Helm, R. Johnson, and J. Vlissides. *Design Patterns: Elements of Reusable Object-Oriented Software.* Addison-Wesley, Reading, MA, 1995.

8. F. Bushmann, R. Meunier, H. Rohnert, P. Sommerlad, and M. Stal. *Pattern-Oriented Software Architecture: A System of Patterns.* Wiley, West Sussex, UK, 1996.

9. C. Alexander, S. Ishikawa, M. Silverstein, M. Jacobson, I. Fiksdahl-King, and S. Angel. *A Pattern Language.* Oxford University Press, New York, 1977.

10. B. Webster. *The NeXt Book,* Second edition, Addison-Wesley, Reading, MA, 1991.

11. Y. Tanaka, and T. Imataki. IntelligentPad: A hypermedia system allowing functional composition of active media objects through direct manipulations. In *Proceedings of IFIP'89,* pp. 541–546, 1989.

12. Micosoft Corporation. *OLE2 Programmer's Reference, Volume One: Working with Windows Objects; Volume Two: Creating Programmable Applications with OLE Automation.* Microsoft Corporation, Redmond, WA, 1994.

13. P. Ackermann. *Developing Object-Oriented Multimedia Software.* dpunkt, Heidelberg, Germany, 1996.

14. K. Sayood. *Introduction to Data Compression.* Morgan Kaufmann, San Francisco, 1996.

15. V. S. Subrahmanian. *Principles of Multimedia Database Systems.* Morgan Kaufmann, San Francisco, 1998.

16. T. H. Nelson. *Literary Machines. Edition87.1.* (self-published), 1987.

17. T. Berners-Lee, R. Cailliau, N. Pellow, and A. Secret. The World-Wide Web Initiative. In *Proceedings of INET'93,* 1993.

18. M. Andreessen. *MCSA Mosaic Technical Summary.* NCSA Mosaic Technical Summary 2.1, 1993.

19. R. Mori and M. Kawahara. Superdistribution: The concept and the architecture. *Transactions of the IEICE, E73*(7): 1133–1146, 1990.

# CHAPTER 3

# AUGMENTATION MEDIA ARCHITECTURES AND TECHNOLOGIES—A BRIEF SURVEY

Marshall McLuhan considered media to be not only communication mediators but also as augmentators of our physical capabilities, i.e., seeing, hearing, speaking, walking, grasping, understanding, and thinking [1]. Today's personal computers are considered to be augmentation media that provide us with various tools for entertainment and thought [2]. They provide tools to augment our individual capabilities. Some are expanding their target of augmentation from individuals to groups to provide group-augmentation media that support collaborative activities. Such systems are called groupware systems [3, 4]. Some others are further expanding their target of augmentation to organizations for the integrated management of resources, projects, and achievements [5, 6]. Their resources include people, money, equipment, and materials; their achievements comprise contracts, products, and profits. Some projects consume certain resources to yield specific achievements, whereas others change their resources and/or their achievements. Enterprise integration systems are examples of organization augmentation systems [7].

Knowledge media such as the Web have further expanded the target of augmentation from groups and organizations to communities or societies. People in a group or in an organization share a definite common goal such as making a decision, designing a system, or solving a problem, but people in a society share their achievements and reuse them to produce new achievements. People in a society share an accumulation of their achievements, which we call their culture. Current Web technologies, however, do not provide direct manipulation operations for reediting and redistributing knowledge resources. When provided with such direct manipulation operations, knowledge media will work as meme media.

This chapter is a survey of past and current research and development (R&D) efforts and technologies that are closely related to meme media and meme pool architectures and technologies. It contains a brief technological history of augmentation media and knowledge media on computers, and a brief survey of current Web technologies as knowledge media technologies. This chapter lists potential applications of meme media technologies. It also clarifies the difference between Web technologies and meme media technologies.

## 3.1 HISTORY AND EVOLUTION OF AUGMENTATION MEDIA

Augmentation media on computers may be divided into four categories based on the targets of the augmentation:

1. Personal-augmentation media
2. Group-augmentation media
3. Organization-augmentation media
4. Social-augmentation media

### 3.1.1 Pioneers

The origin of the personal-augmentation computer-media technologies can be found in Vannevar Bush's article entitled "As We May Think," which was published in *The Atlantic Monthly* in 1945 [8]. He claimed that the progress of research was being stymied by the inability of researchers to find and access relevant information. He proposed the "memex" system, a microfiche-based system of documents and links. Some of the requirements he specified for this system are fast access to information, the ability to annotate, and the ability to link and to store a trail of links.

Doug Engelbart, who found Bush's article and avidly read it in a Red Cross library on the edge of the jungle on Leyte, one of the Philippine Islands, in the fall of 1945, was much influenced by this article. Subsequently, he went back to Stanford University and finished his B.S. in electrical engineering after the war, and worked for the NACA until 1951, when he got fed up with his goalless role. He then formulated the goal for which his later works represent the pursuit vehicle. He started his project at SRI, and in 1962 published his research program in a paper entitled "Augmenting Human Intellect: A Conceptual Framework." This set Engelbart's research agenda for the next 35 years [9]. He sought to define and implement the functionality necessary for computers to augment human abilities. The functions he thought necessary include links between texts, electronic mail, document libraries, separate private space for users' personal files, computer screens with multiple windows, and the facilitation of work done in collaboration with more than one person. He invented the mouse, outline processor, idea processor, and on-line help systems integrated with software. He was responsible for the first substantive implementations of electronic mail, word processing, and shared-screen teleconferencing. His system AUGMENT is marketed by McDonnell Douglas. He now heads the Bootstrap Institute, which aims to build software and hardware prototypes that will help office workers collaborate. He has been focusing his studies not simply on personal augmentation, but seriously on group and organization augmentation. He also focused on the coevolution of augmentation systems and the people who use these environments as users and/or developers. Engelbart made significant contributions to the establishment of current hardware and software architectures of workstations and personal computers, as well as to the establishment of basic ideas of the current personal-augmentation media. At the same time, he was the pioneer who tried to apply augmentation-media technologies to the performance improvement of collaborative work and enterprise activity. He originated the studies on group- and organization-augmentation media.

Ted Nelson coined the word "hypertext" and presented it to the world. Initially, he wanted to develop a system in which fragments of ideas could be written and stored together with the associative, referential, and quotation relationships among them. Each idea fragment might well be relevant to more than one subject. It should be stored in different contexts without making copies, for copies may lose consistency. He insisted that any chunk of information in one text should be quotable at any location in other texts, and that this quotation relationship should be maintained through further reediting and reusing of these texts. Any update of the original should be immediately reflected in its quotations. He called this type of link between two information chunks in different contexts "transclusion links" to distinguish them from associative, referential, and navigational links [10]. In contradistinction to those who came after him, he mainly focused on system models for nonlinear writing. In nonlinear writing, chunks of writing need not be arranged in a linear sequence; each chunk can be related to more than one context without losing the consistency and dependency among them.

One day, Nelson read about the death of a person who, people thought, was writing a book on daily life in New York. No manuscript was found; his life work just disappeared. Nelson attributed this to the difficulty of personally publishing one's own work. This lead him to envision a worldwide electronic publishing reservoir that people could electronically access through their own terminals or the terminals at franchise shops. Anyone could publish his or her works in this reservoir, explore the reservoir to browse some others' works, and purchase any chunks of text from others' works for reuse in his or her own works without violating copyright. He conceived all of the above in the early 1960s. Since then, he has been relentlessly fighting to construct "Xanadu," a worldwide publishing reservoir with "transclusion" and royalty services [11].

In the late 1960s, Nelson advised Andries van Dam and his team at Brown University to develop the Hypertext Editing System on an IBM 360 [12]. This system was intended to serve two purposes: to produce printed documents clearly and efficiently, and to explore the hypertext concept. From 1988 to 1992, Autodesk, Inc. invested in Xanadu and supported Xanadu Operating Co. In 1994, Nelson moved to Sapporo, Japan, to join the Sapporo HyperLab and began joint projects with Yuzuru Tanaka (the author of this book) at Hokkaido University. In 1996, he joined the faculty of Keio University.

His vision has stimulated researchers to develop hypermedia system technologies, the World-Wide Web [13], and HTML browser systems such as NCSA Mosaic [14], Netscape Navigator, and Microsoft Internet Explorer. However, Xanadu has not yet been constructed. Nelson started from personal-augmentation media and continues to aim at social-augmentation media.

Based on the Hypertext Editing System, Andries van Dam conducted his second hypertext project at Brown, completing his File Retrieval and Editing System (FRESS) in 1982 [15]. The latest hypertext project at Brown is called "Intermedia" [16]. His team developed Intermedia-based applications for the teaching and learning of biology and english literature at Brown [17]. This system was used both by professors to develop courseware systems, and by students to learn subjects and to write reports.

Carnegie-Mellon University developed another hypermedia system called ZOG [18], which is the last of what Frank Halasz calls the first-generation hypertext systems [19]. ZOG was specially designed to provide fast response to a large number of people. The first-generation systems were all originally designed to run on mainframes. They only dealt with text, though their model can be equally applied to other media.

The researchers at XEROX PARC inherited these research results achieved in 1960s. Their primary concern was the development of a personal computer and an active media system running on it. Alan Kay, for example, proposed Reactive Engine in 1969 [20], which, renamed "Dynabook" in 1972 [21], motivated the development of the personal computer Alto machine [22] and the interactive object-oriented interpretive language Smalltalk [23].

In 1967, Nicholas Negroponte formed the Architecture Machine Group in the Architecture Department at MIT. Although the initial goal was to use computers for architectural design, a new focus developed: that of making computers easier to use. In 1976, the Architecture Machine Group proposed a research program to the U.S. Defense Advanced Research Projects Agency (DARPA) entitled "Augmentation of Human Resources in Command and Control through Multiple Media Man–Machine Interaction." This proposal resulted in the Spatial Data Management System (SDMS) [24]. The SDMS media room contained an instrumental Eames chair, large projection screen, and side-view video screens. While seated in the chair, the user could use joysticks, a touch screen, or stylus to navigate through the information space viewed on the large screen. The first version organized the space hierarchically, with lower levels reachable via ports. SDMS II [25] used a single global space and zooming could be employed to get more detailed views. Later, voice-based navigation and control were added to the system. DARPA then asked Computer Corporation of America (CCA) to develop a practical version of SDMS [26].

In the late 1970s, Negroponte and his group began the Aspen project [27]. Film shots taken from a moving vehicle traveling through the town of Aspen were stored on videodiscs. They were accessed interactively to simulate driving through the town. A touch screen allowed the user to control the speed and direction of travel. Images of the facades of significant buildings were also stored on videodiscs. The user could stop at any of these buildings and access associated information. From 1980 to 1983, the group also developed a prototype of the electronic book [28]. Pages turned like ordinary books when the user slid his fingers across a touch screen.

In 1985, Negroponte opened the MIT Media Lab [29]. He focused on the multimedia technologies at the intersection of three previously distinct industries: television, publishing, and computers. He aimed at a new emerging medium, characterized by the auditory and visual richness of television, the accessibility and personal quality of books, and the interactivity and expressive potential of computers.

### 3.1.2 Evolution of Personal-Augmentation Media

In early 1980's, the second-generation hypertext authoring products came onto the market with the emergence of workstation-based, research-oriented systems like KMS [30] and Intermedia [16]. These systems ran on workstations that supported more sophisticated user interfaces than earlier systems. KMS, a commercial implementation of ZOG, came onto the market in 1983. It was capable of storing text and graphics in any node.

Around the same time, Peter Brown began to develop the first commercial hypertext authoring system for a personal computer. It was called Guide [31] in 1985 when Office Workstations Limited began to market it for the Apple Macintosh. Guide had less functionality than earlier mainframe and workstation-based hypertext products, but had rich graphical-user-interface capabilities.

In 1986, Xerox PARC released NoteCards [32], which pioneered in the application of a card metaphor to hypertext; each node is represented on-screen as a card. Cards are classified as to their types, such as text, graphics, and animation. NoteCards, KMS, and

Intermedia all support graphics and animation nodes as well as formatted text. They also provide graphical overviews of the link network spanned among nodes to aid navigational access.

In 1987, Bill Atkinson developed HyperCard, which was then released by Apple as bundled software for Macintosh computers. As a hypermedia system, it had the least functionality for linking and navigation among those available at that time. HyperCard imposes a card metaphor on its node. Cards have the same fixed size. No card can be simultaneously displayed with others. A hyperdocument is called a stack, and HyperCard programs are called "stackware." Each card can be linked to others via link anchors that work as buttons on this card. A mouse-click on such a button will replace the current card on the screen with the target card.

HyperCard made two contributions. First, it popularized the hypermedia concept. The second and probably more significant contribution is the fact that it served as a standard multimedia development platform for several years. HyperCard popularized new system design and development methodologies that are not based on how to process information, but on how to put information fragments, together with their functions and interrelationships, into a standard media framework.

Analyst, a commercial product developed at Xerox XSIS Lab., was an integrated hypermedia system. Using a hypermedia framework, it integrated a wide range of object-oriented applications, including word processing, desktop publishing, spreadsheets, forms, graphics, images, databases, and maps, with rule-based organization tools and an expert-system shell. It extensively used a media framework, especially a compound-document framework, for the first time to integrate varieties of applications. The set of these applications was, however, not open for future extension. Analyst was a closed integration OIS (office information system).

During the 1980s, many multimedia research groups were formed. Two notable ones are Olivetti Research Lab and Apple Computer Multimedia Lab. The former has two subgroups: the Cambridge, England, research group, and the California research group. The Cambridge group had two multiyear projects. Pandora, a joint effort with Cambridge University, focused on developing a peripheral box for creating a multimedia workstation test bed. The second project developed a dynamic locator system called Active Badge. By using sensors located throughout the building and sensor badges carried by each individual, anyone could be located. This system is a group-augmentation media system. The California group focused on desktop audio, and developed VOX [33] for managing audio for multimedia conferencing.

Apple Computer Multimedia Lab, on the other hand, focused particularly on the area of education. They developed many interactive multimedia titles by supplementing educational movies with additional documentation, simulation, navigational tools, and activities that involve students in subject matter.

Paralleling the development of hypermedia systems, various visual computing technologies have been developed during the last 15 years. For example, window widgets have been developed to provide construction toolkits for visual presentation of information on display screen windows. These include X-Window (X11) with Xlib and Xt Intrinsics-Based Toolkit [34], OSF-Motif [35], OPEN LOOK Intrinsics Toolkit (OLIT) [36], Xview Toolkit [37], Sun's NeWS [38], NextStep Application Kit [39], HP NewWave [40], Borland ObjectWindows class library [41], and Apple's MacApp [42]. Window systems have also been improved to support flexible linkage with applications, effective redrawing of overlaid windows, and efficient and sophisticated dispatching of user events to window objects. The progress of multimedia technologies and widow systems has allowed us to integrate varieties of media on a single display screen and, furthermore, on a single display window. These technologies encouraged the research and development of visual programming, which in turn, resulted in the extension of window systems and their toolkit systems, enabling users to directly define functional linkage among display objects. These will be detailed in Chapter 5, especially in Section 5.4.

### 3.1.3 The Evolution of Group-Augmentation Media

The rapid progress of computing environments in the last couple of decades has replaced terminals with desktop computers connected by networks, and has provided software tools with WIMP (window, icon, menu, and pointer) user interfaces. These changes were first recognized as a trend toward networked computing for group augmentation and organization augmentation. Computers as personal-augmentation media have enabled people to produce higher-quality documents. Their network connection has enabled people to distribute these documents to each other in less time, and has significantly improved people's office work. These, however, aid each individual to work separately, rather than as a group of people working collaboratively.

Paul Wilson noted in 1991 that the fundamental requirement for supporting group work is two-way communication, which can be used in two ways: to share information, and to share a virtual workspace [43]. In 1984, Irene Greif and Paul Cashman introduced the term computer-supported cooperative work (CSCW) as a way of describing how computing technology can help people to work together in groups [44]. They made it clear that CSCW tools will only work if they reflect and augment the way people actually talk, work, and live together. This is more than just making the tools easy to use. Ellis described CSCW-enabling technology using two main characteristics: the style of interaction and the geographical location of the participants [45]. The former includes synchronous (same-time) cooperation such as brainstorming, and asynchronous (different-time) cooperation such as collaboration through mail.

Potential applications for CSCW cover wide areas in which communication technology is used to coordinate activities by keeping participants advised of what awaits their attention, to help reduce the need for meetings, and to provide a shared information space. Wilson listed the following application types [43]:

1. Collaboration tools help groups agree on missions, allocate tasks and roles, and undertake specific group activities.
2. Meeting room systems support face-to-face meeting activities.
3. Desktop video conferencing enables two or more geographically separated people to work together using a common screen display, video images of other people in separate windows, and an integrated voice connection.
4. Procedure processing or workflow technology automate paper-based forms handling and provide full summary information about status, whereabouts, and overruns.

Among these four, the last one falls in the category of organization-augmentation systems, which will be detailed in the next section.

Tom Rodden classified the enabling technologies for CSCW into four types: message systems, computer conferencing, meeting rooms, and coauthoring and argumentation systems [46].

Message systems evolved from the early electronic mail facility. They are classified into three control models—formal, semiformal, and informal—based on how much their messages are structured and coordinated. The formal control model has the highest degree of task-prescriptivity. It provides a configurable message system to support structured group work. Among those systems using the formal control model are Coordinator proposed by Terry Winograd in 1986 [47], CHAOS by de Cindio et al. in 1986 [48], Domino by Thomas Kreifelts and Gerd Woetzel in 1986 [49], Cosmos by John Bowers and John Churcher in 1988 [50], and Amigo by Thore Danielson et al. in 1986 [51]. Coordinator is based on the principles of speech–act theory. It transposes conversational routines to a networked format in which groupwork team members declare their agreements and commitments. The software asks participants to declare, to promise and commit, and to articulate the conditions of satisfaction of a request. The computer then holds them accountable for the commitments in a public record. The informal control model was adopted by Information Lens, developed by Thomas Malone et al. in 1986 [52]. The Information Lens lets users specify rules that automatically file or reroute incoming messages based on their content. Strudel, proposed by Allen Shepherd et al. in 1990 [53], is an example of a semiformal control model system. The Imail system adds intelligence to the messages themselves [54]. It has a language for attaching scripts to messages. Scripts are sender-specified programs that execute in the receiver's environment to query the receiver, to report back to the sender, or to cause the message to be rerouted.

Computer conferencing systems originated in EMISARI, developed in the United States in the early 1970s [55]. EMISARI consisted of two parts: Party-Line for point-to-point communication between two users, and Discussion for providing on-line file storage of topic-specific messages for all users to access. These two components are building blocks of the traditional conferencing systems that followed, which addressed asynchronous group activities. The progress of high-bandwidth local area networks promoted the development of real-time conferencing systems, which address synchronous group activities and support real-time cooperation and concurrent access to the shared information space.

There are two different basic approaches for implementing real-time computer conferencing systems. The first one embeds an unmodified single-user application in a conferencing environment that multiplexes the application's output to each participant's display. Input comes from one user at a time. A floor-passing protocol exchanges input control among users. The second approach is to design the application specifically to account for the presence of multiple users. RTCAL, proposed by Irene Greif in 1988 [56], supports meeting scheduling among a group of users by providing a shared workspace of information from participants' on-line calendars. Cognoter by Mark Stefik et al. [57] is a real-time group-note-taking system. These systems are based on the first approach.

The progress of multimedia technologies has promoted the development of desktop conferencing systems. There are two fundamental aspects to desktop conferencing systems: telepresence and teleworking. Telepresence can be enhanced by adding live video images of participants on the screen. As Stephen Gale pointed out, the video conferencing capability must be integrated with the teleworking environment, i.e., it must be a shared computing environment [58]. Electronic bulletin boards are early attempts to provide asynchronous shared computing environments. Some provided a real-time electronic version of a chalkboard that multiple users could add to or modify [59].

An example of desktop conferencing is the MMConf system [60], which provides a shared display of a multimedia document, as well as communications channels for voice and shared pointers. Another example is the Bell Labs' Rapport system [61]. Rapport is an experimental groupware system that allows coworkers to jointly edit computer files while discussing them using voice and video. It provides a uniform interface, which allows a favorite word processor, CAD system, or financial planning program to be used on almost any project.

A meeting room system often consists of a screen projector and some networked workstations or terminals, and can be used to conduct decision conferences. These are called Group Decision Support Systems (GDSS). Four software elements are identified for the construction of decision conferencing: decision analysis software, modeling software, voting tally software, and display software. Many GDSSs were implemented as electronic meeting rooms. An example is the Colab system developed at Xerox PARC by Mark Stefik et al. [59]. Text and images can be easily manipulated on the shared electronic chalkboard. Colab provided two kinds of windows: public interactive windows accessible to the entire group and private windows with limited access. Another example is the PlexCenter Planning and Decision Support Laboratory developed at the University of Arizona [62]. The facility provided a large U-shaped conference table with eight personal workstations, a workstation in each of four breakout rooms, and a large screen projection system that could display screens of individual workstations or a compilation of screens. Later, the number of workstations was increased to 24 to support up to 48 people.

Coauthoring and argumentation systems are multiuser hypertext systems, wherein the hypertext document is created by several users. Some of these editors such as ForComment [63] are for asynchronous use, and conveniently separate the text supplied by the author from the comments of reviewers. Real-time group editors allow a group of people to edit the same object at the same time. They usually divide the object into logical segments. They allow concurrent read access to any segment, but only one writer per segment. Examples include Collaborative Editing System (CES) by Irene Greif et al. [56], Shared Book by Lewis and Hodges [64], and Quilt by Robert Fish et al. [65]. The Mercury system by Kaiser et al. is an editor intended for programming teams. It informs users when their code needs to be changed because of program modifications made by others. The DistEdit system by Michael Knister et al. [66] tried to provide a toolkit for building multiple group editors. Idea generation and issue analysis in group discussion were also developed using multiuser hypertext systems as their basic framework.

A large number of groupware products are now available. Some are commercial products, whereas others are experimental systems. Some are classified in one of the abovementioned categories, whereas others have capabilities in more than one category.

### 3.1.4   The Evolution of Organization-Augmentation Media

Group augmentation focuses on both telepresence and teleworking. For small groups, the augmentation focuses more on the telepresence of each participant's personality, whereas for large groups, the augmentation focuses more on teleworking and coordination, rather than on individual personalities. Such augmentation of organizations could involve groups with hundreds or thousands of people. In such cases, we require coordination of a large number of interrelated activities, resource scheduling of people, products, and money, and information management and distribution of all documents.

Coordination systems focus on the integration and harmonious adjustment of individual work efforts toward the accomplishment of a larger goal of a group. These systems allow individuals to view their actions, as well as the relevant actions of others, within the context of the overall goal. They may trigger users' actions. Coordination systems are categorized by one of four types of models: form-oriented models, procedure-oriented models, conversation-oriented models, or communication-structure-oriented models. Of these, only the third type focuses on group augmentation, whereas the remaining three types focus on organization augmentation. Conversation-oriented models are based on the observation that people coordinate their activities through their conversation; they are based on "speech–act theory." Coordinator was such a system.

Form-oriented models focus on the routing of documents and forms in organizational procedures. They model organizational activities as fixed processes. Some systems tried to introduce more flexible process support. In Electronic Circulation Folders (ECF) by Karbe et al., exception handling is addressed through migration specifications that describe all the possible task migration routes in terms of steps to be carried out in processing organizational documents [67]. Some form-based models are called form-flow models; they model organizational activities as flows of forms through varieties of form converters that are triggered by varieties of events [68, 69].

Procedure-oriented models view organizational procedures as programmable processes. The development of process programs is a rigorous process consisting of specification, design, implementation, and testing/verification phases.

Communication-structure-oriented models describe organizational activities in terms of role relationships. In ITT, developed by Anatol Holt et al., a user's electronic work environment is composed of a set of centers; each center represents a function for which the user is responsible [70, 71]. Within the centers are roles that perform the work. Centers and roles have connections to other centers and roles, and the behavior of the connections is governed by the role scripts of the interacting roles.

Workflow-management software is a computer system that manages the flow of work among participants, according to a defined procedure consisting of a number of tasks. It coordinates user and system participants, together with the appropriate data resources, which may be accessible directly or off-line, to achieve defined objectives.

Concurrent engineering is another type of cooperative work used in industry [72]. It is defined as an attempt to optimize the design of a product and manufacturing process to achieve reduced lead times and improved quality and cost by the integration of design and manufacturing activities, and by maximizing parallelism in working practices. Many authors have shown that although there are great advantages to this strategy, it is also risky; some have pointed out that development and production costs are about 100 times as much as research costs. Consequently, because in the concurrent engineering paradigm there is a rapid commitment of resources to any project, a mistake can be expensive if it is not caught very early. If time is lost as a result of these mistakes, the effects can be severe.

Concurrent engineering requires that the old, functionally based department structures, in which the development of products was carried out sequentially, be replaced by product-based teams that combine people from all aspects of the product life cycle, including researchers, designers, engineers, and suppliers' representatives. It is a potential application field of group- and organization-augmentation media technologies.

Chapter 14 will give the architectural details on form-flow and workflow application frameworks based on IntelligentPad, and discuss their applications to concurrent engineering.

### 3.1.5 The Evolution of Social-Augmentation Media

Social augmentation is the most recent augmentation media concept. When we started our project in 1987, we could find only one example of social-augmentation media—Xanadu, proposed by Ted Nelson [11], a system concept that has been awaiting its implementation for 30 years. It is not just a hypertext system. It aims at a worldwide publishing repository. In Xanadu, users all over the world can easily access various documents published by institutes and people all over the world, easily quote any fragment of information from others' publications with automatic royalty arrangement by the system, and easily publish their writings, which may possibly include quotes from others without violating any law. Users of this system share neither decision-making nor performance-achievement goals, but they share the culture accumulated in the Xanadu repository.

During the last decade, we have been experiencing the incredibly rapid evolution of social-augmentation media, namely the WWW (World-Wide Web) [13] and its browser systems: NCSA Mosaic [14], Netscape Navigator, and Microsoft Internet Explorer. WWW is a system for creating and browsing distributed hypertexts. WWW hypertexts link machines around the globe, and contain links to files and newsgroups as well as to Telnet, Gopher, Archie, and ftp servers on the Internet. Within WWW, a document may contain links to other documents, parts of a document, files, Telnet sites, newsgroups, etc. The links can be local or to any machines on the Internet. These links are called URLs (universal resource locators). WWW documents are authored using the HyperText Markup Language (HTML) [73], a subset of SGML [74].

Until the launching of the NCSA Mosaic effort, WWW had primarily been developed by volunteers, since the original team's main concern was supporting high-energy physics research at CERN. The NSF has funded the NCSA Mosaic effort. Mosaic is an extended version of WWW that supports extensions such as support for formatted text with fonts, as well as embedded images, sound, video, and text/voice annotation. In 1995, Netscape Navigator, the further-extended commercial product, almost overtook Mosaic. Then, Microsoft released another browser—Internet Explorer.

HotJava is a Web browser that makes the Internet "come alive." HotJava builds on the Internet browsing techniques established by Mosaic and Netscape, and expands them by implementing the capability to add arbitrary behavior, which transforms static data into dynamic applications. Using HotJava, you can add applications that range from interactive science experiments in educational material to games and specialized shopping applications. HotJava provides a new way for users to access these applications that are written in Java programming language [75]. Software transparently migrates from a server to a client across the network.

Later, Netscape was extended to provide plug-in capability for Java application programs called applets. It is noteworthy that Java applets were originally intended to run only on Web pages at client sites, which is sometimes called "Web-top computing." They were not originally intended to run in local environments of client sites. The classes necessary to run Java objects on a Web page can be managed by the server providing this page. The server can send each client only those classes necessary to run these objects. When we want to run these objects outside the Web page together with local objects, the execution requires two different kinds of objects, i.e., those objects whose classes are defined in the server, and the others whose classes are defined locally. This execution requires the consistent merging of these two different sets of classes, causing the so-called class-migration problem. Though it is not impossible, the migration of Java objects across the network to local environments of client sites requires an additional class-migration management mechanism.

In 1994, IntelligentPad, a meme-media system developed at Hokkaido University, was provided with a meme-pool system using existing Web browser systems as catalogs of media components called pads [76]. This system allowed users to click an arbitrary pad image in such a catalog for downloading this pad into their local environments. In 1996, IntelligentPad was provided with a special Web browser pad that shows HTML files as Web pages, and furthermore allows us to embed arbitrary composite media objects in an arbitrary Web page for publishing through the Internet [77]. Client users opening this page can directly drag out such an embedded media object into their own environments and reuse it locally. This new meme-pool system is now used by Hitachi Software, one of the three providers of commercial IntelligentPad systems, for the free distribution of their sample composite applications through the Internet. These samples run on their shareware version of IntelligentPad, and can be easily decomposed and reused. Unlike HotJava, IntelligentPad, with one of these two meme-pool systems, supports the distribution of interactive multimedia documents, application tools, and services that end-users can easily decompose and reuse in combination with any other media objects composed in IntelligentPad environments.

Chapter 11 will detail the meme-pool architectures based on IntelligentPad. Chapter 12 will discuss the architectural details of how we can introduce business activities into meme pools to make them work as meme markets.

## 3.2 HISTORY AND EVOLUTION OF KNOWLEDGE MEDIA ARCHITECTURES

The first introduction of a paper media concept into a computer system was probably done by Ivan Sutherland in early 1960s. Sketch Pad used a media metaphor of a paper sheet on which users could directly draw pictures [78]. Then came NLS [9, 79] and AUGMENT [79] by Doug Engelbart, who developed and demonstrated, in late 1960s, most of the fundamental software and hardware components that constitute the user interfaces of current workstations. Then Alan Kay proposed Reactive Engine in 1969 [20], which was later renamed as Dynabook [21]. He presented a clear view of computers as media, or as meta-media. Then in 1970s, Xerox PARC developed personal workstations starting with Alto [22], leading to Star [80], and also object-oriented interactive languages such as Smalltalk [23] for the development of a direct-manipulation graphical user interface.

### 3.2.1 Compound-Document Architectures

The adoption of compound-document editing began in the early 1980s with desktop publishing (DTP), and has developed as shown in Figure 3.1. The Star workstation from Xerox is the most typical example [80]. Desktop publishing enabled us to layout various types of media on a single page. This encouraged the development of languages to control printers for various fonts and page layouts. The WYSIWYG (what you see is what you get) concept extended such languages to show print images on display screens. The exten-

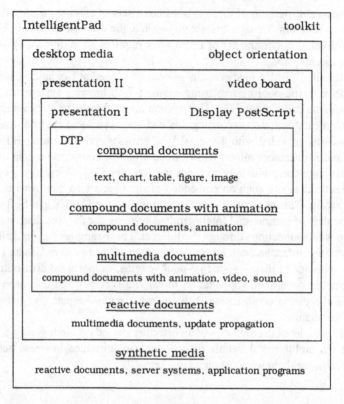

**Figure 3.1**   The development of compound-document editing systems.

sion was not only for the preview of documents, but also for the direct editing of the printed image of documents. Among these languages is a Display PostScript, which enabled us to program animations and to replace some figures in compound documents with animations. This extension is not only the extension of document presentation, but also the extension of document processing and management. Extended documents can be E-mailed, and can be managed by document file systems, both in the same way as conventional documents can be.

Around the mid 1980s, video boards enabled display windows to show video cuts (or clips) with sound, and enabled us to interact with video cuts. In early systems, these video cuts used analog video signals as input signals. The user interaction with such a video cut actually controlled the VCR that supplied its analog video signals. Then the progress of video compression technologies such as JPEG [81, 82] and MPEG [83, 84] allowed computer systems to digitally store video cuts together with sound, and to play them in real time. This progress further extended compound documents to include video cuts as embedded components. This extension opened a door to the multimedia desktop presentation (DTPR). These extended documents can be mailed and managed in the same way as conventional documents.

Next, people began to seek a way to handle different types of components in a uniform way. This encouraged object-oriented system design, which allowed us to embed programs in complex documents. Such documents became reactive media objects. The embedding of a program originated in such documents with command buttons; a click of such a button invoked a script program. Trillium system by Austin Henderson used such buttons to rapidly prototype a control panel for a photocopy machine [85]. In addition to these buttons, Trillium also used several types of display panels that could be pasted on the base panel. Such systems are sometimes called glue systems since they allow users to glue together visual components through direct manipulations.

Some other people further tried to embed display objects of various application programs into compound documents as components. Such an extension allows us to embed a spreadsheet or a drawing tool in a multimedia document as a component. Furthermore, some tried to handle these display objects in the same way that we handle documents. This allows us to paste a chart not only on a document, but also on any visual application tool such as a spreadsheet. Since we are dealing with application tools, we must consider how to define the application linkages. Two kinds of linkages have been proposed: object containment and object wiring. Object containment functionally relates an embedded component object to its base object. Object wiring adopts the direct setting of a graphical link to interrelate two different application objects. HP's NewWave was the first commercial attempt for object containment and wiring [40]. Around 1995, we saw two competitive commercial attempts to integrate compound document architectures with object containment and wiring—Microsoft's OLE (Object Linking and Embedding) [86] and CI (Component Integration) Lab's OpenDoc [87]. CI Lab was established by Apple, IBM, and Novel, but unfortunately soon closed.

### 3.2.2 Media Toolkit Systems

Object-oriented programming allows two different styles of programming. Class-hierarchy programming (or refinement-based programming) defines classes in their hierarchy to allow subclasses to inherit properties of their superclasses. Synthetic programming (or composition-based programming), on the other hand, defines a set of object instances to serve as primitive objects. Programmers can make a copy of any object instance to create a new independent instance with the same property as the original. They can combine several instances of different types to define a new composite object. Class-hierarchy programming originated in program development, whereas synthetic programming originated both in direct manipulation of visible objects, and in prototyping techniques based on the reusability paradigm.

Around the mid-1980s, the synthetic paradigm of object-oriented programming developed such GUI toolkit systems for window systems as Xt of MIT [34], Andrew Toolkit of CMU [88], OPEN LOOK Toolkit [36], and Motif Toolkit [35]. In the beginning of 1987, this trend encouraged our group to apply the toolkit approach to the design of reactive media, which led to our proposal for synthetic media, a media-embedding architecture. This resulted in the development of IntelligentPad as a media toolkit system [89]. Its visual components are called pads. Pads are inherently different from widgets. In any window toolkit, widgets and windows belong to different classes. No widget can serve as a window. Some widgets do not allow others to be pasted on them. Every pad, however, can work both as a window and as a component of a window. Whereas a pad always has its model component in itself as well as its display object, widgets might be considered as display objects without a model. Chapter 7 will describe the architectural details of IntelligentPad, and Chapter 5 will give the preliminaries on object-orientation and the MVC (model-view-controller) programming scheme. Chapter 4 will describe the architectural details of component integration.

Around the late 1980s, database management system (DBMS) providers began to provide each of their DBMS products with a form construction kit, a toolkit for users to construct a form interface to a database. A form interface is a visual interface that provides users with an office-form view of retrieved records. Among these form construction kits are Studio from Ontologics and GainMomentum from Sybase. Section 10.2 will show a form-interface architecture based on our knowledge-media architecture, IntelligentPad.

### 3.2.3 IntelligentPad as a Meme Media System

Toolkits and construction kits focus on easy and rapid construction of graphical user interfaces, but IntelligentPad focuses on easy decomposition of composed objects as well as on easy composition of objects. IntelligentPad was initially developed as a media toolkit system, and later, around 1992, extended to serve as a meme media system. The evolution of a meme pool requires that end-users can easily reedit and redistribute meme media objects. For this reason, meme media need to provide not only ease of composition, but also ease of decomposition.

Neither toolkits nor construction kits for rapid prototyping enable easy decomposition of what is already composed. In these systems, an application linkage between components is either textually described or graphically defined by directly setting a link between them. Some of these systems even request users to textually describe which components are geometrically embedded in what other component. This makes it difficult for us to extract a primitive or composite component from a composite object. If the relationships of the component to the remaining body are textually described, we have to understand these descriptions and modify them to remove the component. If the relationships of the component to be removed are defined by graphical links, we have to find all these links, understand them, and remove them without modifying the remaining web of links. IntelligentPad has solved this problem by restricting the use of functional linkages to only those between each component object and its container object. When we remove a primitive or composite pad from a whole composite pad, we need only to examine a single connection between this pad and its container pad to understand their relationships and both the generic function and interface of the component.

Chapter 7 will detail IntelligentPad architecture. Chapter 6 will give detailed considerations of why we have chosen its restricted functional linkage architecture for component integration.

## 3.3 MEME MEDIA AND THEIR APPLICATIONS

Meme media are defined as new computer media that uniformly handle multimedia documents and application tools; they are easy to edit, to distribute, and to manage. Meme media include the following:

1. Multimedia with intelligence: A meme media object may serve as a multimedia object with some internal intelligent mechanism with which users can interact through direct manipulation of this media object on a screen. Chapter 9 will describe multimedia application frameworks based on IntelligentPad.
2. Directly manipulable and reusable software components: Meme media components

can be used for easy and direct composition of application systems. Chapter 16 will discuss software engineering with IntelligentPad.

3. GUI construction kit: Meme media components can be used to construct a graphical user interface for any application system through direct manipulation of these building blocks. Chapters 9, 10, and 13 include such applications.

4. A framework for integrating documents and tools: Meme media allow users to interrelate varieties of documents and tools, not only through static definition of application linkages, but also through their dynamic definition, which provides an open integrated environment of documents and tools that can be flexibly interrelated. Chapter 9 will provide a detailed discussion.

5. Publication media for multimedia documents and tools: Meme media with multimedia documents and tools can be published on CD-ROMs or through the Internet. Published documents and tools can not only be viewed but also executed on different machines. Chapter 11, especially Section 11.6, will provide a detailed discussion.

6. Reeditable and redistributable media for intellectual resources: Meme media can carry any kind of intellectual resource that computers can handle. They can be used to exchange, distribute, and reedit these intellectual resources. Users can decompose a composite meme media object, and reuse some of its components to compose a new composite meme media object. Chapter 11 will give the architectural details on meme pool architectures. Chapter 12 will integrate them with the idea of superdistribution to propose a meme market system architecture.

In the following subsections we will list potential application areas of meme media.

### 3.3.1  Office-Information Systems

A variety of office-information tools can be represented as meme media objects. Examples include multimedia document editors, multimedia document filing systems, spreadsheets, business chart tools, databases, report generators, schedule managers, form converters, electronic mail systems, statistic analyzers, simulators, expert systems, presentation tools, and various transaction processing systems. These systems and the records they process can all be represented as meme media objects. A database management system, for example, may be represented as a meme media object that can understand query messages and control commands, and send out retrieved records. For example, a media object holding a single record is embedded in a database media object. This record media object interprets the message about the retrieved record, and holds each attribute value in its register. Text output media objects are pasted onto this media object. They are linked one-by-one to different registers of the record media object; these registers hold the values of different attributes. The database media object here represents a database, whereas the record media object with text output media objects represents a record. Users can make a copy of this record media object together with text output media objects. This copy holding a retrieved record can be temporarily pasted on a chart tool media object to input the record value to this chart tool. Users can dynamically interoperate varieties of documents and tools. Users may also a priori define a functional linkage between the record media object and the chart tool media object. In this case, each database access automatically changes the display of this chart tool.

Representation of varieties of documents, records, and tools in office-information processing as meme media objects enables us to integrate them not only through a priori designed functional linkages, but also through interactively specified interoperation linkages among documents and tools.

Meme media provide a framework for developing integrated tool systems like Xerox SIS's Analyst, but, unlike Analyst, meme media provide an open integration environment. Meme media also work as a form construction kit for databases, which requires the development of a database media object specially designed for each specific database management system. Such a meme media object that works as a proxy of some external object like a database management system is called a proxy meme media object. Office-information systems are sometimes modeled by a set of form flows and form conversion processes. This model is called a form-flow model. Meme media can easily represent forms and form conversion tools. They can also easily represent form flows as application linkages among form conversion tools. Therefore, meme media can provide a development framework for form flow systems.

The IntelligentPad system is already used as an open integrated business-tool system and a form-construction kit for databases. Furthermore, our group developed a framework on IntelligentPad for form-flow systems. A commercial version of IntelligentPad was also used to integrate an interactive multimedia catalog of automobiles at distributed sales offices with the central database for planning production and shipping. The customer's interactive selection of models, colors, and optional equipment is directly sent to the central database in order for the production line to immediately respond to this new order.

Chapters 9 and 10 will, respectively, describe multimedia application frameworks and database application frameworks based on IntelligentPad. Chapter 14 will discuss form-flow and workflow frameworks. Section 17.2 will describe a PIM (personal information management) application of IntelligentPad.

### 3.3.2   Scientific Publication

A cut of a film that is removed before it is shown or broadcast is called an out-take. Making a film results in lots of out-takes. Most are removed not because of their quality, but because of time and length restrictions. We have the same situation in scientific publication. Lots of work and data become out-takes. Furthermore, we have no means to publish research papers with large quantities of related data, related video with sound, or software programs developed for these studies. Researchers have been daily repeating the same efforts that others have already made.

The use of meme media will enable scientists to publish their reports together with these out-takes, and related data, movies, and software tools. A formula in a document can be represented as an embedded meme media object, which may contain a program to evaluate this formula. A chart in a document can be also an embedded meme media object that contains a large quantity of raw data. Readers of a document can make a copy of such meme media objects representing a formula or a chart, and make them interoperate with their personal tools that are also represented as meme media objects. You may drag and drop such a formula media object onto your own special chart tool to obtain a chart representation. Or you may drag and drop a chart media object, embedded in some scientific paper, onto your polynomial approximation tool to obtain an approximate polynomial representation of the data in this chart.

Furthermore, if these publications are supported by a marketplace implemented on the

Internet so that users can freely publish their work and access anyone else's, meme media will allow people to recombine others' published tools to create new tools. This marketplace, working as a meme pool for meme media objects, will accelerate the evolution of tools and, furthermore, the development of each scientific area. First, each scientific area will form a meme pool. Then, people will start to exchange documents and tools across different areas. This will bring about a punctuated equilibrium, in which, according to a hypothesis of population genetics, new species appear and displace related species much more rapidly than would be predicted. Formation of interdisciplinary research areas will be much accelerated by the use of meme media.

Chapter 11 will provide the details on meme pool architectures. Section 11.6 will discuss the application of meme media to scientific publications.

### 3.3.3  Education Tools

Meme media allow each multimedia component to include some internal intelligent mechanism. Intelligent multimedia components can react to user operations and/or cooperate with other intelligent multimedia components or tool components. Meme media can provide such intelligent multimedia components with various tools and components, which makes it much easier for users to develop interactive multimedia systems integrated with simulation and analysis tools, or to provide construction kits for end-users to develop such systems by themselves. These features of meme media make them suitable for educational applications.

Meme media can provide all the following facilities necessary for education tools:

1. Interactivity with multimedia documents
2. Dynamic linkage among experimental data, simulation tools, and analysis tools
3. Provision of database management functions for a large number of multimedia documents and data
4. Guiding facilities based on student modeling
5. Microworlds with interoperable objects and tools that users can directly play with
6. Building blocks for constructing interactive objects and tools in microworlds

A microworld is a computer-aided instruction (CAI) system with directly manipulable interactive objects and tools. These objects and tools constitute a virtual world in which the user can play with these objects and tools through direct manipulations to learn the subject of this world through his or her experience. This type of CAI systems was first proposed by Seymour Papert [90]. Meme media enable us to publish education systems with some or all of the facilities mentioned above either on CD-ROMs or through the Internet. Networked multimedia service functions that we will describe next allow the dynamic downloading of documents and tools from remote servers to a user's local environment, and allow some of these tools to cooperate in real time with some functions of remote servers. Remote learning and remote teaching systems represent applications of these functions.

Takafumi Noguchi at Kushiro Technical Collage has used IntelligentPad to develop various CAI systems with microworld construction kits. These systems include not only interactive multimedia documents, but also interoperable experiment tools, simulation tools, and analysis tools. His target areas include basic mathematics, basic mechanics, and basic electronic circuit theory. Subsection 17.3.2 will provide details of his systems and application frameworks. A group of linguists teaching Japanese to foreign college students organized a research group in 1995 to develop CAI systems using IntelligentPad; Shin Nitoguri of Tokyou Gakugei University and Yoshiaki Yanagisawa at The National Language Research Institute are the leaders of this group. Subsection 17.3.1 will descibe their systems and application frameworks.

### 3.3.4  Networked Multimedia Systems

Meme media can provide a special media object working as a URL anchor button; when clicked, it issues a URL to retrieve a file from a remote server. Such a button may be made transparent, and defined to be intelligent enough to change its size and location with time on another meme media. Pasted on a movie media object, such a button can be instructed to always cover a specific object appearing in the movie. This transparent rectangular button would then always minimally cover this object, and would define this moving area as a hot spot. The size and location of such a button can be specified only in certain sample frames of the movie. The changes between these sample frames are interpolated. This framework, then, enables us to develop a networked "hypermovie" system. A hypermovie is a hypermedia using video. Any objects in movies can be specified to work as anchors that link to other movies. These links may point to local objects or remote objects in remote servers. This configuration may also work with video-on-demand systems, which can be applied to a variety of networked video services.

URLs of such anchors may not necessarily point to other movies; they may point to any meme-media objects, including documents and tools. Among the most typical applications are networked museum services and networked library services, in which users can easily navigate through a large remote library of video movies, multimedia documents, and interoperable tools, just by accessing them through their computers. Applications also include interactive movie guide systems for cable TV programs.

Section 9.3 will give the details of the hypermovie framework. Section 11.4 will show how to extend hypermovie links to jump across networks.

### 3.3.5  Geographic Information Systems

Geographical information systems (GISs) deal with interactive maps, their multiple-layer configurations, varieties of interactive objects on these maps, and varieties of viewers of these maps, all of which can be represented as meme media objects. Interactive maps can utilize the interactivity of meme media. Their multiple-layer configuration can be implemented by the overlay of meme media objects and the application linkage mechanisms among them. Interactive objects can be represented as anchors pointing to documents or tools. Viewers of the maps can be also meme media objects that interoperate with interactive maps. The meme media representation of maps also simplifies their interoperation with databases.

Nigel Waters, a professor in the Department of Geography, University of Calgary, pointed out the potential application of IntelligentPad to GIS [91]. His article envisaged a situation where a map display, a traffic simulation model, a video image of an intersection, and a display in graph form are all represented as mutually interacting pads. It pointed out that a system with these pads would not only be a great pedagogical device, but would also be invaluable for planning.

Section 10.6 will give the architectural details of a GIS based on IntelligentPad, and descibe its applications to urban design systems.

### 3.3.6 Design Applications

Designers use a variety of media to externalize their initial design ideas, and to play with them directly, using their hands and eyes for further brainstorming and improvement. Designers of shapes or structures can use a variety of physical materials for their modeling. Designers of physical objects can use either physical models or simulation models for further brainstorming and improvement.

Today, designers are confronted with the design of information [92]: how to present, access, and process varieties of information and knowledge. We do not have sufficient methodologies or notations for this kind of design. For example, we do not have any good general notation or methodology to describe multiple concurrent spatiotemporal motions. In making animated films, for example, artists use lots of sketches. Rough story ideas are often worked out in thumbnail sketches. Group discussion use a storyboard, a large board on which are pinned sketches telling a story in comic strip fashion. Detail design is summarized in a continuity script, which describes each scene in a whole sequence with a sketch and a script [93]. In addition to these, they use layout drawings, and even floor plan drawings. They draw lots of sketches for analysis and suggestion of structures, motions, and colors for each character. A similar situation also holds for live-action films and stage performances.

Edward Tufte has collected, in his three famous books [94–96], varieties of methods used for envisioning information. However, these do not include any good general notation or methodology to describe multiple concurrent spatiotemporal motions. Only a few notational methods are known for such description. One is the musical score; another example is the "labanotation" in choreography [97].

This lack of notation and methodology seriously limit designers' capabilities. Designers have to figure out the overall behavior in their own minds. This is equivalent to the situation of communicating with others without a sufficiently large vocabulary, or of trying to figure out mechanical motion without using mechanical equations and their calculus rules. Designers of information require meme media objects that will enable them to easily prototype their design ideas, and to play with them for the development of additional ideas. Meme media, since they are interoperable, also allow designers to keep their ideas in active forms, and to exchange their active ideas with others.

Subsection 17.5.5 will describe a trial by Takeshi Sunaga of Tama Art Collage of using IntelligentPad as an information design tool.

Meme media might be used to develop CAD systems for the design of physical functional objects. They may also play a significant role for those dynamic physical objects whose design cannot be independent from the understanding and design of their spatiotemporal behaviors.

Subsection 17.5.1 will describe the potential of IntelligentPad and its 3D extension, IntelligentBox, in CAD/CAM applications.

### 3.3.7 DIY Software for Client Systems

Software tools and their components can be also represented as meme media objects.

Some of these components may provide just their logical functions; they are represented as blank sheets on the display screen. They exist on the screen to allow users to directly manipulate them. Meme media representation of these components enables users not only to combine them easily for the composition of new tools, but also to decompose composite tools in order to reuse some of their components. Sample compositions for typical applications work as "patterns" that instruct users how to construct similar tools by themselves. Meme media enable users to distribute and exchange such patterns among themselves.

IntelligentPad was once considered by the mass media as DIY (do it yourself) software, i.e., a new CASE (computer-aided software engineering) tool, that allows us to combine modules for the composition of arbitrary applications as easily as combining Lego blocks for constructing animals, vehicles, and buildings [98].

Meme media representation is not suitable for defining server programs, such as database management systems and numerical simulators, as compositions with primitive components. Users use these server systems as they are through some client applications. Server programs are atomic components in users' environments. Therefore, meme media represent each server system as an atomic meme media object. Client applications, on the other hand, need to be customizable to satisfy varying requirements and tastes of users; they must consist of various components for the customization of functions and user interfaces. Meme media representation is suitable for these components.

The commercially available versions of IntelligentPad have been extensively used by system engineers to develop custom-made client applications. The most important phase in such development is the customer interview, which is necessary to help customers clarify their image about the system's appearance and usability. Conventionally, system engineers have to develop the GUI part of a system on order before implementing its internal mechanism, so that the customer is able to clarify his or her image of the system and provide appropriate comments on the candidate design. The actual development of applications does not start before the completion of such interviews. IntelligentPad has changed this process; instead of using GUI components to develop only the GUI part, system engineers can directly combine meme media components to compose a candidate implementation of the client application system. They can overlap the actual system-development process with the customer-interview phase. This new concurrent engineering method remarkably shortens development time. Furthermore, this approach allows customers to further modify the developed system by themselves. Chapter 16 will focus on software engineering with IntelligentPad.

One frequently mentioned problem of software component systems is the migration of legacy systems [99]. A legacy system means an already existing system developed independently from the component systems and already used by many users. Any legacy system with no GUI can be easily transported into a meme media environment by just developing a special meme media object that works as a proxy for this system. Legacy systems with their own GUI are, however, very difficult to transport into a meme media environment. IntelligentPad Consortium established a mutual membership with CI Labs in 1995 to partially solve this problem. Our plan was to develop a linkage mechanism between IntelligentPad and OpenDoc, and to make legacy systems based on OpenDoc interoperate with knowledge media objects in IntelligentPad. This plan was unfortunately not realized due to the sudden closing of CI Labs. Fujitsu has developed a bilateral conversion tool between ActiveX controls and pads for the same purpose. Takeshi Mori et al. at NEC developed a special ActiveX control that works as a run-time environment for IntelligentPad with which pads can be executed and manipulated. Using this ActiveX control, and assuming that Internet Explorer is used as a Web browser, we can publish pads with their run-time environment by embedding this environment in arbitrary Web pages.

Section 6.7 will discuss in detail the legacy-system migration problem in general. Section 8.6 will show how to migrate legacy systems in the IntelligentPad architecture.

## 3.4  WEB TECHNOLOGIES AND MEME MEDIA

Since 1996, we have seen significant progress in Web technologies. The client-side scripting technologies such as JavaScript [100] and VBScript (Visual Basic Script) [101] introduced dynamic behaviors into Web pages. The server-side scripting technologies such as JSP (Java Server Pages) [102], ASP (Active Server Pages) [103], and Java Servelets [104], as well as CGI (Common Gateway Interface) [105] and its script languages like Perl [106], introduced invocations of Web server programs that update Web pages. J2EE (Java2 Enterprise Edition) [107] introduced component-based application development utilizing components running on different application servers distributed over intranetworks, and has enabled us to embed services defined by the orchestration of distributed application components, including database servers. Web services [108] and SOAP technologies [109] allowed service providers to publish their services as Web services, service brokers to provide inquiry services about Web services, and service requesters to ask service brokers for the retrieval of desired Web services and to invoke the found Web services. Web services and SOAP technologies allowed us to embed a large variety of public Web services and/or their compositions in a Web page.

These Web technologies are tools for Web page designers to compose a complicated application by simply combining public Web services, and making the composed service available on a Web page. Web page designers have to write HTML definitions accessing Web services through SOAP proxies. These tools are definitely not for Web readers. Application of meme media technologies to Web technologies will allow Web readers to extract any components of any Web pages with embedded tools and services, to paste these extracted pads together to combine their functions, to embed the composed pad into a new Web page, and to publish this page not only for their private use but also for others' use. The reediting of Web pages with tools and services using meme media technologies does not require Web readers to rewrite HTML definitions using the knowledge of Web services and SOAP.

### 3.4.1  Open Hypermedia Systems

Up to now, hypermedia research groups have mainly focused their efforts on linking services among intellectual resources for navigation and interoperability. They basically assumed that hypermedia contents were just viewed without making copies, reediting, or redistributing them among people. Over the last several years, the Open Hypermedia Working Group (OHSWG) has been working on a standard protocol to allow interoperability across a range of application software components. The group first focused on the separation of link services from document structures, which enables different hypermedia systems to interoperate with each other, and client applications to create, edit, and activate links that are managed in separate link databases [110]. Microcosm [111] and Multicard

[112] are examples that work as reference systems of link servers. The hypertext community also focused on the interoperability with database systems, which introduced higher-level functionality: for example, HyperBase [113] on a relational foundation, and HBI [114] on a semantic platform. The interoperability with databases also led to the idea of separating component storage, run time, and document content issues. The Dexter Hypertext Reference Model [115] proposed a layered architecture to separate them. As an alternative to such a layered architecture, the open hypertext community collaboratively developed a standard protocol, OHP [116], for different interdependent services to interoperate with each other. These architectures worked as a basis to apply link services to the Web [117]. HyperDisco [118] and Chimera [119] proposed such interoperable service models, which were later applied to the Web [120, 121].

The OHSWG approach was based on the following principles: the separation of link services and the standardization of a navigational and/or functional linking protocol among different applications and services. The standard protocol may rely on either API libraries or an on-the-wire communication model using such a standard transport medium as a socket. The group is further expanding the linking service functionality by introducing collaborative spatial structures [122], computational aspects, or dynamically defined abstract communication channels [123]. Recently, an Israeli venture company, BrowseUp, developed an annotation server and a new browser that allow us to select any portion of any Web page, and to make an annotation on it in a public and/or local file. BrowseUp allows us to use legacy document systems like Word and Excel to make local annotation files.

Meme media research that has been conducted independently from the open hypertext community has been focused on the replication, reediting, and redistribution of intellectual resources. To achieve this goal, our group adopted a visual wrapper architecture. Any component, whether it is an application or a service, small or large, is wrapped by a visual wrapper with direct manipulability and a standard interface mechanism. These wrappers work as media to carry different types of intellectual resources. A media object denotes an intellectual resource wrapped by such a standard wrapper. Our wrapper architecture allows users to define a composite media object by combining primitive media objects. Composite media objects allow further recombination. Users can exchange those composite media objects through the Internet.

Application of meme media technologies to OHS technologies simply means that objects in the latter framework are wrapped by meme media wrappers, which will introduce meme media features to those objects without losing any of their OHS features.

### 3.4.2   Client-Side Web Programs and XML

The evolution of the Web has disseminated the use of HTML for representing compound documents with embedded application programs to interact with users. These embedded application programs are called Web programs. Some Web programs run locally on the Web browser, namely, in the client environment, whereas others invoke server programs in or through Web servers. The former Web programs are called client-side Web programs; the latter ones are called server-side Web programs.

Client-side Web programs are defined either as script programs or as Java applets. They can be embedded in HTML texts. Script programs are written in interpreter languages such as JavaScript [100] and VBScript [101], whereas Java applets are written in Java, and assume that the client platform installs JavaVM (Java Virtual Machine) [124].

Although the client-side Web programming in HTML texts has enabled us to define Web pages with dynamically interacting objects, HTML does not allow script programs to dynamically move an embedded component on a Web page. DHTML (Dynamic HTML) [125] has solved this problem by separating the style definition of each Web page as a style sheet. This allows us to manipulate the Web page style in script programs, which enables us to dynamically move components on Web pages. In 1998, W3C (WWW Consortium) proposed DOM (Document Object Model) [126, 127] to standardize the operations on the structure and components of HTML documents, which standardized the specification of DHTML between two de facto browsers, i.e., Netscape Navigator and Internet Explorer. Style sheets are useful not only to manipulate styles in script programs, but also to apply the same style to more than one Web page. W3C proposed CSS1 (Cascading Style Sheets Level 1) in 1996 and CSS2 in 1998 [128] as the standard specification of style sheets. An HTML file may either embed a style sheet in its header part, specify a style sheet in a tag to which you apply this style sheet, or span a reference link, using a <link> tag, to an independent style sheet file.

The separation of style sheets from HTML documents, together with the introduction of DOM, made people focus on the logical structure of Web page content. HTML does not allow us to identify logical document components such as the title, the list of authors, chapters, paragraphs, and each item in each list. XML (eXtensible Markup Language) has been developed since 1996 to solve this problem, and was released as XML1.0 in 1998 [129]. XML describes the logical structure of documents, whereas XSL (eXtensible Style sheet Language) describes the document styles [130]. XML allows us to use tags with user-defined names to identify logical components of documents. Each component to articulate is identified in the textual definition of the document by enclosing this part with a begin-tag <tag-name> and an end-tag </tag-name>. XML and HTML are both offsprings of SGML (Standard Generalized Markup Language) [131]. HTML discarded the articulation of logical document components and introduced hyperlink capabilities. XML separated the style definition as an independent file, simplified SGML functions, and introduced hyperlink capabilities. To render an XML file using a XSL style sheet file on a browser, we use XSLT (XSL Transformations) to convert this XML file to an HTML file [132]. HTML was also extended to cope with XML capabilities and to merge the advantages of these two languages, which defined XHTML (eXtensible HTML) [133].

An XML document consists of the XML declaration part, the DTD (document type definition) if any, and the XML instance, i.e., the document definition body. The XML declaration part specifies the XML version and character codes. The DTD defines the schema, i.e., the skeleton structure, of the XML document. It specifies the hierarchical structure among tag names to be used in the XML instance. The DTD may be specified as an independent file. In such a case, we call it an external subset. Otherwise, we call the DTD an internal subset. An external subset can be shared by more than one XML document. We call XML documents with DTDs valid XML documents, and those without DTDs well-formed XML documents. Tagged components can be nested in XML documents. Each component in an XML document can be uniquely identified by a concatenation of tag names of all the components including the specified component from the outmost one to the inmost one. We call this concatenation the XPath [134] of the component. When you want to merge two XML documents into a single one, their tag names may cause conflicts, i.e., the same name may be used to identify different components. To solve this problem, XML enables us to define an independent name space for each document. Tags in a merged context can be uniquely identified using name space names as their prefixes.

Some Web page authoring tools such as Dreamweaver [135] enable users to define and embed JavaScript programs without knowing the JavaScript grammar. Java applets are small application programs written in Java. You may embed a Java applet in your Web page specifying a Java applet file name by enclosing it with an HTML tag, <applet code>. When this HTML file is downloaded, the embedded Java applet is also downloaded from a Web server, and executed by the local JavaVM.

Client-side Web programs define Web documents with embedded animation graphics and/or visual tools running on the client computer, but without any embedded services provided by remote servers.

From 1994 to 1998, we introduced different HTMLViewerPads by wrapping three different browsers—Mosaic, Netscape Navigator, and Internet Explorer—with pad wrappers [136]. Each of them works as a pad with the full functionality of each wrapped browser. Sections 11.1 to 11.7 will describe in detail the architectures of these browser pads. Section 11.5 describes a browser pad that enables you to publish a Web page with embedded pads, and allows others to drag them out for reuse while browsing this page [137]. Section 11.7 shows how IntelligentPad technology enables us to annotate Web pages through a browser pad [138]. Sections 11.9 and 11.10 illustrate how meme media technologies enables us to extract some portions of Web pages, including application tools and services, paste them together with slot connections to compose a new compound document, and publish it on the WWW so that other people can browse it using a legacy Web browser. Section 11.9.4 shows how we can use XML to define a pad. Section 11.10 describes how the use of JavaScript for the description of slot connections among pads defined in HTML will define composite pads that we can play on legacy browsers.

### 3.4.3  Server-Side Web Programs

A server-side Web program executes the processing requested by a client on a server machine. It may interoperate with other servers such as database servers to perform advanced services such as querying a database.

Server-side Web programs can be classified into two different types. The first type makes the Web server invoke an external program through, for example, a CGI (common gateway interface) [105]. The second type executes programs using extended functions installed in the Web server. CGI is an interface mechanism for a Web server to invoke a server-side program, and to return the processing result to the client. A CGI program denotes a program used in CGI. CGI programs are written in script languages such as Perl [106] or other development languages. CGI, however, invokes a new process whenever it is accessed by a client. It may generate a lot of processes, consuming a lot of resources, which may significantly lower the system performance. The second type of server-side Web program that utilizes extended functions installed in a Web server includes Web applications using either Java servelets [104] or such server-side scripting technologies as ASP (Active Server Pages) [103] and JSP (Java Server Pages) [102].

A Web application using the JSP technology or a Java servelet executes the processing in a run time environment called a container. A Web application using the ASP technology runs ASPs in a run time environment similar to a container. This environment for ASPs is called an IIS (Internet information server). In such a Web application, each request from a client does not invoke a new process, but creates only a new thread in the same container, namely, in the same process space, to process this request. This multithread processing reduces resource consumption and also improves performance, since the container becomes resident once the Web application is invoked.

JSP programs are converted to Java servelets to be executed. A Java servelet is an independent program file, but a JSP program is inserted in an HTML file using a JSP tag, <% .. %>. A Java servelet needs to explicitly rewrite and print an HTML file to output a new page, but a JSP program is embedded in an HTML file as an element, which simplifies the definition of an output page.

To utilize a server-side Web application from a Web page, you may use a form and/or a link to a CGI program. To access a database Web site, you may enter a keyword in a text box form, and click the start button to invoke the server-side database retrieval program.

More than one client may access a single Web server. A sequence of requests from the same client may be intermingled with other request sequences from different clients. Cookie [139] is a technology for a Web server to identify consecutive requests from the same client. A Web page with a Cookie, when accessed, creates a file in the client computer to store the access date and time and the user-identifying information. When the same Web site is accessed, the Web browser searches for the Cookie file corresponding to this Web site, reads this Cookie if it is found, and sends the read-out information to the Web server. The Web server may use this information to perform the appropriate service for the requesting client.

Java servelets can manage each session with each client. Each servelet container assigns different IDs to different clients. When accessed by a client, each servelet container creates a new object for the session with this Web browser, and assigns a new ID to this browser. A Web page using a Java servelet, when accessed, creates a Cookie storing a new session ID, and stores it as a client file. Requests from different clients may invoke the same servelet, which receive different session IDs as Cookie values from different clients. Using these session IDs, each servelet can return the result to the requesting client.

Server-side Web programs are capable of defining Web documents with embedded services provided by remote servers. These embedded services provide input forms in Web pages for users to input data. An output from such a server is returned to the client as a Web page. ASP and JSP allow us to define Web documents with embedded animation graphics and/or tools running not on the client computers, but on the servers. These embedded components are secure in the sense that they are executed on the server side.

We used server-side Web programming technologies to introduce proxy pads that work as proxies of remote servers such as database servers [140]. Chapter 10 will show how database proxy pads will play essential roles in the database-form interface framework in the meme media architecture. Section 18.6 will describe the 3D extension of our database access framework using database proxy boxes, and propose a component-based database visualization and materialization framework [141].

## 3.5 SUMMARY

Augmentation media on computers can be classified into four categories based on the targets of augmentation; they are personal-augmentation media, group-augmentation media, organization-augmentation media, and social-augmentation media. They have been developed in this order. Knowledge media have expanded the target of augmentation from groups and organizations to communities or societies. Knowledge media with 2D representation have developed compound document architectures. WWW and its browsers work as knowledge media systems. Current Web technologies, however, do not provide direct manipulation operations for reediting and redistributing knowledge resources. When provided with such direct manipulation operations, knowledge media will work as meme media.

When applied to Web content, meme media technologies make the WWW work as a meme pool, wherein people can publish their intellectual resources as Web pages, access some Web pages to extract some of their portions as meme media objects through drag-and-drop operations, visually combine these meme media objects together with other meme media objects to compose new intellectual resources, and publish these resources again as Web pages. Our framework will open a new vista in the circulation and reuse of knowledge represented as multimedia documents, application programs, services, and/or compositions made from them. Meme media technologies provide Web content with reediting and redistributing functions, which are orthogonal to the functions that the rapidly growing Web technologies are focusing on to expand.

# REFERENCES

1. M. McLuhan. *Understanding Media, The Extensions of Man.* McGraw-Hill, New York, 1964.

2. M. von Wodtke. *Mind Over Media: Creative Thinking Skills for Electronic Media.* McGraw-Hill, New York, 1993.

3. R. Johansen. *Groupware: Computer Support for Business Teams.* Free Press, New York, 1988.

4. S. Khoshafian and M. Buckiewicz. *Introduction to Groupware, Workflow, and Workgroup Computing.* Wiley, New York, 1995.

5. W. H. Davidow and M. S. Malone. *The Virtual Corporation: Structuring and Revitalizing the Corporation for the 21st Century.* Harper-Collins, New York, 1993.

6. Y. Jyachandra. *Re-Engineering the Networked Enterprise.* McGraw-Hill, New York, 1994.

7. C. J. Petrie, Jr. (ed.). *Enterprise Integration Modeling.* MIT Press, Cambridge, MA, 1992.

8. V. Bush. As We May Think. *Atlantic Monthly, 176*(1): 101–108, 1945.

9. D. C. Engelbart. A conceptual framework for the augmentation of man's intellect. In P. W. Howerton and D. C. Weeks (eds.), *Vistas in Information Handling: I. The Augmentation of Man's Intellect by Machine.* Spartan Books, Washington, DC, pp. 1–29, 1963.

10. T. H. Nelson. A file structure for the complex, the changing, and the intermediate. In *Proceedings of the ACM National Conference,* pp. 84–100, 1965.

11. T. H. Nelson. *Literary Machines. Edition87. 1.* (self-published), 1987.

12. A. van Dam. Hypertext '87 keynote address. *CACM 31*(7): 887–895, 1988.

13. T. Berners-Lee, R. Cailliau, N. Pellow, and A. Secret. The World-Wide Web Initiative. In *Proceedings INET'93,* 1993.

14. M. Andreessen. *MCSA Mosaic Technical Summary.* NCSA Mosaic Technical Summary 2.1, 1993.

15. N. Yankelovich, N. Meyrowitz, and A. van Dam. Reading and writing the electronic book. *IEEE Computer, 18*(10): 15–30, 1985.

16. N. Yankelovich, B. J. Haan, N. K. Meyrowitz, and S. M. Drucker. Intermedia: The concept and the construction of a seamless information environment. *IEEE Computer, 21*(1): 81–96, 1988.

17. N. Yankelovich, G. P. Landow, and D. Cody. Creating Hypermedia Materials for English literature students. *ACM SIGCUE Outlook, 19*(3–4): 12–25, 1987.

18. C. K. Robertson, D. McCracken, and A. Newell. The ZOG approach to man–machine commu-

nication. *Intl. J. Man–Machine Studies, 14:* 461–488, 1981.

19. F. G. Halasz. Reflections on NoteCards: Seven issues for the next generation of hypermedia systems. *CACM, 31*(7): 836–852, 1988.

20. A. C. Kay. *The Reactive Engine.* Ph. D. thesis, University of Utah, 1969.

21. A. C. Kay and A. Goldberg. Personal dynamic media. *IEEE Computer, 10*(3), 1977.

22. C. P. Thacker et al. Alto: A personal computer. In Siewiorek et al. (eds.), *Computer Structures: Principles and Examples,* Chapter 33, McGraw-Hill, New York, 1982.

23. A. Goldberg and A. C. Kay (eds.). *Smalltalk-72 Instruction Manual.* Xerox Palo Alto Research Center, Techniocal Report No. SSL 76-6, March 1976.

24. N. Negroponte. Media room. In *Proceedings of the Society for Information Display. 22*(2): 109–113, 1981

25. R. Bolt. Put-that-there: Voice and gesture at the graphics interface. *ACM Computer Graphics, 14*(3): 262–270, 1980.

26. C. F. Herot. Spatial Management of Data. *ACM Transactions on Database Systems. 5*(4): 493–514, 1980.

27. A. Lippman, Movie-maps: An application of the optical videodisc to computer graphics. *Computer Graphics, 14*(3): 32–42, 1980.

28. D. Backer. Prototype for the electronic book. In M. Greenberger (ed.), *Media for a Technological Future—Electronic Publishing Plus.* Knowledge Industry Publications, Washington, DC, 1985.

29. S. Brand. *The Media Lab.* Viking Penguin, New York, 1987.

30. R. Akscyn, D. L. McCracken, and E. Yoder. KMS: A distributed hypertext for sharing knowledge in organizations. *CACM, 31*(7): 820–835, 1988.

31. P. J. Brown. Turning ideas into products: The guide system. In *Proceedings of ACM Hypertext'87,* pp. 33–40, 1987.

32. F. Halasz, T. P. Moran, and R. H. Trigg. NoteCards in a nutshell. In *Proceedings of ACM CHI+GI'87,* pp. 45–52, 1987.

33. B. Arons, C. Binding, K. A. Lantz, and C. Schmandt. The VOX Audio Server. In *Proceedings of IEEE 2nd International. Workshop in Multimedia Communications,* 1989.

34. P. Asente, and R. Swick. *The X Window System Toolkit.* Digital Press, Bedford, MA, 1990.

35. D. A. Young. *The X Window System Programing and Applications with Xt: OSF/Motif Edition.* Prentice-Hall, Englewood Cliffs, NJ, 1990.

36. D. A. Young and J. A. Pew. *The X Window System Programing and Applications with Xt: OPEN LOOK Edition.* Prentice-Hall, Englewood Cliffs, NJ, 1992.

37. D. Heller. *Xview Programming Manual.* O'Reilly & Associates, Sebastopol, CA, 1991

38. J. Gosling, D. S. H. Rosenthal, and M. J. Arden. *NeWS Book: An Introduction to the Network/Extensible Window System.* Springer-Verlag, New York, 1989.

39. NeXT. *NextStep Environment: Concepts.* NeXT, Inc.

40. Hewlett-Packard. *HP NewWave Environment General Information Manual.* Hewlett-Packard, Cupertino, CA, 1988.

41. Borland. *ObjectWindows for C++: User's Guide.* Borland, Scotts Valley, CA, 1991.

42. D. A. Wilson, L. S. Rosenstein, and D. Shafer. *C++ Programming with MacApp.* Addison-Wesley, Reading MA, 1990.

43. P. Wilson. *Computer Supported Cooperative Work: An Introduction.* Intellect, Oxford, UK 1991.

44. I. Greif (ed.). *Computer-Supported Cooperative Work: A Book of Readings.* Morgan Kaufmann, San Mateo, CA, 1988.

45. C. A. Ellis, S. J. Gibbs, G. L. Rein. Computer groupware: Some issues and experiences,

*CACM 34*(1):38–58, 1991.

46. T. Rodden. A survey of CSCW systems. *Interacting with Computers. 3:* 319–353, 1991.

47. T. Winograd. A language/action perspective on the design of cooperative work. In *Proceedings of CSCW'86,* pp. 203–220, 1986.

48. F. De Cindio, G. De Michelis, C. Simone, R. Vassalo, and A. M. Zanaboni. CHAOS as coordination technology. In *Proceedings of CSCW'86,* pp. 325–342, 1986.

49. T. Kreifelts and G. Woetzel. Distribution and error handling in an office procedure system. In *Proc. IFIP WG 8.4 Working Conference on Office Systems Methods and Tools,* pp. 197–208, 1986.

50. J. Bowers and J. Churcher. Local and global structuring of computer mediated communication: Developing linguistic perspectives on CSCW in COSMOS, In *Proceedings of CSCW'88,* pp. 125–139, 1988.

51. T. Danielsen, A. Patel, R. Speth, U. Pankoke-Babatz, W. Prinz, P. A. Pays, and K. Smaaland. The AMIGO project—Advanced group communication model for computer-based communications environment. In *Proceedings of CSCW'86,* pp. 115–142, 1986.

52. T. W. Malone, K. R. Grant, and F. A. Turbak. The information lens: An intelligent system for information sharing in organizations. In *Proceedings of CHI'86 Conference on Human Factors in Computing Systems,* 1986.

53. A. Shepherd, N. Mayer, and A. Kuchinsky. Strudel—An extensible electronic conversation toolkit. In *Proceedings of CSCW'90,* pp. 93–104, 1990.

54. J. Hogg. IntelligentMessage system. In D. Tsichritzis (ed.), *Office Automation.* Springer-Verlag, New York, pp. 113–133, 1985.

55. S. R. Hiltz and M. Turoff. *The Network Nation: Human Communication via Computer,* Addison-Wesley, Boston, MA, 1978.

56. I. Greif and S. Sarin. Data sharing in group Work. In I. Greif (ed.), *Computer-Supported Cooperative Work: A Book of Readings,* Morgan Kaufmann, San Mateo, CA, pp. 477–508, 1988.

57. M. Stefik, D. G. Bobrow, G. Foster, S. Lanning, and D. Tatar. WYSIWIS revisited: Early experiences with multiuser interfaces. *ACM Transactions on Office Information Systems, 5*(2): 147–167, 1987.

58. S. Gale. Desktop video conferencing: technical advances and evaluation issues. *Computer Communications, 15:* 517–526, 1992.

59. M. Stefik, G. Foster, D. G. Bobrow, K. Kahn, S. Lanning, and L. Suchman. Beyond the chalkboard: Computer support for collaboration and problem solving in meetings. *CACM, 30*(1): 32–47, 1987.

60. T. Crowley, P. Milazzo, E. Baker, H. Forsdick, and R. Tomlinson. MMConf: An infrastructure for building shared multimedia applications. In *Proceedings of CSCW'90,* pp. 329–342, 1990.

61. S. R. Ahuja, J. R. Ensor, S. E. Lucco. A comparison of application sharing mechanisms in real-time desktop conferencing system. In *Proceedings of COIS'90,* pp. 238–248, 1990.

62. L. M. Applegate, B. R. Konsynski, and J. F. Nunamaker. A group decision support system for idea generation and issue analysis in organization planning. In *Proceedings of CSCW'86,* pp. 16–34, 1986.

63. R. Dalton. Group-writing tools: Four that connect. *Information Week,* March, 62–65, 1987.

64. B. T. Lewis and J. D. Hodges. Shared Books: Collaborative publication management for an office information system. In R. B. Allen (ed.), *Proceedings of Conference on Office Information Systems,* ACM Press, New York, pp. 197–204, 1988.

65. R. S. Fish, R. E. Kraut, D. P. Leland, and M. Cohen. Quilt: A collaborative tool for cooperative

writing. In R. B. Allen (ed.), *Proceedings of Conference on Office Information Systems,* ACM Press, New York, pp. 30–37, 1988.

66. M. J. Knister and A. Prakash. DistEdit: A distributed toolkit for supporting multiple group editors. In *Proceedings of CSCW'90,* pp. 343–355, 1990.

67. B. Karbe, N. Ramsperger, and P. Weiss. Support of cooperative work by electronic circulation folders. In *Proceedings of Conference on Office Information Systems,* pp. 109–117, 1990.

68. M. M. Zloof. QBE/OBE: A language for office and business automation. *IEEE Computer, 14*(5): 13–22, 1981.

69. S. B. Yao, A. R. Hevener, Z. Shi, and D. Luo. FORMANAGER: An office forms management system. *ACM Transactions Office Information Systems, 2*(3): 235–262, 1984.

70. A. W. Holt. Diplans: A new language for the study and implementation of coordination. *ACM Transactions Office Information Systems, 6*(2): 109–125, 1988.

71. A. W. Holt, H. R. Ramsey, and J. D. Grimes. Coordination system technology as the basis for a programming environment. *Electrical Commun., 57*(4): 307–314, 1983.

72. H. -J. Bullinger and J. Warschat (eds.). *Concurrent Simultaneous Engineering Systems—The Way to Successful Product Development.* Springer-Verlag, London, 1996.

73. T. Berners-Lee and D. Connolly. *Hypertext Markup Language—A Representation of Textual Information and Metainformation for Retrieval and Interchange;* Internet draft. WWW, ftp://info.cern.ch/pub/www/doc/html-spec.ps, 1993.

74. C. F. Goldfarb. *The SGML Handbook.* Oxford University Press, Oxford, UK, 1990.

75. D. Flanagan. *Java in a Nutshell.* O'Reilly & Associates, Sebastopol, CA, 1996.

76. Y. Tanaka. From augmentation media to meme media: IntelligentPad and the world-wide repository of pads. In *Information Modelling and Knowledge Bases, VI* (ed. H. Kangassalo et al.), IOS Press, Amsterdam, pp. 91–107, 1995.

77. Y. Tanaka. Meme media and a world-wide meme pool. In *Proceedings of ACM Multimedia 96,* pp. 175–186, 1996.

78. I. Sutherland. Sketchpad: A man–machine graphical communication system. In *Proceedings of the Spring Joint Computer Conference, 23,* pp. 329–346, 1963.

79. D. C. Engelbart. The augmented knowledge workshop. In A. Goldberg (ed.), *A History of Personal Workstations.* Addison-Weley, Reading, MA, pp. 187–236, 1988.

80. D. C. Smith et al. The Star user interface: An overview. In *Proceedings of AFIPS Conference,* pp. 515–528, 1982.

81. G. K. Wallace. The JPEG still picture compression standard. *CACM, 34:* 31–44, 1991.

82. W. B. Pennebaker and J. L. Mitchell. *JPEG Still Picture Compression Standard.* Van Nostrand Reinhold, New York, 1993.

83. ISO/IEC IS 11172. *Information Technology—Coding of Moving Pictures and Associated Audio for Digital Storage Media up to about 1. 5 Mbits/s.*

84. ISO/IEC IS 13818. *Information Technology—Generic Coding of Moving Pictures and Associated Audio Information.*

85. A. Henderson. The Trillium user interface design environment. In *Proceedings of CHI'86,* pp. 221–227, 1986.

86. Micosoft Corporation. *OLE2 Programmer's Reference. Volume One: Working with Windows Objects. Volume Two Creating Programmable Applications with OLE Automation.* Microsoft Corporation, Redmond, WA, 1994.

87. Component Integration Laboratories. *OpenDoc: The New Shape of Software.* Component Integration Laboratories, Sunnyvale, CA, 1994.

88. A. J. Palay. Toward an "operating system" for user interface components. In M. Blattner and R.

Dannenberg (eds.), *Multimedia Interface Design,* ACM Press, New York, pp. 339–355, 1992.

89. Y. Tanaka and T. Imataki. IntelligentPad: A hypermedia system allowing functional composition of active media objects through direct manipulations. In *Proceedings of of IFIP '89,* pp. 541–546, 1989.

90. S. Papert. *Mindstorm: Children, Computers, and Powerful Ideas.* Basic Books, New York, 1980.

91. N. Waters. POGS: Pads of Geographic Software. *GIS World, 8*(11): 82, 1995.

92. R. Jacobson (ed.). *Information Design.* MIT Press, Cambridge, MA, 1999.

93. F. Thomas and O. Johnston. *The Illusion of Life—Disney Animation.* Hyperion, New York, 1981.

94. E. R. Tufte. The Visual Display of Quantitative Information. Graphics Press, Cheshire, CT, 1983.

95. E. R. Tufte. *Envisioning Information.* Graphics Press, Cheshire, CT, 1990.

96. E. R. Tufte. *Visual Explanations: Images and Quantities, Evidence and Narrative.* Graphics Press, Cheshire, CT, 1997.

97. A. Hutchinson. *Labanotation—The System of Analyzing and Recording Movement.* Third Edition, Routledge/Theatre Arts Books, New York, 1977.

98. B. Johnstone. DIY software. *New Scientist. 147,* 1991: 26–31, 1995.

99. M. L. Brodie and M. Stonebraker. *Migrating Legacy Systems: Gateways, Interfaces and The Incremental Approach.* Morgan Kaufmann, San Francisco, 1995.

100. D. Flanagan and P. Ferguson (eds.). *JavaScript: The Definitive Guide.* O'Reilly & Associates, Sebastopol, CA, 2001.

101. P. Lomax and R. Petrusha (eds.). *VB and VBA in a Nutshell.* O'Reilly & Associates, Sebastopol, CA, 1998.

102. S. Brown, L. Kim, J. Falkner, B. Galbraith, R. Johnson, R. Burdick, D. Cokor, S. Wilkinson and G. Taylor. *Professional JSP.* Wrox Press, Chicago, 2001.

103. A. K. Weissinger and R. Petrusha (eds.). *ASP in a Nutshell.* O'Reilly & Associates, Sebastopol, CA, 2000.

104. J. Hunter and W. Crawford. *Java Servlet Programming.* O'Reilly & Associates, Sebastopol, CA, 2001.

105. S. Gundavaram and A. Oram (eds.). *CGI Programming on the World Wide Web.* O'Reilly & Associates, Sebastopol, CA, 1995.

106. L. Wall and M. Loukides (eds.). *Programming Perl,* 3rd ed., O'Reilly & Associates, Sebastopol, CA, 2000.

107. *Java 2 Enterprise Edition.* http://java.sun.com/j2ee/tutorial.

108. W3C Consortium. *Workshop on Web Services.* http://www.w3.org/2001/01/WSWS, 2001.

109. D. Box, et al. *Simple Object Access Protocol (SOAP) 1. 1, W3C NOTE.* http://www.w3.org/TR/SOAP/, 2000 (The latest version is available at http://www.w3.org/TR/ soap12/)

110. L.,Carr, W. Hall, and D. De Roure. The evolution of hypertext link services. *ACM Computing Survey, 31*(4), 1999.

111. A. M. Fountain, W. Hall, I. Heath, and H. C. Davis. Microcosm: An open model with dynamic linking. *Proceedings of ACM European Conference on Hypertext '90 (ECHT '90),* Versailles, pp. 298–311, 1990.

112. A. Rizk and L. Sauter. Multicard: An open hypermedia system, *Proceedings of ACM European Conference on Hypertext '92 (ECHT '92),* Milan, pp. 4–10, 1992.

113. H. Schütt and N. A. Streitz. Hyperbase: A hypermedia engine based on a relational database management system. *Proceedings of ACM European Conference on Hypertext '90 (ECHT '90),* Versailles, pp. 95–108, 1990.

114. J. L. Schase and J. J. Legget, et al. Design and implementation of the HBI hyperbase manage-

ment system. *Electronic Publishing: Origination, Dissemination and Design,* 6(2), 35–63, 1993.

115. F. G. Halasz and M. D. Schwartz. The Dexter hypertext reference model. *Communications of ACM,* 37(2), 30–39, 1994.

116. H. C. Davis, A. Lewis, and A. Rizk. OHP: A draft proposal for an open hypermedia protocol. *ACM Hypertext '96, Open Hypermedia Systems Workshop,* Washington, DC, 1996.

117. K. Grønbæk, N. O. Bouvin, and L. Sloth. Designing Dexter-based hypermedia services for the World Wide Web. *Proceedings of ACM Hypertext '97,* Southampton, UK, pp. 146–156, 1997.

118. U. K. Will and J. J. Leggett. The HyperDisco approach to open hypermedia systems. *Proceedings of ACM Hypertext '96,* Washington DC, pp. 140–148, 1996.

119. K. M. Anderson, R. N. Taylor, and E. J. Whitehead. Chimera: Hypertext for heterogeneous software environments. *Proceedings of ACM European Conference on Hypermedia Technology (ECHT '94),* Edinburgh, pp. 94–106, 1994.

120. U. K. Will, and J. J. Leggett. Workspaces: The HyperDisco approach to internet distribution. *Proceedings of ACM Hypertext 97,* Southampton, UK, pp. 13–23, 1997.

121. K. M. Anderson. Integrating open hypermedia systems with the World Wide Web. *Proceedings of ACM Hypertext '97,* Southampton, UK, pp. 157–167, 1997.

122. O. Reinert, D. Bucka-Lassen, C. A. Pedersen, and P. J. Nürnberg. CAOS: A collaborative and open spatial structure service component with incremental spatial parsing. *Proceedings of ACM Hypertext '99,* Darmstadt, Germany, pp. 49–50, 1999.

123. L. Moreau and N. Gibbins, et. al. SoFAR with DIM agents: An agent framework for distributed information management. *Proceedings of Fifth International Conference and Exhibition on the Practical Application of Intelligent Agents and Multi-Agents,* Manchester, UK, 2000.

124. T. Lindholm and F. Yellin. *The Java Virtual Machine Specification.* Addison-Wesley Longman, Reading, MA, 1999.

125. Microsoft Corporation. Dynamic HTML. http://msdn.microsoft. com/library/ default. asp?url=/workshop/author/dhtml/dhtml.asp.

126. *Document Object Model (Dom): Level 1 Specification,* Vol. 1, iUniverse, Incorporated , 1999.

127. *Document Object Model (Dom): Level 2 Specification: Version 1.0,* Vol. 1. iUniverse, Inc., 1999.

128. E. A. Meyer and L. Lejeune (eds.). *CSS Pocket Reference.* O'Reilly & Associates, Sebastopol, CA, 2001.

129. T. Bray, J. Paoli, and C. M. Sperberg-McQueen, *Extensible Markup Language (XML) 1.0, W3C Recommendation.* http://www.w3.org/TR/1998/REC-xml-19980210, 1998.

130. S. Adler et al. *Extensible Stylesheet Language (XSL) Version 1.0, W3C.* http://www.w3.org/ TR/xsl/, 2000.

131. E. Maler, M., Eve, and J. E. Andaloussi. *Developing SGML DTDs: From Text to Model to Markup.* Prentice Hall PTR, Upper Saddle River, NJ, 1995.

132. J. Clark. *XSL Transformations (XSLT) Version 1.0, W3C Recommendation.* http://www.w3.org/ TR/xslt, 1999.

133. World Wide Web Consortium. *XHTML 1.0: The Extensible HyperText Markup Language.* http://www.w3.org/TR/xhtml1/, 2000.

134. J. Clark and S. DeRose, *XML Path Language (XPATH) Version 10, W3C Recommendation.* http://www.w3.org/TR/xpath.html, 1999.

135. Dreamweaver Macromedia. *Dreamweaver MX.* http://www.macromedia.com/software/ dreamweaver/.

136. Y. Tanaka. Meme media and a world-wide meme pool. *Proceedings of ACM Multimedia 96,*

pp. 175–186, 1996.

137. Y. Tanaka. Meme media and a world-wide meme pool. *Proceedings of the Fourth ACM International Multimedia Conference,* Boston, 175–186, 1996.

138. Y. Tanaka, J. Fujima, and T. Sugibuchi. Meme media and meme pools for re-editing and redistributing intellectual assets. In *Hypermedia: Openness, Structural Awareness and Adaptivity,* Springer L NCS 2266, pp. 28–46, 2002.

139. S. St. Laurent. *Cookies.* McGraw-Hill, New York, 1998.

140. Y. Tanaka. Meme media and databases. *International Symposium on Cooperative Database Systems for Advanced Applications,* Kyoto, 174–183, 1996.

141. Y. Tanaka and T. Sugibuchi. Component-based framework for virtual information materialization. *Discovery Science,* Springer LNAI 2226, pp. 458–463, 2002.

# CHAPTER 4

# AN OUTLINE OF INTELLIGENTPAD AND ITS DEVELOPMENT HISTORY

The previous chapter introduced the concept of meme media and their potentialities. This chapter briefly introduces our approach to the technologies that enables meme media to work on networked computing environments, and proposes 2D and 3D meme media architectures: IntelligentPad and IntelligentBox. It takes a closer look at the development history of IntelligentPad; how our research group has coevolved with IntelligentPad and IntelligentBox to reach the concept of meme media.

## 4.1 BRIEF INTRODUCTION TO INTELLIGENTPAD

Multimedia studies have been focusing on media richness, whereas hypermedia studies have been focusing on associative linkages among multimedia objects. Multimedia systems and hypermedia systems both handle multimedia components, but not software components in general. Our research project has been focusing on a universal media architecture that can uniformly deal with both multimedia components and software components, and provides not only associative linkage but also functional linkage among components. This architecture is called IntelligentPad.

IntelligentPad represents each component as a pad, which looks like a sheet of paper on the screen. IntelligentPad applies a compound-document architecture to both multimedia documents and software components. It defines functional linkage between two component objects by physically embedding one component into the other in the framework of compound documents. Namely, a pad can be pasted onto another pad. This physical containment relationship also defines a functional linkage between these two pads. Component pads can be pasted together to define varieties of multimedia documents and tools as composite pads. Such a composition defines not only the physical layout of components in a composed pad, but also the functional linkage among these components. Unless otherwise specified, composite pads are always decomposable to their component pads.

### 4.1.1 The Motivation for Our Project

Our IntelligentPad project began in early 1987. Around that time, many tools were available on personal computers for office information processing. They included word processors, spreadsheets, drawing tools, and chart tools. Some systems integrated several different kinds of tools for easy exchange of data. Users could readily get a chart representation of data calculated by a spreadsheet. In some advanced systems, users could directly manipulate data on a chart to change the corresponding data in a spreadsheet. These systems were called integrated business software systems. For end-users, personal computers were no longer machines to program, but tools to be used without any programming. However, people were not satisfied with these integrated business software systems. In such systems, no two tools can exchange data unless the system has an a priori defined linkage between them. Furthermore, no tool can be integrated with others unless it has been defined as a part of the original tool set. At that time, users were also unable to reuse any function that was not provided as a member tool, even if it was used by several member tools. For example, we could find a sorting function in almost every member tool in such integrated business software. However, we could not extract this function for use in another context. Each member tool was atomic, and not decomposable. These systems were closed-integration systems. No user-defined tools could be added later as member tools. The demand for an open-integration system was rapidly increasing.

At that time, it seemed that whenever we wanted to do some office work on our computers, we could find all the necessary functions somewhere among the tools we had already installed in our computers. However, in most cases, we could not perform what we wanted since it was difficult or even impossible for us to extract those required functions from the existing tools, combine them, and apply the composed function to perform the required task. This is a typical problem that still bothers users today.

In our daily intellectual activities, whenever we conceive an idea, we try it out, observe the result to evaluate it, and eventually proceed to conceive a new idea. In our intellectual activities, we repeat this process of "think," "try," and "see" as shown in Figure 4.1. When applied to problem-solving contexts, researchers call such a repetitive process a plan–do–see loop. Many feel that computers can be applied to support this process, speeding it up and driving progress around this cycle. This requires seamless support of the three phases: think, try, and see.

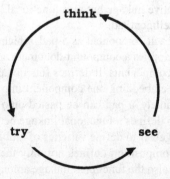

**Figure 4.1** Our intellectual activities repeat thinking, trying, and seeing, in that order.

The first phase is mainly performed by humans. The second phase requires the representation of each idea and its execution. The third phase requires various evaluation and analysis tools. The first and the third phases are the application areas of artificial-intelligence systems and computation-intensive systems, but we do not have appropriate systems that effectively support the second phase.

To solve this problem, we need a system in which end-users can directly manipulate various functions and arbitrarily define functional linkages among them. These functions, however, do not include internal functional modules of server systems such as database-management systems, compilers, and numerical-computation systems. End-users use these server systems as they are provided by their developers. Functions that end-users want to directly manipulate and compose are client-system functions. For example, in order to view the population distribution in a certain geographical area, we may use either a simple table showing the population of each city, or a map with a bar indicator placed at each city to show its population. These two different views, however, access the same database with the same query. They use the same server as it is provided, but they provide different visual representations for the same retrieved data. To satisfy varieties of users' requirements, client systems must be easily customizable by end-users.

Client systems are not GUI (graphical user interface) assemblies: An editor, for example, is a client system that cannot be constructed from GUI tools. It may be thought of as consisting of two subsystems: One is a display object that works as a window showing, for instance, some text or table; the other is an internal program that performs the word processing or the table calculation. To distinguish GUI objects and such composite systems, we call the latter ones media objects (see Figure 2.4).

When the author of this book started the IntelligentPad project in 1987, he had a vague estimate that about one hundred different component pads would be sufficient to define any multimedia document and any tool. Based on this prediction, the project tried to develop both the IntelligentPad kernel system and a "complete" set of component pads as a construction kit [1, 2]. The project termed this system a media-toolkit system.

### 4.1.2 Synthetic Media Architecture

Around 1989, we realized that our prediction was wrong. Pads are combined to define both functions and layout designs. For computable functions, we can list a finite number of primitive functions necessary and sufficient to compose any computable function. For layout designs, however, there is no such concept of computational completeness. You can easily find more than 50 different models of Walkman-style audio cassette players with almost the same set of functions, not only from Sony but also from many others.

Around the same time, we realized that not only multimedia components and tool components, but also various server systems like DBMSs, E-mail systems, application systems, and their environments, can be represented as pads and, therefore, can be combined with other pads. Most of these new pads have no need for GUIs; they may look like blank sheets. The openness of the set of component pads and the expansion of the pad representation scope made it important to define each pad as a generic object independently from the pad it is functionally linked to. Such generic definition of pads requires standardization of the message exchange interface between pads. This led us to the current IntelligentPad architecture in which every pad defines its functional interface as a list of slots, and uses only three standard messages—"set," "gimme" and "update"—to communicate with other pads [3, 4]. This architecture is called a synthetic media architecture.

### 4.1.3   Meme Media Architecture

If there is effectively no limit to the number of different component pads, there arises a question; who provides all these varieties of pads? Can a single provider provide all of them? If the answer is yes, then other competitors will also develop similar competing systems and provide other sets of components. These systems will provide mutually incompatible components, which will then lead to the same troublesome situation we are facing now. We must allow multiple vendors and volunteers to provide this large variety of mutually compatible pads. In addition, to support compatibility in use, we must ensure that the IntelligentPad kernel facilities are standardized across different computing platforms.

Around 1991, these considerations led us to the extension of the IntelligentPad architecture toward a social infrastructure for the exchange and distribution of intellectual resources. Pads can represent various kinds of intellectual resources. The standardization of IntelligentPad systems running on different platforms guarantees the cross-platform transportability of pads. Users can easily exchange pads with each other and use them in their own environments. These considerations finally led us to the concept of "meme media," which we first proposed in 1993. Since then, we have been focusing our research on a marketplace architecture for the distribution, reediting, and redistribution of pads not only by pad developers, but also by end-users. This, then, is an architecture that can realize the concept of the "meme pool" discussed in Chapter 2.

In 1994, we developed a pad publication system on the Internet using either Mosaic or Netscape pages as catalog pages for pads [5, 6, 7]. Users can browse these catalog pages and select pads to download from remote servers into their local IntelligentPad environments.

## 4.2   INTELLIGENTPAD ARCHITECTURE

Instead of directly dealing with component objects, IntelligentPad wraps each object with a standard pad wrapper and treats it as a pad. Each pad has both a standard user interface and a standard connection interface. The user interface of every pad has a card-like view on the screen and a standard set of operations like "move," "resize," "copy," "paste," and "peel." As a connection interface, every pad provides a list of slots, a standard set of messages—"set" and "gimme"—to access each of these slots, and another standard message—"update"—to propagate a state change from one pad to another.

IntelligentPad provides an open-integration framework for multimedia-document components and software components. Once it is wrapped with a standard pad wrapper and defined as a pad, any object can be assimilated into an IntelligentPad environment. It is up to each developer to decide how to wrap his or her object with a pad wrapper.

### 4.2.1   Pad Architecture

In IntelligentPad, a component pad consists of a display object and a model object (Figure 4.2). The display object defines both the view on the display screen and its reaction to user events, whereas the model object defines its internal state and behavior. Wide varieties of documents and tools can be represented as component and composite pads. You may use paste operations in arbitrary ways; for example, to overlay multiple translucent compo-

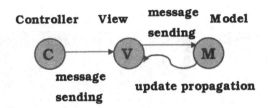

**Figure 4.2** The internal structure of each pad.

nent pads of the same size, or to arrange multiple component pads on the same base component pad. Unless otherwise specified, both component pads and composite pads are just referred to as pads. Component pads are called primitive pads. Users can easily replicate any pad, paste a pad onto another, and peel a pad off a composite pad, all through direct manipulation. These operations can be equally applied to both primitive pads and composite pads. When a pad $P_2$ is pasted on another pad $P_1$, the pad $P_2$ becomes a child pad of $P_1$, and $P_1$ becomes the parent pad of $P_2$. Instead of "child" and "parent," we also use "slave" and "master," respectively. No pad may have more than one parent pad (Figure 4.3). Pads are decomposable persistent objects. You can easily decompose any composite pad by simply peeling off the primitive or composite pad from its parent pad.

### 4.2.2 Paste Operation and Slot Connection

Figure 4.4 shows a bookshelf and books that are all constructed by pasting various primitive pads. The opened book shows text items with scroll bars on both pages, and a map of Japan with several bar meters on the right-hand page. The scroll-bar pads and the bar-meter pads actually share the same function that detects the mouse location and sends the un-

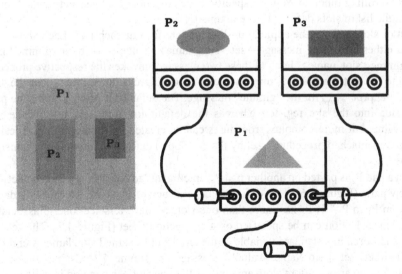

**Figure 4.3** Application linkages in the media-based architecture.

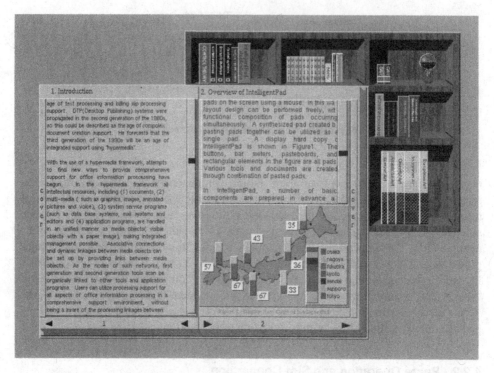

**Figure 4.4** Composite pads define a bookshelf and books.

derlying pad a value between 0 and 1 depending on the detected relative location. There-fore, you could replace the scroll bar with a copy of one of the bar meters (Figure 4.5). When you paste a bar meter onto a text pad, you have to connect this bar meter to the text pad's text-scrolling function. You can specify this connection just by selecting the "scroll" slot from the list of slots defined by the text pad.

A list of slots defines the application-linkage interface of each pad. Each slot can be accessed either by a "set" message—set <slot_name> <value>—or by a "gimme" mes-sage—gimme <slot_name>. Each of these two messages invokes the respective procedure attached to the slot. Each slot $s_i$ may have two attached procedures, $proc_{i,set}$ for the "set" message and $proc_{i,gimme}$ for the "gimme" message. The default for $proc_{i,set}$ stores the para-meter value into the slot register, whereas the default for $proc_{i,gimme}$ returns the slot-register value, but more complex procedures can be created by programming if desired. The slots and attached procedures, set by the developer, define the internal mechanism of each pad.

When a pad $P_2$ is pasted on another pad $P_1$, IntelligentPad constructs a linkage between their view parts (Figure 4.6). This defines a dependency of $P_2$ to $P_1$; we call it "a depen-dency from $P_1$ to $P_2$." If $P_1$ has more than one slot, we have to select one to associate it with $P_2$. This selection can be specified on a connection sheet (Figure 4.7). The selected slot name is stored in a standard variable of the child pad $P_2$ named slotName. A child pad can send either "set ↑ slotName <value>" message or "gimme ↑ slotName" message to its parent. The up arrow before slotName means that the slot name stored in slotName be-comes the real parameter. A pad that is a parent to one or more children can inform the

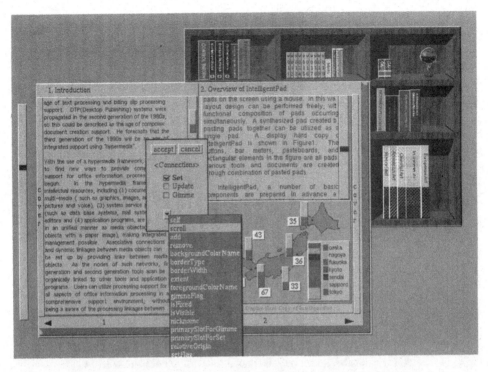

**Figure 4.5**   The replacement of a scroll bar in a text page with a bar meter.

children of changes to its own state by sending the "update" message (which has no arguments). The interpretation of the update message again depends on the implementation of the sender and the receiver pads. It is usually used to inform the child pads of a parent's state change.

In the definition of pads, programmers use "pset <value>" and "pgimme" messages, which the IntelligentPad kernel automatically converts to "set ↑ slotName <value>" and "gimme ↑ slotName" messages. Therefore, programmers can define a pad without specifying which pad it communicates with.

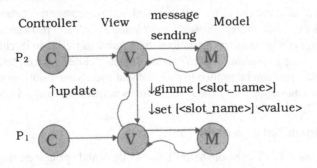

**Figure 4.6**   The standard message interface between pads.

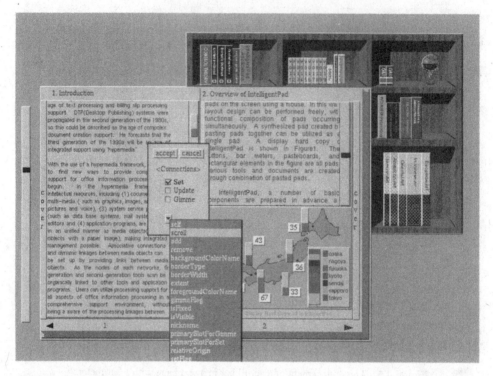

**Figure 4.7** Specification of a slot connection on a connection sheet to connect a bar meter to the scroll slot of the underlying text pad.

IntelligentPad allows us to disable some of the three standard messages, "set," "gimme" and "update," on the connection sheet. If we disable "gimme" and "update," the child pad works as an input device to its parent pad. If we only disable the "set" message, the child pad works as an output device of the parent pad; its output value is automatically updated whenever the parent pad changes its state. If we disable both the "set" and "update" messages, the child pad works as an on-demand output device: Its output is not automatically updated by the parent pad's state change; it reads the parent pad's slot and outputs the value whenever it is requested.

The two messages "set $s$ $v$" and "gimme $s$" sent to a pad P are forwarded to its parent pad if P does not have the slot $s$. We call this mechanism message delegation.

Besides the three slot-related messages mentioned above, any pad can send additional standard messages for geometrical operations to its parent as well as to its child pads. These include "move," "copy," "delete," "hide," "show," "open," "close," "resize," and "paste" messages. These messages can be applied to pads without specifying a slot connection. The set of these standard messages with the slot-related ones defines the standard interface of pads.

### 4.2.3 IntelligentPad as a Meta-Tool

Figure 4.8 shows another example set of pads. Pulleys and springs on the right-hand of Figure 4.8(a) are animated by transparent pads. By pasting these pads together, you can easily connect animated springs and pulleys. When pasted together, two pads automatical-

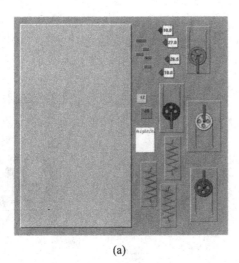
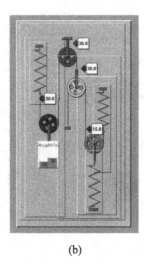

(a)                                                    (b)

**Figure 4.8** Connections of springs and pulleys that are animated by transparent pads. (a) Component pads representing springs and pulleys. (b) A composition with pads from (a).

ly adjust the location of their animated parts so that these parts work as if they are directly connected. These springs and pulleys constitute a construction set for a microworld, wherein learners can play with a given set of objects; furthermore, they can decompose these objects, and recombine their components to create new objects.

Any pad accepts "copy" and "shared-copy" requests. Shared copies of the same pad share the same state. The state of a primitive pad is defined as the state of its model part. Therefore, shared copies of a primitive pad share the same model object. The state of a composite pad is defined as the state of the base pad. Therefore, shared copies of a composite pad share the same model object for their base pads. Shared copies, however, cannot share a user event applied to one of them except insofar as it changes the shared state. A user event may change the pad view without changing its state. For example, it may change only the relative location of a component pad in a composite pad. To share events such as this, we require an event-sharing mechanism. To be applicable to any pad and any event, the event-sharing mechanism should be provided as an independent generic function. In IntelligentPad architecture, every independent generic function should be implemented as an independent pad so that its generic actions can be applied to arbitrary pads according to users' wishes. The base pad of the leftmost pad in Figure 4.9 works as such an event-sharing pad. We call it a FieldPad since it represents a field in which all user events are managed for sharing. In Figure 4.9, the pulley-and-spring pad is pasted on the FieldPad, and the whole composite pad is duplicated by a shared-copy operation. These two copies share every user event applied to either of them.

In Figure 4.10, a campus map of our university has been pulled off the bookshelf. It has pictures of several persons at different sites. Each picture is actually a pad clipped into that shape. This clipping facility is also provided as a shape-mask pad. When a pad is pasted on a shape-mask pad, it is clipped into the shape of this shape-mask pad. Each picture pad on the campus map can transport any pad to an a priori specified IP address. If you want to send one of the shared copies in Figure 4.9 to one of the persons shown on the campus map, you can just drag this copy to the person's picture and drop it there. The

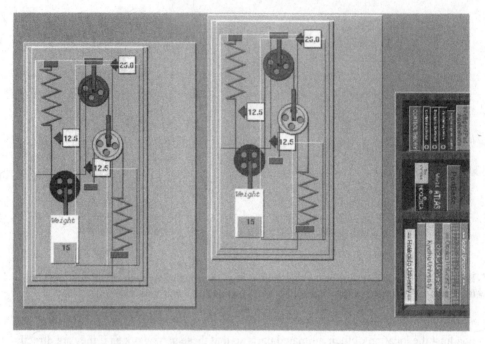

**Figure 4.9**   Shared copies of a FieldPad with arbitrary pads on it share all the user events applied to any one of these copies.

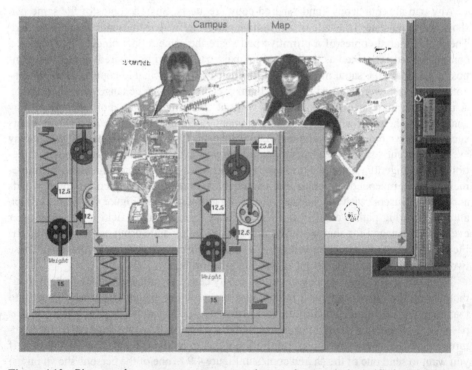

**Figure 4.10**   Picture pads on a campus map can send any pads to a priori specified workstations.

copy is automatically sent to the workstation of that person. Shared copies transported across a network continue to share the same state.

All the pads mentioned above were developed before 1993, and demonstrated at the TED (Technology Entertainment and Design) 4 Conference organized by Richard Wurman in Kobe, Japan in 1993. At this conference, I gave a talk on "From Augmentation Media to Meme Media," in which I first proposed the concept of "meme media."

Figure 4.11 shows toolkit pads for learning elementary functions and geometry. By peeling and pasting function names, parameters, triangles, circles, or scales in these environments, learners can easily design their own experiments and experience the repetitive think–try–see process.

Figure 4.12 shows an industrial plant simulator. By adding copies of component pads, the user can easily change the configuration of the plant. Figure 4.13 shows a form interface to a relational database. IntelligentPad works as a form-construction kit for relational databases and object-oriented databases. The base pad in this figure works as an interface to the database. Such a pad that works as a proxy of some external object is called a proxy pad. Such external objects include industrial plants, databases, computer-controlled devices, and numerical computation programs running on supercomputers. A single proxy pad may relate to more than one external object. A typical example is the view integration of two different databases: the proxy pad issues mutually related queries to respective databases, and combines the two records retrieved from the different databases to define a single record. The proxy pad provides a slot for each attribute of this record. By associating an appropriate pad with each slot that represents an attribute of this composed record type, you can define a single form whose items are actually retrieved from two different databases.

Video pads show video cuts. Various video editing tools are available as primitive or composite pads.

Figure 4.14 shows a research paper. It is, however, not an ordinary static document. In fact, every formula in it is a pad with a program to calculate the formula. Here we made a copy of such a formula pad. Every chart stores the data used to plot the chart. You can make a copy of a formula in such a reactive document and paste it onto your own chart tool pad to evaluate it from your own viewpoint.

These examples include a lot of useful tools. Some are composite pads, some others are component composite pads, and others are primitive pads. The distribution and the exchange of useful tools and documents among users who share the same interests will surely stimulate the evolution of their scientific culture.

### 4.2.4 Pads as Meme Media

Pads can be easily replicated and edited. Furthermore, they can be easily transported from one system to another via networks or off-line media. If the source and destination systems share the same class library, the transport of a composite-pad instance sends the destination system only the pad type ID and the current state of each component primitive pad together with the composition structure; this set of information is called the save-format information of the pad, since it is used to save and load this pad to and from a file. If the systems do not share all the required classes, transportation requires the inclusion of some class definitions.

However, the transportability of pads is not sufficient for the distribution and exchange of pads among users. This in itself will not form a meme pool. We need an open marketplace where each end-user can display, browse, sell, buy, and exchange various pads.

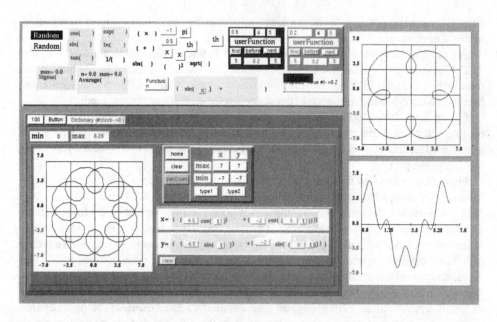

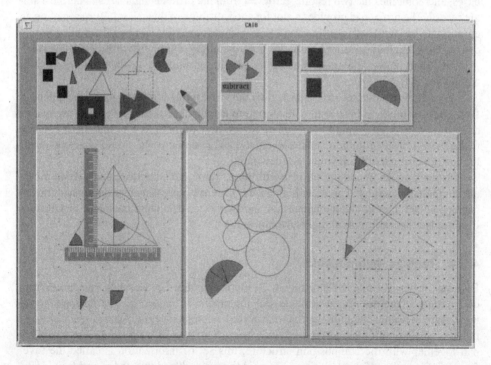

**Figure 4.11**    Microworlds for learning elementary functions and geometry.

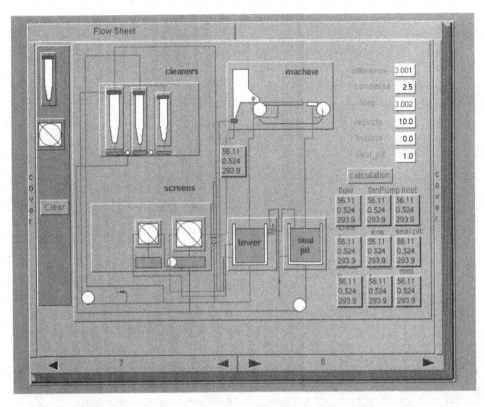

**Figure 4.12** An industrial plant simulator developed as a composite pad.

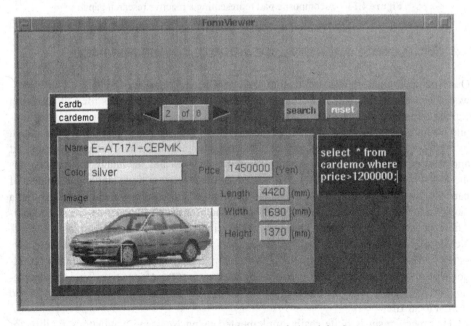

**Figure 4.13** A form interface to a relational database.

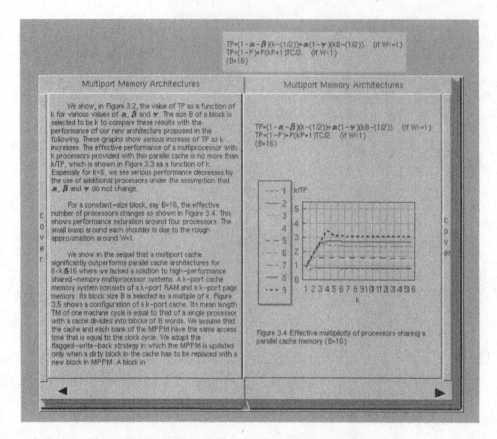

**Figure 4.14**  A composite pad representing a reactive research paper.

## 4.3  WORLDWIDE MARKETPLACE ARCHITECTURES FOR PADS

Our first open-marketplace architecture uses WWW and Netscape Navigator. The WWW works as a worldwide pad repository, and Netscape Navigator provides for a hypermedia catalog of pads to navigate this repository [5, 6]. We assume that every site in the community of our concern installs an IntelligentPad system with the same class library. As shown in Figure 4.15, each page displayed in Netscape Navigator describes some pad using text and images. In addition to the ordinary functions of Netscape Navigator, this catalog has the following extended functions. Pad names in textual descriptions and visual images of pads work as special anchors. A mouse click on one of these special anchors will pop up a new window with a copy of the requested pad. The original of this pad may be stored anywhere in the world, using the save format described above. When an anchor is clicked, Netscape Navigator issues a file transfer request to the WWW server at this remote site. After a while, the local Netscape Navigator receives this file, and then invokes the IntelligentPad system to reconstruct the pad using its save-format information. This reconstruction does not differ from the pad reconstruction process necessary for the loading of a pad from a local file.

This mechanism is quite easily implemented using Netscape Navigator's facility for mapping a customer-defined file-name extension to an invocation of an application pro-

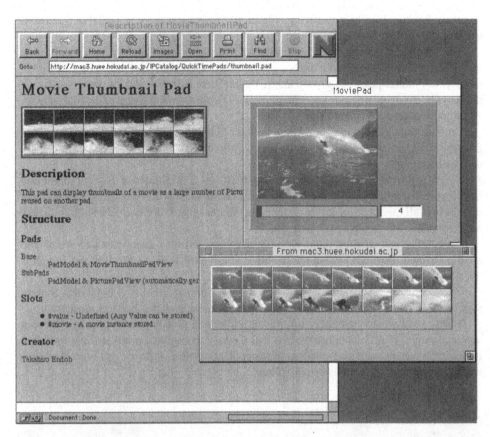

**Figure 4.15** A pad catalog on Netscape, and an IntelligentPad system with a window, including the downloaded pad.

gram. We used "pad" as the customer-defined file-name extension, and mapped this to the invocation of a special file loader in the IntelligentPad system. Although the implementation mechanism is quite simple, it has opened a new vista in the distribution and exchange of knowledge resources.

Our second open-marketplace architecture provides a special web browser pad that shows HTML files as web pages, and furthermore allows us to embed arbitrary composite media objects into any web page to publish them through the Internet [8]. Client users opening this page can directly drag out these embedded media objects into their own environments to reuse them there. Chapter 11 describes the details of these open-marketplace architectures as well as their successors.

## 4.4 END-USER COMPUTING AND MEDIA TOOLKIT SYSTEM

The IntelligentPad architecture has several versions for implementation. It was first implemented in Smalltalk 80, then in SmalltalkAgents, and also in C++ using InterViews. Now we have four more commercially developed versions in C++, three for Windows PC, and the other for Macintosh. Two Windows PC versions are now commercially available and their functions are being actively enhanced. The others are now available free as is, without any further revision.

The Smalltalk 80 version of IntelligentPad has more than 600 primitive pads. Some may differ from others in minor aspects. They are roughly classified into nine categories, namely: (1) model pads, (2) view pads, (3) controller pads, (4) data converter pads, (5) proxy pads, (6) geometrical management pads, (7) generator/consumer pads, (8) pad converter pads, and (9) ornament pads.

A model pad has an application system as its model. Its view has nothing to do with its function. It is either a blank pad or mapped with some texture. Model pads are usually used as base pads.

A view pad works as an input and/or output device. It is connected to a slot of another pad. Figure 4.16 shows a calculator and all of its components. Its base pad is a model pad that defines all the functions of the calculator, whereas the buttons and the digital display are view pads.

A controller pad changes the event-dispatch mechanism; it intercepts user events and applies its own dispatch mechanism to them. The FieldPad is a controller pad, which is usually blank or transparent.

A data converter pad is inserted between two pads to perform the required data conversion between these two pads; data converter pads are also usually blank or transparent.

A proxy pad works as a proxy of an external object; this external object might be an application program, a computer-controlled device, a computer-controlled plant system, or a server system such as a database management system. A proxy pad communicates with its external object, and is usually blank.

**Figure 4.16**   A hand calculator and all of its component pads.

A geometrical management pad manages the geometrical arrangement of its child pads on itself. Usually, geometrical management pads have no slot connection with their child pads. A grid alignment pad is an example of a geometrical management pad: when a pad is pasted onto a grid pad, it moves this pad to align the left top corner of this pad to the nearest grid point. Figure 4.17 shows another geometrical management pad, a tree pad, that arranges its child pads at the nodes of a one-level tree. Since a tree pad can also be put on another tree pad, we can easily construct a tree with an arbitrary number of levels.

A generator/consumer pad either generates a pad on the screen or hides a pad from the screen. For example, an anchor pad, when clicked, pops up its registered pad. When clicked again, it hides this pad. A trash pad eliminates whatever pad is dropped there.

A pad-converter pad accepts a pad as its input and outputs another pad. It processes pads and converts them to new ones.

An ornament pad is pasted on another pad without any slot connection. It decorates its parent pad with some chosen texture or lettering.

From the end-users' point of view, the diversity of the primitive pad library makes it difficult or even impossible to discover the pads necessary for what they want to construct. Each user can use only those primitive pads whose functions are already familiar to him or her. Whenever a user uses a new pad, he or she has to consult the manual. Therefore, a large library of primitive pads by itself will not encourage users to reuse them. For this reason, the IntelligentPad system provides a large number of sample composite pads. Some are included in the initial system file, and others are provided by sample-pad Web pages through the Internet. They cover a variety of application areas, and are indexed with keywords.

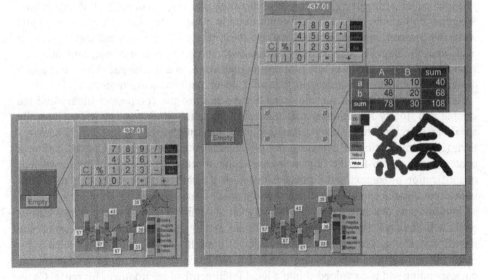

**Figure 4.17** A tree pad arranges its child pads as nodes of a one-level tree. Tree pads can also be put on another tree pad to define a multiple-level tree.

Suppose that you want to construct a form interface to an Oracle database. By searching the library using the keywords "database" and "form interface," you may find a sample composite pad that works as a form interface to some database, say Informix. This sample tells you that you have to use a database proxy pad corresponding to your database-management system as the base pad. It also tells you that a RecordPad should be connected to the #currentRecord slot of the base pad, and that the output form can be defined on this RecordPad using various types of view pads. With these guidelines, you can easily construct your own form interface. Samples work as so-called "patterns." Christopher Alexander, a postmodern architect, introduced "pattern language" into architectural design [9]. He decomposed design and planning problems into a series of components, and listed fundamental "patterns" that can be used to synthesize various architectural forms. Each pattern is associated with the situation in which it can be applied. This idea is recently being applied to object-oriented software development [10, 11]. Sample composite pads provided by the IntelligentPad system play the role of patterns in this sense.

End-users of IntelligentPad are similar to children playing with Lego toy blocks. They need to get used to the available components and their uses. Lego Group releases more than 60 new Lego block kits every year into the market. These kits vary from vehicles to amusement parks, and come with instructions on how to construct them. These kits also work as patterns. Children start by imitating these sample construction patterns. Then they gradually get used to the components and their uses, and start to construct their own original models.

End-users typically are those who do not have the skills, motivation, or resources needed to develop new primitive pads. However, such users can paste and peel existing pads, and can use IntelligentPad's other construction facilities—an end-user pad programming language, an authoring language, and a model description pad. Commercial product versions of IntelligentPad running on Windows PCs adopt Visual Basic as a programming language for end-users to develop new primitive pads. The authoring language uses the metaphor of a stage; it is used to program how to coordinate the behavior of pads on a special pad called a StagePad. A program in this language can manipulate all the pads on a StagePad in the same way as a user might directly manipulate them. It can also read and write the primary slot value of any pad on the StagePad. Users can interact with these pads, and the StagePad can be programmed with actions to perform in accordance with such interaction events. A model description pad works as a model pad. Users can easily describe the relationships among its data slots using mathematical expressions.

The most difficult task for end-users is the search of the component library and the sample pad library for existing pads that can help satisfy their requirements. Generally speaking, search methods can be classified into four categories: (1) browsing, (2) navigation, (3) quantification of contents, and (4) quantification of context. Quantification of contents is a search for the objects whose contents satisfy a given condition, whereas quantification of context is for objects situated in a specified context. IntelligentPad provides basic facilities to develop these four types of search services.

For browsing pads, we have a catalog pad that looks like a book. Its page shows various pads with their descriptions. Some of these are actual pads that can be just copied and reused. Some others are images of pads. Each of these has a URL pointer to a local or remote file storing the corresponding actual pad. When one of these images is clicked, the corresponding pad is downloaded into a local IntelligentPad environment for reuse. Chapter 11 details the pad catalog architecture. Chapter 19 gives a new framework for organizing and accessing a huge number of pads.

Our research group has a special interest in pad catalogs. The situation we will possibly encounter when IntelligentPad becomes a social infrastructure for the distribution and exchange of various intellectual resources will be very similar to our present consumer society. Our society is full of consumer products, increasing day by day. There are often many alternatives available to satisfy a given need; they may have different qualities, different prices, different designs, additional values, or different prestige. How can we find the product that satisfies both our needs and our tastes? Our choice is usually based on the information we obtain about the products, and our society provides various kinds of information about new products. Obviously, such information is fundamental to the evolution of our consumer society. The same is true for pads. The distribution and exchange infrastructure for pads cannot be formed without the coevolution of new information providers to publish catalogs of pads in the market.

IntelligentPad also provides hypermedia facilities for navigational search of pads. An anchor pad can register any pad by holding either the pad itself or a pointer to the pad. When clicked, an anchor pad pops up its registered pad on the screen. When clicked again, it hides this pad. An anchor pad is resizable and can be made transparent. It can be pasted at any location on any pad.

IntelligentPad also provides various database facilities for quantification search of pads. Our group is undertaking projects on this subject, which will be described in Chapter 10.

## 4.5 OPEN CROSS-PLATFORM REUSABILITY

One goal of the IntelligentPad project is to provide a social infrastructure for the general distribution and exchange of intellectual resources. To achieve this goal, the Intelligent-Pad architecture has been designed to satisfy the following four kinds of openness:

1. Open kernel technology: The kernel system is open to the public as shareware together with a basic primitive pad library and sample composite pads for typical applications. In addition, we developed an evaluation version of IntelligentPad and made its source code public for free reference.
2. Open pad-development library: An API (application program interface) library, sufficiently rich for pad developers to develop new primitive pads, is made available to the public.
3. Open set of primitive pads: Newly developed primitive pads can be immediately used in combination with other pads. The set of primitive pads is open for future extension.
4. Cross-platform compatibility: Pads can be transported across different platforms, and reused in different environments.

To achieve the last of these, cross-platform compatibility, we have to solve two problems: how to transport each pad from one IntelligentPad system to another IntelligentPad system, and how to cope with different platforms.

Generally speaking, there are three levels of object migration across different systems. The shallowest level assumes that the two systems share the same class library. In this case, the migration of an object only requires the transportation of the class name and the state of this object. This mechanism cannot be used for sending any object whose class definition is not already installed on the destination system.

The middle level of object migration assumes that the two systems share only the basic common portion of the class library. It is further assumed in this case that each object definition only derives its properties from classes within the basic class library. In this case, the source system can send any object to the destination. The source sends the definition code of each object. Such definition codes refer to only those classes within the basic class library, and can be executed by both of the two systems.

The deepest level of object migration assumes no common class library. In this case, we have to migrate not only the objects but also all the classes used in their definitions. Class migration requires special consideration, and causes a performance problem. This is addressed in later chapters.

The current IntelligentPad systems support the middle level of pad migration and, hence, as a special case, the shallowest level. They cope with pad migration across different platforms by programming at the API level. Our project specified the API of the pad programming. This API includes not only the pad manipulation functions for slot access and geometrical management of pads, but also the event dispatching and the display redrawing functions that are specially defined for user interaction with pads. We jointly developed commercially available versions of IntelligentPad with Fujitsu and Hitachi Software, for Windows PC and Macintosh. They shared the same API and the same basic class library. They were mutually compatible systems. The two most recent versions for Windows PC, available from Hitachi Software and K-Plex Inc., however, are not mutually compatible with each other. Each of them independently supports the middle level of pad migration. Pads in each version can migrate between two machines running this version.

## 4.6 REEDITING AND REDISTRIBUTION BY END-USERS

IntelligentPad was often viewed by the mass media as do it yourself (DIY) software [12]. It is true that we can compose a new tool just by combining existing pads, as long as this composition requires no new components. However, although some versions of IntelligentPad provide an end-user pad programming language, an authoring language, and/or a model description pad, it is still difficult for the majority of end-users to develop new pads. To alleviate this difficulty, various sample composite pads can be provided for typical applications. This will be done by vendors, by volunteers, and even by users themselves. If these samples are distributed among users, users need not always compose their application tools from the basic components. Users can use an appropriate sample as their base, rearrange its component pads, or replace one component with another to compose what they need. This is no longer a programming process; it is an editing process or, more strictly speaking, a reediting process. The reediting of composite pads representing varieties of documents and tools will yield new documents and tools as composite pads. These new composite pads also work as good samples for users' pad composition. So they too should be published by their composers, namely by end-users. Therefore, it is important for IntelligentPad to allow not only pad vendors to distribute their pads, but also end-users to redistribute reedited pads to other users. The facilities for end-users to reedit and to redistribute pads are the most fundamental functions of the IntelligentPad system.

Without them, IntelligentPad could not hope to satisfy its user community. These are fundamental for pads to work as meme media.

Assuming that there emerge just 1000 pad programmers around the world, and that each of them would develop, say, three primitive pads a year. The total number of primitive pads would increase by 3000 pads every year. Within three years, we would have 9000 different primitive pads of a sufficiently large variety. Suppose, then, that we may have 1,000,000 users who can reedit and redistribute pads, and that each of them might compose five different pads a year. Then we will have a 5,000,000 increase of composite pads every year, pads that we will be able to work with and reedit for different uses. This is an enormous number. Furthermore, this is not a dream.

The realization of this, however, presents several problems from the business point of view. How can venders do business? Does this scenario conflict with someone's business strategy? The first issue can be approached by shifting from pay-per-copy billing to pay-per-use billing. Many proposals for the implementation of pay-per-use billing are already emerging, as will be discussed in Chapter 12. The second question causes a much more difficult problem. It is obvious that users desire open systems that allow not only the reuse of objects but also the reediting and the redistribution of objects. The author of this book believes that there are only two possible scenarios. The first scenario assumes the symbiosis of different platform providers, whereas the second assumes the convergence of different platforms to a single one. The author has no answers to the question of which scenario will actually play out. However, he believes that the first scenario is much healthier for the competitive coevolution of our technologies.

Current WWW technologies provide a worldwide publication repository for people to publish their multimedia documents in HTML, to navigate through those published by other people, and to browse any of them. You may embed any tools or services in your published HTML document. To define such services, you may set up servers such as database servers, file servers, and application servers.

Although the current Web technologies have allowed us to browse huge accumulations of intellectual resources published on the Web, we have no good tools yet to flexibly reedit and redistribute these intellectual resources for their reuse in different contexts. We need OHS (open hypermedia system) technologies for the advanced reuse of Web-published intellectual assets. Meme media technologies will work as such OHS technologies to annotate Web-published resources, and to reedit and redistribute some portions of their copies with embedded tools and services, without changing their originals, for their reuse in different contexts together with different applications [23, 24].

In Section 11.9, we apply our 2D meme media technologies for the reediting and redistribution of content in Web pages. These Web contents include live content and Web applications. Live content denotes content that autonomously changes its state. Meme media technologies allow us to reedit and to redistribute live content and Web applications as well as static multimedia content [24]. Users need not edit HTML definitions of Web documents. Users can easily extract any document components through drag-and-drop operations, and paste them together on the screen to define both the layout and the functional linkages among them. Web content extracted from Web documents will become reeditable and redistributable objects when wrapped with pad wrappers. You may send reedited Web content across the Internet by attaching it to an e-mail. Recipients with IntelligentPad installed in their platforms can reuse, further reedit, and redistribute Web content.

## 4.7   EXTENSION TOWARD 3D REPRESENTATION MEDIA

Although pads in IntelligentPad are 2D representation media, the idea and the basic architecture of IntelligentPad can be also applied to develop 3D media components. We call such 3D components "boxes," and have developed a 3D meme media system architecture called IntelligentBox [25, 26]. Chapter 18 of this book will give the details of this system architecture. The ideas of IntelligentPad can be similarly applied to IntelligentBox as follows.

1. Each component is wrapped by a 3D representation wrapper with a list of slots as its standard functional linkage interface to other components.
2. Each component has an MVC architecture.
3. View linkage among components can be used to define composite 3D objects.
4. Each component in a composition has no more than one parent component, and can access no more than one of this parent's slots.
5. The updating of components propagates from each component to its child components.
6. Components and their compositions work as meme media, and their worldwide repository forms a meme pool.

Boxes may have arbitrary internal functions as well as arbitrary 3D visual display functions. Different functions define different boxes. Composite boxes are also simply referred to as boxes, unless this causes any confusion. Just as pads in IntelligentPad can represent not only multimedia documents but also application tools, boxes in IntelligentBox can represent not only computer animation graphics, but also various tools, including server systems, application systems, and their environments. Boxes can also represent information visualization systems and scientific visualization systems as compositions using animation boxes, application system boxes, and proxy boxes for computation servers or database servers. IntelligentBox allows us to integrate computer animation with information visualization and scientific visualization.

The right-hand side of Figure 4.18 shows a simple example of a composite box using some primitive boxes shown in the left-hand side of this figure. In this example, the motor of a car is implemented as a counting process having a cylindrical shape. Its model has an integer-value slot, and works as an incremental counter. The ToggleButtonBox connected to the #startStop slot of the motor works as a toggle-button switch to start and stop this counting process. When the toggle-button is pushed down, and the #startStop slot of the motor therefore becomes true, the motor regularly and continuously increases its slot value in unit steps until the #startStop slot becomes false again. The example composite box has two toothed wheels. Each of them is put in a transparent RotationBox. One of the two RotationBoxes is defined as a child of the motor box, while the other is defined both as a child of the former, and as the parent of the long shaft with two rear wheels. The motor box sends its child, RotationBox, an "update" message whenever it increases its counter value, which makes RotationBox issue a "gimme" message to read out the counter value and rotate itself to the angle proportional to this value. Whenever the first RotationBox rotates, it sends the second RotationBox an "update" message, and makes it also rotate. If these two toothed wheels have different numbers of teeth, we may insert a transparent converter between these two RotationBoxes to change their ratio of rotation speeds.

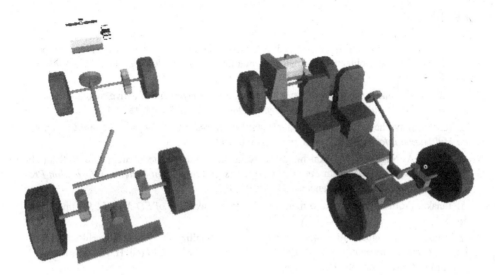

**Figure 4.18**  Primitive boxes in IntelligentBox, and an interactive composite box composed with these primitive boxes.

## 4.8  SUMMARY

This chapter has briefly introduced our approach to the technologies that enable meme media to work on networked computing environments, and has proposed 2D and 3D meme media architectures—IntelligentPad and IntelligentBox.

IntelligentPad represents each component as a pad, which looks like a sheet of paper on the screen. IntelligentPad applies a compound-document architecture to both multimedia documents and software components. It defines functional linkage between two component objects by physically embedding one component into the other in the framework of compound documents, namely, a pad can be pasted onto another pad. This physical containment relationship also defines a functional linkage between these two pads. Component pads can be pasted together to define varieties of multimedia documents and tools as composite pads. Such a composition defines not only the physical layout of components in a composed pad, but also the functional linkage among these components. Unless otherwise specified, composite pads are always decomposable to their component pads.

Although pads in IntelligentPad are 2D representation media, the idea and the basic architecture of IntelligentPad can be also applied to develop 3D media components. We call such 3D components "boxes," and have developed a 3D media system architecture called IntelligentBox.

In these two systems, each component is wrapped by a 2D or 3D representation wrapper with a list of slots as its standard functional linkage interface to other components. Each component has an MVC architecture. View linkage among components can be used to define composite objects. Each component in a composition has no more than one parent component, and can access no more than one of this parent's slots. The updating of components propagates from each parent component to its child components. Components and their compositions work as meme media, and their worldwide repository forms a meme pool.

## REFERENCES

1. Y. Tanaka and T. Imataki. IntelligentPad: A hypermedia system allowing functional composition of active media objects through direct manipulations. In *Proceedings of IFIP '89*, pp. 541–546, 1989.

2. Y. Tanaka. A toolkit system for the synthesis and the management of active media objects. In *Proceedings of Deductive and Object-Oriented Databases*, pp. 76–94, 1989.

3. Y. Tanaka. A synthetic dynamic-media system. In *Proceedings of the International Conference on Multimedia Information Systems*, pp. 299–310, 1991.

4. Y. Tanaka, A. Nagasaki, M. Akaishi, and T. Noguchi. Synthetic media architecture for an object-oriented open platform. In *Personal Computers and Intelligent Systems, Information Processing 92, Vol. III*, North Holland, pp. 104–110, 1992.

5. Y. Tanaka. From augmentation to meme media. In *Proceedings of ED-MEDIA 94*, pp. 58–63, 1994.

6. Y. Tanaka. From augmentation media to meme media: IntelligentPad and the world-wide repository of pads. In *Information Modelling and Knowledge Bases, Vol. VI* (ed. H. Kangassalo et al.), IOS Press, Amsterdam. pp. 91–107, 1995.

7. Y. Tanaka. A meme media architecture for fine-grain component software. In *Object Technologies for Advanced Software* (ed. K. Fuiatsugi and S. Matsuoka), Springer-Verlag, New York, pp. 190–214, 1996.

8. Y. Tanaka. Meme media and a world-wide meme pool. In *Proceedings of ACM Multimedia 96*, pp. 175–186, 1996.

9. C. Alexander, S. Ishikawa, M. Silverstein, M. Jacobson, I. Fiksdahl-King, and S. Angel. *A Pattern Language*. Oxford University Press, New York, 1977.

10. E. Gamma, R. Helm, R. Johnson, and J. Vlissides. *Design Patterns: Elements of Reusable Object-Oriented Software*. Addison-Wesley, Reading, MA, 1995.

11. F. Bushmann, R. Meunier, H. Rohnert, P. Sommerlad, and M. Stal. *Pattern-Oriented Software Architecture: A System of Patterns*. Wiley, Chichester, UK, 1996.

12. B. Johstone. DIY Software. *New Scientist, 147*, 1991, 26–31, 1995.

13. D. Flanagan and P. Ferguson (eds.). *JavaScript: The Definitive Guide*. O'Reilly & Associates, Sebastopol, CA, 2001.

14. P. Lomax and R. Petrusha (eds.). *VB and VBA in a Nutshell*. O'Reilly & Associates, Sebastopol, CA, 1998.

15. S. Brown, L. Kim, J. Falkner, B. Galbraith, R. Johnson, R. Burdick, D. Cokor, S. Wilkinson and G. Taylor. *Professional JSP*. Wrox Press, Chicago, 2001.

16. A. K. Weissinger and R. Petrusha (eds.). *ASP in a Nutshell*. O'Reilly & Associates, Sebastopol, CA, 2000.

17. J. Hunter and W. Crawford. *Java Servlet Programming*. O'Reilly & Associates, Sebastopol, CA, 2001.

18. S. Gundavaram and A. Oram (eds.). *CGI Programming on the World Wide Web*. O'Reilly & Associates, Sebastopol, CA, 1995.

19. L. Wall and M. Loukides (eds.). *Programming Perl*, 3rd edition, O'Reilly & Associates, Sebastopol, CA, 2000.

20. *Java 2 Enterprise Edition*. http://java.sun.com/j2ee/tutorial.

21. W3C Consortium. *Workshop on Web Services*. http://www.w3.org/2001/01/WSWS, 2001.

22. D. Box et al. *Simple Object Access Protocol (SOAP) 1.1, W3C NOTE*, http://www.w3.org/TR/SOAP/, 2000 (The latest version is available at http://www.w3.org/TR/soap12/.)

23. Y. Tanaka, J. Fujima, and T. Sugibuchi. Meme media and meme pools for re-editing and redis-

tributing intellectual assets. In *Hypermedia: Openness, Structural Awareness and Adaptivity,* Springer L NCS 2266, 28–46, 2002.

24. Y. Tanaka, D. Kurosaki, and K. Ito. Live document framework for re-editing and redistributing contents in WWW. In *Proceedings of 12th European–Japanese Conference on Information Modelling and Knowledge Bases,* Krippen, Germany, 2002

25. Y. Okada and Y. Tanaka,. IntelligentBox: A constructive visual software development system for interactive 3D graphic applications. In *Proceedings of the Computer Animation 1995 Conference,* pp. 114–125, 1995.

26. Y. Okada and Y. Tanaka. Collaborative environments of intelligentBox for distributed 3D graphics applications. *The Visual Computer CGS,* special issue *14*(4): 140–152, 1998.

# CHAPTER 5

# OBJECT ORIENTATION AND MVC

Before going into the details of meme media technologies, we need to know basic concepts and frameworks of the object-oriented way of describing and developing software systems. This chapter provides a brief introduction to object orientation based on the author's view, which works as a basis for readers to understand the subsequent chapters.

The large and rapid shift toward object orientation in 1990s was driven by users' unending demands both for more functionality from their computing systems, and for simpler, easier to use computing environments. Computing environments with increased functionality and ease of use require more complex underlying systems, and more lines of code to be organized, managed, and maintained. This calls for software development that is more rapid, less expensive, and more flexible.

Object orientation aims to provide better paradigms and tools for:

1. Modeling a real world as close to a user's perspective as possible
2. Interacting easily with a computational environment, using familiar metaphors
3. Constructing reusable software components and easily extensible libraries of software modules
4. Easily modifying and extending implementations of components without having to recode everything from scratch

Object orientation attempts to satisfy the needs of both end-users and developers of software products. This is accomplished via real-world modeling capabilities.

Chapter 5 gives a brief introduction to object orientation and its generic system architecture. A special object-oriented programming framework is used to define visual objects that interact with their users. This framework is called MVC (model, view, and controller), and is extensively used to define modern window systems. Our meme media architectures described in later chapters are also based on the MVC framework.

## 5.1   OBJECT-ORIENTED SYSTEM ARCHITECTURE—A TECHNICAL INTRODUCTION

In object orientation, a system is not considered as a set of procedures and subroutines invoked by them. Instead, a system is viewed as a model of a real world with entities and events. Entities of a real world such as a memo pad, a pen, and an eraser are all modeled as objects, and each event in this real world is modeled as a message sent from one object to another. Each object can interpret a set of messages and provide appropriate responses. This set is called the interface of the object. Each object responds to a message either by changing its state or by sending further messages to other objects.

Some objects may have their graphical representations on a display screen. User devices such as a mouse and a keyboard are considered resource objects. The object that receives a user event through such a resource object is called the target object of the event. User manipulation of these resource objects either results in messages sent directly to the target object, or causes state changes that the target object can later query to detect the occurrence of this user manipulation. This allows users to directly manipulate graphically represented objects on a display screen. System events are also considered to be messages sent from system-resource objects. The system clock and an interval timer are modeled as system-resource objects. Each of them either interrupts the activity of some other object by sending messages, or responds to messages sent by other objects.

Objects with their GUI (graphical user interface) representations and their direct-manipulation capabilities make it possible to introduce familiar metaphors of real-world objects and object manipulations into computational environments. Examples of such metaphors include document icons, file folders, a printer icon, a postbox, and a mailbox—all accessible through drag-and-drop manipulation. For example, a drag-and-drop operation of a document icon onto a printer icon starts the printing of the document.

Objects are information-hiding modules; they are encapsulated. The user only needs to know their interfaces. Assembling objects to create some system requires only the knowledge of their interfaces. This requires only the specification of message flows among these objects. Each object works as a component of the assembly. The developer of each component object may be different from the developer of other component objects, and also from the person who assembles these objects into some system. Objects can be used as elements of more than one system; they form an extensible library of reusable software components.

Increasing demand for object orientation has spurred the development of a variety of object-oriented languages. Such languages, however, have to deal with object-oriented describing, as well as with object-oriented modeling. Real worlds have only entities as objects, whereas their descriptions may deal not only with entities as objects but also their properties or the descriptions of these properties as objects. The same property might be shared by more than one entity. Entities sharing the same property form a conceptual group. This group has both its extensional meaning as a set of entities and its intentional meaning as a category. A pen, for example, is an entity, whereas the word "pen" denotes a category.

Categories in our conceptual space are related to each other through various relationships such as "*is-a*" relationships. A relationship "*A is-a B*" holds between two categories if the property of $B$ is satisfied by the property of $A$. Many language designers have treated both entities and categories as objects. Entities are called instance objects, or just objects, whereas categories are called class objects, or just classes. Classes allow us to treat properties as objects, which further allows us to reuse not only instance objects but also their classes in programming. Suppose that a relationship "*A is-a B*" holds between two classes. The class *B* is called a superclass of the class *A*, and *A* is called a subclass of *B*. In this case, the description of *A* can reuse the description of *B*, and only needs to specify the additional part of the property. This reuse of property description is called property inheritance.

In object orientation, the property of an object is specified by the set of messages it accepts and its response to each of these messages. The response definition for each message is called the method of the message. The "*is-a*" relation among classes defines a hierarchy of classes with more general classes at higher levels and more specific classes at lower levels. Each class is defined by specifying its set of messages and its method for each of these messages. Property inheritance allows the programming of each object to inherit the specification of some of its messages from its superclass unless otherwise specified in its definition. The specification of each message includes its name, format, and method.

Property inheritance also allows us to define a new class by reusing the definition of an already defined similar class. We can just define this new class as an immediate subclass of the similar class. Then we need to specify only the new additional messages as well as those that are defined by the superclass but need to be modified. The redefinition of some superclass messages by a subclass is called message overloading or, simply, overloading. The addition and the overloading of messages provide an easy way to modify and extend components without having to recode them from scratch.

## 5.2   CLASS REFINEMENT AND PROTOTYPING

As described in the preceding section, object orientation models a real world as a set of instance objects sending messages to each other. These objects work as reusable components. Their accumulation will form an extensible library of components. The majority of object-oriented languages, on the other hand, focus on the intentional description of classes, and the reuse of class descriptions through the property-inheritance mechanism. Property inheritance, however, is not fundamental to object orientation. Furthermore, some object-oriented languages have no concept of classes. Self is such a language [1]. Property inheritance is essentially an object-oriented way of reusing program codes, which need not be identical to the object-oriented way of modeling a real world. The reuse of description is based on an "*is-a*" hierarchy among classes, whereas the reuse of objects as reusable components in a different assembly needs to focus on the composition with instance objects. The former leads to the class-refinement programming paradigm; the latter to the synthetic-programming paradigm, namely, the prototyping paradigm.

Class-refinement programming starts from the definition of a general class, and gradually increases the necessary classes as subclasses of already defined classes. Synthetic programming, namely, the prototyping, uses a library of reusable objects as components, and combines some of them to compose application systems. The definition of a new component object may or may not use an object-oriented language. Even if each component has its corresponding class, a composed application has no corresponding class.

Class-refinement programming can also define a relationship between a class and its component classes. For example, the class of technical reports has component classes including the title class, the author class, the class of abstracts, the class of chapters, and the class of references. Such relations defined in class definitions are, however, static and defined a priori by developers. They cannot be modified by users playing with objects in this application environment. Users can assign different instance objects of the specified class to each placeholder of such a relation. However, they cannot define a new type of composition by themselves.

The prototyping paradigm provides more functionality to users, allowing them to even synthesize new objects by themselves, whereas the refinement paradigm provides users with only those objects and their operations that their developers have defined a priori.

Meme media should exploit the prototyping paradigm so that users can easily replicate any meme media objects, combine them to compose arbitrary meme media objects, and recombine composite meme media objects to make new ones. Static composition defined by a priori described classes cannot cope with the ever-expanding variety of knowledge fragments and their structures.

## 5.3  MODEL, VIEW, CONTROLLER

Object orientation, with the aim of modeling a real world as close to a user's perspective as possible, and of providing users with familiar metaphors for their easy interaction with a computational environment, has developed a special framework for graphical representation and direct manipulation of objects on display screens. Direct manipulation of objects requires these objects to have their GUI representations on a display screen. In the object-orientation paradigm, these GUI representations must be implemented as objects, which we term display objects. An object with its GUI representation may separate its display function as its display object. The remaining portion forms a model object. Even an object without any GUI capability, when paired with an appropriate display object, becomes a directly manipulable object. Such an original object works as a model object. A model object and its display object are functionally combined through the message exchange between them to form a composite object. Each display object can be further considered as a composite object with two component objects. One of these deals with the graphical display output; the other handles the mouse and keyboard events coming from the user to this display object. The former is called a view object; the latter is called a controller object.

### 5.3.1  MVC Construct

The MVC scheme, or the model–view–controller scheme [2], is a standard framework or, in more precise terminology, a standard pattern used to provide any application object with both its graphical view on the display screen and direct manipulation capability. It treats the application object as a "model," and provides this with two other objects, its "view" and its "controller."

The model of an MVC construct can be any object. Its view is responsible for providing this model object with a visual representation. For example, a view designed for displaying binary trees might display the tree graphically. Alternatively, it might display the tree textually, with indentation conventions to indicate the hierarchical relationships. You may even partition the display into several subviews, each designed to display the same model in a different way or to display a different aspect of the same model.

The controller of an MVC construct is responsible for interfacing between the user and the model/view. It interprets keyboard characters along with mouse movements and clicking. It either handles the interactions locally, passing the information directly to the view for processing, or performs some local processing before passing the information along. It is also concerned with activating and deactivating itself. If a view has subviews, each subview has a corresponding controller for handling its own interface interactions.

There are several advantages of using the MVC scheme:

1. The MVC scheme allows a single model object to have more than one view, i.e., more than one display representation.
2. The MVC scheme permits views to be used as parts for assembly into larger units. New kinds of views can be constructed using views as subviews.
3. The MVC scheme permits controllers to be interchanged, allowing different user-interaction modes, for example, ranging from the expert mode to the nonexpert mode.
4. The MVC scheme separates input processing from output processing. An input through one of the multiple views of the same model changes the model state, which updates all these views and their output.

The MVC scheme specifies not only the use of three objects but also the connections among them as shown in Figure 5.1. Views have exactly one controller and one model. They can also have subviews and a superview. Controllers have exactly one view and one model. Models can have many views associated with them. Each view knows explicitly about its model and its controller. Each controller knows explicitly about its model and its view. However, there is no explicit connection from the model to the other two. Nevertheless, they must be connected if a change to the model is to be reflected in all of its views. The simplest solution is for the model itself to explicitly signal the views. This requires each object that works as a model to be able to easily add a field for keeping track of related views. This solution is, however, unreasonable since the MVC scheme aims to allow any object to work as a model.

## 5.3.2 Dependencies in MVC

The MVC scheme uses either of the following two solutions. Assuming that the total number of active models in the system is reasonably small, the first solution keeps all ob-

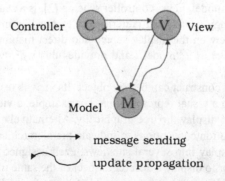

**Figure 5.1**   A basic MVC (model–view–controller) framework.

jects playing the role of models in a global identity dictionary of the system. Each model serves as a key in this dictionary, and associated value is a collection of views on that model. The second solution provides a model object with a local instance variable for maintaining its views. A special protocol is provided whereby a model can signal its views of a change. The model explicitly sends itself a "**changed**" message. Then the system accesses either the global identity dictionary or the local instance variable to retrieve the list of all the views on this model, and then sends each of these views an "**update**" message.

This generic mechanism can be used for arbitrary dependency maintenance. If a change of object *A* may effect a change in object *B*, we say that there is a dependency from object *A* to object *B*. Object *A* is termed a sponsor; object *B* is termed a dependent. Keeping track of dependent views of models is a particular application of this generic mechanism.

The dependency maintenance mechanism above maintains a consistency among multiple views of the same model by propagating its state change to all the views, even if the model is modified only through one of these views or by a separate process.

Sponsors can communicate with their dependents in the following three ways: (1) by broadcasting a zero- or one-parameter message, (2) by indicating that they have changed, or (3) by requesting that they be allowed to make a change. The first and second methods use "**changed**" (and hence "**update**") messages with and without parameters, whereas the third uses "**changedRequest**" (and hence "**updateRequest**") messages with and without parameters. An "**updateRequest**" message to a dependent returns "true" if the sponsor should be allowed to update itself; otherwise, it returns "false." If the message takes a parameter, the recipient takes this into account when returning a value.

Dependents, on the other hand, react either to an "update" command or to a query by a sponsor asking for permission to modify itself.

A complex view may consist of several subviews, each in turn potentially containing additional subviews. The individual views in the hierarchy are explicitly connected as shown in Figure 5.2. If view *B* is above view *A* in such a hierarchy, as shown in this fig-

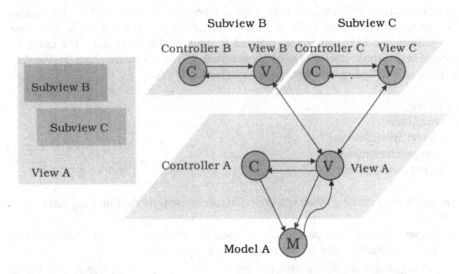

**Figure 5.2** A view hierarchy and its MVC-implementation structure.

ure, *B* is called a subview of *A*, whereas *A* is a superview of *B*. The root view in the hierarchy is the top-level view. Views are provided with operations for extracting subviews and the superview if they have any. Controllers, on the other hand, do not form a hierarchy by themselves. Each of them is associated with a view, and their views may form a hierarchy.

Meme media represent each media object with a simplified version of the MVC scheme. The IntelligentPad architecture uses a dependency not only from the model of each pad to its view, but also from the view of each pad to the views of its child pads.

### 5.3.3   Pluggable VC

Each controller is always paired with a view, and vice versa. Such a pair is sometimes called a display object. Each display object has two functions. One is the graphical display of some aspect of its model, and the other is the response to user events. Many display objects pop up a menu in response to a mouse event, and then detect which entry is selected by the mouse. Many display objects display the same type of objects, but deal with different models, aspects, and menus. There are two ways to cope with this variety. The first method creates specialized classes of the single, more general display object class. The second method uses different instances of the same display object class, but embeds the different data needed for the different applications in these instances; it uses a generic class definition with some parameters to deal with different models, their different aspects, and different menus. The first method is called the specialization approach; the second is called the pluggable VC approach [3]. Earlier versions of Smalltalk were entirely based on the specialization approach, but the pluggable VC approach later became more popular.

As mentioned in the previous subsection, a single model may have more than one display object. Different display objects may have different pop-up menus, and may deal with different aspects of the same model. They graphically display these aspects. Some display objects accept users' input to modify these aspects of the same model. In order to make each display object independent from these differences, we need to move all the information about these differences from these display objects to the model. This defines each display object as a pluggable VC that is parameterized with one model and three message selectors. The model must respond to these message selectors. For example, pluggable text display objects can be created from the same generic class TextView by specifying a model along with three message selectors:

> TextView
>   **on:** aModel
>   **aspect:** aspectSelector
>   **change:** changeSelector
>   **menu:** menuSelector

These selectors (actually symbols) must be designed to perform the following tasks.

1. "**aspectSelector**" (no parameters) is used to specify an aspect of the model. It should return the value of the model's aspect.

2. "**changeSelector**" (one parameter) must update the model in response to a user modification in the display object. Its parameter is the revised value for the model's

aspect. The model has the option to accept or neglect the change. If it accepts, the method should return "true," otherwise "false."

3. "**menuSelector**" (no parameter) must return a menu as an object.

The parameterized class definition for these pluggable display objects can use "model **perform:** aspectSelector" to obtain the model aspect, "model **perform:** changeSelector **with:** newAspect" to modify this aspect with a new value, and "model **perform:** menuSelector" to obtain the menu selector. This definition is generic in the sense that it does not directly use any model-specific messages.

To accommodate the view, the model must be provided with the following methods for these messages, and with some additional ones.

1. An "**aspectSelector**" that returns its specified aspect as an object
2. A "**changeSelector**" that accepts a modified value of the specified aspect as an object, and returns "true" or "false" depending on whether or not the change request was accepted and made
3. A "**menuSelector**" that returns a menu as an object
4. External changes to the model that affect the aspect being viewed should send a "self **changed**: aspectSelector" message. This message is issued only if the model's aspect becomes different from its previous version
5. A method "**changeRequestFrom:** aView" that returns a Boolean indicating whether or not the display object is allowed to change the model's aspect

These mechanisms for pluggable display objects permit application-specific behaviors to be added to these display objects without having to construct specialized classes for these objects. These display objects can be plugged onto any object if it is provided with the above-mentioned methods. In order to plug a pluggable display object onto some model, we only need to specify its model parameter and its three message selector parameters using "**on: aspect: change: menu:.**"

In meme media systems, each primitive meme media object is atomic. Pads are atomic in IntelligentPad. Meme media objects need not exploit the pluggable VC approach. Such exploitation, however, allows the developer to provide the library of display objects independently from the library of model objects, which allows pad developers to combine an arbitrary display object with an arbitrary model object to define a new primitive pad. The pluggable VC mechanism is used only by pad developers, not by pad users. IntelligentPad architecture, however, exploits the pluggable connection between a pad and its child pads. Users can use this pluggable connection to compose and decompose composite pads.

## 5.4 WINDOW SYSTEMS AND EVENT DISPATCHING

Easy interaction with entities in a computational environment using familiar metaphors requires not only their object-oriented graphical representation, but also their reactiveness to user events. Typical user events are mouse events and keyboard events. These should normally be applied to the outermost graphical object at the mouse cursor location. Some objects may be able to grab these events when they are changed to their event-grabbing mode. Such a mode change is also specified by a mouse event. Different events may define different event-grabbing modes. For each type of event-grabbing mode, no more than one object can be simultaneously changed to this mode. While there is one object in some type of event-grabbing mode, all the user events of this type are applied to this object. Both the detection of user events and their application to appropriate objects are summarized as the event dispatching, and performed by event dispatchers.

When you have several tasks to perform concurrently, you must have an independent working environment for each of them. These working environments should be simultaneously opened on the display screen. Each has its own graphical objects. Each of these environments should remember which graphical object is currently grabbing events, even if the mouse cursor temporarily leaves this environment. The graphical representation of such an environment is called a top-level window, i.e., a window that is not subordinate to any others. Each top-level window is given an independent process to run its controller. The activation and deactivation of these processes are coordinated by the window manager.

### 5.4.1   Event Dispatching

When visual objects are all modeled by MVC triples, their controllers work as event dispatchers. The dispatching of events to the outermost graphical object, namely the one without any subviews, is performed by the following method defined for the controllers of graphical objects.

**ControlActivity**
    self **controlToNextLevel**

When this method is invoked, the controller executes the following method to dispatch the current user event it has received to the controller of its subview that has a mouse cursor in it:

**ControlToNextLevel**
|aSubView|
    aSubView ← view **subViewWantingControl**.
    aSubView ~~ nil **ifTrue:** [aSubView **controller startUp**]

The same process is repetitively executed by the controller of the subview, which is defined by the following startUp method:

**startUp**
    self **controlInitialize**.
    self **controlLoop**.
    self **controlTerminate**

where

**controlLoop**
    [self **isControlActive**] **whileTrue:** [self **controlAcitivity**]

Whether the controller is active or not depends on the characteristics of the graphical object. Here we show the two candidate definitions:

**isControlActive**
  "Remains active as long as the mouse cursor is within the view."
  ↑ self **viewHasCursor**

**isControlActive**
  "Remains active as long as no button is pressed outside the view."
    ↑ status == #active and: [
      sensor **anyButtonPressed ifTrue:** [self **viewHasCursor**] **ifFalse:** [true]]

For example, the second definition can be used to grab the keyboard events.

The specific event reactions that are characteristic of each pad are defined by overwriting the "**ControlActivity**" method or the "**controlLoop**" method itself. For example, the typical "**controlActivity**" method is defined as follows:

**controlActivity**
|insideView|
    insideView ← self **viewHasCursor**.
    sensor **redButtonPressed** & insideView
      **ifTrue:** [ ↑ self **redButtonActivity**].
    sensor **yellowButtonPressed** & insideView
      **ifTrue:** [ ↑ self **yellowButtonActivity**].
    sensor **blueButtonPressed** & insideView
      **ifTrue:** [ ↑ self **blueButtonActivity**].
    super **controlActivity**

The "**xxButtonPressed**" method is used to check if the "**xx**" button is pressed, whereas the "**xxButtonActivity**" method defines how to react when the "**xx**" button is pressed. The last line of the above method performs the "**controlActivity**" method for the standard controller.

In the above discussion, we have assumed that the same single process executes these methods. The controllers with these methods are used by graphical objects that are run by the same single process.

Windows are also graphical objects. They are classified into two categories—scheduled windows and unscheduled windows. Scheduled windows are given independent processes, and run independently from other scheduled windows. They correspond to top-level windows, i.e., windows that are not subordinate to any others. Unscheduled windows correspond to subordinate windows in a multilevel window, and execute as part of the process associated with the top-level scheduled window. Scheduled windows have scheduled controllers, whereas unscheduled windows have unscheduled controllers.

Unscheduled controllers are defined similarly to the controllers of graphical objects we have described above. Scheduled controllers, on the other hand, are defined as follows.

The activation and deactivation of the scheduled window controllers are coordinated by the window manager. Whereas the process manager is responsible for all processes in the system, the window manager is responsible for one of them, i.e., the process corresponding to the active window controller. In order for a controller to become active, the window manager creates a process for it and schedules it. The window manager will not permit a second controller to be made active while the first is still executing. It maintains a list of scheduled controllers and chooses one for activation. A process is constructed corresponding to this chosen controller, and it is scheduled for execution. When the process completes, another controller is chosen, and the algorithm is repeated.

A window process is created and activated by sending the window manager the message "**searchForActiveController**." This method yields the following two consequences. (1) One of the scheduled controllers is selected, and a process is created for it. (2) The process sending the activation message is terminated. The process associated with the controller to be activated both starts up the chosen controller and then, after it terminates, chooses a new controller for subsequent activation. The starting-up and the termination of the chosen controller are done by sending the "**startUp**" message described above.

Termination of a scheduled controller occurs when the message "**isControlActive**" to this controller returns a "false" value. A typical case is leaving a mouse cursor off the corresponding view. The condition may vary depending on the definition of this method for each controller. When the active controller is terminated, the "**searchForActiveController**" method searches the list of scheduled controllers for another scheduled controller to activate. This new one should be the one that is requesting the activation. It is detected by the "**isControlWanted**" message, which returns a true value if the receiver controller, for example, has the mouse cursor within its view. This condition may also vary depending on the definition of this method for each controller.

The mechanisms described above activate and deactivate scheduled windows, and dispatch user events appropriately to unscheduled windows or graphical objects on scheduled windows. Most modern window systems exploit these mechanisms, which are based on the MVC framework—X-Windows of MIT [4], Sun NeWS [5], and various versions of Microsoft Windows. Most window systems provide a library of primitive graphical objects, termed widgets; the library is called a window toolkit. Examples of window toolkits include Xt of MIT [6], Andrew Toolkit of CMU [7], OPEN LOOK Toolkit [8], Motif Toolkit [9], and Macintosh ToolBox, Some toolkit systems have object-oriented application development frameworks using these toolkits. Such frameworks include MacApp [10], Actor on top of MS Windows, NeXTStep Application Kit [11], Interface Builder [12], and HP's NewWave with Object Management Facility (OMF) and NewWave Office [13]. Some of these, for example, Interviews [14], its extension Fresco [15], Tcl and the Tk Toolkit [16], Visual Tcl [17], ET++ [18], and Taligent framework [19] provide their frameworks with their own toolkits and powerful programming languages. Some object-oriented application development framework systems with GUI toolkits focus especially on the integration of different media. Such multimedia toolkit systems include MAEstro Multimedia Authoring Environment [20], MADE [21], MediaMosaic Multimedia Editing Environment [22], MediaView [23], CMIFed [24], Mbuild [25], active media approach [26], and MET++ [27].

### 5.4.2 Redrawing of Overlaid Windows

Windows and graphical objects may be overlaid on each other. They may redraw themselves when they update themselves. The redrawing of one object sometimes damages what has been drawn by others, which requires the propagation of redrawing among overlaid objects. Inappropriate redrawing schemes may make the overlaid objects flap on each other.

Suppose that graphical object $A$ partially covers graphical object $B$. Both may change their drawings. Suppose first that the background color of object $A$ is neither transparent nor translucent. Object $A$ needs to save the damage area image of object $B$ so that it may leave this image when it changes its location. When object $B$ changes its display graphics, it also needs to notify object $A$ so that it updates the saved damage-area image of object $B$. This simple redrawing scheme, however, may make objects $B$ and $A$ redraw the overlapped area twice, which may cause flaps of this area. Here the flaps are only caused by the propagation of the redrawing. This can be solved by using the so-called double-buffering technique. Redrawing by each object is not directly drawn on the display screen until the redrawing propagation is completed. Each object redraws itself on an off-the-screen canvas. The final image after the completion of the redrawing propagation is then sent from this off-the-screen canvas to the display screen. Some systems allow us to mask a portion of the redrawing area in order not to redraw this portion. In such a system, object $B$ can redraw itself without using any off-the-screen canvas, masking the area covered by object $A$.

If the background color of object $A$ is transparent or translucent, the above-mentioned masking method does not work. This case requires a double-buffering technique to avoid any flaps of the overlapped area. The damage area also needs to be held by object $A$.

### 5.4.3 From Windowpanes to Visual Objects

The application of the MVC framework is not restricted to windowpanes; it can be applied to any visual objects. Recent versions of IntelligentPad systems also applied the pad framework to arbitrary graphical objects that you may directly put on a desktop or on a Web top. Kamui-Mintara, a recent Windows PC version developed by Hitachi Software, allows you to define pads in any shape, and to put them directly on a desktop. You may paste one of them on another in the same way as in the preceding versions. Plexware, another recent version from K-Plex Inc., allows you to manipulate pads on a Web page.

Among those object-oriented systems using the MVC framework for user-defined graphical objects, the most interesting recent proposal may be Squeak [28], which is an open programming language designed especially for personal computing and multimedia. Using Squeak, you can easily program the behavior of graphical objects, by visually combining slips representing either objects or messages on the display to compose a scenario for these objects. Squeak is a general-purpose programming language, whereas IntelligentPad is a media framework. Definitely, there are lots of potentialities in using Squeak as the base language of an IntelligentPad system, which we plan to do in the future.

### 5.5 SUMMARY

In object orientation, a system is viewed as a model of a real world with entities and events. Entities are all modeled as objects, whereas each event is modeled as a message sent from one object to another. Each object can interpret a set of messages and provide appropriate responses. This set is called the interface of the object. Each object responds to a message either by changing its state or by sending further messages to other objects.

Some objects may have their graphical representations on a display screen. User devices such as a mouse and a keyboard are considered resource objects. The object that receives a user event through such a resource object is called the target object of the event. User manipulation of these resource objects either results in messages sent directly to the target object, or causes state changes that the target object can later query to detect the occurrence of this user manipulation. This allows users to directly manipulate graphically represented objects. A special object-oriented programming framework is used to define visual objects that interact with their users. This framework is called MVC (model, view, and controller), and used to define modern window systems. Our media architectures described in later chapters are also based on the MVC framework.

Objects work as reusable components. Their accumulation will form an extensible library of components. The majority of object-oriented languages, on the other hand, focus on the intentional description of classes, and the reuse of class descriptions through the property-inheritance mechanism. Property inheritance is essentially an object-oriented way of reusing program codes, which need not be identical to the object-oriented way of modeling a real world. The reuse of description is based on an "*is-a*" hierarchy among classes, whereas the reuse of objects as reusable components in a different assembly needs to focus on the composition with instance objects. The former leads to the class-refinement programming paradigm, whereas the latter leads to the synthetic-programming paradigm, namely the prototyping paradigm.

Meme media should exploit the prototyping paradigm so that users can easily replicate any meme media objects, combine them to compose arbitrary meme media objects, and recombine composite meme media objects to make new ones.

This chapter has also given a brief introduction to pluggablity of objects, and event-dispatching/redrawing mechanisms among graphical objects that are overlaid with each other on a display screen.

## REFERENCES

1.  D. Ungar and R. Smith. Self: The power of simplicity. In *Proceedings of the OOPSLA Conference*, pp. 227–241, 1987.
2.  G. Krasner and S. Popo. A cookbook for using the model-view-controller user interface paradigm in smalltalk-80. *Journal of Object-Oriented Programming 1*(3): 26–49, 1988.
3.  W. R. LaLonde and J. R. Pugh. *Inside Smalltalk. Volume II.* Prentice-Hall, Englewood Cliffs, NJ, 1991.
4.  R. Scheifler and J. Gettys. *X Window System: The Complete Reference to X lib, X Protocol, IC-CCM, XLFD,* 2nd edition. Digital Equipment Corp., 1990.
5.  J. Gosling, D. S. H. Rosenthal, and M. J. Arden. *NeWS Book: An Introduction to the Network/Extensible Window System.* Springer Verlag, New York, 1989.
6.  P. Asente and R. Swick. *The X Window System Toolkit.* Digital Press, Bedford, MA, 1990.
7.  A. J. Palay. Toward an "operating system" for user interface components. In M. Blattner and R. Dannenberg (eds.), *Multimedia Interface Design.* ACM Press, New York, pp. 339–355, 1992.
8.  D. A. Young and J. A. Pew. *The X Window System Programing and Applications with Xt: OPEN LOOK Edition.* Prentice-Hall, Englewood Cliffs, NJ, 1992.
9.  D. A. Young. *The X Window System Programing and Applications with Xt: OSF/Motif Edition.* Prentice-Hall, Englewood Cliffs, NJ, 1990.
10. D. A. Wilson, L. S. Rosenstein, and D. Shafer. *C++ Programming with MacApp.* Addison-Wesley, Reading, MA, 1990.
11. NeXT. *NextStep Developer's Library.* NeXT, Inc., 1992.
12. B. Webster, *The NeXt Book,* 2nd edition. Addison-Wesley, Reading, MA, 1991.
13. Hewlett-Packard. *HP NewWave Environment General Information Manual.* Hewlett-Packard, Cupertino, CA, 1988.

14. M. Linton, J. Vlissides, J., and P. Calder. Composing user interfaces with interviews. *IEEE Computer, 22*(2): 8–22, 1989.

15. M. Linton and C. Price. Building distributed user interface with Fresco. *The X Resource, 5,* 77–88, 1993.

16. J. K. Ousterhout. *Tcl and Tk Toolkit.* Addison-Wesley, Reading, MA, 1994.

17. D. H. Young *The Visual Tcl Handbook.* Prentice-Hall PTR, Upper Saddle River, NJ, 1997.

18. A. Weinand, E. Gamma, and R. Marty. ET++—An object-oriented application framework in C++. *Structured Programming, 10*(2), 1989.

19. S. Cotter and M. Potel. *Inside Taligent Technology.* Addison-Wesley, Reading, MA, 1995.

20. G. D. Drapeau. Synchronization in the MAEstro Multimedia Authoring Environment. In *Proceedings of ACM Multimedia '93,* 1993.

21. I. Herman, G. J. Reynolds, and J. Davy. MADE: A multimedia application development environment. In *Proceedings of the IEEE International Conference on Multimedia Computing and Systems,* 1994.

22. J.-K. Lin. MediaMosaic—A multimedia editing environment. In *Proceedings of UIST '92,* 1992.

23. R. L. Phillips. MediaView—A general multimedia digital publication system. *CACM, 34*(7), 1991.

24. G. van Rosum, J. Jansen, K. S. Mullender, and D. C. A. Bulterman. CMIFed: A Presentation environment for portable hypermedia documents. In *Proceedings of ACM Multimedia '93,* 1993.

25. R. Hamakawa and J. Rekimoto. Object composition and playback models for handling multimedia data. In *Proceedings of ACM Multimedia '93,* 1993.

26. S. Gibbs. Composite multimedia and active objects. In *Proceedings of OOPSLA '91,* 1991.

27. P. Ackermann. *Developing Object-Oriented Multimedia Software Based on the MET++ Application Framework.* dpunkt—Verlag fuer digitale Technologie GmbH, Heidelberg, Germany, 1996.

28. M. Guzdial and K. Rose. *Squeak: Open Personal Computing and Multimedia,* Prentice-Hall, Upper Saddle River, New Jersey, 2002.

## CHAPTER 6

# COMPONENT INTEGRATION

Although the highly advanced production technologies in use today depend heavily on computer systems, especially on their software, the production of software today is much like the production of hand-crafted goods in the nineteenth century. Software development is labor intensive; it takes too long to accomplish and costs too much. Once their development has been completed, today's software systems are typically inflexible and difficult to repair or modify. So-called rapid application development is even worse; it typically results in ad hoc software architectures that are difficult to scale up and maintain.

The highly advanced production technologies of today are the result of factoring out frequently used mechanisms as standard components and trying to design systems as compositions with such standard components. Mass production of standard components by specialized component providers results in the uniformity of their qualities, and significantly improves the average quality. The use of components introduces a hierarchy in the process of designing systems. The detailed design of each component is not referred to in the scheme of how to assemble components to compose a product. The assembly line is also concurrently designed in the process of designing each composite product, which allows the designer to optimize the cost performance of the assembling process.

This chapter provides a brief introduction to software components—the necessity to reuse existing software components, architectures for defining and assembling them, frameworks for their visual representation and direct manipulation, and integration of legacy software systems. We will also focus on the maintainability of composed systems; flexible composition structures may provide ease of composition, but may result in poor maintainability.

Components expose only their interfaces, which is usually not sufficient to imagine how to reuse them. The ways of using each component are not independent from its contexts. In this chapter, we will also focus on the use of sample compositions as representations of component contexts.

## 6.1   OBJECT REUSABILITY

Object-oriented programming has opened up two ways of reusing existing software. One is the reuse of defining codes, and the other is the reuse of running object instances as components. Software development based on either or both of these two types of reusing existing software is called component-based software development [1, 2].

The reuse of a code fragment requires knowledge both of its original context and of its reuse context. One mechanism that allows this type of reuse is property inheritance. This mechanism assumes a hierarchy of class definitions. For each class, the subclass inherits its definition code from this superclass with some overriding modifications. Code fragments to be reused are not objects themselves. They are not components since their reuse requires knowledge of its content details. They are not semantically meaningful units. The same is true for any code fragment to be newly added. This implies that this method of reusing codes requires programming expertise. The cost of programming the overriding portion is roughly proportional to the size of this portion with respect to the whole. This type of reuse reduces the programming cost only by a constant factor; it cannot significantly improve application development performance.

Another mechanism that allows the reuse of codes is the definition of a new class as a composite class constructed with existing classes. For example, the class of technical reports may have the following component classes—title, author, abstract, chapter, and reference. Most properties of a composite class are those of the component classes, with some properties additionally defined. Component classes are just called components. Here again, the definition of a composite class requires not only programming expertise, but also knowledge of its components—their messages, message formats, parameter types, and return value types.

The reuse of running object instances, on the other hand, requires no knowledge of their content details. It does, however, require a coherent way to functionally combine these instances to compose a new compound object. Object instances with such a coherent connection mechanism work as application software components, collectively termed component software, or simply componentware. A sufficiently large library of components replaces the programming of codes with the assembly of components.

Furthermore, the composition structures also become reusable if they are appropriately restricted and kept regular enough to discuss their abstract patterns. This leads to architectural patterns and application frameworks for system development with software components.

Meme media should exploit the reuse of running object instances since they are reused not by programmers but by end-users who have no programming expertise. They should be provided with a sufficiently large library of components, which should be open for future extension by many different component providers.

## 6.2   COMPONENTS AND APPLICATION LINKAGE

The reuse of running object instances means either their reuse by program codes or by object compositions. Their reuse by a program code means that some of their functions and properties are utilized by a program; the reuse of running object instances by an object composition means that they can be arbitrarily combined together to define a new composite object. Both cases require each reusable object instance to expose its interface as a list of message names. Such reusable object instances are called components. Some messages invoke methods of components, whereas some others access properties of components. Some messages may work as events to components. Some component systems such as ActiveX Controls [3] and JavaBeans [4] distinguish these different uses of messages. However, these are all essentially nothing but messages. The use of such an exposed message of an application object by a program to invoke its method is called an application linkage between the program and the application object.

In the reuse of components by a program code, the programmer explicitly specifies which components to utilize and which of their exposed messages to send to these components in order to access their functions (Figure 6.1). The programmer needs to know a priori the interface of each component he or she reuses.

In the reuse of components by an object composition, the functional connection of one component to another requires at least that one of them can send a message to the other. This implies that each component needs to expose its interface so that others can access its functions through this interface. Furthermore, the reuse of components by an object composition must guarantee the pluggability of components. Each component in a composition should be easily replaceable with another component having similar functionality. This similar functionality need not be accessed by the same message used to access the original component's functionality. This implies that the program of each component should explicitly specify neither the components it accesses nor the messages it uses to access their functions. The program of each component must be independent from the component it may access and from the message it may send to this component.

The functional connection of one component to another is specified outside of any components' program codes by a component-integration environment, which is called by different names such as authoring tool or construction environment. Some component-integration environments are static, whereas others are dynamic. Static component-integration environments compose a specified composition during the load-and-link time of re-

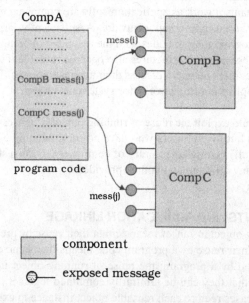

**Figure 6.1** The reuse of components by a program code.

quired components, whereas dynamic component-integration environments can compose a specified composition during the run time of required components.

The pluggability of components requires each component program to implicitly specify which other components it accesses and which messages it uses for each of these accesses. Each component program must define the placeholders for the components it accesses in a specific composition, and also the placeholders for the messages it uses for each of these accesses in this composition (Figure 6.2). Placeholders of the former type are called component placeholders; those of the latter type are called message placeholders. A component-integration environment is used by a composer, i.e., a person who integrates components, to specify the filler for each of these placeholders of the components that are reused in a composition (Figure 6.3).

Suppose that a component accesses $m$ other components with $n$ different messages. The program of this component uses m different component placeholders {$comp(i)$} and $n$ different message placeholders {message($j$)}. Its component access is stated in the program as follows:

*Disp* **send:** *message(j)* **to:** *comp(i)* **with:** parameters

Here, *comp(i)* and *message(j)* are, respectively, its $i$th component placeholder and its $j$th message placeholder, and *Disp* denotes a message dispatcher. These placeholders will be filled in later when a composer specifies a composition using a component-integration environment. The component placeholders provided by a component are called the plugs of this component; the number of plugs is referred to as the connectivity of the component.

The simplest model of pluggable components is obtained by restricting each component to have only one component placeholder and one message placeholder (Figure 6.4). Let us call this simplified composition model a "uniplug" composition model. This sim-

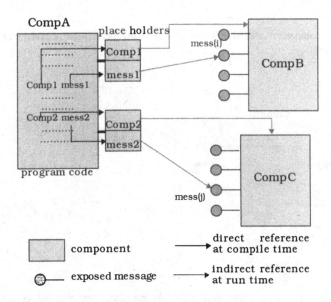

**Figure 6.2**   Pluggable components use pairs of placeholders, one for a component ID and the other for a message.

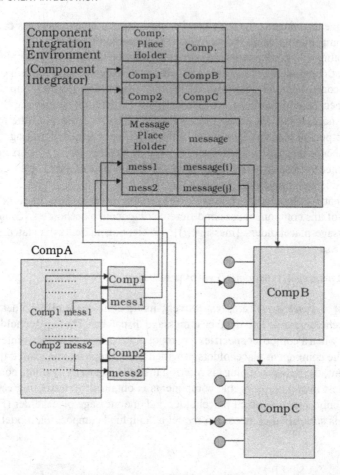

**Figure 6.3** A component integrator is used to specify the place filler for each placeholder of pluggable components.

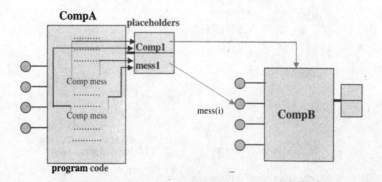

**Figure 6.4** Pluggable components, each with only one component placeholder and only one message placeholder.

plifies composition specification, which is fundamental in the component integration by end-users.

Furthermore, you may consider each pair of a component and one of its exposed messages as an object. Such an object is called a "slot" (Figure 6.5). Now the above-mentioned component access statement is replaced with the following.

*Disp* **send:** ($comp(i)$, $message(j)$) **with:** parameters

This may be further replaced with the following:

*Slot* **of:** ($comp(i)$, $message(j)$) **send:** parameters

Here, "*Slot* **of:** ($comp(i)$, $message(j)$)" becomes a slot when it is evaluated. Now the message "**send:**" is interpreted as a message accepted by any slot. We may further extend the slots to accept more than one standard message as shown in Figure 6.6, where "**send$_i$:**" is the $i$th message accepted by any of the slots.

As a special case of this framework, we may restrict the slot accessing messages to the following two:

Slot **set:** value
Slot **gimme**

A "**set:**" message sends a parameter value to a slot, whereas a "**gimme**" message requests a return value from a slot. A uniplug model that exploits this simplest version of the slot framework is shown in Figure 6.7. As described in the next chapter, our meme media components exploit this model. The parameter of a "**set:**" message and the return value of

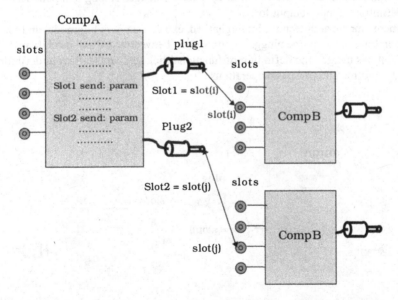

**Figure 6.5** Each pair of a component and one of its exposed messages can be considered as an object called a slot. Now the plugging is the binding between the formal name "Slot" and an actual slot object "slot($i$)."

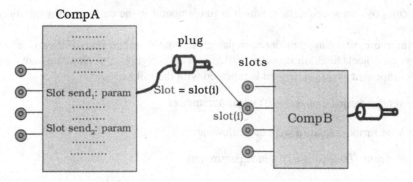

**Figure 6.6** A uniplug model that allows each slot to accept more than one standard message.

a **"gimme"** message may have different value types even if they access the same slot. The pair of these two value types defines the slot type.

Systems for component reuse by program codes do not require component pluggability, and provide no standard framework such as component and message placeholders for the implicit specification of reused components and messages. ActiveX [3] and Java [5] including JavaBeans [4] both fall in this category. JavaBeans, however, has several component integration environment systems such as Java Studio from Sun Microsystems, JBuilder from Borland, and VisualAge from IBM. Java Studio, for example, uses a wiring window to define linkages among components, and another separate window to define the layout of forms corresponding to some components. A form is a display object of a component, and works as an input/output cell. Most component integration environment systems separately treat the definition of functional linkages among components and the layout definition of input/output forms.

Our meme media architecture, IntelligentPad, exploits the uniplug model and the slot-connection framework for the pluggable connection between a pad and its child pads. Furthermore, it has merged the definition of functional linkages and the layout definition of input/output forms into pad paste operations.

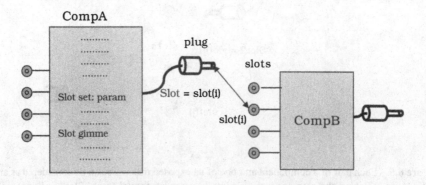

**Figure 6.7** A uniplug model that allows each slot to accept either a "set" or "gimme" message.

## 6.3  COMPOUND DOCUMENTS AND OBJECT EMBEDDING/LINKING

As described in Section 2.1.4, the compound-document model was first adopted on computers by desk-top publishing systems. These allowed us to put images, drawings, tables, and charts into a single text page. Since then, the compound-document model has gradually increased the variety of embedded components to include animations, video cuts, and script programs. Now, the compound-document model can put any object in the object-orientation paradigm into a single document page whenever this object is given an appropriate media-component representation (Figure 6.8). Objects in the object-oriented paradigm are in general reactive. They exchange messages with each other, and some react to users' operations. The model with this extension is called the reactive compound-document model.

We can put an object into a document page in two ways. The document may contain this object, or it may contain only a reference pointer to this object (Figure 6.9). The former is called "object embedding," and the latter is referred to as "object linking." Microsoft's OLE (Object Linking and Embedding) [6] was named after this. Both ways define the view integration based on the compound-document model. By the term "compound-document architectures," we simply denote architectures with this view-integration framework based on

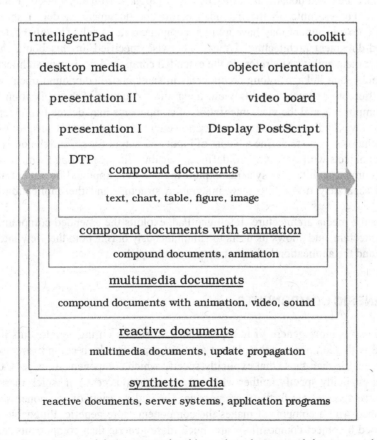

**Figure 6.8**  From compound documents to the object-oriented compound-document architecture.

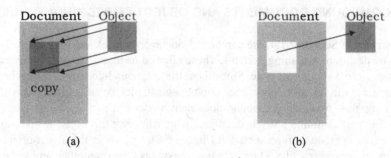

**Figure 6.9**  Two ways of putting an object in a document. (a) Object embedding. (b) Object linking.

the compound-document model. Such compound-document architectures include Microsoft's OLE, its extension ActiveX [3], CI Lab's OpenDoc [7], and HP's NewWave [8].

Although the original compound document model has only two levels—the text document as the first level, and the component objects as the second level—it can be easily extended to allow each component to have other components on itself. Furthermore, the base need not be a text document; it may be any component with a media-component representation. For example, in the extended compound-document model, a spreadsheet placed in a text document may have a video component in its cell. This also extends the compound-document architecture. Unless otherwise specified, in this book, the compound-document architecture refers to the extended compound-document architecture.

The application linkage among components in an extended compound-document may have a different structure from its view integration structure. The application linkage among components and the view integration of components may define two independent structures. Java Studio, a component-integration environment for JavaBeans, for example, has two windows—one to define a layout of input and output forms, and the other to wire JavaBeans objects with each other to define application linkage among them. Most compound-document architecture systems exploit the simple compound-document architecture, and separately define the view integration structure and the application linkage structure.

Our meme media architecture, IntelligentPad, exploits the extended compound-document architecture, and allows its users to simultaneously define both the view integration structure and the application linkage structure among pads.

## 6.4  GENERIC COMPONENTS

A component is more generic if it imposes less restriction on the components it can be combined with. Components that do not explicitly specify which components to access are more generic than those that explicitly specify which components to access. Components that explicitly specify neither which components to access nor which messages to use for these accesses are furthermore generic. The wider variety of components that can be combined with a component makes the component more generic. Pluggable components reused by object compositions are much more generic than components reused by program codes.

Components that do not explicitly specify which components to access but explicitly specify which messages to use for these accesses could be made more generic if we could somehow standardize the message names among components. This may work for some specific application domains, but definitely not in general. The implicit specification of partner components and the messages to access them is fundamental for a component to be generic. The program of such a component uses component placeholders and message placeholders to access other components. These placeholders will be filled in later when a composer specifies a composition using a component-integration environment.

The exploitation of slots with standard slot-access messages allows each component to implicitly access some slots with explicitly specified standard slot-accessing messages. This also makes the components sufficiently generic. The parameter and the return value of such an implicit component-access statement may take different object types for different combinations of place fillers. Components that automatically perform necessary conversions for different types are more generic than those without this function. However, this function may introduce too much overhead to each component.

Components may have some messages that can be accepted by any component. Some components may just neglect some of these messages after accepting them. These messages can be explicitly used in programming a component without making this component less generic. An example of such messages is an "update" message that is used to notify that the sender component has just been updated. This "update" message takes no parameters. The "copy" message is another example. It replicates each component. In a system in which all components have display representation, the "move" message to change their location on the display, and the "resize" message to resize them are also examples of such messages.

## 6.5 WHAT TO REUSE—COMPONENTS OR SAMPLE COMPOSITIONS?

In the following sections, we only consider the reuse of components by object compositions. A composite portion of a composite object may also be considered as a reusable component. Components that are not decomposable are primitive components, whereas those that are themselves composite objects are composite components. The pluggability of a composite component in a composition depends on how many different plugs are used to connect this composite component to the rest. Fewer plugs lead to higher pluggability of the composite component. The simplest case uses no more than one plug to connect a composite component to the rest. Under this restriction, any composition will have a tree-structured connection structure among primitive components. As described in the next chapter, our meme media components basically satisfy this restriction.

Components expose only their interfaces, which is usually not sufficient for us to imagine how to reuse them. Many projects on reusable components have failed in the past for this specific reason. The ways of using each component are not independent of its context. A slider component may scroll texts on a text window, skim a video cut, or change the volume of a sound. Its role may change in different contexts. Furthermore, if two different components used in two different compositions have similar contexts in these compositions, and if one of them is used in another context, it is highly probable that the other can be also used in this new context. Various contexts of a component provide information about varieties of its use.

Contexts of a component can be presented as sample compositions using this component. When provided with sample compositions, component libraries provide much more information about components and the ways to reuse them. Furthermore, instead of providing a component library, we may provide a library of sample compositions. Each component in a sample composition may be associated with those components that may be substituted for the original component in this context. What are reused are not components but sample compositions. In their reuse, sample compositions are partially decomposed, and some composite components are recombined with new components.

When described at a certain level of abstraction, some mutually different components may be considered identical to each other, and, furthermore, some mutually different compositions may be considered identical with each other. We may consider more than one such level of abstraction. Such repetitively appearing abstract structures of compositions are so-called patterns [9, 10] and frameworks [11]. They are also reused to compose new objects. Chapter 16 will discuss patterns and frameworks in detail in the context of our meme media architecture, IntelligentPad.

## 6.6   REUSE AND MAINTENANCE

A large library of reusable generic components allows us to rapidly develop sophisticated applications. However, the rapid prototyping with components does not necessarily lead to good maintainability of the developed applications. The maintainability of a composite application indicates how easy we can replace each of its primitive and composite components with a new version or with a different component that has similar functionality. A component with more plugs to connect itself to the remainder is harder for us to replace with another than a component with fewer plugs (Figure 6.10). Compositions with cyclic connections are also harder for us to maintain than those without cyclic connections (Figure 6.11).

The simplest case is the acyclic uniplug composition model that makes each component provide only one plug to connect itself to another without forming cyclic connections. Suppose we pull out a plug of a component in some composition. When we pull out

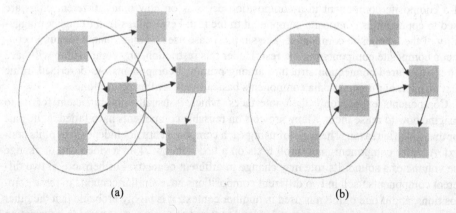

(a)                                                (b)

**Figure 6.10**   A component with multiple plugs to connect itself to the remainder is harder to replace with another than a component with a single plug. (a) Components with multiple plugs (difficult to replace a component). (b) Components with a single plug (easy to replace any component).

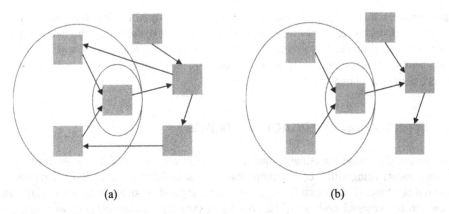

(a)                                                    (b)

**Figure 6.11**  Compositions with cyclic connections are harder to maintain than those without cyclic connections. (a) A composition with cyclic connections. (b) A composition without cyclic connections.

a plug, the component resets its single component placeholder to break its connection to another component. In the acyclic uniplug composition model, pulling out a plug always decomposes any composition to two independent composite components.

The reuse of components should take into account the ease of future maintenance of whatever is composed. The acyclic uniplug composition model provides each composite application with good maintainability. It defines each application as a tree-structured composition with components as its nodes. All the implicit component accesses are performed along the edges of this tree, but some explicit component accesses with standard messages need not be performed along these edges. Explicit component accesses independent from these edges also make the maintenance of composite applications difficult. Their maintenance becomes much easier if we restrict explicit component accesses to those along these edges. The acyclic uniplug composition model that satisfies this further restriction is called the tree composition model. As described in the next chapter, our meme media components basically satisfy the tree composition model.

Because of the simple connection structures among components, the tree composition model is likely to complicate the data structures of parameters and return values that are exchanged between components in compositions. Components with multiple plugs can simplify these data structures, but lead to spaghetti-like connections and seriously reduce maintainability. The complex data structures of connections in the tree composition model, when interpreted as the semantics of each connection, provide useful information for the maintenance of each connection.

Some readers may think that the tree composition model cannot decompose programs with loops into components. Actually, it can decompose such programs in a restricted but desirable way. A single program loop, for example, consists of a loop skeleton and a sequence of procedures in this loop. The tree composition model decomposes such a program loop into a single base component that represents the loop skeleton and as many child components as there are procedures. The base component has as many slots as there are child components. Each child component is connected to the corresponding slot of the base component. The base component periodically invokes these child components in the specified order. The tree composition model does not break the loop structure of the original program, which is desirable from the viewpoint of maintainability. The tree composition model shares the same philosophy as the structured programming. The tree composition model can deal with any programs. In this sense, there is no restriction in its applicability. However, it strongly guides you in decomposing programs into components to achieve better maintainability.

## 6.7    INTEGRATION OF LEGACY SOFTWARE

Generic and pluggable components must expose their interfaces and implicitly access other components using either component/message placeholders or slots. Such components need not be objects if they satisfy these conditions. By adding an additional code, any program can be wrapped with a new exposed interface through which it is accessed, and through which it implicitly accesses other components. Such an additional code is called a wrapper. Components are not necessarily objects defined in some object-oriented system. Although they may not have class definitions or property inheritance, they have to expose their interfaces as lists of messages, and be able to implicitly access each other through component placeholders and message placeholders.

Therefore, in principle, any program becomes a pluggable component when it is wrapped by an appropriate wrapper. The functionality of such a component, however, depends on which functions of the wrapped program the wrapper can expose as messages of this component. Whatever wrappers might be used, functions that are not accessible from the outside of the original program cannot be exposed as messages of the components. Whether the migration of a legacy system into a components environment will succeed or not depends heavily on whether this legacy program allows us to invoke a sufficiently large set of its functions from its outside.

Visual components need to interact with user operations. They expose standard messages for user events. When a user event is applied to a visual component, the event dispatcher detects this event and sends a corresponding appropriate standard message to this visual component. When applied to a wrapped legacy system, such an event is handled either by the wrapper or by the internal legacy system. If the legacy system has no GUI, its wrapper can handle all such events. Otherwise, some events should be dispatched to the GUI of the legacy system. The program of the legacy system must be able to accept such dispatched events as messages. Furthermore, the event interpretation by the GUI of the legacy system should be consistent to the standard event interpretation by visual components. Otherwise, some inherent direct operations of the legacy system may be interpreted as some of the standard operations of visual components. In such cases, we have to redefine the mapping between events and operations of the legacy system, which is usually a difficult task.

Furthermore, the migration of a legacy system with GUI into a visual component environment requires special consideration on its drawing function. The drawing by a visual component may damage, or be damaged by, the drawing by another component, which requires each visual component to have the capability of redrawing and managing damaged areas. The required capability is usually more than what is required for the GUI of the original legacy system. This difference should be programmed when we wrap this legacy system, which is again usually not an easy task. An often-used solution to this problem makes the legacy system draw its display output off the screen, and maps this image as a texture onto its visual component representation. This solution is sometimes called a "shadow copy" mechanism; it was used in HP NewWave architecture [8]. User events on the visual component need to be dispatched to the off-the-screen GUI of the legacy system.

## 6.8 DISTRIBUTED COMPONENT INTEGRATION AND WEB TECHNOLOGIES

Systems using objects distributed over a network as their components need to use a standard protocol for exchange messages among component objects. They also need a lookup service to find out a desired component object from a component repository, and to get its reference as a proxy object, as well as a method to access it through the proxy. Such a lookup service varies from a naming service to a content-addressable lookup service. A naming service accepts an object name and returns its reference; a content-addressable lookup service accepts a quantification condition of desired objects and returns their proxies.

### 6.8.1 CORBA and Application Server Component Technologies

CORBA (Common Object Request Broker Architecture) [12] proposed by OMG (Object Management Group) provides APIs called GIOPs (General Inter-ORB Protocols) for the communication between CORBA objects using ORBs (Object Request Brokers). CORBA uses IIOP (Internet Inter-ORB Protocol) as an intermediate protocol to bridge GIOP and TCP (Transmission Control Protocol). An ORB is a program that enables each distributed object to exchange messages with other distributed objects. CORBA objects may use any language, but each of them needs to install a special interface to send and receive messages through an ORB. Each CORBA object uses two kinds of interface codes, i.e., a stub for sending messages going through an ORB, and a skeleton for receiving messages coming through an ORB. In CORBA, the coding of stubs and skeletons uses a special language called IDL (Interface Definition Language).

JavaBeans [13] is a technology for Java program components called Beans. JavaBeans specifies API between components. In Web applications, when a sever-side Java servlet [14] receives a client request, it invokes the Bean for the requested processing with input parameters. When the Bean completes its processing, the servlet sends back the result to the client. You may use JSP (Java Server Pages) [15] for this output to the client. EJB (Enterprise JavaBeans) [16] is a specification introducing distributed object technologies to JavaBeans. EJB allows us to invoke components stored in different machines through a network. Its components are called Enterprise Beans. They are classified into two categories. Session Beans manage client requests and control the processing; Entity Beans perform database processing.

The execution of EJB requires an EJB server and an EJB container. An EJB server manages EJB containers, and provides Enterprise Bean functions; an EJB container resides in an EJB server and executes services provided by the EJB server. The invocation of Enterprise Beans as well as Beans is performed by a Java servlet executed in a Web server. Such a servlet is called an EJB client application. Each Enterprise Bean can also invoke another Enterprise Bean. Such a caller Enterprise Bean needs to be installed with the EJB client application function. Such invocations may make Enterprise Beans distributed in different servers cooperate with each other.

Each EJB client application accesses an EJB server, and gets information about registered objects using JNDI (Java Naming and Directory Interface) [17]. JNDI provides API to access the naming service that manages distributed objects with their names. Using JNDI, you can invoke any object registered in an EJB server without knowing its location. Each client application, then, asks an EJB container to create a Home object, which is responsible for creating and deleting Enterprise Bean instances. When creating an Enterprise Bean instance, the Home object also creates an EJB object that mediates the method invocation of the Enterprise Bean instance. The EJB client application becomes able to invoke the methods of this Enterprise Bean through this EJB object. The processing result is sent back to the client through this EJB object.

An application server is a software system that provides an execution environment for EJB components. J2EE (Java2 Enterprise Edition) [18] is an extension of Java2 Standard Edition, and includes API for EJB. Several venders provide application servers with J2EE functionalities. These include IBM's WebSphere, BEA WebLogic Server, and Oracle Application Server. In an application server, an EJB container provides various functions for the execution of EJB components. These functions include the interoperation between an EJB component and an EJB server, transaction management, session management for each client, life-cycle management of each EJB component instance, resource management, management of retrieved data as Entity Bean objects, and capability management of users and groups to restrict the access to EJB components.

The interoperation of a Web browser and a Web server over the Internet uses the HTTP protocol. Systems with such interoperation are implemented as either two-layer systems or three-layer systems. A two-layer system uses either a servelet or a JSP, and executes them together with data management on a single computer. A three-layer system uses EJB components to separate the application processing and the database processing from a Web server. The application processing is executed by an independent application server, i.e., an EJB server, whereas the database processing is performed by a database server. These three layers, the Web server layer, the application server layer, and the database server layer are sometimes called, respectively, the presentation layer, the business logic layer, and the data layer.

J2EE provides APIs called RMI (Remote Method Invocation) and RMI/IIOP (Internet Inter-Orb Protocol) for the communication between Enterprise Beans. RMI allows us the use of Java to define the object interface to other distributed objects. Each component uses two kinds of interface codes, i.e., a stub for outgoing messages and a skeleton for incoming messages. RMI/IIOP extends RMI for Enterprise Beans to communicate not only with each other, but also with CORBA objects. The communication between a servelet or a JSP and EJB components uses RMI or RMI/IIOP. For the communication between an application server and a database server, J2EE provides an API called JDBC (Java Database Connectivity) [19].

Microsoft's component technology for Windows is called COM (Common Object Model) [20]. COM components can be used in various languages including Visual Basic, Visual C++, and Visual J++. COM components are stored as EXE or DLL files. A COM library stores information about COM components, helps a client to locate a COM server including the desired COM component, and creates an instance of the COM component. The SCM (Service Control Manager) in the COM library sends back the client the reference information of the created COM object. ActiveX is basically the same as OLE. An ActiveX control or an OLE control is a component based on OLE. Its reference is embedded in an application. It is downloaded to a client through the Internet to execute there.

Different from Java applets, ActiveX controls use native codes. DCOM (Distributed Component Object Model) [21] is an extension of COM to cope with distributed objects. To use a COM component in a server machine, a client uses RPC (Remote Procedure Call) to ask the SCM (Service Control Manager) on the server machine for the instantiation of the COM component and the invocation of this object. In DCOM, the communication between a client and a COM object on different machines use a proxy at the client side and a stub at the server side. A proxy converts the COM object ID and parameters to the transportation format; a stub reconverts the transportation format data for the COM object to understand. These two conversions are called the marshalling and the unmarshalling, respectively.

Windows DNA (Distributed InterNet Application) [22] is a technology used to support application system development using distributed objects over the Internet. It basically provides a framework for three-layer systems, consisting of the presentation layer, the business logic layer, and the data layer. Windows DNA also provides ASP (Active Server Pages) [23] using VBScript, which is similar to JSP using Java.

Application server component technologies allow us to develop complicated application services accessible from Web documents. These application services can access application components distributed over the Internet, and may involve database access and transaction processing. Since the naming service by JNDI just returns the object location for a given object name, application server component technologies are mainly applied to intranetwork systems with definite sets of system components that are managed by their names. These technologies are mainly used to integrate enterprise information systems distributed over the network, and to make some functions accessible from Web browsers.

### 6.8.2   Web Services and Their Integration

Web service [24] is a technology for application programs distributed over the Internet to mutually utilize their services. Web service provides three mechanisms: the publication mechanism for each application to register itself as a Web service in a registry; the inquiry mechanism for a client or a Web service to find another registered Web service based on its provider's name, service name, service category, or service interface information; and the binding mechanism for the requesting client or Web service to invoke the retrieved Web service. UDDI (Universal Description, Discovery and Integration) [25] allows applications to register themselves as Web services in a UDDI directory, and allows clients or Web services to search a UDDI directory for those Web services satisfying the requirements. UDDI is also a Web service. UDDI works as a service broker. The requesting client (or application) and the registering application, respectively, work as service requesters and service providers. The registration of a Web service uses WSDL (Web Service Description Language) [26] to describe its detailed information. WSDL is an XML-based language used to describe, for each Web service, the methods and parameters it accepts, and its output format.

Clients can invoke a Web service in a different machine through a SOAP proxy as if invoking a local program—a program to invoke the Web service—and obtain its processing result. SOAP (Simple Object Access Protocol) [27] is an XML-based standard common interface between components distributed over the Internet. In CORBA and DCOM, components in different specifications cannot communicate with each other. Therefore, these technologies are mainly used in local network environments. The interoperation of components distributed over the Internet requires a standard common API based on both a standard message format and a standard RPC protocol over the Internet, which led to the proposal of SOAP. SOAP uses XML to represent access requests and return value data. Each request message in XML format is sent to a target component using POST method. SOAP allows both COM objects and CORBA objects to communicate with each other.

Web service technologies allows us to define Web documents with embedded services provided by Web servers. These Web services are published to an open repository by service providers. Web service technologies allow us to define a composed embedded service that orchestrates some public Web services using SOAP to perform its service task. Such an orchestration can be also published as a Web service. For example, a traveler agent may publish a flight reservation Web service, which may access flight reservation Web services of mutually competitive airlines to find the best offer. Interoperation of Web services defines integrated services, either for customers or for member companies, in a B2B (business-to-business) alliance. Various software vendors provide visual authoring tools for the composition or orchestration of Web services and its embedding into a Web page. For the composition and/or orchestration part, they provide UML-based visual programming environments and/or text editor environments with wizards, as well as the function to search and bind Web services in these environments. For the embedding of defined services into a Web page, they provide visual form layout editors that allow us to arrange forms on a Web page. These authoring tools also allow us to relate each form and a Web service parameter. Some allow you to specify a parameter in a text editor or in a diagrammatic programming environment to create a new form, which you can drag and drop anywhere on a form-layout editor. Some others allow you to create a form first, and to click it to open a text editor with a wizard, so you can specify which Web service to use. They are basically authoring tools for Web service integrators and Web page designers, and not for Web page readers. Some vendors provide personal portal editors for Web page readers to lay out fragments of different Web pages on a single canvas using frames. Microsoft's Digital Dashboard [28] is such a tool. These tools, however, provide no functional linkage mechanism between fragments of Web pages.

In 2000, a newly established venture company, K-Plex Inc. of San Jose, California, developed a new version of the IntelligentPad system called Plexware. This version uses XML both as the save format of pads and for the message exchange with servers. Plexware uses SOAP to communicate with Web services. Pads in Plexware run on an Internet Explorer browser. Plexware has wrapped Internet Explorer and provides its full function as a standard component pad.

### 6.8.3 The Internet as a Platform and Universal Document Interface

Microsoft.NET [29] is a new technology to make the Internet work as a single platform. Microsoft Windows uses ActiveX technologies for embedding a Windows document in another Windows document of a different type. Windows applications, including Words and Excel, are ActiveX objects. Web documents and applications running on Web pages, however, use XML and SOAP technologies that are different from ActiveX technologies. Microsoft.NET tries to unify these two different worlds of applications and documents.

ActiveX technologies allow us to embed an Excel worksheet in a Word document. A client receiving such a document, however, cannot reuse this document unless it installs all the application software systems required to execute those ActiveX objects used in the document. Web documents do not cause such problems; embedded applications are either downloaded for execution or invoked when required.

Microsoft.NET proposes the universal canvas technology as a unified document interface to replace ActiveX technology. When a universal canvas is used as a document page, the application program corresponding to each displayed data item is automatically invoked through the Internet and provides its function. Microsoft.NET tries to achieve independence from any OSs and programming languages. Programs in Microsoft.NET use class libraries provided by Microsoft.NET Framework. They are compiled to IL (Intermediate Language) codes, which CLR (Common Language Runtime) converts to native codes to execute. These mechanisms are similar to Java programs, Java codes, and JavaVM, but the programming with Microsoft.NET Framework allows us to use various de fact languages including C++, VB, COBOL, Pascal, Smalltalk, and Perl. Microsoft provides Visual Studio.NET and Microsoft.NET Framework SDK to support program development with Microsoft.NET Framework.

IBM Internet Technology Group and IBM Research proposed a new technology called Sash [30] that allows us to use standard Web technologies like HTML, XML, and JavaScript to develop applications utilizing client machines' performance and resources. These applications are called weblications. Sash enables Web application developers to utilize the desktop functions. Weblications run outside of browsers, directly on clients' desktops.

These technologies will unify desktop environments and the Web, which means the unification of applications and documents in these two environments. These documents may include local and remote application tools and services.

### 6.8.4 The Internet as Shared Memory Spaces for Objects

Sun Microsystems proposed a new technology called Jini [31] for various service-providing objects distributed over the Internet to dynamically organize a federation, or a dynamically defined flexible network, of objects. Some of these objects may not need to run on client computers or on servers, but may run in electronic appliances or other devices connected to the Internet by wire or radio.

The essential function of Jini is its Lookup service, which works as a broker between service provider objects and client objects. Neither of them needs to know each other in advance. Jini's Lookup service organizes participating objects into service groups. More than one Lookup service can maintain the same service group. One Lookup service may work as a gateway to another Lookup service.

Jini enables each object that wants to participate in some service group to discover this group. Actually, this discovery process finds a Lookup service that manages some objects in this service group, and makes this Lookup service return its RMI stub, i.e., its proxy, to the requester object for accessing this Lookup service. Through this proxy, the requester object can join the desired service group by registering its RMI interface instance as its proxy to the found Lookup service. This process is called a Join process. The Lookup service identifies each registered proxy with its interface type. A newly participating object sends a presence announcement packet to the network. This packet contains its IP address, its port number, and a name list of service groups it wants to participate in. This packet is multicast to Lookup services in the same domain. Each Lookup service monitors packets to identify each announcement packet. When a Lookup service finds an announcement packet, the service searches the name list in the packet for a service group that matches with one of its service groups. If it finds such a service group, the Lookup service returns its RMI stub as its reference to the sender object of this packet. When an object participating in some service group accesses its services, this object sends a request to the Lookup service, and gets an RMI stub, or a proxy, of a desired service object. Such a request specifies the interface type. This process is called a lookup process. These three processes, a discovery process, a join process, and a lookup process, provide a distributed mechanism for service provider objects and client objects to dynamically organize federations to collaborate for specific purposes.

Sun Microsystems proposed another new technology called JavaSpace [32] for objects on the network. A JavaSpace works as a shared memory defined over the network for reading, writing, and taking out shared objects. Objects stored in a JavaSpace are content-addressable, i.e., you may read or take out objects in a JavaSpace by specifying their template and some of their attribute values. A JavaSpace provides objects on the network with a blackboard system such as those used in AI. Some objects may define tasks and write them in a JavaSpace, whereas others may search the JavaSpace for unfinished tasks that they can process, take them out to perform, and return the result in the JavaSpace. The idea of such a mechanism originates in Linda, proposed by David Hillel Gelernder in 1982. His *Mirror Worlds,* published in 1991 [33], extends the basic idea, and proposed a tuple space, which became the basis of a JavaSpace. In a tuple space, each entry written in this space is a tuple, i.e., a list of attribute–value pairs. Objects can issue an SQL-like query to a tuple space to find desired tuples, read or take out these tuples, and write new tuples in a tuple space.

When applied to meme media, Jini and JavaSpace technologies will make meme media objects dynamically pluggable to various accessible federations of services on the Internet.

### 6.8.5 Distributed-Object Technologies and Meme Media Components

As described in the preceding subsections of Section 6.8, lookup services play the most important roles in distributed-object environments, especially in open environments over the Internet. Such environments consist of service providers, service brokers, and service requesters. Service providers register their services to lookup services. Service brokers orchestrate more than one service to perform sophisticated services. They ask lookup services for desired services, and register their newly defined composite services to lookup services. Service requesters simply ask lookup services for desired services, and invoke them to perform their tasks. Distributed-object technologies assume that all these players—service providers, service brokers, and service requesters—are software objects. Therefore, each lookup service should provide methods for software objects to specify what kind of services they want to access. Some lookup services allow software objects to specify services by their names; some others allow the specification by their interface. Others allow objects to specify services by their templates and attribute values. Lookup services return a reference to the found service, or a proxy of the found service.

In meme media component environments, we assume that users manually combine media components to define composite media objects. Meme media composition means not only layout composition, but also functional composition by defining linkage among components. Meme media component technologies, therefore, focus on an easy direct-manipulation way of arranging components on another component as well as functionally connecting them. It is the user, not a program, who accesses lookup services for primitive and/or composite components satisfying requirements. As opposed to lookup services that are mainly for programs, lookup services for humans require interactive access facilities for navigation, visual definition of queries, and direct manipulation for retrieving and registering visual components. Chapter 19 focuses on this subject for meme media objects.

## 6.9  SUMMARY

This chapter has given a brief introduction to software components: why it is necessary to reuse existing software, architectures for defining and assembling components, frameworks for their visual representation and direct manipulation, and integration of legacy software. We have also focused on the maintainability of composed systems and why flexible composition structures may provide ease of composition, but may result in poor maintainability.

The pluggability of components requires each component program to implicitly specify which other components it accesses and which messages it uses for each of these accesses. Each component program must define the placeholders for the components it accesses in a specific composition, and also the placeholders for the messages it uses for each of these accesses. Placeholders of the former type are called component placeholders; those of the latter type are called message placeholders. Furthermore, you may consider each pair of a component and one of its exposed messages as an object. Such an object is called a slot. As a special case of this framework, we may restrict the slot accessing messages to "Slot **set:** value" and "Slot **gimme.**" A "**set:**" message sends a parameter value to a slot, whereas a "**gimme**" message requests a return value from a slot.

The simplest model of composition allows each component to access only one other component through a single slot. As described in the next chapter, our meme media components exploit this model.

Systems using objects distributed over a network as their components need a lookup service to find a desired component object from a component repository and to get its reference as a proxy object, as well as a method to access it through the proxy. Such a lookup service varies from a naming service to a content-addressable lookup service. In meme media component environments, we assume that users manually combine media components to define composite media objects. It is a user, not a program, who accesses lookup services for primitive and/or composite components satisfying requirements. As opposed to lookup services mainly for programs, lookup services for humans require interactive access facilities for navigation, visual definition of queries, and direct manipulation for retrieving and registering visual components. Chapter 19 focuses on this subject for meme media objects.

## REFERENCES

1. A. W. Brown (ed.). *Component-Based Software Engineering.* IEEE Computer Society Press, Los Alamitos, CA, 1996.
2. O. Nierstrasz and D. Tschritzis. *Object-Oriented Software Composition.* Prentice-Hall, Englewood Cliffs, NJ, 1995.

3. A. Denning. *ActiveX Controls Inside Out.* Microsoft Press, Redmond, WA, 1997.

4. R. Englander. *Developing Java Beans.* O'Reilly & Associates, Sebastopol, CA, 1997.

5. D. Flanagan. *Java in a Nutshell.* O'Reilly & Associates, Sebastopol, CA, 1996.

6. Microsoft. *Object Linking and Embedding Programmer's Reference.* Microsoft Press, Redmond, WA, 1992.

7. J. Feiler, and A. Meadow. *Essential OpenDoc: Cross-Platform Development for OS/2, Macintosh, and Windows Programmers.* Addison-Wesley, Reading, MA, 1996.

8. Hewlett-Packard. *HP NewWave Environment General Information Manual.* Cupertino, CA, 1988.

9. E. Gamma, R. Helm, R. Johnson, and J. Vlissides. *Design Patterns: Elements of Reusable Object-Oriented Software.* Addison-Wesley, Reading, MA, 1995.

10. F. Bushmann, R. Meunier, H. Rohnert, P. Sommerlad, and M. Stal. *Pattern-Oriented Software Architecture: A System of Patterns.* Wiley, Chichester, UK, 1996.

11. A. A. R. Cockburn. The impact of object-orientation on application development. *IBM System Journal, 32*(3), 1993.

12. Object Management Group. *The Common Object Request Broker: Architecture and Specification,* 2.5 edition, September 2001.

13. M. Morrison. *Presenting Javabeans.* Sams, Indianapolis, IN, 1997.

14. J. Hunter, W. Crawford. *Java Servlet Programming.* O'Reilly & Associates, Sebastopol, CA, 2001.

15. S. Brown, L. Kim, J. Falkner, B. Galbraith, R. Johnson, R. Burdick, D. Cokor, S. Wilkinson, and G. Taylor. *Professional JSP,* Wrox Press, Chicago, 2001.

16. R. Monson-Haefel and M. Loukides (Editor). *Enterprise JavaBeans.* O'Reilly & Associates, Sebastopol, CA, 2001.

17. R. Lee and S. Seligman. *The Jndi API Tutorial and Reference: Building Directory-Enabled Java Applications,* Addison Wesley Longman, Reading, MA, 2000.

18. *Java 2 enterprise edition.* http://java.sun.com/j2ee/tutorial.

19. G. Reese and A. Oram (eds.). *Database Programming with JDBC and Java,* Second Edition. O'Reilly & Associates, Sebastopol, CA, 2000.

20. D. Rogerson. *Inside COM: Microsoft's Component Object Model with CDrom.* Redmond, WA, Microsoft Press, 1996.

21. F. E. Redmond. *Dcom: Microsoft Distributed Component Object Model with CDrom.* IDG Books Worldwide, Boston, MA, 1997.

22. S. J. Peterson and L. W. Storms. *Microsoft Windows DNA Exposed.* Sams, Indianapolis, IN, 1999.

23. A. K. Weissinger and R. Petrusha (eds.). *ASP in a Nutshell.* O'Reilly & Associates, Sebastopol, CA, 2000.

24. W3C Consortium. *Workshop on Web Services.* http://www.w3.org/2001/01/WSWS, 2001.

25. UDDI community. *Universal Description, Discovery, and Integration.* http://www.uddi.org.

26. Erik Christensen et al., *Web Services Description Language (WSDL) 1.1,* W3C Note, http://www.w3.org/TR/wsdl, 2001.

27. D. Box, et al. *Simple Object Access Protocol (SOAP) 1.1,* W3C NOTE, http://www.w3.org/TR/SOAP/, 2000 (The latest version is available at http://www.w3.org/TR/soap12/.)

28. Microsoft. *Digital Dashboard Integrating Microsoft Project Central into a Digital Dashboard.* http://www.microsoft.com/office/project/evaluation/ProjCen/digidash.asp, 2000.

29. T. L. Thai and H. Lam. *.NET Framework Essentials.* O'Reilly & Associates, Sebastopol, CA, 2001.

30. *Sash: The Javascript Runtime.* http://sash.alphaworks.ibm.com/.

31. I. Kumaran and S. I. Kumaran. *Jini Technology: An Overview.* Prentice-Hall PTR, Upper Saddle River, NJ, 2001.

32. E. Freeman, K. Arnold, and S. Hupfer. *JavaSpaces Principles, Patterns, and Practice.* Addison Welsey Longman, Reading, MA, 1999.

33. D. Gelernter. *Mirror Worlds: Or the Day Software Puts the Universe in a Shoebox . . . How It Will Happen and What It Will Mean.* Oxford University Press, New York, 1992.

# CHAPTER 7

# MEME MEDIA ARCHITECTURE

Our meme media architecture, IntelligentPad, is based upon the following architectural concepts:

1. Wrapper architecture
2. Frame architecture
3. MVC architecture
4. Update-dependency architecture
5. Compound-document architecture

The first three define the architecture of primitive components, whereas the last two define the composition architecture.

This chapter provides the technical details of IntelligentPad with respect to these five basic architectural concepts.

## 7.1   CURRENT MEGATRENDS IN COMPUTER SYSTEMS

Current computer system environments cannot be discussed without the four keywords (1) networks, (2) open architecture, (3) downsizing, and (4) multimedia. Demands are increasing for new system architectures that allow us to integrate, in a bottom-up way, heterogeneous PCs and workstations through networks, and to easily construct various application systems with sufficient performance without spending too much money. Such systems should be able to easily reconfigure themselves to immediately respond to frequently occurring new requirements for the extension of system functions and application domains. They should allow us to arbitrarily combine and to recombine various data and program resources that are distributed across networks, and to easily construct required systems.

Software development also increases demands for new system development environments in which fundamental functions are provided as functional components and their various combinations define various application systems. Such environments are called component software or, simply, componentware.

From the users' points of view, application systems with sophisticated GUI (graphical user interface) representations are becoming indistinguishable from multimedia compound documents. The distinction between these two is becoming insignificant. This leads to compound-document architectures, in which the application of the compound document framework is extended further to include application systems as components. This trend, together with componentware architectures, is still evolving; examples of compound-document architectures include OpenDoc [1], ActiveX [2], and Webtop computing with Java [3]. In Webtop computing, Web pages that originally represent documents work as desktop environments for running Java applet application objects.

The idea of applying the compound document framework to application systems is not limited to display representation. It can be extended to creation and editing, management and retrieval, publication and distribution, quotation, reediting, and redistribution. Hypermedia research activities in the 1980s such as those described in [4, 5, 6, 7, 8] accelerated this trend. The popularization of the WWW [9] and Web browser systems like NCSA Mosaic [10], Netscape Navigator, and Microsoft Internet Explorer during the last decade, together with the appearance of Java [3] and Web page authoring tools, indicates that the application of the compound-document framework to application systems can already be observed in the publication and distribution of application systems. Various search engine services such as Yahoo, Alta Vista, and Google further indicate that this trend is already seen in the management and retrieval of application systems. Instead of directly searching for application systems, these search engines are used to indirectly search for those Web page documents that include these application systems.

Furthermore, the growing interest in intranet technologies indicates that the renovation of large organizations through restructuring and reengineering [11] has increased the need for new information environments where users can easily access not only data and document resources but also application systems, and easily define application linkages for dynamically constructing arbitrary work flows among different resources. Compound-document architectures for editing, managing, and distributing both multimedia documents and application systems are promising for such intranet information environments.

## 7.2  PRIMITIVE MEDIA OBJECTS

Our meme media architecture, IntelligentPad, satisfies the above-mentioned requirements. It adopted the following architectural concepts:

1. Wrapper architecture
2. Frame architecture
3. MVC architecture
4. Update-dependency architecture
5. Compound-document architecture

The first three define the architecture of primitive components, whereas the last two define the composition architecture. Let us first consider the architecture of primitive components.

### 7.2.1   Wrapper Architecture

Wrapper architectures are commonly used in component software systems. The basic idea is similar to the use of cabinets for AV-system components. All-in-one type AV systems were replaced by AV-system components such as tuners, turntables, cassette tape decks, compact disc players, video cassette recorders, amplifiers, graphic equalizers, TV monitors, and loudspeakers. This replacement allowed each user to configure his or her own system according to desired performance, cost, and taste by arbitrarily combining his or her favorite components selected from a great variety of products made by various companies. This was accomplished by first dividing the overall function of all-in-one-type AV systems into mutually rather independent functions, and then encapsulating each of these functions within a cabinet of standard shape and size. This allowed us to stack these components any way we liked. Each AV-system component allows flexible functional linkage with others by providing a set of connection jacks on the back panel of its cabinet. These connection jacks are all of standard shape and size. One connection jack receives an audio signal and another outputs a video signal. Some may be used for unilateral communication with another component, whereas others may be used for bilateral communication.

The AV-component architecture can be summarized as follows:

1. Components are physically wrapped with standard cabinets, not only to hide their internal circuits, but also to allow flexible physical layout of an arbitrarily selected set of components.
2. Each component provides a set of connection jacks of standard shape and size.
3. Each connection jack receives and/or sends some kind of signals. Every connection jack is labeled with its name. Some connection jacks use a naming convention for their names to note the specifications of what kind of signals they receive and/or send, whereas others require operation manuals for the details of such specifications.
4. These connection jacks are hidden from the front view of system components.

The IntelligentPad architecture wraps each functional component with a wrapper. Such a wrapper provides any content object with a visible shape, and enables its user to directly manipulate it on a display screen. It gives each object a card image. Such cards are called pads. In general, an object wrapped by a wrapper with some media image is called a media object. Pads are examples of media objects. Pads are instances, not classes. They are persistent instance objects. To create a new pad instance that has the same features as an existing one, you may make a copy of it. Copies of the same pad share the same pad type. Pads may have arbitrary planar shapes and sizes. The default shape of pads is a rectangle. A pad can be put on another pad. Multiple pads can be arranged on a single pad to define a layout, or they can be overlaid one over another with some of them being made translucent. Each content object with a GUI can display its graphics on the surface of its wrapper, whereas those without any GUI are represented as blank-sheet pads. Some pads can be resized, whereas others cannot.

### 7.2.2   Frame Architecture of Each Pad

A frame in general is a prototype describing a standard situation or object. A frame holds slots with different aspects, which are described by declarative or procedural facets. Declarative facets associate values to slots, whereas procedural facets introduce so-called reflexes, or daemons, which are procedures activated on slot accesses. Frame-based languages and frame architectures were originally inspired by Marvin Minsky's frame idea [12].

IntelligentPad also exploits a frame architecture for each pad. Each pad provides a set of slots that work as connection jacks. Each slot may receive and/or send some kind of signal. Every slot has a name. A naming convention is used for some slots to indicate their roles and communication data types. In general, an on-line reference manual is required to find the role and the communication data type of each slot. Slots are hidden from the surface view of pads. Any slot of a pad can be selected from the special pop-up menu of this pad.

The content object in each pad can be accessed only through its slots. The Intelligent-Pad architecture provides two types of standard access messages for each slot—"set" and "gimme." Each "set" message takes a single parameter value, whereas each "gimme" message takes no parameters. Corresponding to these two kinds of slot accesses, each slot $s$ is defined by two methods, i.e., the "set" method, $Proc_{s,set}$, to be invoked by a "set" message, and the "gimme" method, $Proc_{s,gimme}$, to be invoked by a "gimme" message. The default method for a "set" message sets the parameter value to a special register dedicated to this slot, whereas the default method of a "gimme" message returns the current value of the same dedicated register. A slot whose methods are both defined as default methods is called a data slot. Its value is the value of its dedicated register. The logical function of each pad is specified by its slots and by the two methods defined for each of these slots.

### 7.2.3 MVC Architecture of Each Pad

Since every media object is visible and can be directly manipulated on a display screen, it has a display object as its component. The remaining part is called the model part of the media object, whereas the display component is further divided into two parts, i.e., its view part and its controller part. The view part defines its visual appearance on a display screen and the controller part defines its reactions to user events through a mouse or a keyboard. The representation of a visible and directly manipulable object with three such components is well known as the MVC (model-view-controller) representation framework [13]. From the users' point of view, every media object is atomic and indivisible.

A pad can define some of its slots in its model part and the others in its view part, called, respectively, the model slots and the view slots of this pad. No slots are defined in controller parts. Some of the view slots define the geometrical properties and the slot-connection properties of the pad. They are just called properties. These include the foreground color, the background color, the extent, the relative origin on the parent pad, the enable/disable flags for "set," "gimme," and "update" messages, the border width, the visibility flag, the nickname, the primary slots for the "set" and "gimme" messages, and the border type. Model slots are public in the sense that they can be accessed from the outside of the pad. The model may have additional slots that can be internally accessed by its view and by itself. These slots are private slots.

The IntelligentPad architecture uses a specialized version of the MVC construct to represent each pad, as shown in Figure 7.1. Different from the well-known MVC structure, this special version has no direct linkage between its controller and its model.

When the controller detects either a mouse event or a keyboard event, it asks its view for the message selector of the corresponding action, and then asks its view to perform the

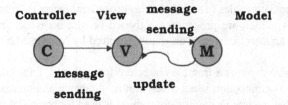

**Figure 7.1** Each pad is represented by a specialized version of the MVC construct.

method for this message. The view must define the methods for the following messages to answer the message selector name:

**blueButtonViewAction** (the action to take when the blue button is down)
**redButtonDownAction** (the action to take when the red button is down)
**redButtonUpAction** (the action to take when the red button is up)
**redButtonWentDownAction** (the action to take when the red button goes down)
**keyboardViewAction** (the action to take when a key is pressed)

Each of these messages may return "nil" if the pad has no special action for its corresponding user event. The methods for these messages return the message selectors of the corresponding actions. For example, the ButtonPadView, used as the view of a button pad, define the **redButtonDownAction** as follows.

**redButtonDownAction**
↑ #selected: "this makes the view to perform '**selected:** aPoint' when the red button is down."

The method for **selected:** is defined as follows in the view.

**selected:** aPoint
"If the 'selected' flag is not already set,"
self isSelected
ifFalse: ["set the 'selected' flag,"
internals at: #isSelected put: true.
"and request to redraw itself."
self invalidate]

To ask the view to perform the corresponding action, the controller sends the following message to the view.

**perform:** action **with:** aPoint

The parameter "action" is the message selector obtained from the view. In the above example, it is the message selector "#selected:."

The view can send its model no other messages than "**set:** data **to:** slotName" and "**get:** slotName," where "slotName" may be any of the public model slots or private model slots. The model can send its view no other messages than "**update:** aSymbol," where the current implementation uses only "nil" for "aSymbol."

The "**set:**" and "**get:**" messages are defined as follows:

Messages to the model

>    **set:** data **to:** slotName
>         (self slotList includes: slotName)
>                   ifFalse: [ ↑ nil].
>         (self respondsTo: ('set', slotName, ':') asSymbol)
>                   ifTrue: [self perform: ('set', slotName, ':') asSymbol with: data]
>         ifFalse: [self setDefault: data to: slotName]
>
>    **setDefault:** data **to:** slotName
>         slots at: slotName ifAbsent: [ ↑ self].
>         (slots at: slotName)=data ifTrue: [ ↑ nil].
>         slots at: slotName put: data.
>         self changed
>
>    **get:** slotName
>         ↑ (self respondsTo: ('get', slotName) asSymbol)
>         ifTrue: [self perform: ('get', slotName) asSymbol]
>         ifFalse: [self getDefault: slotName]
>
>    **getDefault:** slotName
>         ↑ slots at: slotName ifAbsent: [nil]

The first line of the "set" method examines if the slotName is included in the slot list of the model. Let this slotName be a string "index", for example. The third line examines if the model has a method for the message selector "setindex". If it has, the fourth line makes the model perform its method for the message selector "setindex", with data as its parameter. Otherwise, the "index" slot is considered as a data slot, and the entry with the same name "index" is selected from the data slot list, and its value is set to the specified data. Whenever the data slot value is updated, the changed message is sent to the model.

For the same slotName, for example, the first line of the "get" method examines if the model has a method for the message selector "getindex". If it has, the second line makes the model perform its method for the message selector "getindex". Otherwise, the "index" slot is considered as a data slot; the entry with the same name "index" is selected from the data slot list, and its value is used as the return value.

The "**update:**" method is defined in the view as follows:

Messages to the view

>    **update:** aSymbol
>         self viewUpdate
>         self refreshDisplay
>         self padUpdate

The first line performs the necessary updates of the view properties and the view internal variables in correspondence to the model's update. The second line refreshes the display of the view if necessary. When we need to refresh the display, the method for "**refreshDisplay**" is defined as follows:

> **refreshDisplay**
> self invalidate

The third line of the "**update:**" method performs the update of the pads that are functionally combined with this pad. These pads are combined through the slot connection mechanism that will be explained in the next subsection.

> **padUpdate**
> self updateToSlaves.
> self updateToMaster

> **updateToMaster**
> (self setFlag and: [self master notNil])
> ifTrue:
> > [self master set: (Array with: slotName with:
> > (self get: self primarySlotForSet) copy)]

> **updateToSlaves**
> self slaves do: [:pad |(pad isKindOf: PadView) ifTrue: (pad updatePad)]

The method "**padUpdate**" first updates all of its child pads, and then updates its parent pad. The method "**updateToMaster**" updates the parent pad by sending the connection slot of the parent the current value of the primary slot. This corresponds to the execution of a "set" message to the parent pad. Section 7.5 will give a detailed explanation on this mechanism.

The state of a pad is the list of all the variables of this pad, with each variable associated with its current value. This is the state of a pad as a media object. It consists of the states of the three components of this pad, i.e., the model state, view state, and controller state. In addition to its state, every pad defines its logical state, which is a subset of all the variables in its model. It is up to the programmer of a pad to decide which subset to define as its logical state. For example, let us consider a pad that works as a bar meter. This pad may have two variables: one to hold the current value and the other to hold the current range. Its logical state may be defined to include either two of them or only the current value. In the latter case, the current range may be included either in the model state or in the view state. These alternatives define bar meter pads with different semantics.

## 7.3 COMPOSITION THROUGH SLOT CONNECTIONS

The first three of the five architectures that IntelligentPad adopted define the architecture of primitive components. We have discussed these architectures in the previous section. Here we will discuss in detail the last two architectures that define the pad composition

architecture. They are an update-dependency architecture and a compound-document architecture.

### 7.3.1   Distributed Versus Centralized Compositions

Compositions with primitive components are classified into two types: distributed compositions and centralized compositions. Every centralized composition has one distin-
guished primitive component object whose logical state represents the logical state of the
composed object, whereas no distributed composition has such a primitive component object. Such a primitive component object is called the supervisory component of the composed object. It should be noticed that the above definition depends on how we define the
logical state of the composed object. A centralized composition system is a component
software system that only allows centralized compositions.

A centralized composition, when its supervisory component is removed, can be decomposed into a set of compositions with no functional linkage among them. These compositions are called child compositions of the original composition. Child compositions of
a centralized composition have mutually disjoint sets of component objects. Otherwise,
more than one child composition share the same object and, hence, have a functional linkage among themselves. In a centralized composition system, each child composition is
also a centralized composition and, hence, it can be further decomposed by removing its
supervisory component. Therefore, in a centralized composition system, any composed
object has a tree structure composition, which simplifies the management and maintenance of composed objects.

### 7.3.2   Update Dependency in Centralized Compositions

In a centralized composition system, we can define a dependency among the primitive
component objects. For composition $C$, let *components*$(C)$, *supervisor*$(C)$, and *child-com-
positions*$(C)$ denote, respectively, the set of primitive component objects, the supervisory
component, and the set of child compositions of $C$. Obviously, there exists a dependency
from *supervisor*$(C)$ to every primitive component object $o_i$ in *components*$(C)$. We call this
dependency an update dependency among primitive component objects, and denote it as
*supervisor*$(C) \rightarrow o_i$. This terminology will be explained later. If $a \rightarrow b$ and $a \rightarrow c$ both
hold, we simply denote them as $a \rightarrow bc$.

Let $S$ be a centralized composition system. Let us consider a directed graph with all the
primitive component objects in $S$ as its nodes. We define its links as follows. There exists
a link $o_1 \Rightarrow o_2$ from a node $o_1$ to another node $o_2$ if and only if the following three conditions all hold:

1. $o_1 \neq o_2$
2. $o_1 \rightarrow o_2$
3. There exists no such node $o$ $(\neq o_1, o_2)$ that satisfies $o_1 \rightarrow o$ and $o \rightarrow o_2$

We call this graph a composition graph. Obviously, any composition graph is a set of directed trees. Each tree in a composition graph represents a composition, while its root represents the supervisory component of this composition.

Let us now consider how to define a functional linkage between two component ob-
jects $o_1$ and $o_2$ to satisfy $o_1 \Rightarrow o_2$. By definition, the logical state of this composition with

$o_1$ and $o_2$ is the logical state of $o_1$. Therefore, in general, any change of the logical state in $o_1$ should be immediately informed to $o_2$. Of course, this capability need not be utilized by any of such compositions. Anyway, we need to provide a standard message to inform such state changes. We call it an update message. Every component, on the other hand, needs to define a method to react to this update message. The component object $o_2$ need not know the overall logical state information of $o_1$, but may reference some portion of this information. The component object $o_1$, in general, has more than one such component as $o_2$. Instead of informing them with different portions of the updated logical state, we chose the strategy to make $o_1$ send the same message "update" without any parameters.

The component object $o_2$, if it wants, should be able to control or monitor some portion of the logical state of $o_1$. Furthermore, suppose that each component can be accessed only through its slots. Although the component object $o_2$ may access more than one slot of $o_1$, we chose another strategy to restrict this number to one. This choice has several advantages. It simplifies not only composition operations but also the management and maintenance of composed objects. Each component object can hold its right to define which portions of its logical state can be controlled or monitored by the other component objects. This is defined by its design strategy as to what kinds of slots to provide. Furthermore, the definition of the component object $o_2$ need not refer either to the specific component object $o_1$ or to its specific slot. All these specifications can be dynamically defined when we combine these components.

### 7.3.3  Update Dependency Architecture for Compositions

These design choices lead to the following standard interface protocol between component objects. To define a composition $o_1 \Rightarrow o_2$, the component object $o_2$ is connected to only one of the slots of $o_1$. The component object $o_2$ can access this slot by "set" and/or "gimme" messages, whereas its definition need not refer either to the component object $o_1$ or to its slot name. The component object $o_1$, on the other hand, can send only "update" messages to $o_2$. We call such a primitive composition "a slot connection" of two component objects. The component object $o_1$ is the parent or master of this slot connection, and the object $o_2$ is its child or slave. Furthermore, no component object can become a child of more than one parent.

### 7.4  COMPOUND-DOCUMENT ARCHITECTURE

In compound-document architectures, component objects are all represented as document components, and each functional linkage between two components is defined by directly embedding one of their document-component representations into the other on the display screen through mouse operations. This identifies composition operations on components with editing operations on their document-component representations. The embedding of a document component into another by a direct mouse operation is called a "paste" operation. We impose a restriction that the logical state of a compound document is the logical state of its base component, namely, of the bottom one. Under this restriction, the composition graph of each composition becomes isomorphic to the embedding structure of its compound-document representation.

The IntelligentPad architecture adopts a compound-document architecture, and imposes the above-mentioned restriction. You may use paste operations in arbitrary ways; for example, to overlay multiple translucent pads of the same size, or to arrange multiple pads on the same base pad. Users can easily replicate any pad, paste one pad on another, and peel a pad off a composite pad. These operations can be equally applied both to any primitive pads and to any composite pads. When a pad $P_2$ is pasted on another pad $P_1$, pad $P_2$ becomes a child of $P_1$ and is termed its child pad or slave pad. Pad $P_1$ becomes the parent of $P_2$, and is called its parent pad or master pad. No pad may have more than one parent pad. Pads are decomposable persistent objects. You can easily decompose any composite pad by simply peeling off any primitive or composite component pad from its parent pad.

The linkage between a child pad and its parent pad is defined by a "paste" operation, which is more closely related to their view parts than either their model parts or their controller parts. Therefore, their linkage is actually set between their view parts. Later, we will define shared copies of the same pad. Although they share the same model, each of them has its dedicated display object. Different shared copies of the same pad should be able to have different child pads. The linkage between two pads through their view parts satisfies this requirement.

## 7.5   STANDARD MESSAGES BETWEEN PADS

When a pad $P_2$ is pasted on another pad $P_1$, the IntelligentPad system constructs a linkage between their view parts (Figure 7.2). This defines an update dependency from $P_1$ to $P_2$. If $P_1$ has more than one slot, we have to select one of them to associate it with $P_2$. This selection can be specified on a connection sheet (Figure 7.3). The selected slot name is stored in an instance variable slotName of the child pad $P_2$. A child pad can send either a "**set:** data **to:** slotName" message or "**gimme:** slotName" message to its parent, whereas the parent pad, when its state is changed, can send some of its child pads an "**updatePad**" message without any parameter to propagate an update event. The interpretation of the "**updatePad**" message again depends on the implementation of the sender and the receiver pads. It is usually used to inform the child pads of a parent's state change. The slot name stored in the variable slotName becomes the real parameter of "**set:**" and "**gimme:**" messages. In the definition of each pad, its programmer cannot a priori know the name of its parent's slot that will be used for the slot connection. The indirect reference of the connection slot in "**set:**" and "**gimme:**" messages solves this problem. IntelligentPad allows us to disable some of the three standard messages—"**set:**," "**gimme:**," and "**updatePad**"—between a parent pad and a child pad, which can be specified on the connection sheet. The two messages "**set:** data

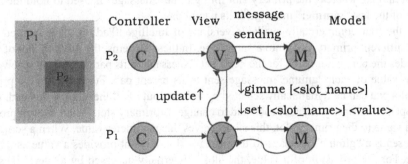

**Figure 7.2**   The pasting of a pad on another defines a functional linkage between these pads.

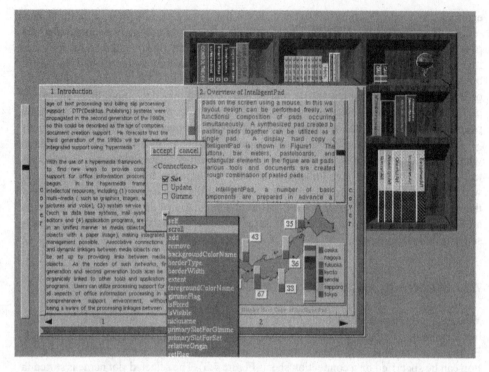

**Figure 7.3**    A bar meter is connected to the scroll slot of the underlying pad. This slot connection is specified by opening the corresponding connection sheet.

**to:** slotName" and "**gimme:** slotName" sent to a pad P are forwarded to its parent pad if P does not have any slot of the name specified by slotName.

Among its data slots, each pad has three special slots—the primary slot, the primary slot for "set" messages, and the primary slot for "gimme" messages. They are obtained by sending, respectively, "**primarySlot**", "**primarySlotForSet**", and "**primarySlot- ForGimme**" messages to the view. The primary slot is used to access a pad using "set" and "gimme" messages without explicitly specifying the slot name. Such accesses are used by script programs of StagePads, which will be detailed in Section 8.3. The primary slot for "set" messages is used to keep the parameter value for the next "**set:**" message to its parent pad, whereas the primary slot for "gimme" messages is used to hold the return value of the last "**gimme:**" message to its parent pad.

In the four commercially available versions of IntelligentPad, we have merged these three different primary slots into a single one. In these systems, the primary slot of a pad provides the parameter value for the next "**set:**" message to its parent pad and receives the return value of each "gimme" message sent to its parent pad. Furthermore, the primary slot of a pad can be dynamically selected by the user out of all the slots of this pad. Users can open the property sheet of each pad to change its primary slot. When a script program sets a value to the primary slot, this slot receives this parameter value. When a script program sends a "gimme" message to the primary slot, the slot provides a value as a return value. For the provision of a value, the slot is internally accessed by a "**get:**" message, whereas, for the reception of a value, the slot is internally accessed by a "**set:**" message.

The method for "**set:**" message is already defined in the previous section. The methods for the remaining two standard messages are defined as follows.

> **gimme:** slotname
>     |data|
>     (self propertyList keys include: slotname)
>         ifTrue: [ ↑ self propertyGet: slotname].
>     (self slotNames includes: slotname)
>         ifTrue: [data:=(self get: slotname) copy.
>                 ↑ data]
>         ifFalse: [self master notNil ifTrue: [ ↑ self master gimme: slotname]].
>     ↑ nil

> **updatePad**
>     |data|
>     self updateFlag
>         ifTrue: [data:= self sendGimme: slotName.
>                 data notNil ifTrue: [self set: data to: self primarySlotForGimme]]

> **sendGimme:** slotname
>     self master isNil ifTrue: [ ↑ nil].
>     ↑ self gimmeFlag
>         ifTrue: [self master gimme: slotname]
>         ifFalse: [nil]

The second line of the "**gimme:**" method examines if the "slotname" refers to properties of the view. If it does, then the value of this referred property is read out as the return value. Otherwise, the fourth line examines if this pad has the specified slot as its slot. If it has, the slot is accessed by a "**get:**" message, and its return value is returned to the sender pad of this message. Otherwise, this "**gimme:**" message is delegated to its parent pad, and its return value is returned to the sender pad of this message.

The method for the "**updatePad**," when the updateFlag is set to enable this message, performs "self **sendGimme:** slotName," which, when gimmeFlag is also set to enable "gimme" messages, sends a "**gimme:**" message to the specified slot of the parent pad. Its return value is then set to the primary slot for "gimme" of this pad.

In a default way of defining a pad, we use "self **sendGimme:** slotName" in the view to send a "**gimme**" message to its parent pad, and "self **setDefault:** data **to:** self **primarySlotForSet**" in the model to send a "**set:**" message to its parent pad. The method for "**setDefault**" is defined as follows.

> **setDefault:** data **to:** slotname
>     slots at: slotname ifAbsent: [ ↑ self].
>     (slots at: slotname) = data ifTrue: [ ↑ nil].
>     slots at: slotname put: data.
>     self changed

The execution of "self **setDefault:** data **to:** self **primarySlotForSet**" causes the model to send an "**update**" message to the view, which then causes the view to perform "self

**viewUpdate**," "self **refreshDisplay**," and "self **padUpdate**," in this order. The last of them executes "self **updateToSlaves**" and "self **updateToMaster**." The latter will send the specified connection slot of its parent pad the "**set:**" message with the current value of the primary slot for "set" messages. The following is the previously given definition of the method "**updateToMaster**." The first two lines check if the "set" message is enabled. The following two lines update the value of the connection slot.

> updateToMaster
>> (self setFlag and: [self master notNil])
>> ifTrue:
>>> [self master set: (Array with: slotName with:
>>> (self get: self primarySlotForSet) copy)]

Of course, you may directly use "self **master set:** data **to:** slotName" to send a "set" message to the parent pad. In this case, you have to define all the necessary updates.

In addition to these three standard messages—"**set:**," "**gimme:**," and "**updatePad**,"—any pad can send some other standard messages for geometrical operations to its parent as well as to its child pads. Among these messages are included the following:

| | |
|---|---|
| **changeRelativeOrigin:** aPoint | to change the relative location on its parent pad |
| **relativeOrigin** | to obtain its relative location on its parent pad |
| **changeExtent:** aPoint | to resize the pad |
| **extent** | to obtain its size |
| **changeBorderWidth:** anInteger | to change its border width |
| **borderWidth** | to obtain its border width |
| **moveTo:** aPoint **offset:** anOffset | to move the pad to the specified location |
| **copyTo:** aPoint **offset:** anOffset | to make its copy at the specified location |
| **setBackgroundColorName:** aSymbol | to set its background color to the specified one |
| **backgroundColor** | to obtain its background color |
| **setForegroundColorName:** aSymbol | to set its foreground color to the specified one |
| **foregroundColor** | to obtain its foreground color |

These are the messages to the wrappers, but not to the contents. Since wrappers are standardized, these messages can be applied to any pads without specifying any slot connection. Unless otherwise specified, geometrical messages have nothing to do with the logical states of pads and, hence, they are independent from the update dependencies among pads. Each pad may send geometrical messages to any pad that is not either its child pad or its parent pad.

Geometrical messages together with the three standard messages—"**set:**," "**gimme:**" and "**updatePad**"—define the standard interface between pads.

## 7.6 PHYSICAL AND LOGICAL EVENTS AND THEIR DISPATCHING

IntelligentPad is an open system that can communicate asynchronously with various resources. Interaction can occur with people, extended devices, other applications and objects (communicating with sockets or OLE), and with server systems (database and

WWW servers). IntelligentPad receives status changes of these asynchronously operating resources as events.

Although two separate resources may be viewed by IntelligentPad as identical in type, differences in the operating systems and resource handlers may prevent IntelligentPad from processing their events in the same manner. Even if pads that could handle multiple platforms were developed, the inability to use the source program across multiple platforms would result in overlapping efforts and increased cost of pad platform development.

The concept of virtual resources and logical events were introduced to overcome the differences in the operating systems and resource handlers. The ability of the virtual resources to handle additional registration, and to define resource types and logical event systems, facilitates the expansion of resources and satisfies the diverse requirements of resource handling.

### 7.6.1   Physical and Logical Events

IntelligentPad can handle various resources as real resources that can become an event-generation source. These include the system clock; an interval timer; input devices such as a mouse, pen, and keyboard; external devices such as sensors and actuators; communication means such as sockets, OLE, DDE, and CORBA [14]; other applications; other objects to communicate with; and information management systems such as databases, WWW, and E-mail. The OS notifies the IntelligentPad system about the events in the real resources as event messages. These raw events are physical events.

Logical events are converted physical events. Although the physical events are in the event-expression format defined by the OS, the logical events are in the expression format defined by the IntelligentPad system. Virtual resources cause logical events. The definition and registration of new virtual resources to an Intelligentpad system expand the resources and logical events that the IntelligentPad system can utilize. A virtual resource receives a physical event generated in a real resource, converts it to a logical event, and then places it in the logical event queue. Pads can request logical events of virtual resources. Pads specify the type of the logical event that they desire to receive by using the parameter of a request. The virtual resource delivers the generated logical event to the pad that requested it.

A pad can also request a logical event grab of a virtual resource. The logical event grab makes it possible to take a logical event prior to other pads, and to decide whether to deliver this particular event to other pads that requested it. Normally, a logical event grab should be avoided because it limits other pads' ability to receive events and affects the operation of other pads. Each virtual resource defines the type of grabbable logical events and the way in which they are specified.

### 7.6.2   Position Events and Their Dispatching

Among various events, position events require special considerations for pads to behave like directly manipulable objects. A position event is an event including the position information. Mouse events are examples of position events. A position event is usually processed by the outermost pad at this position, namely by the pad whose portion at this position is not covered by any other pad. As shown in Figure 7.4, the overlay structure

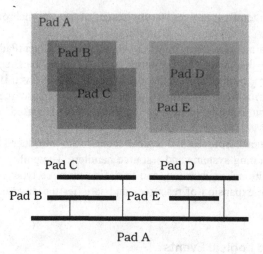

**Figure 7.4**   The overlay structure among pads does not necessarily coincide with the parent–child relationship hierarchy among them.

among pads does not coincide with their parent–child relationships. A pad may be partially or fully covered by another independent pad. Furthermore, a pad may have a child pad that partially or fully covers another child pad.

A special pad, upon receiving an event, can selectively delegate this event to another pad. The target pad need not be placed immediately under the recipient. For example, you may consider a special pad that searches for the outermost pad under its parent pad to delegate mouse events it receives, and to display on itself the target pad's portion it covers. When pasted on some pad, this special pad makes a hole on its parent pad. Every mouse event within the hole is delegated to the target pad.

Unless otherwise specified by each pad, three mouse button events are assigned to the following direct manipulation of pads. The right button, called the blue button, is used to drag a pad, whereas the middle button, called the yellow button, is used to resize a pad. The left button, called the red button, is used by each pad to define its specific operations. When the right button is clicked while pressing of the shift key, the pad pops up an operation menu including the following entries: "move," "resize," "copy," "connection," "shared copy," "property," "primary slot," "free," and "delete." A selection of one of them will invoke its operation method.

### 7.6.3   User-Event Dispatching Mechanism

User events through a mouse and a keyboard are detected by the following methods of the PadController class and its superclass, Controller.

For class Controller:

> **startUp**
>     self controlInitialize.
>     self controlLoop.
>     self controlTerminate

where, for class PadController:

**controlInitialize**
    (view isKindOf: PadView) ifTrue: [view enter]

**controlTerminate**
    (view isKindOf: PadView) ifTrue: [view leave]

**controlLoop**
    |previousState state|
    state := self sensor redButtonPressed.
    state ifTrue: [self redButtonDown: self sensor cursorPoint].
    [previousState := state copy.
        self poll
        state := self sensor redButtonPressed.
        state
            ifTrue: [previousState
                ifTrue: [self redButtonDown: self sensor cursorPoint]
                ifFalse: [self redButtonWentDown: self sensor cursorPoint]]
            ifFalse: [previousState
                ifTrue: [self redButtonWentUp: self sensor cursorPoint]
                ifFalse: [self redButtonUp: self sensor cursorPoint]].
    self isControlActive]
        whileTrue: [self controlActivity].
    (state or: [previousState]) ifTrue: [self redbuttonUp: view bounds center]

When the mouse cursor enters a pad, its controller performs the "**controlLoop**" method to detect various mouse and keyboard events. The loop from the fourth line to the fifteenth line of the "**controlLoop**" method tries to detect the four different events caused by the red button of the mouse. When it detects any of these events, it asks the view if this pad defines the corresponding action, and makes it perform this action (which will be explained later). This loop also repetitively performs the following method.
    For class PadController:

**controlActivity**
    self sensor yellowButtonPressed & self viewHasCursor
        ifTrue: [ ↑ self yellowButtonActivity].
    self sensor blueButtonPressed & (self viewHasCursor & view isFixed not)
        ifTrue: [ ↑ self blueButtonActivity].
    self sensor keyboardPressed
        & (view **keyboardViewAction** notNil & self viewHasCursor)
        ifTrue: [ ↑ self keyboardActivity].
    super controlActivity.
    ↑ nil

This method further examines if any of the remaining mouse-button events and keyboard events has occurred. These would include such events as pressing the yellow button, the blue button, and the keyboard. When this method detects any of these events, it makes the pad perform the corresponding action (which will be explained later). Then the method performs the following method in the while loop of the "**controlLoop**."

For class Controller:

> **controlActivity**
> self controlToNextLevel
>
> **controlToNextLevel**
> |aSubView|
> aSubView←view subViewWantingControl.
> aSubView isNil ifFalse: [aSubView controller startUp]

The execution of "super **controlActivity**" transfers the event management from the current pad to its child pad that includes the mouse cursor. Even during the execution of the "**controlLoop**," the mouse may change its location. This transfer is necessary to dispatch each mouse event to the outermost pad at its cursor location.

The "**controlLoop**" execution exits from its loop when "self **isControlActive**" becomes false. This message performs the following method.

For class PadController:

> **isControlActive**
> ↑ [self viewHasCursor and:
>      [(self sensor blueButtonPressed and: [view isFixed]) not and:
>      [view isVisible]]]

The condition "self **isControlActive**" becomes false if the mouse exits from the pad, the blue button is pressed, or the pad becomes invisible. In this case, the "**controlLoop**" execution exits from its loop, and if the red button is still down, assumes that the red button is released and performs the corresponding action.

When the "**controlLoop**" method detects any mouse event, it performs the corresponding action among the following:

> "self **redButtonDown:** self **sensor cursorPoint**"
> "self **redButtonWentDown:** self **sensor cursorPoint**"
> "self **redButtonWentUp:** self **sensor cursorPoint**"
> "self **redButtonUp:** self **sensor cursorPoint**"

Each pad uses the red button to define its specific operations. For example, the **redButtonDown** method is defined as follows:

> **redButtonDown:** aPoint
> |action|
> (action := view **redButtonDownAction**) isNil
>      ifTrue: [ ↑ self]
>      ifFalse:[view perform: action with: aPoint]

This performs the red button action defined for this pad if any. The other methods are also similarly defined.

The "**controlLoop**" also performs the following in the "**controlActivity**" method:

"self **yellowButtonActivity**"
"self **blueButtonActivity**"
"self **keyboardActivity**"

The "**yellowButtonActivity**" and the "**blueButtonActivity**" methods are defined similarly to the above-mentioned red button activities:

**blueButtonActivity**
　　|action|
　　(action := view **blueButtonViewAction**) isNil
　　　　ifTrue: [self sensor shiftdown
　　　　　　if True: [ ↑ self shiftBlueButtonActivity].
　　　　　　self moveWithDrag]
　　　　ifFalse:[view perform: action with: self sensor cursorPoint]

**yellowButtonActivity**
　　|action|
　　(action := view yellowButtonViewAction) isNil
　　　　ifTrue: [self resizeWithDrag]
　　　　ifFalse: [view perform: action with: sensor cursorPoint]

The blue button is used to drag a pad whereas the yellow button is used to resize a pad. When the blue button is clicked with the pressing of the shift key, the pad pops up an operation menu including the following entries: "move," "resize," "copy," "connection," "shared copy," "property," "primary slot," "free," and "delete." A selection of any one of them will invoke its operation method:

**shiftBlueButtonActivity**
　　|index|
　　index := (PopUpMenu labels: 'move\resize\copy\connection\shared
　　　　　　copy\property\primary slot\free\delete' withCRs) startUp.
　　index > 0 ifTrue:
　　　　[self perform: (#(#moveWithDrag #resizeWithDrag
　　　　#copyPad #changeConnection
　　　　#openPropertySheet #openprimarySlotSheet #free #delete) at:
　　　　index)]

The "**keyboardActivity**" is defined as follows:

**keyboardActivity**
　　|key|
　　[self sensor keyboardPressed]
　　　　whileTrue: [key := self sensor keyboard].
　　(key isKindOf: Character)
　　　　ifFalse: [ ↑ self].
　　self keyIn: key

> **keyIn:** keyChar
> |action|
> (action := view keyboardViewAction) isNil
>     ifTrue: [ ↑ self]
>     ifFalse: [view perform: action with: keyChar]

When a key input occurs, this method asks the view of the pad if it will respond to a keyboard event, and, if it will, tells the view to perform the corresponding action with the input key.

All the above define the event dispatch mechanism for user events applied to pads.

### 7.6.4 Geometrical-Operation Notification

Every geometrical operation applied to a pad notifies its completion to the parent of this pad. Unless otherwise specified, each pad receiving such a notification further propagates this to its parent pad. Such geometrical operations on a pad include its moving, resizing, pasting, peeling, and slot connection; the releasing of its slot connection; its copying, property change, and selection; the releasing of its selection; its deletion and grouping; the releasing of its grouping; and its saving, showing, and hiding. The notification of their completion can be used by another underlying pad such as a stage pad to trigger some of its performance.

These notifications of geometrical operations use the parent–child relationships among pads, which is different from the position event dispatching among pads. These notifications include the following operation completion events: "moved," "resized," "copied," "pasted," "peeled," "mclicked" (mouse clicked), and "keyIn" (key input).

When one of these operations, say moving a pad from (100, 20) to (30, 50), is completed, this pad sends the following message to its parent pad:

> **sendEvent:** "moved" **from:** P **with:** #(100@20 30@50)

The recipient parent pad further forwards this message to its parent pad if it has one. It is up to each recipient pad to utilize this information or not.

### 7.7 SAVE AND EXCHANGE FORMAT

The IntelligentPad system defines both the save format and the exchange format of composite pads. The save-format representation of a pad is used to store this pad in a file. You need not store its pad classes. You only need to store the current state of each of its component pads, all the parent–child relationships among them, and all the slot connections among them. The save-format representation of a pad consists of this set of information, which is necessary and sufficient to reconstruct the original pad using the pad class library.

The exchange-format representation of a pad is used to transport this pad among different IntelligentPad systems sharing the same pad library. The implementation details of the shared library may differ in different systems. The exchange-format representation of a pad consists of all the information necessary and sufficient to reconstruct the same pad at the destination site. It logically provides the same information as the save-format representation of the same pad.

The save format and the exchange format of the same composite pad may be identical. Each prototype version of IntelligentPad uses the same format for these two, whereas the commercially available versions of IntelligentPad use different formats for these two. The exchange format is standardized among mutually compatible different IntelligentPad systems, whereas the save format depends on the specific version and its underlying platform to optimize the save and load performance.

The exchange-format representation of a composite pad is in text format. It consists of the header description, a set of pad descriptions, and the update-propagation order description. The header description includes the creation date, the storing date, the creator, the number of pads, and other descriptions of the context in which this composite pad is created. Each pad description consists of the common area, the model information area, and the view information area. The common area of a pad includes its pad class name; pad version, pad name; pad ID in the exchange-format representation; parent pad ID; model-sharing pad ID; enable/disable flags for "set," "gimme," and "update" messages; connected slot name; origin; extent; show/hide flag; background color; transparency; and operation-protection information. The model and the view information areas contain their state information as lists of pairs (item name and value).

The order of update propagation affects the operation of compound pads. The update-propagation order description consists of the copy-order description and the connection-order description. When the model of a pad is updated, all of its shared copies should receive update propagation in some order. This order is specified by a list of model-sharing pads for each set of shared copies. The copy-order description consists of such lists. When a slot is updated, the update message is issued to all the child pads that are connected to this slot in some order. This order is specified by a list of child pads. The connection-order description consists of such lists.

## 7.8   COPY AND SHARED COPY

For any pad, whether it is primitive or composite, the IntelligentPad architecture allows us to make shared copies as well as nonshared copies. Shared copies of the same object share its logical state. In the IntelligentPad architecture, the logical state of a primitive pad is defined by its model. Furthermore, the logical state of a composite pad is defined as the logical state of its base pad. Therefore, a shared copy P' of a primitive pad P shares its model component with P, but has a dedicated view component and a dedicated controller component (Figure 7.5). Shared copies of a composite pad are defined as sharing the state of their base pad, as shown in Figure 7.6. The IntelligentPad architecture considers the model component of a composite pad to be the model component of its base pad.

The IntelligentPad architecture allows us to electronically send a shared copy of an arbitrary pad to other users at different sites. Its receiver can share the model of this pad with its sender. Shared copies of the same pad distributed across a computer network may concurrently request their model component to update its state. In order to resolve any conflict among them, shared copies at different sites are assigned with different priority numbers. Shared copies with larger priority numbers have higher priorities. IntelligentPad divides the updating process of each pad into three phases, i.e., the update-request phase, the model-update phase, and the view-update phase. Each request is sent to the model component, then updates this component and makes it update all of its view components. With respect to their update, pads are classified into two types, i.e., combinatorial pads

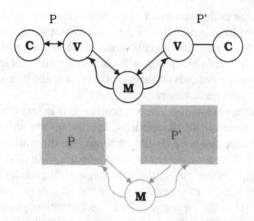

**Figure 7.5** A shared copy P′ of a primitive pad P shares its model component with P.

and sequential pads. A combinatorial pad determines its next state independently from its current state, whereas a sequential pad requires its current state information to determine its next state. A combinatorial pad may accept a new update request with the higher priority, neglecting the preceding one under the processing, if the pad is still in either the update-request phase or the model-update phase. However, if it is already in the view-update phase, it cannot neglect the preceding update under the processing to accept a new one. A sequential pad, on the other hand, can accept a new update request with the higher priority, neglecting the preceding one under the processing, only when the pad is still in the update-request phase. IntelligentPad allows us to associate each shared copy with an arbitrary number as its priority level. An update request from a shared copy with $i$ as its priority level is defined to have the same priority level $i$.

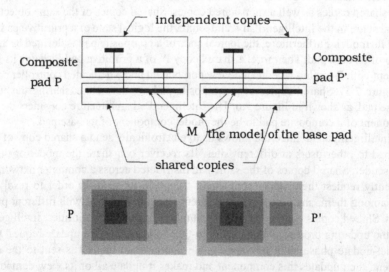

**Figure 7.6** Shared copies of the same composite pad.

## 7.9  GLOBAL VARIABLE PADS

Global variables are variables commonly accessed by more than one pad without using slot connections. If the current time is defined as a global variable, pads can easily refer to the current time in their programs without explicitly connecting themselves to any slot that provides the current time. Global variables are usually used by an application package of pads as shared variables accessible by any of these pads. A package of physical simulation pads, for example, may use global variables to share physical constants.

If all global variables are accessible by any pad, they have a single level of access structure. It is desirable to introduce a hierarchy to the access of global variables. In the case of single-level global variables, we may consider that these global variables are defined in the desktop. Similarly, we may consider a special pad that defines some global variables that can be accessed by any other pads over this pad. Such a pad is called a global-variable pad. Global-variable pads can be pasted on any other pads. They introduce a hierarchy to the access of global variables. This hierarchy observes the so-called scope rule as shown in Figure 7.7. A pad can access a global variable if and only if this variable is defined by a global-variable pad under this pad, and there is no other global-variable pad with the same name variable between these two pads.

A global-variable pad may not have slots or slot connection capability to its parent pad. Furthermore, it may or may not issue an "update" message when its global variable is updated. All these definitions of a global-variable pad are up to its developer. Some global-variable pads may provide only read-only variables.

## 7.10  SUMMARY

Our meme media architecture, IntelligentPad, is based on the following architectural concepts.

1. Wrapper architecture
2. Frame architecture
3. MVC architecture

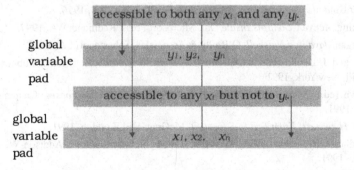

**Figure 7.7**  A hierarchy of global variable pads defines the access-scope hierarchy of their global variables.

4. Update-dependency architecture

5. Compound-document architecture

The IntelligentPad architecture wraps each functional component with a wrapper. Such a wrapper provides any content object with a visible shape, and enables its user to directly manipulate it on a display screen. It gives each object a card image. Such cards are called pads.

IntelligentPad exploits a frame architecture for each pad. Each pad provides a set of slots that work as connection jacks. The content object in each pad can be accessed only through its slots. The IntelligentPad architecture provides two types of standard access messages for each slot—"set" and "gimme."

The IntelligentPad architecture uses a specialized version of the MVC construct to represent each pad.

To define a composition, a component object is connected to only one of the slots of another object. The former object can access this slot by "set" and/or "gimme" messages, whereas its definition need not refer either to the latter component object or to its slot name. The latter component object, on the other hand, can send only "update" messages to the former. The latter component is the parent or master of this connection; the former is its child or slave. Furthermore, no component object can become a child of more than one parent.

The IntelligentPad architecture adopts the compound-document architecture. You may use "paste" operations in arbitrary ways; for example, to overlay multiple translucent pads of the same size, or to arrange multiple pads on the same base pad. Pads are decomposable persistent objects.

IntelligentPad is an open system that can communicate asynchronously with various resources. Although two separate resources may be viewed by IntelligentPad as identical in type, differences in the operating systems and resource handlers can prevent it from processing the events in the same manner. The concept of virtual resources and logical events were introduced to overcome the differences in the operating systems and resource handlers.

## REFERENCES

1. J. Feiler and A. Meadow. *Essential OpenDoc: Cross-Platform Development for OS/2, Macintosh, and Windows Programmers.* Addison-Wesley, Reading, MA, 1996.

2. A. Denning. *ActiveX Controls Inside Out.* Microsoft Press, Redmond, WA, 1997.

3. D. Flanagan. *Java in a Nutshell.* O'Reilly & Associates, Sebastopol, CA, 1996.

4. E. Berk and J. Devlin (eds.). *Hypertext/Hypermedia Handbook.* Intertext Publications, McGraw-Hill, New York, 1991

5. H. Brown (ed.). *Hypermedia/Hypertext and Object-Oriented Databases.* Chapman & Hall, London, 1991.

6. R. Rada. *Hypertext: From Text to Expertext.* McGraw-Hill, London, 1991.

7. N. Woodhead. *Hypertext and Hypermedia: Theory and Applications.* Addison-Wesley, Wilmslow, UK, 1991.

8. J. Nielsen. *Hypertext and Hypermedia.* Academic Press, Cambridge, MA, 1993.

9. T. Berners-Lee, R. Cailliau, N. Pellow, and A. Secret. The World-Wide Web Initiative. In *Proceedings of INET'93,* 1993.

10. M. Andreessen. *MCSA Mosaic Technical Summary.* NCSA Mosaic Technical Summary 2.1, 1993.

11. M. Hammer and J. Champy. *Reengineering Corporation: A Manifesto for Business Revolution.* HarperBusiness, New York, 1993.

12. M. Minski. A framework for representing knowledge. In P. Winston (ed.), *The Psychology of Computer Vision,* pp. 211–281, McGraw-Hill, New York, 1975.

13. W. R. LaLonde and J. R. Pugh. *Inside Smalltalk.* Volume II. Prentice-Hall, Englewood Cliffs, NJ, 1991.

14. Object Management Group. *The Common Object Request Broker: Architecture and Specification.* Wiley, New York, 1992.

# CHAPTER 8

# UTILITIES FOR MEME MEDIA

The previous chapter described the IntelligentPad architecture. This chapter provides the system with basic utility tools for modifying, coordinating, inspecting, managing, or transporting pads. These tools are also implemented as pads. This allows us to apply these tools to any pads, including themselves.

A FieldPad is used to define a shared workspace with arbitrary pads; its copies with all the pads on it share every user event. A StagePad allows users to write a script program for manipulating multiple pads and performing a series of steps. It can manipulate any pads on itself in the same way as we directly manipulate them. It also allows users' interactions. It can associate each user event with a corresponding action. When a user event is applied, it triggers the corresponding action. A proxy pad works as a proxy of an external object such as a database server, a file server, or an application system. It communicates with the external object to integrate the function of this object with other pads.

## 8.1 GENERIC UTILITY FUNCTIONS AS PADS

IntelligentPad treats every manipulable object as a pad. It also tries to treat every generic function as a pad. Furthermore, as a special case, IntelligentPad treats generic functions that are applied to pads as pads, thus allowing us to apply such functions to another copy of the same function. Utility functions for controlling, coordinating, arranging, editing, managing, searching, transporting, and distributing pads are all generic functions that are applied to pads. Once they are implemented as pads, their functions can be applied to any pads, including themselves.

Utility functions for pads are generic functions applicable to all kinds of pads. These functions are classified as follows:

1. Modify a target pad
2. Coordinate a group of pads

3. Inspect a target pad
4. Manage and retrieve pads
5. Transport a target pad

The modification of pads is further classified into the following:

a. Modification of the controller part of a target pad
b. Modification of the view part of a target pad
c. Modification of the model part of a target pad

Controller modification changes user events and their dispatch mechanism. View modification changes the appearance of pads on the display. The clipping of a pad into some shape and the rotation of a pad to some angle are examples of view modification. Model modification changes the internal processing function of a pad. An example is the addition of a new slot to a target pad.

The coordination function is further classified into the following:

a. Spatial coordination
b. Temporal coordination
c. Spatiotemporal coordination

Spatial coordination geometrically arranges pads, whereas temporal coordination controls the timing of the activation of pads. Spatiotemporal coordination controls both the activation and the movement of target pads.

The inspection function examines the structure and the status of a target pad. For example, the inspection of a composite pad structure represents the composition structure as a tree of components.

The management and retrieval functions store a variety of pads, index them, and help us to find the pads we want.

All these utility functions need to be represented as pads. Once represented as pads, these functions are easily applied to any pads through direct manipulations by end-users. They are mostly represented as base pads on which target pads are placed.

When a pad is pasted on another pad, the child pad usually works as an input and/or output device of the parent pad. However, this is not the only relationship we can define between a pad and its parent. Utility function pads used as base pads apply their functions to their child pads.

## 8.2   FIELDPAD FOR THE EVENT SHARING

Shared copies of the same pad share the same state, i.e., the same model object. The state of a composite pad is defined as the state of the base pad. Shared copies, however, cannot share a user event applied to one of them unless it only changes the shared state. A user event may change the pad view without changing its state. For example, it may change only the relative location of a component pad in a composite pad. Hence, we require an event-sharing mechanism as an independent primitive function.

### 8.2.1 How to Share Events

In order for us to collaborate through network connections, we must share the same environment of pads. This requires the sharing of events, including mouse and keyboard events, among the distributed copies of the same environment. Event sharing has the following two ways of implementation. Events need to be detected at each site. The detected events are sent to the central arbiter, and made consistent with each other. This arbitration neglects some events if necessary. Mutually consistent events are applied either to the master copy of the environment, or to all the copies of the environment. The former approach requires each slave copy of the environment to work just as a monitor display of what happens to the original copy. Such slave copies are called view copies. The latter approach requires every copy to have the same set of pads with the same initial states. Every copy of the same environment has the same pads with the same initial states at the same relative locations on this copy, and receives the same sequence of events (Figure 8.1). Therefore, all the environment copies behave in the same way unless some pads exhibit nondeterministic behaviors.

The view copy of a pad can be implemented in either of the following two ways. The first method multiplies the view part of the original pad, and uses copies of the original view part as the view copies (Figure 8.2). The message traffic between each view copy and the original is the same as the traffic between the view part and the model part of the original pad. The second method uses only a copy of the original's display image as a view copy (Figure 8.3). Each copy changes its image whenever the original changes its display image. Such a copy of the original is sometimes called a shadow copy. Whenever it changes its display image, the original pad needs to send its bitmap image to each of its shadow copies.

Event sharing has also two ways of implementation. The first multiplies the controller of the original pad and uses each of these copies to detect events at each site. Detected events are all dispatched to the original pad and arbitrated there to neglect conflicting events. This controller-copy method is combined with the view-copy method to define copies of the same environment. Each copy consists of a view copy of the original, and the

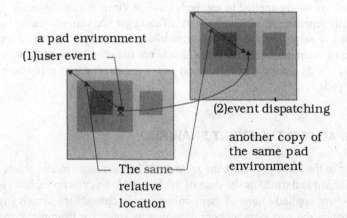

a pad environment
(1)user event

(2)event dispatching

another copy of
the same pad
environment

The same
relative
location

**Figure 8.1** Every copy of the same environment has the same pads with the same initial states at the same relative locations on this copy. Each copy receives the same sequence of user events.

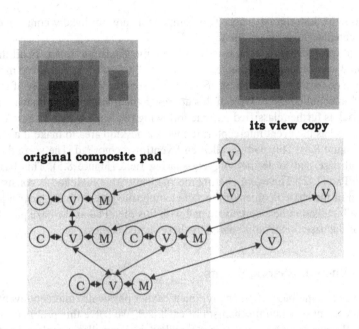

**Figure 8.2**   The first method defines a view copy by providing only the view part for every component of the original pad.

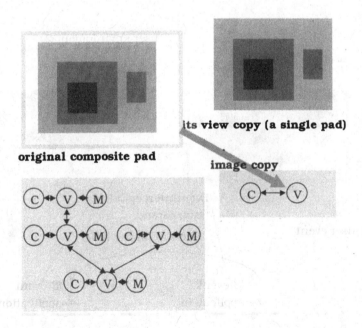

**Figure 8.3**   The second method for the view copy uses only a copy of the original's display image as a view copy.

controller copy of the original. These two components are not locally connected but remotely connected through the original pad.

The second way of sharing events uses a special mechanism to intercept all the events over the shared environment. Intercepted events are arbitrated by a centralized mechanism and then made consistent with each others. They are sent back to every copy of the shared environment and applied there. We call this approach the interceptor approach. The interceptor approach is further classified into the following two approaches. The first one uses a transparent pad as the event interceptor; it covers a desktop area to make it a shared environment (Figure 8.4). This pad is called an EventInterceptorPad. The second approach uses a special base pad to define an event-sharing field (Figure 8.5). This base pad is called a FieldPad [1, 2]. The event-sharing mechanism with a FieldPad is consistent with the definition of the shared copies of the same composite pad if we consider a pad environment on a FieldPad to be a composite pad with this FieldPad as the base pad. Only the model part of the base FieldPad is shared by these shared copies.

### 8.2.2   FieldPad For Sharing Events

A FieldPad used as the base of an environment cannot physically intercept events unless we change the event dispatch mechanism of each pad. We solve this problem as follows (Figure 8.6). Whenever a pad is put over a FieldPad, its controller is replaced with a special controller. When the pad is dragged out from the FieldPad, its controller is changed to the original one. A new controller sends the event information of each event on it to the nearest FieldPad below itself. This FieldPad receives event information through its view

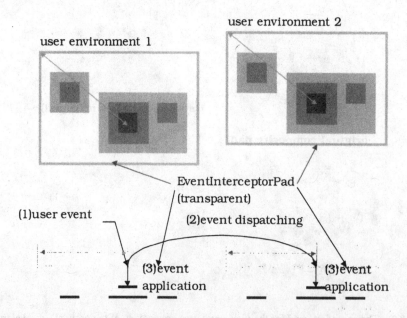

**Figure 8.4**   The first method of sharing events uses a transparent pad as an event interceptor, which covers a desktop area to make it a shared environment.

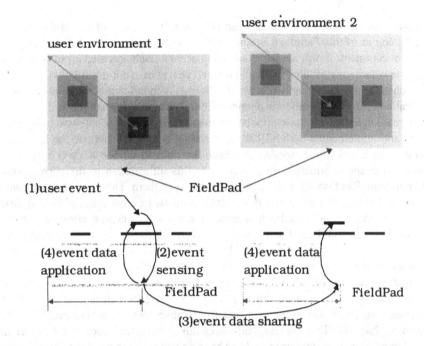

**Figure 8.5**   The second method of sharing events uses a FieldPad to define an event-sharing field.

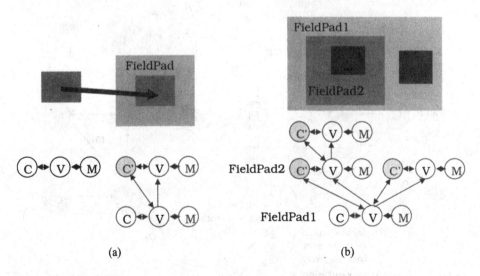

**Figure 8.6**   A FieldPad intercepts all the events applied to those pads over itself. (a) Whenever a pad is put over a FieldPad, its controller is replaced with a special controller. (b) A new controller sends the event information of each event to the topmost FieldPad below itself.

part, which then sends this to its model part (Figure 8.7). The model part is shared by all the shared copies of this FieldPad, and arbitrates events coming from different copies to make them consistent. It may neglect conflicting events. Each accepted event is sent back to every view part copy of this FieldPad. For each arrival of event information, each view then searches for the pad to apply this event. This pad is found as the outermost pad at the event location. The event location is obtained from the event information.

In the real implementation, we divided the function of a FieldPad into two independent functions and implemented each of them as a pad (Figure 8.8). They are the EventSensingPad and the EventApplicationPad. An EventSensingPad intercepts each event, translates it to its event information data, and sends this information to the corresponding EventApplicationPad through a slot connection between them. This EventApplicationPad sends this information to its model part, which arbitrates events coming from different copies to make them consistent. Each accepted event is sent back to every view part copy of the EventApplicationPad. Each view part copy of the EventApplicationPad then searches for the pad to apply this event. This pad is found as the outermost pad at the event location relative to each view of the EventApplicationPad.

Figure 8.8 shows the details. When a user applies a user event to a pad P, its controller sends the corresponding event information to the nearest EventSensingPad below P. This information consists of the event type and the relative location of the event over this EventSensingPad. This EventSensingPad stores this event information in its model slot. Its model notifies its view that its model has been updated. The view of the EventSensingPad reads this slot value and sends this event information to the event slot of its parent pad

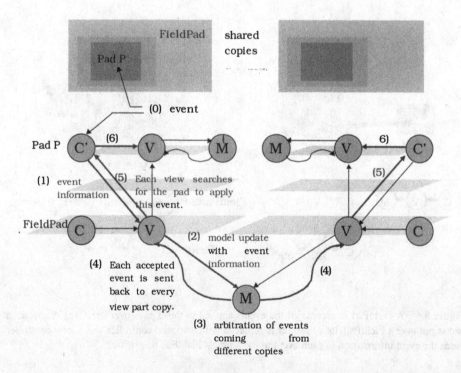

**Figure 8.7** The event-sharing mechanism implemented by shared copies of the same FieldPad.

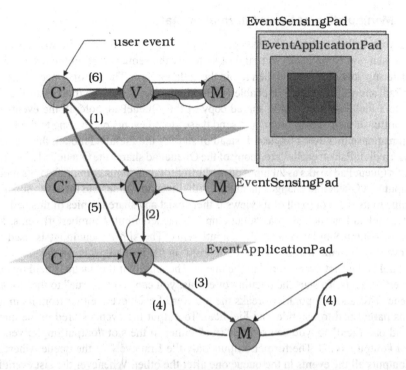

**Figure 8.8**  In the real implementation, we divided the function of a FieldPad into two independent pads—an EventSensingPad and an EventApplicationPad.

EventApplicationPad. The view of the EventApplicationPad stores this event information to the event slot defined in the model part. This model is shared by more than one view of the same EventApplicationPad. The model notifies its update to all of its views. Each of these views then reads out the stored event information and sends it to the controller of the target pad over itself. Then the controller of the target pad sends the corresponding message to the view of the target pad.

Each view of the EventApplicationPad finds the target pad using the relative location of the event. The target pad over each view of the EventApplicationPad is identified as the outermost pad at this relative location over this view. This method of identifying the target pad from its location is based upon the following two assumptions. First, the EventApplicationPad and the paired EventSensingPad have the same size. Second, the relative locations of pads over a pair of these pads are kept the same among their different copies.

The moving of a pad over a FieldPad by means of a mouse may generate a large sequence of mouse events that successively changes the state of the FieldPad, which may seriously deteriorate the performance. Our implementation treats each pad-moving operation as a single event with two locations as its parameters—the origin and the destination of the movement.

The separation of the two functions of a FieldPad as an EventSensingPad and an EventApplicationPad allows us to insert a pad between them to filter or modify events that the EventSensingPad sends to the EventApplicationPad.

### 8.2.3   Manipulation of Event Information Data

During your collaboration with other people, you may have to leave the workspace for a while. When you come back, you might like to see the sequence of all the events that occurred during your absence and then rejoin the collaboration. The use of a special pad called QueuePad, shown in Figure 8.9, enables you to temporarily stop the transfer of the shared events to a FieldPad pasted on a shared copy of this QueuePad, hold all the events in the queue buffer in their arrival order, and send these stored events one by one to the FieldPad later in response to a user's request. Instead of sharing the FieldPad model, this configuration with a FieldPad on each shared copy of the QueuePad shares the QueuePad model. Each view of a QueuePad works as an input queue buffer for data items coming from its model. A new input to a QueuePad changes its model with this input value, and then the model sends this value to its view, or to all of its views if there exist any shared copies of this pad.

A QueuePad has such slots as #queueInput, #queueOutput, #numberOfEvents, #start-ToQueue, #outputSingleEvent, and #outputEvents. The slot #queueInput is used to receive event information from its model or from its parent pad, whereas the slot #queue-Output holds the first event stored in the queue. The length of the queue is held by the slot #numberOfEvents. To start the queuing of events, you can send a "true" to the slot #start-ToQueue. This also temporarily breaks the transfer of each event either from its model or from its parent pad to its child pad FieldPad. To output the events stored in the queue to the child pad FieldPad, you can send a "true" either to the slot #outputSingleEvent or to the slot #outputEvents. The former outputs only the first event of the queue, whereas the latter outputs all the events in the queue one after the other. Whenever the last event in the queue is output, the QueuePad resumes the direct transfer of each input event either from

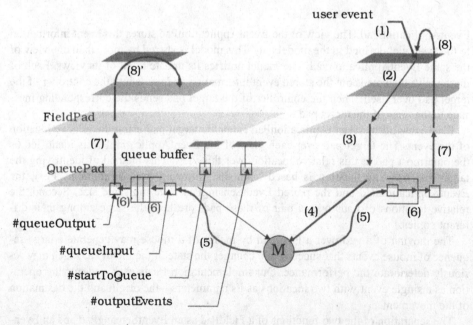

**Figure 8.9**   A QueuePad allows you to leave the shared workspace for a while. It allows you to see the sequence of all the events that have occurred during your absence when you come back, and then to rejoin the collaboration.

its model or from its parent pad to the child pad. Figure 8.9 shows how a QueuePad is used, where the two button pads connected to the slots #startToQueue and #outputEvents can be used, respectively, to suppress and to resume the participation in the collaboration. A FieldPad can be also used with a QueuePad to take an event log.

You may sometimes want to enlarge or to reduce some copies of the shared environment to arbitrary sizes. The configuration shown in Figure 8.10 answers this requirement.

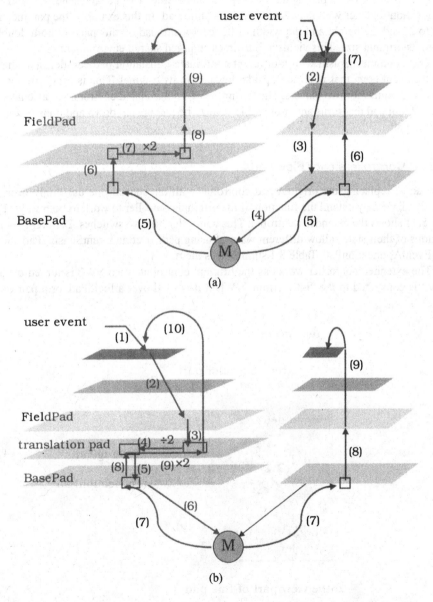

**Figure 8.10** A coordinate translation pad is used between a FieldPad and a BasePad to enlarge or reduce a copy of the shared environment to an arbitrary size. (a) A shared event occurred in the right-hand environment. (b) A shared event occurred in the left-hand environment.

It uses another pad with a slot to store a single event. This pad is used as the base pad to share event information. In Figure 8.10, the right FieldPad is pasted directly on a copy of this pad with its slot connection to this event-holding slot, whereas the left one is connected to another copy of this pad via a coordinate-translation pad. This translation pad multiplies each coordinate of the location in the event information coming from its child pad by a specified parameter value, and sends the translated location together with the event type to its parent pad. It also divides each coordinate of the location in the event information coming from its parent pad by the same specified parameter value, and sends the translated location together with the event type to its child pad. In this example, the parameter is set to 2, and the height and the width of the composite pad on this pad are both doubled from its original size. This yields a four-times enlarged shared environment.

The same mechanism with a different coordinate-translation pad can define a shared environment copy that is turned upside-down from its original. This is especially useful for board games for two players. The definition of such a shared environment also needs a special tool pad that turns any dropped-in composite pad upside-down and pops up the resulting pad.

### 8.2.4 Controllers over FieldPads

Instead of replacing the original pad controller with the special one used only over the FieldPad, we may extend the function of the original controller to work in both ways. Figure 8.11 shows the extended controller. This controller has two switches. Different combinations of their states allow different ways of using pads over an EventSensingPad and/or an EventApplicationPad. Table 8.1 summarizes them.

The extended controller works as the original controller when SW1 is turned off and SW2 is connected to the "int" terminal. When it is used over a FieldPad, or a pair of an

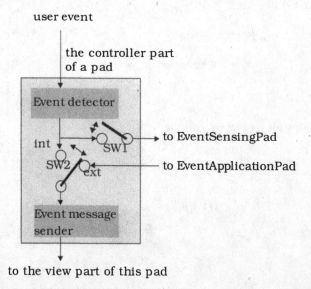

**Figure 8.11** The extended controller has two switches. Different combinations of their states allow different ways of using pads over an EventSensingPad and/or an EventApplicationPad.

**Table 8.1**   Different combinations of the two switches in Figure 8.11 allow different ways of using pads over the EventSensingPad and/or the EventApplicationPad

| SW1 | SW2 | Use |
|-----|-----|-----|
| on  | int | For a pad over an EventSensingPad |
| off | ext | For a pad over an EventApplicationPad |
| on  | ext | For a pad over a FieldPad |
| off | int | For pads other than those above |

EventSensingPad and an EventApplicationPad, its SW1 should be turned on and SW2 should be connected to the "ext" terminal.

If we turn on SW1 and connect SW2 to "int," we can use this controller for all the pads over an EventSensingPad to detect all the user events over this EventSensingPad, and to send their information to somewhere else. You may use this combination to take a log of user events. If we turn off SW1 and connect SW2 to "ext," we can use this controller for all the pads over an EventApplicationPad to apply event information coming from this EventApplicationPad. These pads cannot be directly manipulated. The configuration in Figure 8.12 uses these two different types of controllers over an EventSensingPad and over an EventApplicationPad, respectively. Furthermore, the EventSensingPad is connected to the EventApplicationPad via shared copies of a basic pad. The two environments in this configuration may run on different machines connected through a network. This mechanism allows you to monitor on your own display screen all the operations done by another user on a different display screen.

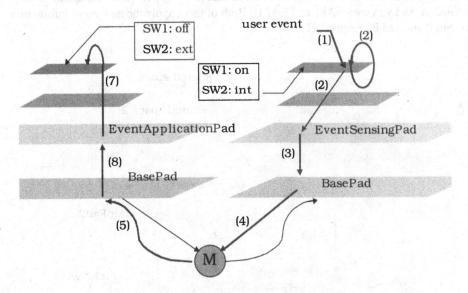

**Figure 8.12**   Two different types of controllers are used over an EventSensingPad and over an EventApplicationPad, respectively, which allows us to monitor on our own display screen all the operations done by another user on a different display screen.

### 8.2.5 Conflict Resolution

The event-sharing mechanism using a FieldPad shares event information through its shared copies. FieldPad is classified among combinatorial pads. Its next state is determined by the new event information and does not depend on its current state. As discussed in Section 7.7, a combinatorial pad may accept a new update request with the higher priority, neglecting the preceding one under the processing, if the pad is still in either the update-request phase or the model-update phase. It cannot accept a new update, neglecting the preceding one under the processing, if it is already in the view-update phase. Therefore, a FieldPad accepts new event information with the higher priority, neglecting the preceding one under the processing, unless its views are being updated with the preceding one. The same is true with the EventApplicationPad.

### 8.2.6 Nested Shared Environments

FieldPads or pairs of an EventSensingPad and an EventApplicationPad can be overlaid as shown in Figure 8.13. Shared copies of this composite pad are defined as shown in Figure 8.14. This allows us to define the nesting of more than one different shared space, as shown in Figure 8.15, where users A and B can interact with all the pads in the nested two shared spaces, whereas a user C can interact only with an internal shared space. Figure 8.16 shows the message-sending paths in a nested shared environment.

When an event occurs over the FieldPad FP1 that consists of the EventSensingPad ESP1 and the EventApplicationPad EAP1, it is detected by ESP1 and its information is sent to the EventApplicationPad EAP0 through the EventSensingPad ESP0. The EventApplicationPad EAP0 updates its model, which then sends back this event information to all of its views. The view of EAP0 then propagates this event information to EAP1, which then updates its model. The model of EAP1 is shared by its two views. Its update is propagated to the two views EAP1 and EAP1′. Both of them apply the new event information to pad P and pad P′, respectively.

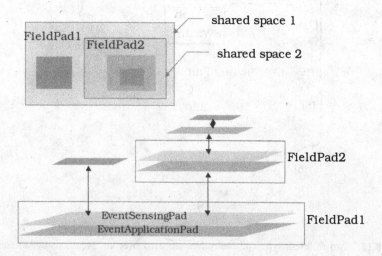

**Figure 8.13** FieldPads or pairs of an EventSensingPad and an EventApplicationPad can be overlaid one over the other.

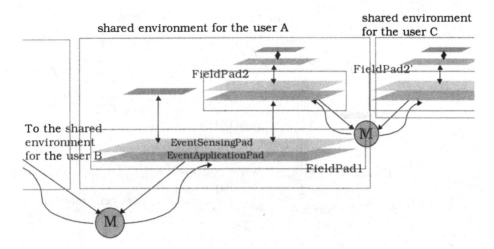

**Figure 8.14** Shared copies of a composite pad with more than one FieldPad.

When an event occurs over the FieldPad FP1′, it is detected by the EventSensingPad ESP1′, and sent to the EventApplicationPad EAP1′, which updates its model with this new event information. Then this model sends this information to its other view FP1, which further sends this information to EAP0 through ESP0. The remaining event application process proceeds in the same way as described above.

Every change of event information goes to the bottommost EventApplicationPad to resolve any event conflict. This process passes the event information from each EventSensingPad to the next underlying EventSensingPad. The application of each event information goes from the bottommost EventApplicationPad to the target pad. This

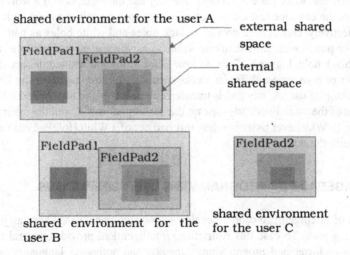

**Figure 8.15** Overlaid FieldPads define the nesting of more than one different shared space. Users A and B can interact with all the pads in the two nested shared spaces, whereas a user C can interact only with an internal shared space.

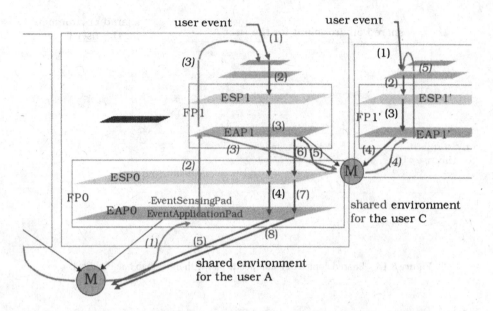

**Figure 8.16** Message-sending paths in nested shared environments.

process passes event information from each EventApplicationPad to the next overlying EventApplicationPad.

### 8.2.7 Wormholes among Different Spaces

Different FieldPads as well as different desktops define different workspaces. We cannot directly move a pad from one workspace to another workspace. We need a special pipe that connects one workspace to another. We may use the metaphor of a wormhole for this pipe, where the entrance and the exit of each pipe may be called a black hole and a white hole, respectively. Our system provides black holes and white holes as pads. Each black hole may be paired with more than one white hole, whereas each white hole is paired with only one black hole. Figure 8.17 shows how black holes and white holes are used to allow the transfer of pads across different workspaces. If you drop a pad on the BlackHolePad on the desktop of user A, this pad is transferred to each of the two WhiteHolePads on the two copies of the same FieldPad—one on the desktop of user A, and the other on the desktop of user B. Whichever user may drag this pad out of a WhiteHolePad onto a FieldPad, it is moved into the shared space.

### 8.3 STAGEPAD FOR PROGRAMMING USER OPERATIONS

End-users of IntelligentPad cannot develop a new component pad. They can just paste and peel existing pads. To ease this restriction, IntelligentPad provides several facilities, including an end-user pad programming language, an authoring language, and a model-description pad. Commercial product versions of IntelligentPad running on Widows PCs adopt Visual Basic as their end-user programming language for end-users to develop new component pads. A model description pad works as a model pad. Users can easily de-

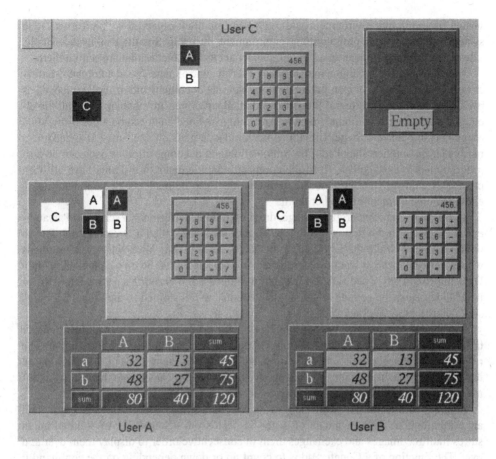

**Figure 8.17**  A pair of a BlackHolePad and a WhiteHolePad defines a wormhole between two different spaces to transport pads from one space to the other.

scribe the relationships among its data slot values using expressions. A Fujitsu commercial product version of IntelligentPad running on Windows PCs provides a procedure pad that allows us to define the relationship among its slot values using an interpreter programming language whose syntax is similar to C++. The authoring language uses the metaphor of a stage, and coordinates the behavior of pads on a special pad called StagePad. It provides a generic function to manipulate multiple pads and to perform a series of steps. It can manipulate any pads on the StagePad in the same way as we directly manipulate them. It can also read and write the primary slot value of any pad on the StagePad. It also allows user interactions. It can associate each user event with a corresponding action. When a user event is applied, it triggers the corresponding action. At present, only the Smalltalk version of IntelligentPad provides the StagePad utility.

## 8.3.1  An Outline of StagePad

StagePad uses a drama metaphor. Other attempts at using a drama metaphor have been made before by several groups. One such system is the Rehearsal [3] system that offers a visual programming environment and regards a Smalltalk object as a "performer." The system offers a visual programming environment by using Smalltalk objects visually. These "performers" appear on a "stage" and act according to cues that are sent to them.

StagePad applies the drama metaphor in order to control pads. It can automate whatever tasks a user can do by manipulating more than one document and/or tool composed as pads. The distinctive feature of StagePad is that all structures are standard since all the elements that comprise a drama are pads. Any composite pad can become a performer on a StagePad, and hence a StagePad with some composite pads on itself may also become a performer on another StagePad. The composition and decomposition of pads can be also programmed in a StagePad. Thus, the compositional elements of a drama have all been created as components. Furthermore, a drama itself can be made as a component, i.e., a compositional element of another drama

A drama is organized around a stage, dressing rooms, performers, a script, and an audience. The stage in the drama is a StagePad and has a pad called a DressingRoomPad to hold performers while they are not on the stage. Performers, called actor pads, are pads whose performance we want to coordinate. An actor pad must be on a StagePad or on a DressingRoomPad. A pad called a TextEditorPad is used to describe a script. The TextEditorPad describes the actions of actors. Its contents are transmitted to the StagePad via its slot connection to the StagePad.

The StagePad transmits messages to every actor as directed to by the script whenever there happens to be a pad action or a user event such as a mouse or keyboard input. The respective pads begin their actions as directed. In this way, actor pads unfold a drama on the StagePad. The user is not simply a passive audience, but can change the flow of a drama by writing a script or generating user events.

Figure 8.18 illustrates a simple application that uses a StagePad. It shows a counter and an AnimationPad with an image of a gorilla pasted on a StagePad. An AnimationPad stores multiple images and exchanges them in consecutive order to display them over and over. The function of a CounterPad is to count up or down depending on the command it receives. ButtonPads for sending commands and a DisplayPad for displaying the count are combined together, and the resulting composite pad and the AnimationPad are pasted on top of a base pad having no specific functions. The directions written in the script are "when the gorilla is clicked, delete the gorilla and click the count-up button," and "when the gorilla moves, move it right first for 20, and then left for 10." When the gorilla is moved or is clicked, the contents of the script are enacted. A simple gorilla hunt game is implemented in this way.

In Figure 8.19, a KeyboardPad is pasted onto a StagePad. The music keyboard has the function of playing a sound that corresponds to the command it receives. ButtonPads are pasted on the keyboard. The directions written in the script are "when 'do' is clicked, click in 'mi,' then click in 'so,'" and "when 'ti' is clicked, click in 're,' then in 'so.'" Thus, the script is enacted if "do" or "ti" is clicked.

## 8.3.2  Scripts and Casting

A script is one of the elements that comprise a drama. Scripts describe procedures and constraints for acting out user's intentions on every pad placed on a StagePad. Every pad on a StagePad follows actions written in a script. A relationship between role names and pads that actually put on a performance with those actors must be defined in order to use

**Figure 8.18** A gorilla-hunting game implemented with a StagePad.

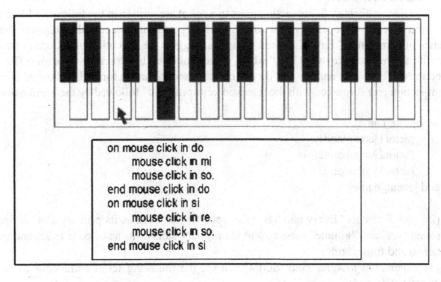

**Figure 8.19** The automatic playing of a keyboard implemented with a StagePad.

role names in a StagePad script and to indirectly designate pads. A CastingList provides relationships corresponding to designated role names and the actual pads listed within a script. Scripts and CastingLists are described in detail below.

**A. Scripts.** StagePad scripts are written to be independent of pads used as actor pads that perform on a StagePad. Thus, any pad can be used as an actor pad independent of the script. Furthermore, a script written under the assumption that it would be used by a certain stage can be used by a different stage without changing a word. Scripts and actors are reusable components due to the independence of scripts and actor pads. The following method is used in StagePad to preserve the independence of scripts. First, pad references within scripts use role names, and the mapping between role names and actor pads are explicitly and independently specified on a special pad called a CastingList. The commands that can be used in the script are restricted to those fundamental operations users can directly carry out on pads. If a script uses commands that only specific pads can understand, it turns out that the types of pads that can be assigned a given role name become limited and the independence of scripts is not preserved. Therefore, scripts are restricted to use only those fundamental-operation commands that every pad understands. In order to send some command other than fundamental operations to some target pad on a StagePad, you can paste on this pad a CommandButtonPad whose click sends this command to the target pad. In the script program, you only need to click this CommandButtonPad.

A StagePad performs its script program based on an event-driven mechanism. A drama progresses as it is triggered by certain events, and then directs to every pad a series of actions to occur. The script is written as a set of event–action pairs, each of which specifies a triggering event and a sequence of consecutive actions to follow this event.

**B. Script Description**

(1) *Description Format.* Event–action pairs in a script are written in the following format: "When a given event occurs, make each specified performer execute the following sequence of commands." First, the event name that triggers the execution of actions is written after the reserved keyword "on," which is then followed by directions to actors. These directions refer to role names, and do not directly refer to any actor pads. The end of an event–action pair is marked with the reserved keyword "end" followed by the event name:

```
on [event_name]
      [actor1]command1.
      [actor2]command2.
      [actor3]command3.
end [event_name]
```

(2) *Slot Reference.* Every pad has a slot specified to work as its primary slot. Scripts can send "set" and "gimme" messages to the primary slots of its actor pads to set and get values to and from them.

(3) *Commands to Actor Pads.* Scripts can use the following set of commands to perform actions on pads:

move to <destination>          move the pad
copy <location>                copy the pad

| | |
|---|---|
| delete | delete the pad |
| hide | hide the pad |
| show | show the pad |
| open | open the pad icon |
| close | iconify the pad |
| resize to <new size> | change the pad size |
| paste on <actor> | paste the pad on the specified pad |
| assoc <new slot> | change the pad connection |
| mclick | send the pad a click event |
| mdrag to <destination> | send the pad a drag event with the specified destination |
| mkey <key> | send the pad the specified key input |

(4) *Constraints between Pads (Constraints on Pad Positions)* Scripts enable us to impose some constraints on pads. Pads with attached constraints regulate actions by always meeting those constraints. In Figure 8.20, a constraint is attached to keep PadA a distance $x$ away from PadB. Based on this constraint, whenever PadB is moved, PadA will always change its location to meet that constraint:

| | |
|---|---|
| <actor1> is <x> from <actor2> | actor1 maintains a distance $x$ from actor2 |
| <actor1> is touching <actor2> | actor1 touches actor2 |
| <actor1> is <x> overlapping <actor2> | actor1 overlaps actor2 by a distance $x$ |

(5) *Control Statements.* The following control statements are used when writing a series of actions for a pad:

```
if <condition> then <action> else <action> end if
while <condition> <action> end while
until <condition> <action> end until
repeat <n> <action> end repeat
```

**C. Casting List.** Role names are used within a script to refer to actor pads. The relationship between a role name and an actor pad must be defined in order for a StagePad to manipulate this actor pad. The linking of these two items is done in a CastingList. A Cast-

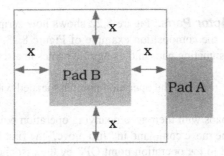

**Figure 8.20**  A constraint is attached to keep PadA a distance $x$ away from PadB. Based on this constraint, whenever PadB is moved, PadA will always change its location to meet this constraint.

ingList is an association list formed from a list of role names and relative locations on the StagePad called operation points:

$$CastingList(\ (role\_name1\ (OP_{11}\ OP_{12}\ OP_{13} \ldots))$$
$$(role\_name2\ (OP_{21}\ OP_{22}\ OP_{23} \ldots))$$
$$\ldots\ldots\ldots\ldots\ldots\ldots\ldots),$$

where each $OP_{ij}$ is an operation point.

When a user uses the mouse to perform an operation on a pad to click, move, or copy this pad, the user first moves the mouse cursor into the region of the pad where he or she intends to perform any operation. The location of the mouse cursor at the time of this operation is called its operation point. An operation point holds a location point on some pad over the StagePad. When a script executes a command on a role name, this command is actually applied to the operation point that is associated with this role by the CastingList. If the command is a pad operation, it is applied to the pad with this operation point on itself.

Each operation point is assigned to a pad over the StagePad in advance. The pad assigned to the operation point becomes the actor pad. As a result, actor pads can be directed via operation points from the StagePad to perform the same variety of pad operations that users can directly apply to these pads using a mouse. Operation points are used to handle both pad operations by a user and those by a StagePad in a uniform manner.

The independence of actor pads from the script can be preserved by the CastingList that associates each role name to an operation point. When operations via a StagePad manipulate primitive and composite pads on a StagePad, the functions held by those pads are not lost since both pad operations by a user and those by a StagePad are handled in a uniform way. For example, when the music keyboard is placed on a StagePad as in Figure 8.21, the keyboard pad maintains its function as a keyboard while following the directions from the StagePad via operation points. The keyboard does not change its operation of playing sounds for a pressed key, whether it is on the StagePad or peeled off the StagePad. Figure 8.21 also shows the CastingList and the operation points. Because they use operation points, StagePads have the advantage of being able to use all pads created in the IntelligentPad system without losing any of their functions.

Pads can be made to perform their roles as written in the script through the use of a CastingList that links role names with these pads. By assigning the same role to different pads or allocating more than one role to the same pad, the same script can develop different dramas on the same StagePad. Various dramas can be realized by changing assignments.

**D. References to Actor Pads.** Figure 8.22 shows how script commands are transmitted to actor pads in the composition example of Figure 8.23. The following conventions are used when designating pads and using role names in a script:

(1) <RoleName>   the pad with the operation point associated with this role name

Figure 8.23 shows pads with their accompanying operation points that have been allocated to role names. The move command in "Jiro move," the first line of the script in Figure 8.22, is transmitted to the operation point OP2 by the association {Jiro: OP2} in the CastingList. The operation point OP2 sends this move message to pad PadB, the pad on which this operation point is defined, and pad PadB executes the move command.

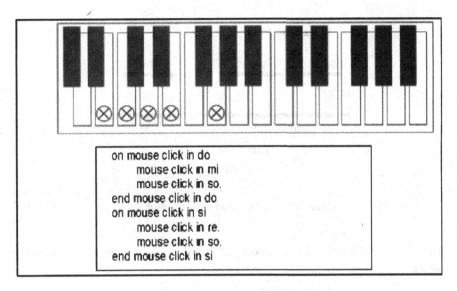

**Figure 8.21**   The independence of actor pads from a script is preserved by a CastingList that associates each role name to an operation point.

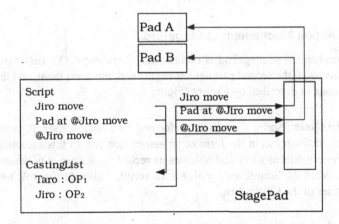

**Figure 8.22**   The transmission of script commands to actor pads in the composition shown in Figure 8.23.

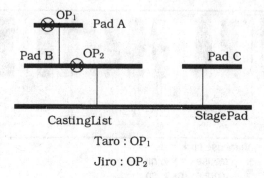

**Figure 8.23**   A StagePad and a CastingList.

(2) Pad at @<RoleName>   the outermost pad at the operation point associated with this role name

The command in the second line of the script in Figure 8.22, "Pad at @Jiro move," is transmitted to the operation point OP2 by the association {Jiro: OP2} in the CastingList. The operation point OP2 uses its own location information to search for the outermost pad at this location, and sends this pad PadA a move message. Pad PadA then executes this move command.

(3) @<RoleName>   the operation point associated with this role name

The command "@Jiro move," the third line of the script in Figure 8.22, is transmitted to the operation point OP2 by the association {Jiro: OP2} in the CastingList. The operation point OP2 moves itself.

Convention (1) can always refer to a particular pad, (2) can refer to a pad from location information, and (3) refers to the operation point itself.

### 8.3.3   The Action Mechanism of StagePad

The action mechanism of StagePad is divided into three parts. The first part reads in a script and analyzes it, the second part detects events and interprets them, and the third part directs actor pads as described by a script (Figure 8.24).

***A. Script Analysis.***  Script analysis is performed by a ScriptParser. A parsed script is then stored in the StagePad in the form of an association list. In this association list, the name of an event works as a key and holds as its record the sequence of actions triggered by this event. When the ScriptParser analyzes the script, it also extracts role names to create all the entries of the CastingList.

***B. Event Interpretation.***  StagePads handle two types of events. The first type includes user events such as mouse clicks and drags. The second type includes events generated through the actions of pads. For each basic pad operation, the corresponding pad-event type exists.

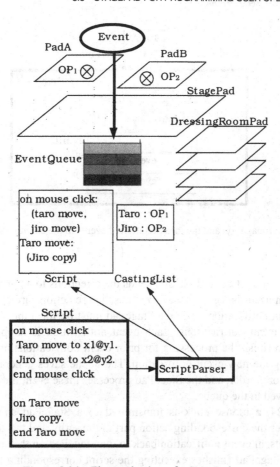

**Figure 8.24** The mechanism of a StagePad.

StagePads start a drama when triggered by events. Thus, all events on a StagePad must be detected. In the IntelligentPad system, regardless of whether a pad generates an event or a pad detects a user event, the notification about this event and the pad where it occurred is propagated successively to all the pads under this pad. StagePads utilize this mechanism to detect events.

Furthermore, StagePads need to interpret each transmitted event notification, and to convert its related pad to the corresponding role name. This is necessary because StagePads can refer to actor pads in the scripts only through role names. Figure 8.25 shows an example of moving pad PadA in the situation shown in Figure 8.23. When an event notification [PadA move] is transmitted from PadA, the StagePad interprets this event notification as [Pad at @ Jiro move] and also as [Taro move] because the pad PadA is referred to in the script as [Pad at @Jiro] and [Taro].

**C. Script Execution.** When an event is generated on a StagePad, its event notification is transmitted to the StagePad. The event notification triggers a search of the script for the event–action pair that the StagePad must enact. Once the StagePad finds the event-action pair to be enacted, it follows the directions described in its action part, gets the operation

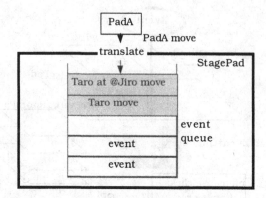

**Figure 8.25** The propagation and the interpretation of events in the example shown in Figure 8.23.

points referred to in the CastingList, and sends the directions to actor pads through them. Actor pads act in accordance to those directions. Those actions are also sent back to the StagePad as event notifications, and the StagePad must perform the above process in response to those event notifications. Each event notification is temporarily stored in a queue in order to finish the processing for prior event notifications in a sequential order before processing the new event notification. The queue saves generated event notifications in the temporal order, and the StagePad processes these event notifications in the order they were saved to the queue.

In Figure 8.24, a mouse click is transmitted to a StagePad as a user event. The StagePad executes the corresponding action part in the script and the corresponding actor pad then transmits an event notification back to the StagePad on the completion of its action. When the StagePad finishes executing the script corresponding to the mouse click, the following two events, "Taro move" and "Jiro move," are stored in the queue. Next, the action part corresponding to the event "Taro move" is executed. The queue then holds "Jiro move" and "Jiro copy" as event notifications. Since no event–action pair exists for either of these two events, the StagePad deletes those events from the queue without sending any other directions, and completes its operation.

**D.  Scripting Function.** StagePads provide a scripting function, which allows us to describe script commands by manually demonstrating a sequence of operations on pads using the mouse. For example, when pad PadA in Figure 8.26 is moved, the script command "Taro move to x@y" is automatically generated by this function and displayed on the editor screen. By using this function, users can actually move pads and verify their actions while creating script commands.

### 8.3.4  Dramas within Dramas

In an IntelligentPad system, pads are handled as components. Primitive pads and application pads created through the combination of primitive pads are used as components when building new composite pads. StagePad is also a primitive pad in this system. Application pads created using StagePads can compose a drama, which in turn can be used as a component. All the pads on a StagePad can be manipulated without changing their indepen-

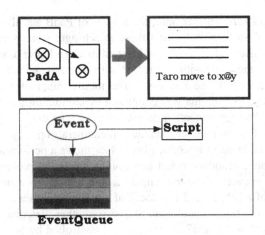

**Figure 8.26** The automatic script-generation mechanism.

dence. Thus, application pads using StagePads can use particular StagePads as building blocks while still maintaining their independence. In other words, dramas within dramas can be composed by pasting StagePads on top of other StagePads.

Dramas within dramas are smaller dramas that exist within larger dramas. Smaller dramas are themselves independent dramas and can work as components of a larger drama. Dramas created using StagePads can be combined into other dramas since they are represented as pads and work as modular components. Hence, the script that accompanies each combined drama does not have to be rewritten. Scripts within such StagePads are enacted independently, but dramas are developed as if the scripts were combined into a single script. In other words, combining StagePads is the same as combining scripts.

Figure 8.27 shows a combined drama in which StagePadA is pasted on StagePadB. The corresponding two CastingLists are shown as CastingListA and CastingListB in the figure. In this situation, the actions of PadA are interpreted as the actions of "Taro" and of "Pad at @Jiro" in StagePadA, and triggers some scripts in StagePadA. Similarly, the actions of PadB are interpreted as the actions of "Jiro" in StagePadA, and these trigger some

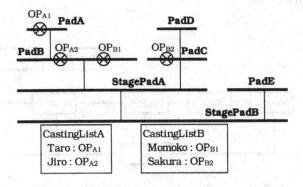

**Figure 8.27** A hierarchy with two stage pads.

other scripts in StagePadA. Furthermore, the actions of PadB are also interpreted as the actions of "Momoko" in StagePadB, and these also trigger some scripts in StagePadB. Actors in small dramas can also perform a different role in a larger drama.

Figure 8.28 shows the composition structure with seven StagePads for a CAI application called "The Training of the Fox-Boy". The total number of pads used, including StagePads, is 112. The total drama was composed by combining individual independent dramas. Every StagePad implements a drama using various existing pads as actor pads such as an AnimationPad, an EnumerationPad that enumerates pads pasted on itself, and a pad to calculate the addition of integers. Figure 8.29 shows a performance of this drama, which is a story about a Buddhist priest explaining calculation problems to the fox boy. StagePads are used in every scene to compose a story. Stage2 is a scene in which a fox boy takes the form of a boy. Stage3 is a scene of a dialogue between the fox boy and the priest. Stage4 is the fox boy's monologue. Stage5 is another dialogue with the priest and contains scenes Stage6 and Stage7. Every scene is controlled by Stage1. If this application were created using a single StagePad, a script would have to be written to cover dozens of events, and would have to handle more than 100 role names. The composition shown in Figure 8.28 is much easier to handle since there are at most 20 role names per each StagePad, and the script has to respond only to a few triggering events per each StagePad. Furthermore, in the case of a single StagePad, each pad would have to search through more than 100 role names at run-time, beginning with the actor pads, and have to select the required event–action pair from among the dozens available. Compared with Figure 8.28, the programming burden increases phenomenally and the execution speed becomes quite slow. Furthermore, the composition of Figure 8.28 can be freely modified while developing a drama by changing part of the script and/or the allocation of role names to actor pads, in contrast to the rather hard work of modifying an entire drama consisting of a single StagePad.

### 8.3.5 Dressing Rooms

A large number of miscellaneous pads are used when developing applications with complex motion. Some device is needed for handling these pads efficiently to simplify authoring on a limited screen. At each moment of a drama, some actors are on the stage, while others are not. Those actors who are not temporarily on the stage are waiting outside the stage. Dressing rooms are such places for actors. Similarly, we can introduce DressingRoomPads in StagePads.

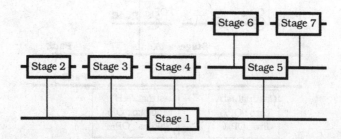

**Figure 8.28** Layers of StagePads used in "The Training of the Fox-Boy."

The fox boy asks you to pick up two strawberries.

The user is requested to input an answer in this small square.

The master checks your calculation by moving two baskets onto a calculation tool.

**Figure 8.29** Snapshots from "The Training of the Fox-Boy" that were created using seven StagePads.

A DressingRoomPad has multiple pages. Pads can be pasted on every page. The StagePad can use these pages to keep pads to be used later, or to temporarily hide pads from the stage. Different pads are kept on different pages.

Actor pads are moved between a StagePad and a DressingRoomPad by directly dragging and dropping them, or by executing a script command that contains the keyword "DressingRoom($i$)" or "@DressingRoom($i$)" as the parameter of a move command, where an index $i$ specifies a page.

### 8.3.6 Applications for Improving Pad Operability

StagePads can be also used to customize the operability of existing pads. For example, consider the operability of copy operations on pads. Usually, when a pad is copied, a user opens a menu using the mouse and selects the copy command. This operation can be changed by using a StagePad in such a way that only a double click on a pad can create a copy. The script of the StagePad shown in Figure 8.30 realizes this modification. It contains the statement "When 'pad' is double-clicked, copy 'pad.'" When the pad assigned to the role name "pad" is double-clicked, this statement creates a copy of the pad. This modification of the operability does not require any redefinition of the pad.

The script of the StagePad shown in Figure 8.31 contains the description "When 'button1' is clicked, repeat the click operation of 'button2' twice." The role name "button2" is allocated to the count-up button $P_2$ on a CounterPad, while the role name "button1" is allocated to the button pad $P_1$ which is pasted on the count-up button $P_2$. $P_1$ and $P_2$ are made to be the same size. Since $P_1$ is on top of $P_2$, users cannot see the count-up button. Although $P_2$ actually sends two count-up commands to the CounterPad, only $P_1$ is recognized by the user as the count-up button pad. Thus, a new CounterPad can be implemented that increments in steps of two for every mouse click.

Usually, we have to rewrite the pad definition program to customize its operability. StagePads allow us to customize the pad operability without redefining the pad.

StagePad is generically defined. It can use any kinds of pads as actor pads. Furthermore, StagePad is also a pad, which allows us to use StagePads on various utility pads whose functions can be applied to any pad. These utility pads include StagePad itself and FieldPad. StagePads with actor pads can be easily reedited, published through networks, and managed by database systems.

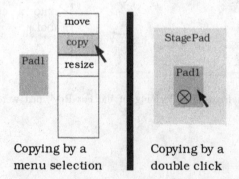

Copying by a
menu selection

Copying by a
double click

**Figure 8.30**   A customization of a copy operation.

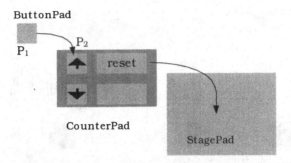

**Figure 8.31**   A customization of a counter operation.

A stage play consists of a stage, a backstage, actors and actresses, scenery, a script, and an audience. The stage is represented by a StagePad that may have DressingRoomPads working as a backstage. Any pad can be considered as either an actor/actress or scenery on the stage. The script corresponds to a script program that is input to a StagePad through a text editor pad. The audience may interact with a stage play. The audience of a StagePad corresponds to its user. Our StagePad allows its user to interact with its pads during the performance.

## 8.4  GEOMETRICAL MANAGEMENT OF PADS

Most drawing tools in use today can define a grid on a drawing sheet. They allow us to specify an arbitrary length for the grid interval. Such a grid has gravity at each grid point. Every point specified by a user is automatically adjusted to its closest grid point. This helps users to align graphical objects to horizontal and/or vertical lines. This grid is an example of geometrical management tools for graphical objects.

Such a grid sheet is also useful for geometrical arrangement of pads. In IntelligentPad, such a sheet is also considered a pad. A geometrical management pad arranges pads in some regular geometrical pattern. Some arrange pads in a grid pattern, whereas others arrange them in a hierarchy. In order to add a pad to the arrangement, you may drop the pad at any location sufficiently close to one of the regular positions defined on the geometrical management pad. Since geometrical management pads are themselves pads, they can be dropped together with other types of pads on another geometrical management pad. Figure 8.32 shows such an example; a grid alignment pad is used to regularly arrange four pads, each using a tree arrangement pad.

Geometrical management pads will be detailed in Chapter 13.

## 8.5  PROXY PADS TO ASSIMILATE EXTERNAL OBJECTS

From the viewpoint of the client–server model, IntelligentPad provides a WYSIWIG client environment that merges a development environment and a runtime environment. You can easily develop various client tools and use them through direct manipulation. The connection of these tools to various servers running on different machines, however, requires a new mechanism. To access a server from an IntelligentPad environment, we need

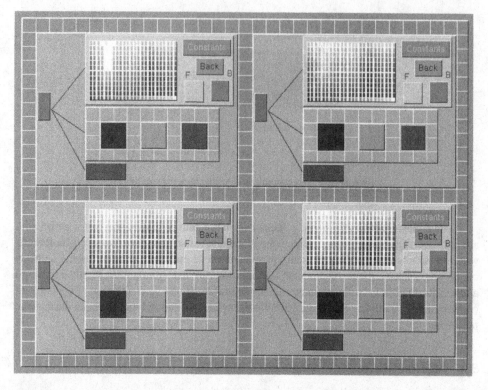

**Figure 8.32** A geometrical management pad is used to arrange pads regularly on another pad.

an object in this environment that communicates with this external server. Every access to this server passes through this object to reach the server. This object, hence, works as a proxy of this external server.

Since every manipulable object in an IntelligentPad system is represented as a pad, we represent this proxy object as a pad. We call such a pad a proxy pad. Physically, a proxy pad has a pad view. Logically, it has a list of slots that are necessary and sufficient to access various functions of the corresponding server. When an access of a function is requested through one of its slots, the proxy pad communicates with its remote server, and possibly changes its state depending on the response from the server.

A proxy pad can be provided for any kind of external object including servers; these servers include database servers, file servers, mail servers, number crunching servers, VOD (video-on-demand) servers, and HTTP servers. External objects that are not servers are computer-controlled and/or computer-monitored systems, including industrial plant systems, measurement tools, sensor systems, robots, audiovisual devices, and music synthesizers.

Let us first start with a simple example, a computer-controlled VCR. Our design goal is a console panel as shown in Figure 8.33. We implement this as a composite pad. This console consists of a base, a set of buttons, and a frame number indicator. These are all independent primitive pads. The base pad works as a proxy to the VCR. Different VCRs may require different control protocols, which require different proxy pads. Other component pads can be reused for different VCRs.

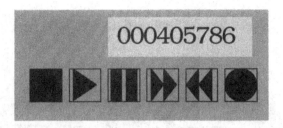

**Figure 8.33** A console panel of a computer-controllable VCR.

The proxy of a VCR is required to provide at least the following slots: #play, #stop, #pause, #fastForward, #rewind, #record, and #frameNumber (Figure 8.34). We assume that the video is displayed on a dedicated monitor display. The first six slots are data slots with logical binary values. The first five of them work in a similar way. When accessed by a "set" message with "true" as its parameter value, each of them sets itself to "true," resets the other four to "false," and sends its corresponding signal to the VCR. The slot #play starts to play the tape. The slot #stop stops playing, fast forwards, or rewinds the tape. The slots #fastForward and #rewind fast-forward and rewind the tape, respectively. The slot #record, when accessed by a "set" message with "true" as its parameter value, changes the VCR mode from the playing mode to the recording mode, and vice versa. The slot #play, when accessed by a "set" message in the recording mode, starts to record the input video on the tape. You may paste a light pad with its connection into each of these slots. A light pad, when it receives an "update" message, reads the connected slot value. If the value is "true," it turns its light on. Otherwise, it turns its light off. These light pads work as indicator lights. The slot #frameNumber is also a data slot. It always indicates the frame number of the current frame. An integer display pad is pasted on the proxy pad with its connection to the slot #frameNumber. This display pad works as a frame number indicator.

Now we will show another example of a proxy pad. Figure 8.35 shows an interface of a relational database. We implement this as a composite pad, consisting of a base and two windows: one to input a query text, and another to show a form representation of a retrieved record. It also has several buttons to start searching the database, and to show the

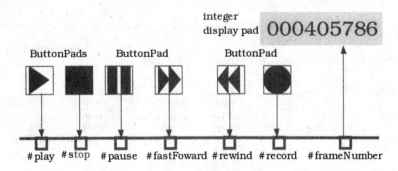

**Figure 8.34** A proxy pad for a computer-controllable VCR is used with ButtonPads and a display pad.

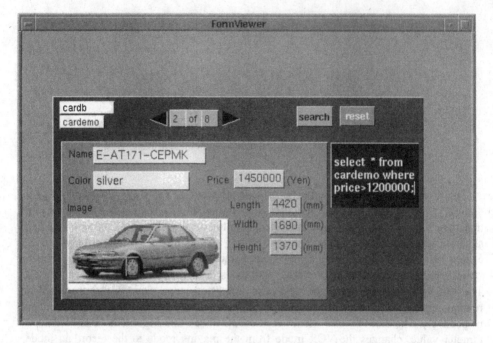

**Figure 8.35** A form interface to a relational database.

next or the previous candidate record. These are all independent primitive pads. The base pad works as a proxy to the database system.

The proxy of a database system must provide at least the following slots: #search, #insert, #query, #result, #currentRecord, #nextCandidate, and #previousCandidate (Figure 8.36). These slots perform the following functions. The slot #search, when accessed by a "set" message, sends a query in the slot #query to the database and starts the search. The slot #insert, when accessed by a "set" message, inserts a record in the slot #currentRecord

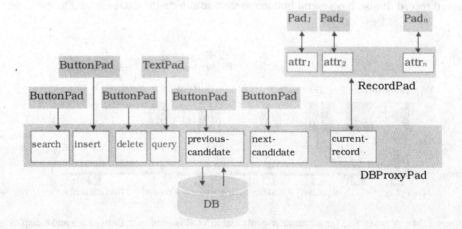

**Figure 8.36** The composition structure of the database-form interface shown in Figure 8.35.

into the database. The slot #query holds an SQL query, which is input to this slot by a "set" message. The slot #result holds a list of records obtained as a retrieval result. The proxy of a database has a current record cursor that points to one record in the retrieved record list. The pointed record is held in the slot #currentRecord. The slot #nextCandidate, when accessed by a "set" message, advances the pointer to the next record, whereas the slot #previousCandidate, when accessed by a "set" message, moves the pointer to the previous record. We paste button pads with their connections into the slots #search, #insert, #nextCandidate, and #previousCandidate. The query input uses a text input pad with its connection to the slot #query. Each record is represented as a form with several entries corresponding to its different attributes. This form itself is a composite pad, which we paste on the database proxy pad with its connection to the slot #currentRecord.

Proxy pads are powerful means to integrate various external objects with an environment of pads. They enable end-users to define such integration through direct manipulation.

When applied to an industrial plant, the proxy pad and the plant simulation pad with the same slot list can mutually substitute for each other. You may start with a simulator pad to develop and debug a console panel as a composite pad. If its slots are compatible with the proxy pad for the real plant, you can simply replace the simulator pad in the developed system with this proxy pad to obtain the final product. The simulator pad may have more slots than the proxy pad to enable us to debug the system easily.

## 8.6  LEGACY SOFTWARE MIGRATION

Legacy software signifies application systems that had been widely used by a community of users, or frequently by an individual user, before the introduction of a new system paradigm. Legacy software migration refers to making these legacy systems usable in a new system paradigm. IntelligentPad is an example of a new system paradigm. It forces each manipulable object to be a pad. Hence, legacy software migration in IntelligentPad means to either wrap a legacy system with a pad wrapper or to provide it with its proxy pad.

Any legacy software system, if it has no GUI, can be easily assimilated into an IntelligentPad environment just by developing its proxy pad. If it has its own GUI, its migration into an IntelligentPad environment is not an easy task. In this case, we use a pad wrapper to make the legacy system behave like a pad.

The simplest generic way of wrapping a legacy system uses a shadow copy and an event dispatching mechanism. A pad wrapper logically works as a proxy pad. A pad wrapper is a pad that makes its size the same as the display area size of the original legacy system. It makes a legacy system display its GUI off the screen, and maps the display bit map image onto itself. The wrapper detects all the events including mouse events and keyboard events, and dispatches them to the same relative location on the off-the-screen display of the legacy system. This method requires that each legacy system allows us to take its shadow copy and dispatch any detected events to it. If legacy systems are developed based on some standard development framework satisfying these requirements, they can be easily migrated into IntelligentPad environments.

OLE, ActiveX, and OpenDocs are all such frameworks. Fujitsu's version of IntelligentPad provides a converter that helps us to convert any ActiveX object to its pad representation. It also provides a reverse converter that helps us to convert any composite pad to its ActiveX object representation. Since the development of tools that can be defined as combinations of existing pads is much easier in IntelligentPad than with the ActiveX framework, this reverse converter is quite useful for Microsoft Windows users and application developers.

## 8.7 SPECIAL EFFECT TECHNIQUES

### 8.7.1 The Clipping of a Pad

Pads need not be rectangular. The shape of a pad defines both its view area and its event detection area. Pads may be circular or triangular. Furthermore, we may consider shapes as generic functions applicable to any pads. A shape as a generic function clips pads in this shape. The IntelligentPad paradigm considers such shape functions also as pads. These pads are called shape-mask pads. When a pad is put on a shape-mask pad, it is clipped to the defined shape. Its view and its event detection area are both clipped to this shape. Some shape-mask pads have regular shapes such as a triangle, circle, or star (Figure 8.37). They are also resizable. A special shape-mask pad allows us to draw a shape freehand using a mouse. A pad put on this shape-mask pad is cut out in this shape (Figure 8.38).

### 8.7.2 Alpha Channel

Alpha channel is a special hardware mechanism that makes some display objects translucent in order not to hide their underlying objects. Alpha channel software simulates this function. Alpha channel allows us to set the translucency rate. This parameter is denoted by $\alpha$. Alpha channel is applied to the background of each pad. When applied to a composite pad, alpha channel treats it as a single pad. It does not show a portion of its component pad that is covered by another component.

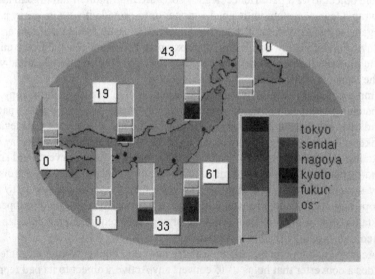

**Figure 8.37**  An oval shape mask pad cuts a composite pad into an oval shape.

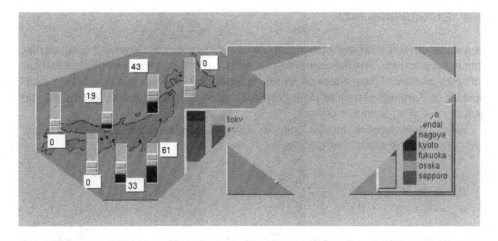

**Figure 8.38**  A pad put on a shape-mask pad can be cut into an arbitrary shape.

Alpha channel is used in IntelligentPad to put a large number of pads on a limited display area. Instead of considering alpha channel as a function of each pad, we consider it to be a generic function that can be applied to any pad, and define it as a pad. When a pad is put on it, the alpha channel pad makes this pad translucent. You may put an arbitrary number of pads on an alpha channel pad with some of them overlapping with each other. They are all made translucent.

### 8.7.3  Zooming, Tilting, and Panning

We may also consider a pad working as a pad environment that can be zoomed in and out, tilted up and down, and panned left and right. It consists of several buttons and a pad that works as a scope window to see this environment. You may put any pads on this scope window pad. The scope window shows only a small portion of a huge environment with a large number of pads on it. The left and right panning moves the ground to the right and left respectively. You may zoom in on any pads on the ground to obtain its close-up view. When you put a new pad into this environment through the scope window, the size of the pad is automatically adjusted to the current zooming rate. When you drag a pad out of the scope window, its size is changed to the original.

### 8.7.4  Dissolution

Dissolution is an effect that gradually changes the end of one video cut to the beginning of another cut. The same technique is used to change slides from one to another. A dissolution pad works as a base pad that holds pads on itself. When clicked or sent an "update" message, the dissolution pad dissolves itself as well as all the pads on it, and disappears. It provides various types of dissolution patterns. This dissolution pad with some pads on it can be put on another composite pad to completely cover this pad. This underlying pad may also be another dissolution pad with some pads on it.

## 8.8 EXPRESSION PAD

A pad may have slots whose relationship is so simple that we can describe it using mathematical expressions. An ExpressionPad is a generic pad that can be specified to have an arbitrary number of data slots with arbitrary names. For each of its slots, it allows us to specify its "gimme" procedure as an expression of slots. This expression determines the return value of a "gimme" message.

For example, suppose that the "gimme" expressions of an ExpressionPad with three data slots, #A, #B, and #C, are defined as

#A: ←#A
#B: ←#B
#C: ←#A+#B

This pad adds the values of the two slots #A and #B and stores the result in #C whenever a "gimme" message accesses the slot #C. Suppose that the "gimme" expressions of another ExpressionPad with three data slots, #A, #B, and #C, are defined differently as

#A: ←#C-#B
#B: ←#C-#A
#C: ←#A+#B

Whenever a "gimme" message accesses one of these slots to read its value, this new pad maintains the relationship among these three slots to satisfy #C=#A+#B. The left arrow in front of each expression means that the evaluated value also updates the corresponding slot.

The ExpressionPad with the second definition works as follows. Suppose that three number pads $P_1$, $P_2$, and $P_3$ are respectively connected to these three slots #A, #B, and #C. You can specify the input/output mode of each of these three pads through the setting or resetting of the three flags that respectively specify the enabling and disabling of the three standard messages to/from the ExpressionPad. If we enable the "update" message only to $P_3$, the ExpressionPad performs the substitution #C := #A+#B. In this case, a new input to $P_1$ or $P_2$ will send this input value to the ExpressionPad to change its state, which issues an "update" message to $P_3$. The pad $P_3$ then issues a "gimme" message to the slot #C, which returns the value #A+#B. If we enable the "update" message only to $P_1$ (or $P_2$), the ExpressionPad performs the substitution #A := #C-#B (or #B := #C-#A). In this case, a new input to $P_2$ (or alternatively $P_1$) or $P_3$ will send this input value to the ExpressionPad to change its state, which issues an "update" message to $P_1$ ($P_2$). The pad $P_1$ ($P_2$) then issues a "gimme" message to the slot #A (#B), which returns the value #C-#B (#C-#A). The pad to which the update propagation from its parent ExpressionPad is enabled is said to be floating, whereas the other two pads are said be fixed.

When specifying expressions, an ExpressionPad opens a dialog sheet for you to specify the expressions.

## 8.9 TRANSFORMATION PADS

Some applications require geometrical linear transformations or the rotation of pads. Some versions of the IntelligentPad system provide these generic functions as pads. These

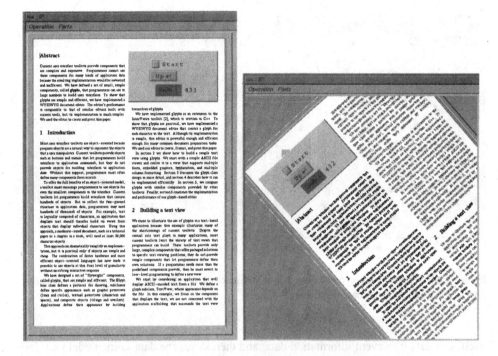

**Figure 8.39** An example transformation applied to a text pad.

transformations need to transform not only the display images of pads from the original to the transformed one, but also the event-location coordinates from the transformed one to the original. When a pad is put on a transformation pad, it is transformed by the stored transformation matrix. When a pad is dragged out of the transformation pad, it returns to its original view. Transformations can be multiply applied to the same pad. The pad is first put on the first transformation pad. Then this composite pad is put on the second transformation pad. Similarly, an arbitrary number of transformations can be applied to a single pad.

Figure 8.39 shows an example transformation applied to a text pad. The transformed pad still works as a pad.

Using such transformation pads, you can define a clock hand as a pad. This pad rotates around one of its edges. Its angle is determined by the value read from its parent pad. Figure 8.40 shows an example clock composed with hand pads. It is further transformed by a transformation pad.

## 8.10 SUMMARY

In IntelligentPad, utility functions for controlling, coordinating, arranging, editing, managing, searching, transporting, and distributing pads are all implemented as pads. This allows us to apply these tools to any pads, including themselves.

A FieldPad is used to define a shared workspace with arbitrary pads; its copies with all the pads on it share every user event. A FieldPad detects every user event that occurs over

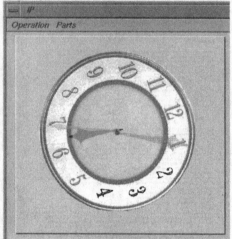

**Figure 8.40** Transformation pads allow you to define clock needles as pads, and further to transform a whole clock using these needles.

itself, converts it to event information data, and then stores the data in its model part. Its model informs its view of the update. If its shared copies exist, their views are all informed of the update. Each view, then, individually applies the event to the target pad that exists over itself.

A StagePad allows users to write a script program for manipulating multiple pads and performing a series of steps. It can manipulate any pads on itself in the same way as we directly manipulate them. It also allows users' interactions. It can associate each user event with a corresponding action. When a user event is applied, it triggers the corresponding action.

A proxy pad is a blank sheet that works as a proxy of an external object such as a database server, a file server, or an application system. It communicates with the external object to integrate the function of this object with other pads.

Since utility pads are also pads, they can be put in a utility environment defined by any of these utility pads.

## REFERENCES

1. Y. Tanaka, A. Nagasaki, M. Akaishi, and T. Noguchi. Synthetic media architecture for an object-oriented open platform. *Personal Computers and Intelligent Systems, Information Processing 92,* Vol III, Madrid. North Holland, Amsterdam, pp. 104–110, 1992.

2. Y. Tanaka. From augmentation to meme media. In *Proceedings of ED-MEDIA 94,* Vancouver, pp. 58–63, June, 1994.

3. W. Finzer and L. Gould. Programming by Rehearsal. *Byte,* June 1984, pp. 187–210.

# CHAPTER 9

# MULTIMEDIA APPLICATION FRAMEWORK

Typical application functions are also generic functions. They form an application library. Once these functions in the application library are implemented as pads, they can be combined with other pads to easily develop sophisticated applications. For a typical application, we can extract generic functions as pads and specify their typical construction structure. For each typical application, a set of generic pads and their typical construction structure form the development framework, called an application framework. This chapter shows frameworks for multimedia and hypermedia applications. These frameworks include pads to represent texts, images, tables, charts, and movies. They also include pads that allow a user to cover a portion of a multimedia pad in order to articulate an object shown in this area.

## 9.1 COMPONENT PADS FOR MULTIMEDIA APPLICATION FRAMEWORKS

Multimedia processing and management have various typical and well-defined technologies that can be provided as application frameworks [1, 2, 3, 4]. These have typical components and constructions. IntelligentPad can provide these basic components as primitive pads, and these typical constructions as sample composite pads.

### 9.1.1 Text Processing Pads

Typical word processors consist of a base window, a text window, a scroll bar, a margin scale, a command button area with many command buttons, and a menu bar with several pull-down menus. These can all be provided as pads, including two pads working as the base window and the text window, respectively, that provide complicated functions. Although these two pads provide complicated functions, they need not be further decomposed to simpler pads.

Instead of separating the text window from the other areas, we may also consider a single primitive pad that works as a word processor. Such a text pad provides all the basic word processing commands as its slots. To scroll the text, you can paste a scroll bar on this text pad with its connection to the scroll slot. To insert some object at the current cursor location, you can paste a pull-down menu pad with varieties of object type names with its connection to the insert slot of the text pad. A click on the pull-down menu pad will open its list, from which you can select one object type. The selected object type is sent to the insert slot of the text pad, which then opens another pad for you to specify the object.

We may also consider another text pad that works as a text viewer without word-processing capabilities. The HTMLViewerPad we will discuss in Section 11.5 is such a pad.

Text processing pads are among the most complicated primitive pads. They deal with a large number of objects that cannot be represented as individual pads, such as characters, words, phrases, paragraphs, sections, and chapters. Unfortunately, most versions of IntelligentPad have no component pads yet that work as word processors. All versions, however, provide text editor pads.

### 9.1.2 Tables and Figures

A spreadsheet is implemented in IntelligentPad either as a primitive pad or as a composite pad. A primitive spreadsheet pad is a single pad that works as an ordinary spreadsheet system. It has a slot for each of its entry cells, which allows us to connect other pads to the values of its entry cells. You may, for example, paste a database access pad with its connection to one of the entry cells. The database access pad accesses a database to retrieve a value, which is directly input to this entry cell.

A spreadsheet as a composite pad consists of a base pad and an entry pad for each cell entry. The base pad is a blank pad with a slot for each cell entry. Instead of using a regular entry pad for each cell, you may use any pad whose value is compatible with the entry value. You may also arrange cells in any layout pattern. Figure 9.1 shows such a composite spreadsheet with a hand calculator for one of its entry cells.

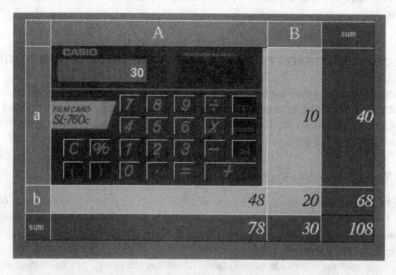

**Figure 9.1**  A composite spreadsheet with a hand calculator used for one of its entry cells. The calculation result becomes the cell value. When the cell changes its value, the calculator reads this value to set its accumulator.

A chart tool is also considered either as a primitive pad or as a composite pad. A primitive chart pad looks like an ordinary chart tool. It has a slot to specify the name of the chart, a slot for a data table, a slot for each of the table entries, a slot to add a new table row, a slot specifying the name of each table row, a slot for the value list of each table row, a slot to add a new table column, a slot specifying the name of each table column, a slot for the value list of each table column, and some more slots to specify, for the chart representation of each table row, the minimum value, the maximum value, the value range, and the line color.

The composite pad representation of a chart tool depends on the type of the chart. A bar graph can be considered to consist of a base pad and a bar meter pad for each bar. A line chart consists of a base pad, and, for each line, a transparent pad that is the same size as the base pad.

Instead of using an ordinary bar meter, you may use a pad as shown in Figure 9.2. This allows you to register a pad that is associated with the value unit it represents. The figure shows a pad with a car image, which is used as a unit to measure values in a chart.

A drawing tool is also considered a pad. This pad may look like an ordinary drawing tool with an operation menu on its left side, or it may just work as a canvas without any menu. In the latter case, primitive drawing objects such as a line, a spline curve, a circle, and a rectangle are all represented as pads. When you drop a copy of such an object at some location on a drawing tool pad, this pad is absorbed, and the corresponding object is drawn at this location on the drawing tool. Once it is drawn, you can select this object to move it, copy it, or resize it. The painting of an area with a color is also specified by dropping a color pad in this area.

Drawing tool pads are also some of the most complicated primitive pads. They deal with a large number of objects that cannot be represented as pads. These are lines, curves, circles, rectangles, colors, and shades. Unfortunately, most versions of IntelligentPad still have no component pads that work as drawing tools. This problem, however, is not a technological matter but a business matter. If IntelligentPad becomes widely accepted, the provision of such a drawing-tool pad will become a good business.

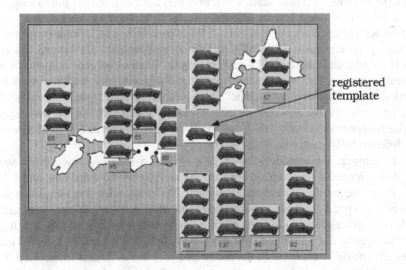

registered
template

**Figure 9.2**  A pad with a car image is used as a unit to measure values in a chart.

### 9.1.3  Multimedia Pads

Multimedia pads include image, sound, and video pads. An image pad stores an image in some format, and displays this image on itself. Different image formats define different types of image pads. Each has at least a data slot through which another pad can input and output an image in the specified format. When a new image is input to this slot, it displays this image on itself and issues a "set" message to its parent pad with this image data as its parameter value. When it receives an "update" message from its parent pad, it issues a "gimme" message to read out new image data from its parent pad, sets this image in its image slot, and displays this image on itself. These are the basic functions of all image pads. Different functions may define different image pads with different sets of slots. Some may have a slot to hold a color table, and others may have a command slot to invoke an edge-detection procedure on the stored image.

Various image processing functions can also be implemented as independent primitive pads. For example, an edge-detection function can be implemented as a primitive pad with a command slot to start the processing, another command slot to make it transparent, and two data slots to hold the original image and the resulting image. When the start slot is accessed by a "set" message, an edge-detection pad reads the underlying image it covers, and applies its edge-detection processing to display the result on itself. Since it does not use any slot connection to read its underlying image, its function can be applied not only to image pads but also to any other pads and any display areas on the screen.

Sounds are also treated as pads. Each sound pad stores a sound record in some format. When clicked, it makes a sound. Different sound formats define different types of sound pads. Each of them has at least a data slot #sound through which another pad can input and output a sound in the specified format. When a new sound is input to this slot, it makes this sound and issues a "set" message to its parent pad with this sound data as its parameter value. When it receives an "update" message from its parent pad, it issues a "gimme" message to read out new sound data from its parent pad, sets this sound in its #sound slot, and makes this sound. These are the basic functions of all the sound pads. Different functions may define different sound pads with different sets of slots. Some may have a slot to change the time scale, and others may have a command slot to suspend their sounds when their sound data are updated.

MIDI sounds are also treated as pads. A MIDI pad stores a MIDI code sequence. When clicked, it plays the music. Each MIDI pad has at least one data slot through which another pad can input and output a MIDI code sequence. When a new code sequence is input to this slot, it issues a "set" message to its parent pad with this code sequence as its parameter value. When it receives an "update" message from its parent pad, it issues a "gimme" message to read out the new code sequence from its parent pad, and sets this sequence in its code sequence slot. Every MIDI pad has these basic functions. Different functions define different MIDI pads with different sets of slots.

Video clips are also considered to be pads. A video pad stores a video clip in some format. It has command slots to play, fast forward, and rewind the video clip, and a data slot to input and output the current frame number. Different video formats define different types of video pads. Each has a data slot through which another pad can input and output a video clip in the specified format. When a new video clip is input to this slot, it issues a "set" message to the parent pad with this video clip as its parameter value. When it receives an "update" message from the parent pad, it issues a "gimme" message to read out the new video clip from the parent pad, and sets this video clip in its video slot. Every video pad provides these basic functions. Different functions may define different video pads with different sets of slots.

## 9.2 ARTICULATION OF OBJECTS

### 9.2.1 Articulation of Multimedia Objects

In multimedia systems, we have to deal with various types of objects. They should be first classified into two categories, i.e., container objects and content objects. Container objects are container media that carry content information. Books, pages, cards, display windows, and communication packets are all examples of container objects. They provide the respective structures and operations of these containers. A media object is defined as a container object with its content objects. Content objects are further classified into two categories. Some of them are clearly articulated, i.e., easily machine-identifiable from their representations, whereas others are not (Table 9.1) [5]. Machine-readable texts have such content objects as characters, words, phrases, sentences, paragraphs, sections, and chapters. They are all articulated objects. Tables have such content objects as entries, columns, and rows. Tabulation tools clearly articulate these objects. Each table format itself is a container object. Charts have such content objects as items, item values, and curves. A curve is considered here as a sequence of item value objects. Chart tools articulate these objects. Each chart type itself is a container object. Figures drawn by drawing tools have such content objects as points, line segments, shapes, and their composites. Drawing tools articulate these objects. The ground of each figure is a container object. All the content objects of drawing tools are articulated, whereas most content objects in images, movies, and sounds are not articulated.

A photograph of a town may show people, roads, cars, and buildings. Images have such nonarticulated content objects. They are not easily machine-recognizable. Movies have

**Table 9.1** Multimedia objects and their articulation

| | Container object | Articulated content object | Nonarticulated content object |
|---|---|---|---|
| Marked-up machine readable text | Page, book | Characters, words, phrases. Sentences, paragraphs, sections, chapters | n.a. |
| Table | Table format | Entries, columns, rows | n.a. |
| Chart | Chart type, format | Items, item values, curves | n.a. |
| Figure | Canvas | Points, line segments, shapes, their composites | n.a. |
| Image | Frame | n.a. | Physical objects shown |
| Coded sound | Score | Notes, bars, instruments | n.a. |
| Natural sound | Tape | Time frame | Notes, bars, instruments |
| Movie | Frame | Cuts | Cuts, scenes, physical objects shown |

both articulated and nonarticulated objects. Frames are articulated container objects, whereas cuts are either articulated or nonarticulated content objects, depending on whether or not the cut-change signal is available. Physical objects shown in movies are all nonarticulated content objects. As to sounds and voices, we have to distinguish coded ones from recorded ones. Coded sounds have such articulated content objects as notes, bars, and instruments. These content objects are hard to recognize in recorded music. However, we often want to identify a priori specified time segments of music or speech. They are inherently nonarticulated content objects, but the a priori given time frames to identify them are articulated objects.

Our main concern here is how to articulate nonarticulated multimedia objects. Multimedia systems should allow us to directly select and manipulate not only articulated objects but also nonarticulated content objects. The most widely used general solution is the use of a reference-frame object for each content object. For recorded music or speech, a reference-frame object defines the shortest time segment that includes one of the music or speech portions you want to identify. This reference-frame object indirectly specifies the corresponding music or speech portion. For an image, a reference-frame object defines the minimum rectangular area that covers one of the content objects you want to identify in this image. This reference-frame object indirectly specifies the corresponding area of the image. Reference-frame objects are articulated objects. Time segments work as temporal reference frames, whereas rectangular areas work as spatial reference frames. A reference-frame object for a cut in a movie defines a time segment. For an object appearing in a movie, its reference-frame object defines a mobile variable-size rectangular area that minimally covers this object in every video frame showing this object.

Pads in IntelligentPad are suitable for the representation of container objects, media objects, and reference frames in multimedia systems. Pads represent multimedia containers as windows or window widgets. They can be easily combined to graphically represent books, pages, cards, and compound document frameworks. Since pads can hold any kind of information and can provide slots to access the contents in various ways, they can easily represent media objects with sufficient interface to access their content objects. For the access of nonarticulated content objects in a media object, we can provide this media object with a special slot named #referenceFrame that receives the location and size of a reference frame and returns the corresponding portion of its content information (Figure 9.3). If the content is an image, then the return value is the portion of this image specified by the reference frame. A "set" message with the location and size of a reference frame as its parameter value is used to send this parameter to the #referenceFrame slot. After this operation, a "gimme" message is used to read the corresponding portion of the content information.

Spatial reference frames can be represented as transparent pads that cover the target content objects. They can be pasted on top of their target media object pads to minimally cover their target content objects. These reference-frame pads provide slots to interface to the target contents. These slots include the #name slot to hold the name of the content object, #location slot to hold its relative location on its parent pad, and #extent slot to hold its size. The oid (object identifier) of this reference-frame pad semantically works as the oid of the corresponding content object. Any pads with the above-mentioned functionality can work as reference-frame pads. IntelligentPad, however, provides some standard pads for usage as reference-frame pads. These include anchor pads and viewer pads. An anchor pad allows us to register a reference pointer to any composite pad. When mouse-clicked, it loads this registered pad and pops it up on the screen (Figure 9.4). Anchor pads without any further functionality are not connected to any of the slots provided by their parent me-

ReferenceFramePad (ViewerPad)

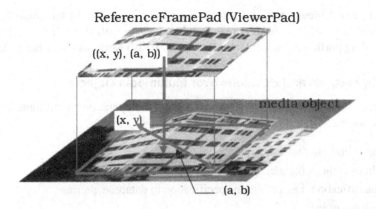

ReferenceFramePad (ViewerPad)

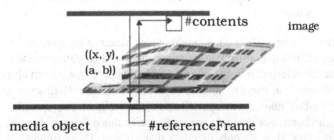

**Figure 9.3** For the access of nonarticulated content objects in a media object, we can provide a media object with a special slot named "#referenceFrame" that receives the location and size of a reference frame and returns the corresponding portion of its content information.

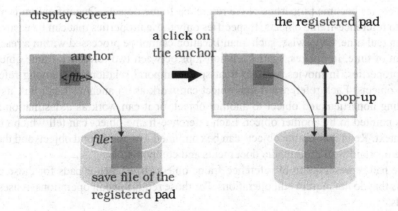

**Figure 9.4** An anchor pad allows us to register a reference pointer to any composite pad. When mouse-clicked, it loads this registered pad and pops it up on the screen.

dia object pads. A viewer pad, on the other hand, is connected to the #referenceFrame slot of its parent media object pad (Figure 9.3). It has the #contents slot to hold the copy of the corresponding portion of the content information. It also works as an anchor pad.

### 9.2.2   Operations and Relations over Multimedia Objects

Articulated objects are units of operations. Among the operations in multimedia systems are the following [5]:

1. File operations (save, load)
2. Edit operations (create, delete, edit)
3. Quantification, i.e., condition specification in database queries
4. Link operations
5. Context specification
6. Composition operations
7. Overlay operations

Edit operations are applied to each single object, whereas composition operations are applied to a set of multiple objects to combine them and to obtain a compound object. Each object may be referred to in specifying some of its properties. Each object may work as an anchor. It may link itself to another object or work as a destination anchor that is pointed to by another object. The specification of an object also specifies its context, which is also an object. For example, we can specify those figures showing a square as one of its components. Here we only specify a shape object. Those figures are specified as the contexts of such objects. Multimedia documents and components can be overlaid in multiple layers using the α-channel technology.

These operations are applicable not only to articulated objects, but also to reference frames of nonarticulated objects. Original images, movies, and sounds are kept unchanged in files. File operations save and load only reference-frame objects. Edit operations are applied only to the copies of the portions selected by reference-frame objects. These copies become properties of the reference-frame objects. Quantification is also applied to reference-frame objects. It specifies only those properties that can be easily calculated in real time. Otherwise, such quantification cannot be processed within a reasonable amount of time. In images, spatial relationships between two reference-frame objects are such properties. In movies, we can treat spatiotemporal relationships among reference-frame objects. Each reference-frame object can work as an anchor. It can link its corresponding nonarticulated object to another object, or it can work as a destination anchor that is pointed to by another object. Each reference-frame object can tell which object is its context. Reference-frame objects can be combined to a compound object, and they also can be overlaid with multimedia documents and components.

The pad representation of reference-frame objects uses anchor pads for those content objects that do not require edit operations. For those requiring edit operations, it uses viewer pads.

### 9.2.3   Application Linkage

Application linkages in object-oriented systems are represented by either the object containment or the object wiring. The object containment embeds a media object in another media object. It just defines a geometrical containment relationship or further defines functional linkage between the two media objects. The object containment can be easily defined in IntelligentPad by the paste operation. The pasted child pad may just sit on the parent pad without any functional linkage, or it may be connected to one of the slots provided by the parent pad to establish a functional connection. An extreme case of the object containment in IntelligentPad is the pasting of one translucent pad, defined as a pad whose background color is set to translucent, on another pad of the same size. IntelligentPad allows us to make any pad translucent. This extreme case is used to overlay multiple layers of information that are mutually geometrically related with each other. Computer mapping systems conventionally use such overlay representation.

The object wiring uses wiring links to connect two spatially separated objects. Navigation links (cold, warm, and hot links) in hypermedia and transclusion in Xanadu are examples of object wiring. In general, messages can be exchanged between the two objects through object wiring. IntelligentPad uses the shared copy operation for the object wiring. It also provides the wiring pad. Its shared copy works together with the original as two terminals connected by a cable. These two terminals transport any value from one to the other. The cable may work as either a bidirectional channel or a unidirectional channel. These two modes can be easily selected by the specification of the #mode slot. Anchor pads implement cold navigation links, i.e., links without functional linkage facility. Wiring pads implement warm and hot navigation links. Hot navigation links provide automatic update propagation, while warm navigation links propagate updates only when requested.

## 9.3 HYPERMEDIA FRAMEWORK

A hypermedia system consists of a set of nodes and a set of links. Each node is a compound document, whereas each link relates a component object in one node either to another node or to another component in another node. The source component of a link is called its source anchor, or simply its anchor; its destination component is called its destination anchor. Either users or application system providers span these links to define associative, quotational, annotative, or referential relationship between nodes. Users use these links to navigate from one node to another. In hypertext systems, forerunners of hypermedia systems, nodes were just simple text documents, and their components were words and phrases. In conventional hypermedia systems, nodes are compound multimedia documents, and their components are words and phrases in texts, various kinds of embedded multimedia objects, and their articulated objects. These embedded multimedia objects include charts, tables, figures, images, movies, and sounds. Reactive hypermedia systems are those with reactive nodes. Their nodes may include components that change their states against user operations. Interactive charts and spreadsheets are such reactive components. The introduction of reactive nodes has extended the roles of links. A cold link is a navigational link. A hot link is used not only to navigate from its source component to its destination node, but also to automatically propagate the state change of its source to its destination. A warm link is also used both for navigation and for update propagation, but it performs the update propagation only when it is requested by the destination node.

IntelligentPad has completely removed the distinction between multimedia documents and application tools based on the compound document architecture. Here we consider reactive hypermedia systems in which any composite pad works as a node. The introduction of reactive nodes also requires that the function of their links be extended. These functional links should be objects. In the IntelligentPad architecture, all the objects that we can directly manipulate should be basically provided as pads. Therefore, links should be basically provided as pads. There are, however, articulated objects that cannot be represented by pads. These include character strings on text pads, composite objects drawn on a drawing pad, and lines, points, and bars on a chart pad. In order to make them work as source anchors of links, the linking function must be provided by their base pads, i.e., by their text pads, drawing pads, and chart pads. When considered as nonarticulated objects, some of these articulated objects that cannot be represented by pads can be indirectly treated by the use of transparent reference-frame pads that minimally cover these objects. Figure 9.5 shows a case in which a phrase in a text document is covered by three transparent anchor pads linked to the same destination pads. Figure 9.6 shows another case in which some objects on a chart are covered by transparent anchor pads. This technique, however, does not work for editable texts in which target strings may change their relative locations, nor for figure components whose areas overlap each other. Anchors that cannot be represented by anchor pads need to be managed for their creation and activation by container media pads such as text, image, drawing, table, chart, sound, and video pads.

Here we only consider anchors represented by pads. An anchor pad has a slot to hold a file name, which specifies the file storing the exchange format representation of its destination pad. To set a file name to this slot you can temporarily paste a text input pad on this pad with its connection to this slot, and input the file name to this text pad, which might be peeled off after the input. When it is mouse-clicked, an anchor pad accesses the specified file to read out the stored exchange format representation, and pops up the converted composite pad on the desktop. Anchor pads can be resized, and be made transparent. When pasted, anchor pads do not establish a slot connection to their parent pads. They are functionally independent from their parent pads.

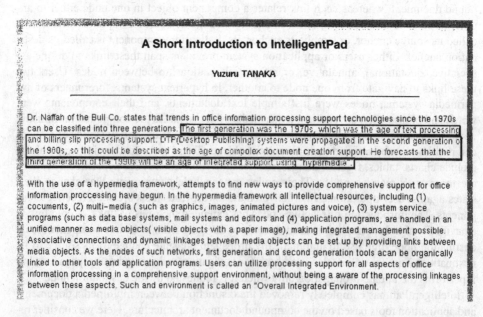

**Figure 9.5**   A phrase in a text document can be covered by three transparent anchor pads linked to the same destination pads.

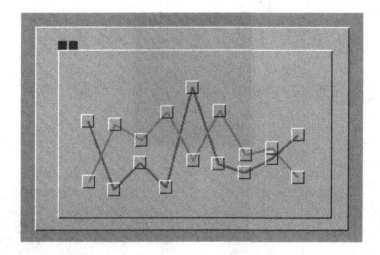

**Figure 9.6**  Some objects on a chart can be covered by transparent anchor pads.

Figure 9.7 (a) shows a composite pad with an anchor pad, which is intentionally made visible. When mouse clicked, this anchor pad pops up another composite pad, as shown in Figure 9.7 (b).

For a nonarticulated object in a movie, the anchor pad should be able to change its size and location to cover this object wherever it appears. Such an anchor needs to know the frame changes of the underlying movie. We call such an anchor pad a hypermovie anchor pad [6]. The state of a movie pad is the frame number. A movie pad has a slot to hold the current frame number. Whenever a frame change occurs, a movie pad issues an "update" message to its child pads. Hypermovie anchor pads can use this "update" message to read out the current frame number from its parent movie pad. In order to change its size and location for different frames, a hypermovie anchor pad keeps a table that stores its size and location in some sampled frames. It linearly interpolates its size and location in the other frames. This table is constructed by step-by-step manual instructions to this hypermovie anchor pad regarding of its size and location in all the sampled frames. In each sampled frame, the hypermovie anchor pad is manually adjusted with respect to its size and location to minimally cover the target object in the movie. Each frame may contain more than one hypermovie anchor pad.

This architecture is however not efficient in its performance. The improved architecture uses an anchor table pad that keeps all the information of hypermovie anchors used on a single movie pad. This information includes, for each hypermovie anchor, a table of its size and location in sampled frames and the name of the file storing its destination pad. This anchor table pad is made transparent and overlaid on the movie pad. Its size coincides with the movie pad. When mouse-clicked at some location, this pad gets the current frame number from the underlying movie pad, searches its tables to find out the anchor whose interpolated area in this frame includes this location, and finally pops up the pad stored in the file specified by this anchor. The tables in this anchor table pad are constructed through step-by-step manual instruction regarding the size and the location of each anchor pad in all sampled frames. In each sampled frame, the hypermovie anchor pad is manually adjusted on the transparent anchor table pad that covers the movie pad so

(a)

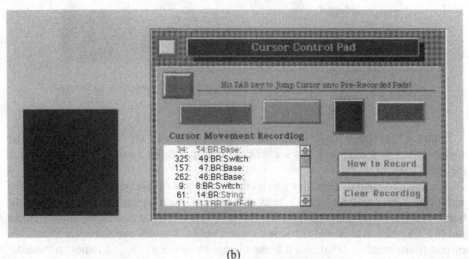

(b)

**Figure 9.7**   When an anchor pad is mouse-clicked, it pops up another composite pad. (a) A composite pad with an anchor pad. (b) The anchor pad pops up another composite pad.

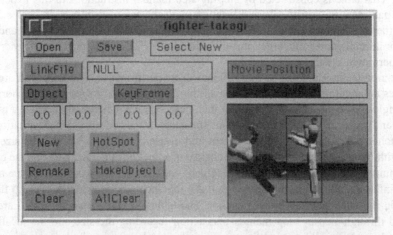

**Figure 9.8**   A composite tool pad is used to manually adjust the location and size of each hypermovie anchor pad in each sampled frame of a movie.

that the anchor pad minimally covers the target object in the movie. Each frame may contain more than one hypermovie anchor pad. Figure 9.8 shows a composite tool pad that can be used to perform such instruction. Its user first puts a movie pad on this tool and covers it with an anchor table pad. The user can put an arbitrary number of anchor pads on the anchor table pad in any frame. When a new anchor pad is first put on the anchor table pad, its link information is automatically input to the anchor table pad. The user of this tool can forward the movie to the next sample frame by shifting the slide lever, and then change the size and location of each anchor pad in the new frame. When the instruction is completed, the movie pad with the anchor table pad can be peeled from this tool to be used as a hypermovie system.

Figure 9.9 (a) is an example of hypermovies thus defined. The first movie shows a corridor of some university laboratory. Each door in this movie is minimally covered by an an-

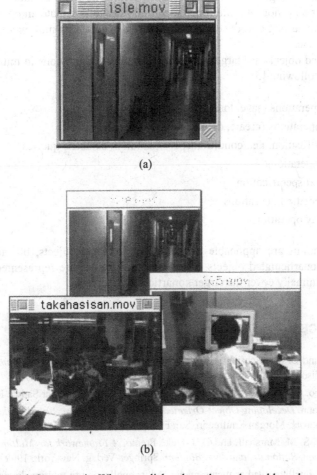

(a)

(b)

**Figure 9.9**  An example hypermovie. When we click a door, the anchor-table pad pops up another movie that enters the selected room. (a) An example hypermovie. (b) A mouse click on a door pops up the lower-right hypermovie showing the inside of the room. A mouse-click on a student in this room pops up the lower left hypermovie featuring him.

chor that changes its size and location to trace this door in the movie. Anchors are all a priori registered in a transparent anchor table pad that fully covers the movie. When we click a door, the anchor table pad identifies which anchor is clicked and pops up the destination pad. In this example, this pad plays another movie that enters the room and shows the interior [Figure 9.9(b)]. Here again, each student in this movie is covered by an anchor. A mouse click on one of these students opens up a different movie featuring this student.

## 9.4 SUMMARY

Multimedia processing and management have various typical and well-defined technologies that can be provided as application frameworks. These have typical components and constructions. IntelligentPad can provide these basic components as primitive pads, and these typical constructions as sample composite pads. These frameworks include pads to represent texts, images, tables, charts, and movies. They also include pads that allow a user to cover a portion of a multimedia pad in order to articulate an object shown in this area. Such a pad that covers some nonarticulated object on a multimedia pad is called a reference frame.

Articulated objects are targets of operations. These operations in multimedia systems include the following [5]:

1. File operations (save, load)
2. Edit operations (create, delete, edit)
3. Quantification, i.e., condition specification in database queries
4. Link operations
5. Context specification
6. Composition operations
7. Overlay operations

These operations are applicable not only to articulated objects, but also to reference frames of nonarticulated objects. Such reference frames are represented as transparent pads that minimally cover the target nonarticulated objects.

## REFERENCES

1. S. Gibbs and D. C. Tsichritzis. *Multimedia Programming: Objects, Environments, and Framework.* Addison Wesley Longman, Inc., Reading, MA, 1994.
2. L. deCarmo. *Core Java Media Framework.* Prentice-Hall PTR, Upper Saddle River, NJ, 1999.
3. P. Ackermann. *Developing Object-Oriented Multimedia Software: Based on the Met++ Application Framework.* Morgan Kaufmann, San Francisco, 1997.
4. I. Herman, S. M. Marshall, and D. J. Duke Premo. *A Framework for Multimedia Middleware: Specification, Rationale, and Java Binding.* Springer-Verlag, New York, 1999.
5. Y. Tanaka. IntelligentPad as meme media and its application to multimedia databases. *Information and Software Technology, 38:* 201–211, 1996.
6. Y. Tanaka. Meme media and a world-wide meme pool. In *Proceedings of ACM Multimedia 96,* pp. 175–186, 1996.

# CHAPTER 10

---

# INTELLIGENTPAD AND DATABASES

---

The easy composition of new pads will bring a rapid accumulation of a large number of different pads. It will become seriously difficult for us to find an appropriate pad out of such an accumulation. We will need a new technology for the management and retrieval of pads. In this chapter, we will consider how to manage and search a large set of pads, and how the required technologies are related to relational database and object-oriented database technologies. We will consider two alternative ways of storing pads. If we have to manage a large number of pads of a few different forms, we can keep the form information outside the databases; we only need to store the state information of pads in the databases. Such a database is called a form base. If we have to manage composite pads of a large number of different forms, we need database facilities not only to manage the states of the pads but also to manage their different forms. In such cases, there is no reason to separately manage the state and the form of each pad. Such a database is termed a pad base. This chapter will provide both a framework for form bases and a foundation for pad bases.

## 10.1 RELATIONAL DATABASES, OBJECT-ORIENTED DATABASES, AND INSTANCE BASES

In the relational model of databases, each database is represented as a set of relations [1]. Each relation is a set of records with the same set of attributes, each attribute taking an atomic value. Records are called tuples in this model. Each tuple in a relation can be uniquely identified by the value of a set of attributes. One such minimal attribute set is specified as the primary key of the relation. Relational database systems manage tuples in each relation by providing them with identifiers called tuple identifiers. In each relation, a one-to-one correspondence holds between the primary key values and the tuple identifiers. Relational database systems provide indices for some attributes in order to improve their search performance. An index for an attribute of a relation maps each existing value of this attribute to a list of identifiers of those tuples that take this specified value for this specified attribute. In each relation, the attributes with indices are called indexed attributes.

In the object-oriented database (OODB) model [2–7], each database is a set of classes. A class in this model plays two roles. First, it defines an object type. Second, it represents a set of objects of the defined type. Objects of the same type accept the same set of messages. Objects in an OODB are uniquely identified by their object identifiers, and persistent in the sense that they continue to exist unless explicitly deleted. Classes in OODBs correspond both to relations and to relation types in relational databases, whereas objects and the messages accepted by them, respectively, correspond to records and their attributes.

One of the most serious problems in OODBs is their performance. OODBs allow us to write message-sending sentences even for the specification of query conditions, which means that these messages are sent to all the objects in a target class in order to select those satisfying these conditions unless this message-sending can be a priori evaluated. If a message to an object just returns a value and does not cause any other side effects, i.e., if it works as an attribute of this object, this message sending can be a priori evaluated. If a message we use in query specifications works as an attribute, and if its return values can be indexed, then we can a priori provide an index file for this message to map each existing return value of this message to a list of object identifiers of those objects that return this specified value when receiving this message. The provision of such an index file for every message that is used in the condition specification part of the queries can improve the performance of query processing to the performance level of relational databases.

OODBs are roughly classified into two categories, structural OODBs and behavioral OODBs. In a structural OODB, all the messages used in the condition specification part of queries work as attributes, i.e., none of them cause any side effects other than returning values. Their return values may be simple or complex. They might even be multimedia documents including images, video movies, maps, and charts. The quantification of objects uses only those messages whose return values can be indexed. Structural OODBs can provide each class with indices for all of the messages used in the condition specification part of the queries. Their performance, therefore, is comparable to that of relational database systems. Structural OODBs whose messages all work as attributes are sometimes called extended relational databases. They are extended from relational databases by allowing attributes to take complex and/or composite values. Examples of structural OODBs include Postgress [8] and UniSQL. [9]. Postgress was later marketed as Illustra [10], which was then integrated with Informix.

Behavioral OODBs are those OODBs that are not structural. Since these cannot take advantage of the indexing technique, they inherently suffer in their search performance when applied to large databases. For this reason, a behavioral OODB is sometimes considered as an extension of an object-oriented programming language through the introduction of object persistency. Such an extended language is called a DBPL (database programming language). Such behavioral OODBs are called DBPL databases. From a practical point of view, behavioral OODB systems, namely DBPL database systems, are only applicable to either small databases or to object-by-object retrieval systems that do not extensively use complicated set operations. Examples of behavioral OODBs include ObjectStore [11], using an extension of C++; GemStone [12], using an extension of Smalltalk; ODMG model [4]; Orion [13], with its model patterned on Smalltalk and Lisp; and $O_2$ [3].

Object-oriented programming, as you know, includes two different programming paradigms, the refinement paradigm and the composition paradigm. In the refinement paradigm, we define objects starting from general objects and proceeding to more specific ones by adding new properties to the previously defined objects. Objects are defined by their properties. A set of properties defines a type of objects. This is called an object class, or simply a class. Each class is defined as a refinement of a previously defined class. To distinguish objects from their classes, they are called instance objects. In the refinement paradigm, each new instance object can be created only through sending a message, **new**, to some class.

In the composition paradigm, on the other hand, a new instance object is defined by combining some existing instance objects. Combined instance objects are functionally linked together to define a composite instance object. Although primitive objects may have their corresponding classes, composite ones have no corresponding classes. This is quite different from the situation of the refinement paradigm. The composition paradigm is extensively used especially in GUI toolkit systems.

Most object-oriented languages are based on the refinement paradigm with the programming capabilities of the composition paradigm. Some exceptional object-oriented languages, however, strictly observe the composition paradigm. They have no concept of classes.

Instance bases are databases that are object-oriented. They are, however, quite different from OODBs. An OODB is a set of classes, i.e., a set of object sets, and is based on the refinement paradigm of the object-oriented programming. An instance base, on the other hand, is based on the composition paradigm of the object-oriented programming, and stores various composite objects. The composition paradigm, together with the gradually widening exploitation of the componentware approach to software engineering, is rapidly increasing the importance of instance bases. Instance bases in this sense, however, are not yet well developed or even well studied with respect to their storage schemes and their search algorithms.

Let us now consider how the management of pads relates to these different types of databases. We will first consider what to store in the databases. A composite pad only needs to store its exchange format representation; no other information needs to be stored in databases. The exchange format representation of a composite pad includes two kinds of information. One is the form information that describes what kinds and sizes of component pads are used, how they are geometrically pasted, and which slot is used in each connection between component pads. The other is the state information of this pad. The state information needs to be sufficient to specify the current values of all of its internal variables whose values are not specified by its form information. Composite pads with the same form information but with different states are said to share the same form. Without loss of generality, we can assume that the state information is of the record type, i.e., it can be represented as a list of attribute–value pairs for the ordered attribute set that is determined by each form.

Let $P$ be a composite pad, $F$ and $S$ be its form and state information, respectively. To guarantee mutual convertibility between $P$ and $(F, S)$, we must provide procedures to compute the following three functions:

1. $f: P \rightarrow F$
2. $s: P \rightarrow S$
3. $g: (F, S) \rightarrow P$

These functions satisfy $P = g[f(P), s(P)]$. Instead of using the function $f$, you may use another function $f'$ that maps the exchange format representation $r(P)$ of $P$ to the form information of $P$, i.e., $f'[r(P)] = f(P)$. Furthermore, the function $g$ can be replaced with a new function $g'$, defined as $\lambda xy. r[g(f'(x), y)]$. For any composite pad $P'$ sharing the same form with the pad $P$, it holds that $g'[r(P'), s(P)] = r\{g[f(P), s(P)]\}$. The function $r$ and its inverse are both provided by the IntelligentPad kernel. The function $s$ can be also replaced with a new function $s'$ defined as $s'[r(x)]=s(x)$. Instead of providing procedures to compute $f$, $s$, and $g$, we can provide procedures for $f'$, $s'$, and $g'$.

Now we may consider two alternative ways of storing pads. If we have to manage a large number of pads of a few different forms, we can keep the form information outside the databases; we only need to store the state information of pads in the databases. Such a database is called a form base. If the state information of a record type has only atomic and simple values for its attributes, we can use a relational database system to store these pads. If some attributes allow variable-length data, continuous data such as movies and sounds, or complex data such as compound documents and other relations, we can use an extended relational database system or a structural OODB system. In this case, we can even deal with a composite pad storing other composite pads in some of its state attributes.

If we have to manage composite pads of a large number of different forms, we need database facilities not only to manage the states of pads but also to manage their different forms. In such cases, there is no reason to separately manage the state and the form of each pad. Such a database is termed a pad base. Pad bases should be instance bases by their nature. Because the R&D of instance bases is at an early stage, pad bases require lots of pioneering studies and development efforts.

Behavioral OODBs, namely DBPL databases, have no direct relations with the management of pads. IntelligentPad is a system that tries to keep its users as far away as possible from writing programs by themselves. It provides users with direct operations to compose new objects from existing ones. Therefore, it is inherently a different approach from DBPL databases.

## 10.2 FORM BASES

Form bases deal with the management of a large number of composite pads with a rather small variety of different forms. They assume management of these forms outside their database systems. Their databases store and manage only the state information of composite pads.

### 10.2.1 Database Proxy Pads

Any relational or object-oriented database system $\Delta$, when provided with its proxy pad DBProxyPad($\Delta$), can be easily integrated with other tools in the IntelligentPad environment. Its proxy pad looks like a blank-sheet pad, and provides a list of slots including #query slot, #result slot, #currentRecord slot, #search slot, #insert slot, #delete slot, #nextCandidate slot, and #previousCandidate slot. The slot #query receives an SQL or an object-oriented SQL query. When the proxy pad receives "true" in its #search slot, it sends the SQL query stored in #query slot to the database system to perform this search. When a search result is sent back from the database, the proxy pad stores this list of records in its #result slot. At the same time, it makes its internal variable "cursor" point to the first record in the record list, and stores this record in #currentRecord slot. When the proxy pad receives "true" in its #nextCandidate slot or in its #previousCandidate slot, it respectively changes its variable "cursor" to point to the next or to the previous record, and replaces the record in #currentRecord slot with this new record.

### 10.2.2  Form Bases With a Single Form

Let us first consider a simple case in which all pads share the same single form. The database only stores their state information as records of a relation. Database function can be brought into this environment by a database proxy pad, DBProxyPad. For the time being, let us assume that queries are textually specified. Each retrieved record corresponds to a composite pad with this specified form. To convert each record to the corresponding pad and vice versa, we need a special pad. We call this a PadGeneratorPad. This conversion also requires the form information. We assume that instead of this form information, this PadGeneratorPad is given an example composite pad of this form. This PadGeneratorPad performs two conversions. It can apply the function $g'$ to the given two inputs to obtain the exchange format representation of the corresponding composite pad. The two inputs are the exchange format representation of an example pad of this form and a record retrieved from the database. It can also apply the function $s'$ to the exchange format representation of any composite pad of this form to obtain its state information that is stored in the database as its record.

The PadGeneratorPad has the following two slots, #padSlot and #padGeneratorSlot. The slot #padSlot is used to input the exchange format representation of an example pad of this form. This slot is connected to a SaverPad as shown in Figure 10.1. To register a

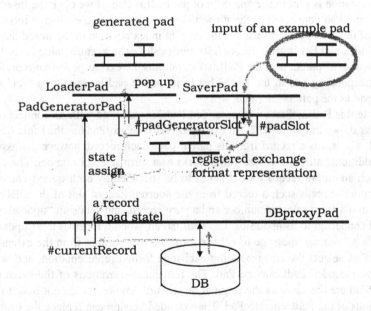

**Figure 10.1**  A pad-generator pad has the following two slots: the pad slot and the pad generator slot. The pad slot is used to input the exchange-format representation of an example pad of this form.

form as the database form interface, you can just drag and drop an example pad of this form on this SaverPad. When sent an update message from a DBProxyPad, this PadGeneratorPad reads the #currentRecord slot of the DBProxyPad to get the next candidate record as the state information of the next pad to output. Using this information together with the exchange format representation stored in its #padSlot, the PadGeneratorPad generates the exchange format representation of the next pad to output, and stores this result in its #padGeneratorSlot. When the generation is completed, the PadGeneratorPad issues an "update" message to a LoaderPad connected to its #padGeneratorSlot. The LoaderPad, when sent an "update" message, deletes any pads on itself, reads the #padGeneratorSlot of the PadGeneratorPad to obtain an exchange format representation, and generates the corresponding composite pad on itself.

When we click the button pad connected to the #nextCandidate slot of the DBProxyPad, a new record is set to the #currentRecord slot of the DBProxyPad, which then sends an "update" message to the PadGeneratorPad to generate the next pad and to replace the previous pad with this new one.

### 10.2.3  Form Bases With Multiple Forms

When we need to deal with multiple forms, we can extend the architecture discussed in the preceding section as follows.

First, we need a new pad to store the exchange format representations of multiple pads. We call this a PadListPad. This pad has several slots including #padSlot, #indexSlot, #insertSlot, and #deleteSlot. It stores an ordered list of pads with index numbers. A SaverLoaderPad is pasted on the PadListPad with its connection to the #padSlot. Two ButtonPads are connected to the #insertSlot and the #deleteSlot, respectively. The #indexSlot holds the current index number. If we drop a pad on the SaverLoaderPad, its exchange format representation is sent to the #padSlot of the PadListPad. If we click the insert button, i.e., the ButtonPad connected to the #insertSlot, at this time, the exchange format representation of this new pad is inserted at the current index position in the stored list of pads. When an index number is given through its #indexSlot or as a return value of its "gimme" message sent to its parent pad, the PadListPad outputs the exchange format representation of the corresponding pad in the stored list to its parent pad by sending a "set" message with this pad as the parameter value.

We paste this PadListPad on an extended PadGeneratorPad with its connection to the #padSlot as shown in Figure 10.2. An extended PadGeneratorPad has the same slots as the original. It also reads a record from its parent pad. Each record, however, is assumed to have an additional attribute whose value works as a form selector number. The construction of such an output record format needs to be specified by each query. The extended PadGeneratorPad reads such a record from the #currentRecord slot of the DBProxyPad, divides it into a form selector number and a pure record, and sends an "update" message to the pad connected to its #padSlot. The PadListPad, when it receives this "update" message, sends a "gimme" message to get the form selector number from the extended PadGeneratorPad, selects the corresponding exchange format representation, and sends this back to the extended PadGeneratorPad. The remaining operations of the extended PadGeneratorPad are the same as the original ones. Furthermore, we do not have to provide both versions of the PadGeneratorPad. The extended version can replace the original one with some minor alterations.

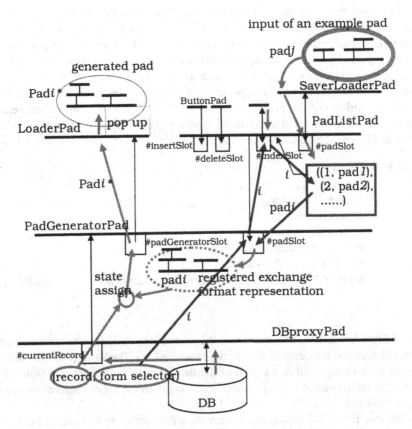

**Figure 10.2** In order to deal with multiple forms, the architecture in Figure 10.1 can be extended as shown here.

### 10.2.4 Form Interface to Databases

In the preceding two sections, we tried to provide the most general frameworks for form bases. The most typical form bases, on the other hand, are those with a single form that works as a form interface to some relational database.

A database proxy pad, DBProxyPad, performs all the details necessary to access a database. You may easily paste various pads on this DBProxyPad with their connection to the #currentRecord slot to define a visual representation of each retrieved record. You may also paste pads with their connections to the #result slot to visually present the distribution of retrieved records or to arrange visual representations of records. Here we first consider the case in which we visually present each retrieved record one at a time.

The whole set of pads available in IntelligentPad works as a form construction kit for the visual interface of this database. A RecordPad is a blank-sheet pad. When it receives an "update" message, it reads out a record-type value, i.e., an association list, from its parent pad and holds this record. Some versions of IntelligentPad call a RecordPad a DictionaryPad. A RecordPad allows us to add an arbitrary number of special slots called attribute slots. For this function, it has a special slot, #addSlot. When it is accessed by a "set" message with a new slot name as its parameter, the "set" procedure of this slot adds a new slot with this name to the list of attribute slots in this RecordPad. A RecordPad has another special slot, #removeSlot, that is used to remove a specified slot from its list of attribute slots. Each attribute slot, when requested to send back its value, reads out the stored record and gets the value of the attribute having the same name as this attribute-slot name. If the record does not have the same attribute name, this attribute slot returns the value "nil." When a record pad is pasted on the DBProxyPad with its connection to the #currentRecord slot of this proxy pad, it works as a base pad to define a form representation of each record that will be retrieved from the DBProxyPad (Figure 10.3). This composite pad is represented by our notation as

DBProxyPad($\Delta$)
 [#query: . . . ,
 #search:$\text{ButtonPad}_1$,
 #insert:$\text{ButtonPad}_2$,
 #delete:$\text{ButtonPad}_3$,
 #previousCandidate:$\text{ButtonPad}_4$,
 #nextCandidate:$\text{ButtonPad}_5$,
 #currentRecord:RecordPad[$\#\text{attrb}_1$:$\text{Pad}_1$, $\#\text{attr}_2$:$\text{Pad}_2$, . . . , $\#\text{attr}_n$:$\text{Pad}_n$]
 . . .
 ].

The pad $\text{Pad}_i$ is a display pad that shows the value of the attribute $\text{attr}_i$. Some examples of such a display pad are TextPad, ImagePad, MoviePad, and BarMeterPad. A mouse click of the pad $\text{ButtonPad}_1$ invokes a search of the database. A click of the pad $\text{ButtonPad}_5$ advances the record cursor to the next candidate record in the list of retrieved records stored in the result slot.

Different from GUI forms, this form with a RecordPad as its base pad can be easily copied and sent to other users or to some tool pads. This copy holds the record that its original had when we made this copy.

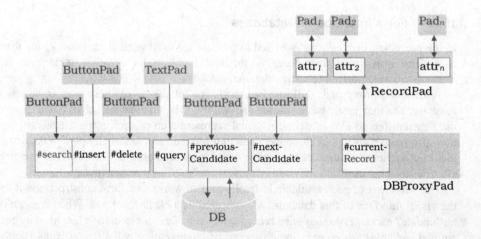

**Figure 10.3** A RecordPad that is pasted on the DBProxyPad with its connection to the #current-Record slot of this proxy pad works as a base pad to define a form representation of each retrieved record.

In its typical use on a DBProxyPad, a RecordPad divides each retrieved record into a set of attribute–value pairs. Each attribute value is set to the slot with the same name as its attribute name. Depending on the value type of each attribute slot, you may connect a text viewer pad, an image viewer pad, a drawing viewer pad, or a video viewer pad to this slot. You may arbitrarily design the layout of these viewer pads on the RecordPad. A DBProxy-Pad with a RecordPad pasted with some viewer pads is called a form-based DB viewer, or a form interface to a database. Figure 10.4 shows an example of a form-based DB viewer.

Instead of pasting a RecordPad on a DBProxyPad, you may paste some type of relation viewer pad and connect it to the #result slot of the DBProxyPad. A relation viewer pad visually presents records in the relation. A table representation pad is an example of a relation viewer pad.

For the setting of a query in the #query slot of a DBProxyPad, you can simply use a text-input pad, TextInputPad. A TextInputPad is pasted on the DBProxyPad($\Delta$) and connected to the #query slot of the DBProxyPad($\Delta$), i.e., DBProxyPad($\Delta$)[#query:TextInput-Pad]. An SQL query q written on this TextInputPad is sent to the #query slot of the proxy pad, i.e., DBProxyPad($\Delta$)[#query←q]. Instead of using such a simple TextInputPad, you may use any composite pad to generate an SQL query. For example, you may consider a pad, Q(#department, #comparator, #salary), which generates a parameterized SQL query $Q(x, \theta, y)$:

$$
\begin{array}{ll}
\text{select} & \text{name, age, photo} \\
\text{from} & \text{Employee} \\
\text{where} & \text{department} = x \\
\text{and} & \text{salary } \theta\, y.
\end{array}
$$

You may paste three TextInputPads on this pad with their connection to these three slots, and paste this composite pad on the proxy pad to connect itself to the #query slot of the proxy, i.e.,

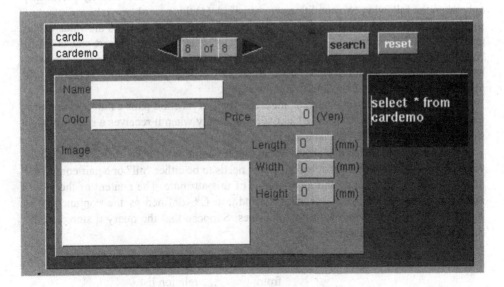

**Figure 10.4** An example of a form-based DB viewer.

DB ProxyPad($\Delta$) [#query: Q[#department: TextPad1,
#comparator: TextPad2,
#salary: TextPad3)]].

This allows you to simply specify a department name, a comparison operator, and an amount of salary for the retrieval of employees' information.

A restriction on the DB proxy pad makes it represent a view relation. This requires one more slot named #view slot. This slot is used to store a view definition. This view definition also specifies the structure of records stored in the #currentRecord slot. The attributes of these records are those defined by this view. When a query is issued through the #query slot, this pad modifies this query with the view definition and sends the modified query to the database system. To avoid the view update problem, the translation of an update request on this view to a DB update request should be clearly defined in this pad. Such a restricted DB proxy pad is called a DBViewPad. A text pad can be used to input a view definition sentence, viewDefinition, to the #view slot, i.e., DBViewPad($\Delta$)[#view$\leftarrow$viewDefinition]. This Pad works as a proxy pad to a database $\Delta_{view}$ with the view relation as its only one relation, i.e.,

$$\text{DBViewPad}(\Delta)[\#\text{view}\leftarrow\text{viewDefinition}] = \text{DBProxyPad}(\Delta_{view})$$

## 10.2.5  QBE on Form Interface

In the preceding sections, we have been assuming that the #currentRecord slot of a DBProxyPad is a data slot. Actually, it is not. Its access by a "gimme" message invokes its "gimme" procedure, which reads out the record pointed to by the cursor from the record list stored in the #result slot, and returns this record value. Its access by a "set" message, on the other hand, sets its parameter value to a special internal variable, "input-record," of the DBProxyPad. The record stored in this input-record variable is used to insert and delete records into and from the database. These operations are successfully performed only when the following two conditions are satisfied: (1) this record type is a projection of some relation R in the database, and (2) this record completely specifies the value of the primary key of R. Otherwise, these operations will fail. When its #insert slot is set to "true," a DBProxyPad tries to insert the record in the input-record variable into the database. When its #delete slot is set to "true," the DBProxyPad tries to delete the record of R identified by the record in the input-record variable.

A DBProxyPad issues an "update" message to all of its child pads connected to either its #result slot or its #currentRecord slot when and only when it receives a result relation from the database or its cursor changes.

The input-record variable is also used in search operations. In this case, each attribute value of the record in the input-record variable needs to be either "nil" or a pair comprised of a comparison operator $\theta_i$ and any value $v_i$ of this attribute. The content of the input-record variable, in this case, specifies a condition C*, defined as the conjunction of $A_i.\theta_i.v_i$ for all the attributes with nonnil values. Suppose that the query q stored in the #query slot of the DBProxyPad is

| q: | select | attribute list |
|---|---|---|
|  | from | relation list |
|  | where | C |

We define a new query q(C*) as

$$
\begin{array}{lll}
q(C^*): & \text{select} & \text{attribute list} \\
        & \text{from}   & \text{relation list} \\
        & \text{where}  & C \text{ and } C^*
\end{array}
$$

When its #search slot is set to "true," the DBProxyPad reads out both the query q in its #query slot and the condition C* from its input-record variable, generates a new query q(C*), and sends this to the database to retrieve the result relation.

The input-record variable is initially set to a record with "nil" for each of its attributes. The insert and delete operations both reset the input-record variable to its initial value when they complete their execution. The condition C* corresponding to this initial value is defined to be logically true.

This extension of the DBProxyPad allows us to construct a QBE (query-by-example) [14] type form interface without making any more changes to the preceding discussion. We use a RecordPad not only for the output display of the retrieved records but also for the QBE type specification of a query. A RecordPad has a special slot called the #setRecord slot. When set to "true," the "set" procedure of this slot sends a "set" message to its parent pad together with its #record slot value as the message parameter. When connected to the #currentRecord slot of a DBProxyPad, a RecordPad with a ButtonPad connected to its #setRecord slot works as a QBE-based input form. When its button is clicked, it sends its record value, which actually specifies a query based on the QBE convention, to the input-record variable of the DBProxyPad, which, in turn, generates a modified query q(C*) from the query q specified by its #query slot. Figure 10.5 shows a composite form-based DB viewer that allows the QBE-based query specification.

## 10.3   PADS AS ATTRIBUTE VALUES

In Section 10.2, we saw that a database service can be represented as a pad. Here, we will see that pads can be treated as database values. Each composite pad has its exchange format representation, which is just a variable-length string. This string can be stored in databases as an attribute value if this attribute allows a variable-length string as its value. This means that any object that can be represented as a composite pad can be stored in those relational databases that allow variable-length data as attribute values [15]. These objects include interactive multimedia objects such as images, movies, and sounds; interactive charts and tables; interactive maps; database access forms, various application tools; and compound documents embedding any of these objects.

Figure 10.6 shows a form interface to a database with an interactive image pad as an attribute value. The corresponding slot of the record pad stores the exchange format representation of an interactive image pad as its value. To generate a composite pad from its exchange format representation, and vice versa, a special pad, SaverLoaderPad, is pasted on the record pad and connected to this slot (Figure 10.7). When it receives an "update" message, a SaverLoaderPad issues a "gimme" message to retrieve an exchange format representation value from its parent, and generates the corresponding composite pad on itself. It also works as a saver. When a composite pad is dragged and dropped on it, a SaverLoaderPad converts this composite pad to the exchange format representation and issues a

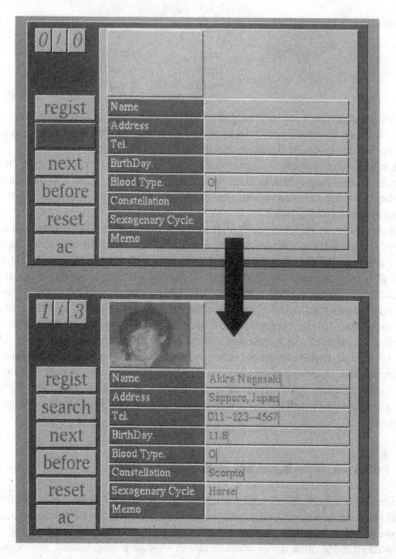

**Figure 10.5**   A composite form-based DB viewer that allows QBE-based query specifications.

"set" message with this representation as a parameter value to store this representation into the connected slot of its parent pad.

The database in Figure 10.6 stores information about cars for sale. Clients can specify a query to retrieve the full information on any specified cars, including photos. This system, however, treats each image as a composite pad with some transparent anchor pads pasted on an image pad. Each anchor pad is a priori associated with a form-based DB viewer, i.e., each anchor pad, when clicked, pops up the registered form-based DB viewer. Each DB viewer has an a priori registered SQL query in its query slot. This query may be issued either to the same database or to a different database. When mouse-clicked, each anchor pad pops up the registered form-based DB viewer and instructs this pad to issue its registered query. The retrieved result will be shown on this form-based DB viewer. If you

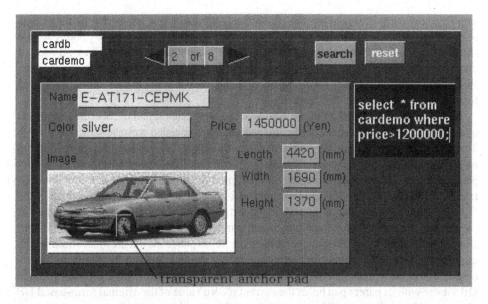

**Figure 10.6** This form interface treats each car image as a composite pad with a transparent anchor pad pasted on an image pad.

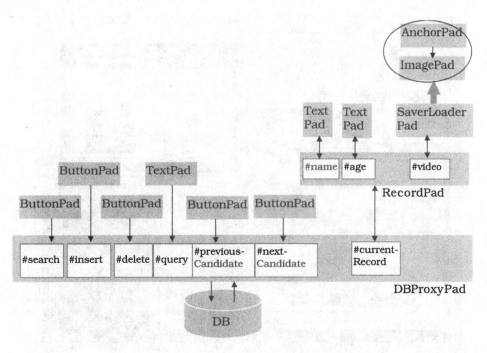

**Figure 10.7** To generate a composite pad from its exchange-format representation, and vice versa, a special pad, SaverLoaderPad, is pasted on the record pad and connected to the slot storing the exchange-format representation of a pad.

want to show users of this automobile database various options on several items such as body colors and wheel covers, you can just paste two anchor pads on the photo pad and store this composite pad in the photo attribute of the database. A mouse-click on each of these anchor pads will pop up the corresponding form-based DB viewer showing the possible choices of the selected item. Figure 10.8 shows such a photo pad and a popped-up form showing options of wheel covers.

In this application, we want to use copies of the same anchor pad to cover all the wheels of different automobiles. These copies are necessarily associated with the same DB viewer. Therefore, this form-based DB viewer needs to modify its registered query depending on which specific car model we are viewing on the original form-based DB viewer. This dependency between the current record in the original form-based DB viewer and the registered form-based DB viewer is implemented as follows. Instead of registering a form-based DB viewer alone to an anchor pad, we register it together with a record-holding pad as its parent pad. We also use a special anchor pad with its connection slot name set to #record slot. When clicked, this special anchor pad on the photo pad reads out the #record slot of the underlying RecordPad to get the current record value, and pops up the registered form-based DB viewer with its parent pad holding this record value. The popped-up form-based DB viewer with its parent pad holds the current record value of the original form-based DB viewer, and hence it can modify its query depending on this record value.

Figure 10.9 shows another form interface to a database. This system has the same composition architecture as shown in Figure 10.7. This form interface shows a stage pad as an

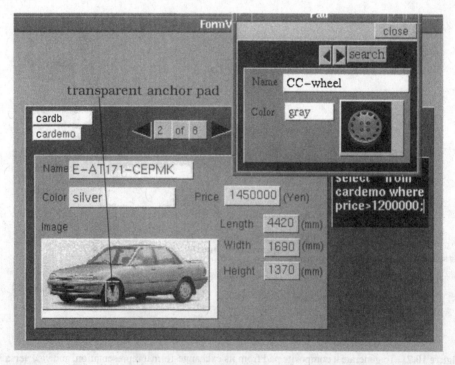

**Figure 10.8** A mouse click on a transparent anchor pad that covers a wheel cover portion of the car image pops up the corresponding form-based DB viewer showing the possible choices of the selected item.

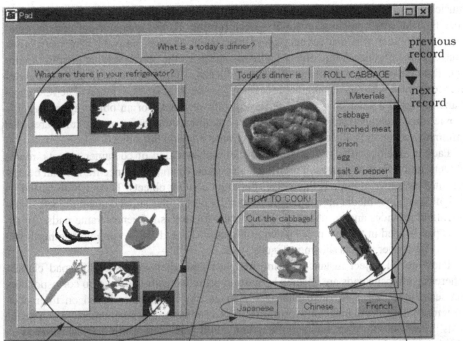

query specifications   a retrieved record   A stage pad shows how to cook this.

**Figure 10.9**   This form interface shows a stage pad as an attribute value. When activated, this stage pad together with its actor pads gives a step-by-step instruction on this cooking recipe. Different recipes can be retrieved from the database by appropriately selecting meat or fish, which vegetables to use, and the cooking style.

attribute value. When activated, this stage pad together with its actor pads gives step-by-step instructions for this cooking recipe. Different recipes can be retrieved from the database together with their instructions by appropriately specifying queries.

## 10.4   MULTIMEDIA DATABASE

Multimedia databases [16–18] have to deal with several different categories of objects— container objects, media objects, articulated content objects, and reference frames for nonarticulated content objects. IntelligentPad represents media objects and container objects as primitive pads. Reference frames are represented as anchor pads or viewer pads. Here we consider a multimedia database architecture based on an object-oriented database and IntelligentPad.

### 10.4.1   Articulation of Objects by Pads

Section 9.2 showed how to articulate nonarticulated multimedia objects. The most widely used general solution is the use of a reference-frame object for each content object. For recorded music or speech, it defines the shortest time segment that includes one of the music or speech portions you want to identify. This reference-frame object indirectly specifies the corresponding music or speech portion. For an image, it defines the minimum rectangular area that covers one of the content objects you want to identify in the image. This reference-frame object indirectly specifies the corresponding area of the image. Reference-frame objects are articulated objects. Time segments work as temporal reference frames, whereas rectangular areas work as spatial reference frames. The reference-frame object for a cut in a movie defines a time segment. For an object appearing in a movie, the reference-frame object defines a mobile variable-size rectangular area that minimally covers this object in every video frame showing this object.

Pads in IntelligentPad are suitable for the representation of container objects, media objects, and reference frames in multimedia systems. Spatial reference frames can be represented as transparent pads that cover the target content objects. They can be pasted on top of their target media object pads to minimally cover their target content objects. IntelligentPad provides anchor pads and viewer pads for use as reference-frame pads. An anchor pad is used in the example shown in Figures 10.6 and 10.7 to pop up another form-based DB viewer pad, as shown in Figure 10.8.

Pads are all object instances. Primitive pads have their corresponding pad classes, whereas composite pads are defined by pasting primitive pads and have no corresponding classes. Since object-oriented databases manage object instances based on their class structures, they can manage only primitive pads as objects, and cannot manage composite pads. They can, however, manage the parent–child pad relationship between pads as an object relationship. Furthermore, the save format string representation of a composite pad can be stored in databases as a string value.

Here we consider a multimedia database architecture based on an object-oriented database and IntelligentPad. For each primitive pad class, our database has a corresponding relation that has attributes corresponding to all the data slots of this pad class. This relation stores all the pads of this class. This relation also has another attribute to store oids (object identifiers) of pads. The parent–child pad relation stores all the parent–child pad pairs of oids with their child pad's locations on the corresponding parents.

Since articulated content objects have their corresponding classes, they can be managed by such databases. IntelligentPad, however, cannot represent them as pads. It treats them as slot values of primitive pads representing the corresponding media objects.

## 10.4.2  Movie Databases

In this section, we discuss movies to show how their objects are represented as pads and managed by a database [19]. IntelligentPad represents each movie as a pad. This pad shows a QuickTime movie. It has a data slot that always indicates the current frame number. A reference frame for a physical object shown in a movie is a transparent pad that changes its size and location to minimally cover this same object in each frame of this movie pad. Users can specify its location and size in some sample frames using such a tool as shown in Figure 9.8. This tool itself is defined as a composite pad. It enables you to specify the location and the size of each reference-frame pad in arbitrarily selected sample frames of an arbitrarily given movie pad. Each reference-frame pad interpolates its location and size in other frames from the given values in sample frames. Reference-frame pads have the following data slots: #objectName, #cutNumber (for the cut number), #frameNumber, #location, and #size.

The database includes two relations, one for movie pads and the other for reference-frame pads. We assume that movies are a priori segmented into cuts, and that reference-frame pads have both #frameNumber slot and #cutNumber slot:

> Movie(oid, title, author, date, location),
> MovieReference(oid, #objectName, movieOid, #cutNumber,
> #frameNumber, #location, #size)

where oid in MovieReference is the oid of the reference-frame pad. Figure 10.10 shows example cuts of movies and the corresponding relations. Reference-frame pads are used here to articulate butterflies and flowers appearing in these cuts. For simplicity, it is assumed that all the frames that show the same object are recorded in the relation MovieReference. In a practical system, it is sufficient to store sample frames in MovieReference.

This rather simple system architecture provides large capabilities for the manipulation of movies. These include the following operations, both on articulated content objects and on reference frames covering nonarticulated content objects:

1. File operations (save, load)
2. Edit operations (create, delete, edit)
3. Quantification, i.e., condition specification in database queries
4. Link operations
5. Context specification
6. Composition operations
7. Overlay operations

File operations are obviously supported. Edit functions are also supported if we use viewer pads for reference-frame objects.

Our system architecture allows various kinds of quantification on various objects. While the quantification on articulated objects needs no further explanation, our system architecture also allows us to quantify nonarticulated objects. Suppose that there are lots of movies showing butterflies and flowers as shown in Figure 10.10, and that we want to find all the movie cuts in which a swallowtail is flying over a dandelion. We assume that butterflies and flowers are all minimally covered with reference-frame pads. This retrieval request can be described by the following SQL query:

> select   movie.oid, mref1.#cutNumber, mref1.oid, mref1.#frameNumber
> from     movie in Movie; mref1, mref2 in MovieReference
> where        movie.oid=mref1.movieOid=mref2.movieOid
>   and        mref1.#frameNumber=mref2.#frameNumber
>   and        mref1.#objectName='swallowtail'
>   and        mref2.#objectName='dandelion'
>   and        mref1.#location.y+mref1.#size.y < mref2.#location.y
>   and        mref1.#location.x+mref1.#size.x > mref2.#location.x
>   and        mref2.#location.x+mref2.#size.x > mref1.#location.x.

We show this result in Figure 10.11(a) for the example relations shown in Figure 10.10. This result can be grouped by movie.oid, mref1.#cutNumber, and mref1.oid to obtain

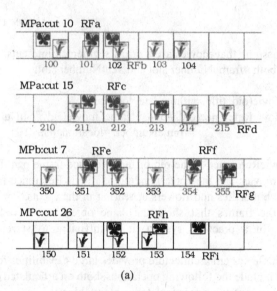

(a)

**MovieReference(oid, #objectName, #movieOid, #cutNumber,
#frameNumber, #location, #size)**

| oid | #object Name | #movie Oid | #cut Number | #frame Number | #location | #size |
|-----|-------------|-----------|-------------|---------------|-----------|-------|
| RFa | swallowtail | MPa | cut10 | 100 | ... | ... |
| RFa | swallowtail | MPa | cut10 | 101 | ... | ... |
| RFa | swallowtail | MPa | cut10 | 102 | ... | ... |
| RFb | dandelion | MPa | cut10 | 100 | ... | ... |
| RFb | dandelion | MPa | cut10 | 101 | ... | ... |
| RFb | dandelion | MPa | cut10 | 102 | ... | ... |
| RFb | dandelion | MPa | cut10 | 103 | ... | ... |
| RFb | dandelion | MPa | cut10 | 104 | ... | ... |
| RFc | swallowtail | MPa | cut 15 | 211 | ... | ... |
| RFc | swallowtail | MPa | cut 15 | 212 | | |
| RFd | dandelion / | MPa | cut 15 | 211 | | |
| RFd | dandelion | MPa | cut 15 | 212 | | |
| RFd | dandelion | MPa | cut 15 | 213 | | |
| RFd | dandelion | MPa | cut 15 | 214 | | |
| RFd | dandelion | MPa | cut 15 | 215 | | |
| RFe | swallowtail | MPb | cut 7 | 351 | | |
| RFe | swallowtail | MPb | cut 7 | 352 | | |
| RFf | swallowtail | MPb | cut 7 | 354 | | |
| RFf | swallowtail | MPb | cut 7 | 355 | | |
| RFg | dandelion | MPb | cut 7 | 350 | | |
| RFg | dandelion | MPb | cut 7 | 351 | | |
| RFg | dandelion | MPb | cut 7 | 352 | | |
| RFg | dandelion | MPb | cut 7 | 353 | | |
| RFg | dandelion | MPb | cut 7 | 354 | | |
| RFg | dandelion | MPb | cut 7 | 355 | | |
| RFh | swallowtail | MPc | cut 26 | 152 | | |
| RFh | swallowtail | MPc | cut 26 | 153 | | |
| RFh | swallowtail | MPc | cut 26 | 154 | | |
| RFi | dandelion | MPc | cut 26 | 150 | | |
| RFi | dandelion | MPc | cut 26 | 151 | | |
| RFi | dandelion | MPc | cut 26 | 152 | | |
| RFi | dandelion | MPc | cut 26 | 153 | ... | ... |

(b)

**Figure 10.10** Example cuts of movies, and the corresponding relation. Reference frame pads are used here to articulate butterflies and flowers appearing in these cuts. (a) Example cuts of movies. (b) The corresponding relation.

| movie. oid | mref1. #cut Number | mref1. oid | mref1. #frame Number |
|---|---|---|---|
| MPa | cut 10 | RFa | 101 |
| MPa | cut 10 | RFa | 102 |
| MPa | cut 15 | RFc | 211 |
| MPa | cut 15 | RFc | 212 |
| MPa | cut 15 | RFc | 213 |
| MPb | cut 7 | RFe | 351 |
| MPb | cut 7 | RFe | 352 |
| MPb | cut 7 | RFf | 354 |
| MPb | cut 7 | RFf | 355 |
| MPc | cut 26 | RFh | 152 |
| MPc | cut 26 | RFh | 153 |

| movie. oid | mref1. #cut Number | $t1$ | $t2$ |
|---|---|---|---|
| MPa | cut 10 | 101 | 102 |
| MPa | cut 15 | 211 | 213 |
| MPb | cut 7 | 351 | 352 |
| MPb | cut 7 | 354 | 355 |
| MPc | cut 26 | 152 | 153 |

(a)                                                     (b)

**Figure 10.11**   The result relation obtained by the query is grouped by movie.oid, mref1.#cutNumber, and mref1.oid to obtain two attributes movie.oid and mref1.#frameNumber/(movie.oid, mref1.#cutNumber, mref1.oid). From the second set-value attribute, we can calculate the minimum min(mref1.#frameNumber/(movie.oid, mref1.#cutNumber, mref1.oid)) and the maximum max(mref.#frameNumber/(movie.oid, mref1.#cutNumber, mref1.oid)) of this set. t1 = min(mref. #frameNumber/(movie.oid, mref1.#cutNumber, mref1.oid)). t2 = max(mref.#frameNumber/ (movie.oid, mref1.#cutNumber, mref1.oid)). (a) Retreived result. (b) Movie scene.

three attributes: movie.oid, mref1.#cutNumber, and mref1.#frameNumber/(movie.oid, mref1.#cutNumber, mref1.oid), where A/B means the grouping of A values with respect to different B values. From the third set-value attribute, we can calculate the minimum *min*(mref1.#frameNumber/(movie.oid, mref1.#cutNumber, mref1.oid)) and the maximum *max*(mref.#frameNumber/(movie.oid, mref1.#cutNumber, mref1.oid)) of this set, which are shown in Figure 10.11(b). Let *pad* be a function from a pad oid to its corresponding pad. Then the movie cuts we want are obtained as *pad*(movie.oid)|[*t1*,*t2*], where *t1* = *min*(mref.#frameNumber/(movie.oid,      mref1.#cutNumber,      mref1.oid)),      *t2*      = *max*(mref.#frameNumber/(movie.oid, mref1.#cutNumber, mref1.oid)), and |[*t1*,*t2*] denotes the selection of the cut between these two frame numbers. This gives us a subsequence of the cut selected by the retrieved combinations of movie.oid and mref1.#cutNumber. Such a subsequence may include frames without either dandelions or swallowtails. However, it starts and ends with frames including both of them in the specified spatial relationship, and includes no cut changes. By concatenating these subsequences in the order of movie.oid and mref1.#cutNumber, we will obtain a single movie sequence.

Our architecture also allows us to span a link from any nonarticulated object in any movie to another pad. An anchor pad is used as a reference frame to cover this nonarticulated object. The specification of a reference frame also specifies its underlying movie pad and some of its frame numbers. Therefore, our architecture provides context-specification functions. Composition operations and overlay operations are both provided by IntelligentPad itself.

Our system architecture can also deal with images and sounds in a similar way.

### 10.4.3   Articulated Objects in Media Objects

Our architecture uses its object-oriented database to manage articulated objects in media objects. Here we examine texts to show how our architecture manages articulated objects in texts.

IntelligentPad represents each text as a text pad. A text pad is associated with a text file storing its text string and works as a screen editor of its text file. Users can easily move its cursor, scroll the text, and specify any portion of the text, all through direct manipulations using a mouse. A text pad also allows its user to register hypertext link anchors and to invoke them by a mouse operation. It provides a special slot, #edit, to access any articulated object. Its access by a "set" message with a parameter (ref <loc1> <loc2>) makes this text pad update its currentObject register to the text portion between two locations <loc1> and <loc2>. A "set" message with (insert <loc> <text>) makes this pad insert the text string <text> at the location <loc>. A "set" message with (del <loc1> <loc2>) makes this pad delete the text portion between <loc1> and <loc2>. An access of this #edit slot by a "gimme" message makes this pad return the value of its currentObject register.

In our multimedia database architecture using IntelligentPad and an object-oriented database, texts are stored not in text files, but in the database. Each text pad is therefore modified so that it can read and write the text contents to and from the database.

Such architecture supports file operations, quantification, link operations, and context specification on articulated content objects. Furthermore, since text pads can be pasted together with any pads, they allow composition operations and overlay operations.

Similarly, articulated content objects in figures and tables are all managed by our database, whereas figures and tables themselves are represented as pads that access the database to display and to edit their contents.

## 10.5   HYPERMEDIA DATABASE

As shown in Section 9.3, IntelligentPad provides all the functions necessary to construct hypermedia documents as pads. In this section, we will consider such cases in which the number of nodes and links become so large that we need a database to manage them.

### 10.5.1   Management of a Large Hypermedia Network

We assume that pads that work as hypermedia nodes are stored by a database, and that they are identified in this database by their pids (pad identifiers). This database called a hypermedia database stores pads as a relation, Pad(PID, PadExchangeFormat). The attribute PID holds the pid of a pad, whereas the attribute PadExchangeFormat holds the exchange format representation of this pad.

For reasons of simplicity, here we only consider anchors that are represented as pads. Different from anchor pads that keep the file name of their destination pads, these pads, which are linked to certain pads in the hypermedia database, use their surrogates. Such pads are called DBAnchorPads. When clicked, DBAnchorPads issue the following SQL query to the hypermedia database:

```
select   PadExchangeFormat
from     Pad
where    PID=pid
```

where *pid* is the pid that the DBAnchorPad keeps in itself. The DBAnchorPad then converts the exchange format representation thus obtained to a composite pad and pops it up on the desktop.

New nodes and new links can be added to this hypermedia system as follows. Figure 10.12 shows a tool that saves and loads pads to and from a hypermedia database. This tool uses a DBProxyPad, a SaverLoaderPad, and a PidExtractorPad. This SaverLoaderPad is connected to the exchange format slot of the PidExtractorPad. The PidExtractorPad is connected to the #currentRecord slot of the DBProxyPad. When a single record is retrieved from the relation Pad, it is stored in the #currentRecord slot. The proxy pad issues an "update" to the PidExtractorPad, which reads the #currentRecord slot of the proxy pad. The readout record consists of a pid and a exchange format string of a pad. The PidExtractorPad separates these values and makes them independently accessible through its #pid slot and its #exchangeFormat slot. This PidExtractorPad then propagates the update to the SaverLoaderPad, which reads the #exchangeFormat slot of the PidExtractorPad to convert its value to a composite pad. The resulting pad is popped up on the SaverLoaderPad. When a composite pad is dropped on it, the SaverLoaderPad converts this composite pad to its exchange format representation and sends this value to the PidExtractorPad, which extracts its pid and sets this pid to its #pid slot.

The DBAnchorGeneratorPad that is connected to the #pid slot of the PidExtractorPad in Figure 10.12 generates a DBAnchorPad with its destination pid set to the readout #pid slot value. When a DBAnchorPad is dropped on it, this DBAnchorGeneratorPad extracts its destination pid and sends this to the #pid slot of its parent pad.

Suppose we want to span a new link from one composite pad to another composite pad, both of which are already stored in the hypermedia database. In this case, we can drop the destination pad on the SaverLoaderPad, which converts it to its exchange format representation and sends the result to the PidExtractorPad. This pad then extracts the pid of the

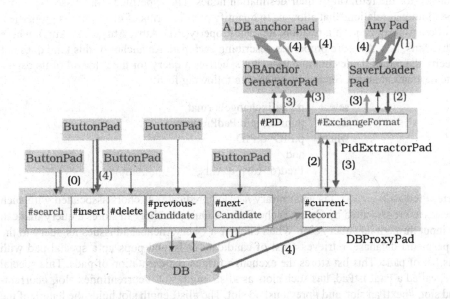

**Figure 10.12** A tool that saves and loads pads to and from a hypermedia database uses a DBProxyPad, a SaverLoaderPad, and a PidExtractorPad.

new destination pad and holds this in its #pid slot. We use another special pad called a DBAnchorGeneratorPad. This pad is pasted on the PidExtractorPad with its connection to the #pid slot. When it receives an "update" message from the PidExtractorPad, it reads out a pid from the the #pid slot and generates a new DBAnchorPad with this pid as its destination. You can paste this generated DBAnchorPad on the source pad to cover its source anchor object. Since the source pad is added with a new anchor, we have to replace its exchange format representation stored in the database with its updated version. For this purpose, we use the tool in Figure 10.12 again. We drop this updated version of the source pad on the SaverLoaderPad, which sends its exchange format representation together with its pid to the #currentRecord slot of the DBProxyPad through the PidExtractorPad. When we click the button connected to the #insert slot of the DBProxyPad, this proxy pad updates the database by replacing the corresponding record of this pad with its new version.

Suppose that we want to span a new link from a node in the database to a new node that is not in the database. We use the same tool shown in Figure 10.12. First, we register this new pad into the database. At this time, we also obtain a new DBAnchorPad with the pid of this new pad. Then we paste this anchor on the source pad and replace the record of this source pad with its updated version.

To delete a node, we can just delete its record from the database using the same tool shown in Figure 10.12. As the result of such deletion operations, a DBAnchorPad may fail to search the database for its destination pad. In this case, the DBAnchorPad pops up nothing. To delete a link, we delete its source anchor, namely the DBAnchorPad pasted on the source pad. Since this updates the source pad, we have to update the database by replacing the old record for this source pad with its new version.

### 10.5.2 Hyperlinks as Queries

The use of a hypermedia database allows us to specify some of its links as queries to this database for the retrieval of their destination nodes. The hypermedia database may store any additional relations that allow us to quantify pads in terms of their various properties. Let PadProperty be such a relation, i.e., PadProperty(PID, $Attr_1$, $Attr_2$, . . . , $Attr_n$), where $Attr_1$, $Attr_2$, . . . , $Attr_n$ are properties describing each pad. An anchor of this kind does not specify the pid of its destination node, but specifies a query for the retrieval of its candidate destination nodes. Such a query has the following form:

$$\begin{array}{ll} \text{select} & \text{p.PadExchangeFormat} \\ \text{from} & \text{p inPad, q in PadProperty} \\ \text{where} & \text{p.PID=q.PID} \\ & \text{and} \\ & \text{Pred(q.Attr}_1\text{, q.Attr}_2\text{, . . . . . , q.Attr}_n\text{)} \end{array}$$

Here, $Pred(x_1, x_2, . . ., x_n)$ is an arbitrary $n$-place predicate. Anchors associated with such queries are represented by QueryAnchorPads. A QueryAnchorPad stores a query that can be input through its #query slot. When clicked, a QueryAnchorPad issues its query to the hypermedia database, retrieves a list of candidate pads, and pops up a special pad with this list of pads. This list stores the exchange format representation of pads. This special pad, called a PadListPad, has such slots as #listLength slot, #currentIndex slot, #currentPad slot, #nextPad slot, and #previousPad slot. The #listLength slot holds the length of the stored list. The #currentPad slot holds one of the pads in this list as the current pad, while the #currentIndex slot holds the index number of the current pad in the list. The #current-

Pad slot is connected to a SaverLoaderPad. The #nextPad slot and the #previousPad slot, respectively, increase and decrease the #currentIndex slot value by one. Figure 10.13 shows the pad composition structure of a hypermedia database system using QueryAnchorPads. A destination node of a query anchor is not a single pad, but a list of pads. To browse pads in this list one after another, you can click the button pad connected to the next pad slot of the pad list pad.

The above discussion assumed that the destination pad specification does not depend on properties of the source pad. For hyperlinks that depend on both the source and destination pad properties, we can extend both QueryAnchorPads and the queries to the pad database as follows. An extended QueryAnchorPad, when clicked by a user, first sends a message to its parent pad to obtain the parent's pid. This parent pad's pid (or master pid), *mpid*, is used in the following extended query to the pad database:

> select    p.PadExchangeFormat
> from     p inPad, q1, q2 in PadProperty
> where        p.PID=q2.PID
>     and    q1.PID=*mpid*
>     and    $\text{Pred}'(q1.\text{Attr}_1, \ldots, q1.\text{Attr}_n, q2.\text{Attr}_1, \ldots, q2.\text{Attr}_n)$

where $\text{Pred}'(x_1, x_2, \ldots, x_n, y_1, y_2, \ldots, y_n)$ is an arbitrary $2n$-place predicate.

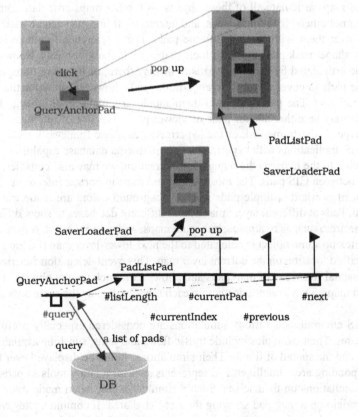

**Figure 10.13**  An example use of a QueryAnchorPad and its composition structure.

## 10.6 GEOGRAPHICAL INFORMATION DATABASES

GIS (Geographical Information System) is no doubt one of the most potential application fields of IntelligentPad. Nigel Waters, who is a professor at the Department of Geography, University of Calgary, pointed out the potential application of IntelligentPad to GIS in an article published in *GIS World* [20]. His article, entitled "POGS: Pads of Geographic Software," envisaged a situation in which a map display, a traffic simulation model, a video image of an intersection, and a display in graph form are all represented as mutually interacting pads. He indicated that a system with these pads would not only be a great pedagogical device, but would be invaluable for planning. Furthermore, he pointed out that one of the GIS functions, which is becoming increasingly important, is providing software patches to carry out operations the software does not address in its existing form. Sometimes, if the patch is extremely useful and becomes popular, it may be incorporated into a later software version. Waters envisaged a situation, however, in which the patches are all in the form of pads that would be passed around among the members of list, evolving and merging to meet the needs of a variety of different users.

GIS is still evolving with respect to its functional capabilities. Therefore, it is not yet possible to provide a standard framework for GIS. Here we consider only a small portion of its basic pads and their interactions.

A map shows various objects. They include roads, rivers, railways, intersections, areas, buildings, and names. Some maps do not articulate any of these; such maps are just images. Other maps articulate all of these objects. Still other maps articulate some of these objects, but not others. Buildings, areas, and intersections in a map can be easily articulated if we cover them with reference-frame pads. These reference-frame pads might be masked by shape-mask pads to match their shapes to the target objects. Names on a map can also be articulated by using text pads to display them, or by using transparent reference-frame pads to cover them. Reference-frame pads, however, do not articulate roads, rivers, or railways. The pad that draws them should articulate these objects. Reference-frame pads may be either anchor pads or viewer pads. The use of reference-frame pads with the hypermedia framework or the hypermedia database framework makes it easy to develop GIS applications with hypermedia or hypermedia database capabilities.

In addition to the hypermedia navigation interaction, we may also consider various interactions between GIS pads. The most simple and most important interaction is the view integration of overlaid multiple pads whose background colors are made transparent or translucent. Pads at different layers may access different databases to show different maps of the same area, such as roadmaps, bus route maps, and subway maps. A mouse event on a map to pick up some object is delegated to the next-lower-layer map if there is no object at the specified location on the current layer map. This event delegation function is one of the fundamental functions of map pads and allows us to pick up any objects at any layers of overlaid maps. They communicate with each other to display the same area at the same scale.

In a GIS environment, various simulations are considered especially useful for planning purposes. Their examples include traffic flows and jams, sunshine availability, flows of people, and the spread of floods. Their simulations should be displayed over the map of the corresponding area. IntelligentPad represents such simulation tools as pads that visualize the simulations on themselves. Such a simulation pad, when made translucent, can also be overlaid on a map pad showing the simulated area. It communicates with the underlying map pad to adjust its location, size, and scale with those of the underlying map.

Figure 10.14 shows a sunshine-simulation pad overlaid on a map pad. Wataru Kowaguchi of Hitachi Software Engineering Co. developed this system together with the accessing of a map database during his stay in our laboratory as a visiting researcher in 1994. This simulation pad accesses the same database that is accessed by the underlying map pad, and extracts information about the height of each building to calculate shadow areas at a given time on a given day of the year. This simulation pad has two slots to specify the time and the day of the year. If we paste a clock and a calendar with their connections, respectively, to the time slot and the day slot, we will be able to directly specify these values through this clock and the calendar.

Some urban designers consider IntelligentPad to be a competent platform system for the development of urban design systems. They want to use GIS in combination with so-called "what-if" queries and simulations. For example, they want to simulate how modified configurations of streets, crossings, parking lots, and/or shops may affect the flows of pedestrians and cars. This requires the original geographical information, its modification with respect to a new configuration of streets, crossings, parking lots, and/or shops, and a simulation system that uses all this information. If their component objects are represented as pads, they can be overlaid to communicate with each other.

Sapporo Electronic Center, an external organization of Sapporo City Government to promote R & D activities in Sapporo, has developed an experimental GIS system for the urban design and administration of Sapporo City using IntelligentPad in cooperation with three major IPC members: Fuji Xerox, Hitachi Software Engineering, and Fujitsu. This project is planning to extend the prototype system for practical use by all the departments and ward offices of Sapporo City Government. The interoperability and exchangeability of pads allow these departments and offices to exchange various types of geographical in-

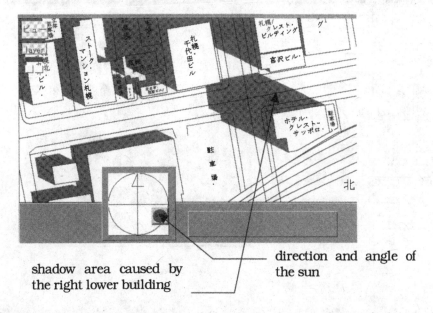

shadow area caused by the right lower building

direction and angle of the sun

**Figure 10.14**  A sunshine-simulation pad overlaid on a map pad accesses the same database that is accessed by the underlying map pad and extracts information about the height of each building to calculate shadow areas at a given time on the given day of the year.

formation, to reuse them in different contexts, and to make them functionally linked with different kinds of administrative information.

Figure 10.15 shows a display hard copy of the IntelligentPad-based GIS that has been developed during the preliminary studies for the above-mentioned project. The map is retrieved from a GIS database through a proxy pad. The system uses a legacy GIS engine for the management of GIS databases. In this example scene, the translucent square pad over the map allows you to specify a region within a specified distance from a specified location. This pad extracts all the buildings within the specified region as independent objects, and displays them on itself. You can move this pad to another tool, and drop its content information about the selected buildings into the tool. This GIS system provides various types of region specification pads. Another example is a pad that extracts objects within a specified distance from a river or a street. The system is also capable of evaluating what-if queries.

Another interesting interaction between pads in a GIS environment is the one between a map pad and a movie pad, as shown in Figure 10.16. A movie pad has a slot whose value is the ratio of the current frame number to the total number of its frames. This slot is called the #frameRatio slot. If we connect a slider pad to this slot, we can forward or rewind the movie by sliding the slider lever right and left. A TrajectoryPad is a special pad that can only move along a specified trajectory on an arbitrary pad. It has a slot whose value changes from 0 to 1.0 in proportion to its distance along the trajectory from the source end to its current location. This value becomes 1.0 when the TrajectoryPad reaches

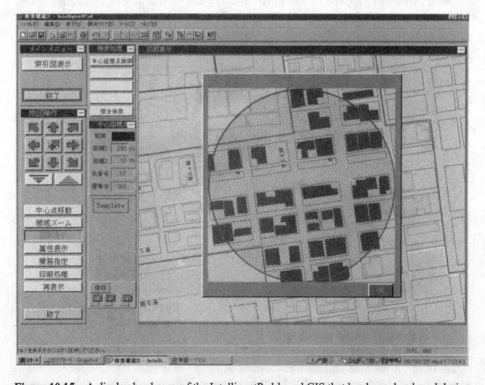

**Figure 10.15** A display hard copy of the IntelligentPad-based GIS that has been developed during the preliminary studies for the urban-planning project.

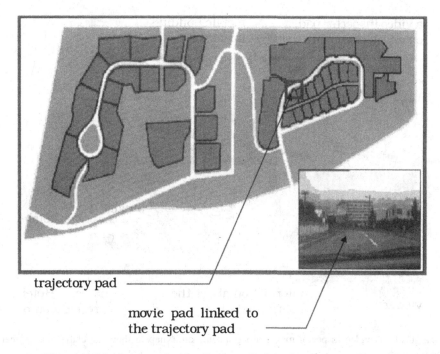

trajectory pad ——————

movie pad linked to
the trajectory pad ——————

**Figure 10.16** A map pad with a TrajectoryPad that is wired to a video pad.

the destination end. This slot is called the #distanceRatio slot. Furthermore, if we change this slot value, the TrajectoryPad moves to the corresponding location on the trajectory. Its trajectory can be specified by sample locations on the trajectory. It interpolates these points to obtain the trajectory. When we try to drag a TrajectoryPad using a mouse, it only moves along the specified trajectory. When used on a map pad, any route between two locations on a map can be set to a TrajectoryPad as its trajectory. Suppose that we paste two shared copies of a WiringPad, one on a TrajectoryPad with its connection to the #distanceRatio slot and the other on a movie pad with its connection to the #frameRatio slot. Suppose also that the TrajectoryPad is a priori instructed to move along a route on a map, and that the movie shows the change of scenery along this route. If we move the TrajectoryPad on a map along the route, the movie pad shows the corresponding change of scenery along the same route. Furthermore, if we forward or rewind the movie by means of a slider pasted on it, the TrajectoryPad also moves forward or backward along the route to tell us the location of the current movie scene on the map. In Figure 10.16, a TrajectoryPad on a map pad is wired to a video pad.

A movie pad can get a frame number from its parent pad to show this frame. An UpwardRangeConverterPad has a #nominator slot, #denominator slot, #ratio slot, and a #value slot. The value of the #ratio slot is the ratio of the #nominator slot value to the #denominator slot value. Each value coming from its parent pad is multiplied by its #ratio slot value and stored in its #value slot value. Suppose that we have a movie of some route on a map. Let the length of the movie be $L$ frames. Suppose also that we have a TrajectoryPad for this route on the map, and that we paste an UpwardRangeConverterPad with its #nominator and #denominator slots, respectively, set to $L$ and 1.0. Then this composite pad moves along the route on the map and changes its slot value from 0 to $L$. Suppose further

a video inspector pad
on a trajectory pad

mobile building
inspector

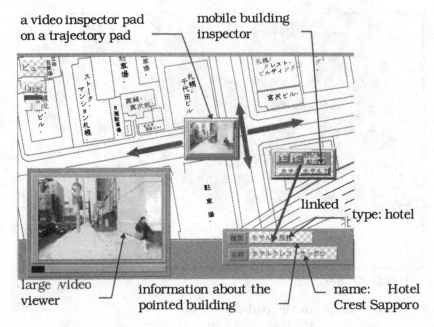

linked

type: hotel

large video
viewer

information about the
pointed building

name: Hotel
Crest Sapporo

**Figure 10.17** A video inspector moves along a route on a map to show the changes of scenery along this route.

that we paste the movie pad on this composite pad. Then we obtain a video inspector as a composite pad that we can move along the route on the map to see the change of scenery. Figure 10.17 shows such a video inspector on a map pad.

Figure 10.17 also shows a mobile building-inspector pad, which you may move around on the map to get the name of and additional information on the underlying building. This pad, whenever it stops, accesses the GIS database to retrieve the information about the underlying building.

## 10.7 CONTENT-BASED SEARCH AND CONTEXT-BASED SEARCH

When we search for something, we may browse through the target area, navigate through related things along some relationship, or ask someone to take over the search by specifying what to search for. The same situation holds for objects stored in computers. There are three ways of searching for objects: search by browsing, navigation search, and quantification search. The browsing of a catalog to find some objects is an example of the search by browsing. The navigation search navigates along links that are a priori spanned among objects to associate each object with its related objects. The quantification search specifies a condition that uniquely characterizes those objects we want to get. There are two ways of characterizing objects. We may quantify either their properties or the contexts in which they exist. A search with the former type of quantification is called a content-based search, whereas one with the latter type is called a context-based search.

In the case of pads, their properties are their pad types, sizes, background colors, slot name list, and slot values, where the value of a slot means the return value of a "gimme" message sent to this slot. If a slot is a data slot, its value is the one stored in the associated register in the pad. The context of a pad is the environment in which this pad exists. This environment includes all the pads and their connection structures under or over this pad. The properties of such a context include all the properties of the pads under or over this pad and the connection structures among them. Since the desktop is also considered to be a pad that provides slots for the user ID, the current time, and the system version, these values are also properties of the context for any pad on the desktop.

The content-based search is the ordinary quantification search we perform in database systems. The context-based search is not widely used, and hence not yet well studied. Only a few research groups have recognized its importance and potential, and studied it from its application side. These research studies, however, are mainly focused on the retrieval of objects through the quantification of the past user operation sequences applied to these objects. For example, Euro PARC's Forget-me-not system [21] was developed as a subsystem of their Ubiquitous Computing Project. The Forget-me-not system records for each user activity all the information about when and where he or she did what operation on which object. Users are allowed to select only some of these records to archive in the system. Later, they can retrieve these activity records by partially specifying when, where, and who did what operation on which object. This kind of search is based on personal memory. It cannot be applied to those objects that the user has never seen. Although the object retrieval based on user's personal history is also an interesting research topic, here we will consider a different type of context-based search.

In Section 10.1, we classified the management of pads into two cases: one with a rather small number of different forms, and the other with a large number of different forms. In the former case, pads can be stored and managed by form bases developed on top of conventional database management systems, as shown in Section 10.2. In the latter case, however, we require a new type of database management system. The former case quantifies the states or the contents of the pads to be retrieved, and has no need to quantify their forms. It performs the content-based search. The latter case, however, needs to quantify the contents and the forms of the pads to be retrieved. The quantification of contents leads to the content-based search, but the quantification on forms requires the context-based search.

In the latter case, forms of pads cannot be managed separately from the states of pads for two reasons. First, the management of a large number of different forms requires another database. Second, the pad states of different forms have different record types and require a huge number of different relations to store them. There is no advantage to the separate management of forms and states. We need a new database to directly manage and retrieve a large variety of composite pads.

As discussed in Section 10.1, each composite pad has no corresponding object class. The present OODB technologies cannot be applied to the management of pads since they assume both the existence of a class definition for each object and each class has a large number of instances. Their efficient search processing mainly depends on the indexing of objects, which also assumes the existence of a class definition for each object.

Therefore, the required new database for the direct management and retrieval of a large variety of composite pads cannot be implemented based on the current OODB technologies.

Let us further consider how we can quantify composite pads we want to search for. Suppose we want to search a database for a pad with elementary calculation functions. How can we specify such a pad? We do not know its name or its pad type. We have no idea about its slot names, its size, or its color. We cannot specify any of its properties. However, it is quite probable that such a pad may be used as a base pad of a composite pad that works as a hand calculator. Then the next question arises. How can we specify such a hand calculator? Can we specify it by its name? That may work sometimes, but not always. Several different names may be used for the same object. Some objects may not have popular names. Which of the remaining properties can we specify if its name does not work? Can we specify its function? The same functions can be specified differently. It is hard to retrieve objects with specified functions. However, its function is partially embodied by its composition structure. Any hand calculator has more than 10 buttons and at least one digital display. We can use this knowledge to specify the target pad as a pad having on itself more than 10 button pads as well as at least one digital display pad. This is nothing but a partial specification of the context in which a copy of the target pad exists. The search for a calculation pad as a pad used by a hand calculator resolves itself into a context-based search.

Another way to specify a pad uses its user's memory about where it was, how it was used, and/or when it was used. Suppose that you remember that you used a hand calculator on a video editing tool with its connection to a frame number slot of a movie pad. Suppose that you used this calculator to calculate the length of two concatenated movies between 17:00 and 18:00 yesterday. In this case, the calculation pad in this calculator can be specified as a pad that was pasted on a movie pad and then peeled off between 17:00 and 18:00 yesterday. If the system keeps the event log and the snapshots of the environment, this specification may be sufficient to retrieve the target pad from the stored snapshots. Such retrieval is also an example of a context-based search that has already been developed in our laboratory on the Smalltalk-80 version of the IntelligentPad system [22].

## 10.8 MANAGEMENT AND RETRIEVAL OF PADS

When managing and retrieving pads with a large variety of forms, we cannot manage their forms separately from their states. We should directly store, manage, and retrieve pads, which requires pad bases, i.e., a new kind of database to manage pads. Pad bases are instance bases required to perform not only content-based searches, but also context-based searches.

The performance of the content-based search can be easily and remarkably improved by providing an indexed file for each content property of the pads in a pad base. The relation between each object and a value of each of its properties is represented by a well-known object-attribute–value triple $(oid, a, v)$, where $oid$, $a$, and $v$ are respectively an object identifier, a property of this object, and its value of this object. The indexed file for this property $a$ is a list of pairs, $(v_1, oid_1)$, $(v_2, oid_2)$, . . . , in ascending order of the first component values. It may use some tree-structured file organization to speed up its access for the retrieval of the object identifiers paired with the specified values. This is a well-known method. We will not go into further detail here.

The context-based search, however, requires new methods to improve its performance.

### 10.8.1 Search for Pads with Partially Specified Composition Structure

The context-based search for pads retrieves from pad bases those pads that contain a specified composition structure as a substructure of its composition. Figure 10.18 shows a composite pad that performs such search jobs. The base pad is a DB proxy pad that com-

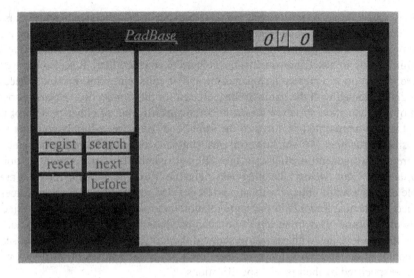

**Figure 10.18** This composite pad retrieves from a pad base those pads that contain a specified composition structure as a substructure of their composition.

municates with a GemStone object-oriented database management system. On this base pad, there are two big pads working as windows to contain composite pads. The smaller one on the base pad accepts a composite pad as a query specification, and sends its composition structure to the DB proxy pad. This composition structure is used as a partial specification of the composition structure of the pads to retrieve. The larger pad on the base pad is a pad loader pad. It pops up the retrieved candidate pads on itself one by one. You can drag each of them out of this pad to use it for your own purposes.

By the composition structure of a composite pad we mean both its view composition structure and its slot connection structure (Figure 10.19). Its view composition structure

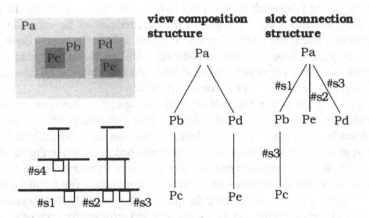

**Figure 10.19** By the composition structure of a composite pad we mean both its view-composition structure and its slot-connection structure.

describes what kinds of primitive pads are used and how they are pasted together. It is represented as a tree with its node representing a pad name and its edge representing a relation between a pad and its parent pad. The slot connection structure describes what kind of primitive pads are used and which slots are used to connect them. It is also represented as a tree with its node representing a pad name and its edge representing a slot connection. Each edge is labeled with the name of the slot used for this connection. A partial specification of a composition structure means a partial specification of either or both of these trees. It is also represented as a tree of the same kind. Here we will only consider view-composition structures. We can, however, treat slot-connection structures in the same way.

There are two general methods for the efficient search of a large amount of objects. One uses index files, whereas the other uses signature files. The indexing methods are applicable only to a set of objects with an a priori defined set of attributes whose values are specified by queries. Records in the same relation in a relational database and object instances of the same class in an object-oriented database both satisfy this condition. We can use their index files with respect to some of their attributes for their efficient search. View-composition structures, however, have no a priori defined set of attributes whose values are specified by their partial specifications.

A signature of an object is a bit string that partially characterizes this object. It is obtained by encoding the corresponding object. Each property is mapped to one or several bit positions in such bit strings. If the object satisfies the property, all the selected bits of its signature are set to "1." Starting from a bit string with all of its bits reset to "0," we set all the selected bits for every property that is satisfied by the object to obtain the signature bit string of this object. Different sets of properties may degenerate into the same signature. Instead of searching a set of objects, a search for an object searches all of their signatures. Since the size of a signature is much smaller than its object, a search of a signature file can be much more efficiently performed than a search of objects. A query partially specifies the target objects by specifying some properties they satisfy. A set of these properties can also be encoded to a bit string using the same encoding function. This bit string is called a query signature. The query processing searches the signature file for those signatures that have "1" at every bit position where the query signature has "1."

The success of the signature file search depends on the design of the encoding function. In general, there are two measures for search quality: the hit–miss ratio and the false-drop ratio. Signature file search does not fail to find any objects satisfying the specified query. Its hit–miss ratio is zero. Because of the degeneration of the encoding, the pads whose signatures match the query signature may not satisfy the query. These pads are called false drops, whereas the retrieved pads that truly satisfy the query are called true drops. The ratio of false drops to the total of false and true drops is the false-drop ratio. The false-drop ratio should be kept as small as possible.

When applied to the search for pads with partially specified view-composition structures, signatures of pads are defined by encoding their view-composition structures. The database stores both composite pads and their signatures. A partial specification of view-composition structures is given by a sample composite pad, as shown in Figure 10.20. The signature of this sample composite pad works as the query signature. Figure 10.21 shows the search process. The query processing searches the signature file for those signatures that have "1" at every bit position where the query signature has "1." The system obtains the identifiers of pads from the matched signatures and retrieves for each of these identifiers the corresponding pad to see if it satisfies the query. This examination process is called false-drop resolution.

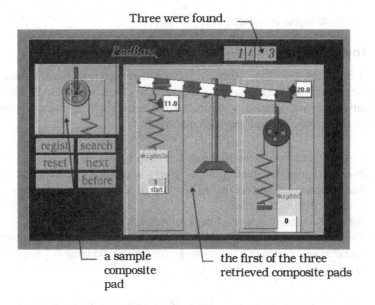

Three were found.

a sample
composite
pad

the first of the three
retrieved composite pads

**Figure 10.20**  A partial specification of view-composition structures is given by a sample composite pad.

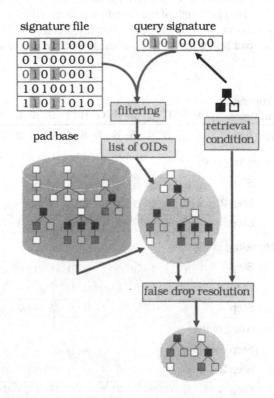

**Figure 10.21**  The query processing searches the signature file for those signatures that have "1" at every bit position where the query signature also has "1." The system obtains the identifiers of pads from the matched signatures, and retrieves for each of these identifiers the corresponding pad to determine if it really satisfies the query.

### 10.8.2 The Encoding of View-Composition Structures

We use the following encoding function to obtain the signature of each composite pad. This method is based on superimposed coding [23, 24]. Let $L$ be the fixed length of signatures. Primitive pads are assumed to be ordered and identified by its index number. We denote by $P_k$ the primitive pad with an index number $k$.

(Step 0) Reset all the bits of a new bit map $S$ of length $L$.

(Step 1) For every primitive pad $P_k$, in the given composite pad, compute h1($k$) using a hash function h1, and set the (h1($k$)+1)st bit of the signature $S$, where

$$h1(k) = ak \bmod L$$

for some constant integer $a$ that is prime with $L$.

(Step 2) For every primitive pad $P_i$ in the given composite pad and its parent primitive pad $P_j$ if any, compute h2($j$, $i$) using another hash function h2, and set the (h2($j$, $i$)+1)st bit of the signature $S$, where

$$h2(j, i) = bj + ci \bmod L$$

for some constant integers $b$ and $c$. The integers $b$, $c$ and $L$ are mutually prime.

Figure 10.22 shows two example composite pads, the bits of their signatures set by step 1 and 2, and the resultant signatures. Uppercase characters from A to P represent pads whose oids are from 1 to 16. The length of the signature is assumed to be 16. The constant integers $a$, $b$, and $c$ are chosen as 1, 3, and 5, respectively. Let us consider the first composite pad, $P_1$. The base pad N sets the 14th bit, whereas its child pad G sets the 7th bit of

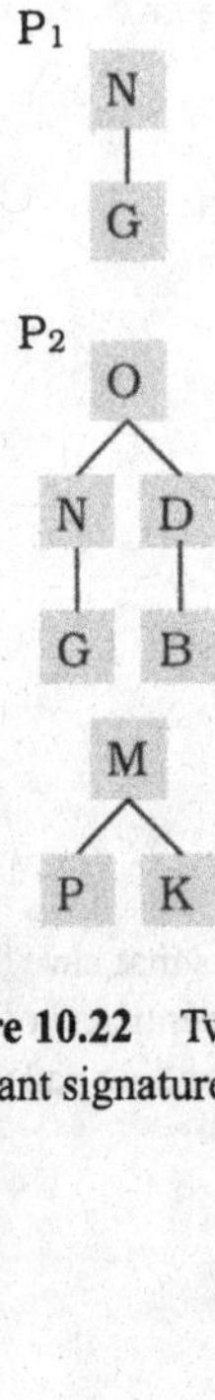


| component pad types | A | B | C | D | E | F | G | H | I | J | K | L | M | N | O | P |
|---|---|---|---|---|---|---|---|---|---|---|---|---|---|---|---|---|
| type No. | 1 | 2 | 3 | 4 | 5 | 6 | 7 | 8 | 9 | 10 | 11 | 12 | 13 | 14 | 15 | 16 |
| **the coding of $P_1$** | | | | | | | | | | | | | | | | |
| Step 1 | 0 | 0 | 0 | 0 | 0 | 0 | 1 | 0 | 0 | 0 | 0 | 0 | 0 | 1 | 0 | 0 |
| Step 2 | 0 | 0 | 0 | 0 | 0 | 0 | 0 | 0 | 0 | 0 | 0 | 0 | 1 | 0 | 0 | 0 |
| Step 3 | 0 | 0 | 0 | 0 | 0 | 0 | 1 | 0 | 0 | 0 | 0 | 0 | 1 | 1 | 0 | 0 |
| **the coding of $P_2$** | | | | | | | | | | | | | | | | |
| Step 1 | 0 | 1 | 0 | 1 | 0 | 0 | 1 | 0 | 0 | 0 | 0 | 0 | 0 | 1 | 1 | 0 |
| Step 2 | 1 | 0 | 1 | 0 | 0 | 1 | 0 | 0 | 0 | 0 | 0 | 0 | 1 | 0 | 0 | 0 |
| Step 3 | 1 | 1 | 1 | 1 | 0 | 1 | 1 | 0 | 0 | 0 | 0 | 0 | 1 | 1 | 1 | 0 |
| **the coding of $P_2$** | | | | | | | | | | | | | | | | |
| Step 1 | 0 | 0 | 0 | 0 | 0 | 0 | 0 | 0 | 0 | 0 | 1 | 0 | 1 | 0 | 0 | 1 |
| Step 2 | 0 | 0 | 0 | 0 | 0 | 0 | 1 | 0 | 0 | 0 | 0 | 0 | 0 | 1 | 0 | 0 |
| Step 3 | 0 | 0 | 0 | 0 | 0 | 0 | 1 | 0 | 0 | 0 | 1 | 0 | 1 | 1 | 0 | 1 |

**Figure 10.22** Two example composite pads, the bits of their signatures set by step 1 and 2, and the resultant signatures.

the signature. The parent–child relation between G and N sets the 13th bit of the signature. As a result, we obtain a signature "0000001000001100" with three set bits. Similarly, we obtain the signature "1111011000001110" for the second composite pad $P_2$. The view composition structure of $P_1$ is a substructure of that of $P_2$. All the bits that are set in the signature of $P_1$ are also set in the signature of $P_2$. This property allows us to search a signature file instead of a file of pads. Figure 10.22 also shows another pad, $P_3$, whose signature is computed as "0000001000101101." The signature of $P_3$ includes all the set bits in the signature of $P_1$. Therefore, the search of the signature file for the signature of $P_1$ as a query signature retrieves not only $P_2$, but also $P_3$. The latter pad, $P_3$, however, does not include $P_1$ as its substructure. Such a pad as $P_3$ in this case is a false drop. The removal of false drops that are possibly included in the retrieval result requires direct comparison of each of them with the query pad.

## 10.9  SUMMARY

This chapter has shown two alternative ways of storing pads. If we have to manage a large number of pads of a few different forms, we can keep the form information outside the databases; we only need to store the state information of pads in the databases. Such a database is called a form base. If the state information of a record type has only atomic and simple values for its attributes, we can use a relational database system to store these pads. If we have to manage composite pads of a large number of different forms, we need database facilities not only to manage the states of the pads but also to manage their different forms. Such a database is termed a pad base. Pad bases should be instance bases by their nature.

A form base uses a database proxy pad as a proxy to a database management system. This pad looks like a blank-sheet pad and provides a list of slots including #query slot, #result slot, #currentRecord slot, #search slot, #insert slot, #delete slot, #nextCandidate slot, and #previousCandidate slot. You may paste a RecordPad on a database proxy pad with its connection to the #currentRecord slot. The RecordPad provides each attribute of a retrieved record as its slot. You may connect an appropriate output pad to each slot of the RecordPad to compose a form interface of the database. The whole set of pads available in IntelligentPad works as a form construction kit for the visual interface of this database.

IntelligentPad allows us to treat any composite pad as a database value. Each composite pad has its exchange format representation, which is just a variable-length string. This string can be stored in databases as an attribute value if this attribute allows a variable-length string as its value. This means any object that can be represented as a composite pad can be stored in relational databases. These objects include interactive multimedia objects such as images, movies and sounds, interactive charts and tables, interactive maps, database access forms, various application tools, and compound documents embedding any of these objects.

A pad base is a new type of OODB. We cannot always specify a pad with its name, its pad type, its slot names, its size, or its color. However, it is quite probable that we can specify a part of its composition structure. For example, a pad that is able to calculate elementary functions may be used by a hand calculator as its base pad. A hand calculator has more than 10 buttons pasted on some of its component pads, and at least one digital display.

This chapter has proposed a basic algorithm for this kind of search. The algorithm exploits superimposed coding of pad structures to define signatures of pads, and search these signatures for those matched with a query signature.

## REFERENCES

1. E. F. Codd. A relational model of data for large shared data banks. *CACM, 13*(6): 377–387, 1970.

2. D. Maier. Why isn't there an object-oriented data model? In *Proceedings of the IFIP 11th World Computer Conference,* 1989.

3. F. Bancilhon, C. Delobel, and P. Kanellakis (eds.). *Building an Object-Oriented Database System: The Story of O₂.* Morgan Kaufmann, San Francisco, CA, 1992.

4. R. G. G. Cattel. *Object Data Management, Version 2.* Addison-Wesley, Reading, MA, 1994.

5. A. Kemper and G. Moerkotte. *Object-Oriented Database Management.* Prentice-Hall, Englewood Cllifs, NJ, 1994.

6. C. Delobel, C. Lecluse, and P. Richard. *Databases: From Relational Systems to Object-Oriented Systems.* International Thompson Publishing, London, 1995.

7. R. G. G. Cattel, and D. K. Barry (eds.). *The Object Database Standard: ODMG 2.0.* Morgan Kaufmann, San Francisco, 1997.

8. M. Stonebraker and L. A. Rowe. The design of postgres. In *Proceedings of ACM-SIGMOD International Conference,* 1986.

9. UniSQL. *Next-Generation Software Solutions,* UniSQL, Austin, TX, 1992.

10. Illustra Information Technologies. *Illustra Object-Relational Database Management Systems.* Illustra, Oakland, CA, 1994.

11. T. C. Lamb, G. Landis, J. Orenstein, and D. Weinreb. The ObjectStore database system. *CACM, 34*(10): 50–63, 1991.

12. P. Butterworth, A. Otis, and J. Stein. The GemStone object database management System. *CACM, 34*(10), 1991.

13. W. Kim. *Introduction to Object-Oriented Databases.* MIT Press, Cambridge, MA, 1990.

14. M. M. Zloof. Query-by-Example: A Database Language, *IBM System Journal, 16*(4): 324–343, 1977.

15. Y. Tanaka. Meme Media and Databases. In *Cooperative Databases and Applications. (Proceedings of the International Symposium on Cooperative Database Systems for Advanced Applications, 1996).* pp. 22–31, 1997.

16. C. Faloutsos. *Searching Multimedia Databases by Content.* Kluwer Academic Publishers, Boston, MA, 1996.

17. B. Thuraisingham, K. C. Nwosu, and P. B. Berra. *Multimedia Database Management Systems: Research Issues and Future Directions.* Kluwer Academic Publishers, Boston, MA, 1997.

18. V. S. Subrahmanian. *Principles of Multimedia Database Systems.* Morgan Kaufmann, San Francisco, CA, 1998.

19. Y. Tanaka. IntelligentPad as meme media and its application to multimedia databases. *Information and Software Technology, 38:* 201–211, 1996.

20. N. Waters. POGS: Pads of geographic software. *GIS World, 8*(11): 82, 1995.

21. M. Lamming and M. Flynn. "Forget-me-not" intimate computing in support of human memory. In *Proceedings of FRIEND21 '94 International Symposium on Next Generation Human Interface.* 1994.

22. Tanaka, Y. A Toolkit system for the synthesis and the management of active media objects. In *Proceedings of of Deductive and Object-Oriented Databases*. pp. 76–94, 1989.

23. C. Faloutsos and S. Christodoulakis. Signature files: An access method for documents and its analytical performance evaluation. *ACM Transactions on Office Information Systems, 2*(4): 267–288, 1984.

24. S. Stiassny. Mathematical analysis of various superimposed coding methods. *American Documentation, 6:* 155–169, 1960.

# CHAPTER 11

# MEME POOL ARCHITECTURES

In order to make pads work as memes in a society, we need a publication repository of pads where people can publish composite pads, download published pads into their own local environment for their own use, recombine these downloaded pads with each other or with their own pads to compose new pads, and replicate these composed pads to publish them for other people's use. The more useful or more interesting pads are likely to be replicated more frequently and distributed more widely. Here we can see all the genetic operations necessary for genetic evolution, namely, replication, recombination, mutation, and natural selection. In this sense, this repository works as a meme pool of pads that work as meme media. In this chapter, we will propose several different architectures for the publication and reuse of pads through the Internet. These architectures provide different levels of pad publication facilities, ranging from a pad catalog on a Web page to a marketplace of pads. The former provides a catalog of pads in which a click of a pad picture leads to the download of the corresponding pad from a remote pad server. The latter provides a virtual marketplace where people can upload and download pads to and from the corresponding server through drag-and-drop operations. This chapter also shows how meme media technologies can be directly applied to Web content to make the Web work as a meme pool.

## 11.1 PAD PUBLICATION REPOSITORY AND THE WWW

The evolution rate of a meme pool depends on the frequency and the variety of memetic recombination, which are ruled by several factors. These factors include the number of people accessing this pool, how easy it is for them to recombine memes, and how often they encounter interesting memes. There are three corresponding ways to accelerate meme pool evolution. To increase the number of people accessing the pool, we need to establish a worldwide repository of memes, and to make it easy to access this repository. For the ease of meme recombination, we need to develop a user-friendly editing system for end-users to compose, decompose, and recombine memes. Finally, to increase the chance for people to encounter interesting memes, we need to develop a good browser or a good reference service system for people to search the repository of memes for what they are interested in.

The second requirement is fulfilled by the meme media architecture, but the first and the third require a worldwide repository of memes, a good browser, and/or a good reference service system to access this repository. In other words, we need to organize a marketplace where people can publish their achievements as pads, browse through all the pads published by other people, and reuse any of these pads for their own use in their own IntelligentPad environments. Pads as meme media require another medium that works as their marketplace.

In addition to the above-mentioned three ways of accelerating meme-pool evolution, we should not forget the fourth way, which is based on the hypothesis of "a punctuated equilibrium" [1] in population genetics. This was discussed in Section 2.1.2. This hypothesis can be interpreted in the context of memes as follows. For the acceleration of meme-pool evolution, it is not a good strategy to provide a single, monolithic large meme pool. Instead, it is better to provide a meme pool that enables people to dynamically develop smaller subpools for subcommunities, to cultivate a local culture in each of them, and to dynamically merge some of them. The WWW fits this strategy due to its nonmonolithic complex web structure.

To bring a punctuated equilibrium to the meme pool of pads, this marketplace needs to have a nonmonolithic complex structure such as the Web. Our IntelligentPad project set up the following four subgoals in 1993 to develop such marketplace systems. The first system uses the WWW and its browsers such as Netscape Navigator or Microsoft Internet Explorer. Although the WWW works as a worldwide pad repository, Netscape Navigator and Internet Explorer provide a hypermedia catalog of pads to navigate this repository. Each Web page describes various pads using texts and images. Pad names in textual descriptions and display-snapshot images of pads work as special anchors. A mouse click on one of these special anchors will pop up an IntelligentPad window with a real working copy of the requested pad. The original of this pad may be stored anywhere in the world. It is stored there using the exchange format representation. When the anchor is clicked, the browser issues a file transfer request to the HTTP server at this remote site. After a while, the local Web browser receives this file, and then invokes the IntelligentPad system to reconstruct the pad using its exchange format representation.

The second system provides a special pad called a URLAnchorPad. When mouse-clicked, a URLAnchorPad directly issues a URL (Universal Resource Locator) to the HTTP server to retrieve another composite pad from a remote site. A URLAnchorPad, when pasted on another pad, works as a link anchor in a hypermedia network spanned across the Internet.

The third system provides a new Web browser that basically works similarly to Netscape Navigator and Internet Explorer. This browser is also a pad called a HTMLViewerPad. It allows us to publish any composite pads by embedding them in arbitrary Web pages. You can publish any documents and tools as composite pads embedded in Web pages. You may even publish a database client tool on a Web page. Since a HTMLViewerPad is also a pad, you may embed a Web page in another Web page. Different from Java applets [2], embedded pads can be copied and locally reused. Different from ActiveX controls [3], embedded pads, after dragged out into a local environment from a Web page, can be decomposed and hence locally reused in recombination with other local pads, or even with those embedded in other Web pages. New pads thus composed in recombination of the original with local pads can be further redistributed through the Internet.

The fourth system integrates the accounting, billing, and payment mechanism with the preceding three different pad distribution systems; this will be discussed in the next chapter.

We developed all these system technologies between 1994 and 1998. In 1998, we developed another architecture for forming a marketplace, in which a large public space is provided for people to freely open their own stores. This system allows us to define a network of marketplaces where each marketplace allows us to upload and to download pads to and from the corresponding server through drag-and-drop operations.

These systems open up a new vista to a wide range of applications. Among those applications, we are especially interested in the publication, exchange, and reuse of scientific knowledge. Section 11.7 takes nuclear reaction physics as an example field, and shows how our system allows researchers in this field to publish both experimental data and analysis tools together with their related documents, to browse the resources published by others, to exchange them, and to reuse some of them.

## 11.2   PAD PUBLICATION AND PAD MIGRATION

IntelligentPad aims at the provision of social infrastructure for the distribution and exchange of various knowledge resources. To achieve this goal, we have to provide cross-platform reusability of pads. Pads should be transportable across different platforms and reusable in different environments. To achieve this cross-platform reusability, we have to solve two problems, i.e., how to migrate each pad from one IntelligentPad system to another, and how to cope with different platforms.

As explained in Section 4.5, there are three levels of object migration across different systems. The shallowest-level object migration assumes that the two systems share the same class library. In this case, the source system cannot send the destination any object whose class definition is not in the destination. The middle-level object migration assumes that the two systems share only the basic common portion of the class library. It is further assumed in this case that each object definition only inherits its property from those classes in the basic common class library, but not from any classes outside of the basic portion of the class library. In this case, the source system can send any object to the destination. The deepest-level object migration assumes no common class library. In this case, we have to migrate not only this object but also all the classes used in the definition of this object.

The Smalltalk 80 version IntelligentPad system supports the shallowest-level pad migration. It assumes that the source and the destination systems share the same class library of objects. Two systems may, however, have different pad libraries. To transport a pad from one system to another, the IntelligentPad system sends only the exchange format representation of this pad.

The four commercially available versions of IntelligentPad also support the shallowest-level pad migration across different platforms. They assume that the source and the destination systems share the same class library of objects. Furthermore, they allow the programming at the API (application program interface) level. The API library includes not only the pad manipulation functions for slot accesses and geometrical management of pads, but also the event dispatching and the display redrawing functions that are specially defined for user interaction with pads. Therefore, the source code definition of each pad can be transported across different systems for its reuse. We have developed two old versions among these four in cooperation with Fujitsu and Hitachi Software Engineering for two different platforms, Windows PC and Macintosh. These two old versions share the same API library and the same basic object class library. They are mutually cross-platform compatible systems. These two old versions, as well as the other two developed by Hitachi Software Engineering and K-Plex Inc., support the middle-level pad migration across different systems by transporting pads together with the required DLL definitions for them.

## 11.3 WEB PAGES AS PAD CATALOGS

The existing Web browsers such as Netscape Navigator and Internet Explorer allow us to publish multimedia documents throughout the world. They allow us to publish pad catalogs that show, for each pad, its features and hard copy image. The worldwide publication repository of pads can use this catalog publication function for its users to browse through pads published into this repository.

We assume that every site in the community of our concern installs an IntelligentPad system with the same class library. As shown in Figure 11.1, each Web page of a pad catalog describes various pads using texts and images. In addition to the ordinary functions of

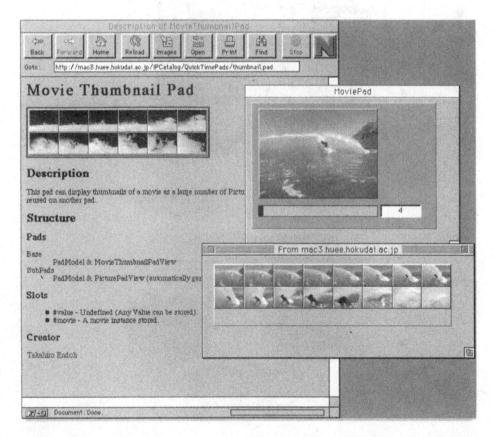

**Figure 11.1** A mouse click on the image of a movie thumbnail pad in this web page of a pad catalog has popped up a new window with its copy downloaded from a remote server. In this example, the downloaded movie thumbnail pad has been applied to a local movie pad to show its thumbnail.

Web pages, this catalog has the following extended functions. Pad names in textual descriptions and visual images of pads work as special anchors. A mouse click on one of these special anchors will pop up a new window with a copy of the requested pad. The original of this pad is stored in the destination file specified by the URL. This file may exist anywhere in the Internet. The pad is stored in this file using its exchange format representation. When the anchor is clicked, the Web browser issues a request to the Web server to transfer the destination file from a remote site. When the Web browser at the client site receives this file, it invokes a special file loader in the local IntelligentPad system to reconstruct the pad using its exchange format representation. This reconstruction does not differ from the pad reconstruction process necessary for the loading of a pad from a local file.

Such invocation requires a special mechanism to associate different types of anchors with different application programs (Figure 11.2). The existing Web browsers have this fa-

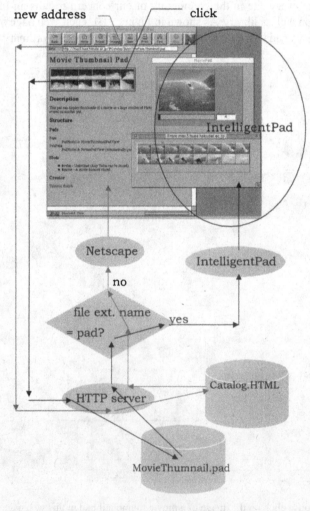

**Figure 11.2**   A special mechanism associates different types of anchors with different application programs to be invoked.

cility. To identify each type of anchor, they use the file name extension of the destination file. When registered to a Web browser, a file name extension works as an anchor type called a "mime" type. Each mime type can be associated with an application program.

Each pad catalog uses "pad" as the file name extension of pad files, and registers this extension to its Web browsers as their mime type to associate this type with an invocation of the special file loader in the IntelligentPad system. When invoked, this loader pops up a new IntelligentPad window with a reconstructed copy of the requested pad [4, 5].

The current version of IntelligentPad assumes that every site shares the same class library. This assumption requires periodic updating of the class library in each site. This update can be manually performed by accessing the on-line IntelligentPad system journal that is managed at a special site called the class-library-manager site. The WWW also simplifies this manual update procedure (Figure 11.3). You can just open the home page of the class-library-manager site and click the version-update button on this page. This anchor button specifies the URL of the system-update difference file. When clicked, this anchor fetches this file and invokes the system-update program. This invocation uses another file name extension "ip" as its mime type.

The WWW and its Web browsers also make it easy for end-users to publish pads into the worldwide repository (Figure 11.4). IntelligentPad provides a special pad called a

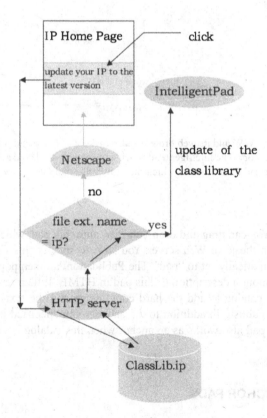

**Figure 11.3**  The WWW also simplifies the periodical manual update of the class library at each site.

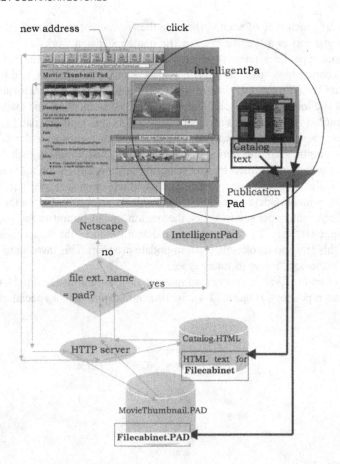

**Figure 11.4**   The WWW and its web browsers also make it easy for end-users to publish pads into the worldwide repository. The IntelligentPad provides a special pad called a PublicationPad. You can drag and dröp your pad onto this pad, which then saves this pad into a new file in the local WWW server.

PublicationPad. You can drag and drop your pad onto this pad, which then saves this pad into a new file in the local Web server. You have to specify this file name, whereas its extension is automatically set to "pad." The PublicationPad then pops up a text input pad and asks you to input a description of this pad in HTML. It then rewrites the HTML file storing your pad catalog to add the hard copy image and the textual description of the pad you want to publish. In addition to the anchors you specified in the description, the hard copy of the pad also works as an anchor when this catalog is viewed through a Web browser.

## 11.4   URL-ANCHOR PADS

Instead of using Web browsers, we can directly span hypermedia links among pads distributed across the Internet. As described in Section 9.3, anchors of links can be represented as pads. Section 9.3 assumes that nodes are all stored in local files, whereas Section 10.5 assumes some nodes are stored in a local database. Anchor pads described in Section 9.3 use file names to specify their destination pads; DB anchor pads described in Section 10.5 use pids (pad identifiers) for the destination specification. Here we consider the case in which nodes are distributed across the Internet. Each node is stored in a file located somewhere in the world. To specify such a file, we can use a URL. IntelligentPad provides a new anchor pad called a URLAnchorPad that specifies its destination pad using the URL of its file.

When mouse-clicked, a URLAnchorPad directly issues an URL to an HTTP server to retrieve a specified composite pad from a remote site. This resizable pad, when pasted on another pad, works as a link anchor in a hypermedia network spanned across the Internet. It can be made transparent and can be pasted at an arbitrary location on an arbitrary pad.

Figure 11.5 shows an application of a URLAnchorPad. It is a city guide of Sapporo for tourists. It shows a bird's-eye view movie of the city. Every sight-seeing spot appearing in this movie is covered by a transparent URLAnchorPad, which changes its size and location to trace this spot. This figure shows another pad showing a picture of the old prefec-

**Figure 11.5**  A city guide of Sapporo shows a bird's-eye view movie of the city. Every sight-seeing spot appearing in this movie is covered by a transparent URLAnchorPad, which changes its size and location to trace this spot.

tural government house. This pad was popped up by clicking on this government house in the movie.

Other typical applications of this pad are networked museum systems and networked libraries. A networked museum system provides remote users with various movies showing exhibition rooms and various exhibits. While you view a movie showing some exhibition room, you may click on any exhibit to retrieve its movie or its detailed description.

A networked library provides remote users with various multimedia documents. A networked library may use the HTMLViewerPad to publish multimedia documents with embedded URL anchors. It may use URLAnchorPads on any composite pads to retrieve HTMLViewerPads. Or it may publish Web pages with embedded pads.

## 11.5 HTMLVIEWERPAD WITH EMBEDDED ARBITRARY COMPOSITE PADS

In 1995, we developed a new Web browser as a pad. This pad is called an HTMLViewerPad. It basically works similarly to Netscape Navigator and Internet Explorer. It allows us to publish any composite pads by embedding them in arbitrary Web pages [Figure 11.6(a)] [6]. Our pad distribution system uses the exchange format representation to embed arbitrary composite pads into HTML text files. Each composite pad to be embedded is first stored in a file at an arbitrary site in the Internet using its exchange format representation. The file name extension of this file must be specified as "pad." Then a URL pointer to this file is embedded in an HTML text, and this text is published as a Web page. Figure 11.6(b) shows the HTML text for the Web page shown in Figure 11.6(a).

When an HTMLViewerPad accesses a Web page without any embedded pads, it works as a conventional browser such as Netscape Navigator and Internet Explorer. When an HTMLViewerPad accesses a Web page with some embedded pads, it treats each embedded pad as follows. When it receives the save format representation file of an embedded pad from a remote site, it first treats this pad as a blank figure of the same size. This figure makes a space of this size in the Web page. Then the HTMLViewerPad constructs the corresponding composite pad, and puts this pad in the saved space in the Web page. Any page scroll of this Web page also moves this pad on the HTMLViewerPad so that it always sits exactly in the space saved for this pad.

You can publish any documents and tools as composite pads embedded in Web pages. You may even publish HTMLViewerPads accessing different Web pages by embedding them in another Web page. You may also publish a database client tool on a Web page. Figure 11.6(a) shows a Web page with an embedded composite pad that works as a form interface to a remote database server. The site of this database server may be different from the Web page site. You can specify a query on this form interface to access this database [Figure 11.7(a)]. The retrieved picture of a car in this example is not a simple image. It is actually a composite pad whose exchange format representation is stored in the database as an attribute value. This composite pad has a transparent pad to cover the wheel cover portion of the underlying picture. This transparent pad works as a link anchor of a hypermedia spanned across the Internet, which was detailed in the previous section. When mouse-clicked, this pad will pop up another form interface to the same database, and allow you to retrieve all the choices for the wheel covers of this car [Figure 11.7(b)].

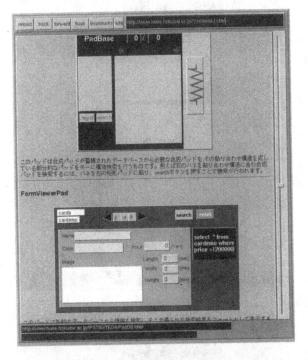

(a)

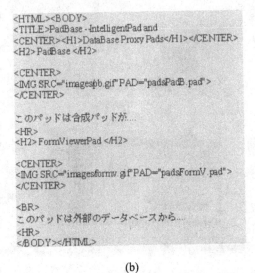

```
<HTML><BODY>
<TITLE>PadBase - IntelligentPad and
<CENTER><H1>DataBase Proxy Pads</H1></CENTER>
<H2> PadBase </H2>

<CENTER>
<IMG SRC="imagespb.gif" PAD="padsPadB.pad">
</CENTER>

このパッドは合成パッドが....
<HR>
<H2> FormViewerPad </H2>

<CENTER>
<IMG SRC="imagesformv.gif" PAD="padsFormV.pad">
</CENTER>

<BR>
このパッドは外部のデータベースから....
<HR>
</BODY></HTML>
```

(b)

**Figure 11.6** An HTMLViewerPad basically works similarly to Netscape Navigator, and allows us to publish any composite pads by embedding them in arbitrary Web pages. (a) An HTMLViewerPad showing a Web page with two embedded composite pads. (b) The HTML text defining the Web page shown in (a).

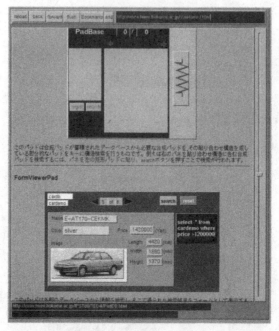

(a)

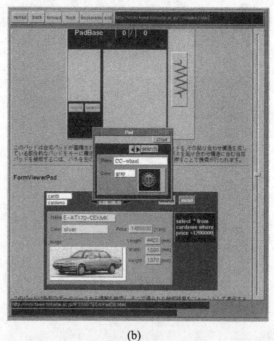

(b)

**Figure 11.7**   An access of a database through a database access tool embedded in a Web page. (a) A database accessed through an embedded form-interface pad. The retrieved picture of a car is actually a composite pad whose save-format representation is stored in the database as an attribute value. This composite pad has a transparent anchor pad to cover the wheel-cover portion of the underlying picture. (b) A mouse click on the anchor pad that covers the wheel-cover portion of the underlying picture pops up another form interface to the same database, and allows you to retrieve all the choices for the wheel covers of this car.

## 11.6 NEW PUBLICATION MEDIA

The HTMLViewerPad allows us to publish and acquire any objects as composite pads to and from Web servers. These servers form worldwide publication repositories. Objects to publish include multimedia documents, application programs working as interactive tools, client tools accessing remote servers, and client tools communicating with remote application programs.

When applied to scientific publications, this new publication repository allows us to publish scientific papers together with reusable related data, reusable related tools, and remotely accessible related database services by embedding all of them in the documents.

### 11.6.1   An Application to Scientific Publication

The Web page shown in Figure 11.8(a) was made in 1995 for Masaki Chiba, who is responsible for the charged particle nuclear reaction database in Japan. He stayed in our laboratory for one year and developed several database access tools as composite pads. This page shows a copy of his research paper reporting these tools. We have embedded his tool pads in his documents. The tool on the right-hand side of this page is just a display-snapshot image of his tool pad, whereas the left-hand one is an actual tool pad that is connected to a remote database server through the Internet. Chiba and Kiyoshi Kato are working on an extended system to introduce it to the international research society as a standard framework for the exchange, publication, and reuse of nuclear reaction data and their analysis tools.

The nuclear reaction database stores a collection of data sets. Each data set is defined as a data table from a series of nuclear reaction experiments. Data sets have attributes. Different data sets may have different sets of attributes. To store these data sets in a relational database, we have to represent each data set as a set of triples consisting of its data set ID, one of its attributes, and its value of this attribute. This set includes all the triples for all of its attributes. We used the UniSQL database management system [7] and defined on it a single relation with three attributes, i.e., data set ID, attribute name, and attribute value, to store all these triples for all the data sets.

Researchers in nuclear reaction physics use this database to pick up some set of data sets satisfying some condition of their attributes such as the reaction type, the incident particle, the target nucleus, etc. Then they analyze the picked-up data sets using some tools, or compare them with others.

The composite pad in Figure 11.8(a) allows you to access the remote nuclear reaction database through the Internet. It gives you the distribution of data sets with respect to two arbitrarily selected attributes [Figure 11.8(b)]. In this example, the X coordinate represents a set of different incident particles and the Y coordinate represents a set of different target nuclei. Each dot in this chart is actually a pad. We call it a data-set pad. You may click one of these data-set pads to show its detailed information, as shown in the display-snapshot image of this tool.

Researchers can easily select one of these data-set pads and retrieve its content from the same database using another tool pad. The HTMLViewerPad in Figure 11.9(a) shows another page of Ciba's research paper that includes this tool pad. You may drag and drop the selected data-set pad into this tool pad. This tool accesses the same remote database and retrieves its content as a pad [Figure 11.9(b)]. You may open one more different Web page to the right of this Web page [Figure 11.10(a)]. This new Web page shows another re-

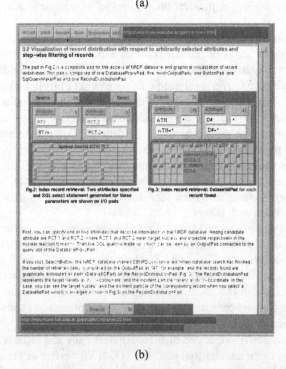

**Figure 11.8** An access tool for a nuclear-reaction database is published through the Internet together with a related research paper by embedding its pad representatioin in a Web page. (a) An access tool for a nuclear-reaction database is embedded in a research paper. (b) The database access tool in (a) gives you the distribution of data sets with respect to two arbitrarily selected attributes.

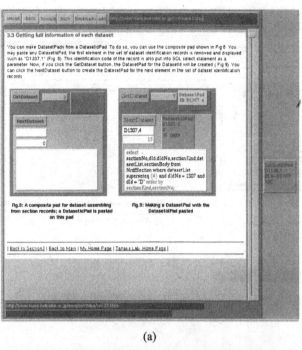

(a)

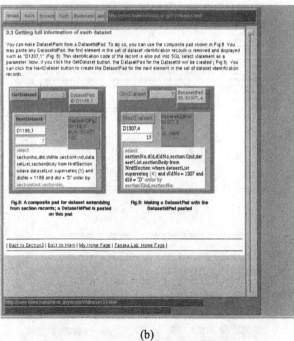

(b)

**Figure 11.9** The data set that has been selected by the tool in Figure 11.8 can be dropped on another tool embedded in a different Web page to retrieve its content from the same nuclear-reaction database. (a) Another page of the same research paper embeds another tool to retrieve the content of a selected data set from the same nuclear reaction database. (b) The retrieved contents of the selected data set is obtained as a gray pad.

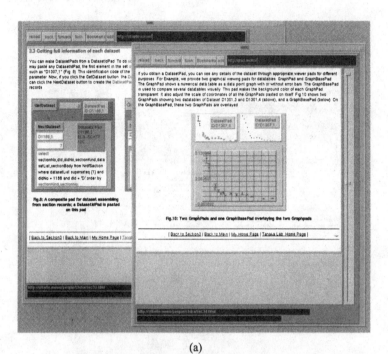

(a)

(b)

**Figure 11.10**   A transfer of data as a pad across different Web pages. (a) Another Web page with an embedded chart tool is opened. (b) A data-set content pad is dragged and dropped into the chart tool pad to show its data's angular distribution of the reaction cross-sections.

searcher's document that includes a chart-drawing tool pad. You may move the data-set content pad from Chiba's Web page to this chart tool in the different Web document to plot its content data [Figure 11.10(b)]. This chart shows an angular distribution of reaction cross-sections.

As shown in this example, our pad distribution architecture allows you to publish arbitrary composite pads as embedded components of Web pages. The HTMLViewerPad allows you to browse the worldwide repository of Web pages in your IntelligentPad environment, and to reuse any composite pads embedded in Web pages in your own environment of pads.

You may even open two Web pages side by side. They may be, for example, two different research papers published by different researchers in different countries. You may retrieve experimental data as a pad through a database client pad in one of them, and drag and drop it on a data analysis tool pad in the other research paper, or you may get two composite pads, one from each of the two papers, and recombine them to construct a new tool for your own use.

Different from Java applets [8] and ActiveX controls, embedded pads can be copied and locally reused in combination with other local pads. The recombination of media objects in the market with local pads is fundamental for them to work as meme media. Java and ActiveX inherently lack this function.

## 11.6.2   Publication and Reuse of Documents, Tools, Services, and Agents

The HTMLViewerPad allows us to publish and acquire any objects as composite pads to and from Web servers. These servers form a worldwide publication repository. Objects to be published include multimedia documents, application programs working as interactive tools, client tools accessing remote servers, and client tools communicating with remote application programs. The first and the second kind of objects may require no further explanation. The third kind of objects can be regarded as services. Remote servers provide these services. Their users can access these services through their client tools published as pads. An object of the fourth kind works as an agent. The person who published this agent provides an application program. The published pad that works as an agent works as a proxy of this application program. It communicates with this program through Web servers by using CGI commands. Such an agent pad, when its page is opened, requests its user for a reply, or for some operation on this agent pad. For example, it may ask the user to drag out itself and to drop itself on a specified local pad to acquire local information through this pad. The agent pad can send back this acquired information to its remote application program. It may even be able to delete itself when its mission is completed.

Service publication can even publish computer-controlled hardware facilities. Suppose that your institute has a fully computer-controlled material-synthesizer system with various measurement tools to analyze synthesized materials. Its synthesis process is fully controlled by a computer through a large number of parameters. Its measurement tools are also fully controlled by the same computer through their parameters, and the measured results are monitored by the same computer. If you develop proxy pads to communicate with the control and monitor programs of this system and its measurement tools, you can compose console panels for these facilities as composite pads, and publish them by embedding them in your Web pages. This allows people all over the world to utilize your facilities, and allows material scientists to use various public facilities distributed all over the world one after another to conduct their research projects. A researcher in Singapore may synthesize a new material using a facility in the United States, measure their characteristics, and then analyze the measured data on a supercomputer installed in Japan. The measurement data are also transported as a pad from one site to another site, from one Web page to another Web page, or to a local environment. Researchers may even pick up some components of these published facilities, recombine them to compose new facilities for their use, and publish these new tools for their reuse by others.

## 11.7   ANNOTATION ON WEB PAGES

The publication and the reuse of various knowledge resources through the WWW will lead to the encounter of a huge number of knowledge resources everyday. We may forget most of them. However, some of them may become significantly important for our future activities. In our everyday book reading, we annotate some pages with comments and marks. Some of these annotations help us to get a summary when we read the same page again. Some others, especially marks, help us to find some information by skimming the book. Other annotations provide references and comments for our second reading. Among various tools for the personal management of knowledge resources, annotation tools are no doubt among the most useful.

Some annotation tools are already proposed for electronic publishing over the Web. ComMentor allowed readers to add and share annotations on character strings in HTML Web pages [9, 10]. An inserted, customizable, character-sized icon acts as both an annotation cue and a link to the annotation text. Annotation content can be shown either as a separate page, in which case links or further annotations can be included and activated, or in context as a temporary pop-up window when the middle mouse button is depressed. DLS provided open hypermedia links on HTML Web pages [11, 12]. To distinguish between inserted and original links, DLS offered a form for the user to select how added links should be presented in a document. The Webvise system [13] and the related Arakne Environment [14] included the possibility for collaborative annotations on character strings as well as new links directly in an HTML Web page. Microsoft Office Web Discussion [15] allows readers to add shared comment to selected paragraphs chosen by the author or an entire HTML document on the Web. Readers use a small cue icon inserted at the end of an annotated paragraph to expand or collapse its annotations in context within the page, pushing later paragraphs downward. Multiple annotations can be expanded at once for comparison. Readers cannot insert links in an annotation or in the body of the document. iMarkup is a commercial Internet Explorer plug-in that allows readers to share annotations with widely varying appearances to HTML Web pages [16]. Handwritten strokes and Post-it®-like notes of many styles can be overlaid on the page and can be shrunk to minimize occlusion. Character strings can also be highlighted and given hidden textual annotations to be shown later in a pop-up ToolTip window. WEBTOUR [17] allows readers to create active tours through HTML Web pages that include dynamic mouse gestures, handwriting, and synchronized audio or video playback, and link traversals among pages. BrowseUp developed an annotation server and a new browser that allow us to select any portion of any Web page, and to make an annotation on it in a public and/or local file. BrowseUp allows us to use legacy document systems like Word and Excel to make local annotation files.

Most of them, however, do not allow us to overlay annotations directly on original pages. Digital technology potentially allows us to overlay a transparent or translucent sheet for annotation on the original text, which may protect both the original text and its appearance from any damage. In the IntelligentPad system architecture, the development of such a transparent or translucent pad for annotation is an easy task.

Figure 11.11 shows a Web annotator composed with an IEPad and a WebAnnotation-Pad. An IEPad is a pad that is obtained by wrapping Internet Explorer with a pad wrapper. It has a #URLaddress slot to hold the URL of the current page. A WebAnnotationPad has a double-layered structure with its base layer and its surface layer. It has three URL slots, #originalURLaddress slot (which works as the primary slot), #annotationURLaddress slot, and #associationURL slot that respectively hold the original page's URL address, the URL of the current annotation file, and the URL address of a URL conversion service converting each original page's URL to the URL of the corresponding annotation file. A WebAnnotationPad has three different operation modes: the transparent mode, the translucent mode, and the hiding mode. The surface layer works as a transparent or translucent film covering the base layer and its child pads, if any. In its transparent mode, a WebAnnotationPad makes its surface layer inactive and the background of this layer transparent only show what is drawn or pasted on this layer. Every user event, including pad pasting events, passes through the surface layer. You may use this mode to paste an IEPad directly on the base layer of a WebAnnotationPad with its connection to #originalURLaddress slot; this IEPad is inserted between the base layer and the surface layer. In its translucent mode, a WebAnnotationPad makes its surface layer active, and the background of this layer translucent. Only those user events that are not processed by this layer pass through the surface layer. In its hiding mode, a WebAnnotationPad makes its sur-

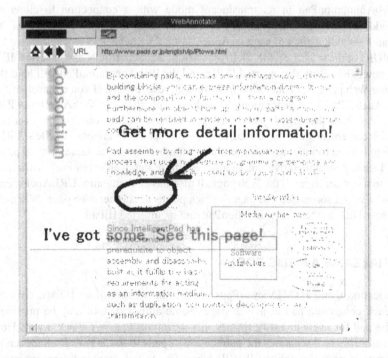

**Figure 11.11**   A WebAnnotatorPad with an inserted IEPad, an annotative anchor pad, and an annotative drawing.

face layer, together with all the child pads of this layer, inactive and invisible; every user event passes through the surface layer.

In its translucent mode, a WebAnnotationPad allows you to paste any pad on its surface layer. The pasted pad works as a child pad of the surface layer. Any pad pasted on a WebAnnotationPad in its transparent or hiding mode becomes a child of the topmost pad at this location under the surface layer. The surface layer also works as a drawing tool. This function allows you to draw any figures as annotations to the Web page shown by the inserted IEPad. When an inserted IEPad scrolls its page, the WebAnnotationPad also scrolls its surface layer for the same distance so that every child pad and every figure on the surface layer keep their original relative locations on the Web page shown by the inserted IEPad.

Each WebAnnotationPad has its associated local or remote file specified by the URL address stored in #annotationURLaddress slot, and allows you to save its annotation information there, including its child pads and annotation figures, together with the URL of the Web page shown by the inserted IEPad. Each WebAnnotationPad has another slot #register for an external event to make it save its current state to its file. When we change the URL of the inserted IEPad, this new URL is informed by this IEPad to the base layer of the WebAnnotationPad through #originalURLaddress. Then the WebAnnotationPad accesses the URL conversion service specified by #associationURL slot with the value of #originalURLaddress slot, sets the returned address, if any, in the #annotationURLaddress slot, and accesses this address to obtain the current annotations on this original page.

A reference to any object as an annotation may use an AnnotationURLAnchorPad with the URL of this object. You may paste such an AnnotationURLAnchorPad at any location on a WebAnnotationPad in its translucent mode with a connection to either #originalURLaddress slot or #associationURLaddress slot. For the selection of #originalURLaddress slot, a click of such an AnnotationURLAnchorPad sets its content URL to #originalURLaddress slot of the WebAnnotationPad, which tells the inserted IEPad to read the new URL. Both the inserted IEPad and the WebAnnotationPad will load the corresponding Web page and annotation information, respectively. If you connect an AnnotationURLAnchorPad to #associationURLaddress slot, then the WebAnnotationPad uses the URL sent from the anchor pad to access a different URL conversion server for converting the current original page's URL to a corresponding annotation file's URL. This mechanism is used to jump to a different user's annotation on the same original page. Figure 11.11 shows an annotative comment "Get more detail information!" with an arrow pointing to a system name in the Web page. It also has an AnnotationURLAnchorPad with a caption "I've got some. See this page," which points to another Web page. When clicked, it sets a new URL to the WebAnnotationPad and its inserted IEPad.

## 11.8 PIAZZA AS A MEME POOL

Pad publication using HTMLViewerPads require the writing of an HTML definition to embed each composite pad in a Web page. Some authoring tool may be provided as a composite pad for users to easily specify this definition in a WYSIWYG way. However, such an authoring tool separates the publication of pads to the WWW from the navigation and retrieval of pads through the WWW. Users like to use drag-and-drop operations not only to retrieve pads from the WWW but also to publish pads to the WWW. They like to use a modeless browser to perform both the retrieval and publication seamlessly without changing the system mode.

Furthermore, the HTMLViewerPad as well as other currently available Web browsers does not allow a user to publish his or her own information in another's Web pages, nor to span any links from another's Web pages to his or her own Web pages. There is no way to do so. Each user has to ask the owner of the Web page by sending, say, an e-mail to include his or her own information there or to span a link from this page to his or her own Web page. This relation between users who want to publish their information and the owners of Web pages is similar to the relation between tenants and owners. Each tenant is required to make a contract with the owner of the building in which he or she wants to open his or her store. Although the owner–tenant system works well by allowing owners to supervise the clustering of similar information content, there is another way of forming a marketplace, in which a large public space is provided for people to freely open their stores. We would like to provide this kind of worldwide publishing repository of pads in which people can freely publish their pads for others to freely reuse them.

"Piazza Web" is a world-wide web of marketplaces, or piazzas, each of which works as such a marketplace [19]. We can browse through Piazza Web, using a PiazzaBrowserPad as shown in Figure 11.12. Each piazza has a corresponding file that stores a set of pads together with their geometrical arrangement. Such files are stored in special remote servers called piazza servers. Each piazza is also represented as a pad called a PiazzaPad. Pads can be dragged and dropped to and from a PiazzaPad to upload and download pads to and from the associated remote server file. When a PiazzaPad is opened, all the pads registered to the associated server file are immediately downloaded onto this pad, arranged in their registered locations, and made available. A PiazzaPad has a slot to specify a piazza server with its URL address. When given an update message, a PiazzaPad saves all the pads on itself with their current states and current locations into the corresponding server. When given a new URL address, a PiazzaBrowserPad either generates a new PiazzaPad

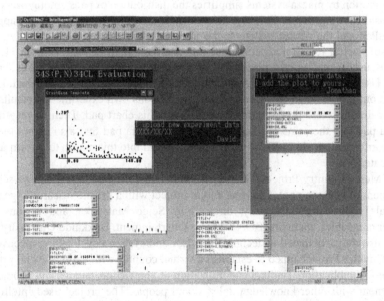

**Figure 11.12**  International distribution and reuse of nuclear reaction data and analysis tools by using a PiazzaBrowserPad at the left top corner.

on itself or uses the old PiazzaPad, depending on its specified mode, and sets this URL address to the file address slot of the PiazzaPad to download the registered pads. An entrance link to a piazza is represented by an AnnotationAnchorPad, and can be put on another piazza to define a link, with its connection to the file address slot of the PiazzaPad. When clicked, the AnnotationAnchorPad sends its stored URL address to the file address slot of the underlying PiazzaBrowserPad, which then opens this piazza. A PiazzaBrowserPad has a save slot, which, when accessed by a set message from, say, a buttonPad connected to this slot, sends an update message to its child PiazzaPad to make it save its child pads to the server. Users are welcome to install their piazza servers anywhere, anytime, and to publish their client pads. A piazza enables end-users to open their own gallery of pads on the Internet, or to exhibit their pads in some other private or public space. Such pad galleries work as flea markets, shops, shopping centers, community message boards, community halls, or plazas. Some piazzas may be for personal use, whereas some others may be shared by communities. Some piazzas may be shared by more than one community, whereas some others may be open to the public.

Transportation of pads undefined at their destination requires their cross-platform migration; their execution on the destination platform requires that all the libraries necessary for their execution be available there in advance. These libraries include pad definition libraries, API libraries, and class libraries. These are defined as DLLs (dynamic link libraries), and dynamically called on when required. Migration of a new pad to a different platform requires migration of all the required DLLs that the destination lacks. Pads that someone has uploaded to a PiazzaPad can be downloaded from the same PiazzaPad and executed if and only if the destination platform has all the required DLLs. Each PiazzaPad allows privileged users to upload a new pad together with its required DLLs. When another user opens this PiazzaPad, it checks to see if the destination platform has all the required DLLs. If it does, this user can drag this pad out of the PiazzaPad. If it does not, the PiazzaPad asks the user if he or she wants to download the missing DLLs. Only after the required downloading, he or she can drag this pad out of this PiazzaPad. The automatic DLL migration by piazza systems simplifies the distribution of pads among users.

Kiyoshi Kato's group at Graduate School of Physics, Hokkaido University, applied IntelligentPad and the piazza system to the international availability, distribution, and exchange of nuclear reaction experimental data and their analysis tools (Figure 11.12). For example, user A may open a piazza and drag and drop a chart showing his experimental results. User B later accesses the same piazza to see what user A has published. He drags this pad out into his own environment, and overlays his own experimental results on this chart by dragging and dropping his data pad onto this chart pad. Then he may drag this updated pad into the same piazza together with the data pad that also shows the bibliographic information. He may also drop a message pad into this piazza to inform user A of this update.

The Meme Country Project that started in late 1999 became the first large-scale field experiment of a meme pool. This was a joint project with a private research organization, Editorial Engineering Laboratory, directed by Seigo Matsuoka, and various content provider companies, including SONY Music Entertainment. Hokkaido University and Hitachi Software participated as technical advisor and system developer, respectively. The Meme Country Project aimed to establish a virtual country with various social infrastructures for the publication, finding, and utilization of knowledge, talents, and people, and to match them with other knowledge, talents, and people. The project used IntelligentPad technologies both for the construction of its infrastructures and for the representation of knowledge, talents, and people in this virtual country. During this one-year experiment, more than 1500 people accessed the system to attend courses such as rhetoric, industrial design, comics, animation, and Japanese poetry. Participants in each course were initially all nonprofessionals. More than a hundred of them were very active, and about 20 of them improved themselves to the professional level. Among them, five people received job offers. EEL's report says that meme media and meme pool technologies worked more effectively in finding new talent over the Internet than expected. Editorial Engineering Laboratory is now enhancing the functionality of this system, and will start a new business service based on the revised Meme Country system.

In 1999, IPC (IntelligentPad Consortium) started a new project, "Hijiri," which works as a community education tool to encourage people not only to learn their community culture but also to add new information about their own culture. This project is supported by the Sapporo City Government and will be initially widely used at elementary schools in Sapporo. This system basically uses the piazza system together with the same system framework used by "Miyako" system, which will be described in Subsection 17.5.4. All the multimedia contents are stored and managed by relational database management systems. It provides not only the same quality of presentation as those multimedia presentations using Macromind Director, but also full interactivity so that users can navigate through any path. The front-end interface of the system uses IntelligentPad to provide an interactive interface to the multimedia database content. Each jump from one presentation stage to another is specified by a query to the back end relational database. Its evaluation retrieves all the content necessary to construct the target presentation stage, including not only archived multimedia content, but also both functional components such as hyperlink anchor buttons and composition structures among these components. IPC extended Miyako's framework to allow users to add new information to databases through drag-and-drop operations on the front-end system. Furthermore, we put the different presentation stages of the front-end system on different piazzas to allow people to share the different stages of the Hijiri environment over the Internet. Users at different sites can access the whole contents of Hijiri through the Miyako-like interface, and add new content to the system through drag-and-drop operations. IPC completed the Hijiri Project in the spring of 2002. Sapporo City has already used prototype versions of Hijiri for social studies in some elementary and junior high schools. Students collect multimedia information about their community areas through interviews and legwork, make their pad representations, and place these pads at appropriate locations on the area maps drawn over different piazzas.

## 11.9 REEDITING AND REDISTRIBUTING WEB CONTENT AS MEME MEDIA OBJECTS

Meme media and meme pool architectures will play important roles when they are applied to a reasonably large accumulation of intellectual resources. The current situation of the Web satisfies this condition. This section focuses on how to convert the intellectual resources on the Web to meme media objects, whereas the preceding sections in this chapter focused on how to convert Web technologies to implement meme pools for the intellectual resources represented as pads. In the latter approach, we cannot deal with legacy Web content objects as memes, i.e., as reeditable and redistributable objects. In the former approach, on the other hand, we can extract any components of Web pages, including multimedia, application tool, and/or service components, recombine them to define a new layout and a new composite function, and publish the result as a new Web page.

### 11.9.1   Web Content as Memes

Research topics of science and technology are becoming more diversified and segmented into more and more categories. The number of interdisciplinary research topics has also increased. With increasingly sophisticated research in science and technology, there is a growing need for interdisciplinary and international availability, distribution, and exchange of the latest research results, in reeditable and redistributable organic forms, including not only research papers and multimedia documents, but also various tools developed for measurement, analysis, inference, design, planning, simulation, and production. Similar needs are also growing for the interdisciplinary and international availability, distribution, and exchange of ideas and works among artists, musicians, designers, architects, directors, and producers. This content, including multimedia documents, application tools, and services, is being accumulated on the Web at a remarkable speed that we have never experienced with other kinds of publishing media. Large amounts of content are now already on the Web, waiting for their advanced reuse and reediting, including the recombination of their components for new layouts and new composite functions.

Current Web technologies provide a worldwide publication repository for people to publish their multimedia documents in HTML, to navigate through those published by other people, and to browse any of them. You may embed any tools or services in your published HTML document. To define such services, you may set up servers such as database servers, file servers, and application servers. Although the current Web technologies have allowed us to browse the huge accumulation of intellectual resources published on the Web, we have no good tools yet to flexibly reedit and redistribute these intellectual resources for their reuse in different contexts. We need OHS (open hypertext system) technologies for the advanced reuse of Web-published intellectual resources. Meme media and meme pool technologies will work as such OHS technologies to annotate Web-published resources, and to reedit and redistribute some portions of their copies with embedded tools and services, without changing their originals, for their reuse in different contexts together with different applications.

In this section, we apply our two-dimensional meme media technologies for the reediting and redistribution of content in Web pages. This Web content includes live content objects and Web applications. A live content object denotes a content object that autonomously changes its states. You may also embed an IntelligentBox environment with composite boxes in a HTML document to publish in the Web. Such IntelligentBox environments also become components of Web documents. Meme media technologies allow us to reedit and to redistribute live content objects and Web applications as well as static multimedia content objects. Users need not edit HTML definitions of Web documents. They can easily extract any document components through drag-and-drop operations, and paste them together on the screen to define both the layout and the functional linkages among them. Web content extracted from Web documents will become reeditable and redistributable objects when wrapped with pad wrappers. You may send reedited Web content across the Internet by attaching it to an e-mail. Recipients with IntelligentPad installed in their platforms can reuse, further reedit, and redistribute this Web content. Our framework also provides for the flattening of pads to HTML documents, which allows you to publish reedited Web content as new Web pages.

Meme media technologies, when applied to Web content, also open new vistas in the circulation and reuse of scientific knowledge. In bioinformatics, for example, there are already many different kinds of database services, analysis services, and related reference information services; most of them are available as Web applications. However, they are serviced by independent groups and are hard to interoperate with each other. Therefore, even gene annotations with information available from some public service requires either manual operations or a program code to automate them. Meme media technologies enable researchers in this field to dynamically extract and combine public services, such as homology search of gene databases and other related information services, and to make them interoperate with each other.

### 11.9.2   Application of Meme Media Technologies to Web Content

Current Web technologies do not fully allow you to arbitrarily reedit and redistribute published documents with embedded services. You may select any textual or image portion of a Web page by mouse operation to make its copy, and paste this copy in your local document, for example, in the MS Word format. However, you cannot extract arbitrary portions of Web pages and combine them together to compose a new document. If a portion to be extracted from a Web page has dynamic content that may change values whenever the page is refreshed or accessed, we would like to keep its copy alive by periodically updating its content. Such a copy is called a live copy, whereas a copy whose value is frozen at the time it is created is called a dead copy. We call such dynamic content live content. Examples of live content include stock prices in stock market information pages and the space-station location information published in the International Space Station home page.

The reediting of Web content requires the following capabilities:

1. Easy extraction of an arbitrary Web-document portion together with its style
2. Keeping live content objects alive after arbitrary reediting
3. Easy reediting of Web content objects that may be extracted from different Web pages by combining them to define both a new layout and a new functional composition.

Web content objects may include not only multimedia content, but also live content and/or Web applications. A Web application denotes a client man–machine interface that accesses an HTTP server from a Web page.

In addition to these, the redistribution of reedited Web documents requires

4. Easy redistribution of reedited Web content across the Internet.

The publication of reedited Web content as a new Web page further requires

5. Easy conversion of reedited Web content to HTML format
6. Easy registration of an HTML document to an HTTP server

Here, we will propose the use of meme media technologies to achieve the first four of the above capabilities. Meme media technologies provide the following capabilities:

a. The wrapping of an arbitrary object with a standard visual wrapper to define a media object having a two-dimensional representation on a display screen. A wrapped object may be a multimedia document, an application program, or any combination of them.

b. The reediting of meme-media objects. You can visually combine a meme-media object with another meme media object on the display screen by mouse operations, and define a functional linkage between them. You may take out any component meme media object from a composite meme media object.

c. The redistribution of meme media objects. Meme media objects are persistent objects that you can send and receive for their reuse, for example, by e-mail across the Internet.

Here we use IntelligentPad technologies to achieve the first four of the abovementioned six capabilities. Now our goal can be paraphrased as follows:

i. How to extract any portion of a Web document and to wrap it with a pad wrapper with some slot definitions

ii. How to incorporate periodic server-access capabilities in the wrapping of live Web content

Once we have solved problem (i), IntelligentPad will give solutions both to the easy reediting of Web content objects together with their functional linkages, and to the easy redistribution of reedited Web content objects across the Internet. The publication of reedited Web content objects as new Web documents further requires solving the following problem:

iii. How to convert a composite pad to an HTML document and to register this to an HTTP server

We call such a conversion a flattening operation.

### 11.9.3   Related Research

Some user-customizable portal sites such as MyYahoo provide another way to personalize Web pages. If you have a priori registered your interests, the system will customize the Web page only to show what you are interested in. Such a system allows you to customize only limited portions of Web documents in a restricted way. Furthermore, such a service allows you to access only those documents it manages.

HTML4.01 provides a special HTML tag <iframe>, or inline frame, that allows us to embed an arbitrary Web document in a target Web page. However, it does not allow us to directly specify either a Web document portion to be extracted or a location in the target document at which to insert the extracted document. We need to edit HTML definitions.

Turquoise [20] and Internet Scrapbook [21] adopt programming-by-demonstration technologies to support the reediting of Web documents. You may change the layout of a Web page on the screen to define a customized one, and apply the same editing rule whenever the Web page is accessed for refreshing. They enable us to change layouts, but not extract any components or to functionally connect them together. Transpublishing [22] allows us to embed Web documents in a Web page. It also offers license management and charge accounting technologies. The embedding uses a special HTML tag to embed a document.

Example tools for extracting a document component from a Web document include W4F [23], DEByE [24], and WbyE [25]. W4F provides a GUI support tool to define an extraction. Users, however, still need to write some script programs. The system creates a wrapper class written in Java from user's manipulations. To use this wrapper class, users need to write program codes. DEByE provides a more powerful GUI support tool. However, it outputs the extracted document components in XML format. Its reuse requires some knowledge on XML. WbyE is an extention of DEByE. These systems, however, do not provide any tools for the user to visually combine two wrapped Web application and to compose a single tool with an integrated function. There are also several research studies about recording and playing a macro operation on a Web browser. Such approach also requires users to have expertise to customize recorded operation sequences described in some language.

As detailed in Section 3.4, hypermedia research groups have mainly focused their efforts on the linking services among intellectual resources for the navigation and interoperability among them. They basically assumed that hypermedia content was just viewed without making copies, reediting, or redistributing them among people. Over the last seven years, the Open Hypermedia Working Group (OHSWG) has been working on a standard protocol to allow interoperability across a range of application software components. The OHSWG approach was basically based on the separation of link services and the standardization of a navigational and/or functional linking protocol among different applications and services. The standard protocol may rely on either API libraries or an on-the-wire communication model using such a standard transport medium as a socket.

Meme media research that has been conducted independently from the open hypertext community has been focused on the replication, reediting, and redistribution of intellectual resources. To achieve this goal, our group adopted a visual wrapper architecture. Any component, whether it is an application or a service, small or large, is wrapped by a visual wrapper with direct manipulability and a standard interface mechanism. Application of meme media technologies to OHS technologies simply means that objects in the latter framework are wrapped by meme media wrappers, which will introduce meme media features to those objects without loosing any of their OHS features.

During the last several years, we saw significant progress in Web technologies, including client-side scripting technologies, server-side scripting technologies, and Web service technologies. These Web technologies are tools for Web page designers to compose a complicated application by simply combining public Web services and making the composed service available on a Web page. Web page designers have to write HTML definitions accessing Web services through SOAP proxies. These tools are definitely not for Web readers. Application of meme media technologies to Web technologies will allow Web readers to extract any components of any Web pages, to paste these extracted pads together to combine their functions, to embed the composed pad in another Web page, and to publish this page not only for their private use but also for others' use.

### 11.9.4  XML and Pads

The conversion of Web document components to pads requires a way to represent HTML or XHTML documents as pads. Although the HTMLviewerPad can represent any HTML document as a pad, we still need a way to make any HTML component of such a pad work as a slot. The value of such a slot is the value of the corresponding HTML component.

The display object and the model object of a primitive pad are usually defined in C++ code, which makes it difficult for nonprogrammers to develop a new pad. Some pads have very simple internal mechanisms that require no coding. These include multimedia documents with some parameters exported through their pad slots. For the definition of such a document, we may use XHTML or a pairing of XML and XSL to define its content and style, which requires no programming expertise. You may specify any of its phrases enclosed by a begin-tag and an end-tag to work as a slot value [26]. An IEPad, a special HTMLviewerPad, when provided with document content in XML and a style in XSL, generates the corresponding XHTML text to view on itself. It also generates a slot for each specified phrase in the original XML or XSL texts. For the development of an IEPad, we wrapped Microsoft Internet Explorer with a pad wrapper and provided it with slot-definition capability.

Figure 11.13 shows a parameterized XHTML that displays any text string in the specified orientation. Two parameters are parenthesized with tags to specify that they work as slots. Figure 11.14 shows its viewing by an IEPad, which has two child pads: one used to input a string and the other to specify the angle. In addition to these functions, an IEPad allows us to embed any composite pad in an XHTML text using a special tag, and gener-

```xml
<?xml version="1.0" ?>
<html xmlns="http://www.w3.org/1999/xhtml" xml:lang="en" lang="en"
    xmlns:ip="http://ca.meme.hokudai.ac.jp/IntelligentPad">
  <head>
      <title>IEPad example</title>
      <script language="VBScript">
          <![CDATA[
          Sub func_caption(caption)
                  lblActiveLbl.Caption = caption
          End Sub

          Sub func_angle(angle)
                  lblActiveLbl.Angle = angle
          End Sub
      ]]>
      </script>
      <ip:slotlist>
          <ip:slot name="caption" func="func_caption">Meme Media Lab.</ip:slot>
          <ip:slot name="angle" func="func_angle">90</ip:slot>
      </ip:slotlist>
  </head>
  <body>
      <h2>This is an IEPad viewing a XHTML text that defines two slots and embeds one
          composite pad.</h2>
      <object classid="clsid:99B42120-6EC7-11CF-A6C7-00AA00A47DD2" id="lblActiveLbl"
          width="250" height="250">
          <param name="FontSize" value="20" />
          <param name="angle" value="90" />
          <param name="caption" value="Meme Media Lab." />
      </object>
      <object id="ipclock" classid="clsid:7D4FE1B3-05AC-463C-A30D-930194AA4D58" />
  </body>
</html>
```

**Figure 11.13** An XHTML text defining two slots and one embedded pad.

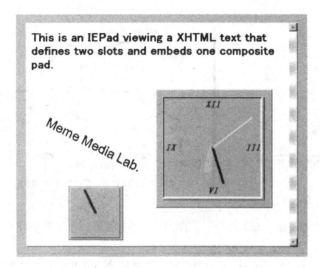

**Figure 11.14**   The viewing of the parameterized XHTML text in Figure 11.13.

ates this pad on itself when viewing this XHTML text. The XHTML text in Figure 11.13 embeds a composite pad working as an analog clock, whereas Figure 11.14 shows the composite analog clock pad embedded in the document viewed by an IEPad.

### 11.9.5   Extraction of Arbitrary Web Content as Two-Dimensional Meme Media Objects

Web documents are defined in HTML format. An HTML view denotes an arbitrary HTML document portion represented in the HTML document format. The pad wrapper to wrap an arbitrary portion of a Web document needs to be capable of both specifying an arbitrary HTML view and rendering any HTML document. We call this pad wrapper an HTMLviewPad; it is different from the HTMLviewerPad discussed in Section 11.5. Its rendering function is implemented by wrapping a legacy Web browser such as Netscape Navigator or Internet Explorer. In our implementation, we wrapped Internet Explorer. The specification of an arbitrary HTML view over a given HTML document requires the capability of editing the internal representation of HTML documents, namely, DOM trees. The DOM tree representation allows you to identify any HTML-document portion, which corresponds to a DOM tree node, with its path expression. Figure 11.15 shows an HTML document with its DOM tree representation. The highlighted portion in the document corresponds to the highlighted node whose path expression is /HTML[0]/BODY[0]/TABLE[0]/TR[1]/TD[1]. A path expression is a concatenation of node identifiers along a path from the root to the specified node. Each node identifier consists of a node name, i.e., the tag given to this node element, and the number of its sibling nodes located to the left of this node.

Sometimes you may need to specify, among sibling nodes, a node with a specific character string as a substring of its textual content. You may specify such a node as tag-name[MatchingPattern:index], where MatchingPattern is the specified string, and index selects one node among those siblings satisfying the condition.

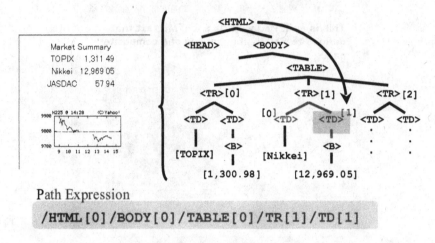

Path Expression

`/HTML[0]/BODY[0]/TABLE[0]/TR[1]/TD[1]`

**Figure 11.15** An HTML document with its DOM tree and a path expression.

You may need to extract some character string in a text node. Its path expression locates this node, but does not locate such a substring. We will extend the path expression to use a regular expression for locating such a substring in a text node. For the DOM tree in Figure 11.16(a), the node /HTML[0]/BODY[0]/P/txt(.* (\d\d:\d\d).*) specifies the virtual node shown in Figure 11.16(b).

The definition of an HTML view consists of the specification of the source document and a sequence of view editing operations. The specification of a source document uses its URL. Its retrieval is performed by the function "getHTML" in such a way as

doc = getHTML("http://www.abc.com/index.html", null)

The second parameter will be used to specify a request to the Web server at the retrieval time. Such requests include POST and GET. The retrieved document is kept in DOM format. The editing of an HTML view is a sequence of DOM tree manipulation operations selected from the following:

1. EXTRACT: Delete all the nodes other than the subtree with the specified node as its root [Figure 11.17(a)].
2. REMOVE: Delete the subtree with the specified node as its root [Figure 11.17(b)].
3. INSERT: Insert a given DOM tree at the specified relative location of the specified node [Figure 11.17(c)]. You may select the relative location out of CHILD, PARENT, BEFORE, and AFTER (Figure 11.18).

An HTML view is specified as follows:

defined-view = source-view.DOM-tree-operation(node)

where source-view may be a Web document or another HTML document, and node is specified by its extended path expression. The following is an example view definition with the nested use of the above syntax:

```
view1 = doc
    .EXTRACT("/HTML/BODY/TABLE[0]/")
    .EXTRACT("/TABLE[0]/TR[0]/")
    .REMOVE("/TR[0]/TD[1]/");
```

You may also specify two subtrees extracted either from the same Web document or from different Web documents, and combine them to define a view:

```
doc = getHTML("http://www.abc.com/index.html", null);
view2 = doc
    .EXTRACT("/HTML/BODY/TABLE[0]/")
    .EXTRACT("/TABLE[0]/TR[0]/");
```

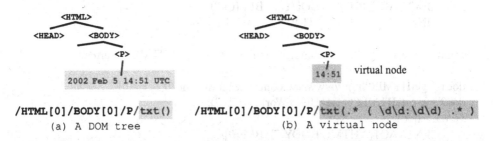

**Figure 11.16** A DOM tree and the path expression of a virtual node.

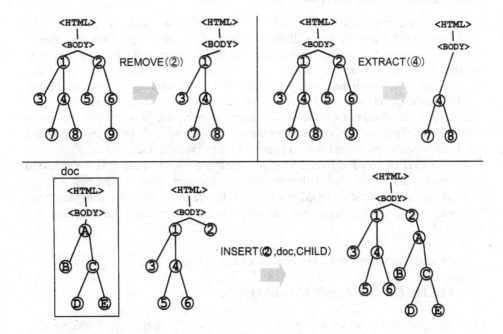

**Figure 11.17** REMOVE, EXTRACT, and INSERT operations on DOM trees.

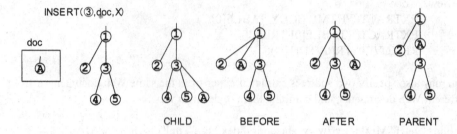

INSERT(③,doc,X)

CHILD          BEFORE          AFTER          PARENT

**Figure 11.18**   Different insertion locations.

```
view1 = doc
     .EXTRACT("/HTML/BODY/TABLE[0]/")
     .INSERT("/TABLE[0]/TR[0]/", view2, BEFORE);
```

You may create a new HTML document and insert it into an HTML document:

```
doc1 = getHTML("http://www.abc.com/index.html", null);
doc2 = createHTML("<TR>Hello World</TR>");
view1 = doc1
     .EXTRACT("/HTML/BODY/TABLE[0]/")
     .INSERT("/TABLE[0]/TR[0]/", doc2, BEFORE);
```

### 11.9.6   Direct Editing of HTML Views

Instead of specifying a path expression to identify a DOM tree node, we will make the HTMLviewPad dynamically frame different extractable document portions for different mouse locations so that its user may move the mouse cursor around to see every extractable document portion (Figure 11.19). This method, however, cannot distinguish different HTML objects with the same display area. To identify such objects, we use an additional console panel with two buttons and a node specification box. The node specification box changes its value while you move the mouse to select different document portions. The first button is used to move to the parent node in the corresponding DOM tree, whereas the second is used to move to the first child node.

When the HTMLviewPad frames what you want to extract, you can drag the mouse to create another HTMLviewPad with this extracted document portion. The new HTML-viewPad renders the extracted DOM tree on itself. Figure 11.20 shows an example extraction using such a mouse-drag operation, which internally generates the following edit code:

```
doc = getHTML("http://www.abc.com/index.html", null);
view = doc
     .EXTRACT("/HTML/BODY/TABLE[0]/");
```

The HTMLviewPad provides a pop-up menu of view–edit operations, including EXTRACT, REMOVE, and INSERT. After you select an arbitrary portion, you may select ei-

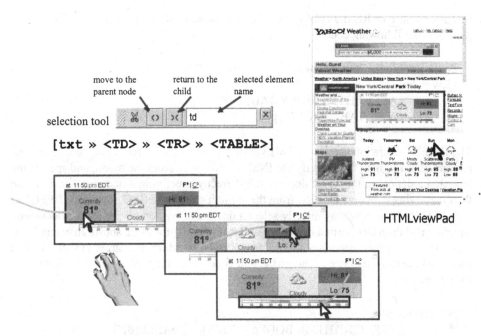

**Figure 11.19**   The mouse movement changes the extractable element marked with a frame.

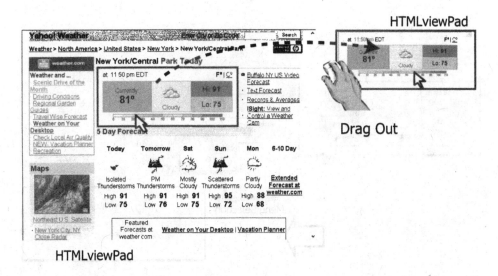

**Figure 11.20**   Live extraction of an element using a mouse-drag operation.

ther EXTRACT or REMOVE. Figure 11.21 shows an example remove operation, which generates the following code:

```
doc = getHTML("http://www.abc.com/index.html", null);
view = doc
    .EXTRACT(("/HTML/BODY/TABLE[0]/")
    .REMOVE("/TABLE[0]/TR[1]/");
```

The INSERT operation uses two HTMLviewPads showing a source HTML document and a target one. You may first specify the INSERT operation from the menu, and specify the insertion location on the target document by directly specifying a document portion and then specifying a relative location from the menu including CHILD, PARENT, BEFORE, and AFTER. Then, you may directly select a document portion on the source document, and drag and drop this portion on the target document. Figure 11.22 shows an example insert operation, which generates the following code, in which the target HTMLviewPad uses a different name space to merge the edit code of the dragged-out HTMLviewPad to its own edit code:

```
A::view = A::doc
        .EXTRACT("/HTML/BODY/. . ./TD[1]/. . ./TABLE[0]")
        .REMOVE("/TABLE[0]/TR[1]/");
view = doc
        .EXTRACT("/HTML/BODY/. . ./TD[0]/. . ./TABLE[0]/")
        .REMOVE("/TABLE[0]/TR[1]/")
        .INSERT("/TABLE[0]", A::view, AFTER);
```

The dropped HTMLviewPad is deleted after the insertion.

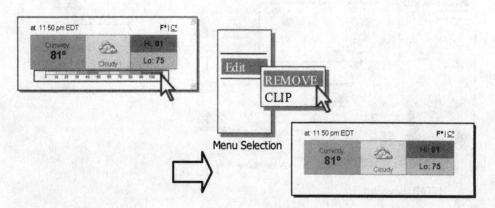

**Figure 11.21** Direct manipulation for removing an element from a view.

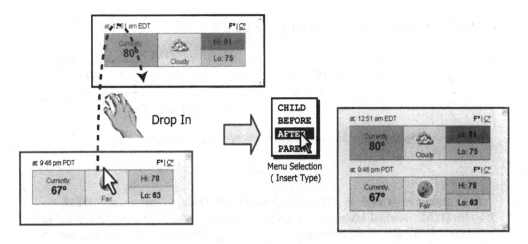

**Figure 11.22**   Direct manipulation for inserting a view in another view.

### 11.9.7   Automatic Generation of Default Slots

The HTMLviewPad allows you to map any node values of its view and any events on its view to its newly defined slots. The definition of such a node-slot mapping takes the following form:

MAP(<node>, NameSpace)

where <node> is specified by its path expression and NameSpace defines a slot name. An example of such a mapping is as follows:

MAP("/HTML/BODY/P/txt( )", "#value")

Depending on the node type, the HTMLviewPad changes the node value evaluation to map the most appropriate value of a selected node to a newly defined slot. We call these evaluation rules node-mapping rules. Each node-mapping rule has the following syntax:

```
target-object => naming-rule(data-type)<MappingType>
naming-rule    :    naming rule for the new slot
data-type      :    data type of the slot
MappingType    :    <IN|OUT|EventListener|EventFire>
```

Slots defined with the OUT type are read-only ones. The IN-type mapping defines a rewritable slot. The rewriting of such a slot may change the display of the HTML view document. The EventListener-type mapping defines a slot that changes its value whenever an event occurs in the node selected on the screen. The EventFire-type mapping, on the other hand, defines a slot whose update triggers a specified event in the node selected on the screen.

MAP("/HTML/BODY/.../P/txt()", "Value1")

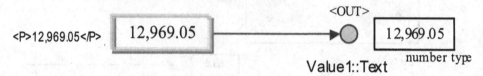

**Figure 11.23** The mapping of a text-string node to define a slot.

For a general node such as </HTML/.../txt( )>, </HTML/.../attr( )>, or </HTML/...
/P/>, the HTMLviewPad automatically defines a default slot, and sets the text in the selected node to this slot. If the text is a numerical string, it converts this string to a numerical value, and sets this value to the slot (Figure 11.23):

    a text in the selected node (character string)
    => NameSpace::#Text(string)<OUT>
    a text in the selected node (numerical string)
    => NameSpace::#Text(number)<OUT>

For a table node such as </HTML/.../TABLE/>, the HTMLviewPad converts the table value to its CSV (comma-separated value) representation, and automatically maps it to a newly defined default slot of text type (Figure 11.24).

For an anchor node such as </HTML/.../A/>, the HTMLviewPad automatically performs the following three mappings to define three default slots (Figure 11.25):

    a text in the selected node
    => NameSpace::#Text(string, number)<OUT>
    href attribute of the selected node
    => NameSpace::#refURL(string)<OUT>
    URL of the target object
    => NameSpace::#jumpURL(string)<EventListener>

MAP("/HTML/BODY/.../TABLE", "Stock")

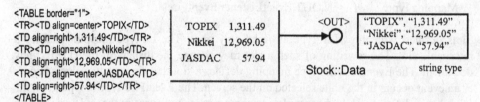

**Figure 11.24** The mapping of a table node to define a slot.

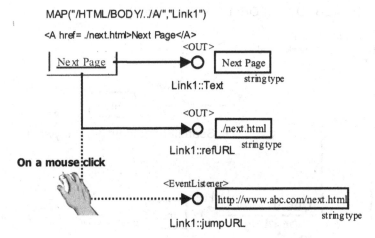

**Figure 11.25** The mapping of an anchor element to define three slots.

For example, let us consider a case in which we extract an anchor defined as follows:

&lt;A href = ./next.html&gt;
Next Page
&lt;/A&gt;

The first mapping sets the text "Next Page" to a string- (or number-) type default slot, NameSpace::#Text. The second mapping sets the href "./next.html" to a string-type default slot, NameSpace::#refURL. The third mapping is of the EventListener type. Whenever the anchor is clicked, the target URL is set to a string-type default slot, NameSpace::#jumpURL.

For a form node such as &lt;/HTML/. . ./FORM/&gt;, the HTMLviewPad automatically performs the following three mappings to define three default slots (Figure 11.26):

the value attribute of the INPUT node with the name attribute in the selected node
=&gt; NameSpace::#Input_type_name(string, number)&lt;IN, OUT&gt;
Submit action
=&gt; NameSpace::#FORM_Submit(boolean)&lt;EventFire&gt;
the value obtained from the server
=&gt; NameSpace::#FORM_Request(string)&lt;EventListener&gt;

type = &lt;text|pasword|file|checkbox|radio|hidden|submit|reset|button|image&gt;
name = &lt;name&gt; attribute in the INPUT node

For example, let us consider a case in which we extract a form defined as follows:

&lt;FORM action="./search"&gt;
&lt;INPUT Type=txt name=keyword&gt;

MAP(" /HTML/BODY/.../FORM/ ", "SearchForm")

```
<FORM action="./search">
<INPUT Type=txt  name=keyword >
<INPUT Type=submit value="search">
</FORM>  ,
```

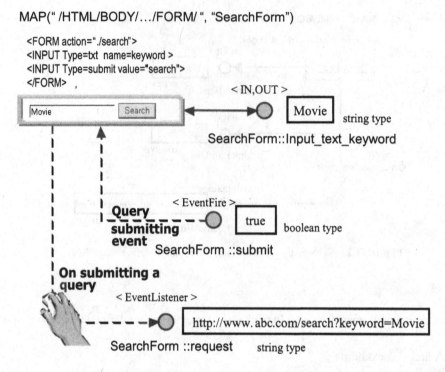

**Figure 11.26**    The mapping of a form element to define three slots.

```
<INPUT Type=submit value="search">
</FORM>
```

The first mapping rule for a form sets the input keyword to a string- (or number-) type default slot, NameSpace::#Input_text_keyword. The second mapping rule is an EventFire-type mapping. Whenever a TRUE is set to a Boolean type default slot, #FORM_Submit, the HTMLviewPad triggers a form-request event. The third mapping is of the EventListener type. Whenever an event sending a form request occurs, the HTMLviewPad sets the corresponding query to a string-type default slot, NameSpace::#FORM_Request.

Each HTMLviewPad has the additional following four default slots. The #UpdateInterval slot specifies the time interval for the periodical polling of referenced HTTP servers. A view defined over a Web document refreshes its content by periodically retrieving this Web document in an HTTP server. The #RetrievalCode slot stores the code to retrieve the source document. The #ViewEditingCode slot stores the view definition code. The #MappingCode slot stores the mapping definition code. The HTMLviewPad updates itself by accessing the source document. Whenever either the #RetrievalCode slot or the #ViewEditingCod slot is accessed with a set message, the interval timer invokes the polling, a user specifies its update, or it becomes active after its loading from a file. In addition to these four slots, the HTMLviewPad automatically creates slots defined by the mapping code that is set to the #MappingCode slot.

### 11.9.8  Visual Definition of Slots for Extracted Web Content

Our HTMLviewPad also allows users to visually specify any HTML node to work as a slot. In its node-specification mode, an HTMLviewPad frames different extractable document portions of its content document for different mouse locations so that its user may change the mouse location to see every selectable document portion. This method, however, cannot distinguish different HTML objects with the same display area. To identify one out of different HTML objects with the same display area, we use the same console panel used to extract Web content. When the HTMLviewPad frames what you want to work as a slot, you can click the mouse to pop up a dialog box to name this slot. Since each extracted Web component uses an HTMLviewPad to render its content, it also allows users to specify any of its portions to work as its slot. We call such a slot thus defined an HTML-node slot. The value of an HTML-node slot is the HTML view of the selected portion. The HTMLviewPad converts ill-formed HTML into well-formed HTML to construct its DOM tree. Therefore, you may connect an HTMLviewPad to an HTML-node slot to view the corresponding HTML view. If the HTML-node slot holds an anchor node, the HTMLviewPad connected to this slot shows the target Web page.

Figure 11.27 shows an HTMLviewPad showing a Yahoo Japan's Web page with an embeded Web application to convert U.S. dollars to Japanese yen based on the current exchange rate. On this pad, you can visually specify the input form for inputting the dollar amount and the output text portion showing the equivalent yen amount to work as slots. The HTML path of the input form is represented as

$$\text{HTML[0]/BODY[0]/DIV[0]/FORM[0]/INPUT[0]/text[(.*)]}$$

whereas the HTML path of the selected output text portion is represented as

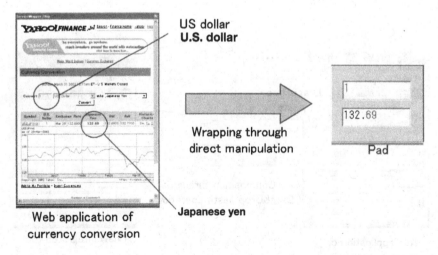

US dollar
**U.S. dollar**

Wrapping through
direct manipulation

Pad

Web application of
currency conversion

**Japanese yen**

**Figure 11.27**    A Web application to convert U.S. dollars to Japanese yen and its wrapping with two slot definitions.

HTML[0]/BODY[0]/TABLE[0]/TR[0]/TD[1]/A[0]/attr[href]

You may name the corresponding HTML-node slots as #dollarAmount, and #yenAmount respectively. The HTMLviewPad allows you to suspend the rendering of its content. In this mode, you may use an HTMLviewPad with an HTML view as a blank pad with an arbitrary size. Figure 11.27 shows, on its right hand side, a currency rate converter pad. We have defined this pad from the above-mentioned Web page just by defining two slots, resizing the HTMLviewPad, and pasting two text IO pads with their connections to the #dollarAmount and #yenAmount slots.

Such a pad wraps a Web application, providing slots for the original's input forms and output text strings. We call such a pad a wrapped Web application. Since a wrapped Web application is a pad that allows you to change its primary slot assignment, you may specify any one of its slots to work as a primary slot.

Figure 11.28 shows an HTMLviewPad with a Lycos Web page for a real-time stock-price browsing service. We have wrapped this page defining a slot for the current stock price. Then we pasted the wrapped currency conversion Web application with its #dollarAmount specified as its primary slot on this wrapped Lycos stock-price page. We connected the conversion pad to the newly defined current stock-price slot. The right-hand side of this figure shows a composite pad combining these two wrapped Web applications. For the input of different company names, we used the input form of the original Web page. Since this Web application uses the same page layout for different companies, the same path expression correctly identifies the current stock-price information part for every different company.

### 11.9.9  Example Applications

The HTMLviewPad allows us to extract an arbitrary HTML element from the Web document it displays. The direct dragging out of this portion creates another HTMLviewPad

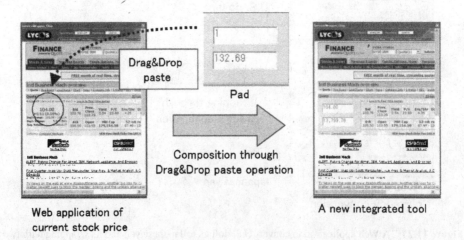

Web application of
current stock price

A new integrated tool

**Figure 11.28**   The wrapping of a stock-price information service and the pasting of the wrapped currency conversion service in Figure 11.27 on this wrapped service.

showing the extracted portion. The periodic polling capability of the latter HTMLviewPad keeps the extracted document portion alive. You may paste such a live copy in pad form on another pad with a slot connection for functional composition. You may also paste a pad on such a live copy in pad form and connect the former pad to one of the slots of the latter. Using such operations, you may compose an application pad integrated with live copies of document portions extracted from different Web pages.

Figure 11.29 shows the plotting of the NASA Space Station's orbit and Yohkoh Satellite's orbit. We used a world map with a plotting function. This map has a pairing of a #longitude[1] slot and a #latitude[1] slot, and creates, on user's demand, more pairs of the same type slots with different indices. First, you need to access the home pages of the space station and the satellite. These pages show the longitude and the latitude of the current locations of these space vehicles. Then, you may make live copies of the longitude the latitude in each Web page, and paste them on the world map with their connection to the #longitude[i] and #latitude[i] slots, respectively. The live copies from the space station Web page use the first slot pair, whereas those from the satellite Web page use the second slot pair. These live copies update their values every 10 seconds by polling the source Web pages. The independent two sequences of plotted locations show the orbits of the two space vehicles.

Figure 11.30 shows an application to the real-time visualization of stock-prices changes. First, you need to access the Yahoo Finance Web page showing the current Nikkei average stock price in real time. Then, you may make a live copy of the Nikkei average index and paste it onto a DataBufferPad with its connection to #input slot. A DataBufferPad associates each #input slot input with its input time, and outputs this pair in CSV format. We pasted this composite pad on a TablePad with its connection to the #data slot. A TablePad adds every #data slot input at the end of the list stored in CSV format. You need to change the primary slot of the TablePad to the #data slot to paste this pad on a GraphPad with its connection to the #input slot. A GraphPad adds a new vertical bar proportional to the input value whenever it receives a new #input slot value.

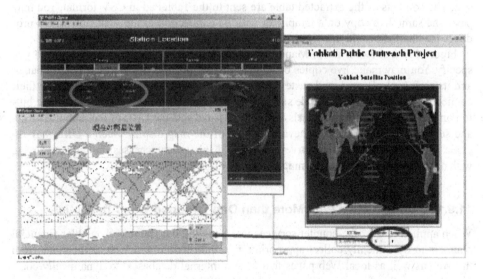

**Figure 11.29**  The plotting of the NASA Space Station's orbit and Yohkoh Satellite's orbit.

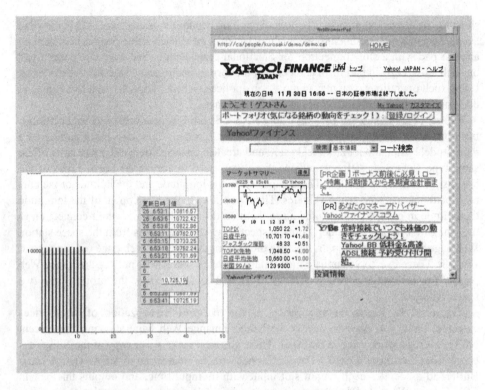

**Figure 11.30**    The real-time drawing of a stock-price chart using a live copy.

Figure 11.31 shows another page of the Yahoo Finance service. This page shows, for a specified company, the time series of its stock prices over a specified period. You may make a live copy of this table and paste it on a TablePad with its connection to the #input slot. The contents of the extracted table are sent to the TablePad in CSV format. You may paste the same live copy on a GraphPad with its connection to the #list slot, which produces the chart shown in this figure.

Figure 11.32 shows a Yahoo Maps Web page. You can obtain a map for a location you specify. You may make live copies of its map display portion, its zooming control panel, and its shift control panel, and paste the two control panels on the map display with their connections to the #RetrievalCode slot of the map display. Whenever you click some button on either of these control panels, the control panel sets the URL of the requested page and sends this URL to the #RetrievalCode slot of the map display. Such a URL may include a query to the specified server. The map display then accesses the requested page with a new map and extracts the map portion to display.

### 11.9.10  Composition With More than One Wrapped Web Application

When applied to over-the-counter services in e-banking, our framework enables financial planners to dynamically collect appropriate live information and Web applications from the Web as well as local Web pages that access internal databases, to dynamically combine them together for composing customized portfolios of live stock-market information,

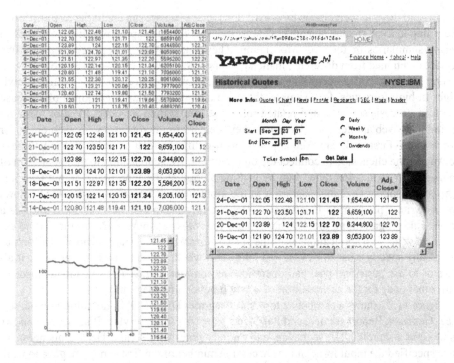

**Figure 11.31**   The real-time drawing of a stock-price chart using a live copy of a table element.

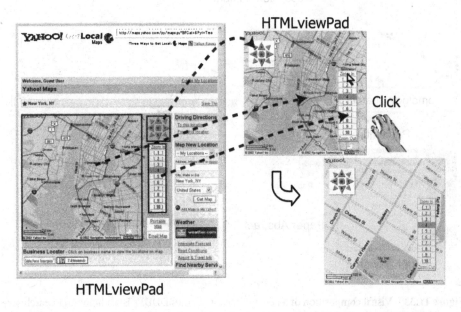

**Figure 11.32**   Composition of a map tool using a map service and its control panels.

and to send them to their clients by e-mail. Financial planners can reedit the live portfolios according to their clients' demands. Clients can also reedit the proposed live portfolios to define summaries or focused information. They can also combine more than one live portfolio obtained from different financial planners to define a cross-comparison view.

Our framework also opens a new vista in the circulation and reuse of scientific knowledge. In bioinformatics, for example, there are already many different kinds of database services, analysis services, and related reference information services. Most of them are available as Web applications. However, they are hard to interoperate with each other, for two reasons. First, different Web applications use different data formats. Second, there is no way on the client side to connect the output of one Web application to the input form of another Web application other than by making a copy of the appropriate output text portion on the source page and pasting it in the input form of the target page. SOAP allows you to write a program to functionally integrate more than one Web services, but it is a server-side programming tool and hard to use for nonprogrammers. Our framework to extract and wrap Web applications uses the HTML format for the data exchange. It allows us to visually specify what to extract and wrap, and which portions to export as slots. It allows us to use paste-and-peel pad operations to combine extracted Web contents together with other pads for the composition of a new functionally integrated tool.

Figure 11.33 shows a composite tool that integrates DDBJ's Blast homology search service, GenBank Report service, and PubMed's paper reference service. Blast service allows us to input a sample DNA sequence, and outputs genes with similar DNA sequences. We have specified the input form and the accession number of the first candidate gene to work as slots. The accession number works as an anchor linking to a GenBank Report Web page

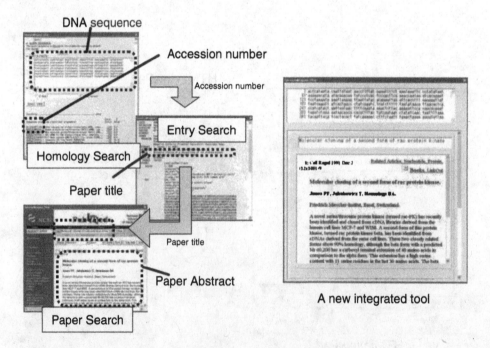

**Figure 11.33** Visual composition of a new tool that integrates DDBJ's Blast homology search service, GenBank Report service, and PubMed's paper reference service.

containing the detailed information about this gene. Its corresponding slot contains the URL to the target GenBank Report page. We have pasted an HTMLviewPad with its connection to this second slot. As a result, this child HTMLviewPad shows the corresponding GenBank Report page. This page contains bibliographic information about the related research papers. We have visually specified the title portion of the first research paper to work as a slot of this pad. We have also wrapped the PubMed service with its input form to work as a slot. PubMed service returns a list of full documents that contain given keywords. We have made this slot work as the primary slot. By pasting this wrapped PubMed service on the HTMLviewPad showing a GenBank Report page with its connection to the title slot, you will obtain a composite tool that functionally integrates these three services.

## 11.10   REDISTRIBUTION AND PUBLICATION OF MEME MEDIA OBJECTS AS WEB CONTENT

Whenever you save a wrapped Web-document portion extracted from a Web page, the system saves only the pad type, namely "HTMLviewPad," the values of the two slots, #RetrievalCode slot and #ViewEditingCode slot, and the path expression and name of each user-defined slot. Copies of such a live copy share only such meta-information with the original. They access the source Web page whenever they need to update themselves. This is an important feature from a copyright point of view, since every update of such a copy requires a server access. The redistribution of a live copy across the Internet requires only the sending of its save-format representation. When a live copy is activated on the destination platform, it invokes the retrieval code stored in the #RetrievalCode slot, executes the view editing code in the #ViewEditingCode slot to display only the defined portion of the retrieved Web document, and defines every user-defined slot. You can further extract any of its portions as a live copy.

For the reediting of extracted Web contents, our framework provides two methods. One of them allows you to insert an HTML view into another HTML view without any functional linkage. The other allows you to paste an HTML view as a pad on another HTML view as a pad with a slot connection between them. The former composition results in a new HTML view, whereas the latter composition is no longer an HTML view. In order to publish composed documents and/or tools as HTML documents in the Web, we need to convert non-HTML view compositions to HTML views. We call such a conversion a flattening operation. There may be several different methods to flatten composite pads but we chose the simplest one—to use Active X representation of composite pads. As shown in Figures 11.13 and 11.14, composite pads can be embedded in an HTML view. Using the same visual operation to insert an HTML view in another HTML view, you can visually insert a composite pad as a new HTML element in an arbitrary HTML view. Our system also provides a tool to lay out more than one composite pad in a single page, and to convert this page to an HTML view. Figure 11.34 shows the flattening of a special pad pasted with more than one composite pad. Our system also provides a tool to easily register an arbitrary HTML view to a specified HTTP server for its publication in the Web.

Although the use of ActiveX controls to embed composed pads in a Web page enables Internet Explorer users to browse this page without losing any functionality of the embedded composed pad except its decomposability, Netscape Navigator users cannot browse this page to use this pad. Here, we propose another way of flattening non-HTML view composition of more than one HTML view. Non-HTML view composition treats HTML views as pads, and

**Figure 11.34** The flattening of a spatial arrangement of composite pads with extracted Web content, and the viewing of the result with Internet Explorer.

combines them through slot connections. Our basic idea is the use of script programs to define both slots of each HTML view and the slot connection between two HTML views.

For the HTML representation of an HTML view working as a pad, we use script variables to represent its slots, its primary slot, its parent pad, the parent's slot it is connected to, and the list of child pads. As shown in Figure 11.35, we use JavaScript to define the SetValue function to set a new value to a sepcified slot, the GimmeValue function to read out the value of a specified slot, and the UpdateValue function to update the primary slot value and to invoke every child pad's UpdateValue function. To update the primary slot value, we define a script program to invoke the parent's GimmeValue function with the connection slot as its parameter, and to set the return value to its own primary slot. Figure 11.35 shows an HTML view defined with two slots—#increment and #number—and the three standard functions. This HTML view works as a counter with a number display and a button to increment the number. The HTML view defines these components in HTML.

Figure 11.36 shows an HTML view composition with three HTML views; two work as

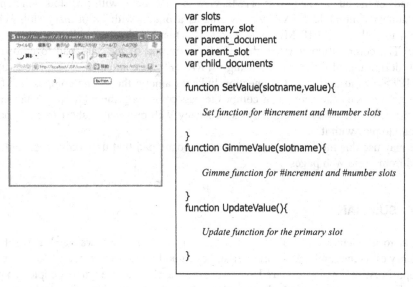

```
var slots
var primary_slot
var parent_document
var parent_slot
var child_documents

function SetValue(slotname,value){

      Set function for #increment and #number slots

}
function GimmeValue(slotname){

      Gimme function for #increment and #number slots

}
function UpdateValue(){

      Update function for the primary slot

}
```

**Figure 11.35**   A JavaScript program to define slots in an HTML view.

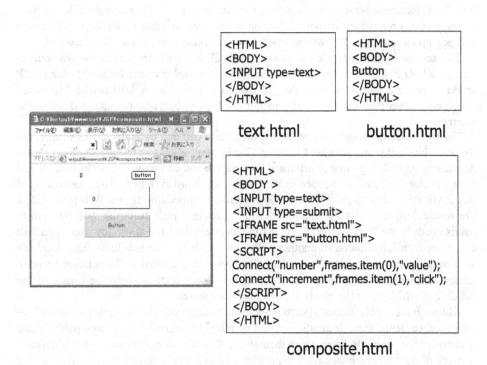

```
<HTML>
<BODY>
<INPUT type=text>
</BODY>
</HTML>
```
**text.html**

```
<HTML>
<BODY>
Button
</BODY>
</HTML>
```
**button.html**

```
<HTML>
<BODY >
<INPUT type=text>
<INPUT type=submit>
<IFRAME src="text.html">
<IFRAME src="button.html">
<SCRIPT>
Connect("number",frames.item(0),"value");
Connect("increment",frames.item(1),"click");
</SCRIPT>
</BODY>
</HTML>
```
**composite.html**

**Figure 11.36**   Use of a JavaScript program for an HTML-view composition with three HTML views.

child pads of the other. The parent HTML view is the counter with two slots, #increment and #number. One child HTML view works as a button with its primary slot, #click, whereas the other child HTML view works as a number display with its primary slot, #value. The composition rewrites the HTML definition of the base pad to embed the HTML definitions of the other two using <IFRAME> tags, and adds a script code using <SCRIPT> tags to define slot connection linkages among them. The composed HTML view works exactly the same as a composite pad combining the pad representations of these three HTML views. Users may use a legacy Web browser to show this composite view and to play with it.

We may use this mechanism to flatten a composite pad that uses only those pads extracted from some Web pages.

## 11.11  SUMMARY

In order to accelerate the evolution of memes in a meme pool, we need a worldwide repository of memes and a good browser and/or a good reference service system to access this repository. In other words, we have to organize a marketplace where people can publish their achievements as pads, browse through all the pads published by other people, and reuse any of them for their own use in a local IntelligentPad environment.

Since 1993, our IntelligentPad project has developed four different types of marketplace systems. The first system uses the the WWW and its existing browsers such as Netscape Navigator and Internet Explorer. Whereas WWW works as a worldwide pad repository, Netscape Navigator or Internet Explorer provide a hypermedia catalog of pads to navigate this repository. A mouse click on a pad name or a pad image in such a catalog will pop up an IntelligentPad window with a real working copy of the requested pad.

The second system provides a special pad called a URLAnchorPad. When mouse-clicked, a URLAnchorPad directly issues a URL (universal resource locator) to the HTTP server to retrieve another composite pad from a remote site. A URLAnchorPad, when pasted on another pad, works as a link anchor in a hypermedia network spanned across the Internet.

The third system provides a new Web browser as a pad that basically works similarly to Netscape Navigator and Internet Explorer. This browser allows us to publish any composite pads by embedding them in arbitrary Web pages. You can publish any documents and tools as composite pads embedded in Web pages. The third system requires the writing of an HTML definition to publish a composite pad by embedding it in a Web page. Users like to use drag-and-drop operations not only to retrieve pads from the Web but also to publish pads to the Web. Furthermore, the third system does not allow any user to publish his or her own information in another's Web pages, or to span any links from another's Web pages to his or her own Web pages. This relation is similar to the relation between tenants and owners. Each tenant is required to make a contract with the owner of the building in which he or she wants to open his or her store.

Although the owner–tenant system works well to supervise the clustering of similar information contents, there is another way of forming a marketplace—a large public space is provided for people to freely open their stores. The fourth system allows us to define a network of piazzas in which each piazza allows us to upload and to download pads to and from the corresponding server through drag-and-drop operations.

Meme media and meme pool architectures will play important roles when they are applied to a reasonably large accumulation of intellectual resources. The current situation of the Web satisfies this condition. Although current Web technologies have already allowed us to access a huge accumulation of intellectual resources, we have no good tools yet to flexibly reedit and redistribute these intellectual resources for their reuse in different contexts. The latter half of this chapter proposed a wrapped-Web-content framework for reediting and redistributing content in Web pages. This content includes live content objects and Web applications. Our framework allows us to reedit and to redistribute live content objects and Web applications as well as static multimedia content objects. They need not edit HTML definitions of Web documents. They can easily extract any document components as pads through drag-and-drop operations, and paste them together to define both the layout and the functional linkages among them.

You may send reedited Web content across the Internet by attaching it to an e-mail. Recipients with IntelligentPad installed in their platforms can reuse, further reedit, and redistribute these live documents. Our framework also provides for the flattening of pads to HTML documents, which allows you to publish reedited Web content as new Web pages.

Our wrapped-Web-content framework makes the Web work as a meme pool, in which people can publish their intellectual resources, retrieve some of them, extract some of their portions as pads, combine these pads together with other pads to compose new intellectual resources, and publish these resources again as Web pages. Our framework will open a new vista in the circulation and reuse of knowledge represented as multimedia documents and/or application programs, especially in the fields of science and engineering.

## REFERENCES

1. N. Eldredge and S. J. Gould. Punctuated equilibrium: An alternative to phyletic gradualism. In *Models in Paleobiology* (J. M. Schopf, ed.), pp. 82–115. Freeman Cooper, San Francisco, 1972.

2. D. Flanagan. *Java in a Nutshell.* O'Reilly & Associates, Sebastopol, CA, 1996.

3. A. Denning. *ActiveX Controls Inside Out.* Microsoft Press, Redmond, WA, 1997.

4. Y. Tanaka. From augmentation media to meme media: IntelligentPad and the world-wide repository of pads. In *Information Modelling and Knowledge Bases, VI* (H. Kangassalo et al., eds.), pp. 91–107. IOS Press, Amsterdam, 1995.

5. Y. Tanaka. A meme media architecture for fine-grain component software. In *Object Technologies for Advanced Software*, (K. Fuiatsugi and S. Matsuoka, eds.), pp. 190–214. Springer-Verlag, New York, 1996.

6. Y. Tanaka. Meme media and a world-wide meme pool. In *Proceedings of ACM Multimedia 96*, pp. 175–186, 1996.

7. UniSQL. *Next-Generation Software Solutions*, UniSQL, Austin, TX, 1992.

8. D. Flanagan. *Java in a Nutshell.* O'Reilly & Associates, Sebastopol, CA, 1996.

9. M. Roscheisen, C. Mogensen, and T. Winograd. Interaction design for shared World-Wide Web annotations. In *CHI'95 Conference Companion*, pp. 328–329, 1995.

10. M. Roscheisen, C. Mogensen, and T. Winograd. Beyond browsing: Shared comments, SOAPs, trails, and on-line communities. In *Proceedings of the 3rd World Wide Web Conference*, 1995.

11. L. A. Carr, D. DeRoure, W. Hall, and G. Hill. The distributed link service: A tool for publishers, authors and readers. In *Proceedings of the 4th International World Wide Web Conference*, 1995.

12. W. Hall, H.C. Davis, and G. Huutchings. *Rethinking Hypermedia: The MicroCosm Approach*, Kluwer Academic, Norwell, MA, 1996.

13. K. Grønbæk, L. Sloth, and P. Ørbæk. Webvise: Browser and proxy support for open hypermedia structuring mechanisms of the World Wide Web. In *Proceedings of the 8thWorld Wide Web Conference*, pp. 253–267, 1999.

14. N. O. Bouvin. Unifying strategies for Web augmentation. In *Proceedings of ACM Hypertext 1999*, pp. 91–100, 1999.

15. J. J. Cadiz, A. Gupta, and J. Grudin. Using Web annotations for asynchronous collaboration around documents. In *Proceedings of CSCW 2000*, pp. 309–318, 2000.

16. *iMarkup: Annotate, Organize and Collaborate on the Web.* http://www.imarkup.com/products/annotate_page.asp.

17. C. Sastry. D. Lewis, and A. Pizano. WEBTOUR: A system to record and play back dynamic multimedia annotations on Web document content. In *Proceedings of ACM Hypretext '96*, pp. 140–148, 1996.

18. Y. Tanaka, J. Fujima, and T. Sugibuchi. Meme Media and Meme Pools for Re-editing and Redistributing Intellectual Assets. *Hypermedia: Openness, Structural Awareness and Adaptivity.* Springer L NCS 2266, 28–46, 2002.

19. Y. Tanaka and J. Fujima. Topica framework for organizing and accessing intellectual assets on meme media. In *Proceedings of the 11th European–Japanese Conference on Information Modelling and Knowledge Bases*, 2001.

20. R. C. Miller, and B. A. Myers. Creating dynamic World Wide Web pages by demonstration. *Carnegie Mellon University School of Computer Science Technology Report*, CMU-CS–97–131, Pittsburgh, 1997.

21. A. Sugiura, and Y. Koseki. Internet Scrapbook: Automating Web Browsing Tasks by Demonstration. In *Proceedings of the ACM Symposium on User Interface Software and Technology (UIST)*, pp. 10–18, 1998.

22. T. H. Nelson. *Transpublishing for Today's Web: Our Overall Design and Why It Is Simple.* http;//www.sfc.keio.ac.jp/ted/TPUB/Tqdesign99.html, 1999.

23. A. Sahuguet and F. Azavant. Building intelligent Web applications using lightweight wrappers. *Data and knowledge Engineering, 36*(3): 283–316, 2001.

24. B. A. Ribeiro-Neto, A. H. F. Laender, and A. S. Da Silva. Extracting semistructured data through examples. In *Proceedings of the 8th ACM International Conference on Information and Knowledge Management (CIKM'99)*, pp. 91–101, 1999.

25. P. B. Golgher, A. H. F. Laender, A. S. da Silva, and B. A. Ribeiro-Neto. An example-based environment for wrapper generation. In *Proceedings of International Workshop on the World Wide Web and Conceptual Modeling*, pp. 152–164, 2000.

26. Y. Tanaka and J. Fujima. Meme media and Topica architectures for editing, distributing, and managing intellectual assets. In *Proceedings of Kyoto International Conference On Digital Libraries: Research and Practice*, pp. 208–216, 2000.

# CHAPTER 12

# ELECTRONIC COMMERCE FOR PADS

Chapter 11 has shown how we can publish pads through the Internet, upload or download them to and from a worldwide publication repository of pads, reuse them as they are, and reedit them for different reuses. These publication systems provide free worldwide distribution and exchange of intellectual resources. However, they need to be combined with some license management and royalty service to encourage people in the business world to play significant roles in providing and distributing intellectual resources. This chapter proposes a way of integrating the pay-per-use billing scheme with the worldwide publication repository of pads. This method is based on Ryoichi Mori's idea of superdistribution. It extends the original idea so that the provider and the distributor of each object are guaranteed to get the reasonable payment even if some component of this object is combined with other objects and reused by some user after its redistribution. This mechanism introduces business competition in providing and distributing intellectual resources, which will significantly enrich their variety and promote their distribution. The introduction of business activities changes a meme pool to a meme market.

## 12.1 ELECTRONIC COMMERCE

Electronic commerce means advertising, selling, and shopping for goods or services electronically through the Internet [Figure 12.1(a)] [1, 2]. In some cases, it also means paying money electronically through the Internet [Figure 12.1(b)] and/or shipping goods or services to the customers electronically through the Internet [Figure 12.1(c)]. Both Internet malls and Net catalogs provide electronic commerce with electronic advertising and ordering functions. Some of them send invoices by traditional mail to request remittance. Others electronically request the buyer for his or her credit card number. The credit card company performs the remittance function by transferring some amount of money from the buyer's bank account to the seller's bank account.

Physical goods are shipped to the customer by various methods. Some nonphysical goods can be electronically shipped through the Internet. They are called electronic

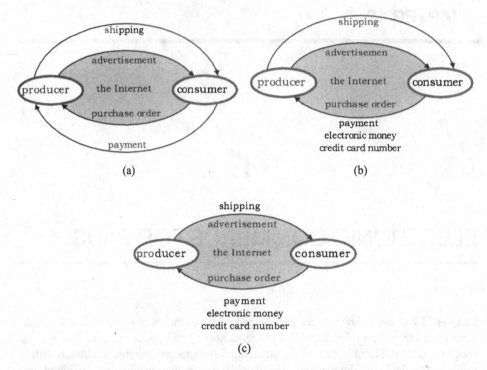

**Figure 12.1**   Various types of electronic commerce. (a) Electronic commerce dealing with physical goods. (b) Use of electronic money or credit cards. (c) Electronic commerce dealing with information, software, and services.

goods. They include multimedia documents and software products. It is difficult to produce copies of physical goods. The production of a copy costs as much as making the original. The situation is, however, quite different for information and software. Just a selection of the copy operation from an operation menu will immediately replicate the information or software electronically in a computer. It costs the downloader nothing to do this. Therefore, providers protect their products from illegal copies using various copy protection mechanisms.

Multimedia creators use various photos, video clips, sounds, and music to develop new multimedia products. Their variety is too large for each creator to produce by himself or herself. Creators purchase the right to reuse these materials from their providers. The purchasing of the right to reuse some content is different from the purchasing of their copies with copy protection. The latter is based on the pay-per-copy billing scheme, whereas the former requires a new, different billing scheme called the pay-per-use billing scheme [3] (Figure 12.2). The pay-per-use billing allows us to reuse information and software.

Pads are also software. Their electronic advertising, selling, shopping, and shipping will definitely grow their market and their variety. Pads can carry whatever computers can store and manipulate. These include multimedia documents, application programs, numerical data, records, rules, and mathematical expressions; their access and manipulation environments; and various services for searching, accessing, processing, managing, delivering, and purchasing these goods, including database services, mail services, and catalog-shopping services. Pads work as universal media for editing, managing, and distribut-

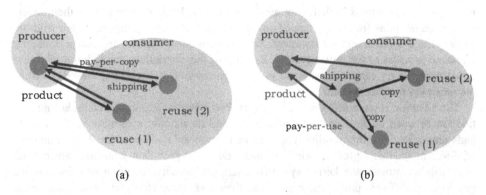

**Figure 12.2**  The pay-per-copy billing scheme (a) and the pay-per-use billing scheme (b).

ing all these electronic goods and services. Pads can be easily replicated. The copy protection of pads will deprive them of their roles to work as meme media. Their electronic commerce requires a pay-per-use billing system.

## 12.2  FROM PAY-PER-COPY TO PAY-PER-USE

Pay-per-copy billing charges money for each copy of a product. It assumes that users cannot make the copies by themselves. Once you have purchased a product, you can do anything you like with it. You may decompose it to reuse some of its parts for your own purpose, or you may even sell it to another user. Since you cannot make the copies by yourself, you cannot reuse the same part simultaneously for more than one purpose, nor can you sell the same product to more than one person. For this reason, the provider of the product can protect his or her rights. The only possible violations of the provider's rights are the production of an imitation and reverse engineering by other providers.

When applied to software, the pay-per-copy billing must protect each product against illegal copying. Software is easy to copy at no cost. Software providers have to protect their products with copy protection mechanisms. Copy protection, however, prohibits each user from reusing the same product simultaneously for more than one purpose. Components of a toolkit system or a componentware system, however, must be easily replicated and simultaneously reused in different constructs. If each of them were protected against copying, they would not work as components. Toolkit and componentware product providers today protect their development environments against copy operations. They allow us to replicate each component and to reuse its copies simultaneously in their development environments, but they prohibit us to replicate the development environments. Such providers are selling their development capabilities as total systems, but not individual components. Additional sets of components are sold as system extensions, but not as individual component packages independent from the system in which they are used. The price of these development environment systems is usually high.

Some of these system providers also charge for each copy of their runtime environment, whereas others do not. The former also protect runtime environments from copy operations, whereas the latter do not. Both types of system providers, however, do not allow us to compose new tools in their runtime environments. Both of them protect their development capabilities from copy operations. Furthermore, initial components are sold together with a development environment. Add-on component libraries are also provided by the same provider of the initial system. Because of this restriction, the addition of a new component library can be considered as a system revision to keep their customers from moving away to other systems.

The situation is quite different in IntelligentPad systems. IntelligentPad makes no distinction between its development environment and its runtime environment. Composite pads retain their decomposability. They can be transported to other users. A large number of different providers provide primitive pads. Different providers who maintain mutual compatibility provide the kernel systems. Users can combine component pads that are provided by different providers to compose their own composite pads. They may make their own copies and send them to other users for their reuse. Pads can be replicated, reedited, and redistributed by end-users. The pay-per-copy billing system does not protect their providers' rights in this case.

Furthermore, some pads carry services instead of electronic contents. Examples of these are database services, information retrieval services, and computation services. The charge for providing such a service cannot be charged on the purchase of its carrying pad. These pads usually work as proxy objects communicating through the Internet with their servers at different sites. The charge should be calculated based on the amount of the service provided to the user through this pad.

These considerations require a paradigm shift from the pay-per-copy billing scheme to the pay-per-use billing scheme. The latter is mainly used for selling services and supplies such as water, gas, and electricity. Their charge is calculated by measuring the amount of services and supplies consumed. This measuring, when applied to software, is called information metering. Pay-per-use billing requires mechanisms for information metering, billing, and remittance.

In case of IntelligentPad, pay-per-use billing should be applied to both the use of each component pad and the use of each composition structure. The latter is also a proprietary product of a system integrator. Different from the pay-per-copy billing, the pay-per-use billing introduces micropayment, i.e., payment of a small amount of money. This also implies a significant increase in payment transactions. Providers cannot deal with such a huge number of micropayment transactions by themselves, which implies the involvement of brokers, credit companies, and banks.

## 12.3 DIGITAL ACCOUNTING, BILLING, AND PAYMENT

Once the pay-per-use billing system is established, providers can publish their pads on their web pages or piazzas. Users can open these pages or piazzas, and drag out the pads they want. No charge is imposed at this stage. When a user uses each pad, a special mechanism that is partly implemented in each pad and partly implemented in each IntelligentPad kernel system will meter the amount of use. The billing and the remittance are executed in several different ways. These include three major methods: the prepaid-card scheme, the credit-card scheme, and the real-time-payment scheme.

The prepaid-card scheme uses prepaid cards issued by brokers. Users have to buy these cards from the issuer prior to the use of pads. These cards are also pads. They are protected against illegal copies. Therefore, they can be sold through the conventional pay-per-copy billing scheme. When you use a pad, you have to a priori provide your system with the prepaid card issued by one of its brokers. The same pad may be sold by more than one broker. When you use a composite pad, you have to provide your system with more than one prepaid card to cover all the components. During the use of each pad, it dynamically requests the corresponding prepaid card to deduct the corresponding charge. When the deduction becomes impossible, the pad will suspend its operation.

The credit-card scheme uses similar cards to charge for the amount of use. Each use of a pad adds the corresponding charge to the corresponding credit card. Users have to dial up the credit company each month, for example, to send the charge record for the clearing of their account. If they fail to do so, or if the accumulated charge exceeds an a priori set limit, the pad will suspend its use of this credit card.

The real-time payment scheme assumes a line connection with the broker during the use of pads. The metered charge is immediately sent to the broker for necessary remittance whenever a pad is used. The remittance may be collected either by the transfer between bank accounts or by using electronic money.

## 12.4  ECOLOGY OF PADS IN THE MARKET

The distribution market of pads requires at least three kinds of players: providers, brokers, and users (Figure 12.3). Each provider provides several brokers with various primitive pads and composite pads. Brokers distribute these pads to users through various distribution channels. Each user may freely make copies of any of the pads in the distribution market, use them as they are or recombine them, and redistribute some of the pads. Dif-

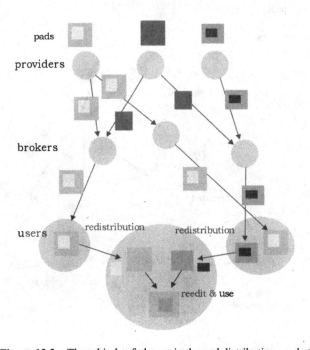

**Figure 12.3**   Three kinds of players in the pad distribution market.

ferent brokers may deal with the same pad of the same provider. They may charge different amounts for the same use of the same pad.

A composite pad in the distribution market may consist of pads that are provided by different providers and/or distributed by different brokers. Its use activates its various component pads. Use of some component pads causes providers and/or brokers to charge the user certain amounts of money. The charged amount should be paid to the provider and the broker of each component pad.

In addition to the three basic kinds of players, we may also have to consider two other kinds of players in the business environment, namely pad integrators and package providers (Figure 12.4). Pad integrators uses primitive pads provided and distributed by others, combine them to compose their own composite pads, and provide these composite pads to the distribution market through brokers. They may or may not make a contract with the provider and/or the broker of each primitive pad they use. Suppose that an integrator I uses a pad Pa, which is provided by a provider P and distributed by a broker B, to compose a composite pad Pb. When a user uses the pad Pb and hence the pad Pa, he should be charged for his use of Pa, and his payment should finally go both to its provider and to its broker. This should be always guaranteed whether or not the use of Pa by the integrator I is based upon any contract with P and B. If the integrator I wants to provide Pa with a special discount charge for its use under a special contract with its provider P and/or its broker B, he must be able to do that. This discount-rate use of Pa should be limited to its use in Pb. Furthermore, the integrator should be able to charge users for their use of the composition Pb even if he provides none of the components of Pb.

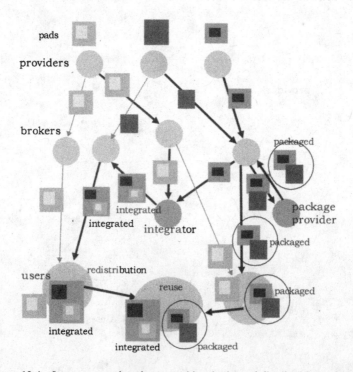

**Figure 12.4** Integrators and package providers in the pad distribution market.

A package provider provides sets of primitive and composite pads as package software. These sets may include no pads developed by the package provider. Similar to pad integrators, package providers may or may not make contracts with the provider and/or the broker of each primitive pad they use. The selected collection of the pads that are provided by different providers and distributed by different distributors is itself considered as the property of the package provider. If the package provider wants to provide each member of a package with a special discount charge for its use under a special contract with its provider and/or its broker, he must be able to do that. This discount-rate use of each pad in a package should be limited within any environment of this package.

## 12.5  SUPERDISTRIBUTION OF PADS

Superdistribution means secure distribution of software and/or multimedia content based on the pay-per-use billing scheme. Ryoichi Mori first proposed this scheme in 1983 [4]. Similar concepts were also proposed by others. Brad Cox first discussed this concept in the context of software components [3].

Mori and the author of this book both believe that the IntelligentPad architecture and the superdistribution scheme will play mutually complementary roles to establish an infrastructure for the exchange and the reuse of knowledge resources in our society. IPC (IntelligentPad Consortium) has been also discussing how to introduce the superdistribution mechanism into the IntelligentPad system architecture. The following is an outline of our consensus. IPC implemented a simplified version of the pad superdistribution system for feasibility studies in 1998 with the support of IPA (Information-technology Promotion Agency), using a commercially available version of IntelligentPad.

The key point of the superdistribution system is how to implement an information metering mechanism. The information metering meters the use of each primitive pad.

The metered amount is then deducted from a prepaid card, or charged to a credit card. Here we consider only these two types of payment. Prepaid cards and credit cards are both independent objects. Each person may have more than one prepaid card and more than one credit card. Since IntelligentPad treats every manipulable object as a pad, it should treat both prepaid cards and credit cards as pads. The information metering should be performed between each primitive pad and the corresponding prepaid or credit card.

The information metering requires an account module that keeps the information about how much each pad is used. Before using each pad, users have to install the account module that is provided by one of this pad's brokers. Once installed, each account module resides in the system, and keeps its account information in a file. This file should be securely protected from rewriting. Different brokers need to provide different account modules. Each pad communicates with its broker's account module to meter the amount of its use. This communication should be securely protected and use different protocols for different brokers. The same pad must use different protocols for different account modules if it is distributed by more than one broker. Furthermore, this protocol should not be known to anyone other than the broker who uses it. To satisfy these requirements, the information metering requires two modules (Figure 12.5). The first one is the account module. The second one is the request module. A request module is provided by a broker and used by a pad provider who has contracted with this broker for the distribution of this pad. A request module is built into a pad by the pad provider under contract with the broker. Different

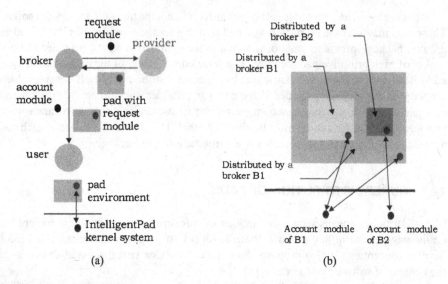

**Figure 12.5** Information metering by two modules provided by each broker. (a) Each broker provides an account module and a request module, whereas each pad provider embeds a request module in his pads. (b) Each request module of a broker can securely communicate with the account module of the same broker.

brokers provide different request modules. The request module of a broker can securely communicate with the account module of the same broker.

The charging strategies may differ for different providers and for different pads. Using its built-in request module, each pad can securely send a charge amount to the account module. It is up to its provider how to meter the use of a pad. For example, a pad may send corresponding charge information whenever its "update" procedure or either the "set" or the "gimme" procedure of one of its slots is invoked [Figure 12.6(a)]. A pad that carries a picture image may send corresponding charge information whenever its printing procedure is invoked [Figure 12.6(b)]. Such an image pad is free to view on the screen, but charges for its printout.

The account module may have an independent account for each provider, or a single account. In the former case, the broker can later use this information to divide the profit among all the contractor providers. In the latter case, the broker needs some other information to fairly divide the profit among all the contractor providers. In the latter case, brokers can simply sell a prepaid card to a user, who then loads this card pad in his or her system to add its credit amount to the account of the corresponding account module. In the former case, the independent account for each provider may be further divided into subaccounts for different pad groups with different charging policies. The variety of charging policies available for brokers depends on the business strategy of each broker. The wider variety of charging policies leads to the larger overhead in exchanging messages among pads. Some providers may prefer better performance of their products to the wide selection of charging policies. Some others may have the opposite preference. A pairing of an account module and a request module can define a set of charging policies. Some pairs can even change their charging policy depending on the use history of the pads and their messages. It may offer a new discount rate for a pad after a certain

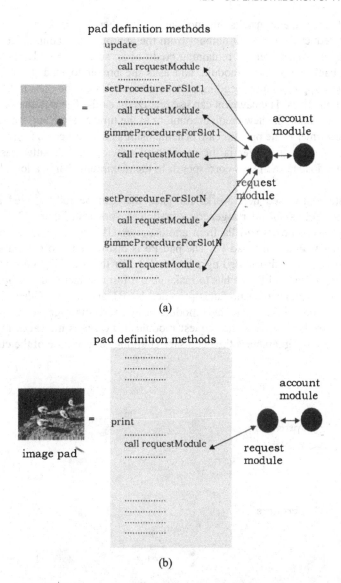

Figure 12.6  Using its statically bound request module, each pad can securely send a charge amount to the account module. (a) A pad may send a corresponding charge information whenever its "update" procedures or either the "set" or the "gimme" procedure of one of its slots is invoked. (b) A pad that carries a picture image may send corresponding charge information whenever its printing procedure is invoked.

amount of its use. Different pairs define different sets of charging policies. This mechanism allows each broker to provide pad providers with a wide variety of charging policies.

Fair division of profit requires each account module to report its information periodically, say every month, to the broker. The simplest solution to satisfy this requirement is as follows. Each user first makes a contract with a broker to get its account module with some credit amount, and installs this module in his or her system. Every use of a pad automatically deducts some credit amount from the appropriate account of the appropriate account module. Whenever the remaining credit of an account module reaches zero, the user sends back the account module, and asks the broker to load it with some credit amount. The shipping and the sending of account modules can be done through the Internet or telephone lines. The payment can use real credit cards. The remittance may be done at the time of loading the new credit amount, or at the time of reporting the account information. The former is the prepaid card scheme using real credit cards for purchasing prepaid cards, whereas the latter is the credit card scheme. In the latter case, the credit amount that is loaded each time corresponds to the maximum charge allowed on the credit card.

The system proposed here works for pads that can be redistributed and reedited by end-users. Let us consider a general situation as shown in Figure 12.7. Here, a user U2 obtained a composite pad Pa from another user U1, and U2 uses a component Pb of Pa together with another pad Pc. The pad Pb is distributed into the market by a broker B1, whereas Pc is distributed by a broker B2. For the user U2 to use the composite pad consisting of Pb and Pc, he has to make an a priori contract with the brokers B1 and B2 to install all the account modules provided by B1 and by B2. Otherwise, the composite pad will not work. The request module in Pb sends messages to the account module provided by B1, whereas the request module in Pc sends messages to the account module by B2. This guarantees the necessary charging for each use of the composite pad by U2.

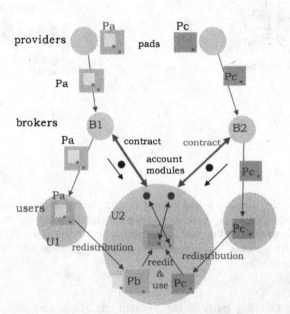

**Figure 12.7**    A user U2 obtained a composite pad Pa from another user U1, and U2 uses a component Pb of Pa together with another pad Pc. The pad Pb is distributed into the market by a broker B1, whereas Pc is distributed by a broker B2. For the user U2 to use the composite pad consisting of Pb and Pc, he has to a priori make contracts with the brokers B1 and B2 to install all the account modules provided by B1 and B2.

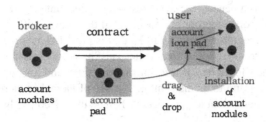

**Figure 12.8**   When a user makes a contract with a broker, he will receive an account pad from this broker. He can just drop this pad on the account icon pad in his IntelligentPad system to install all the account modules provided by this broker in the user's IntelligentPad environment.

Whenever a user makes a contract with a broker, he will receive an account pad from this broker (Figure 12.8). He can just drop this pad on the account icon pad in his IntelligentPad system to install all the account modules provided by this broker in the user's IntelligentPad environment. You can open this account icon pad to see all the registered account pads.

## 12.6   PAD INTEGRATION AND PACKAGE BUSINESS

Pad integrators who use pads developed by others to compose integrated systems should be also able to claim payment for the use of the integration structures. We propose a special pad for this requirement. This pad, called a ChargingPad, can be inserted between any two pads that are pasted together and also between the bottom pad and the desktop (Figure 12.9). The same pad is also used to cover the topmost pads. Although it passes all the user events and messages without any changes, it detects each passing of these events and is able to send a charge through its request module to the corresponding account module. Furthermore, if a user tries to peel or move this pad, the invoked procedure of this pad

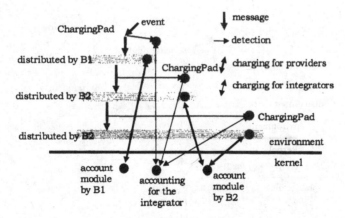

**Figure 12.9**   A ChargingPad can be inserted between any two pads. It passes all the user events and messages without any changes, but detects their passing and is able to send a charge through its request module to the corresponding account module.

sends a high charge as a penalty to the corresponding account module. System integrators can insert this pad at some appropriate positions of their composite pads.

Suppose that an integrator I uses a pad Pa that is provided by a provider P and distributed by a broker B to compose a composite pad Pb. When a user uses the pad Pb and hence the pad Pa, he should be charged for his use of Pa, and his payment should finally go both to its provider and to its distributor. The use of Pa makes its request module send a message to an account module provided by B. The user is correctly charged for his use of Pa.

If the integrator I wants to provide Pa with a special discount charge for its use under a special contract with its provider P and/or its broker B, he must be able to do that. This is guaranteed by the inserted ChargingPads (Figure 12.10). To reduce the charge for using Pa, the integrator can use its child pad ChargingPad and/or its parent pad ChargingPad. These ChargingPads take certain amounts from the account of the provider P and/or the broker B, and add some amount to the account of the integrator I. The charge to the accounts of P and B are based upon the contract of I with P and B. The ChargingPad allows each integrator to charge users for their use of the composition Pb even if he provides none of the components of Pb.

A package provider who provides sets of primitive and composite pads as package software should be also able to claim payment for the use of these packages. We can also use ChargingPad for this requirement. Each pad in a package is put on a ChargingPad and covered by another ChargingPad (Figure 12.11). The request modules in these Charging-Pads allow the package provider to charge users for their use of each pad in the package, whereas the request module in the member pad allows the provider and/or broker of this pad to charge users for their use of this pad.

If the package provider wants to provide each member of a package with a special discount charge for its use under a special contract with its provider and/or its broker, he

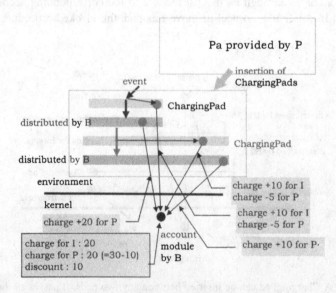

**Figure 12.10**   ChargingPads allow the integrator I to provide Pa with a special discount charge for its use under a special contract with its provider P and/or its broker B.

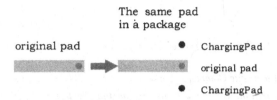

**Figure 12.11** Each pad in a package is put on a ChargingPad and covered by another Charging-Pad.

must be able to do that. This is also guaranteed by ChargingPads. To reduce the charge for using a member pad, the package provider can use its child pad ChargingPad and/or its parent pad ChargingPad. These ChargingPads take certain amounts from the account of the pad provider and/or the pad broker, and add some amount to the account of the package provider. The charge to the accounts of the pad providers and pad brokers are based on the contract of the package provider with them. The ChargingPad allows each package provider to charge users for their use of his or her package even if he or she provides none of its member pads.

## 12.7 SUMMARY

Electronic commerce means advertising, selling, and shopping for goods or services electronically through the Internet. Physical goods are shipped to the customer by various vehicles. Some nonphysical goods can be electronically shipped through the Internet. They include multimedia content and software. Pads are also software. Pads can be easily replicated. The copy protection on pads will deprive them of their roles to work as meme media. Their electronic commerce requires a pay-per-use billing system.

The distribution market of pads requires at least three kinds of players: providers, brokers, and users. A composite pad in the distribution market may consist of pads that are provided by different providers and/or distributed by different brokers. Its use activates its various component pads. Use of some component pads causes their providers and/or brokers to charge the user certain amounts of money. The charged amount should be paid to the provider and the broker of each component pad. Pay-per-use charging requires two modules. The first one is the account module. The second one is the request module. A request module is provided by a broker and used by a pad provider who has contracted with this broker for the distribution of this pad. A request module is built into a pad by the pad provider under contract with the broker. Different brokers provide different request modules. The request module of a broker can securely communicate with the account module of the same broker to update the account information kept in the account module. The account module may have an independent account for each provider. The broker can later use this information to divide the profit among all the contractor providers. Fair division of profit requires each account module to report its information periodically, say every month, to the broker.

This mechanism introduces business competition in providing and distributing intellectual resources, which will significantly enrich their variety and promote their distribution. The introduction of business activities changes a meme pool to a meme market.

## REFERENCES

1. R. Kalakota and A. B. Whinston. *Frontiers of Electronic Commerce*. Addison-Wesley, Reading, MA, 1996.
2. C. A. Jardin. *Java Electronic Commerce Source Book*. Wiley, New York, 1997.
3. B. Cox. *Superdistribution: Objects as Property on the Electronic Frontier*. Addison-Wesley, Reading, MA, 1996.
4. R. Mori and M. Kawahara. Superdistribution: The concept and the architecture. *Transactions of IEICE, E73*(7): 1133–1146, 1990.

# CHAPTER 13

# SPATIOTEMPORAL EDITING OF PADS

When a pad is pasted on another pad, the child pad usually works as an input and/or output device of the parent pad. However, this is not the only relationship we can define between the two pads. In this chapter, we will consider the case in which the parent controls the spatiotemporal arrangement of its child pads. We will begin with geometrical arrangements, then consider time-based arrangements and spatiotemporal arrangements. Then we will apply these arrangement functions to the information visualization of database records and Web documents.

## 13.1 GEOMETRICAL ARRANGEMENT OF PADS

Most drawing tools in use today can define a grid on a drawing sheet. They allow us to specify an arbitrary length for the grid interval. Such a grid has gravity at each grid point. Every point specified by a user is automatically adjusted to its closest grid point. This largely helps users to align graphical objects to horizontal and/or vertical lines. This grid is an example of geometrical management tools for graphical objects.

In this section, we will first consider geometrical management tools for spatial arrangement of pads. In the IntelligentPad architecture, these tools should also be defined as pads. Such pads are called geometrical management pads. In the following, we will show examples of geometrical management pads.

### 13.1.1 Tree Arrangement

Let us start with a tree as shown in Figure 13.1. This tree has a pad at each of its nodes. We want to dynamically add and delete its node pads. A closer observation of this tree tells us that it has a recursive construction structure as shown in Figure 13.2. This gives us a hint on what kinds of pads are necessary for this kind of geometrical management.

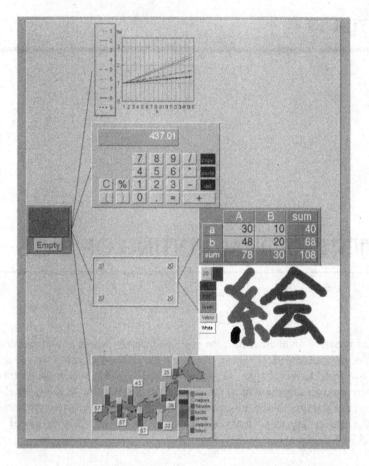

**Figure 13.1**  A tree with a pad at each of its nodes.

We require only one new primitive pad. Figure 13.3 shows this pad, called a TreePad. It accepts the pasting of one pad at the left center on itself, and an arbitrary number of pads at the right-hand side on itself. When a pad is pasted on it, a TreePad automatically enlarges its size to accommodate this pad as its new node [Figure 13.3(a)]. Pads pasted at the right-hand side are vertically arranged with either their left or right edges aligned [Figure 13.3(b)]. There are two types of TreePads, depending on whether their left or right edges are aligned. This process defines a two-level tree. A TreePad has slots to specify two intervals: one between the right edge of the root pad and the leftmost edge of the other pads, and the vertical interval between the two node pads. A TreePad has another slot to specify its orientation from its root to its leaves. There are four possible orientations: left-to-right, right-to-left, top-to-bottom, and bottom-to-top. The first two define horizontal trees, whereas the last two define vertical trees.

Since a TreePad is also a pad, it can be pasted at the right-hand side on another TreePad. This increases the number of levels of the base tree, as shown in Figure 13.4. Each TreePad can hide its borders when instructed through its slot to do so. A tree such as the one in Figure 13.1 can thus be obtained.

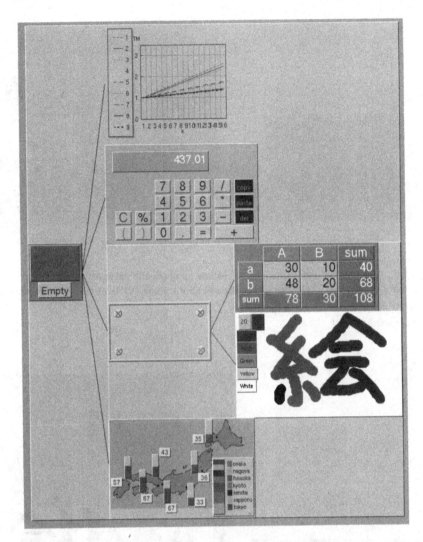

**Figure 13.2**   Closer observation of the tree in Figure 13.1 tells us that it has a recursive construction structure.

Figure 13.5 shows an application example of a TreePad. This tool has two windows side by side. When an arbitrary composite pad is dropped into the left window, this tool produces a composition structure comprised of a tree of primitive pads. This tool uses TreePads to construct this tree.

Figure 13.6 shows another type of tree arrangement. This base pad, called a RadiationalTreePad, arranges its child pads on a circle line whose radius is specified by one of its slots. When too many pads are pasted, they may overlap. Since this base pad is also a pad, it can be pasted on another pad with the same function. Figure 13.7 shows such a case, in which the child RadiationalTreePad with a smaller radius is made transparent.

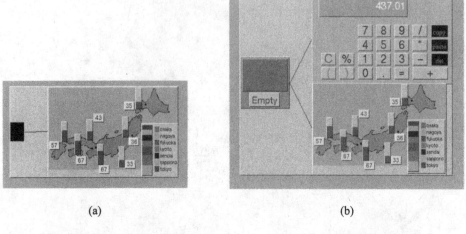

**Figure 13.3** When pasted with some pad, a TreePad automatically enlarges its size to accommodate this new node. (a) One composite pad is placed to form a leaf. (b) Two other pads are placed to form the root and a leaf.

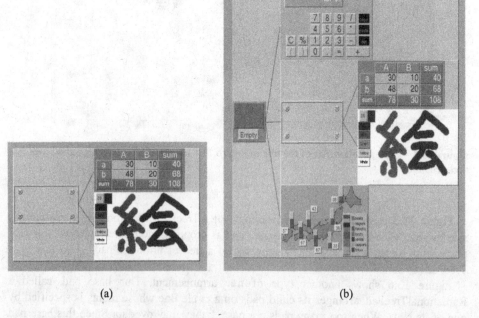

**Figure 13.4** Since a TreePad is also a pad, it can be pasted as a leaf on another TreePad. (a) An example tree. (b) A tree in (a) is embedded as the second leaf of the tree in Figure 13.3(b).

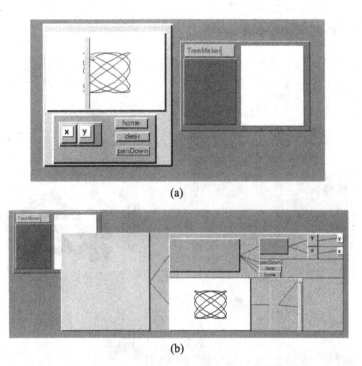

**Figure 13.5** When an arbitrary composite pad is dropped into the left window, this tool yields composition structure of a tree of primitive pads. It uses TreePads to construct this tree. (a) A composite pad working as an X–Y plotter will be dropped into the left window of the tool. (b) The tool pops up the composition structure of the input composite pad.

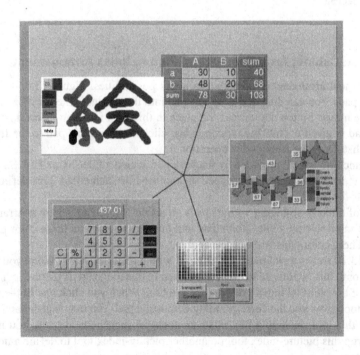

**Figure 13.6** A RadiatinalTreePad arranges its slave pads on a circle whose radius is specified by one of its slots.

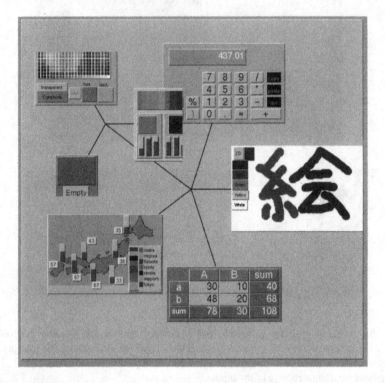

**Figure 13.7**    Another RadiationalTreePad with a smaller radius is made transparent and put on a RadiationalTreePad.

### 13.1.2   Pad Cabinet Arrangement and Picture Index Arrangement

The geometrical arrangement of pads has many possibilities. Figure 13.8 shows a file cabinet for pads. You can drag and drop any pad into this cabinet. The location where you released the mouse button determines the place in this list of pads to insert this new pad. The new pad is given a white tag, which, when clicked, moves this pad to the front position of the list. Only the front pad is operational.

These functions are all provided by the base pad, called a FileCabinetPad. Since this is also a pad, it can be dragged and dropped on another FileCabinetPad. This defines nested file cabinets for pads.

Instead of directly arranging various pads on a FileCabinetPad, you may arrange color pads of the same size on a FileCabinetPad and put various pads on these color pads (Figure 13.9). These color pads work as file folders.

Figure 13.10 shows a pad management tool with a pictorial index. When you drag and drop a pad onto this picture-index tool, it is stored in this tool, and its picture icon is added at the end of the pictorial index provided by this tool. When you click one of these picture icons, this tool gives you the corresponding composite pad. You may register any composite pads in this tool, including any other geometrical management pads. You may even drag and drop this picture-index tool on another picture-index tool to define a nested picture-index tool.

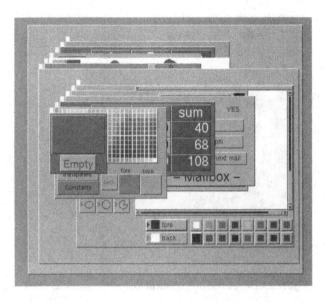

**Figure 13.8**  A file cabinet for pads allows you to drag and drop any pad into this cabinet.

## 13.2 TIME-BASED ARRANGEMENT OF PADS

The time-based arrangement of pads controls the hiding and showing of pads with respect to the current time or the elapsed time. Functions of this kind should be also provided as generic pads. These pads are called temporal arrangement pads. We will discuss some of them below.

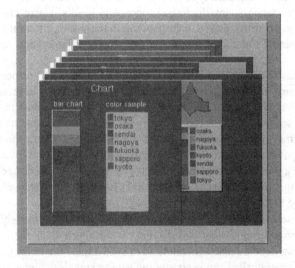

**Figure 13.9**  Instead of directly arranging various pads on a FileCabinetPad, you may arrange color pads of the same size on a FileCabinetPad to put varieties of pads on these color pads.

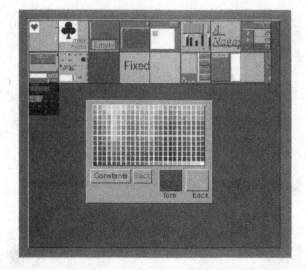

**Figure 13.10**  A pad management tool with a pictorial index.

Temporal arrangement requires a clock. We may consider four types of clocks.

1. Clocks that tell the current time
2. Clocks that tell an a priori specified time
3. Clocks that measure how much time has elapsed
4. Clocks that neither tell nor measure time, but provide pulses at a constant interval

Clocks of the first type are just called clocks, whereas those of the second type are called alarm clocks. Clocks of the third type are called timers, whereas clocks of the fourth type are called pulse generators. IntelligentPad represents clocks, alarm clocks, timers, and pulse generators as primitive pads. Corresponding to these four different types, it provides four different types of pads: ClockPads, AlarmClockPads, TimerPads, and PulseGeneratorPads.

A ClockPad has the following slots. The #date and #time slots, respectively, when accessed by a "gimme" message, return the date and time registered in these slots. The date consists of the year, the month, and the day, whereas the time consists of the hour, the minute, and the second. A ClockPad provides all these components as slots. When accessed by a "gimme" message, each of these component slots returns the value of the corresponding component by extracting this component from either the #date or the #time slot value. A clock pad provides one more slot. The #clock slot, when accessed by a "set" message, makes this pad get the current date and time from the system clock and send an "update" message to its child pads.

A ClockPad itself is passive in the sense that it does not autonomously change its state without any message from another pad. To make it work as a clock that changes its value at every second, we need a PulseGeneratorPad to send a message to the ClockPad at every second. A PulseGeneratorPad can keep sending trigger signals at a constant time interval.

A PulseGeneratorPad, when activated, invokes a process to make this pad keep issuing both an "update" and a "set" message at a specified constant time interval. Its #timeInterval slot specifies the time interval, which is set by a "set" message with a new time interval as its parameter. When accessed by a "set" message, its #start and #stop slots, respectively, activate and deactivate its process. A PulseGeneratorPad, when combined with a ClockPad as shown in Figure 13.11(a), forms both a digital clock and an analog clock as shown in Figure 13.11(b, c). The digital clock uses NumericalDisplayPads. Whenever it receives an "update" from the PulseGeneratorPad, each NumericalDisplayPad sends a "gimme" message to a time component slot in the ClockPad. The PulseGeneratorPad keeps sending an "update" message every second. Therefore, our digital clock changes its display every second. The analog clock uses three transparent circular meters whose value ranges for one rotation are 12, 60, and, 60. These three pads work as the hour, minute, and second needles.

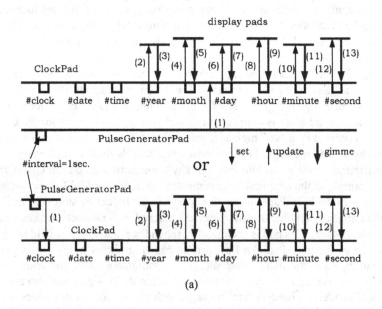

(a)

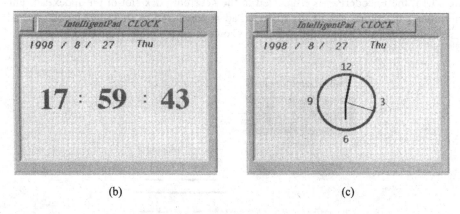

(b)                                          (c)

**Figure 13.11**   A PulseGeneratorPad, when combined with a ClockPad, forms both a digital clock and an analog clock. (a) A pulse generator is combined with a Clock pad to define a clock. (b) a digital clock composed as shown in (a). (c) An Analog clock composed as shown in (a).

An AlarmClockPad, when activated, invokes a process to make this pad issue both an "update" and a "set" message when it reaches an a priori specified time. Its #start and #stop slots, respectively, when accessed by a "set" message, activate and deactivate its process. Its alarm time is set by "set" messages through its slots. Depending on what kinds of slots are provided, we can have several kinds of AlarmClockPads. A DailyAlarm-ClockPad has a #time slot, which is set by a "set" message with a new signaling time as its parameter. Unless deactivated, it issues a signaling message at the specified time every day. A WeeklyAlarmClockPad has a #dayOfTheWeek slot and a #time slot. Unless deactivated, it issues a signaling message at the specified time on the specified day of the week every week. A MonthlyAlarmClockPad has a #dayOfTheMonth slot and a #time slot. Unless deactivated, it issues a signaling message at the specified time on the specified day of the month every month. An AnnualAlarmClockPad has a #dayOfTheYear slot and a #time slot. It works similarly on the specified day every year. A general AlarmClockPad has a #date slot and a #time slot. Unless deactivated, it issues a signaling message at the specified time on the specified day. Each of these pads also provides a slot to specify both day and time through this single slot.

Figure 13.12 shows an example application of AlarmClockPads to a very simple kind of temporal arrangement of pads. It uses two DaylyAlarmClockPads with 6:00 and 12:00, respectively, as their signaling time. The former is connected to the open slot of an Open-ClosePad, whereas the latter is connected to its close slot. This OpenClosePad, when its #open slot is accessed by a "set" message, reveals itself. It hides itself when its #close slot is accessed by a "set" message. This composite pad reveals itself at 6:00 every morning, and hides itself at 12:00 noon. You may put any composite pads on the OpenClosePad. This is an example of the temporal arrangement of pads. Figure 13.13 shows another example. This uses an IndexPad and an EncoderPad. An IndexPad stores an ordered sequence of an arbitrary number of pads. They are indexed with numbers. It shows only one of these pads on itself. This pad is specified by the index number that is held by the #currentIndex slot of the IndexPad. An EncoderPad has an arbitrary number of signal slots. They are numbered as #signal(1), #signal(2), . . . , #singnal(n). This pad allows us to increase or to decrease the number of signal slots. When its $i$th signal slot receives a "set" message, an EncoderPad issues a "set" message with the integer $i$ as its parameter. In Figure 13.13, the EncoderPad is connected to the #currentIndex slot of the IndexPad. Furthermore, each signal slot of the EncoderPad is connected to an DailyAlarmClockPad. This composite pad changes the pad that is shown at each a priori registered time.

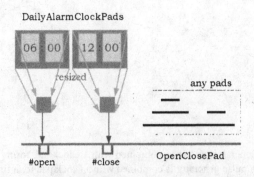

**Figure 13.12**   AlarmClockPads are used to show and to hide the same pad at specified times.

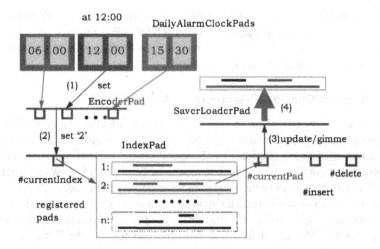

**Figure 13.13**   This composite pad stores some pads and changes the pad to show at each a priori registered time.

A TimerPad, when activated, invokes a process to make this pad issue both an "update" and a "set" message in a specified time length. It stops (kills) the process when the specified time has passed. Its #timeInterval slot specifies the time interval, which is set by a "set" message with a new time interval as its parameter. Its #start and #stop slots, respectively, when accessed by a "set" message, activate and deactivate its process. Figure 13.14 shows a game pad sitting on a KillerPad. A KillerPad deletes itself with all the pads on itself when its #kill slot is accessed with a "set" message. In Figure 13.14, a TimerPad is connected to the #kill slot of the KillerPad. The game in Figure 13.14 will disappear at the end of the time interval.

## 13.3   SPATIOTEMPORAL EDITING OF PADS

There are several ways to combine temporal control with geometrical arrangement. Clock pads can be used to control the geometrical arrangement. A MotionPad, whose motion can

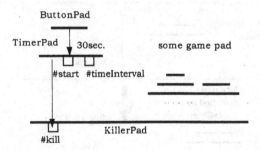

**Figure 13.14**   A game pad sitting on a KillerPad. A KillerPad deletes itself with all the pads on itself when its #kill slot is accessed with a "set" message. Here, a TimerPad is connected to the #kill slot of the KillerPad.

be a priori instructed in a step-by-step manner, can be used to make some pad change its location and size on its parent pad whenever this MotionPad receives an "update" or a "set" message to its clock slot. The hypermovie framework discussed in Section 7.3 is also an example of spatiotemporal editing of pads.

### 13.3.1   Temporal Control of Geometrical Arrangement

Here we will show how to make clock pads control geometrical arrangement. The pasting of an object pad on a geometrical arrangement pad invokes various geometrical arrangement functions discussed in Section 13.1. Temporal control of paste operations can equivalently specify temporal control of such invocations. Figure 13.15 shows a PasteControlPad, which controls when to paste a registered pad on its parent pad. A PasteControlPad has a #pad slot and a #timing slot. The #pad slot is used to register a composite pad into the PasteControlPad, whereas the #timing slot is used to connect a signaling pad such as an AlarmClockPad. The signal from the signaling pad triggers the PasteControlPad to paste the registered pad onto its parent pad.

Figure 13.16 shows the use of a PasteControlPad together with a TreePad. Let us first start with a single TreePad. For the root of this tree pad, we may directly paste any pad on the root. For each of its leaves, we use a PasteControlPad with a registered pad and an AlarmClockPad. The PasteControlPads are resized to their minimum size, and pasted on the TreePad as its leaf pads [Figure 13.16(a)]. When each AlarmClockPad triggers the pasting, the TreePad grows as shown in Figure 13.16(b). Since a TreePad is also a pad, it can be registered into a PasteControlPad, and indirectly pasted on another TreePad. Figure 13.16(b) shows the budding process of a pad tree that is a priori thus defined.

### 13.3.2   Moving Pads

Another type of spatiotemporal control of pads uses a MotionPad. This pad changes its location and size on its parent pad whenever it receives an "update" or a "set" message to its

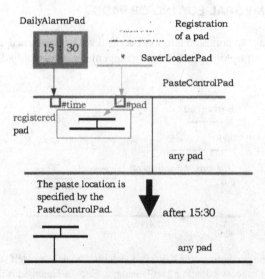

**Figure 13.15**   A PasteControlPad is used to control when to paste a registered pad on its master pad.

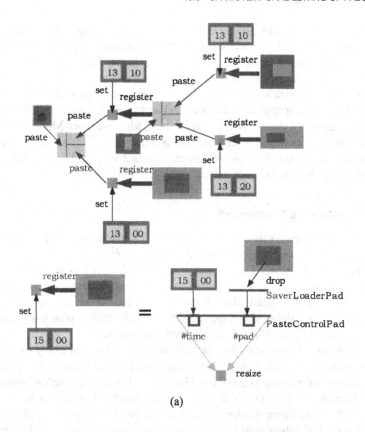

(a)

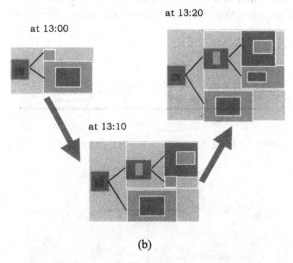

(b)

**Figure 13.16** PasteControlPads are used to control the budding of a tree with pad leaves. (a) For each leaf, we use a PasteControlPad with a registerd pad and an AlarmClockPad. Each PasteControlPad is resized to its minimum size and pasted on a TreePad as its leaf pad. (b) When each Alarm-ClockPad triggers the pasting, the TreePad grows as shown here.

#clock slot. Its motion can be a priori instructed in a step-by-step manner. The instruction may skip some steps. The size and location at these skipped steps are interpolated from the remaining steps using the spline interpolation scheme. The size and location are defined relative to the underlying pad. Therefore, the resizing of the underlying pad will proportionally change the size and location of the MotionPad. To provide a clock signal for a MotionPad, you may connect a PulseGeneratorPad to the #trigger slot of the MotionPad. A MotionPad can carry any composite pad on itself. More than one MotionPad can be put on the same pad. For example, several MotionPads that carry different movie pads may be put on another movie pad. An "update" message issued at each frame by the base movie pad provides each MotionPad with a clock signal.

### 13.3.3 Hypermovie Framework

The hypermovie framework discussed in Section 9.3 is also an example of spatiotemporal editing of pads. Here, we further extend the hypermovie framework.

The discussion in Section 9.3 assumed that each movie is played from its beginning. Therefore, we stored each movie segment as a file, and accessed it through an anchor pointing to this file. We assume that all the movie segments are concatenated to form a single movie, and that the movie player can immediately start to play this movie from an arbitrarily specified frame. QuickTime supports this function.

Anchors can be extended to point, not to another movie file, but to any frame of the underlying movie. When clicked, such an anchor makes the movie seamlessly jump to the specified frame to continue, as shown in Figure 13.17. In its general definition, such an anchor is defined by a function $f$ that maps a frame number i to another frame number $j$, i.e., $j = f(i)$. The input frame number of this function identifies the current frame in which the anchor is clicked, whereas its output frame number specifies the destination frame to which the clicked anchor makes the movie seamlessly jump. We can define such a func-

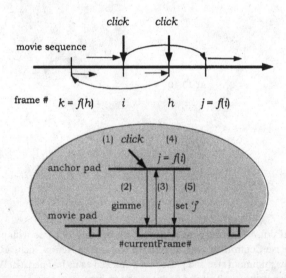

**Figure 13.17** When clicked, a hypermovie anchor makes the movie seamlessly jump to the specified frame to continue.

tion in several different ways. We may use an expression, a program, or a table to calculate the function.

Although it is simple, this framework works for various applications using different functions. Figure 13.18 shows some example functions. The first example divides the movie into two segments of the same length $n$. It uses the function $f(i) = i + n \bmod 2n$, where $i$ is the current frame number. Figure 13.19 shows frame jumps caused by this function. Suppose that the first and the second halves of this movie both show the same rotation of the same machinery, but with and without its exterior cover, respectively. When you click the movie during the rotation of the exterior view, you can immediately remove its cover to observe its internal mechanism. When clicked again, the movie shows the exterior again.

The second example in Figure 13.18 divides the movie into $k + 1$ segments of different lengths. The first of them has $k$ mutually disjoint parts. The function is defined as shown in the figure. If you click the movie in the $i$th part of the first segment, the movie jumps to the first frame of the $i + 1$st segment. On the other hand, if you click the movie in the $i + 1$st segment, the movie jumps to the beginning of the $i$th part of the first segment. An example application of this framework is as follows. The first segment shows a left-to-right pan of panoramic scenery. You can specify $k$ mutually disjoint sequences of frames in this segment. Each of them shows some significant object. For the $i + 1$st segment, you can use a movie shot that zooms in on the $i$th significant object. While you see a panoramic view, you can click the movie to zoom in. If the zoom-in sequence is a priori provided, you will see the zoom-in view.

Hypermovie anchor pads discussed in Section 9.3 can be also extended to specify jumps within a single movie. Instead of a local file name or a URL, an extended hyper-

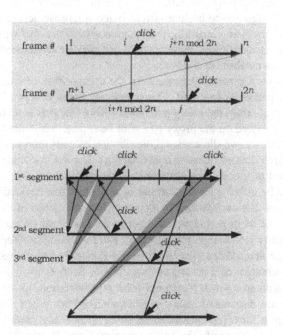

**Figure 13.18**  Various jump functions for hypermovies.

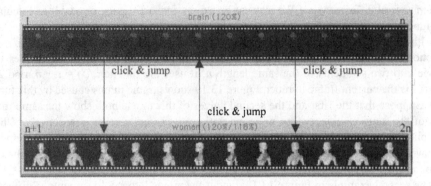

**Figure 13.19** The example application of the frame jump function $f(i) = i + n$ mod $2n$.

movie anchor pad holds a function that maps a current frame number to a destination frame number.

## 13.4 INFORMATION VISUALIZATION

A spatiotemporal arrangement of pads defines an interactive space. For pads representing various kinds of information, their arrangement defines an interactive space of information. Some people call such an environment "an information visualizer" or "a data visualizer" [1, 2], and its design "information visualization." Some others call its design methodology "the information architecture" [3]. The information architecture is the engineering of how to design and to build a virtual space where we access and interact with various kinds of information. Generally, information visualizers deal with a large number of records and data. In most cases, these records and data are dynamically retrieved from a repository such as a database or the Web.

Figure 13.20 shows a general framework for the composition of information visualizers. It uses a proxy pad as its base pad. This proxy pad works as a proxy to a database or the Web. As a retrieval result, the proxy pad holds a list of records in its result slot. A DistributionChartPad is pasted on the proxy pad with its connection to the #result slot of the proxy. This pad defines a two-dimensional distribution of pads representing records. This distribution uses three slots of a DistributionChartPad. The #xCoordinate and the #yCoordinate slots are used to specify two numerical value attributes of records. Each of these two attributes may be either a basic attribute or a derived one defined as a function of some basic attributes. For each record in the result list, the values of its selected two attributes are used to locate its pad representation on the DistributionChartPad. The #recordRepresentation slot is used to register a template pad for the #recordRepresentation. This template pad for the #recordRepresentation uses a RecordPad as its base. It may define such a form representation of a record as described in Section 10.2, or it may be just a small anchor pad with an a priori registered form representation. In the latter case, only small square pads are distributed on a DistributionChartPad. When clicked, each small square pad pops up a form representation of its corresponding record. A DistributionChartPad has also slots to specify the value range of X and Y coordinates. You may use this framework to show a two-dimensional distribution of cars with respect to their prices

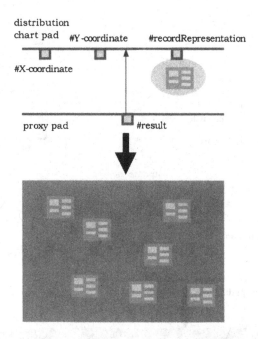

**Figure 13.20** A general framework for the composition of information visualizers with pads.

and production years. You may use the same framework to show the geographical distribution of birds whose locations are periodically updated by the data received through a satellite from the transmitters attached to them. In this application, the DistributionChartPad is made transparent, and a map pad is used under the distribution chart pad without specifying any slot connection.

Instead of a DistributionChartPad, you may use a SequencerPad, or both of these. A DistributionChartPad spatially arranges record-representing pads on itself, but a SequencerPad temporally arranges the display timing of each record in the retrieved record list. This temporal arrangement of record-representing pads uses five slots of a SequencerPad. The #timeAxis slot is used to specify one numerical value attribute of records. This attribute may be either a basic attribute or a derived one. For each record in the result list, the value of its selected attribute is used to calculate the time to display its pad representation on the SequencerPad. The #displayDuration slot is used to specify the duration time to display each record. The #ready slot indicates the readiness of the sequential display of a record list, and the #play slot is used to start this sequential display of records. The #recordRepresentation slot is used to register a template pad for the record representation. This template pad for the record representation uses a record pad as its base. As in the case of a DistributionChartPad, this template pad may define a form representation of a record, as described in Section 10.2.

Spatiotemporal arrangement of record distribution uses a DistributionChartPad and other two special pads. They are an AlarmClockPad and a HideAndShowPad. A HideAndShowPad alternatively hides and shows its child pads whenever it receives an "update" message, or a "set" message through its #switch slot. As shown in Figure 13.21, we insert three tiers of pads between a RecordPad and its child pads. They are of the same

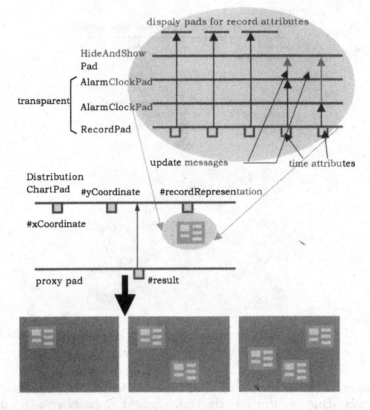

**Figure 13.21** Spatiotemporal arrangement of record distribution uses a DistributionChartPad, an AlarmClockPad, and a HideAndShowPad.

size as the RecordPad. They are a HideAndShowPad at the top, and two AlarmClockPads as the second and the third tiers. Two AlarmClockPads are connected to two attribute slots of the RecordPad. These two attribute values determine when to show and when to hide the record representation pad. The RecordPad and the lower two tiers of pads are all made transparent. This composite pad is registered into the record representation slot of a DistributionChartPad. When a database is accessed, the retrieved records are stored in the #result slot of the DBProxyPad, which sends an "update" message to the DistributionChartPad to read this record list. The DistributionChartPad arranges the pad representation of each record on itself. Each record-representation pad shows itself when the first "update" message comes from one of its AlarmClockPads, and hides itself when the second "update" message comes from the other AlarmClockPad. This visualizes the retrieved records in a spatiotemporal space.

Another type of spatiotemporal visualization of retrieved records represents each record as a pad whose motion also depends on some of its attribute values. The pad representation of a record in this case uses a composite pad as shown in Figure 13.22. The base is again a RecordPad. On top of it, we paste a MotionControlPad with its connection to one of the attribute slots. A MotionControlPad moves its parent pad over its grandparent pad. Its motion is specified by the relative location on the grandparent pad and does not change the relative locations of its child pads on itself.

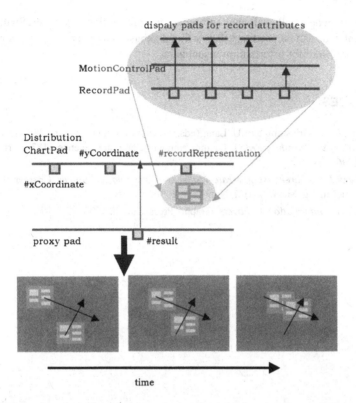

**Figure 13.22**  Another type of spatiotemporal visualization of retrieved records represents each record as a pad whose motion also depends on some of its attribute values. The pad representation of a record in this case uses such a composite pad as shown here.

## 13.5  SUMMARY

IntelligentPad provides special pads for the spatiotemporal arrangements of pads. As to the geometrical arrangements of pads, it provides a TreePad for the tree arrangement and a FileCabinetPad for the pad cabinet arrangement.

Temporal arrangement requires a clock. We may consider four types of clocks. IntelligentPad represents clocks, alarm clocks, timers, and pulse generators as primitive pads, i.e., a ClockPad, an AlarmClockPad, a TimerPad, and a PulseGeneratorPad. These pads are combined with an OpenClosePad to hide and show pads on this pad at predefined times.

There are several ways to combine temporal control with geometrical arrangement. Clock pads can be used to control the geometrical arrangement. A MotionPad whose motion can be a priori instructed in a step-by-step manner can be used to make some composite pad change its location and size on another pad whenever the MotionPad receives an "update" or a "set" message to its #clock slot. The hypermovie framework discussed in Section 9.3 is also an example of spatiotemporal editing of pads.

A spatiotemporal arrangement of pads defines an interactive space. For pads representing various kinds of information, their arrangement defines an interactive space of information. Some people call such an environment an information visualizer. Spatiotemporal arrangement pads can be used together with a database proxy pad to define a generic application framework for information visualizers.

## REFERENCES

1. A. Wierse, G. G. Grinstein, and U. Lang (eds.). *Database Issues for Data Visualization. (IEEE Visualization '95 Workshop Proc.)*. Lecture Notes in Computer Science 1183. Springer-Verlag, Berlin, 1996.
2. R. Mattison. *Data Warehousing: Strategies Technologies and Techniques*. Chapter 19. Visualization in Data Mining. McGraw-Hill, New York, 1996.
3. R. S. Wurman. *Information Architects*. Graphis Press, Zurich, 1996.

# CHAPTER 14

# DYNAMIC INTEROPERABILITY OF PADS AND WORKFLOW MODELING

Computer systems today must satisfy various application requirements through the bottom-up, cross-platform, and right-sized integration of system components distributed across networks. They are requested to immediately adapt themselves to the rapid changes of system requirements and component technologies. They should enable their users to easily build various systems just by dynamically combining varieties of data and application resources distributed across networks. The increasing demand for management flexibility in business organizations is accelerating this trend in computer systems. This chapter will propose application frameworks for such demands based on the IntelligentPad architecture.

## 14.1 DYNAMIC INTEROPERABILITY OF PADS DISTRIBUTED ACROSS NETWORKS

IntelligentPad represents both data and application resources as pads. The dynamic combination of distributed resources requires both dynamic interoperability of pads and the reference of a remote pad. This remote reference itself should take the form of a pad in the IntelligentPad Architecture. We call it a meta-pad.

IntelligentPad provides only two operations to define interoperations of pads. They are "paste" and "drag-and-drop" operations. A "paste" operation dynamically defines a static functional linkage between two pads. Once the linkage is defined, it exists until it is broken by a "peel" operation. A "drag-and-drop" operation, on the other hand, dynamically applies the function of a target pad to an object pad. This function is applied only once to the object pad when it is dropped on the target pad. The interoperation defined by a "paste" operation is said to be static, whereas the one defined by a "drag-and-drop" operation is said to be dynamic.

The target pad of a "drag-and-drop" operation should be an annihilator pad, which receives the dropped pad, stores this pad in itself, and hides this pad from the surface of itself. The target pad may access any slots of the object pad. The target pad needs to know the slot name before it accesses this slot.

The output of a pad from a tool pad should pop up this pad on a pad that works as an output port of the tool, which allows the user to directly drag this output pad for further manipulations. Such a pad that works as an output port receives a pad as its new stored value either from another pad or from an external system, generates this pad as a visual object, and pops it up on itself. We call such a pad a generator pad.

Figure 14.1 shows a composite pad with one annihilator pad and two generator pads. They are connected to an input slot and two output slots of the base pad, which, when an object is input to its input slot, outputs two of its copies through its two output slots. When you drop an arbitrary pad on the annihilator pad, you will obtain two of its copies on the two generator pads. To use these copies, you can just drag them out of the two generator pads. The annihilator pad absorbs the dropped pad and sends this pad to the underlying

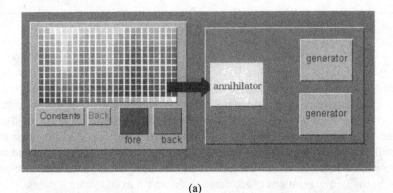

(a)

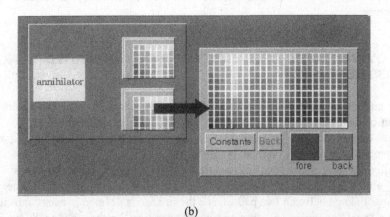

(b)

**Figure 14.1** A composite pad with one annihilator pad and two generator pads replicates any pad that is dropped onto the annihilator pad, and pops the two copies upon the generator pads. (a) A composite pad with a single annihilator pad and two generator pads, and a pad to feed into the annihilator pad. (b) The input pad is replicated and the two copies are popped up on the generator pads.

base pad, which then makes its copy and sends this copy together with the original to the two output slots. These output slots are connected to the two generator pads. The base pad sends an "update" message to the generator pads to fetch the current value of their connected slots, which then makes these generator pads pop up the fetched copies of the input pad.

In IntelligentPad, any processing service, when considered as an independent object, should take the form of a composite pad. The same is true for its input and output objects, whether they are data, texts, figures, images, or programs. They should all take the form of pads. The drag-and-drop operation is the only way for end-users to dynamically associate each processing service with its input and output objects. The end-user computing with various types of processing services needs to make these service tools defined as pad converter pads that convert dropped pads to pop up result pads as outputs.

Our architecture for dynamic interoperability aims at the step-wise, bottom-up integration of already existing systems, i.e., integration of personal environments into a group environment, group environments into a department environment, department environments into a company environment, and company environments into an enterprise environment. We assume here that all these environments are implemented in IntelligentPad systems. They are all assumed to consist purely of pads. We have no plan to integrate legacy software without a priori wrapping each of them to work as a pad. Bottom-up integration aims to integrate already running systems to work interactively and consistently without changing these systems.

The most difficult problem in bottom-up integration is how already existing systems that are distributed across networks can know each other in order to communicate. To solve this problem, we introduce the concept of meta-pads. A meta-pad works as a proxy of some primitive pad, which we call the referent of this meta-pad. A meta-pad can be sent to any machine different from the machine with its referent. Meta-pads are different from proxy pads. A proxy pad works for an external object, whereas a meta-pad works for a remote primitive pad. A pad may have more than one copy of its meta-pad. Meta-pads and their referent always know how to access each other even if some of them travel across networks. Each meta-pad holds the address of its referent pad, and the referent holds an address list of its meta-pads. Here we classify referent primitive pads into five categories: pad annihilators, pad generators, pad converters, pad gates, and others. The functions of their meta-pads differ from each other.

A meta-pad for a pad annihilator is used to drop a locally available pad onto a remote annihilator pad. When a pad is dropped on it, the meta-pad transports this pad to its referent annihilator, and drops it there (Figure 14.2). A meta-pad for a pad generator is used to retrieve a new pad that is popped up on the pad generator at a remote site. When a pad is popped up on its referent, the meta-pad receives a meta-pad of this newly generated pad and pops it up on itself (Figure 14.3).

A pad converter performs some conversion of pads. It has input-port slots and output-port slots. Each input-port slot has its corresponding queue buffer. When it receives a "set" message with some pad as its parameter, an input-port slot adds this pad to the corresponding input queue. Each output-port slot, when accessed by a "gimme" message, gets the pad stored in the corresponding register, and returns it to the message sender; if the corresponding register is empty, this output-port slot returns "nil." A pad converter starts its execution as an independent process whenever the preceding conversion has been completed, and all the new inputs necessary for the new conversion are available in input queues. For each output slot, this conversion process sets the corresponding register

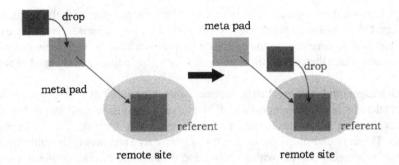

**Figure 14.2**   A meta-pad for a pad annihilator is used to drop a locally available pad onto a remote pad.

with a new pad, and sends an "update" message to the child pads connected to this slot. Each conversion is considered complete when all the output slots have been accessed by "gimme" messages to return new pads to their senders.

To input a pad into an input-port slot by a drag-and-drop operation, we need to paste an annihilator pad called an InputPortPad with its connection to this slot. Similarly, to pop up a pad in an output-port slot, we need to paste a generator pad called an OutputPortPad with its connection to this slot. Each OutputPortPad, when it receives an "update" message, sends its parent pad a "gimme" message to get the next output pad, and pops this pad up on itself.

A meta-pad for a pad converter has a subset of those slots in its referent pad converter. It has input-port slots and output-port slots. These ports, however, have no queue buffers. Each of its input-port slots, when receiving a pad or its meta-pad, inputs this pad to the corresponding input-port slot of the referent pad converter. Every meta-pad that is input to a pad converter autonomously retrieves its referent to replace itself with its referent when required by the pad-conversion process. Each of its output-port slots, when accessed by a "gimme" message, sends this message to the corresponding slot of the referent; if the referent returns a pad, this output port slot returns a meta-pad of this read out pad to the message sender; otherwise, it returns "nil." A meta-pad of a pad converter allows a user to use this pad converter from a remote site (Figure 14.4).

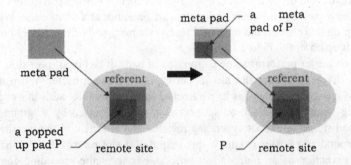

**Figure 14.3**   A meta-pad for a pad generator is used to retrieve a new pad that is popped up at a remote site.

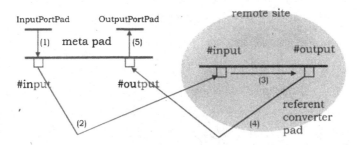

**Figure 14.4** A meta-pad of a pad converter allows a user to use this pad converter from a remote site.

A pad gate works as a queue buffer of pads. It has two modes—the output-enabled mode and the output-disabled mode. It is a pad with a single input-port slot, a single output-port slot, and a control slot. Pads are input through the input-port slot and stored in the queue. When its queue is empty, a pad gate pad stays in the output-disabled mode. Otherwise, when a "set" message accesses its control slot, a pad gate changes its mode to the output-enabled mode. If a "gimme" message accesses its output-port slot during its output-enabled mode, a pad gate outputs the first pad in the queue as the return value, and changes its mode to the output-disabled mode. If a "gimme" message accesses its output port slot during its output-disabled mode, it returns "nil." A pad gate pad issues an "update" message to its child pads whenever it changes its mode from the output-disabled mode to the output-enabled mode.

A meta-pad for a pad gate has three slots: an input-port slot, an output-port slot, and a control slot. It has, however, no queue buffers. Its input-port slot, when receiving a pad or its meta-pad, inputs this pad to the input-port slot of the referent. Its output-port slot, when accessed by a "gimme" message, sends this message to the output-port slot of the referent. If the referent returns a pad, this output-port slot returns a meta-pad of this read-out pad to the message sender; otherwise, it returns "nil." Pad gates do not convert input meta-pads to their referents. They treat their inputs as tokens without referring to the contents. An access of the control slot of a meta-pad is transferred to its referent pad-gate pad. A meta-pad of a pad gate allows a user to use this pad gate from a remote site (Figure 14.5).

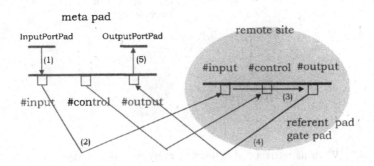

**Figure 14.5** A meta-pad of a pad gate allows a user to use this pad gate from a remote site.

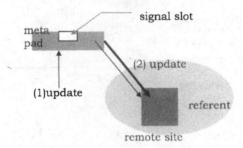

**Figure 14.6** When receiving an "update" message, every meta-pad makes its referent pad invoke the "update" method. This function is used to detect a local signal and to invoke the "update" procedure of a remote pad.

In addition to the functions described above, every meta-pad has a signal slot and the following functions. When receiving an "update" message, every meta-pad makes its referent pad invoke the "update" method (Figure 14.6). This function is used to detect a local signal and to invoke the "update" procedure of a remote pad. When its referent pad is updated, every meta-pad changes its signal slot value to "true," and issues both an "update" message and a "set" message with "true" as the parameter (Figure 14.7). This function is used to locally detect an update of a remote referent pad. The signal slot can be reset to "false" by sending a "set" message with "false" as its parameter.

For every meta-pad, its copies work for independent copies of the same referent, whereas its shared copies work for the same referent.

Instead of directly dragging and dropping a pad to and from another pad, we can use their meta-pads. If these referent pads exist at different sites, their interoperability cannot be directly specified without using their meta-pads.

## 14.2 EXTENDED FORM-FLOW SYSTEM

The form-flow model is a kind of workflow model. It was intensively studied in the latter half of 1970s and early 1980s [1, 2]. Recent advances in object-oriented modeling tech-

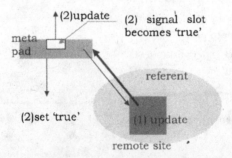

**Figure 14.7** When its referent pad is updated, every meta-pad changes its signal slot value to "true," and issues both an "update" message and a "set" message with "true" as the parameter. This function is used to locally detect an update of a remote referent pad.

nologies have simplified the systematic modeling of forms and their flows, and have recently revitalized its study. The IntelligentPad architecture has further simplified form-flow modeling. It can directly define forms as composite pads.

### 14.2.1 Form-Flow Model in IntelligentPad

The form-flow model consists of several different kinds of components. They include forms, form converters, form generators, form annihilators, triggers, distributors, mergers, inspectors, gates, detectors, and flow definitions (Figure 14.8).

Forms visually represent information. A single form has an arbitrary number of entry cells. They are arbitrarily arranged on the base sheet of the form. Some entry cells may contain smaller forms. Users cannot change the formats of forms. Some forms, however, may allow users to fill in or rewrite some entry cells.

A form converter receives input forms and converts them to a single form or a sequence of forms of the same output format that is different from the input format. It reads out some entry cells of the input forms to compute each entry cell of the output forms. A form generator generates a form. It is a special type of form converter. The information necessary to generate a form does not come from any other forms, but from an external system such as a database, an e-mail system, a fax machine, an industrial plant, or a user interaction system. A form annihilator receives input forms and deletes them from the system; it outputs their contents information to an external system such as a database, an e-mail system, a fax machine, an industrial plant, or a user interaction system.

A trigger is a module to generate a control signal that opens or closes a gate to control a form flow from one module to another. Triggers may be various objects. A system alarm clock, for example, is a trigger that issues a control signal at some specified time and date.

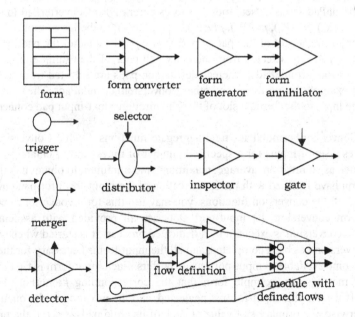

**Figure 14.8** Components of the form-flow model.

A distributor has a single input port and multiple output ports. Depending on its selector signal, it selects one of its output ports to output the form it receives. A merger merges more than one input flow to a single output flow.

An inspector receives each input form and outputs either a control signal or a selector signal whose value depends on whether the input form satisfies the specified condition. Its output signal is used to control a gate or a distributor.

A detector, when receiving an input form, immediately outputs this form and issues a trigger signal.

The IntelligentPad architecture implements these components as composite pads. A form uses a RecordPad as its base pad. Entry cells of a form may use various pads including text, numerical, chart, image, sound, and video pads. They are pasted on a RecordPad to compose a form.

A FormConverterPad is a blank-sheet pad with several slots including the #conversion-Formulae slot, #inputForm slots, #outputForm slots, #inputFormFormat slots, #output-FormFormat slots, and #reset slot. Its #conversionFormulae slot is used to specify formulas to calculate the output-form entries from the input-form entry values. Each #inputForm slot is used to input a form to the form converter, whereas each #outputForm slot is used to output a converted form. Each #inputFormFormat slot and each #output-FormFormat slot are used to maintain pointers to example input and output forms that work as the input and output form templates, respectively. The slot #reset is used to initialize the form converter.

ConversionFormulaPads are all connected to the single same #conversionFormulae slot of a FormConverterPad. Each conversion-formula pad enables us to specify its source pads for each of its input variables, its destination pad for its single output variable, and the formula to compute its output variable value from its input variable values. Suppose that a ConversionFormulaPad defines a conversion function $f(x_1, x_2, \ldots, x_n)$, and associates each input variable $x_i$ with a pad $P_i$, and its single output variable with $P_o$. This ConversionFormulaPad sends a "set" message to its parent FormConverterPad to add a tuple $[f(x_1, x_2, \ldots, x_n), pid(P_0), pid(P_1), pid(P_2), \ldots, pid(P_n)]$ to the list of tuples stored in the #conversionFormulae slot of this parent pad, where $pid(P)$ denotes the pad identifier of a pad P. Source pads are selected from the entry-cell pads of the example input forms and other ConversionFormulaPads, whereas destination pads are selected from the entry-cell pads of the example output forms and other ConversionFormulaPads. The conversion formula can be input to the formula slot of this pad through a text-input pad connected to this slot.

Some ConversionFormulaPads treat aggregate functions. Such a ConversionFormulaPad receives a set of inputs for a specified number of times, and calculates an aggregate function such as summation, average, maximum, and minimum to obtain its output value.

Once you have finished with the specification of the input-form formats, output-form format, and all the conversion functions, you may use this form converter to perform the defined form conversion. Its input-port slots are all provided with associated queue buffers. The conversion is executed by a dedicated process. It is started whenever the preceding conversion has been completed, and all the input forms necessary for the next conversion become available in input-port queue buffers. Each input form is first examined if its format matches the example form that the corresponding #inputFormFormat slot points to. If it fails, this input form is neglected, and the next one in the queue is examined. Otherwise, the primary slot value of each of its child pads is set to the primary slot of the corresponding child pad of the example form that the corresponding form-format slot points to. These primary slots are the primary slots for the "gimme" message. Then each function stored in the #conversionFormulae slot is applied.

A FormConverterPad interprets the list in its #conversionFormulae slot as a data-flow program, and execute this program. Its execution of an instruction $[f(x_1, x_2, \ldots, x_n),$ $pid(P_0), pid(P_1), pid(P_2), \ldots, pid(P_n)]$ reads, from each source pad, its primary slot for the "gimme" message, uses these values to compute the function value, and sends this value to the destination pad through its primary slot for the "set" message. Let a terminal pad in such a data-flow program denote a pad that appear as an output destination of some instruction, but never as an input source of any instruction. When all the terminal pads are set with new values, a FormConverterPad makes a copy of the form pointed to by the #outputFormFormat slot, then stores this pad in the #outputForm slot, and issues an "update" message to its child pads. When its #outputForm slot is accessed by a "gimme" message, and returns a converted form, this FormConverterPad completes a conversion. If an OutputPortPad is connected to this slot, it then issues a "gimme" message to get the form in the #outputForm slot and to pop up this form on itself. Some form converter may require more than one input form coming through the same input port to complete a conversion. Some others may generate more than one output forms of the same format in a single conversion process.

Figure 14.9 shows a form converter with one form input and one form output. This converter outputs a single form as a summary for every consecutive five input forms. The left ConversionFormulaPad reads two cells of each input form, multiplies these two, and outputs the product. The right ConversionFormulaPad receives this product, adds it to its current sum, and outputs this sum for every five consecutive inputs. This sum is reset to zero after every output. Whenever the summation function outputs a new value to a cell of the output-form template, the template with this value is copied and stored in the #outputForm slot as a new output form.

The implementation of form generators and form annihilators will be detailed later.

As trigger components, IntelligentPad provides various trigger-signal generators. They include alarm-clock pads and interval-timer pads. A gate pad can be used as a first input first output (FIFO) queue of forms; its control signal is used to enable a single output from this queue.

A FlowDefinitionPad works as a circuit board on which various tool pads are connected with each other. It allows us to draw a cable from a primitive pad $P_1$ of one composite tool pad on itself to a primitive pad $P_2$ of another composite tool pad on itself (Figure 14.10). This wiring adds a tuple $(P_2, P_1)$ to the list stored in the FlowDefinitionPad. For each tuple $(P_i, P_j)$ in this list, a FlowDefinitionPad sends a "gimme" message to $P_j$ to read

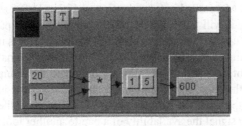

**Figure 14.9**  A form converter that outputs a single form as a summary for every consecutive five input forms.

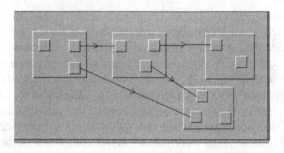

**Figure 14.10**   A FlowDefinitionPad works as a circuit board on which various tool pads are connected with each other.

its primary slot for the "gimme" message whenever $P_j$ issues an "update" message. This FlowDefinitionPad then sends a "set" message to $P_i$ to write this read out value to its primary slot for the "set" message. The tool pads include form converters, queue buffers, distributors, mergers, and detectors. These composite tool pads use FormConverterPads, PadQueuePads, PadDistributorPads, MergerPads, and PadDetectorPads as their base pads, respectively.

A PadQueuePad has a #input slot, a #output slot, and a #outputRequest slot, and works as a queue buffer. When a pad is input to the #input slot, it is added to the end of the pad queue in the buffer. When a request signal is input to the #outputRequest slot, a PadQueuePad outputs the first pad in its pad queue to its #output slot. If it has no pad to output, it will immediately output the next input pad when it comes. A PadQueuePad issues an "update" message whenever its #output slot is updated. A PadQueuePad implements a gate that opens/closes the output gate of a queue buffer depending on its control signal.

A PadDistributorPad has a #input slot, several output slots, and a #selector slot. It has also an input queue, not only for the #input slot, but also for the #selector slot. When a pad is input through its #input slot, it is added to the pad queue. When a selector number is input to the #selector slot, it is added to the selector queue. If the selector queue is not empty, a PadDistributorPad outputs the first pad in the pad queue to the output slot that is selected by the first selector in the selector queue. If a PadDistributorPad has no pad to output, it will immediately output the next input pad to the next selected output slot when a new pad is input to the pad queue. A PadDistributorPad issues an "update" message whenever one of its output slots is updated.

A MergerPad has several input slots, a #output slot, and a #outputRequest slot. It has also a single input pad queue and an output request queue. When a pad is input through one of its input slots, it is added to the pad queue. When a request signal is input to the #outputRequest slot, a MergerPad outputs the first pad in its buffer to its #output slot. If it has no pad to output, it will immediately output the next input pad when it comes. A MergerPad issues an "update" message whenever its #output slot is updated.

A PadDetectorPad has a #input slot, a #output slot, and a #signal slot. When a pad is input to the #input slot, this pad is immediately output to the #output slot, the Boolean value "true" is set to the #signal slot, and an "update" message is issued. When a pad is read out from the #output slot, the Boolean value "false" is set to the #signal slot. A PadDetectorPad is used to signal the availability of a pad to another tool pad.

In addition to these pads, any composite pads can be used as tool pads on FlowDefinitionPads.

Instead of using FlowDefinitionPads, we may use wiring pads to transport forms from an output-port slot of some pad to an input-port slot of another pad. Wiring pads send the value of a slot of one pad to a slot of another pad whenever the source slot changes its value. To use a wiring pad, you can paste a wiring pad on the source pad with its slot connection to the source slot, and also paste a shared copy of this wiring pad on the destination pad with its slot connection to the destination slot. Different from ordinary shared copies, a shared copy of a wiring pad can receive any update of the original, but cannot propagate its update to the original.

### 14.2.2  Virtual Forms to Assimilate Transaction-Based Systems

In form-flow systems, it is hard to maintain consistency among the contents of forms. IntelligentPad provides a shared-copy operation to maintain the consistency among copies of the same form. This, however, does not work for maintaining the integrity of the contents of different forms. Some forms will have such integrity, while others may not. This can be resolved by the use of a database to maintain the integrity of such forms. This is the main reason why the form-flow model attracted mainly database researchers' attention during late 1970s and early 1980s.

We introduced the concept of virtual forms for this purpose. Virtual forms are kept consistent with the databases. Each virtual form represents a record of some view relation defined over a database. They access their related databases to fill in their unspecified entries, or to insert their records to the databases. Their programs define their ways of accessing databases. Here we define two special types of virtual forms: reader forms and writer forms. A reader form distinguishes some of its entries from others, and allows its users or form converters to fill in only those entries. We call these entries input entries. The reader form automatically fills in the remaining entries by accessing the database. A writer form, when all of its entries are filled in, inserts this record into the database.

Virtual forms can be considered proxies of the database views discussed in Section 10.2. An example of a reader form is an employee-record form. It has entries such as ID#, name, age, sex, address, salary, etc. If employee records are kept in a database, it is not necessary for either users or form converters to specify any entry values other than the ID#. The remaining entry values can be retrieved from the database using the given ID#. Furthermore, this reader form always presents the up-to-date entry values, consistent with the database, whenever these values are requested to be read.

When a reader form is input to a form converter as its input form, the form converter requests this reader form to present all the required entry values. This request makes the reader form access its related database to retrieve those values. A reader form may also be registered as an output form of a form converter. In such a case, the form converter fills in only its input entries. When a copy of the reader form is output, it fills in its remaining entries by accessing the related database.

Writer forms are only used as output forms of form converters. They are not used as input forms of any form converter. When a form converter has filled in all of its entries, a writer form accesses the related database to insert the record it holds to the database. Then the converter outputs this form, which will not be further rewritten and will work as a real form.

Virtual forms may also work as proxies for any other transaction-based systems and external devices. They include production-line control systems, delivery-control systems, warehouse-control systems, shipping-control systems, fax machines, e-mail systems, and user-interaction systems. The rewriting of a writer form means that it controls a production line, a delivery system, a warehouse system, or a shipping system. When applied to a fax machine or an e-mail system, it means the transmission of a letter constructed from the form record and an a priori registered letter template. Its destination might also be determined from some entry values of the form record. When applied to a user-interaction system, it means the presentation of the form record to a user.

The accessing of a transaction-based system or external device by a reader form, on the other hand, means the monitoring of this system. When applied to a production line, a delivery system, a warehouse system, or a shipping system, it means the monitoring of their states. When applied to an e-mail system, it means the access of the first message in the message queue. When applied to a user-interaction system, it prompts the user to input requested values.

We can monitor and control any transaction-based systems and any user-interaction systems through their virtual forms. Furthermore, these virtual forms can be manipulated by an integrated form-flow system. Virtual forms extend the form-flow model to integrate not only office work, but also all the enterprise activities that office workers control and monitor. Furthermore, this integration completely encapsulates those transaction-based subsystems and hides their details from users of the form-flow system (Figure14.11).

### 14.2.3  Form Generators and Form Annihilators

Form generators and form annihilators also work as proxies of external objects such as a database, an e-mail system, a fax machine, an industrial plant, or a user-interaction system. Different from virtual forms, they do not travel through a form-flow system by them-

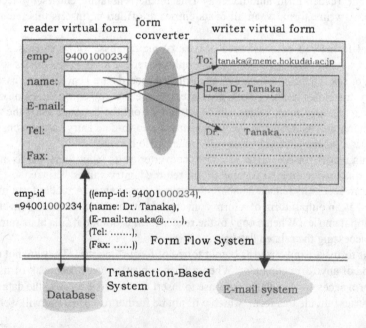

**Figure 14.11**  Virtual forms are used to integrate various transaction-based systems with form-flow systems by encapsulating them and hiding their details from users.

selves. Instead, they generate or consume forms that travel. A form generator allows us to register a reader form. A reader form accesses the external system when it receives a read request. A form generator, on the other hand, is triggered by its associated external system to request its registered virtual form to access this external system. The form generator then generates a form with the same format and the same contents as the result of this registered virtual form. The generated form may or may not be a virtual form. Form generators for e-mail systems can transform any messages they receive to forms, and forward them to various tools in form-flow systems. Every form generator also issues an "update" message and a "set" message as ready signals when it has generated a form. These signals can be used as trigger signals.

A form annihilator allows us to register a writer form. It accepts as its input a real form with the same format of the registered form. When an input form arrives, it maps the contents of this form to the registered writer form, deletes the input form, and tells this writer form to output its message to the corresponding external system. When applied to an e-mail system, a form annihilator can automatically generate an e-mail text and its destination address from each input form, and send this text to this destination. Every form annihilator also issues an "update" message and a "set" message as ready signals when it completes its execution. These signals can be used as trigger signals.

Form generators and form annihilators together with some virtual forms can integrate external communication systems and transaction-based systems with form-flow systems.

## 14.3  PAD-FLOW SYSTEMS

The form-flow system architecture in IntelligentPad can be further extended to a pad-flow system architecture, which deals with flows of various pads instead of form pads. In pad-flow systems, form converters are extended to pad converters. Form annihilators and form generators are extended to pad annihilators and pad generators, respectively. Other component pads for form-flow systems are used in the same way in pad-flow systems. They are triggers, distributors, mergers, inspectors, gates, detectors, and flow definitions.

Pad-flow systems can model flows of objects through various processing services. They can treat any objects that can be represented as pads. The connection of an output port of one service to an input port of another service can be defined either by a FlowDefinitionPad or by a wiring pad.

Processing services are represented by pad converters. A pad converter has some number of input-port slots, a #outputPort slot, and a #reset slot. It has a queue for each of its input ports. Different from form converters, pad converters do not have input-form format slots, output-form format slots, or conversion-formulae slots.

The conversion is executed by a dedicated process. It is started whenever the preceding conversion has been completed, and all the input pads necessary for the next conversion become available in input-port queue buffers. Each conversion computes an output pad from the input pads; it sends this output pad to the #outputPort slot, and makes this pad converter issue an "update" message to its child pads. When its #outputPort slot is accessed by a "gimme" message and returns a converted pad, this pad converter completes a conversion. If an OutputPortPad is connected to this #ouputPort slot, it issues a "gimme" message to get the output pad in the #outputPort slot, and pops up this pad on itself.

For example, we may treat an input image as an image pad, and consider an edge-detection program as a pad converter. Then the converter outputs the processed image as a pad. An InputPortPad and an OutputPortPad are pasted on this pad converter with their connection to the input-port slot and the output-port slot, respectively. This composite pad allows users to drag and drop any image pad on its InputPortPad, and pops up the edge-detected image as a pad on its OutputPortPad.

Pads to flow through pad-flow systems might be proxy pads of some external objects. Proxy pads in pad-flow systems play the same role as virtual forms in form-flow systems. The details on how a pad converter, a pad annihilator, or a pad generator process their input and output proxy pads are left to the definition of its processing function.

## 14.4 DYNAMIC INTEROPERABILITY ACROSS NETWORKS

Form-flow systems as well as form converters define form-processing services. More generally, pad-flow systems and pad converters, respectively, define complex and simple object-processing services. As discussed in Chapter 11, these systems as pads can be published through the Internet or intranets by embedding them in web pages. This type of publication, however, transports the processing services themselves to client machines. There should be another type of publication, i.e., the publication of service ports. Each service has its input and output ports. Instead of publishing a service program itself, we may only publish its input and output ports. When a service has published its input and output ports by embedding its pad representations in a Web page, we can open this page and drag and drop an object pad into the input-port pad to request its processing. When the processing completes, the result will be popped up on the output-port pad on the same page. We can drag out this pad for further local use.

### 14.4.1 Network Publication of Form-Flow and Pad-Flow Systems

The publication of service ports uses InputPortPads, OutputPortPads, and their meta-pads. InputPortPads are pad annihilators, whereas OutputPortPads are pad generators. These meta-pads, when published through their embedding in Web pages, can be used by remote users to input and output pads to and from the services with their referent input- and output-port pads. The publication of service ports allows us to open several Web pages one after the other or simultaneously to drag and drop pads from one service to another across the Internet to perform a sequence of pad conversions. It allows us to dynamically link several processing services distributed around the world to perform a complex job.

When more than one user simultaneously accesses the same service, the publication of service ports fails to distinguish the set of inputs and outputs of each user from those of others. To solve this problem, we can publish a meta-pad of a pad converter, and use its different copies for different users. This also replicates the service program running on the service site. It is also possible to extend a pad converter and its meta-pads for a single-service program to process more than one request. This extension can use the colored token technique that is well known in data-flow programming.

### 14.4.2 Bottom-up Integration across Networks

Pads for form-flow systems and pad-flow systems provide an easy way for end-users to define flows of work in an office, a laboratory, a factory, a bank, an enterprise, and, fur-

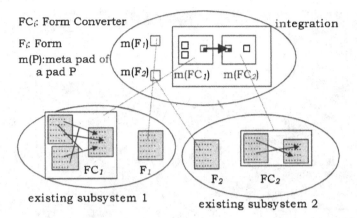

**Figure 14.12**  The publication of meta-pads and their connection at a client site provides a remote patch board for pads and pad converters.

thermore, across these organizations. These works are, however, inherently distributed through a local area network or even through a global area network.

Meta-pads provide a method to integrate more than one form-flow or pad-flow system distributed across networks. Instead of directly connecting forms and form converters, or pads and pad converters, we can connect their meta-pads on a flow-definition pad. The resulting composite pad works as a remote controller of forms and form converters, or of pads and pad converters. If the meta-pads are published on a Web page through the Internet or an intranet, we can define the connection of remote pads and remote converters in our own local environment. Furthermore, these pads and converters may be distributed across networks; their meta-pads can be published through the Internet by embedding them in arbitrary Web pages. By dragging these meta-pads out of different Web pages, we can wire the output of one of them to the input of another. The publication of meta-pads and their connection at a client site provide a remote patch board for pads and pad converters. Figure 14.12 shows such a definition. This example integrates two existing systems using meta-pads. These two may run on different sets of machines. The remote controller can be defined either on a machine in one of these two sets or on another machine.

We can also use a meta-pad for a flow-definition pad on which a form-flow or pad-flow network is already defined. This allows us to integrate more than one subsystem that is also an integration of smaller subsystems.

Figure 14.13 shows a display screen copy of an example form-flow system. The top middle composite pad defines a form flow using meta-pads. This flow has meta-pads for three form converters. It also shows these three form converters, one in the left middle window, and two others in the bottom window. Some example input forms and their corresponding output forms are shown in the right middle window.

## 14.5  WORKFLOW AND CONCURRENT ENGINEERING

Workflow is a metaphorical view of activities in an organization as a set of jobs flowing through various processing services [3]. Some services are provided by software systems,

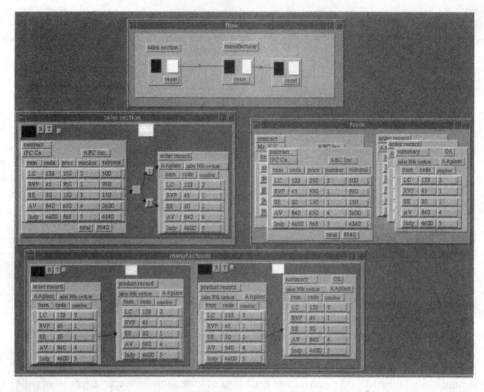

**Figure 14.13** A display screen copy of an example form-flow system. The top middle composite pad defines a form flow using meta-pads.

whereas others are provided by people. Workflow systems seek to assist, automate, and control the processing of work. They can play pivotal enabling roles for the successful implementation of reengineered business processes or the incremental quality improvement gains in business transactions.

## 14.5.1 Workflow Systems

Workflow systems connote the framework for automating and enhancing the flow of work activities or task activities between workers and processes. A workflow application automates the sequence of actions, activities, or tasks used to run the process, including tracking the status of each process instance, as well as tools for managing the process itself. Workflow does not have to be structured. Its primary function is to facilitate the fulfillment of projects and deliverables by a team. Workflow software is the tool that empowers individuals and groups in both structured and unstructured environments to automatically manage a series of recurrent or nonrecurrent events in a way that achieves the business objectives of the company. It actively manages the coordination of activities among people in general business processes. Whether used primarily as a tool to enhance existing infrastructures or as a tool to implement business reengineering, we have to remember that workflow means tools. Workflow technologies themselves do not have inherent solutions to solve business-process problems. There must be a design step, which is a major strategic business evaluation of the processes in the organization, the culture within the organization, and the adoption of the proper technology to bring about the change or improvement. The workflow system must support groups and collaboration. The groups and individuals involved can be either local users or remote users. The collaboration capabilities of the workflow system must specify the scope of collaboration. Workflow systems often support cases, forms, tracking, approval, and decision trees. All these functions involve collaboration by workers with different roles. The workflow system must have specific targets, goals, and deliverables.

Workflow systems have their roots and initial implementations in document imaging. The primary purpose of these systems was to convert existing paper documents and office procedures using paper-based information into digitized documents and automated information flow. The converted paper documents appear either as images, editable forms, or free text. When they are introduced into a document imaging system, they become objects with attributes and content. For efficient retrieval and manipulation of document images, both attribute-based indexing and content-based indexing are supported. The images, forms, or generated text documents can either be viewed or updated by office workers. The update can be in the form of annotations on top of the image documents or through updating keywords and attribute values of the objects. Often, the processing of the images follows well-defined procedures in a corporation.

Now, however, with the proliferation of various electronic interchange mechanisms for documents, forms, spreadsheets, and other types of objects, a substantial amount of information is generated digitally to start with. The new generation workflow systems have similar goals as their document imaging applications, namely to replace paper-based business processes with their computerized electronic counterparts.

One distinction that is often made between various workflow solutions is whether they are message-based or server-based [4]. The former systems are basically e-mail-based with extensions to cope with notifications, receipts, forms, rule-base forwarding, advanced filing, and digital signatures. Some of them incorporate flow capabilities to automate the flow of messages of frequently used business transactions. The latter systems are implemented on top of a commercial database management system or a proprietary DBMS. Most of the workflow-engine functionality is executed on the server node. The engine is responsible for handling workflow activation, tracking, notifications, rules, and so on. The workflow engine interfaces with transport engines to deliver the objects on a workflow's route. The client node handles the graphical user interface of the workflow.

Workflow systems are often classified into three categories—transaction- or production-based, ad hoc, and administrative [4].

With transaction or production workflow systems, there is typically a very involved policy or procedure described and imposed by a corporation. They are at the very heart of the business of the corporation. The tasks carried out by production workflow systems are followed day by day with little change. These procedures and processes usually involve various departments within an organization.

Many tasks and activities in corporation, however, are more project-oriented and do not use extensive processes and procedures. Ad hoc workflow applications have goals and deliverables whose steps and the dynamics between users are more difficult to define in detail and to any degree of predictability. Ad hoc workflow systems tend to involve more creative and usually higher-level knowledge workers. They do not require elaborate project-management systems, which are just overkill. However, they need to provide some sort of control for making sure the various tasks and responsibilities of participants are delivered on time, and that the deliverables are acceptable. They also need to constantly communicate intermediate results for approval, recommendation, and so on.

Administrative workflow systems handle routine administrative tasks. Most systems that deal with routing of forms fall into this category. They provide the facilities for the creation of simple forms, the routing of forms, iteration of form completion by approval personnel and workers, and the control over deadlines including notifications and alarms to remind people to perform tasks.

### 14.5.2   Pad Flow as Workflow

Pads have enabled us to edit, distribute, manage, and, of course, interact with various intellectual resources in the same way as we deal with paper documents. These intellectual resources include multimedia documents, forms, maps, drawings, programs, rules, application tools, client tools to access various servers, and whatever else we can treat as pads. Pad-flow systems allow us to automate well-defined flow of all these kinds of intellectual resources and their processing, which is also represented as pad converter pads, and can be treated as a kind of intellectual resource. They can also track the status of each process instance by monitoring #signal slots of PadDetectorPads; each of these PadDetectorPads is used to detect a pad transfer from an output port of one pad converter to an input port of another pad converter.

The message-based workflow systems can be easily implemented using the pad mail system, which can cope with notifications, receipts, forms, rule-base forwarding, advanced filing, and digital signatures. The server-based workflow systems can also be easily implemented using database proxy pads as well as other kinds of server proxy pads.

Workflow systems must be able to integrate the two types of services: services by application programs and services by people. The pad-flow framework can integrate those distributed services that are provided by pad converters. It connects the meta-pads of their input and output ports to define flow paths among them. This framework can also integrate various human activities into these flows. Each human activity accesses either an input port or an output port in these flows. The pad-flow framework represents these ports as slots. Furthermore, an InputPortPad and an OutputPortPad with their connections to an input-port slot and an output-port slot, respectively, allow us to access these ports by drag-and-drop operations. The meta-pads for these two IO port pads enable us to access these ports from a remote site, which means that any human activities can be integrated into pad flows through various pad converters. The publication of these meta-pads through the Internet by embedding them in Web pages would further allow any authorized people anywhere in the world to get involved in the workflow system. Therefore, the pad-flow framework can integrate the two types of distributed services, those by software systems and those by people. With these capabilities, pad-flow systems can cope with all the three types of workflow systems—transaction- or production-workflow systems, ad hoc workflow systems, and administrative workflow systems.

Furthermore, pad-flow systems can support not only the flow-based cooperation model, but also various other cooperation models including check-out/check-in client/server models, smart container models, hot linking with other data and applications, and various shared work space models. In the check-out/check-in client/server model, collaborative workers lock and check out a version of an object in the project, process it, then check the object back in, and unlock this object. The checked-in object is a new version. This model can be easily implemented using database proxy pads. Smart containers such as smart folders or smart compound documents determine which objects they should contain. Virtual forms work as smart containers. The proxy pads of data and applications realize hot linking with them. For various kinds of shared spaces, IntelligentPad provides the shared copy mechanism and the event sharing mechanism.

### 14.5.3  Concurrent Engineering

During the last 10 years, the life cycle time of products from different branches of industry decreased dramatically while the time spent on product development greatly increased. Due to these changes, the pay-off period between market entry and amortization increased as well. Companies have to cope with a tremendous shift from a seller's to a buyer's market, i.e., the supply of products is higher than the demand. The customer's expectations have become more integrated and demanding. Standard products are rejected in favor of individual solutions to problems that meet the specific wishes of the customer. A variety of products in the market and short reaction time at a low-cost level must be ensured.

Each company has to reduce the time to market to raise market share, improve the overall quality that meets the needs and wishes of the customers, and reduce product- and process-development costs to decrease the pay-off period. Concurrent engineering is an attempt to improve efficiency in the product-development process to meet these requirements [5]. The improvement of efficiency requires the optimization of the three factors—costs, quality, and time. The target can be reached by the following three approaches—parallelisation of subprocesses and tasks to eliminate delays, integration of departments and persons to improve communication, and standardization of the product-development process to improve understanding and to minimize confusion and misunderstanding.

Parallelisation in the product-development process implies the cutting and optimization of time. Processes that do not have any dependencies on the other processes can be carried out simultaneously. Even processes that have dependencies on the others may sometimes start their processing without waiting for the full completion of all the preceding processes.

Standardization is applied at two different levels. Standardization of processes means the definition of particular orders of activities to structure processes that are often repeated. Standardization of products, on the other hand, means the structuring of products in terms of their systems, elements, and construction kits. The objectives of standardization are to avoid repetition and needless work as well as to learn from the existing experience of the company. The form of standardization can vary from guidelines to compulsory arrangements and rules, or to fixed detailed operations.

Integration means working in interdisciplinary teams, thinking and behaving in a process-oriented way, and realizing a common objective instead of advancing the interests of departments. Another important aspect of integration is data integration within a company. CALS (continuous acquisition and life-cycle support) is such an attempt to integrate data and documents within a company.

Parallelisation requires controlled and concurrent access to distributed data and information, multiple project management, visualization of information/data flow from and to another process, the structuring of the project/product into distinct interrelated or independent work packages, the possibility of dividing the project into its components, support of parallel access to different tasks of an installed project, and mechanisms to free information/data in time for other users to enable concurrent and simultaneous work on a project.

Standardization requires cross-platform compatibility, distributed database access capability, standard interfaces to exchange data between different tools and frameworks, the facility to reuse results and work packages in different projects, libraries of reusable results and work packages, and tools to detect and to evaluate similarities between products.

Integration must integrate different kinds of users, provide each of them with their own customized version of the integration platform, provide a common graphical user interface, support users in controlling the processes, allow users to access different tools, enable users at different sites to communicate with each other and to share the same resources, manage the status of results, keep track of their consistency, manage all interdependencies between work packages, and inform the participants of the effect of the work.

These requirements can be fulfilled by pad-flow systems if appropriate pads are newly developed and added to the current varieties of pads. Concurrent engineering is no doubt one of the most challenging application fields of IntelligentPad. Pads allow us to exchange and to share not only information and data, but also any kinds of intellectual resources. Pads with standard forms can be efficiently managed by conventional databases. Database proxy pads and their publication through the WWW allow distributed access to these databases. Pad-flow systems can standardize repetitive processes to automate them without excluding ad hoc intervention of project members. Pads provide project members with a uniform integrated environment in which every manipulable objects, including not only deliverables but also processes and projects, are all represented as pads.

### 14.5.4 Web Technologies and Workflow Systems

During the last decade, we saw significant progress in Web technologies. These include client-side scripting technologies, server-side scripting technologies, component-based application development utilizing application servers, and Web service. Web service is a technology for application programs distributed over the Internet to mutually utilize their services. Web service provides three mechanisms: the publication mechanism for each application to register itself as a Web service into a registry, the inquiry mechanism for a client or a Web service to find another registered Web service, and the binding mechanism for the requesting client or Web service to invoke the retrieved Web service. Clients can invoke a Web service in a different machine through a SOAP proxy as if it invokes a local program. The interoperation of components distributed over the Internet requires a standard, common API based on both a standard message format and a standard RPC protocol over the Internet, which led to the proposal of SOAP.

Web service technologies allow us to define a Web document with a composed embedded service that orchestrates some public Web services using SOAP to perform its service task. Such an orchestration may define a workflow, and can be also published as a Web service. For example, a traveler agent may publish a flight reservation Web service, which may access flight reservation Web services of mutually competitive airlines to find the best fare. Interoperation of Web services defines integrated services, either for customers or for member companies, in a B2B (business-to-business) alliance. Such a workflow system that is defined as an orchestration of Web services may include as its component a Web page through which a worker may receive a task, perform it, and return the result to the workflow. Various software vendors provide visual authoring tools for the composition or orchestration of Web services and its embedding into a Web page. They are basically authoring tools for Web service integrators and Web page designers, and not for Web page readers.

Plexware, a new version of the IntelligentPad system developed by K-Plex Inc. in 2000, uses SOAP to communicate with Web services. Pads in Plexware run on an Internet Explorer browser. Plexware has wrapped Internet Explorer and provides its full function as a standard component pad. Plexware allows us to treat Web documents as pads. Recent technologies described in Sections 11.9 and 11.10 enable Web page readers to extract multimedia content, application tools, and services from Web pages as pads, and to paste them together to compose new pads. Such technologies together with the framework described in this chapter enable us to easily construct workflow and/or pad flow systems, utilizing services embedded in different Web pages.

## 14.6 SUMMARY

The dynamic combination of distributed resources requires both dynamic interoperability of pads and the reference of a remote pad. This remote reference takes the form of a pad called a meta-pad. IntelligentPad provides only two operations to define interoperations of pads: "paste" and "drag-and-drop" operations. A "paste" operation dynamically defines a static functional linkage between two pads, whereas a "drag-and-drop" operation dynamically applies the function of a target pad to an object pad.

A meta-pad works as a proxy of some primitive pad, which is called the referent of this meta-pad. A meta-pad can be sent to any machine different from the machine with its referent. Different from proxy pads working for some external objects, a meta-pad works for a remote primitive pad. Each meta-pad holds the address of its referent pad; the referent holds an address list of its meta-pads.

A meta-pad for a pad converter has a subset of those slots in its referent pad converter. It allows a user to use this pad converter from a remote site. When receiving an "update" message, every meta-pad makes its referent pad invoke the "update" method. When its referent pad is updated, every meta-pad changes its signal slot value to "true," and issues both an "update" message and a "set" message with "true" as the parameter.

This chapter also proposed an application framework for the extended form-flow model. It is an extended model since it can assimilate any transaction-based system as a virtual form. A virtual form for a database, for example, works as a form that is always kept consistent with the database contents. This extended model of form flow can be further extended to deal with flows of pads instead of flows of forms. This pad-flow model works as a generic model of workflow systems. These flows can be implemented across networks using meta-pads.

## REFERENCES

1. M. M. Zloof. QBE/OBE: A language for office and business automation. *IEEE Computer, 14*(5): 13–22, 1981.

2. S. B. Yao, A. R. Hevener, Z. Shi, and D. Luo. FORMANAGER: An office forms management

system. *ACM Trans. Office Information Systems, 2*(3): 235–262, 1984.

3. G. Poyssick, and S. Hannaford. *Workflow Reengineering.* Adobe Press, Mountain View, CA, 1996.

4. S. Khoshafian, and M. Buckiewicz. *Introduction to Groupware, Workflow, and Workgroup Computing.* Wiley, New York, 1995.

5. G. Sohlenius. Concurrent enginering. *Ann. CIRP, 42*(2): 645, 1992.

# CHAPTER 15

# AGENT MEDIA

Although IntelligentPad is basically a single-thread system, it can be extended to a multiple-thread system to deal with concurrent processing of pads. Such a system with concurrently operating pads may work as a multiple-agent system. This chapter will introduce a concurrent IntelligentPad architecture, and show some of its applications.

In a distributed environment, a single-thread IntelligentPad may concurrently work with other ones running in different sites. The latter half of this chapter will introduce a framework for developing mobile-agent systems in IntelligentPad.

## 15.1 THREE DIFFERENT MEANINGS OF AGENTS

Software agents date back to the early days of artificial intelligence (AI) work and Carl Hewitt's concurrent actor model [1]. Since then, the word "agent" in computer science and software engineering has had several different meanings [2]. First, it is used in the context of distributed AI systems [3] and/or emergent computing systems. Each of these systems tries to model a complex intelligent system as a system of a large number of mutually communicating autonomous processing modules with much simpler capabilities. They call these modules collaborative agents, or simply agents. Collaborative agents emphasize autonomy and cooperation with other agents. Their examples include MII [4], Archon [5], and OASIS [6].

Second, agents in the context of human–computer interaction are interface agents. They are computer-generated virtual creatures that can interact with users in natural languages to aid in their access to various documents and applications. In 1987, Apple Computer produced a videotape narrated by John Sculley, showing scenarios of how future versions of their personal computers would look. Their visionary system called "Knowledge Navigator" uses an intelligent agent in its interface [7]. Studies on interface agents include those at MIT's Media Lab [8, 9].

Third, agents may be mobile. Mobile agents are software modules that can travel through networks to interact with other modules at different sites. They partially execute themselves at different sites. Different from remote-procedure calls that send messages to invoke some remote procedures residing at different sites and communicate with them, mobile agents send themselves to remote sites, execute their codes there to interact with other native objects, and possibly return to their home sites. Mobile agents can deliver messages to distributed remote objects, and/or collect information from distributed remote objects. Studies on mobile agent systems led to development of their programming languages. Telescript from General Magic is the most famous one. Java is also used to program mobile agents, but it does not provide specific protocols for them.

Mobile agents are becoming increasingly significant, especially in the context of electronic commerce [10, 11]. They will play important roles both in the secure delivery of information content, software products, and services, and in the secure payment for their use.

The fourth type of agents are information/Internet agents. They perform the role of managing, manipulating, or collaborating with information from many distributed sources, especially from those on the WWW. They could be mobile. However, this is not the norm as yet. They are sometimes called Internet robots or Internet sofbots (software robots) [12]. Jasper agents developed at BT Laboratory are examples of such agents [13].

The fifth type of agents are reactive agents. Reactive agents represent a special category of agents that do not process internal, symbolic models of their environments. Instead, they respond in a stimulus–response manner to the present state of the environment in which they are embedded. Studies on such agents date back to the research of Brooks in 1986 [14], and the later work by Maes [15], Brooks [16], Connah [17], and Ferber [18].

Other types of agents are hybrid agents and heterogeneous agent systems. Hybrid agents refer to those whose constitution is a combination of two or more agent philosophies within a single agent [19], whereas heterogeneous agent systems refer to integrated set-ups of at least two or more agents that belong to two or more different agent classes [20].

In this chapter, we will focus on two types of agents, collaborative-and-reactive agents, and mobile agents. We will discuss how they are implemented as pads.

## 15.2   COLLABORATIVE-AND-REACTIVE AGENTS AND PADS

IntelligentPad can be extended to run more than one pad concurrently. The extended version is called Concurrent IntelligentPad, which we developed using Smalltalk Agents in 1995. When sending a "set" or an "update" message, each pad need not wait for the completion of the invoked procedures in the target pads. It can proceed its execution concurrently with the execution of these invoked procedures. When sending a "gimme" message, however, each pad waits for the return value. The "gimme" procedure of the recipient pad can continue its execution even after sending back the return value. Concurrent IntelligentPad provides several concurrency control pads for the synchronization among pads. They control the synchronization of messages among pads. Here we will list only some of them.

A pair of a PrecedentPad and a FollowerPad controls the order of two independent messages. Each of them is inserted between two pads that are connected through a slot connection. A PrecedentPad detects a message that passes through itself. It signals its FollowerPad when it detects some message. A FollowerPad has a slot to suspend and to hold an incoming message. If it has already been signaled by its PrecedentPad, a FollowerPad passes the incoming message to its recipient pad. Otherwise, it holds this message until it is signaled. The FollowerPad forwards the suspended message to its recipient when it is signaled. Shared copies of the same PrecedentPad signal their common FollowerPad when all the copies detect some messages. Shared copies of the same FollowerPad are simultaneously signaled.

Figure 15.1(a) shows an example use of these pads, where Pp is a PrecedentPad instructed to detect a "set" message as the preceding message, and Pf is a FollowerPad instructed to suspend an "update" message as the follower message. In this example, the FollowerPad receives an "update" message before the PrecedentPad receives a "set" message. Therefore, the "update" message is suspended before reaching the pad Pc. If the two messages are received in the opposite order, the "update" message that is received later than the "set" message is immediately transferred to the pad Pc. Figure 15.1(b) shows how these pads control the concurrent execution of component pads.

A VerticalUpdatePad sends "update" messages to its child pads in either ascending or descending order of their top-edge y coordinate [Figure 15.2(a)], whereas a HorizontalUpdate Pad sends "update" messages to its child pads in either ascending or descending order of their left-edge x coordinate [Figure 15.2(b)]. These pads sequentially activate concurrently operational pads using their geometrical relationships.

Concurrent IntelligentPad also introduces active pads. A pad is active if it continues to execute its code unless explicitly killed. Otherwise, it is passive. Active pads can communicate with each other through slot connections. They are autonomous modules that can be combined to compose more complex functions. They might be called autonomous agents.

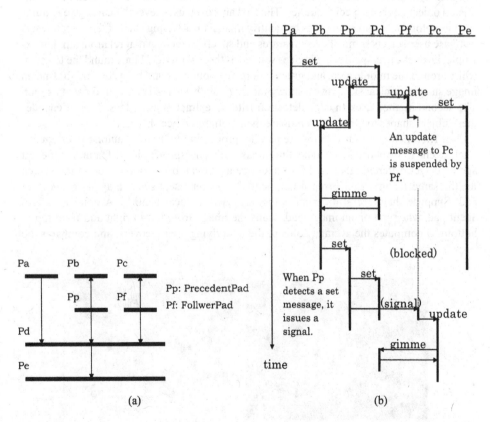

(a)                                                   (b)

**Figure 15.1**  A pair of a PrecedentPad and a FollowerPad controls the evaluation order between two messages among pads. (a) An example use of a PrecedentPad and a FollowerPad. (b) Message control by a PrecedentPad and a FollowerPad.

(a) (b)

**Figure 15.2** Geometrical control of the child-pad-activation order. (a) VerticalUpdatePad sends "update" messages to its child pads in either the ascending or descending order of their top-edge y coordinate. (b) HorizontalUpdatePad sends "update" messages to its child pads in either the ascending or descending order of their left-edge x coordinate.

The remarkable advances in digital image and video technologies and their network distribution technologies are significantly increasing their presence in the market. We are confronted by the difficulty of how to find the images and videos we want from the huge number available. Research studies on image and video databases aim to solve this problem. They are mainly based on two different approaches. The first one uses local image features and their spatial relationships to specify queries, whereas the second uses the shapes of extracted object edges to specify queries. The first approach uses several local image features such as colors or textures, and tries to identify image areas having each of these features. A database user selects some of these features and specifies their spatial relationship. For example, he or she may qualify the images wanted as those with light blue around the top area, white around the middle area, and green around the bottom area. The system might find an image showing a clear sky above a snowy mountain with a spread of green forest at its foot. The second method uses an edge detection filter to extract object edges. Then it encodes these object shapes to efficiently compare them with reference shapes.

The first method is suitable for the parallel processing with many autonomous agents. Each agent is responsible for detecting areas with one specific local feature. Different agents detect different features. More than one agent can be used to concurrently search for the same feature. Concurrent IntelligentPad can represent such an agent as an agent pad. Suppose that several different colors are used as local features. A color detection agent pad, when put on an image pad, scans the image from left to right and from top to bottom. It computes the average color of the underlying area it covers, and compares the

**Figure 15.3** Each color-detection agent pad replicates itself to cover all the areas of its designated color.

**Figure 15.4** A visual query to an image database, in which the features of stored images are extracted by placing color-detection agent pads on these images.

average with its given color. When the difference is within the allowance, it leaves its copy there and proceeds. Otherwise, it just proceeds to the next cell area. For each of the colors of your concern, you may put more than one color detection agent pad on this image. They will concurrently scan mutually disjoint areas.

Figure 15.3 shows an original image on the left. When we put several color detection agent pads on this image, we will obtain the result shown on the right. Here, for better visibility, the result is shown separately from the underlying image. If you calculate, for each color, the first- and the second-order moment of the spatial distribution of agent pads that detect this color, this pair will work as a signature of the spatial distribution of this color. A query can be specified either by putting several color pads of arbitrary sizes on a blank pad, or by using a sample image on which various color pads are already in place, as shown in Figure 15.4. This specifies a spatial distribution of colors. The latter method is used to retrieve images whose color distributions are similar to the sample image. The system will calculate, for each of these colors, the first- and second-order moment of the spatial distribution of this color. This pair is called a signature of the query for this color. The search compares, for each color, the color signature of each stored image with the color signature of the query. If their difference is small enough for each of the colors in the query, the compared stored image will be output as a candidate image.

## 15.3 MOBILE AGENTS AND PADS

Mobile agents travel through networks to visit various sites and to interact with objects there. Some return to their home sites, whereas others do not. Each mobile agent must have capabilities to specify the following, and to execute the specified mission:

1. Travel course:   Which sites to visit in what order?
2. Interaction objects:  Which objects to interact with at each visited site?
3. Interaction operation: How to interact with each of them?

If mobile agents can interact with any objects at any sites through any operations, then even a network virus can be easily implemented as a mobile agent. We therefore need to introduce appropriate and reasonable restrictions on them.

Here we present an application framework of IntelligentPad for the implementation of mobile agents. In IntelligentPad, a mobile agent should be also a pad. Mobile agent pads must dynamically interact with other pads. We assume that the interaction between a traveling agent pad and pads in each local site is coordinated by a special pad that is a priori installed at this local site under an agreement between the owner of the agent and the user of this local environment. This special pad is considered as an example of the pad converters we discussed in Section 14.1 (Figure 15.5). A pad converter is used with an InputPortPad and an OutputPortPad that are connected to its #input and #output port slots, respectively. When a pad is dropped on the InputPortPad, it is input to the pad converter and processed there. For example, when an agent pad is dropped on the InputPortPad, it is absorbed, and the pad converter may make some local pads that are kept under its supervision communicate with this agent pad by accessing its special slot with "set" and "gimme" messages. After the completion of such communication, the same agent pad with a different state will be popped up on the OutputPortPad. The use of such special pad converters to coordinate the agent's interaction at each destination site simplifies and standardizes the interaction of agent pads with local pads.

In this simplified framework for agent pads to interact with local pads, the local processing is governed by special pad converters, and not by agent pads. Agent pads are passively accessed through their special slots by these pad converters, and cannot actively access slots of any local pads. We could, of course, propose different frameworks in which agent pads take the initiative in the local processing. However, we intentionally propose this passive agent interaction with local pads for security reasons. Although the local pad takes the initiative in the interaction with an agent pad, this interaction is itself invoked by the arrival of the agent pad. In this model, a special pad converter is a priori installed in each local system under an agreement with its owner. Agent pads cannot perform any operations in each local system other than those agreed to by its owner.

The remaining problem we have to solve for agent pads is how to specify their travel courses. Since we use pad converters as local interaction objects, we can use meta-pads of InputPortPads, OutputPortPads, and FlowDefinitionPads. Suppose that we want to make an agent pad visit pad converters $P(1)$, $P(2)$, ..., $P(n)$, in this order. Let MetaIn($i$) and

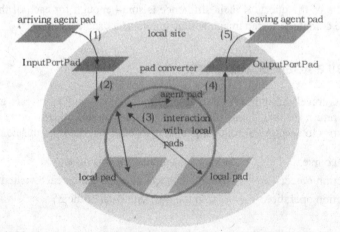

**Figure 15.5**   The interaction between a traveling agent pad and pads at each local site is coordinated by a special pad converter that is a priroi installed at this local site under an agreement between the owner of the agent and the user of this local environment.

MetaOut($i$) be meta-pads for the InputPortPad and the OutputPortPad on P($i$). The travel route of this agent pad is specified by FlowDefinitionPads that connect MetaOut($i$) to MetaIn($i + 1$) for each $i$. These FlowDefinitionPads need to travel together with the agent pad. Furthermore, we want to activate the $i$th FlowDefinitionPad that specifies a connection from MetaOut($i$) to MetaIn($i + 1$) only when the agent is visiting the pad converter P($i$). Otherwise, whenever the agent visits a new site, each meta pad MetaOut($i$) needs to inform its original output port pad of its new site address. This is necessary to maintain the communication channel from each OutputPortPad to its meta pad. In order to avoid the unnecessary rewriting of site addresses, we need to activate MetaOut($i$) only when it needs to be used.

Pads become active when they are loaded onto the desktop. Therefore, the agent pad needs to store all the FlowDefinitionPads as inactive pads in itself. While the agent pad is visiting the $i$th pad converter, it only loads the $i$th FlowDefinitionPad on itself as an active composite pad. For this purpose, we use a special pad called an IndexedPadManager that can store more than one composite pad. It indexes the stored pads in the order of their registration. When it receives an "update" message, this pad replaces its current child pad with its next stored pad.

Figure 15.6 shows an overall composition structure of an agent pad. The base pad has a function to issue an "update" message whenever it is put on an input port pad. The agent body is a pad that communicates with each pad converter. The IndexedPadManager holds FlowDefinitionPads. When visiting the $i$th pad converter, only the $i$th FlowDefinitionPad becomes active on the IndexedPadManager. After its interaction with local pads through the $i$th pad converter, the agent pad pops up on MetaOut($i$), which the $i$th FlowDefinitionPad, then sends to the next input meta pad MetaIn($i + 1$). This transfers the agent pad to the next pad converter that may exist at a different site.

The agent body may be a composite pad, which allows us to replace its components with other pads, and also to extend its function by pasting some other pads on it. Therefore, a whole agent pad is also reeditable, and its components are reusable.

The client site of this agent pad can send it out by just dropping this pad onto the pad MetaIn(1), i.e., a meta-pad of the InputPortPad connected to the #inputPort slot of the first pad converter.

The owner of each pad converter that coordinates the interaction between a traveling agent pad and pads in each local site can publish its meta-pad together with the meta-pads

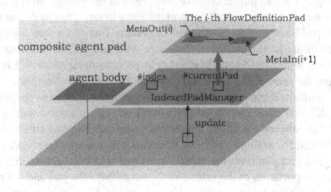

**Figure 15.6**  Overall composition structure of an agent pad.

of IO port pads pasted on this pad converter through the Internet by embedding them in a Web page.

The IntelligentPad approach to mobile agents has a large spectrum of application areas. Under the coordination of pad converters provided by destination sites, agent pads can interact with any types of local pads in each destination site they visit. These local pads might be data holding pads, multimedia document pads, application tools, database proxy pads, or proxy pads of industrial plant systems, computer-controlled devices, data acquisition systems, or transaction-based systems such as shipping and inventory management systems. Agent pads may only extract content data from some local pads of these types, or they may acquire some local pads as they are. At each site it visits, an agent pad may further process what it acquires there. An agent pad may also process itself to change its state or its composition structure.

The use of mobile agent pads allows us to provide typical mobile agent applications with application frameworks that consist of component pads and generic pad-composition structures. Each of these frameworks provides a construction kit including component pads and sample compositions for nonprogrammers to easily define the functions of both the mobile agents and the local pad converters.

## 15.4 PAD MIGRATION AND SCRIPT LANGUAGES

Agent pads require the migration of pads across different systems. As discussed in Section 11.2, there are three levels of pad migration across different systems. The shallowest-level pad migration assumes that the two systems share the same class library. In this case, the migration of a pad only requires the transportation of its exchange format representation. The middle-level pad migration assumes that the two systems share only the basic common portion of the class library. It is further assumed in this case that each primitive pad definition only inherits its property from those classes in the basic common class library, but not from any classes outside of the basic portion of the class library. In this case, the source system can send any object to the destination. The source sends the definition code of this object. The deepest-level object migration assumes no common class library. In this case, we have to migrate not only this object but also all the classes used in the definition of this object. Class migration requires special consideration, and causes a performance problem.

Our strategies for pad migration have converged to the middle-level pad migration. In other words, we use a hierarchically organized class library only to define the kernel and the primitive pad library of the IntelligentPad system. Two of the four commercially available versions of the IntelligentPad system cope with pad migration across different platforms including Windows PC and Macintosh by programming at the API level. These two versions share the same API library and the same basic object class library. They are mutually cross-platform compatible systems. Although the middle-level pad migration works well across different machines of the same platform type, it causes some problems if the platforms differ between the target and source machines. The two different commercially available systems, for example, use C++ to define pads. Since object codes cannot be executed on a different platform, the middle-level pad migration across different platforms requires the transportation of the source code that defines the pad and the recompiling of this source code on the target machine. This means that the providers cannot protect their source codes. To solve this problem, we need a new programming language and its interpreter. Its program codes should be able to be encrypted, and decrypted by its interpreters when they are executed. We call such a language a script language for cross-platform migration. IPC (IntelligentPad Consortium) is not yet working on such a language.

## 15.5 SUMMARY

The word "agent" in computer science and software engineering has several different meanings. First, it is used in the context of distributed AI systems and/or emergent computing systems to denote mutually communicating autonomous processing modules called collaborative agents. Agents in the context of human–computer interaction are interface agents. They are computer-generated virtual creatures that can interact with users. The third type are mobile agents. They are software modules that can travel through networks to interact with other modules at different sites. The fourth type are information/Internet agents. They perform the role of managing, manipulating, or collaborating information from many distributed sources, especially from those on the WWW. The fifth type are reactive agents. Reactive agents represent a special category of agents that respond in a stimulus–response manner to the present state of the environment in which they are embedded.

This chapter has focused on two types of agents, collaborative-and-reactive agents and mobile agents, and discussed how they are implemented as pads.

## REFERENCES

1. C. Hewitt. Viewing control structures as patterns of passing messages. *Artificial Intelligence,* *8*(3): 323–364, 1977

2. H. S. Nwana and D. T. Ndumu. A brief introduction to software agent technology. In N. R. Jennings and M. J. Wooldridge (eds.), *Agent Technology: Foundations, Applications, and Markets.* Springer-Verlag, Berlin, 1998.

3. M. N. Huhns and M. P. Singh. *Distributed Artificial Intelligence for Information Systems.* CKBS-94 Tutorial, University of Keele, UK.

4. C. S. Winter, R. Titmuss, and B. Crabtree. Intelligent agents, mobility and multimedia information. In *Proceedings of the First International Conference on the Practical Application of Intelligent Agents and Multi-Agent Technology '96,* pp. 22–24, 1996.

5. T. Wittig (ed.). *ARCHON: An Architecture for Multi-Agent Systems.* Ellis Horwood, London, 1992.

6. A. S. Rao and M. P. Georgeff. BDI agents: From theory to practice. In *Proceedings of the First International Conference on Multi-Agent Systems.* pp. 312–319, 1995.

7. J. Sculley. The Relationship between business and higher education: A perspective on the 21st century. *CACM, 32*(9): 1056–1061, 1989.

8. P. Kozierok and P. Maes. A learning interface agent for scheduling meetings. In *Proceedings of ACM-SIGCHI International Workshop on Intelligent User Interfaces,* pp. 81–93, 1993.

9. H. Lieberman. Letizia: An agent that assists Web browsing. In *Proceedings of IJCAI 95,* AAAI Press, Menlo Park, CA, 1995.

10. P. Wayner. *Agents Unleashed: A Public Domain Look at Agent Technology.* AP Professional, Chestnut Hill, MA, 1995.

11. C. A. Jardin. *Java Electronic Commerce Source Book.* Wiley, New York, 1997.

12. O. Etzioni and D. Weld. A softbot-based interface to the Internet. *CACM, 37*(7): 72–76, 1994.

13. N. J. Davies and R. Weeks. Jasper: Communicating information agents. In *Proceedings of the Fourth International Conference on the World Wide Web,* 1995.

14. R. A. Brooks. A robust layered control system for a mobile robot. *IEEE J. Robotics and Automation, 2*(1): 14–23, 1986.

15. P. Maes. *Designing Autonomous Agents: Theory and Practice from Biology to Engineering and Back.* MIT Press, London, 1991.

16. R. A. Brooks. Intelligence without representation. *Artificial Intelligence, 47:* 139–159, 1991.

17. D. Connah. The design of interacting agents for use in interfaces. In M. D. Brouwer-Janse and T. L. Harringdon (eds.), *Human–Machine Communication for Educational System Design.* NATO ASI Series F, Vol. 129. Springer-Verlag, Berlin, 1994.

18. J. Ferber. Simulating with reactive agents. In E. Hillebrand and J. Stender (eds.), *Many Agent Simulation and Artificial Life,* pp. 8–28. IOS Press, Amsterdam, 1994.

19. J. P. Muller, M. Pishel, and M. Thiel. Modeling reactive behavior in vertically layered agent architectures. In M. Wooldridge and N. Jennings (eds.), *Intelligent Agents.* Lecture Notes in Artificial Intelligence, Vol. 890, pp. 261–276. Springer-Verlag, Berlin, 1995.

20. M. R. Genesereth and S. P. Ketchpel. Software agents. *CACM 37*(7): 48–53, 1994.

# CHAPTER 16

# SOFTWARE ENGINEERING
# WITH INTELLIGENTPAD

In this chapter, we will review IntelligentPad from software engineering points of view. First of all, IntelligentPad is a middleware system. When used as a software development system, it provides a lot of concurrent collaborations among requirements analysts, interface designers, system architects, system programmers, debuggers, and system evaluators. IntelligentPad can deal with both coarse-grain components and fine-grain components. They are all equally treated as pads.

When experts work on a problem arising in some situation, it is quite unusual for them to try to solve it without using their knowledge on how they themselves or others in the same or related domains have ever solved similar problems in similar situations. Such knowledge, when described as a rule, is called a pattern. A typical pad composition for a typical application works as a pattern in this sense.

In the latter half of this chapter, we will use object-oriented software development methods to compose a pad from its specification. Then we will provide a formal approach to this problem.

## 16.1  INTELLIGENTPAD AS MIDDLEWARE

Middleware introduces a middle layer between the layer of operating systems and the layer of application programs [1]. It aims to hide the difference of underlying platforms including their hardware and operating systems, by setting up a standard middle layer. From the application development point of view, it aims to provide standard frameworks for the development of typical application programs, a standard library of application components, and standard infrastructures for developing, distributing, managing, accessing, and using these components and frameworks.

Middleware treats each server as an atomic object, and provides its proxy object as a standard component. A proxy object communicates with its server. It hides the detailed mechanism of the server, and provides only the input and output functions of the server. Middleware focuses on client application systems and their composition. It provides a standard linkage mechanism to combine application components. Some middleware systems provide some of their components with their views on the display screen. Some others provide every component with its view. Some allow us to embed visual components into compound documents. The physical embedding does not necessarily imply functional linkage between the embedded component and its base component.

Middleware has become increasingly important since the remarkable success of the WWW and its browsers. It allows us to plug in application systems in Web pages. These application systems can be easily downloaded at any client site. If it is compatible with the client platform, a downloaded system can be executed there. This capability opens up a new vista toward the distribution of reusable components across platforms. Furthermore, a plugged-in client application system can communicate with its remote server. Distributed-object technologies such as CORBA [2] support the communication among distributed objects. The WWW and its browsers have introduced a third tier between the tier of servers and the tier of clients (Figure 16.1). This model of system architectures is called a three-tier model [1, 3], whereas the conventional client–server model is called a two-tier model. The three-tier model makes clients, servers, and their connections network-transparent. They are liberated from their home locations. This technology trend will liberate any components from their home locations. The publication of client applications results in the publication of services provided by their servers. The distribution of components across networks realizes the distribution of documents, tools, and services.

IntelligentPad has already achieved all the above-mentioned goals of middleware. Its standard API library hides the difference between platforms. Its pads work as reusable components. Their connection is simplified and standardized. They can be transported across different platforms, and can be published by embedding them in Web pages. Documents, tools, and services are all represented as pads, and therefore can be published through the Internet.

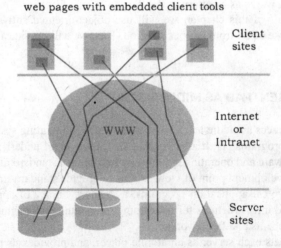

**Figure 16.1**  The three-tier architectural model.

## 16.2   CONCURRENT ENGINEERING IN SOFTWARE DEVELOPMENT

In Section 14.5, we observed that pad flow systems can provide basic frameworks for concurrent engineering systems. Here we focus on concurrent engineering in software development, especially development of client software systems. As intended since its birth, IntelligentPad can cover the development of most client software systems, which implies that pad flow systems can deliver not only documents and data products, but also client software products as pads. Various versions of products and their components can be delivered to and from workers and systems with different responsibilities and different functions.

These workers include requirement analysts, interface designers, system architects, system programmers, system integrators, component debuggers, system debuggers, and system evaluators. A requirement analyst interviews customers to extract their requirements, and clearly specifies the requirements. An interface designer also interviews customers and designs a satisfactory user interface. A system architect divides the whole system into component modules so that the connection structure among them may satisfy the user's design framework. A system architect also specifies the interface protocols among these component modules. A system programmer develops those components that are not available from the library of reusable components. A system integrator combines components to compose a required system. A component debugger debugs the newly developed components, whereas a system debugger debugs a composed system. A system evaluator evaluates the performance and the usability of the developed system.

Automated processing systems include a system-documentation tool and a system-analysis tool. A system-documentation tool draws a connection-structure diagram of a given composite system. A system-analysis tool examines the statistics of a given composite system, and reports what kinds of components constitute the system, how many copies of each component are used, how many other components on the average are connected to each component, and so on.

Concurrent engineering is an attempt to introduce concurrent activities among these workers and processing systems. The most familiar conventional life cycle model of software development is the well-known "waterfall" life cycle model, which consists of a sequence of six steps—the software-concept step, the requirement-analysis step, the architectural-design step, the detailed-design step, the coding-and-debugging step, and the system-testing step (Figure 16.2). The waterfall model allows no concurrent activities among different stages, although it may allow backing up to the previous stage. A project review is held at the end of each step to determine whether it is possible to advance to the next phase. The waterfall model is document-driven, which means that the main work products that are carried from one step to another are documents. In the pure waterfall model, the steps are also discontinuous. They do not overlap. The waterfall model performs well for product cycles in which you have a stable product definition and when you are working with well-understood technical methodologies. In such cases, the waterfall model helps you find errors in the early, low-cost stages of a project. The waterfall model also helps to minimize planning overhead because you can do all the planning up front. The disadvantages of the waterfall model arise from the difficulty of fully specifying requirements at the beginning of a project. This contradicts modern business needs; the goal is often not to achieve what you said you would at the beginning of a project, but to achieve the maximum possible within the time and resources available.

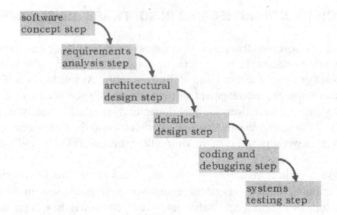

**Figure 16.2**   Waterfall life cycle model of software development.

When pads are used to develop client software products, different workers and various kinds of automated processing can exchange various versions of intermediate development results as pads. In IntelligentPad, a client software system is either a composite pad, or a set of composite pads that are mutually connected by wiring pads. An interface designer first draws a rough sketch of the GUI, which is passed to a system architect. A system architect designs the composition structure of the system, and specifies the slot list of each component pad. The result is a composition diagram as shown in Figure 16.3, with functional specification of each slot and the data type specification of each slot-access message. More than one system architect can share this information to collaborate. If the overall system can be divided into several subsystems, each system architect may work on an individual subsystem. The architectural design results are passed to a system programmer. He or she first searches the library of reusable pads for necessary component pads, and develops each unfound pad by himself or herself. System programmers sometime develop a dummy pad for some required component. Although a dummy pad does not completely provide the required internal mechanism, it can partially mimic the required pad. Some dummy pads mimic only the slot connections of the required pads; others partially simulate the IO operations of the required pads. More than one programmer can work on different component pads. Interface designers may use both nonfunctional pads and functional pads such as buttons, sliders, and display pads to design the GUI. They can sometimes use dummy pads, which provides more reality in the process of interaction design. IntelligentPad further allows an interface designer to modify the developed product. He or she may change the layout of components, or even replace some of them with an alternative pad of the same function. A system integrator combines the pads from the library and the newly developed pads, in the same structure as the composition diagram, to compose a system that satisfies the system requirements. A component debugger debugs each component pad independently from other components. A system debugger may use dummy pads to test the connection of each component pad with the other components. A system evaluator may also sometimes use dummy pads to evaluate the usability of a component pad or a component composite pad.

The processes mentioned above indicate that there is much concurrency among themselves. Similarly there is also much concurrency between these workers' processes and

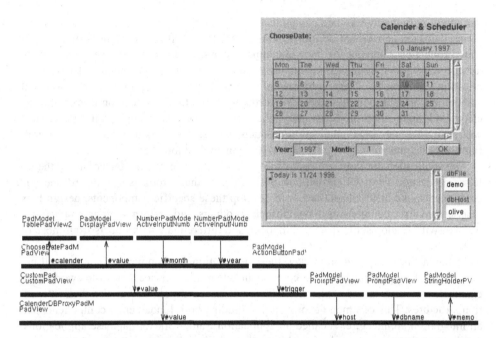

**Figure 16.3**  A composition diagram shows the composition structure of a system with the specification of the slot list for each component pad.

various kinds of automated processing. The sharing and exchange of such intermediate development results and their documents, both as pads, by using the pad flow system framework enable both these workers and processing tools at distributed remote locations to collaborate in the development of client software systems.

## 16.3  COMPONENTS AND THEIR INTEGRATION

The granularity of components ranges from a complex database server to a simple button. The IntelligentPad architecture can deal with different sizes of components. It can deal with both coarse-grain components and fine-grain components. They are all equally treated as pads. Furthermore, the grain size of a component has nothing to do with its pad size. A coarser-grained component pad can be pasted on a finer-grained component pad.

Componentware inherently involves three waves. In the first wave, components are developed and utilized inside the same software production company and its subcontractors. They are utilized only by application developers to reduce production time and cost. The reduction of production time and cost will encourage software production companies put more emphasis on customer satisfaction. User taste will push software production companies to increase the variety of products that essentially provide the same function, which will lead them to develop customization technologies and to increase the variety of components for customization. This change will develop in a very short time, which will make each software production company unable to develop all the necessary components by themselves. Some existing software companies have their specialties. Demands for a large variety of high-quality standard components will grow these specialized companies to become dedicated component developer companies. They will supply components to software production companies. They will compete with each other in their specialties. Some may produce good digital video components, whereas others may be good at database application components. Their components will be licensed to application development companies, or sold to application users through distributors. Application users will purchase both application products and application components through distributors. They will customize purchased application products with components they have. No distribution flow of components is legally allowed among application users.

The application development companies will shift their roles from the coding to the integration design. They will design how to decompose their products to standard, specific components, ask their subcontractors to develop these specific components, design how to assemble these components to compose the products, and perform their assembly. Each of them will develop some special components to differentiate its products from those of others.

In the business application market, these application development companies sell not only application products but also component integration services and frameworks. For example, various database applications share not only components but also their integration structures. This common denominator, including both fundamental components and an integration architecture, is called an application framework for database applications. Application frameworks can be found in many typical applications.

In the end-user market, components will become consumer products and their variety will increase. The same function will be provided by different components with different tastes. This variety will synergistically enlarge their market. This phenomenon is commonly observed in the consumer product market. Sony's Walkman portable CTRs synergistically enlarged their market with their followers by the variety of colors and designs brought by these followers. Components as consumer products must be frequently revised. Components as consumer products should be considered expendable. Because of their repetitive revision, their life cycles are very short. This is true even for end-user application systems such as word processors and drawing tools. These application systems are frequently revised to maintain customers' satisfaction. If not, new systems will replace them. Most of them are not durable for more than a year without any revision. The purchase price of components will become remarkably lower to encourage users to keep buying new components. Some suppliers will even distribute free application products and components to enlarge their market, which will allow users to exchange these products and components.

The increased variety of application components will stimulate the creativity of end-users, and encourage them not only to customize purchased products with optional components, but also to recombine them to compose new custom products. This causes no license problems. This change will bring us a new possibility of viewing end-users as application developers. Their potentiality to enrich the variety of available application software is remarkably high. Without the distribution of these custom products among users, however, this potentiality will not be realized.

The third wave will arrive when even end-users will become able to distribute and exchange application components among themselves. This change requires a shift from the purchase of products to the purchase of product usage, i.e., from the pay-per-copy billing to the pay-per-use billing. The pay-per-copy system requires copy protection, but the pay-per-use system allows users to make copies of products. Furthermore, in the pay-per-use system, users can recombine products to compose custom products, and redistribute them among themselves. The redistributed custom products may include components and assembly structures that are both some other developers' property. Each use of them should be appropriately metered, and the corresponding charge should be paid to their owners. We have seen in Chapter 12 that the pay-per-use billing scheme can be well integrated with the reediting and redistributing capabilities of pads.

## 16.4 PATTERNS AND FRAMEWORKS IN INTELLIGENTPAD

When experts work on a problem arising in some situation, it is quite unusual for them to try to solve it without using their knowledge of how they themselves or others in the same or related domains have ever solved similar problems in similar situations. Such knowledge consists of rules, each of which is represented by a triple consisting of

1. A situation or a context
2. A problem arising in this context
3. Its solution

The architect Christopher Alexander called such a group of rules a pattern [4, 5]. He defines this term as follows: Each pattern describes a problem that occurs over and over again in our environment, and then describes the core of the solution to that problem in such a way that you can use this solution a million times over without ever doing it the same way twice.

Contexts and problems can be described at various different levels of abstraction. Their description at different levels of abstraction defines different levels of their similarities. Whichever domains they are working in, experts repeatedly encounter similar situations and similar problems. The similarities may range from abstract ones to concrete ones, and from functional ones to structural ones. The level at which we discuss similarities affects our interpretation of what is and isn't a pattern.

### 16.4.1 Architectural Patterns, Design Patterns, Idioms, and Frameworks

Patterns can be also found in various levels of software architecture. Experts in software engineering know these patterns from their experience and reuse them in developing applications. The pioneers of patterns in software development are Ward Cunningham and Kent Beck who came up with five patterns dealing with the design of user interfaces [6]. The first published work about the use of patterns in software engineering was Erich Gamma's doctoral thesis in 1991. Later with Richard Helm, Ralph Johnson, and John Vlissides, he extended his work and published a seminal work *Design Patterns—Elements of Reusable Object-Oriented Software* [7], which extensively dealt with patterns at a certain abstraction level, i.e., design patterns.

A design pattern provides a scheme for refining the subsystems or components of a software system, or the relationships between them. It describes a commonly recurring structure of communicating components that solves a general design problem within a particular context [7].

In 1992, James Coplien published the book *Advanced C++ Programming Styles and Idioms* [8]. Some other pioneers of patterns are Douglas Schimidt, who focused on industrial communication systems [9], Peter Coad, who presented about two hundred patterns in his book [10], and Wolfgang Pree, who focused on structural principles of design patterns for framework development [11]. In 1996, Frank Bushmann, Regine Meunier, Hans Rohnert, Peter Sommerlad, and Michael Stal published the book *Pattern-Oriented Software Architecture—A System of Patterns* [12] to deal with patterns at more levels of abstraction than those dealt with by *Design Patterns* [7]. They grouped patterns into three categories—architectural patterns, design patterns, and idioms.

According to them, an architectural pattern expresses a fundamental structural organization schema for software systems. It provides a set of predefined subsystems, specifies their responsibilities, and includes rules and guidelines for organizing the relationship between them. Architectural patterns help in structuring a software system into subsystems. Design patterns support the refinement of subsystems and components, or the relationships between them. An idiom is a low-level pattern specific to a programming language. It describes how to implement particular aspects of components or the relationships between them using the features of the given language [12].

A framework is a partially complete software system that is intended to be instantiated on its use. It defines the overall architecture for a family of systems, and provides its basic components and the relationships between them. These remain unchanged in instantiation. A framework also defines its parts that can be adapted to specific application needs.

### 16.4.2 Sample Composite Pads as Architectural Patterns

Around 1994, when Fujitsu and Hitach Software Engineering developed the first commercially available versions of IntelligentPad and their system engineers began to use it internally for the development of various different application systems, these system developers also became aware of the frequent use of similar composition structures of pads in the development of different application systems. Students in my laboratory had the same experience around 1992.

One of the most typical example of such frequently used composition structures can be found in business applications using databases. These applications require form interfaces to databases. As detailed in Section 10.2, a form interface to a database uses a DBProxyPad as the base pad, and, on top of it, a RecordPad with its connection to the #currentRecord slot of the DBProxyPad. To each attribute slot of the RecordPad is connected a TextPad, an ImagePad, a VideoPad, or some other display pad depending on the type of this attribute value. This description is an example of architectural patterns, or more precisely, an application architectural pattern. It describes the solution part of a pattern. In IntelligentPad however, we do not need to textually describe the solution part of this pattern as above. Instead, we can provide a sample composite pad that works as a form interface to a sample database. We can further provide several different proxy pads for several widely used DBMSs.

Such a sample composite pad works as a pattern, or more precisely, as its solution scheme. It satisfies the following definition of patterns for software architecture:

A pattern for software architecture describes a particular recurring design problem that arises in specific design contexts, and presents a well-proven generic scheme for its solution. The solution scheme is specified by describing its constituent components, their responsibilities and relationships, and the way in which they collaborate [12].

A form interface is a particular recurring design problem that arises in specific design contexts, i.e., business application systems accessing databases. The composition structure of a sample form interface pad presents a well-proven generic scheme for the solution to this problem. This composition structure as a solution scheme is specified by describing its constituent component pads, their responsibilities and relationships defined by slot connections, and the way in which they collaborate by exchanging standard messages with various types of parameters.

Our Web browser pad enables us to make a catalogue of such sample composite pads, which describes each pattern with textual descriptions of its context and problem, and contains an embedded sample composite pad we can play with. A sample composite pad may be used as a component of another sample composite pad. Patterns are mutually related. Each pattern in this catalogue is associated with its related patterns by navigation links. For example, a sample form interface composite pad in our pattern catalogue should be related to a sample QBE (query-by-example) DB interface, and various kinds of sample information-visualization tool pads in this pattern catalogue. This sample form interface composite pad may also be related to the form-flow framework described in the framework catalogue for IntelligentPad users. These are linked by bilateral links. Suppose that a sample form interface has an ImagePad to display an image-type attribute. The pattern catalogue may provide this ImagePad with an annotation and several link anchors that jump to a Video Pad, a SaverLoaderPad, and an ImagePad having several anchor pads on it. These are the pads that can replace the original ImagePad in the sample form interface.

### 16.4.3  Pad Packages with Sample Compositions as Application Frameworks

Applications of a certain typical class often share a large number of primitive pads as commonly used components. Furthermore, they often share the same set of composition structures to combine these commonly used components. These commonly used components and composition structures are what we call the framework of such applications. A sample composite pad and its basic primitive pads constitute an application framework in IntelligentPad systems. A framework may include optional component pads that can replace some components of the sample composite pad. The framework for a form-flow system, for example, provides several example form-flow systems as sample composite pads, and a set of component pads including sample forms, sample virtual forms, sample form converters, sample form generators and consumers, meta-pads, and all the primitive pads for form-flow systems. It provides these pads together with the textual description of their functions, their slots and composition structures, and how to use each of them. Our Web browser pad enables us to make a catalogue of frameworks that includes all these pads and their descriptions. Pads and their descriptions in this catalogue may be associated through navigation links with related frameworks in the same catalogue, and also with related patterns in the pattern catalogue.

In IntelligentPad, an application package means a family of primitive and composite pads whose slots are standardized with respect to their names and the types of data that are sent and obtained through the slots. This allows us to easily combine components without knowing the detail semantics of each slot. Similar situation can be observed among AV components, in which not only the shape of their connection jacks and pinplugs are standardized, but also the various signals that go through these connection jacks. Video devices are connected by three cables—yellow, red, and white—which send video and left and right sound signals, respectively. The corresponding connection jacks are labeled with "video," "left," and "right." Once we have learned this convention, we do not need any instruction to connect a TV monitor to a laser disc player, or a video camera to a VCR. The same is true for a package of pads in IntelligentPad. More than one package may share the same convention. They are said to belong to the same package family. More than one package family may coexist in the same application field. They correspond to different communities with different cultures. Although pads in different package families may not be mutually compatible, the introduction of appropriate converter pads by either of these communities or by the third vender may make them interoperable with each other.

Takafumi Noguchi at Kushiro Technical Collage has used an IntelligentPad system to develop a package family of CAI tools in basic physics and mathematics. He developed several packages for various fields, including basic mechanics, basic electronic circuitry, and basic mathematical functions. Their pads, however, exploit the same convention with respect to their slot names and slot data types, and can be easily combined based on the naming convention of their slots.

### 16.4.4   Slot List as a Pattern

The architecture of pads itself is considered as a design pattern or as an architectural pattern. Each primitive pad is represented as a simplified version of MVC. A pad pasted on another pad is linked through the connection between their views. Each primitive pad provides a list of slots, each of which can be accessed only by either a "set" or a "gimme" message. Furthermore, each pad accepts "update" messages. These three messages can be issued only through the view-connection links among pads. An "update" message goes from a parent pad to its child pad, whereas the other two go from a child pad to its parent.

The process of developing a new primitive pad also has a common pattern. We first specify a list of its slots, then specify for each of these slots its "set" procedure and "gimme" procedure, and also specify its "update" procedure. Furthermore, we specify event handlers that are invoked when some events occur. These include the handler that is invoked when we put this pad on another, and the one that is invoked when another pad is put on this pad. Using this standard pattern of programming new pads, we can develop a wizardry system that guides our pad development. Fujitsu's commercially available version of IntelligentPad provides such a wizardry system. For the definition of each procedure, it first provides its default definition, and allows us to rewrite it. If its default definition satisfies our requirements, we do not need to rewrite it.

### 16.5   FROM SPECIFICATIONS TO A COMPOSITE PAD

Various kinds of software development methods can be applied to pad development, with some customization to the IntelligentPad Architecture. In this book, we will show two methods for the application specification and its translation to a composite pad. The first method describes an application using an action diagram, and translates this diagram to a composite pad. The second method is a semiformal method. It provides a formal way to describe an application as a list of slots. Each slot is associated with its access dependency relationship. In this method, we initially assume that the total application can be implemented as a single pad. The method then gives alternative ways to replace this single pad with an equivalent composite pad. This method can maximally reuse existing pads. Here in this section, we will discuss the first method. In the next section, we will discuss the second one.

### 16.5.1   Use-Case Modeling

Any description of a single way of using a system or application is called a use case. A use case is a class of top-level usage scenarios that captures how a black-box application is used by its users. They are used to recognize different scenarios of interaction between a system and its user and also between subsystems, and then to elicit, understand, and define functional requirements of the system. A resultant diagram that documents a system's behavior as a set of use cases, actors, and the communication arcs between them, is called a use-case model [13]. Actors represent whatever communicates with the system. The user is also an actor.

A use-case model can be decomposed into subsystems. The top-level system describes the whole behavior of the system. System X in Figure 16.4 represents the top-level system. The requirements of each subsystem are described as a set of lower-level use cases. The use cases b1 and b2 in the figure are lower-level use cases of the use case b for System X.

As a method to describe use cases from the user's view point, we can use task analysis. The task analysis is used to elicit, understand, and define functional requirements, and to construct an interactive system model [14]. A task model is represented as a tree with tasks as its nodes. A task describes a job independently from its implementation from the user's point of view. A task model thus obtained represents requirements of the user interface of the system.

Figure 16.5 shows a task model. Each task is identified by its identifier. A task constructed with subtasks is provided with such a task process as "do (2.5.1), (2.5.2), (2.5.3)," "optionally, do (2.5.1), (2.5.3)," which specifies which subtasks are executed, which of them are optionally executed, and in which order they are executed. The first one in this figure is a generic task model that generalizes more than one task model with the same task hierarchy but with different types of generated objects.

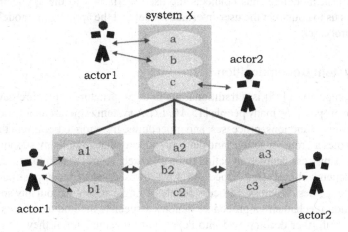

**Figure 16.4**   A use-case model can be decomposed into subsystems.

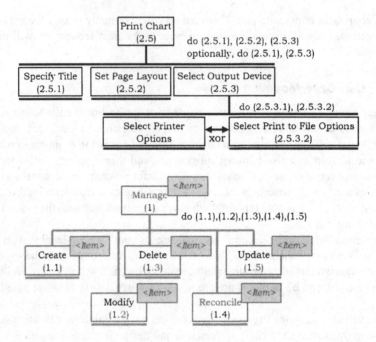

**Figure 16.5** In a task model, a task constructed with subtasks is provided with such a task process as "do (2.5.1), (2.5.2), (2.5.3), optionally, do (2.5.1), (2.5.3)," which specifies which subtasks are executed, which of them are optionally executed, and in which order they are executed.

The initial stage of the task analysis extracts and identifies some tasks. The second stage organizes these tasks in a task hierarchy, and refines each task to its subtasks. The extraction and recognition of tasks are subjective matters, and where to stop further refinement must be considered. A general criterion for this decision is to stop further decomposition whenever we reach a task that specifies its execution method. The purpose of the task modeling is to specify what kind of activities the user requires. The refinement of tasks in the task modeling thus connects the use-case model to the application model, which allows us to construct the user-interface model and the application model as two independent processes.

### 16.5.2 System Decomposition

System decomposition [15] is a traditional method for structured software development, and has been proposed by many people [15, 16, 17]. A system is hierarchically decomposed into three levels—functions, processes, and procedures, from top to bottom in this order. A function denotes a group of actions and decision-making that completely support an aspect of a system. A process denotes an action to be executed. A process can be further decomposed into dependent processes. Processes at the lowest level of decomposition are called elementary processes. Whereas a process denotes a single action without any specification of its execution mechanism, a procedure denotes a specific method to execute a process. Procedures are further decomposed into dependent procedures until they as a whole describe an executable program structure. Figure 16.6(a) shows a concept of system decom-

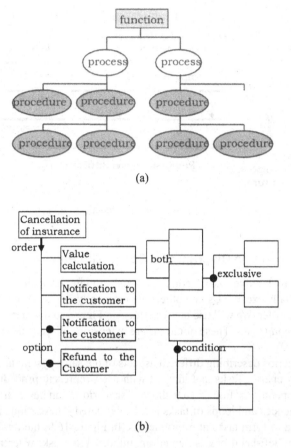

(a)

(b)

**Figure 16.6**   System decomposition and a decomposition diagram. (a) System decomposition. (b) A decomposition diagram.

position, whereas Figure 16.6(b) shows a decomposition diagram that is used to describe system decomposition. Decomposition diagrams can use constructs to represent optional branches, conditional branches, exclusive branches, and ordered sequences.

Figure 16.7 shows a structure of a composite pad. The outermost (i.e., topmost) pads in a composition are GUI components that receive user inputs, or output data to a user. These pads directly interact with a user. Those pads closer to the bottom implement subsystem functions and mutually connect with each other through slots. Those pads closer to a user mainly perform interactions with users, whereas those closer to the bottom perform interactions between subsystems. The former pads perform use cases, and their composition structures may be considered to embody task hierarchies, whereas the composition structure of the latter pads can be interpreted to describe a system decomposition structure.

This observation leads us to the pad development method described in the next subsection, where tasks are hierarchically decomposed into subtasks based on given scenarios of how the system is used by its user, and the relationships among these tasks are analyzed to decompose the system. This decomposition structure will tell us how to compose a pad to satisfy the specifications.

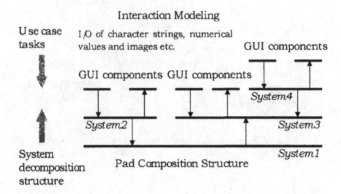

**Figure 16.7**   The composition structure of a composite pad.

### 16.5.3   From an Action Diagram to a Composite Pad

A scenario of an interactive system consists of tasks to interact with users. Some of these tasks are sequentially executed, some others are optionally executed, and some are executed in an arbitrary order. We will use the constructs in Figure 16.8 to represent different execution orders among tasks. These notations are extensions of those used by the action diagram method.

Different scenarios describing different aspects of the same system are finally integrated into a single scenario. Tasks that interact with users represent procedures necessary to respond to user operations. Figure 16.9 shows a scenario for an automatic teller machine, from which sequences and loops of tasks can be extracted. These sequences and loops of tasks are grouped to form tasks at higher levels. In Figure 16.9, the total task consists of two subtasks. The left-hand one is named an authorization task, whereas the right-hand one is named an accounting task.

Instead of vertically arranging tasks in optional execution and in random execution, we will horizontally arrange tasks even in these cases. The three subtasks in the accounting subtasks can be given the following names: deposit, withdrawal, and completion. Figure 16.10 shows a task hierarchy thus obtained.

This hierarchy can be interpreted as a pad composition structure. Tasks are interpreted to represent pads. The topmost tasks represent input and/or output pads, whereas the lower pads define internal mechanism. Now we have to specify what kinds of slots to provide

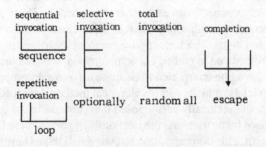

**Figure 16.8**   Notations used for scenario description based on the action diagram.

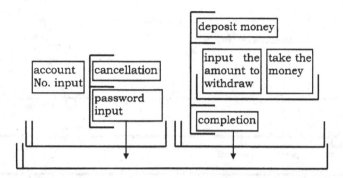

**Figure 16.9**   An extended action diagram that describes a scenario for an automatic teller machine. The deposit and the withdrawal of money are simulated by drag-and-drop operations of money pads.

for each task, and which slot to use in each linkage between tasks. The specification of these should proceed upward from the bottom level, since the specifications of internal mechanisms are more stable than those for the user interactions.

Let us first consider an interface between authorization and accounting. Since the accounting task must record "who did what operation," it must get information from the authorization task about who was authorized. On the other hand, the authorization task must know about the completion of the accounting task. Therefore, these two tasks should be able to exchange the user ID and the execution completion flag. Furthermore, only authorized users should be allowed to access the accounting task. We need a mechanism to block user interaction with the accounting task. We may use a SlideCoverPad for this blocking.

The authorization task prompts the account number input and the password input in this order. These inputs can be considered as the inputs to the authorization subsystem. Both the account number input and the password input may use text input pads, whereas the canceling may use a button pad. The authorization needs to wait for the completion of the accounting, and requires more than one state, which means that the modeling by a state transition machine may work well for the authorization subsystem.

The accounting task processes the deposit task, the withdrawal task, and the completion task of the system. Both the deposit task and the withdrawal task access the account

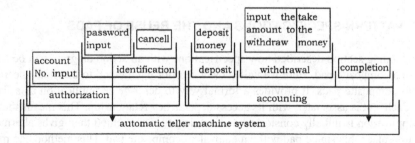

**Figure 16.10**   A task hierarchy of the system described in Figure 16.9.

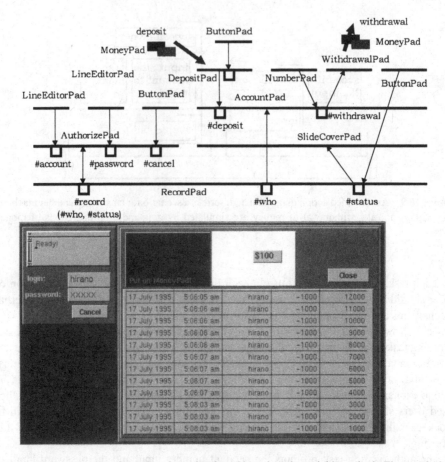

**Figure 16.11**   A composite pad we have developed based on the task hierarchy in Figure 16.10.

record. The deposit task reports to the accounting task how much money comes in, whereas the withdrawal task not only reports how much money goes out, but also has to check first if the balance is greater than the withdrawal request.

Figure 16.11 shows a composite pad we have developed based on the task hierarchy in Figure 16.10. In this figure, we simulate the deposit and withdrawal of money by drag-and-drop operations of money pads.

## 16.6   PATTERN SPECIFICATIONS AND THE REUSE OF PADS

The preceding section described how specifications with an action diagram can be translated to a composite pad. Here we will show a semiformal method to translate specifications to composite pads. It provides a formal way to describe an application as a list of slots. Each slot is associated with its access dependency relationship. This means that the total application is initially considered as a single pad. The method then gives alternative ways to replace this single pad with an equivalent composite pad. This method can maximally reuse existing pads

### 16.6.1 Application Specification and Pattern Description for Primitive Pads

In this method, we first assume that an application to develop can be implemented as a single pad. We can use this assumption without loss of generality. Based on this assumption, we specify this pad at a certain level of abstraction. When we develop a pad, we usually start by listing all the slots, then we specify for each of these slots the functions of its "set" and "gimme" procedures, and, finally, we specify the "update" procedure. Our abstract specification of a pad follows this development process. We first specify a list of slots with their names and their types. The type of each slot is specified by a pair of two data types—one for the parameter of its "set" message, and the other for the return value of its "gimme" message.

The function of each slot procedure is specified in an abstract way using a dependency relationship among slot accesses. If a "set" access to a slot #x further causes a "set" access to another slot #y, and if this update propagation requires all the return values of "gimme" accesses to some slots $#z_1$, $#z_2$, ..., $#z_n$, we say that there is a slot-update dependency from #x to #y with references to $#z_1$, $#z_2$, ..., $#z_n$, and represent this dependency as $#x \rightarrow #y$ ($#z_1$, $#z_2$, ..., $#z_n$). The list of slots $#z_1$, $#z_2$, ..., $#z_n$ may include either #x or #y, or both of them. This dependency describes two facts. First, it tells us that there is an update dependency from a slot #x to #y. Second, all of the slots $#z_1$, $#z_2$, ..., $#z_n$ need to be referenced simultaneously. We call this set $\{#z_1, #z_2, ..., #z_n\}$ a reference base.

Let us consider a form interface to a database as an example application. Suppose that the records we want to visually show have three attributes: name, age, and photo. Our first step in this method specifies all the slots in this application. This list of slots may include the following slots:

| | |
|---|---|
| #search: | (bool, bool) |
| #query: | (text, text) |
| #result: | (record list, record list) |
| #cursor: | (integer, integer) |
| #record: | (record, record) |
| #previous: | (bool, bool) |
| #next: | (bool, bool) |
| #name: | (text, text) |
| #age: | (integer, integer) |
| #photo: | (image, image) |

The slot access dependencies are given as follows, where #changed(P), #set(P), and #gimme(P) are three dummy slots that represents the issuing of an "update" message, a "set" message, and a "gimme" message from this pad P, respectively.

#search → #set(P) (#query)
> When a search is requested, the query is read and sent out to the database using a "set" message.

#result → #record, #changed(P) (#result, #cursor)
> When a new retrieved result is obtained, the current record is also updated, which requires accesses of #cursor and #result. An "update" message is issued.

#cursor → #record, #changed(P) (#result, #cursor)

> When a cursor is updated, the current record should be also updated, which requires accesses of # result and #cursor. An "update" message is issued.

#record → #name, #age, #photo, #changed(P) (#record)

> When a record is updated, its attribute values should be all updated. An "update" message is issued.

#previous → #cursor, #changed(P)(#cursor)

> When the previous record is requested, the cursor should be updated using its current value. An "update" message is issued.

#next → #cursor, #changed(P) (#cursor)

> When the next record is requested, the cursor should be updated using its current value. An "update" message is issued.

#gimme(P) → #result, #cursor, #changed(P).

> When the pad reads the retrieved result from its parent, it updates #result, and resets its #cursor. An "update" message is issued.

These dependencies, when neglecting their reference parts, are transitive. If two dependencies #s1 → #s2 and #s2 → #s3 both hold, then the third dependency #s1 → #s3 also holds.

The specification of the "update" procedure is also given as a slot access dependency using a dummy slot #update(P). In the above example, this dependency is given as follows:

#update(P) → #gimme(P).

> When an "update" message is received, the pad issues a "gimme" message to its parent pad to read the retrieved result.

Thus, a single pad is specified with its slot list S and its slot-update dependency set D. The set S does not include any dummy slots. This pair (S, D) can be considered as a pattern description of this pad. In the following subsections, we call this pair the pattern of a primitive pad.

The slot-update dependency relation, neglecting its reference part, defines a partial order among slots, including dummy slots, which allows us to obtain a Hasse diagram for a given set of dependencies. Two slots satisfying #s1 → #s2 and #s2 → #s1 are said to be equivalent. Mutually equivalent slots are merged to a single node in a Hasse diagram. Figure 16.12 shows the Hasse diagram for the above example with each maximal reference base being enclosed by a circle. If a reference base is a proper subset of another reference base, the former one is not shown in the Hasse diagram. We call this diagram an extended Hasse diagram.

### 16.6.2  Pattern Description of Composite Pads

Now we consider the pattern description of composite pads. Let us consider a composition P1[#s: P2], which means that a pad P2 is pasted on another pad P1, and that P2 is connected to a slot #s of P1. Let (S1, D1) and (S2, D2) be pattern descriptions for P1 and P2, respectively. Without loss of generality, we can assume that S1 and S2 are mutually disjoint. Otherwise, they can be easily renamed to satisfy this assumption. Then the pattern description (S, D) for this composite pad is given as follows:

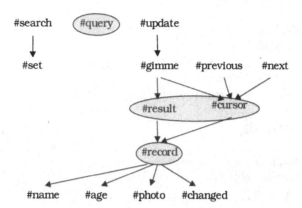

**Figure 16.12**   An extended Hasse diagram for the update dependencies in the example, with each reference base enclosed by a circle.

$$S = S1 \cup S2,$$
$$D = D1 \cup D2 \cup Ds \cup Dg \cup Du,$$

where Ds, Dg, and Du are given as follows:

Ds = {#set(P2) → #s} if the slot connection enables "set" messages, φ otherwise

Dg = {#gimme(P2) → φ(#s)} if the slot connection enables "gimme" messages, φ otherwise

Du = {#changed(P1) → #update(P2)} if the slot connection enables "update" messages and if these "update" messages are sent to all the child pads,

        {#s → #update(P2)} else if the slot connection enables "update" messages and if each slot update issues "update" messages only to those child pads connected to this slot,

    φ otherwise

Here, the dependency #gimme(P2) → φ(#s) in Dg only states that the set {#s} is a reference base.

Now let us consider a single pad that is equivalent to this composite pad. This single pad should have S as its slot list. Its dummy slots include #set(P) [= #set(P1)], #gimme(P) [= #gimme(P1)], #update(P) [= #update(P1)], and #changed(P), where #changed(P) merges the two dummy slots #changed(P1) and #changed(P2). Other dummy slots such as #set(p2), #gimme(P2), and #update(P2) do not communicate with other pads, and hence can be removed. However, before removing these dummy slots, we have to calculate the transitive closure of the dependency set D.

Let us consider the two pads whose pattern descriptions are given as follows:

(1) CounterPad (S1, D1)
slots:
  #up : (bool, bool)
  #down : (bool, bool)
  #count : (integer, integer)

dependencies:
    #up → #count(#count)
    #down → # count(#count)
    #count → #changed(CounterPad), #set(CounterPad)(#count)
    #gimme(CounterPad) → #count
    #update(CounterPad) → #gimme(CounterPad)

(2) CollectionPad (S2, D2)
slots:
    #collection : (list, list)
    #currentItem : (object, object)
    #index : (integer, integer)
dependencies
    #collection → #currentItem (#index, #collection)
    #index → #currentItem (#index, #collection)
    #gimme(CollectionPad) → #collection, #index
    #update(CollectionPad) → #gimme(CollectionPad)

Suppose that they are combined as CollectionPad[#index: CounterPad] with all three messages enabled. We also suppose that an update in CollectionPad issues an "update" message only to those child pads connected to those updated slots. Then the pattern description (S, D) of the composite pad becomes as follows:

S = S1 ∪ S2
D = D1 ∪ D2
    ∪ {#set(CounterPad) → #index, #gimme(CounterPad) → $\phi$(#index), #index
        → #update(CounterPad)}

The dependency closure of the equivalent single pad is obtained as follows:

    {#up → #up, #count, #index, #currentItem, #changed(P),
    #down → #down, # count, #index, #currentItem, #changed(P),
    #count → #count, #index, #currentItem, #changed(P),
    #collection → #currentItem, #changed(P),
    #index → #count, #index, #currentItem, #changed(P)
    #gimme(P) → #gimme(P), # count, #index, #collection, #currentItem,
                #changed(P),
    #update(P) → #update(P), #gimme(P), # count, #index, #collection,
                #currentItem, #changed(P)}

Figure 16.13 shows the extended Hasse diagram for this dependency set. A glance at this extended Hasse diagram tells us it is similar to the previous extended Hasse diagram shown in Figure 16.12. If we neglect #name, #age and #photo slots, and rename slot names appropriately, the current diagram coincides with one of the two parts in the previous diagram. This means that the current composite pad can possibly be used to implement a part of the previous specification.

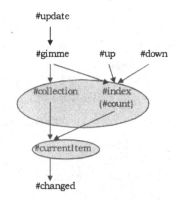

**Figure 16.13** An extended Hasse diagram for the update dependencies in the composed pad.

## 16.6.3 Composition and Decomposition of Patterns

Let H1 and H2 be the extended Hasse diagram representations of two pads P1 and P2, and H be the extended Hasse diagram representation of the pattern description of the composite pad P1[#s: P2]. We express this relationship as

$$H = H1 *_{\#s} H2$$

We define another operator $/_{\#s}$ as

$$H1 = H /_{\#s} H2$$

Let H2' be the extended Hasse diagram representation of the pattern description (S2', D') satisfying that H2' has the extended Hasse diagram H2 as its subgraph. Suppose further that the difference set S2' − S2 and S are mutually disjoint. The division operator $/_{\#s}$ can be extended as

$$H1 = H /_{\#s} H2'$$

The division operator depends on which of the three messages are enabled, and also on whether the parent pad broadcasts or selectively sends update operations to its child pads. For simplicity, here we assume that each pad issues an "update" only to those child pads connected to those slots whose values are updated. In the default implementation of pads, they issue updates to all of their child pads. However, when a pad receives an "update," it sends a "gimme" message to read the parent's slot to which it is connected, and examines if the read out value is the same as the last read out value it holds. If they are the same, the pad considers that there has been no update in this slot. In the default implementation, each pad initially holds a reference value as the last read out value. Therefore, the default implementation of pads does not contradict with the above assumption.

The decomposition of an extended Hasse diagram H into H1 and H2 requires that H has a node #s whose removal divides H into two parts. We call such nodes division nodes. Figure 16.14 shows an extended Hasse diagram that has only one division node, #collec-

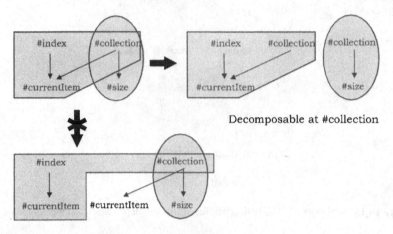

Decomposable at #collection

Not decomposable at #currentItem

**Figure 16.14** A correct decomposition and an incorrect decomposition of an extended Hasse diagram.

tion. The node #currentItem is a division node of the corresponding Hasse diagram, but not a division node of this extended Hasse diagram.

Suppose that a pad P is equivalent to a composite pad with P' as its base pad. Then "set" and "gimme" messages from the pad P should correspond to those from P', and "update" messages to P should correspond to those to P'. Therefore, for an arbitrary single pad P, the extended Hasse diagram H of its pattern description can be divided into three parts $H_{upper}$, $H_{middle}$, and $H_{lower}$, as shown in Figure 16.15, so that the middle part includes all of the three dummy slots, #set, #gimme, and #update. Each of the other two parts may be null. Let #s1 and #s2 be the two division nodes in this division. Let us rename their copies in the upper and the lower parts #s1' and #s2', respectively, as shown in Figure 16.15. The middle part includes the dependencies from #update(P) and #gimme(P), and the dependency to #set(P). These are the interface to its parent pad, and hence should be implemented by the base pad after any possible decomposition. Let $P_{upper}$, $P_{middle}$, and $P_{lower}$ denote the pads corresponding to these three parts of the Hasse diagram. Their composition, which is equivalent to P, is given by $P_{middle}$[#s1: $P_{upper}$][#s2: $P_{lower}$] (Figure 16.16).

Since the dummy slots #set, #gimme, and #update should reside in the same component after any possible division, the Hasse diagram as shown in Figure 16.17 cannot be further decomposed, although it has a division node.

The slot connection [#s2: $P_{lower}$] must implement an access dependency from the slots in the parent pad $P_{middle}$ to its child pad $P_{lower}$, which implies that the connection should enable both "update" and "gimme" messages. If #s2' has any incoming edges, then accesses of #s2' may need to propagate to #s2 in $P_{middle}$, which implies that the connection should also enable "set" messages. In this case, we have to add dependencies #gimme($P_{lower}$) → #s2', #update($P_{lower}$) → #gimme($P_{lower}$), and #s2' → set($P_{lower}$). Otherwise, we can just replace #s2' with # gimme($P_{lower}$).

The other slot connection [#s1: $P_{upper}$] needs to implement an access dependency from the slots in the child pad to its parent pad, which implies that the connection should enable

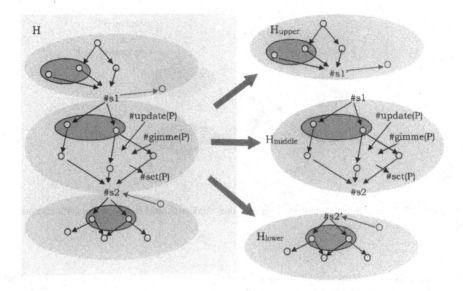

**Figure 16.15** For an arbitrary single pad P, its extended Hasse diagram may be divided into three parts.

"set" messages. If #s1′ has any outgoing edges, then accesses of #s1 may need to propagate to #s1′ in $P_{upper}$, which implies that the connection should also enable both "update" and "gimme" messages. In this case, we have to add dependencies #gimme($P_{upper}$) → #s1′, #update($P_{upper}$) → #gimme($P_{upper}$), and #s1′ → set($P_{upper}$). Otherwise, we can just replace #s1′ with # set($P_{upper}$).

Figure 16.16 shows all these possibilities of decomposition.

### 16.6.4 Pattern Descriptions and the Reuse of Pads

The reuse of pads requires specification matching between the required function and reusable existing pads. We can use the pattern descriptions as signatures of the specifications both for the required function and for reusable pads. Their extended Hasse diagrams give their canonical representations. If an extended Hasse diagram coincides with another

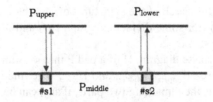

**Figure 16.16** A composite pad corresponding to the decomposition shown in Figure 16.15. The left gray arrow representing a pair of "update" and "gimme" messages is required if #s1′ has any outgoing edges in Figure 16.15. The gray arrow representing a "set" message is required if #s2′ has any incoming edges in Figure 16.15.

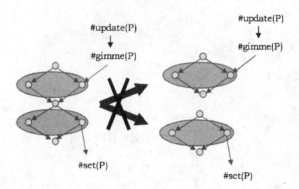

**Figure 16.17**   The dummy slots #set, #gimme, and #update should reside in the same component after any possible division.

extended Hasse diagram after renaming its slots, they are said to match each other. This coincidence includes both the matching of their structures and the node types of each corresponding pair. We express this matching as H1 = $\sigma$H2, where $\sigma$ denotes a renaming function. The relation that H1 is a subgraph of $\sigma$H2 is expressed as H1 $\subseteq$ $\sigma$H2.

Suppose that we are given a specification P. Let H be its extended Hasse diagram. Suppose that H is divided into two parts H(1) and H(2) as H = H(2)$*_{\#s(1)}$ H(1). Suppose further that there exists a reusable pad P(1) whose extended Hasse diagram H(1)$'$ satisfies H(1) $\subseteq$ $\sigma$(1) H(1)$'$ for some renaming function $\sigma$(1). Then it holds that H $\subseteq$ H(2)$'_{\#s(1)}$ $\sigma$(1)H(1)$'$. Similarly, suppose that H is divided into $n$ parts H(1), H(2), . . . , H($n$) as

$$H = \{(\ldots [H(n)*_{\#s}(n-1) \ H(n-1)] * \ldots)*_{\#s(2)} \ H(2)\}*_{\#s(1)} \ H(1)$$

Suppose further that, for each $i$, there exists a reusable P($i$) whose extended Hasse diagram H($i$)$'$ satisfies H($i$) $\subseteq$ $\sigma$($i$) H($i$)$'$ for some renaming function $\sigma$($i$). Then it holds that

$$H \subseteq ((\ldots (H(n)'*_{\#s(n-1)} \ \sigma(n-1)H(n-1)') * \ldots)*_{\#s(2)} \ \sigma(2)H(2)')*_{\#s(1)} \ \sigma(1) \ H(1)'$$

Then the specification using reusable pads is likely to be implemented as follows:

$$P \subset \sigma(1) \ldots \sigma(n-1)\{(\ldots (P(n)[\#s(n-1): P(n-1)]) \ldots)[\#s(2): P(2)]\}[\#s(1): P(1)].$$

This process requires the search of the signatures of reusable pads for such H($i$)$'$ that satisfies H($i$) $\subseteq$ $\sigma$($i$) H($i$)$'$ for some divider subgraph H($i$) and for some renaming function $\sigma$($i$).

Given an extended Hasse diagram H of a pad P that we want to implement, we can divide this into three parts, $H_{upper}$, $H_{middle}$, and $H_{lower}$. The middle part, $H_{middle}$, cannot be further divided, whereas the remaining two parts, if any, can be further divided at their division nodes to atomic components as shown in Figure 16.18(a). Suppose that the pad P can be composed using reusable pads as

$$P \subset \sigma(1) \ldots \sigma(n-1)\{(\ldots (P(n)[\#s(n-1): P(n-1)]) \ldots)[\#s(2): P(2)]\}[\#s(1): P(1)]$$

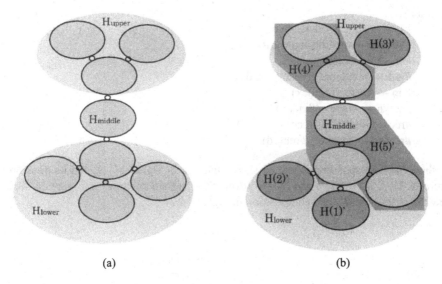

(a)                                                (b)

**Figure 16.18**  Decomposition of an extended Hasse diagram, and its coverage with extended Hasse diagrams of some reusable components. (a) Decomposition of an extended Hasse diagram to atomic components. (b) Some set of reusable pads covers the given extended Hasse diagram with their extended Hassse diagrams.

Then, for every component $H_i$ in Figure 16.18(a), there always exists one and only one pad $P(j)$ in this composition, as shown in Figure 16.18(b), such that the extended Hasse diagram $H(j)'$ of $\sigma(j)P(j)$ includes $H_i$ as its subgraph.

The efficient algorithm for this kind of search requires further research.

### 16.6.5  An Example Development Process

Here we consider a client application system for library services. Its specification is given as follows.

slots:

        #key (string, string)
        #template (string, string); Several different queries are stored.
        #query (string, string)
        #search (bool, bool)
        #dbFile (fileName, fileName)
        #result (recordList, recordList)
        #total (integer, integer); Total number of retrieved records.
        #up (bool, bool)
        #down (bool, bool)
        #index (integer, integer)
        #record (record, record)
        #title (string, string)
        #author (string, string)

dependencies:

#key → #query (#key, #template)
#search → #result (#query, #dbFile)
#result → #total(#result)
#index → #record (#result, #index)
#up → #index (#index)
#down → #index (#index)
#record → #title (#record)
#record → #author (#record)

We show the corresponding extended Hasse diagram in Figure 16.19, and its division in Figure 16.20. Our primitive pad library covers this diagram as shown in Figure 16.20. We show the corresponding pad composition in Figure 16.21.

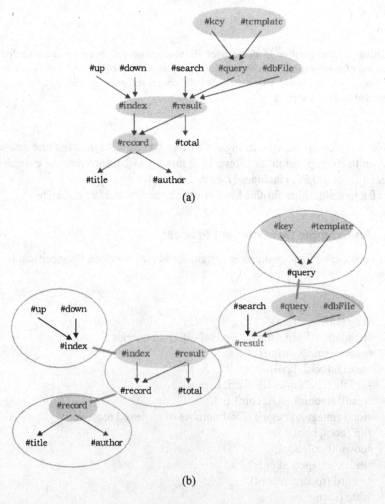

**Figure 16.19** An example extended Hasse diagram and its division. (a) An extended Hasse diagram of the example pad specification. (b) Division of the extended Hasse diagram.

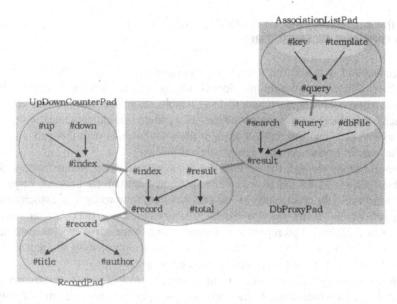

**Figure 16.20**  Our primitive pad library covers the diagram in Figure 16.19 as shown here.

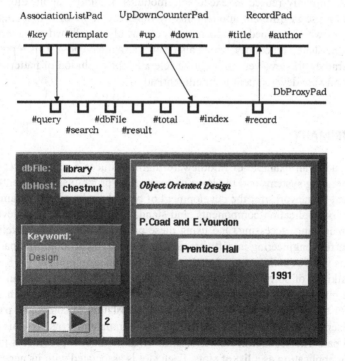

**Figure 16.21**  A composite pad that has been developed from the example specification using our pad library.

## 16.7   INTELLIGENTPAD AS A SOFTWARE DEVELOPMENT FRAMEWORK

When considered as a software development environment, IntelligentPad is an evolving environment. The current version provides hundreds of components and some number of sample composite pads. Unfortunately, these sample composite pads are not well related with each other. Each sample composite pad, as a pattern, should be related to other sample composite pads that can replace some of their components with this pad, and also to those that can be used as optional components of this pad.

When published through the WWW, the catalogues of patterns and frameworks described in Sections 16.4.2 and 16.4.3 can be distributed through the Internet. Anyone anywhere in the world can publish his or her patterns and frameworks with association links to other patterns and frameworks published by others at different sites. Anyone can access and reuse each of them. This repository of patterns and frameworks evolves itself through the publication of new patterns and frameworks by the people sharing this repository, and through the spanning of new links among them by people.

Such a repository will help us to form a pattern-and-framework community whose members add new patterns and frameworks to this repository, relate them to the already registered ones, and retrieve some of these patterns and frameworks to reuse in different but related applications. Since patterns and frameworks in IntelligentPad systems are provided as executable and decomposable composite pads, they themselves or their components can be directly reused as executable modules in similar applications, and easily modified to reuse in different applications by replacing some of their components with other pads. Newly developed composite pads can be also published as patterns or frameworks into the shared repository, which also works as a meme pool. This repository of patterns and frameworks evolves itself and accelerates the evolution of patterns and frameworks for software development in IntelligentPad.

## 16.8   SUMMARY

IntelligentPad is an example of middleware that introduces a middle layer between the layer of operating systems and the layer of application programs. IntelligentPad provides standard pad frameworks for the development of typical application programs, a standard pad library of application components, and standard infrastructures for developing, distributing, managing, accessing, and using these pads and frameworks. IntelligentPad allows concurrent engineering in software development. Typical composite pads for typical applications work as architectural patterns in application developments.

Various kinds of software development methods can be applied to pad development with some customization to the IntelligentPad architecture. This chapter has shown two methods for application specifications and their translation to composite pads. The first method describes an application using an action diagram, and translates this diagram to a composite pad. The second method is a semiformal method. It provides a formal way to describe an application as a list of slots. Each slot is associated with its access dependency relationship. This means that the total application is initially assumed to be a single pad. The method then gives alternative ways to replace this single pad with an equivalent composite pad. This method can maximally reuse existing pads.

# REFERENCES

1. D. T. Dewire. *Second-Generation Client/Server Computing.* McGraw-Hill, New York, 1997.

2. Object Management Group. *The Common Object Request Broker: Architecture and Specification.* Wiley, New York, 1992.

3. T. W. Ryan. *Distributed Object Technology: Concepts and Applications.* Prentice-Hall PTR, Upper Saddle River, NJ, 1997.

4. C. Alexander. *The Timeless Way of Building.* Oxford University Press, New York, 1979.

5. C. Alexander, S. Ishikawa, M. Silverstein, M. Jacobson, I. Fiksdahl-King, and S. Angel. *A Pattern Language.* Oxford University Press, New York, 1977.

6. J. O. Coplien. *The History of Patterns.* See *http://c2.com/cgi/wiki?HistoryOfPatterns,* 1995.

7. E. Gamma, R. Helm, R. Johnson, and J. Vlissides. *Design Patterns: Elements of Reusable Object-Oriented Software.* Addison-Wesley, Reading, MA, 1995.

8. J. O. Coplien. *Advanced C++—Programming Styles and Idioms.* Addison-Wesley, Reading, MA, 1992.

9. D. C. Schmidt. *ACE—The ADAPTIVE Communication Environment.* See *http:/siesta.cs.wustl. edu/~schmidt/ACE.html,* 1996.

10. P. Coad, D. North, and M. Mayfield. *Object Models—Patterns, Strategies, and Applications.* Yordon Press, Prentice Hall, Upper Saddle River, NJ, 1995.

11. W. Pree. Meta Patterns—A means for capturing the essentials of reusable object-oriented design. In *Proceedings of ECOOP '94,* pp. 150–162, 1994.

12. F. Bushmann, R. Meunier, H. Rohnert, P. Sommerlad, and M. Stal. *Pattern-Oriented Software Architecture: A System of Patterns.* Wiley, Chichester, UK, 1996.

13. I. Jacobson, M. Ericsson, and A. Jacobson. *The Object Advantage: Business Process Reengineering with Object Technology.* ACM Press, New York, 1955.

14. B. Kaplan and J. Goodsen. *Task Analysis.* Technical Report The Dalmatian Group Inc., 1995.

15. J. Martin, and C. McClure. *Diagramming Techniques for Analysts and Programmers.* Prentice-Hall, Englewood Cliffs, NJ, 1985.

16. A. S. Fisher. *CASE Using Software Development Tools.* Wiley, New York, 1988.

17. J. Martin and C. McClure. *Action Diagrams,* Prentice-Hall, Englewood Cliffs, NJ, 1985.

# CHAPTER 17

---

# OTHER APPLICATIONS
# OF INTELLIGENTPAD

---

In Chapters 9 and 10, we showed applications of IntelligentPad to multimedia systems and database systems, and the generic frameworks for these applications. Chapter 14 showed application frameworks for form-flow systems and workflow systems. Chapters 8, 11, 12, 13, and 15 showed utility pads for defining a shared workspace, coordinating a group of pads, defining a meme pool, introducing economic activities to a meme pool to make it a meme market, and defining mobile agents as pads. With these frameworks and utilities, IntelligentPad can cover a large range of interactive applications.

This chapter will show some potential application examples of IntelligentPad. They are classified as follows:

1. Tool integration environments and PIM (personal information management)
2. Educational applications
3. Web page authoring
4. CAD/CAM applications
5. GIS with planning capabilities
6. Financial applications
7. Information kiosk
8. Electronic libraries/museums and digital archives
9. Exchange of scientific and technological data and tools
10. Matchmaking place among creators, connoisseurs, and buyers

Some of these applications were described in preceding chapters. Section 10.6 discussed applications to GIS with planning capabilities, and Sections 11.6 and 11.8 described aaplications to the exchange of scientific and technological data and tools. Section 11.8 also introduced Seigo Matsuoka's Meme Country Project, which aimed to establish a virtual country with various social infrastructures for the publication, finding, and utilization of knowledge, talents, and people, and for their matching with other knowledge, talents, and people. This chapter shows some of the applications of IntelligentPad that have not been referred to in the preceding chapters.

## 17.1 CAPABILITIES BROUGHT BY THE IMPLEMENTATION IN INTELLIGENTPAD

IntelligentPad has versatile application fields. It has the capability of covering all kinds of client application systems that use two-dimensional graphical representations. Each application may require the development of new primitive pads. Some primitive pads may be too complicated to be called primitive pads, and require professional programmers to develop them. Application development in an IntelligentPad system introduces the following five significant capabilities to the developed systems:

1. User-definable dynamic linkage among different systems
2. What-if trials without destroying original resources or processes
3. User customizability
4. Reuses of components, patterns, and frameworks
5. Distribution of components through the Internet, and their reediting and redistribution by end-users

IntelligentPad allows us to easily combine existing applications and/or their components by dynamically defining linkages among any of them. Furthermore, it allows us to execute what-if trials without destroying original resources or processes. A what-if trial examines what will happen if something is assumed. What-if trials are especially important in trial-and-error jobs. Such jobs include design, planning, simulation, and decision making. System products provided as pads can be made totally or partially user-customizable. The product provider can control the decomposability of each connection among the product's components. This also allows us to reuse components of products, composition patterns of products, and frameworks provided by package products. Composite pads can be distributed through the Internet, and reused at the destination sites. They can be further reedited there just by peeling off some pads and pasting some new pads. The resulting composite pad can be redistributed again through the Internet.

## 17.2 TOOL INTEGRATION ENVIRONMENTS AND PERSONAL INFORMATION MANAGEMENT

The very first reason for developing IntelligentPad was to make various tools interoperable through direct manipulations by their users. Once various system libraries, whether they have graphical user interfaces or not, have been represented as primitive pads with appropriate slots, they can be easily and dynamically combined to perform more complex jobs. Command-based utilities of operating systems are good candidates for pad applications. For example, a file browser can be represented as a pad. Each file can be also represented as a pad with a slot returning its contents when accessed by a "gimme" message.

PIM (Personal Information Management) consists of various tools, including a schedule calendar, a to-do list, an address list, memos, and tools to communicate with other computers and PDAs (personal data adapters). These tools should be able to exchange whatever objects we select with each other whenever we need them. If the objects they deal with are represented as pads, they can be easily dragged and dropped from one tool to another.

Pads and their anchor pads can be pasted at any locations on any pads. Let us consider a pad that allows you to input a person's name. Suppose that its click will pop up another pad that retrieves a photo, the address, the phone number, and the e-mail address of this person from a database to present them as pads on itself. If such a pad is used in a schedule calendar to memorize the person to meet at some time on some day, you can click this pad to obtain his e-mail address pad, and stick this address pad on an e-mail pad to send this mail to him. Or you can just click such a pad on a schedule calendar to obtain his phone number pad, and click this phone number pad to put yourself through to this person. On a schedule calendar, you may use a special alarm-clock pad whose alarm time is automatically set to the day and the time determined by its location on the schedule calendar pad. From this alarm time you may subtract arbitrary years, months, weeks, days, hours, and minutes by dropping special pads on this alarm-clock pad. This makes it possible to activate an alarm clock some minutes, hours, or days ahead of the scheduled time. Anchor pads pasted on such an alarm-clock pad will pop up the associated pads at its alarm time.

A to-do list as a pad may also hold various pads on itself. Furthermore, its anchor pad can be pasted on an alarm-clock pad that is pasted on an appropriate location of the schedule-calendar pad. This to-do list will be popped up at the specified time on the specified day. You can easily drag and drop any job represented as a pad from one to-do list pad at some location on the calendar to another to-do list pad at another location on the calendar.

Memo pads can be also represented as pads. You may put any pads on them. Memo pads and their anchors can be pasted on any pads, including alarm-clock pads, a schedule calendar, to-do list pads, other memo pads, maps, and text pads.

Figure 17.1 shows a PIM system developed by C's Lab. Inc. using an IntelligentPad system. Here you can see an address list on the right, a calendar on the left, and an e-mail system at the center. The format of the address table entries can be easily customized

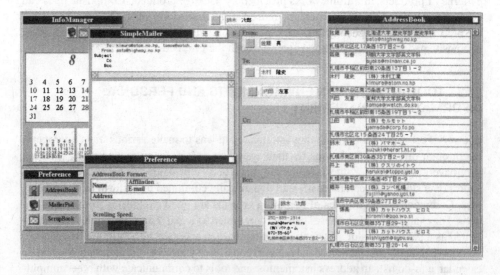

**Figure 17.1** A PIM system developed by C's Lab. Inc. using an IntelligentPad system.

through the editing of the pad shown in the "Preference" window below the e-mail system. If you click an entry of the address list, the address-list pad will pop up a slip pad as shown at the center top. This slip pad shows only the name of the selected person, but contains all the detailed information. When you click its left button, such a slip expands itself to show its details as shown at the left-bottom corner of the address list. When dropped on the address entries of the e-mail system, such a slip pad sends the e-mail address part of its content information to the corresponding entries of the e-mail system.

Figure 17.2 shows a scrapbook for pads at its center top. The same company that developed the above-mentioned PIM utility also developed this scrapbook. Any composite pad can be put on this pad. Only the reduced image of the original pad is visually registered on this pad. When you click this image, the scrapbook will pop up its original pad. The right-top pad is also a scrapbook, which is registered at the left-top corner in the previous scrapbook. This figure shows two more pads popped up from this scrapbook.

## 17.3   EDUCATIONAL APPLICATIONS

IntelligentPad provides all kinds of facilities necessary for education tools:

1. Interactivity with multimedia documents
2. Dynamic linkage among experimental data, simulation tools, and analysis tools
3. Provision of large reference databases of multimedia documents and data
4. Guiding facility based on student modeling and/or monitoring
5. Microworlds with interoperable objects and tools that users can directly play with
6. Building blocks for constructing objects and tools in microworlds

**Figure 17.2**   A scrapbook for pads developed by C's Lab. Inc. using an IntelligentPad system.

IntelligentPad enables us to publish education systems with some or all of these facilities either on CD-ROMs or through the Internet.

### 17.3.1  Teaching Japanese to Foreign Students

A group of linguists teaching Japanese to foreigners organized the first user community of IntelligentPad around 1994. The community now includes not only teachers but also their students in Asia, Europe, America, and Oceania. They were not satisfied with previously available systems such as Directors and HyperCards. They wanted to provide arbitrary functional modules with arbitrary shapes and textures, and to put them at arbitrary locations on a card, without writing a single line of code. They asked Hitachi Software Engineering Corp., one of the most active IPC members, to help them use IntelligentPad. They found that most of their worksheets could be classified into a rather small number of different types.

One such type, for example, asks a student to select one out of many choices. It answers "correct" if he or she selects the correct one. Otherwise, it answers "incorrect." These selection buttons are laid out differently for different problems. We need to provide only two types of buttons. A correct button answers "correct," whereas an incorrect button answers "incorrect." A group of problems of this type starts with a single sentence telling you to select one out of several sentences that follow. All these sentences can be written on a single pad. A correct sentence is covered by a transparent correct button, whereas incorrect sentences are covered by incorrect buttons. Once these two buttons are provided, this authoring becomes a foolproof job. Another group of problems of this type have a single sentence telling you to select one out of the several pictures that follow. The sentence and these pictures may be images on a single pad. You can just cover these pictures with appropriate transparent buttons. No more work is required for the authoring. Figure 17.3 shows two worksheets that can be easily authored using the above-mentioned single framework.

One of the most difficult things in the Japanese language is the proper use of postpositional particles after subjects, objects, locations, and times. A sentence with several postpositional particles left unspecified works as a good exercise for students to select

**Figure 17.3**   Various worksheets that can be easily authored using the same framework.

the most appropriate postpositional particle out of many candidates to fill in in each of the positions left unspecified. This type of exercise begins with an instruction telling you to fill in each empty box in the given sentence with the most appropriate candidate selected out of the given candidates. Each empty box and each candidate are both represented as pads. If the most appropriate candidate pad is put on an empty-box pad, the candidate pad will stay there. Otherwise, the candidate pad will be returned to its original position. This worksheet uses a base pad to hold other component pads on itself—a text pad showing a sentence with several postpositional particles left unspecified, empty-box pads to cover each position of the unspecified postpositional particles, and a set of candidate pads to fill in empty boxes (Figure 17.4). The same framework can be used in various different worksheets. An example is a picture of animals with name tags. It asks you to put an appropriate name tag on each of the animals in this picture. Each animal is covered by a transparent empty-box pad, whereas each name tag is represented by a candidate pad.

Each empty-box pad is a single PlaceHolderPad with a #index slot storing a positive integer, whereas each candidate pad may be a composite pad with a PlaceFillerPad as its base pad. A PlaceFillerPad has also a #index slot, and remembers its previous position. When put on another pad, it checks to see if the underlying pad is a PlaceHolderPad, sends this PlaceHolderPad a "gimme" message to read its #index slot, and compares this value with its own #index slot value. If the underlying pad is not a PlaceHolderPad or these index numbers do not match each other, the PlaceFillerPad will return to its original position. Otherwise, the PlaceFillerPad will stay there. You may paste an image pad or a text string pad on top of each PlaceFillerPad to make various types of candidate pads. The grouping operation can protect such composite pads from decomposition.

Shin Nitoguri of Tokyo Gakugei University, in cooperation with Hitachi Software Engineering Corp., has developed several frameworks and provided each of them with necessary primitive pads and some sample composite pads. He published a Japanese language textbook for foreign students together with a CD-ROM including many worksheets developed in IntelligentPad.

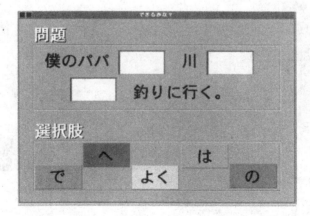

**Figure 17.4** A worksheet teaching how to use postpositional particles in Japanese after subjects, objects, locations, and times.

### 17.3.2  CAI in Physics and Mathematics

Takafumi Noguchi of Kushiro Technical Collage has developed several CAI systems in elementary mechanics, elementary electronics, and elementary mathematical functions (Figure 17.5).

Figure 17.6 shows a mechanical system with pulleys and springs connected together. Probes are used to measure the tension of some ropes, and the values of two probes are sent to an XY plotter using wiring pads to show the functional relationship between them. The plotter shows that the value of the upper probe is always twice as large as the value of the lower probe when we change the weight in the weight box. Each of these pulleys and springs is animated on a separate transparent pad. Figure 17.7 shows primitive pads representing springs, two types of pulleys, a weight box, weights, and latches. It also shows a composite system with these components.

Figure 17.8 shows how components are pasted together to define a mechanical system. Figure 17.8(a) shows the situation just after the pasting of the upper spring onto the other one. At this instance, components are not yet functionally linked together. Figure 17.8(b) shows how component pads are pasted and connected together. The starter pad starts the coordination of all the components over itself whenever it receives event information about the pasting or the moving of a pad over itself. It coordinates the components so they

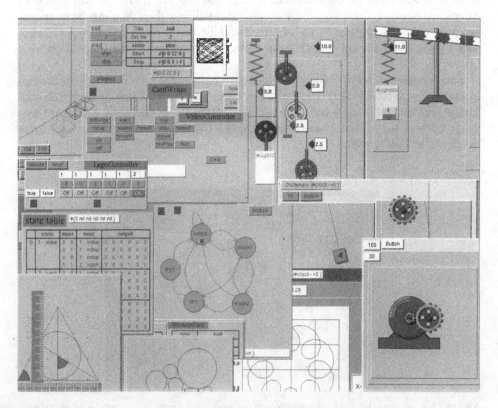

**Figure 17.5**  CAI systems in elementary mechanics, elementary electronics, and elementary mathematical functions.

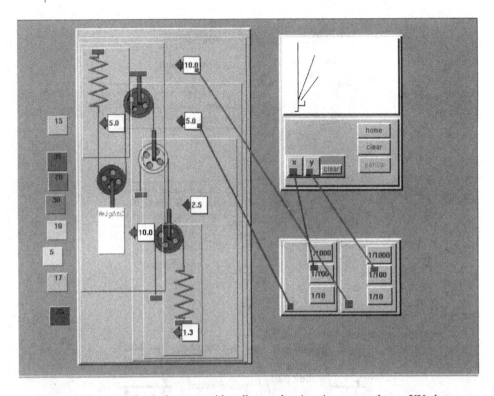

**Figure 17.6**   A mechanical system with pulleys and springs is connected to an XY plotter.

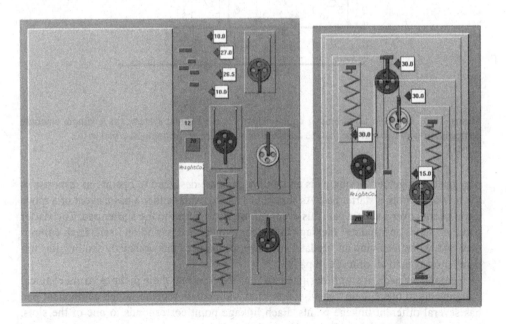

**Figure 17.7**   A composite pad and its decomposition to primitive component pads.

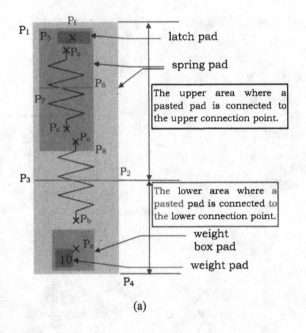

(a)

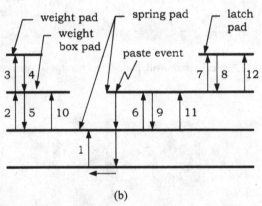

(b)

**Figure 17.8**   Message flows among components of a mechanical system. (a) A simple example composition with two springs. (b) The composition structure of the composite pad in (a).

may operate together. Spring pads and pulley pads are designed to operate in response to the messages from a starter pad. As shown in 17.8(b), when either a paste event or a move event occurs over a starter pad, this event information is sent to the starter pad. The starter pad then sends an "update" message to the component pad pasted on itself. Each component pad, when receiving an "update" message, propagates this update by sending its "update" messages to all of its child pads.

Component pads are well designed so that they redraw their pictures of mechanical components to make them visually connected and operate together. Each component pad has several different linkage points. Each linkage point corresponds to one of the slots. When you paste another pad around one of these linkage points, the parent pad automatically connects the child pad to the corresponding slot. Each latch as well as each weight box has one linkage point at its center. Each spring has two linkage points at its two ends. Each pulley has three linkage points—two at the two ends of its rope, and one at the end of the harness mounting the wheel. Each spring pad divides its area into the upper and the lower areas at the center of its displayed spring. These two areas include the upper and the lower linkage points, respectively. They are called linkage areas of the spring pad.

When a spring pad outputs information about its linkage points, it outputs an information pair for these two points. Each component on top of a spring pad receives such an information pair, and selects only the portion related to itself.

In Figure 17.8, up arrows represent "update" messages, whereas down arrows represent "set" messages. When a component receives an "update" message, it reads the connected slot of its parent pad to get the necessary information. Each parameter value sent to or read from component pads is represented as an association list of the following structure:

$$[(<\text{message}_1>.\textit{value}_1), (<\text{message}_2>.\textit{value}_2), \ldots, (<\text{message}_n>.\textit{value}_n)],$$

where $<\text{message}_i>$ is a keyword and $\textit{value}_i$ is its value. In the following, we show the details of the linkage mechanism using the example in Figure 17.8, where it is assumed that the displacement coefficient of each spring is 1, and that each of the weights and the weight box weighs 10 grams.

1. Messages 1, 2, 3, 6, and 7 are "update" messages that request the recipient pads for their statuses. Message 1 triggers messages 2 and 6, which then further trigger messages 3 and 7. Each sender pad of theses messages stores in its connection slot an association list of the form [(<giveData>.true)]. Any physical constant, such as the gravitational constant, that all the components must use can be delivered to them if we add its information to this association list to store [(<giveData>.true), (<gravity>.9.8)] in the connection slot.

2. Sending the "update" message 3 to the weight pad makes this pad to read the list [(<giveData>.true), (<gravity>.9.8)], which requests this pad to send back the "set" message 4 with its state. This state is represented as [(<weight>.10)].

3. The weight box pad that has received the "set" message 4 reads the association list that has been sent to its connection slot, gets the value 10 of the keyword <weight>, adds its own weight 10 to this value to obtain the total weight 20, and sends the "set" message 5 to its parent pad. Its parameter is also an association list [(<free>.true), (<point>.Pe), (<weight>.20)], where the first item (<free>.true) denotes that the weight box is not fixed, the second item (<point>.Pe) shows the position of its linkage points, and the last item shows the total weight.

4. The latch that has received the data request message through an "update" message immediately sends the "set" message 8 with an association list [(<fix>.true), (<point>.Pf), (<constant>.0)] as its parameter, where the first item (<fix>.true) denotes that the latch is fixed, the second item shows the position of its linkage point, and the last item shows its displacement coefficient. Since the latch is not a spring, its displacement coefficient is 0.

5. The spring pad that has received the message 8 reads out the association list [(<fix>.true), (<point>.Pf), (<constant>.0)] from its slot, uses these values to calcu-

late its state, and sends the "set" message 9 with an association list [(<fix>.true), (<point>.Pd), (<constant>.1)] as its parameter. The first item of this list denotes that the spring is fixed to the latch. The second item shows the position of the spring's lower linkage point after the upper linkage point has been fixed to the linkage point Pf of the latch. The last item denotes that its displacement coefficient is 1.

6. The lower spring pad that has received the set messages 5 and 9 reads out the two association lists from its two slots connected to its child pads. From the first association list [(<fix>.true), (<point>.Pd), (<constant>.1)] and the <weight> part of the second association list [(<free>.true), (<point>.Pe), (<weight>.20)], the lower spring pad knows that its upper linkage point must satisfy $P_a = P_d + (0, 20)$, where the displacement 20 is obtained by multiplying the displacement coefficient 1 by the weigh 20. The lower spring pad also knows that its length is expanded by 20, which is the product of its own displacement coefficient 1 and the weight 20 applied to it. Therefore, the lower spring pad can calculate the position of its lower linkage point as $P_b = P_a + (0, 20) = P_d + (0, 40)$. The lower spring pad sets the association list [(<point>.[((P_1, P_2), P_a) ((P_3, P_4), P_b)]), (<weight>.[(20) (20)])] to the two slots connected to its child pads, where [a b] denotes an array of data. The list $((P_1, P_2), P_a)$ denotes that the upper linkage point is at $P_a$, and that the upper linkage area is a rectangle defined by two diagonal nodes $P_1$ and $P_2$. The item (<weight>.[(20) (20)]) denotes that a downward force of magnitude 20 is applied to each of the two linkage points $P_a$ and $P_b$. This spring pad then issues "update" messages 10 and 11 to its child pads.

7. The weight box pad that has received the "update" message 10 reads the slot of its parent by a "gimme" message. It knows that there are two linkage areas $(P_1, P_2)$ and $(P_3, P_4)$ defined in its parent pad, selects the $(P_3, P_4)$ including its own linkage point $P_e$, gets the position $P_b$ that is paired with this selected area $(P_3, P_4)$, and moves itself so that $P_e$ coincides with the position $P_b$.

8. The upper spring pad that has received the "update" message 11 reads the slot of its parent by a "gimme" message. It knows that there are two linkage areas $(P_1, P_2)$ and $(P_3, P_4)$ defined in its parent pad, selects the $(P_1, P_2)$ including its own floating linkage point $P_d$, gets the position $P_a$ that is paired with this selected area $(P_1, P_2)$, and redraw its picture of a spring so that $P_c$ and $P_d$ coincide with the positions Pf and $P_a$, respectively. This spring pad then stores the association list {(<point>.[((P_5, P_6), P_c) ((P_7, P_8), P_d)]), (<weight>.[(20) (20)])} in its two connection slots, and sends an "update" message to its child pad. The latch pad receiving this message does not move since it is fixed.

Figure 17.9 shows a motor with gears and XY plotters. Here again, each component such as a motor and a gear is a pad. Each XY plotter is also composed with primitive pads. The motor rotates at a constant angular velocity triggered by its underlying clock-pulse-generator pad. Each gear pad has a reference position at its edge and two slots representing the X and Y coordinate values of this point. The rotation of a gear moves its reference point and changes these slot values. Each of the two left XY plotters plot the value of one of these slots as a function of time to draw a sine curve.

Figure 17.10 shows a pad environment developed for the learning of elementary functions. Here you can easily define a complex composite function by pasting together function pads, constant pads, and variable pads as shown in Figure 17.11. Such a composite

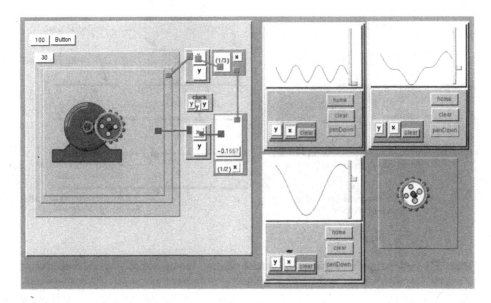

**Figure 17.9** A motor with gears and XY plotters. They are all composed with component pads.

pad is pasted on top of another pad with its connection to a slot of its parent pad. This parent pad can request the composite pad to evaluate the function value and send this value to this connection slot. Any pad that requests its child pad to send a value to its slot can be used as the parent of such a composite pad. The message flows in this composition are similar to those in the mechanical system example described above.

When a pad in such a composition wants to request its child pad to evaluate the func-

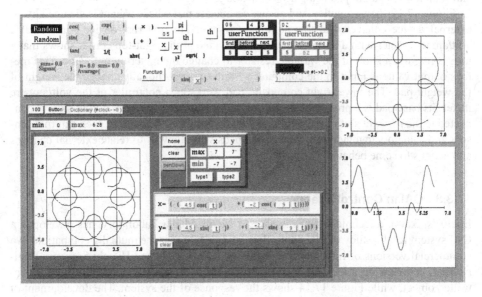

**Figure 17.10** A pad environment for leaning elementary functions.

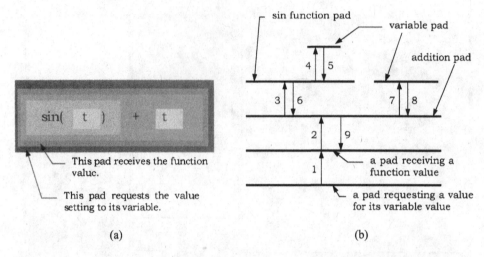

(a)  (b)

**Figure 17.11** Message flows among component pads for playing with elementary functions. (a) An example composition of a mathematical function. (b) Message flows in the composition in (a).

tion value, it sends an association list of the form [(<giveData>.true)(<variable>.*v*)] to its slot that is connected to the function-evaluating child pad, and sends this child pad an "update" message, where *v* denotes the value of the variable. The recipient child pad sends a "gimme" message to its parent to read out this association list. In such a composition, association lists of this type are sent from every pad to its child pads, starting from the bottommost pad, and proceeding toward the topmost constant or variable pads. Each topmost pad returns to its parent pad either its constant value or its variable value depending on whether it is a constant pad or a variable pad. Its recipient can evaluate its function value, and send it to its parent pad using a "set" message.

Figure 17.12 shows a pulley-and-spring composite pad whose weight is changed by an external device connected to this computer system. This external device consists of a volt/ampere meter with a variable resistor. The video at the right-top corner shows that a user is rotating a knob of the variable resistor to change the meter output value. This meter's output value is input to the computer system to proportionally change the weight of the weight pad. The lower-right composite pad works as a controller of the volt/ampere meter. Its base pad is a proxy pad of the volt/ampere meter. One of its output slots is connected to the #weight slot of the weight pad by a wiring pad. The use of such external sensors and actuators together with their proxy pads will allow us to relate external changes and actions to some behaviors of pads.

### 17.3.3 CAI in Control Theory

Eiichi Ishikawa, a technical staff member of Meme Media Laboratory, has developed a CAI system for the study of PID controllers. His system uses the mutually compatible two commercial versions of IntelligentPad available from Fujitsu and Hitachi Software Engineering, and runs on a PC and Macintosh. Figure 17.13 shows a controller and a controlled object, while Figure 17.14 shows the response of the system. The development of this whole system did not require any coding except the program defining the controlled

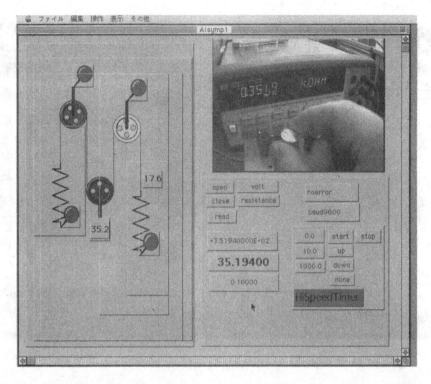

**Figure 17.12** A pulley-and-spring composite pad whose weight is changed by an external device connected to this computer system.

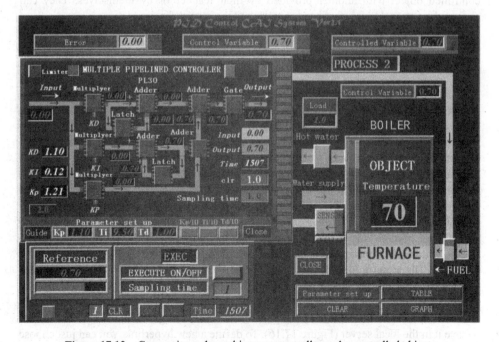

**Figure 17.13** Composite pads working as a controller and a controlled object.

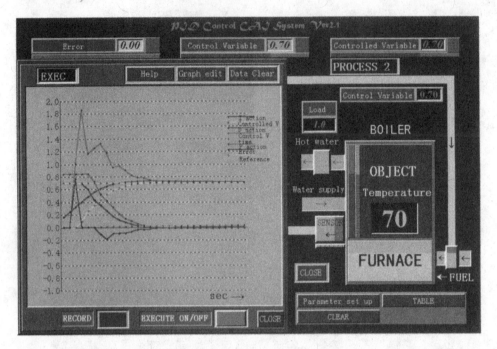

**Figure 17.14**   Composite pads showing the response of the system in Figure 17.13.

object. Students can replace this controller with a new one they design, or replace this controlled object with another provided by their teacher or by themselves. They can change the external noise, the input signals, and the output display.

## 17.4   WEB PAGE AUTHORING

Tokyo Electric Power Company has been publishing lots of information about their research and development activities, nuclear power technologies and operations, as well as their service information through the WWW. However, they found it difficult to update their home-page contents in a timely manner because the writing in HTML requires time-consuming manual operations to enter and edit texts, numbers, and multimedia data such as photos and graphs, and to handle hyperreferences for making scenarios.

Masaki Nakamura and Morihiro Shiozawa of Tokyo Electric Power Company and Keizo Uchiyama of Tokyo Electric Computer Service solved this problem by using IntelligentPad technologies. Their system allows us to define a web page just by pasting together texts, photos, videos, tables, graphs, and other data objects. If you want to insert an image, you can first paste an image pad at a desired location, resize it, and then open its associated file selector to select an image file as shown in Figure 17.15. The selected image is displayed on this image pad. This system automatically generates the HTML description of your contents, which can be published through the World Wide Web or intranets. You can just click the "HTML generation" button to generate the HTML file and to save it in the local server (Figure 17.16). To define a new hyperlink, you can just choose a character string for an anchor, and select the destination page from the file selector.

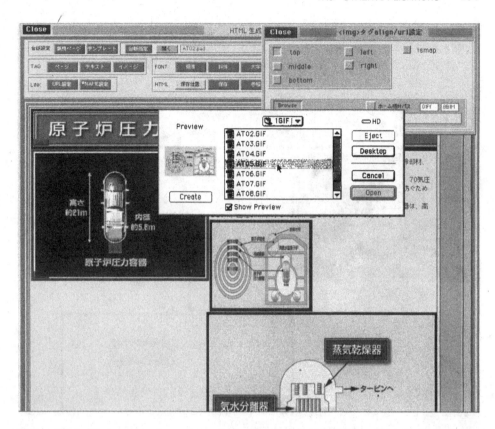

**Figure 17.15** If you want to insert an image, you can first paste an image pad at a desired location, resize it, and then open its associated file selector to select an image file.

## 17.5 OTHER APPLICATIONS

Other applications that some IPC members are interested in include CAD/CAM systems, financial analysis systems, information kiosk systems, and electronic library and museum systems. Takeshi Sunaga of Tama Art Collage is interested in using IntelligentPad as a tool for information design.

### 17.5.1 CAD/CAM Applications

Drawings in CAD/CAM can be treated as pads, which enable them to exchange data and messages among themselves. Objects in a drawing can be also treated as pads pasted on the base drawing pad, which enables each component to communicate with the total system modeled by the base pad. The paste and peel of components also change the system model or its parameters stored in the base pad.

The base models and these components in CAD/CAM systems are usually managed by database systems to maintain coherency among replicated uses of the same model and the same component by different drawings. Each of these drawings not only refers to these models and components, but also updates them. Their management by a data-

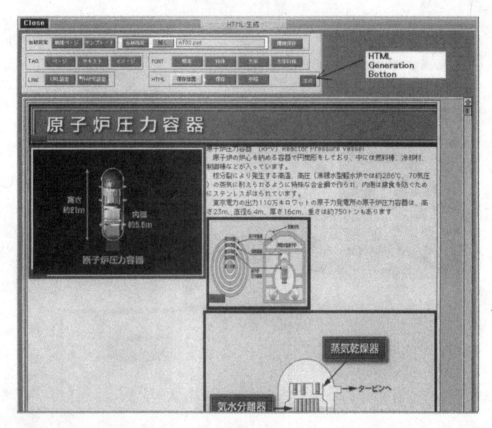

**Figure 17.16** You can just click the "HTML generation" button to generate an HTML file and to save it in the local server.

base maintains not only their integrity, but also the coherency among their replicated references in different systems. Every modification of a base model or a component in one system updates its representation in the database. Every reference of a base model or a component accesses the database to retrieve its most recent version. Every object reference is updated on demand. This mechanism is quite similar to the use of virtual forms instead of real forms. To achieve this goal you may extend each drawing pad and each component pad to retrieve their contents from a database and to update them by updating the database.

The above mechanism guarantees coherency among replicated references on demand. The real-time coherency among them can be also achieved by treating them as shared copies of the same pad.

CAD/CAM systems also require what-if trial capabilities that allow us to observe, without destroying any resources or any processes, what happens if we try something. IntelligentPad makes it easy to provide application frameworks capable of performing what-if trials. However, special considerations are necessary to replicate proxy pads and shared copies of pads. In CAD/CAM systems without either the on-demand coherency mechanism or the real-time coherency mechanism, what-if trials can simply use independent copies of drawings and components. In CAD/CAM systems with the on-demand coherency mechanism, what-if trials should be related to the version control mechanism of databases.

### 17.5.2 Financial Applications

Financial applications are also considered prospective application areas of IntelligentPad. Stock market analysis and portfolio management both require visual presentation and various capabilities including the exchange of their contents with other systems, what-if simulation over themselves, and direct access to transaction services through themselves. Furthermore, they must be presented on clients' computer through the Internet, and clients should be able to access various services through these presentation sheets. It is quite natural to represent these as pads.

### 17.5.3 Information Kiosk Systems

Information kiosk systems help visitors to cities, towns, museums, libraries, company offices, department stores, and malls to find how to access what they want to see, to visit, to read, to buy, or whom they want to meet. Information kiosk systems are naturally suited to the capabilities of IntelligentPad. A typical information kiosk system consists of a map with some recommended tour routes, guided tour presentations, access entrances to other pages, an automatic dial-up service, service-request-form pages, and information-presentation pages. The first page is a map with several anchors working as access entrances to other pages. A click on one of them pops up a new page, which may be also a map or a service page. A service page enables us to communicate with a service or a person through an input/output form or a phone connection. All these pages and their component objects can be represented as pads.

### 17.5.4 Electronic Libraries and Museums

Electronic museum and/or library systems are also systems of increasing importance to which IntelligentPad can be directly applied. They deal not only with multimedia documents, but also with scientific tools, data, facts, and rules, all in a unified manner. They should have the capabilities of network publication of these contents and their search services. IntelligentPad represents these contents and services as pads. Its HTMLViewerPad can publish all of them through the Internet by embedding them in arbitrary Web pages. Old manuscripts are published as images. Their pad representation allows us to overlay annotations to them as an independent pad. A single manuscript page may have more than one annotation pad. These annotation pads can make their annotation texts visible when requested. Otherwise, they hide their texts. URL anchor pads can be pasted on annotation pads to span links among document and tool pads across the Internet.

Seigo Matsuoka of Editorial Engineering Laboratory Inc. and Ken-ichi Imai of Kyoto Stanford Research Institute applied IntelligentPad to the production of a digital archive system, "The Miyako," of Kyoto's cultural heritage with the support of MMCA (Multimedia Contents Association) (Figure 17.17). "Miyako" in Japanese means an old capital, especially Kyoto. The design of this system had the following requirements:

1. All the multimedia contents should be stored and managed by a relational database management system.

**Figure 17.17**  A digital archive system, "The Miyako," of Kyoto's cultural heritage used IntelligentPad to develop its fully interactive front-end system and an RDB as its back end to store digital content.

2. It should provide the same quality of presentation as those multimedia presentations using Macromind Director.

3. It should provide full interactivity so that users can navigate through any path.

In order to satisfy these requirements, the development team exploited IntelligentPad to develop the front-end interface of the system. Each jump from one presentation stage to another is specified by a query to the back-end relational database. Its evaluation retrieves all the content necessary to construct the target presentation stage, including not only archived multimedia content, but also both functional components such as hyperlink anchor buttons, and composition structures among these components.

This system has various features. One of them is the association search using the archetype of each item. Temples, for example, are classified into several categories, each of which has an archetype for the layout of buildings and gardens. The Miyako allows you to retrieve associated information through these archetypes. Another feature is the navigation through associative relationships among motifs appearing in various items. For example, a pine tree often appears with a crane in paintings. Japanese culture has rich associative relationships among flowers, trees, insects, animals, mountains, rivers, and seasons. The Miyako allows you to pick up one motif appearing in a retrieved multimedia item, to obtain all the possible motifs in some associative relationships, and to pick up one to find other items having the selected motif.

### 17.5.5 Information Design Tools

Today, designers are confronted with the design of information: how to present, access, and process varieties of information and knowledge. We do not have sufficient methodologies or sufficient notations for this kind of design. Takeshi Sunaga of Tama Art Collage started his career as a product designer and established a new department of information design. This was the first establishment of such a department in Japan, and it encouraged many followers.

In his information design course, he first sets up some goal such as designing a tool to support travel planning. Students then brainstorm on this subject in groups, using idea sketches. Each group presents their design idea to other groups to obtain comments and further discussion. Then each group further elaborates on the details of their design through the mock-up development using Macromind Director.

Takeshi was confronted with two problems. First, they had no tools to complete their designs. Macromid Director enabled them to present the flows of operations and the corresponding state changes of the tool they wanted to design, which they could not well present with idea sketches. However, Macromind Director enabled them only to develop mock-ups. With Macromind Director, they could not develop fully interactive systems accessing various servers. This is a serious problem since, in information design, we design not only the visual appearance of the system, but also the process of users' interaction with the system. Mock-ups developed with Macromind Director do not allow designers to flexibly change their design of users' interaction processes in a trial-and-error manner. Second, Macromind Director separates the script programming phase from the presentation phase, which makes it difficult for designers to use this tool in their brainstorming. Designers have to finish with the design of both users' interaction processes and the system's state changes before using Macromind Director.

Takeshi started to use IntelligentPad in his design course. He asked pad developers at Hokkaido University and IPC to collaborate in his design course. Using IntelligentPad, pad developers and designers can collaborate from the very first stage of the design process. Furthermore, design with IntelligentPad removes the difference between mock-ups and real interactive systems, which allows designers to use pads even in their brainstorming. This kind of collaboration also stimulated pad developers a lot. Using conventional system development, they have never participated in the brainstorming phase of information design. They observed in such collaboration a remarkable reduction of system development time and cost.

## 17.6  SUMMARY

IntelligentPad has the capability of covering all the client application systems that use two-dimensional graphical representations. Their implementation in an IntelligentPad system introduces the following five significant capabilities:

1. User-definable dynamic linkage among different systems
2. What-if trials without destroying original resources or processes
3. User customizability
4. Reuses of components, patterns, and frameworks
5. Distribution of components through the Internet, and their reediting and redistribution by end-users

These functions are especially required by such applications as PIM (personal information management), Web page authoring, CAD/CAM applications, GIS (Geographical Information System) with planning capabilities, financial applications, information kiosk systems, electronic library/museum applications, and the exchange of scientific and technological data and tools.

# CHAPTER 18

# 3D MEME MEDIA

Both the concept of meme media and the IntelligentPad architecture can be extended to three-dimensional (3D) representation media. This chapter will discuss IntelligentBox, a 3D extension of IntelligentPad. IntelligentBox provides some components that Intelligent-Pad does not. These components include, for example, a shape deformation box that deforms a wire-frame model that is put in this box. IntelligentBox provides application frameworks not only for interactive 3D animation but also for interactive information visualization and interactive scientific visualization.

## 18.1 3D MEME MEDIA INTELLIGENTBOX

Pads in IntelligentPad are two-dimensional (2D) representation media, but the idea and the basic architecture of IntelligentPad can also be applied to 3D representation media. The idea of IntelligentPad consists of the following:

1. Each component is wrapped by a 2D representation wrapper with a list of slots as its standard functional linkage interface to other components.
2. Each component has an MVC architecture.
3. View linkage among components defines a composite object as a compound document.
4. Each component in a composition has no more than one parent component, and can access no more than one of this parent's slots.
5. Each slot can be accessed by one of the two standard messages, "set" and "gimme." Each slot defines two different methods for these two messages.
6. The updating of components propagates from each parent component to its children.
7. Components work as meme media, and their worldwide repository forms a meme pool.

Exactly the same idea can be applied to 3D representation media, with some small modifications to the first and third principles.

1. Each component is wrapped by a 3D representation wrapper with a list of slots as its standard functional linkage interface to other components.
3. View linkage among components defines a composite 3D object.

The result is the 3D meme media architecture called IntelligentBox. Its components are called boxes.

Boxes may have arbitrary internal functions as well as arbitrary 3D visual display functions. Different functions define different boxes. Composite boxes are also simply referred to as boxes unless this causes any confusion. Just as pads in IntelligentPad can represent not only multimedia documents but also application tools, boxes in IntelligentBox can represent not only 3D computer animation graphics but also various application tools including 3D information visualization systems and 3D scientific visualization systems. Furthermore, IntelligentBox allows us to integrate 3D computer animation with 3D information visualization, 3D scientific visualization, and 3D application systems.

## 18.2  3D APPLICATION SYSTEMS

3D application software is in great demand for various application fields including medical science, mechanical engineering, architecture, molecular biology, genome informatics, electromagnetism, fluid dynamics, statistical data analysis, other scientific and business fields requiring scientific visualization and/or information visualization, and entertainment business such as computer animation production and 3D arcade/TV game production.

There already exist a lot of 3D application software development toolkit systems available in the market. They include virtual reality toolkit systems, 3D computer-animation development toolkit systems, and 3D GUI toolkit systems.

Virtual reality toolkit systems include WorldToolkit [1], WalkThrough [1], VREAM [1], SUPERSCAPE VRT [1], REND386 [1], MR Toolkit [2], SilTools [3], and MERL [4]. SUPERSCAPE VRT, for example, consists of two individual parts, i.e., an editor and a visualizer. Developers design 3D scenes using the editor. It also provides developers with SUPERSCAPE Control Language. Using this language, developers define the behaviors of each 3D object in a virtual world. The visualizer is the run-time software that works as an interpreter to interpret user-defined programs and to execute them. The SilTools is an integrated simulation system used to justify manufacturing processes of industrial products. Other systems are more or less similar to the SUPERSCAPE VRT. Their users have to write script programs using a script language to define behaviors of objects in virtual worlds. The standardization of VRML (Virtual Reality Modeling Language) [5] has encouraged development efforts in this area. VRML-based virtual reality toolkit systems include Virtual Studio 97 and VRCreator. Java is also extended by various groups to cope with 3D graphics capabilities. Java 3D is such an example. VRML Consortium used Java to add intelligent interactivity to VRML animation objects.

Computer-animation development toolkit systems provide a modeling tool and a rendering tool for the creation of 3D scenes. None of them treats every 3D object appearing in a 3D scene as a reactive object, nor provides any mechanism that allows us to dynamically combine individual reactive 3D objects into a reactive composite 3D object.

3D GUI toolkit systems include 3D Widget [6] and IRIS Inventor [7]. Both of them provide 3D components that have 3D shapes to be changed by direct manipulations on the screen. They enable developers to edit these 3D components to create 3D scenes. The definition of 3D components and their mutual relations in these systems, however, requires programming by developers.

Different from these systems, every 3D object in IntelligentBox has its own function and reacts to user events. IntelligentBox provides a dynamic functional composition mechanism that enables us to directly combine 3D objects on the screen to compose a complex 3D object. Only primitive component boxes need to be programmed by their developers. We do not assume that there exists a sufficiently large closed set of primitive components to cover various applications. Instead, we assume that market competition will encourage box developers to provide new primitive components.

## 18.3 INTELLIGENTBOX ARCHITECTURE

The IntelligentBox system architecture has inherited three basic mechanisms from the IntelligentPad system architecture [8]. They are (1) Model-View-Controller (MVC) modeling, (2) parent-child relationships, and (3) the message-sending protocol through the slot-connection mechanism. The following three subsections explain these basic mechanisms briefly.

### 18.3.1 The Model-View-Controller Modeling

Each box in IntelligentBox systems consists of three individual objects: a model, a view, and a controller. Its model defines an internal mechanism of each box. Its view defines the 3D graphical appearance of each box, and its controller defines how each box reacts to user events. The controller decodes such a user event as a mouse drag, a mouse click, and a keyboard input, and sends an appropriate message to its corresponding view, which, if necessary, sends another message to the corresponding model. Whenever a model changes its state, this update information is propagated to the corresponding view.

Each box is logically modeled as a list of slots, each of which can be accessed by each of the two standard messages, a "set" message and a "gimme" message. Corresponding to each slot, a box has two procedures that are respectively invoked by a "set" and a "gimme" message. When default definitions are used for these procedures, the corresponding slot works as a data slot, namely as a data register to read and write a value. Some slots are defined in the model part, whereas the others are defined in the view part.

In addition to slots, each box has properties such as dimension, orientation, its angle, and so on. A box may define some of these properties as slots, which allows other boxes to change those properties through their slot connection linkages to this box. A Rotation-Box has a cylinder shape, and rotates itself corresponding to user operations. It has a slot named #ratio whose value changes from 0.0 to 1.0 in proportion to its rotation angle. An ExpandBox expands and shrinks its height corresponding to user operations. It has also a slot named #ratio whose value changes from 0.0 to 1.0 in proportion to its height. These boxes change their shapes when their #ratio slots are set with new values. Direct manipulation of these boxes changes not only their shapes but also their #ratio slot values.

### 18.3.2    Parent–Child Relationship between Boxes

In any composition, each component box can be connected to a single slot of no more than one other box. The former becomes a child box or a slave box of the latter, whereas the latter is called a parent box or a master box of the former. Each child box is managed by the coordinate system defined by its parent box. In the case of IntelligentPad, the corresponding constraint between a pad and its parent pad naturally coincides with the constraint of paste operations: each pad cannot be pasted on more than one pad. In the case of IntelligentBox, this constraint between a box and its parent box naturally coincides with the constraint of embedding operations; each box cannot be embedded in more than one coordinate system. However, because of the invisibility of each coordinate system, it may look as if there is no such natural constraint on the box composition operations. IntelligentBox provides a linkage viewer to show parent–child relationships among all the component boxes in a selected composite box. The viewer shows these relationships as a tree with component box names as its nodes.

A rendered image of a composite box is naturally defined as the combination of the rendered images of its component boxes. Sometimes, it is required to hide some components in a composition, along with their functions contributing to the composite boxes. IntelligentBox allows us to make any box transparent.

### 18.3.3    Message-Sending Protocol for Slot Connections

The slot connection connects a child box to a single slot of its parent box. The child box can access this slot of its parent box by either a "set" message or a "gimme" message. A "set" message takes one parameter, whereas a "gimme" message has no parameter. The parent box can send an "update" message to its child boxes. This message takes no parameter. In their default definitions, a "set" message writes its parameter value into the corresponding slot register in the parent box, whereas a "gimme" message reads the value of this slot register. An "update" message tells the recipient that a state change has occurred in the sender box. The developer of each box may overload the definition of the two slot access procedures of each slot and the "update" procedure to change the default interpretation of these three standard messages.

In addition to these three standard messages, each box can accept geometrical messages such as "resize," "move," "copy," "hide," and "show."

### 18.3.4    Shared Copies

Shared copies of a box are also defined in the same way as in IntelligentPad. Shared copies of a primitive box share their model. Shared copies of a composite box share the model of the base box, i.e., its component primitive box that has no parent. Shared copies are often used to temporarily connect more than one composite box in a manner similar to the use of wiring pads. For this purpose, IntelligentBox provides a wiring box whose two shared copies work as two terminals of a connection cable. It can be connected to any type of slots.

### 18.4    EXAMPLE BOXES AND UTILITY BOXES

The IntelligentBox system provides basic primitive boxes used as input devices or output devices [8]. They include, for example, a push button, a rotary controller, and a slide-bar

**Figure 18.1**    A simple example of a composite box using some primitive boxes.

meter. It also provides various converters that adequately convert slot values of other boxes. Figure 18.1 shows a simple example of a composite box using some primitive boxes.

In this example, the motor of a car is nothing but a counting process having a cylinder shape. Its model has an integer-value slot. It works as an incremental counter. The toggle button connected to the #start/stop slot of the motor works as the switch to start and stop this counting process. Once the toggle button is pushed down, and the #start/stop slot of the motor becomes "true," the motor keeps increasing its slot value incrementally until the start/stop slot becomes "false" again.

The example composite box has two toothed wheels. They have geometrical shapes, but no functionality. Each of them is defined as a child of a transparent RotationBox, which embeds this toothed wheel in the coordinate system of the RotationBox. The RotationBox rotates together with the internal toothed wheel. One of the two RotationBoxes is defined as a child of the motor box, whereas the other is defined both as a child of the former and the parent of the long shaft with two wheels. The motor box sends its child RotationBox an "update" message whenever it increases its counter value, which makes this child RotationBox issue a "gimme" message to read out the counter value and to rotate itself to the angle proportional to this read out value. Whenever the first RotationBox rotates, it sends the second RotationBox an "update" message, and makes it also rotate. If these two toothed wheels have different numbers of teeth, you can insert a transparent converter box between these two RotationBoxes to change their units of rotation.

The following list shows some of the currently available primitive boxes.

1. General purposes reactive boxes. These include boxes to be used as input and/or output devices. They include RotationBox, ExpandBox, SliderMeterBox, ToggleSwitchBox, ScalingBox, AutoDirectingBox, 3D-RotationBox, PushButtonBox, and MoverBox.

2. Filtering boxes. These are boxes to be inserted between two message-exchanging boxes for the data conversion between them. They include RangeBox, FilterBox, MinmaxBox, and VectorRangeBox.

3. Storage boxes. These work as data registers and hold some data shared by more than one box. They include IOBufferBox, ListBox, VectorBox, and DictionaryBox.

4. Motion-constraint boxes (detailed in the next section): TrajectoryBox, TrajectoryMoverBox, CreepingBox, etc.

**Figure 18.2**   A car-driving simulator composed with primitive boxes. The window at the top left corner provides the driver's view.

5. Shape deformation boxes (detailed in the next section): FFDControlBox, Mesh-Box, RFFDControlBox, etc.

6. Boxes for creating CG animation: KeyFrameAnimationBox, CameraBox, Light-Box, etc.

7. Boxes for coloring and labeling other boxes: ColorBox, StringBox, etc.

8. Boxes for developing distributed applications: RoomBox, TranslationBox, etc.

9. Boxes for playing sound files: SfplayerBox, SfvolumeBox, etc.

10. Other functional boxes: ProcessBox, CommandBox, SceneSwapBox, System-FunctionBox, OperationBox, CollisionCheckBox, EnvironmentBox, etc.

IntelligentBox is an open system; its component library is open for future extension. Using some of the boxes listed above, you can develop, for example, a car-driving simulator as shown in Figure 18.2, and distributed 3D graphic applications presented in later sections. All of them can be simply composed by combining primitive boxes without writing any programs.

## 18.5   ANIMATION WITH INTELLIGENTBOX

Our IntelligentBox Project is focusing on three major application fields—interactive computer animation, interactive information visualization, and interactive scientific visualization. Among them, interactive computer animation is the most direct application of IntelligentBox. Shapes as well as motions and shape transformations can be all treated as generic components. Furthermore, lights and cameras can be also treated as generic components. IntelligentBox can provide all these generic components as primitive boxes, and allow us to easily combine them through slot connections [8].

### 18.5.1   Motion Constraint Boxes

Any box that moves or rotates itself also moves or rotates its child boxes attached to itself. Such a box imposes various motion constraints on its child boxes. A TrajectoryBox and a

TrajectoryMoverBox introduce a motion constraint that restricts the motion of any box to an a priori defined trajectory. A TrajectoryBox specifies a trajectory, whereas a TrajectoryMoverBox is constrained to move along the trajectory defined by its parent TrajectoryBox. The shape of the TrajectoryBox is not a polyhedron but a 3D curve. When a TrajectoryMoverBox becomes a child of a TrajectoryBox, such a constraint is imposed on this TrajectoryMoverBox. Any composite box that is defined as a child of this TrajectoryMoverBox moves together with this TrajectoryMoverBox. For example, the space shuttle in Figure 18.3 is defined as a child of a TrajectoryMoverBox, which is constrained to move along the trajectory defined by a TrajectoryBox.

A TrajectoryBox has a slot called a #trajectorySlot. This slot holds a set of vertices defining a trajectory. Its child TrajectoryMoverBox reads this slot to obtain the trajectory data, which determines the motion of this TrajectoryMoverBox. A TrajectoryMoverBox has a slot named a #currentPositionSlot. This slot takes a value between 0.0 and 1.0, and indicates at which position on its trajectory this TrajectoryMoverBox is located. Direct manipulation of a TrajectoryMoverBox to move along its trajectory changes this slot value. On the other hand, the change of this slot value moves this TrajectoryMoverBox to the location on its trajectory determined by this slot value.

A CreepingBox introduces another motion constraint. It restricts itself to move around on the surface of its parent box. A CreepingBox imposes a constraint on its child box to move only on the surface of its parent box. The relationship between a CreepingBox and its parent box is the same as the relationship between a TrajectoryMoverBox and its parent TrajectoryBox.

Figure 18.4 shows an example use of a CreepingBox, where an insect moves around on a wooden block. The CreepingBox used here is defined as a child of the wooden-block box, and also as a parent of a composite box modeling a moving insect. A CreepingBox

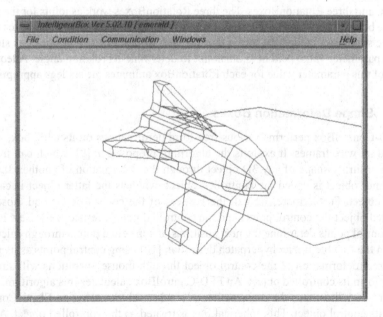

**Figure 18.3** A space shuttle that is defined as a child of the TrajectoryMoverBox is constrained to move along the trajectory defined by the TrajectoryBox.

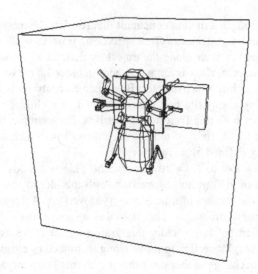

**Figure 18.4** An example use of a CreepingBox, in which an insect moves around on a wooden box.

has a #creepingFaceSlot. This slot indicates one of the parent box faces on which the CreepingBox currently sits on. A CreepingBox has also a #speedSlot. Direct manipulation of this slot value through some value-changing box connected to it moves the Creeping-Box at the speed determined by this slot value.

The insect in Figure 18.4 is simply composed from a few kinds of primitive boxes, though it looks rather complicated. Its body consists of three boxes that form its head, tho-rax, and abdomen. Each of its six legs consists of the three boxes that form the thigh, shank, and foot, and three RotationBoxes. The three RotationBoxes work as joints for the remain-ing three boxes. They share the same slot value by using the remaining three boxes to prop-agate the single slot value held by the thorax. Each RotationBox multiplies this slot value with its parameter value held in another slot to determine its rotation angle. Adequate se-lection of this parameter value for each RotationBox animates the six legs appropriately.

### 18.5.2 Shape Deformation Boxes

An FFD-ControlBox performs various free-form deformations on its child box, which is modeled by wire frames. It exploits the algorithm proposed in [9], which can freely de-form an arbitrary shape of any 3D object through the deformation of another 3D object. The former object is called the controlled object, whereas the latter object is called the control object. Furthermore, we call the vertices of the control object and those of the controlled object the control points and the controlled points, respectively. New locations of the control points determine the new positions of controlled points through calculations based on the tricubic Bézier hyperpatch definition [10] using control points as its parame-ters. Direct deformation of the control object through mouse operations will simultane-ously deform its controlled object. An FFD-ControlBox calculates this algorithm.

Figure 18.5 illustrates the deformation of a spherical box using an ElasticController-Box as its control object. This spherical box is treated as the controlled object. An FFD-

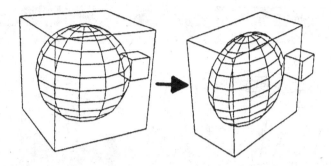

**Figure 18.5** A deformation of a spherical box using an ElasticControllerBox as its control object.

ControlBox is used as its parent box. User manipulation of the ElasticControllerBox can change its horizontal length, which simultaneously expands or squeezes the spherical box based on the FFD function calculated by the FFD-ControlBox.

As shown in Figure18.6, the FFD-ControlBox has two slots: #controlledPointsSlot and #controlPointsSlot. The slot #controlPointsSlot holds the set of vertices of the control box, whereas the slot #controlledPointsSlot holds the set of vertices of the controlled box. For the control box, you may use any box that issues "set" messages with its current set of vertices. An ElasticControllerBox is such an example. For the controlled box, you may use any box that issues "gimme" messages to read out its new set of vertices and changes its shape. Wire-frame-modeled boxes are all such examples.

For an arbitrary box to be used as a control box, you may use a VertexBox. When its #valueSlot is accessed by a "set" message, a VertexBox reads the set of vertices of the sender box using one of the standard geometrical messages, and sends this set of vertices to its parent box. Any box can be specified as a child of a VertexBox that is connected to #controlPointSlot of an FFD-ControlBox. Whenever this box changes its shape and issues a "set" message with some value as its parameter, its parent VertexBox will read the set of vertices of this sender box and sends this set to #controlPointSlot of an FFD-ControlBox.

This further allows us to use any composite box as a controller object, as shown in Figure18.7, where three transparent blocks are connected by three RotationBoxes working as

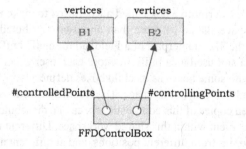

**Figure 18.6** An FFD-ControlBox has two slots: a #controlledPointsSlot and #controlPointsSlot. The #controlPointsSlot holds the set of vertices of the control box, whereas the #controlledPointsSlot holds the set of vertices of the controlled box.

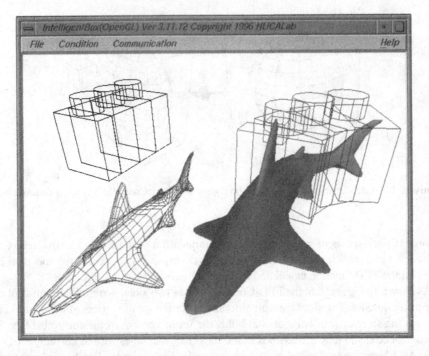

**Figure 18.7** Three transparent boxes are connected by three RotationBoxes working as joints. These three RotationBoxes always share the same slot value using slot connections among them and, hence, share the same rotation angle. Direct manipulation of this composite box imitates the tail fin motion of a shark.

joints. These three RotationBoxes always share the same slot value using slot connections among them, and hence share the same rotation angle. Direct manipulation of these RotationBoxes imitates the tail fin motion of a shark. This composite box covers the tail fin portion of a wire-frame-modeled shark, which is connected to the #controlledPointsSlot of the FFD-ControlBox.

### 18.5.3 A RoomBox for Defining a 3D Shared Workspace

IntelligentBox provides a primitive box called a RoomBox to make it easy to construct an interactive 3D workspace shared by more than one user distributed through the Internet [11]. A RoomBox is the 3D counterpart of a FieldPad in IntelligentPad.

A RoomBox has a slot used as a buffer to store each user event within this box as its value. A RoomBox with some boxes as its child boxes define a workspace to be shared; its child boxes are the only objects in this space. The RoomBox works as the base box of this composite box. Shared copies of this composite box can be distributed across the network. They share every user event within this shared workspace. Different users at different sites may view different copies from different positions, and at different angles. Any user event of any one of these users is applied to all these copies. The conflict resolution is performed based on the comparison of the priority numbers associated with these shared copies. Shared spaces can be nested by nesting more than one RoomBox. The event-dispatching mechanism in such a nested environment is exactly the same as that of nested FieldPads. Similar to a BlackHolePad and a WhiteHolePad, IntelligentBox provides a BlackHoleBox and a WhiteHoleBox. These are used to transport boxes between different workspaces, i.e., among different shared workspaces and different desktop spaces.

### 18.5.4  A CameraBox for the Interactive Viewing of a Box World

IntelligentBox also provides a primitive box called a CameraBox for the interactive viewing of a box world (Figure 18.8). A CameraBox works as a video camera in a world of boxes. In Figure 18.8, the camera view is shown in the separate window placed at the upper-right corner. Camera parameters such as the zoom rate can be controlled through the slots of a CameraBox. You may connect some value-changing boxes to these slots, and directly manipulate them to change these slot values. In order to control the camera motion, you can use motion constraint boxes. The real-time view of a camera is shown in a separate window. This view is computed using the position and the direction of the CameraBox. Boxes in this view are not just their images. They are still manipulable boxes. Their manipulation through a camera view will be applied to the original boxes. Furthermore, the live view of a CameraBox can be texture-mapped in real time onto a surface of an arbitrary box in a different box world. As pointed out in [12], the introduction of a CameraBox is especially useful for interactive 3D simulators such as flight simulators and car-driving simulators (Figure 18.2), where it is put at the pilot's or the driver's eye position in a vehicle to give his or her view of the external environment defined by other boxes.

Figure 18.9 illustrates a simple use of a CameraBox together with a RoomBox. They are two display snapshots of two different sites taken at the same time. The upper right small view of each snapshot is a CameraBox view. The larger window in each snapshot is the main IntelligentBox window. IntelligentBox allows us to exchange the roles of these two windows whenever necessary.

Suppose that we want to construct a car-driving simulator. Its user should be able to sit in a car as if driving. The car goes forward, backward, and makes a turn when its user directly manipulate its gear shift and steering wheel. These actions should also change the

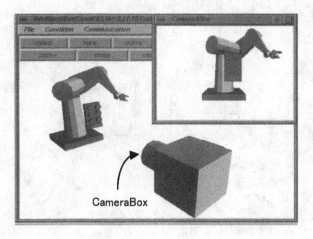

**Figure 18.8**   A CameraBox works a video camera in a world of boxes.

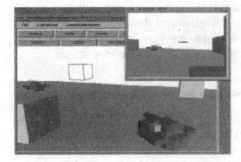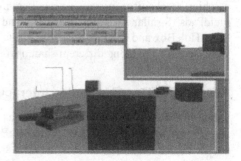

**Figure 18.9** A simple use of a CameraBox together with a RoomBox.

user's view. A CameraBox can be simply set at the driver's-eye position to obtain this view. We have developed an avatar box in the shape of a human. Wearing a motion-capture system, you can make this avatar mimic your body motion. You can easily obtain your avatar's view by setting a CameraBox at the avatar's-eye position.

IntelligentBox also provides a LightBox as a generic component. Its parameters such as the intensities of red, green, and blue (RGB) color components and its wideness are all controlled through its corresponding slots by other boxes. To control its motion, you can use motion-constraint boxes. Using multiple LightBoxes, you can simultaneously control multiple lights in an easy way. Figure 18.10 shows an example use of a CameraBox and a LightBox. Both of them move around a flying eagle. They keep shooting the flying eagle. A pair of special boxes is used to satisfy such a constraint; one is attached to the flying eagle, and the other is attached to the CameraBox. Another pair is used to satisfy the constraint between the flying eagle and the LightBox.

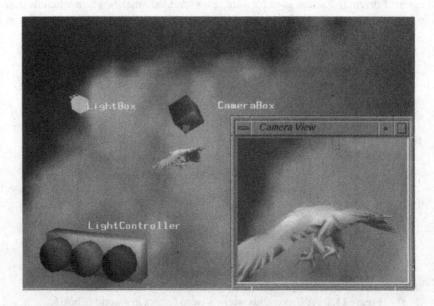

**Figure 18.10** A flying eagle with a CameraBox and a LightBox.

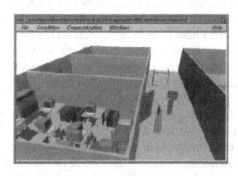 

**Figure 18.11**  A distributed virtual reality application. The left-hand snapshot shows a virtual 3D space with two mobile robots, whereas the two right-hand snapshots are the camera views of these robots. These robots are controlled by different users at different sites on the Internet.

### 18.5.5  An Example Animation Composition

Figure 18.9 shows the display snapshots of two different machines sharing the same workspace. This workspace defines an interactive tank-battle game environment. The user who operates the left-hand system controls one of the two tanks. The other user operates the right-hand system to control the other tank. The upper-right small view in each snapshot is a camera view. Each CameraBox is set on the left side of the battery on each tank. A wireframed cube is a RoomBox, which can be made invisible if necessary. All the 3D objects are defined as descendant boxes of the RoomBox. They are shared by these two users. Each tank is a MoverBox that moves forward/backward or turns left/right responding to its user's mouse operation. Each user can control his own tank manually, observing the battlefield through his own camera view.

Figure 18.11 shows a distributed virtual reality application. This snapshot shows a virtual 3D space with two mobile robots. They are controlled by different users at different sites on the Internet. Each robot is a MoverBox with a CameraBox at its head. The upper-right small view is a camera view of one robot, whereas the lower-right small view is the camera view of the other robot. Each user can move his own robot, observing the shared field through his own camera view. Each user can manipulate any reactive objects in this field. He or she can directly open or close the door of each room.

IntelligentBox allows us to construct these types of distributed interactive 3D graphic applications just by directly combining primitive boxes on a screen without writing any programs.

The tank-battle game and the robot environment were originally developed as single-user systems. Use of a RoomBox simply extended these applications to multiuser systems.

### 18.6  INFORMATION VISUALIZATION WITH INTELLIGENTBOX

Our research group defines information visualization not only as the 3D visual presentation of a large set of data or records, but also as an architectural design of an interactive

3D space in which we virtually materialize a large set of data and records and interact with them. Information architecture denotes these two aspects of information visualization. Conventional information visualization systems have been focusing only on the former aspect. We will propose in this section a generic visualization framework that virtually materializes records as interactive 3D objects. The componentware architecture of IntelligentBox, developed by my group, provides the basis of this application framework. The materialization may use any interactive composite object defined in IntelligentBox as a virtual materialization template. You can associate the parameters of this composite object with arbitrarily selected attributes of the record. We will further extend this framework to use more than one template depending on some attribute values, and also to materialize the coordinate systems in which we materialize records so that users can easily change the view of record distribution to possibly find a significant structure among them. We will also show some applications including interactive animation of gene expression profiles in the process of cell division.

### 18.6.1 Basic Functions for Interactive Information Visualization

Interactive information visualization of a large set of data or records is one of the most promising applications of interactive 3D graphics. Recently, many papers have been published on information visualization. They are extensively surveyed by Stuart K. Card, Jock D. Mackinlay, and Ben Shneiderman in [13]. Visualization of data objects or records maps some of their attributes to their visual representation parameters and some others to their arrangement parameters. As to the object representation, these systems use a multimedia document card representation [14, 15, 16], a colored texture representation [17], or a combination of 2D primitive boxes or 3D primitive blocks that change each of their sizes and colors [18, 19, 20, 21]. As to the arrangement of visualized objects, some use 1D [14, 17], 2D [15, 18], or 3D [16, 19, 22] arrangements, or their nesting [21,23, 24] for multidimensional arrangement, whereas others use hierarchical [25, 26] or network [27, 28] arrangements. Some information visualization tools use a specially designed multidimensional data representation called a parallel coordinates representation, in which each data object is represented as a line in a line graph, and X and Y coordinates represent multiple coordinates and the value of each object in each coordinate, respectively [29].

Each of these systems, however, proposes a specific way of viewing a large set of data using 3D graphics and animation technologies. Each of them provides no more than a couple of a priori designed ways of representing each object and of arranging objects. In other words, these systems focus on proposing new visualization schemes. Different applications, however, deal with different data or records, and require different visualization schemes, i.e., different record-representation schemes and different record-arrangement schemes. Data analysts in each application are potentially the best designers of visualization schemes. This is especially the case in scientific research fields such as astrophysics, geophysics, nuclear-reaction physics, genome informatics, and molecular biology, in which researchers are developing new data analysis tools. We believe that the next generation of information visualization systems should allow these data analysts to design their own information visualization schemes, and to develop their own information visualization tools. This requires a toolkit system, i.e., a component-based generic application framework, for the information visualization of data and records.

Furthermore, the current systems also lack a generic framework to associate each datum with an arbitrarily defined fully interactive 3D object. They provide only limited ways of interacting with visualized objects and their environment. Their interactivity allows users only to change viewpoints [30], to distort [15, 21, 31, 32, 33, 34] or to zoom [35, 36, 37] a viewing space for seamlessly controlling levels of details, to select some visualized objects to change their visualization properties [20], to request additional, detailed, or related information by issuing a new query [38, 39], or to navigate through different views. These operations are closely tied to the proposed visualization schemes. Users are allowed to interact with the systems only through these a priori designed operations. Visualized objects in these systems allow users only to select some of them, to change their properties or the levels of their detail, or to click on some of them to pop up related objects or views. Their visual objects do not materialize records as interactive 3D animation objects in a virtual world. For example, users cannot make copies of a visual object to reuse them in a different virtual reality (VR) environment. Suppose that we visualize records as humans walking at different speeds proportional to the values of some attribute. We want to put them on streets in an a priori defined virtual town. This requires an extension of information visualization to virtual materialization of records as interactive animation objects.

This section proposes a generic framework for developing virtual materialization systems based on a componentware architecture for 3D applications. Our approach visualizes a large set of data by materializing each record as a fully interactive animation object, and allows data analysts to develop their own visualization schemes and tools by combining reusable components. Data analysts can share their visualization tools with each other as reusable and decomposable composite objects.

Virtual materialization of data or records must provide the following five functions:

1. Retrieval of source data or records
2. Association of each of the retrieved data or records with its visual presentation
3. Visual presentation of each datum or record as an interactive virtual object
4. Geometrical arrangement of visualized records in a 3D space
5. Scope control to visualize a limited number of records among the retrieved ones

For the retrieval of source data, we have to specify conditions on data or records; the system retrieves only those data or records satisfying these conditions out of a huge information repository such as databases or the WWW.

For the association of each of the retrieved data or records with its visual presentation, we need to register a composite 3D object as a representation template of each record. For each of the retrieved data or records, the system uses an independent copy of this registered composite object, and makes this copy represent this record.

The visual presentation of each data or record is defined by a composite 3D object. Users should be able to associate some of its parameter values with some attributes of records. Some attribute may determine the size of the composite 3D object, whereas some other may specify its shape. Some may specify its texture, its orbit, or its interaction.

For the geometrical arrangement of these visual objects, we can use one, two, or three attributes of retrieved records to determine their positions in a specified one-, two-, or three-dimensional arrangement

The scope of visualization selects some of the retrieved records. This selection is performed based on the value of some attribute. Several different selection schemes can be used. One selection scheme uses one numerical attribute of records, and selects, out of all the retrieved records, only a specified number of records. They are the first records when they are arranged in the ascending order of the values of this attribute, neglecting those whose values of this attribute are less than a specified value. This specified number and the specified threshold value are called the scope width and the scope bottom, respectively. Another selection scheme also uses one numerical attribute of records, and selects out of all the retrieved records only those whose values of this attribute fall between two specified boundary values. These boundary values are called the scope bottom and the scope top, respectively.

This section proposes application frameworks for the visualization and the virtual materialization of database records. We use as their basis the IntelligentBox system architecture. Our visualization and virtual materialization of database records uses a composite box as a template to represent each record, and makes each visualized record an interactive animation object.

### 18.6.2   3D Visualization and Virtual Materialization of a Single Retrieved Record

Before giving the details of the information visualization and virtual materialization framework, let us extend the form interface framework from 2D representation to 3D representation. This requires two of the above-mentioned five basic functions of information visualization and virtual materialization. They are the retrieval of source data or records, and the visual presentation of each datum or record.

The retrieval of source data or records from a database is performed by a DBProxy-Box. This box works as a proxy of a database. A proxy box in general has both a 3D physical shape and a list of slots, and works as a proxy of some external object such as a server, an application program, or a plant system monitor. A proxy box is used to integrate the corresponding external system into an IntelligentBox environment. A DBProxyBox has a slot list including #query, #search, #insert, #delete, #result, #previousCandidate, #nextCandidate, and #currentRecord. When the #search slot is accessed by a "set" message, the DBProxyBox issues the query held by the #query slot to the Database. The retrieved result is stored in the #result slot. The DBProxyBox has a cursor that points to one of the records in the #result slot. The pointed record is held by the #currentRecord slot. The two other slots, the #previousCandidate slot and the #nextCandidate slot, when accessed by a "set" message, move the cursor backward and forward. Different DBMSs require different DBProxyBoxes. A DBProxyBox performs all the details necessary to access a database. You may easily connect various boxes to this DBProxyBox with their connection to the #currentRecord slot to define a 3D visual representation of each retrieved record, or with their connection to the #result slot to visually present the 3D distribution of retrieved records. Here we first consider the case in which we visually present one retrieved record at a time.

Similar to the framework of form interfaces to databases, you can connect a RecordBox to a #currentRecord slot of the DBProxyBox. This RecordBox reads this slot, and holds the read out current record. The whole set of boxes available in IntelligentBox works as a 3D record-representation construction kit for the visual interface to this database. The RecordBox can take any shape and any texture. When it receives an "update" message, it reads out a record from its parent box and holds this record. It allows us to add an arbitrary number of special slots called attribute slots. For this function, it has a special slot #addSlot. When it is accessed by a "set" message, its "set" procedure pops up a dialog box, asks the user to type in a new slot name, and then adds a new slot with this name to the list of attribute slots in this RecordBox. A RecordBox has another special slot, the #removeSlot, that is used to remove a specified slot from its list of attribute slots. The "set" procedure of this special slot pops up a menu list of slots, and asks the user to specify which one to remove. Each attribute slot, when requested to send back its value, reads out the stored record and gets the value of the attribute having the same name as this attribute-slot name. If the record does not have the same attribute name, this attribute slot returns the value "nil." When a RecordBox is connected to a DBProxyBox with its connection to #currentRecord slot of this proxy box, it works as a base box to define a 3D representation of each record that will be retrieved from the DBProxyBox (Figure 18.12). This composite box is represented by our notation as

DBProxyBox($\Delta$)
        [#query: . . . ,
        #search:PushButtonBox$_1$,
        #insert: PushButtonBox$_2$,
        #delete: PushButtonBox$_3$,
        #previousCandidate: PushButtonBox$_4$,
        #nextCandidate: PushButtonBox$_5$,
        #currentRecord:RecordBox [#attr$_1$:Box$_1$, #attr$_2$:Box$_2$, . . . , #attr$_n$:Box$_n$]
        . . .
        ].

The box Box$_i$ is a 3D display box that shows the value of the attribute attr$_i$. Some examples of such a display box are TextBox, ImageBox, MovieBox, RotationBox, ExpandBox, SliderMeterBox, and MoverBox. A mouse click on the box ButtonBox$_1$ invokes a search of the database. A click on the box ButtonBox$_5$ advances the record cursor to the next candidate record in the list of retrieved records stored in #result slot.

Different from 3D GUI representation, this 3D representation with a RecordBox as its base box can be easily copied and sent to other users or to some tool boxes. This copy holds the record that its original had when we made this copy.

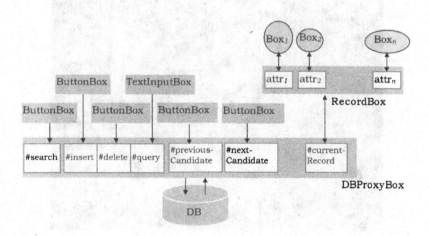

**Figure 18.12**   A 3D visualization framework for records retrieved from databases.

In its typical use on a DBProxyBox, the RecordBox divides each retrieved record into a set of attribute-value pairs. Each attribute value is sent to the slot with the same name as its attribute name. Depending on the value type of each attribute slot, you may connect a text, image, video viewer, rotating, or moving box to this slot. You may arbitrarily design the geometrical arrangement of these viewer boxes within or around the RecordBox. A DBProxyBox with a RecordBox combined with some viewer boxes is called a 3D DB viewer, or a 3D interface to a database. Figure 18.13 shows an example of a 3D DB viewer.

Instead of connecting a RecordBox to a DBProxyBox, you may connect some type of relation viewer boxes to the #result slot of the RecordBox, which works as a 3D information visualizer of retrieved records. A relation viewer box visually presents records in the relation. The details are discussed in Subsection 18.6.5.

For the setting of a query in the query slot of a DBProxyBox, you can simply use a text-input box called TextInputBox. The text-input box is connected to the #query slot of the proxy box DBProxyBox($\Delta$), i.e., DBProxyBox($\Delta$)[#query:TextInputBox]. An SQL query q written on this text-input box is sent to the #query slot of the proxy box, i.e., DBProxyBox($\Delta$)[#query$\leftarrow$q]. Instead of using such a simple text-input box, you may use any composite box to generate an SQL query. For example, a parameterized SQL query Q(x, $\theta$, y),

```
select    name, age, photo
from      Employee
where     department = x
and       salary θ y
```

can be generated by a box Q-Box(#department, #comparator, #salary). You may combine three text-input boxes on this box with their connection to these three slots, and connect this composite box to the query slot of the proxy, i.e.,

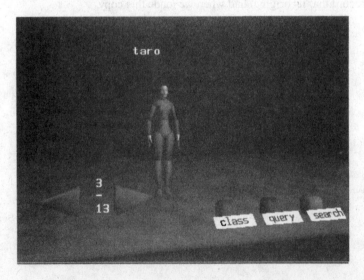

**Figure 18.13**   An example 3D database viewer.

> DBProxyBox($\Delta$) [#query:  Q-Box[#department: TextBox1,
> #comparator: TextBox2,
> #salary: TextBox3)]].

This allows you to simply specify a department name, a comparison operator, and an amount of salary for the retrieval of employees' information.

A restriction on the DB proxy box will make it represent a view relation. This requires one more slot named #view slot. This slot is used to store a view definition. This view definition also specifies the structure of records stored in the #currentRecord slot. The attributes of these records are those defined by this view. When a query is issued through the #query slot, this box modifies this query with the view definition and sends the modified query to the database system. To avoid the view update problem, the translation of an update request on this view to a DB update request should be clearly defined in this box. Such a restricted DBProxyBox is called a DBViewBox. A text box can be used to input a view definition sentence, viewDefinition to #view slot, i.e., DBViewBox($\Delta$)[#view←viewDefinition]. This box works as a proxy box to a database $\Delta_{view}$ with the view relation as its only one relation, i.e.,

$$DBViewBox(\Delta)[\#view \leftarrow viewDefinition] = DBProxyBox(\Delta_{view})$$

### 18.6.3  QBE Using a 3D Interface to a Database

In the preceding section, we have been assuming that the #currentRecord slot of a DBProxyBox is a data slot. Actually, it is not. Its access by a "gimme" message invokes its "gimme" procedure, which reads out the record pointed to by the cursor from the record list stored in the #result slot, and returns this record value. Its access by a "set" message, on the other hand, sets its parameter value to a special internal variable "input-record" of the DBProxyBox. The record stored in this input-record variable is used to insert and delete records to and from the database. These operations are successfully performed only when the following two conditions are satisfied: (1) this record type is a projection of some relation R in the database, and (2) this record completely specifies the value of the primary key of R. Otherwise, these operations will cause the so-called view update problem. When its #insert slot is set to "true," the DBProxyBox tries to insert the record in the input-record variable into the database. When its #delete slot is set to "true," the DBProxyBox tries to delete the record of R identified by the record in the input-record variable.

The DBProxyBox issues an "update" message to all of its child boxes connected to either its #result slot or its #currentRecord slot when and only when it receives a result relation from the database or its cursor changes.

The input-record variable is also used in search operations. In this case, each attribute value of the record in the input-record variable needs to be either nil or a pair of a comparison operator and any value of this attribute value type. The content of the input-record variable, in this case, specifies a condition C* on some of its attributes. Suppose that the query q stored in #query slot of the DBProxyBox is

> q:    select    attribute list
> from    relation list
> where    C.

We define a new query q(C*) as

$$
\begin{array}{lll}
q(C^*): & \text{select} & \text{attribute list} \\
& \text{from} & \text{relation list} \\
& \text{where} & C \text{ and } C^*.
\end{array}
$$

When its #search slot is set to "true," the DBProxyBox reads out both the query q in its #query slot and the condition C* from its input-record variable, generates a new query q(C*), and sends this to the database to retrieve the resulting relation.

The input-record variable is initially set to a record with "nil" for its every attribute. The insert and delete operations both reset the input-record variable to its initial value when they complete their execution. The condition C* corresponding to this initial value is defined to be always "true."

These extensions of the DBProxyBox allow us to construct a QBE (query-by-example) type 3D interface without making any more changes to the preceding discussion. We use a RecordBox not only for the output display of the retrieved records but also for the QBE-type specification of a query. The RecordBox has a special slot called the #setRecord slot. When set to "true," the "set" procedure of this slot sends a "set" message to its parent box together with its #record slot value as the message parameter. When connected to the #currentRecord slot of a DBProxyBox, the RecordBox with a PushButtonBox connected to its #setRecord slot works as a QBE-based input tool. When its button is clicked, it sends its record value, which actually specifies a query based on the QBE convention, to the input-record variable of the DBProxyBox, which, in turn, creates a modified query q(C*) from the query q specified by its #query slot.

### 18.6.4  Boxes as Attribute Values

In Subsection 18.6.2, we saw that a database service can be represented as a box. Here, we will see that boxes can be treated as database values. Each composite box has its exchange format representation, which is just a variable-length string consisting of a description of its composition structure and the current state of each component box. The composition structure description describes both geometrical configuration and slot connections. This string can be stored in databases as an attribute value if this attribute allows variable-length strings as its values. This means any objects that can be represented as composite boxes can be stored in those relational databases that allow variable-length data as attribute values. Those objects include interactive multimedia objects such as images, movies, sounds, interactive charts and tables, interactive maps, database access forms, various application tools, interactive 3D animation systems, interactive 3D models in CAD/CAM application systems, interactive 3D simulators, walkthrough 3D environments, interactive information visualization and virtual materialization tools, interactive scientific visualization tools, and compound 3D applications that embed any of these objects.

Let us consider a 3D interface to a database with an interactive 3D car-modeling box as an attribute value. The corresponding slot of the record box stores the exchange format representation of an interactive animation box as its value. To generate a composite box from its exchange format representation, and vice versa, a special box SaverLoaderBox is connected to this slot of the RecordBox (Figure 18.14). When it receives an "update" message, a SaverLoaderBox issues a "gimme" message to retrieve an exchange format

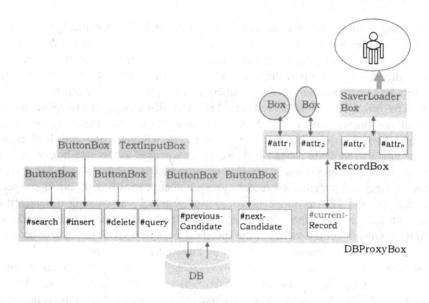

**Figure 18.14**   A composition framework for a database viewer to cope with boxes as attribute values.

representation value from its parent, and generates the corresponding composite box. It also works as a saver. When a composite box is dragged and dropped on it, a SaverLoaderBox converts this composite box to the exchange format representation, and issues a "set" message with this representation as a parameter value to store this representation into the connected slot of its parent box.

Such a composite box that is popped up by a RecordBox through a SaverLoaderBox may have some transparent button boxes. Each of these button boxes may hold a URL. When clicked, it issues this URL to retrieve another box from somewhere on the Internet or from a local file. This box may work as another database viewer to the same or a different database to retrieve related information as a composite box or as a set of composite boxes.

### 18.6.5   Information Visualization and Virtual Materialization Framework Using IntelligentBox

Our information visualization and virtual materialization framework using IntelliegntBox provides five basic functions: the retrieval of source data or records, the association of each of the retrieved data or records with its visual presentation, the visual presentation of each datum or record, the geometrical arrangement of visualized records in a 3D space, and the scope control of visualization.

The visual presentation of each datum or record can use arbitrary boxes and their arbitrary compositions, and need not be provided by the framework. Here we will only deal with the visualization and virtual materialization of records retrieved from a database. The association of each of the retrieved data or records with its visual presentation requires an authoring tool described later.

The retrieval of source data or records is performed by a DBProxyBox as described in the preceding sections. The information visualization and virtual materialization of retrieved records uses the #result slot of this box. This slot holds all the retrieved records.

The geometrical arrangement of visualized records in a 3D space can be performed in two different ways. You may embed a geometrical displacement box in the template composite box, and associate its displacement parameters with some attributes of each retrieved record. When each retrieved record is materialized using this template, the displacement box displaces the materialized record at a location determined by its parameter values. Instead, you may materialize each record without using any displacement box, but with a RecordBox instead. This RecordBox is used as the base box of the template composite box, and is made invisible when records are materialized. The geometrical arrangement of materialized records uses an arrangement box. It has three special slots—#X, #Y, and #Z—to define its coordinate system by associating one record attribute with each of these three slots. Such an arrangement box reads each materialized record it contains to get the values of the specified three attributes, and locates each materialized record at the position determined by these attribute values.

The scope control of the visualization uses a ScopeWindow box, which has among its slots a #result slot, #recordList slot, #attributeSelection slot, #scopeBottom slot, and #scopeWidth slot (Figure 18.15). A ScopeWindow box is used with its connection to the #result slot of a DBProxyBox. When it receives an "update" message, the ScopeWindow box reads this list from the #result slot of the DBProxyBox and stores this list in its #result slot. Its #attributeSelection slot is set with the name of a numerical value attribute. Its #scopeBottom slot is set with a value $v_0$ of this attribute, whereas its #scopeWidth slot is set with a natural number $n$. The ScopeWindow selects only the first $n$ records whose value of this selected attribute is greater than or equal to the value $v_0$, and stores the list of these selected records in its #recordList slot. The specification of $v_0$ and $n$ may use RotationBoxes with appropriate value range conversion boxes. These can be connected to the #scopeBottom slot and the #scopeWidth slot of the ScopeWindow box.

The association of each of the retrieved records with its visual presentation uses a

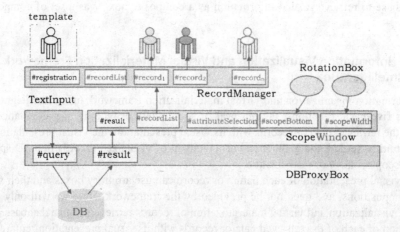

**Figure 18.15**  A 3D information-visualization framework for records in databases.

RecordManager box. This box has among its slots a #registration slot and a necessary number of #record slots. Its #record slots are indexed with integers. It is used with its connection to the #recordList slot of a ScopeWindow box. When it receives an "update" message from its parent, the RecordManager box reads out a record list from its parent, generates as many #record slots in itself as the length of this list, and distributes each record value in this read out list to one of these #record slots. Its #registration slot can hold an arbitrary composite box. When the ScopeWindow generates as many #record slots in itself as the length of the record list, it also makes the same number of copies of the registered composite box, and connects each of them to each of these generated #record slots. When it completes the distribution of the records to these slots, the ScopeWindow issues an "update" message to each copy of the registered composite box, which reads each #record slot to change its properties such as shape, size, texture, and motion.

The composite box to be registered should use a RecordBox as its base box. Any composite box can be defined as its child. Each component of this composite box can access any attribute slot provided by the base RecordBox, which allows us to associate each record attribute with some component's function of the composite box used to represent each record.

Figure 18.16 shows an example virtual materialization of database records. It uses a 3D doll as a 3D representation of each record. The height of each doll and the name label are associated with the two attributes of records. You may even model this doll to stamp and to change its pace, and associate this stamping speed with another record attribute (Figure 18.17).

Since each 3D record representation is a composite box, it can also be modeled to respond to user events. This allows us to easily develop interactive information visualization and/or virtual materialization systems.

Instead of using a single template to materialize each retrieved record, you may use different templates for different values of a specified attribute. Figure 18.18 shows such an example using two different dolls for different genders to materialize personnel records. You can use the same framework as shown in Figure 18.15 even for the virtual materialization that uses multiple templates. We use a special box SelectorBox to merge multiple templates into a single template. A SelectorBox allows you to register more than one template as its child boxes. It gives an index number to identify each registered template. A SelectorBox also allows you to pick up one record attribute, and to associate its different values or different value intervals with different index numbers. When it is connected to one attribute slot of a RecordBox, a SelectorBox reads this slot value, obtains the corresponding index number, and selects the corresponding template.

These basic boxes including a DBProxyBox, a ScopeWindow box, and a RecordManager box may take any shape. In Figure 18.19, their composition forms a treasure chest. Its lid works as a search button. The two RotationBoxes on the front face of this box specify the scope bottom and the scope width. The balls and cubes flying out of this treasure chest represent retrieved records. Their video textures and orbits are determined by the specified record attributes. This capability allows us to naturally embed database accesses and their resulting visualization and materialization in arbitrarily designed interactive 3D environments.

Figure 18.20 shows a virtual materialization of the solar system using planet and satellite data stored in a database. When the database is accessed, the system generates all the planets moving around the sun. Each planet includes, in its representation, a database ac-

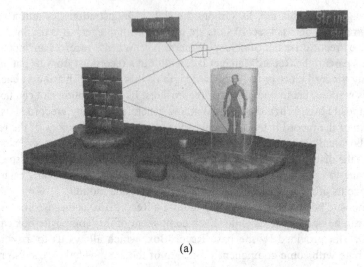

(a)

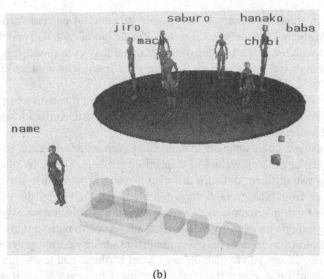

(b)

**Figure 18.16**  An example information visualization of a database access that uses a 3D doll as a 3D representation of each record. (a) Association of some attributes with slots of a composite box. (b) 3D representation of retrieved records.

cess mechanism. The Earth can be further clicked to show the moon moving around it. Different from visualization of records, the materialization of records using 3D interactive objects allows us to interact with the visualized result. For example, you may put a camera box at an arbitrary location on an arbitrary planet or satellite as shown in the figure, and open its camera-view window to observe not only the motion of the sun and the other planets and satellites, but also various eclipses.

Instead of embedding a geometrical displacement box in the template composite box to geometrically distribute materialized records depending on their values of specified at-

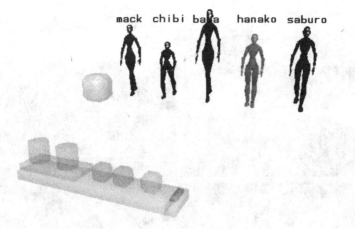

**Figure 18.17**  Virtual materialization of records in databases, using a stamping doll as the record template.

**Figure 18.18**  Virtual materialization using multiple different templates.

**Figure 18.19**  A composition with three basic boxes—a DBProxyBox, a ScopeWindow box, and a RecordManager box—may take any shape such as a treasure chest. Each record is represented as a flying ball whose video texture and orbit are determined by the specified record attributes.

**Figure 18.20**    Interactive animation of the solar system generated from a database allows you to put a camera at arbitrary locations on arbitrary planets and/or satellites.

tributes, you may use an arrangement box to geometrically distribute materialized records. The composite template does not use any displacement box, but a RecordBox as its base box instead. This RecordBox provides a slot for each attribute of the retrieved records. An arrangement box is a rectangular wire-frame box, and may contain an arbitrary number of composite boxes in this rectangular area. It has three special slots—#X, #Y, and #Z—to define its coordinate system by associating one record attribute to each of these three slots. Such an arrangement box reads each materialized record it contains to get the values of the specified three attributes, and locates each materialized record at the position determined by these attribute values.

Figure 18.21 shows the virtual materialization of 7000 fixed stars retrieved from the HIPPARCOS (HIgh-Precision PARallax COllecting Satelite) catalog database. This materialization represents each star record as a tiny ball, and uses a standard arrangement box to distribute materialized star records in a 3D coordinate system. You can see the template composite box on top of the arrangement box. Instead of this tiny ball representation, you may use any composite box to materialize each star record. All the other boxes in our materialization framework are made invisible in this example. Figure 18.21(a) shows the initial situation immediately after the record retrieval from the database. It shows all of the 7000 materialized records at the origin of this arrangement box. Figure 18.21(b) shows how the introduction of three coordinate-axis components that are represented as arrows defines a 3D coordinate system in an arrangement box and distributes these 7000 materialized star records in this space. Each coordinate-axis box allows you to specify one record attribute. For each record, the value of this attribute determines the displacement of this record along this coordinate axis. In this example, we

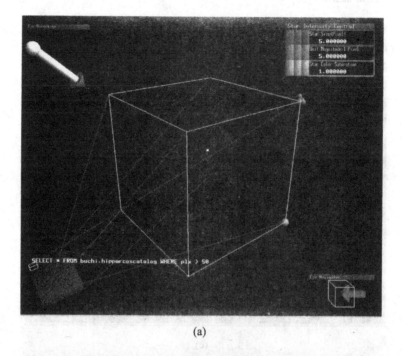

(a)

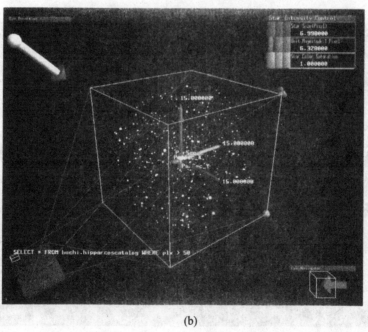

(b)

**Figure 18.21** HIPARCOS catalog database and the virtual materialization and arrangement of its records. (a) All the stars are materialized at the origin. (b) The introduction of three coordinate components defines a coordinate system, and distributes stars at their relative cosmic locations from the Earth.

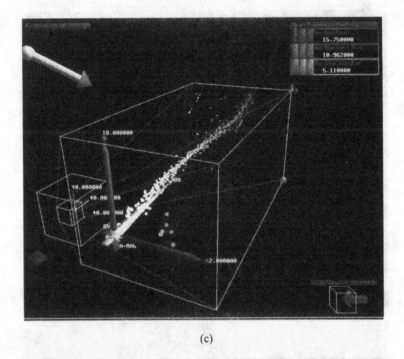

(c)

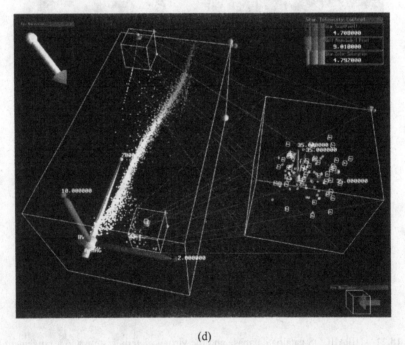

(d)

**Figure 18.21** *(continued)* HIPARCOS catalog database and the virtual materialization and arrangement of its records. (c) Some area in (b) is picked up, copied, and enlarged with a different coordinate system. (d) Those stars deviating from the characteristic structure are picked up by two rectangular boxes, and mapped again in the coordinate system in (b) to place them at their relative cosmic locations from the Earth.

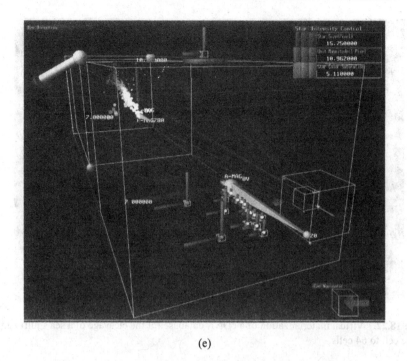

(e)

**Figure 18.21** *(continued)* HIPARCOS catalog database and the virtual materialization and arrangement of its records. (e) A set of stars is selected and arranged in a different coordinate system with different record representation.

used the coordinate system in which stars are placed at the relative cosmic location from the Earth. As shown in Figure 18.21(c), you can select a rectangular subarea using another arrangement box, and make a shared copy of this arrangement box. You may put a different coordinate system into this copy. This allows you to inspect some portion of records through a different view. In this example, the new X coordinate axis represents the primary colors of stars, the Y coordinate axis the ordinal number of each star arranged in descending order of brightness, and the Z coordinate axis the inverse of the brightness. This new coordinate system arranges most of the materialized stars in a characteristic structure as shown in (c). There are some exceptional stars deviating from this characteristic structure. As shown in Figure 18.21(d), you can easily select these exceptional stars by enclosing them with several rectangular boxes, send their content stars to a single arrangement box, and introduce again the original coordinate system used in Figure 18.21(b), which shows us relative locations of these exceptional stars from the Earth. As shown in Figure 18.21(e), you may select a subset of stars from the arrangement in Figure 18.21(c), and arrange this set of records in a different coordinate system using a different representation for each star record. Here, each star record is represented by a combination of two orthogonal variable-length bars.

As an application of our framework, we have been collaborating with Gojobori's group at the National Institute of Genetics in Japan to develop an interactive animation interface to access the cDNA database for the cleavage of an ascidian (sea squirt) egg from a single cell into 64 cells. The cDNA database stores, for each cell and for each gene, the expression intensity of this gene in this cell. Figure 18.22 shows the system we

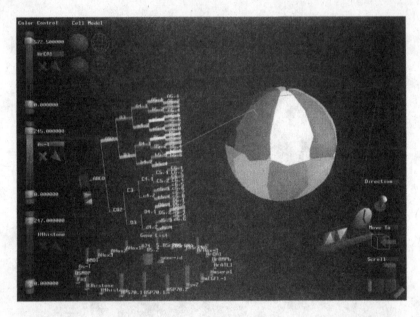

**Figure 18.22**   Virtual materialization of a cDNA database for the cleavage of a sea squirt egg from a single cell to 64 cells.

developed for Gojobori's group. First of all, it animates the cell division process from a single cell to 64 cells. It has two buttons to forward or to reverse the division process. When you click an arbitrary cell, the system shows the expression intensity of each of a priori specified genes as shown in the left lower part of this figure. You may also arbitrarily pick up three different genes to observe their expression intensities in each cell. The expression intensities of these three genes are associated with the intensities of three color components (red, green and blue) to highlight each cell of the cleavage animation. The wire-frame cube that encloses the whole egg performs this function. Keeping this highlighting function active, you can forward or reverse the cell-division animation. The development of this system took only several hours using the geometrical models of cells that were designed by other people. The cDNA database is stored in an Oracle DBMS, which IntelligentBox accesses using Java JDBC.

### 18.6.6   3D Information Visualization of the WWW

Information visualization of the WWW is increasing its importance. It will provide not only a 3D interface to the WWW and a 3D representation of Web pages, but also a 3D representation of its linkage structures. These are the current major focuses of the Information Visualization Project in my research group.

Most of them are still ongoing projects. Here we will show only one of them (see Figure 18.23). In this figure, some walls in a museum show Web pages with embedded composite pads. You can interact with any of these Web pages. Each embedded pad is also active, and can be dragged out and dropped on any wall. An embedded pad, when clicked, pops up a composite box.

**Figure 18.23**   Some walls in this museum show Web pages with embedded composite pads.

## 18.7   COMPONENT-BASED FRAMEWORK FOR DATABASE REIFICATION

Various research fields in science and technology are now accumulating large amounts of data in databases, using recently developed computer-controlled, efficient data-acquisition tools for measurement, analysis, and observation. Researchers believe that such extensive data accumulation in databases will allow them to simulate various physical, chemical, and/or biological phenomena on computers without carrying out any time-consuming and/or expensive real experiments. Information visualization for DB-based simulation requires each visualized record to work as an interactive object. Current information visualization systems visualize records without materializing them as interactive objects. Researchers in these fields develop their individual or communal mental models from their target phenomena, and often like to visualize information based on these models. We will propose here a generic component-based framework for developing virtual materialization of database records, i.e., database reification. This framework provides visual interactive components not only for (1) accessing databases, and (2) defining an interactive 3D object as a template to materialize each record in a virtual space as shown in the previous section, but also for (3) specifying and modifying database queries, and (4) defining a virtual space and its coordinate system for such information materialization. These components are all represented as boxes, i.e., components in the IntelligentBox architecture.

### 18.7.1   Flexible Definition of Visualization Schemes

Recently, extensive application of information technologies in various social activities such as production, distribution, sales, finance, communication, transportation, education, and welfare has enabled us to file large amounts of personal records on these social activities and to store them in databases. Information visualization technologies as well as data mining technologies aim to support people in extracting such knowledge resources. Most of the current information visualization systems propose various specific visualization schemes, assuming typical application fields and typical analysis methods in these fields. However, they allow us to visually specify queries to a database to retrieve data for visualization. Some of them even allow us to dynamically change parameters of queries to change visualization results.

Ahlberg and Shneiderman proposed starfield displays [40] that plot items from a database as small selectable spots (either points or small 2D figures) using two of the ordinal attributes of the data as the variables along the display axes. The displayed information can be filtered by changing the range of displayed values on each axis. A query that is dynamically defined by users' manipulation of sliders and toggles is called a dynamic query. IVEE [41] and its commercialized version, Spotfire, support dynamic queries. IVEE imports database relations and automatically creates environments holding visualizations and query devices. IVEE offers multiple visualizations such as maps and starfields, and multiple query devices, such as sliders, alphasliders, and toggles. Arbitrary graphical objects can be attached to database objects in visualizations. Multiple visualizations may be active simultaneously. Users can interactively lay out and change different types of query devices. Users may retrieve details on demand by clicking on visualization objects.

Semiologies of graphic representation methods have been developed by various researchers to gain understanding of the visualization design space. Among these, A Presentation Tool (APT) [42], BOZ[43], and SAGE [44] use knowledge-based approaches for synthesizing appropriate visualizations by combining common business visualizations such as bar charts and XY charts. APT create visualization based on a characterization of the underlying data and of the user's choice of the relations to be visualized. APT checks by means of formal criteria which information may be conveyed via a particular graphical technique (the criterion of expressivity) and how effectively such a technique may present the information to be communicated (the criterion of effectiveness). These criteria were used in 2D mappings, but can also be applied to 3D mappings. In such systems, a ranked list of possible mappings is usually used for each data type; the best set of mappings for the whole data set is then chosen as a constraints satisfaction problem. Whereas APT generates visualization presentation from data description, BOZ uses task description for the automatic generation of the presentation. In addition to automatic generation of the presentation, SAGE provides computer-supported-data graphic design tools, in which users can interactively specify and/or search and choose from a library of previously created graphics.

AVS [45] and IBM DataExplorer [46] are commercially available visualization environment systems with object-oriented visual components for computation and graphics. They provide visual programming environments for users to easily construct data-flow programs for visualization.

Multiple coordinated visualization uses multiple views of the same data, keeping their contents synchronized. It enables users to rapidly explore complex information. Users often need unforeseen combinations of coordinated visualizations that are appropriate for their data. Snap-Together Visualization [47] enables data users to rapidly and dynamically mix and match visualizations and coordinations to construct custom exploration interfaces without programming. Snap-Together's conceptual model is based on the relational database model. Users load relations into visualizations, then coordinate them based on the relational joins between them. Users can create different types of coordinations such as brushing, drill down, overview and detail view, and synchronized scrolling of different views. DEVise [48] is another visualization system that allows us to create coordinated multiple visualizations by specifying links among them. DEVise supports several different link types for us to specify different coordination types including brushing-and-linkage, drill down, aggregation, etc. Visage [49] generalizes such coordination, allowing users to drag and drop and then brush tabular data elements among many types of visualizations, including charts and geographical maps. Visage is information-centric, which means that data objects are represented as first-class interface objects, which can be manipulated using a common set of basic operations, such as drill down and roll up, applicable regardless of where they appear: in a hierarchical table, a slide show, a map, or a query. Tioga 2 (Tioga DataSplash) [50] is a system that supports visualization of database information. Visualization is specified via a boxes-and-arrows data-flow diagram in which the arrows represent data and the boxes represent operations. There are facilities for making composites and groups and for zooming in to obtain more details. Tioga DataSplash is a direct manipulation semantic zoom system in which users can construct and navigate visualizations. This system has been implemented on top of the POSTGRES object-relational database management system.

Various research fields in science and technology are now accumulating large amounts of data in databases, using recently developed computer-controlled, efficient data-acquisition tools for measurement, analysis, and observation of physical, chemical, and biological phenomena. Data analysis and knowledge-extraction methods in these fields are still the targets of research and development efforts. Researchers in these fields currently focus on the accumulation of all the data they can now acquire for their future analysis. They believe that such an extensive data accumulation in databases will allow them to simulate various physical, chemical, and biological phenomena on computers without carrying out any time-consuming and expensive real experiments. Here, we call such a new way of research in science "data-based science." Information visualization will no doubt be one of the most powerful tools in data-based science. Current information visualization technologies, however, do not satisfy the requirements of data-based science for the following reasons.

Information visualization for DB-based simulation requires each visualized record to work as an interactive object. It should be easy enough for these researchers, who are not necessarily computer experts, to define the functionality of each visualized record as well as the spatial record arrangement. Current information visualization systems visualize records without materializing them as interactive objects in a virtual environment. Instead of information visualization systems, we need an information materialization framework that allows us to materialize each record as an interactive visual object in a virtual space. Furthermore, researchers in these fields develop their individual or communal mental models from their target phenomena, and often like to visualize information based on these models. We need to provide these researchers with a new visualization environment in which they can easily define their own visualization schemes as well as various query conditions.

This section shows a generic component-based framework for developing virtual materialization of database records. This framework provides visual interactive components for (1) accessing databases, (2) specifying and modifying database queries, (3) defining an interactive 3D object as a template to materialize each record in a virtual space, and (4) defining a virtual space and its coordinate system for the information materialization. These components are represented as boxes, i.e., components in the IntelligentBox architecture.

### 18.7.2 Information Materialization through Query Composition

Figure 18.24 shows an example composition for information materialization. It specifies the above-mentioned four functions as a flow diagram from left to right. The leftmost box

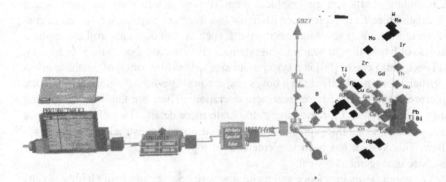

**Figure 18.24**  An example composition for information materialization.

is a TableBox, which allows us to specify a database relation to access; it outputs an SQL query with the specified relation in its "from" clause, leaving its "select" and "where" clauses unspecified:

> select
> from      *specified_relation*
> where

The database is stored in a local or remote database server running, for example, an Oracle DBMS. When cliked, a TableBox pops up the list of all the relations stored in the database, and allows us to select one of them. To obtain the list of all the accessible relations in the database, the TableBox issues an SQL query through JDBC (Java Database Connectivity) to query the DDD (Data Dictionary and Directory) storing information about all the relations in the database.

The second box is a TemplateManagerBox, which allows us to specify a composite box used as a template to materialize each record. It allows us to register more than one template, and to select one from those registered for record materialization. When we select a template named Ball, for example, the TemplateManagerBox adds a virtual attribute, "Ball" as TEMPLATENAME, in the "select" clause of the input query, and outputs the modified SQL query. For an input query

> select    X
> from      Y
> where     C

it outputs a modified query

> select    X, "Ball" as TEMPLATENAME
> from      Y
> where     C

The database has an additional relation to store the registered templates. This relation TEMPLATEREL has two attributes; TEMPLATENAME and TEMPLATEBOX. The second attribute stores the template composite box specified by the first attribute. The specified SQL query is later joined with the relation TEMPLATEREL to obtain the template composite box from its name. When this join is performed, the virtual attribute "Ball" as TEMPLATENAME works as a selection operation TEMPLATENAME = "Ball" on the relation TEMPLATEREL, and makes the attribute name TEMPLATEBOX refer to the composite box named Ball. When we register a new template composite box, the TemplateManagerBox accesses the database DDD to obtain all the attributes of the relation specified by the input SQL query. It adds slots for these attributes to the base box of the template composite box, defining a one-to-one relation between these attributes and newly defined slots. The record materialization later assigns each record value to a copy of this template box, which decomposes this record value to its attribute values and stores them in the corresponding attribute slots of the base box.

The third component in the example is a RecordFilterBox, which allows us to specify an attribute *attr*, a comparison operator $\theta$, and a value $v$. This specification modifies the input query by adding a new condition *attr* $\theta$ $v$ in its "where" clause. The RecordFilterBox accesses the database DDD to know all the accessible attributes.

The last component in this example is a ContainerBox with four more components: an OriginBox, and three AxisBoxes. A ContainerBox accesses the database with its input query, and materializes each record with the template composite box. Whereas an OriginBox specifies the origin of the coordinate system of the materialization space, each AxisBox specifies one of the three coordinate axes, and allows us to associate this with one of the accessible attributes. When you click a button at the center of each AxisBox, it pops up a list of accessible attributes by accessing the database DDD. Each AxisBox also normalizes the values of the selected attribute by evaluating the database for the minimum and maximum values of the specified attribute. Suppose that *attr* and $\alpha$ denote the selected attribute name and the normalization factor for this attribute, respectively. You may not put an AxisBox in parallel with one of the three coordinate axes of the ContainerBox. Let *lx*, *ly*, and *lz* denote the projected lengths of the AxisBox to the X, Y, and Z axes of the ContainerBox, respectively. OriginBoxes and AxisBoxes also use query modification methods to perform their functions. An OriginBox, when put in a ContainerBox, gets its relative location (*ox*, *oy*, *oz*) from the ContainerBox, and adds three derived attributes—*ox* as Xcoordinate, *oy* as Ycoordinate, and *oz* as Zcoordinate—in the "select" clause of the input query. Each AxisBox, on the other hand, converts the current query

```
select   ..., xexpr as Xcoordinate,
         ..., yexpr as Ycoordinate,
         ..., zexpr as Zcoordinate, ...
from   ...
where   ...
```

to the following modified query:

```
select   ..., xexpr +lx×α×attr as Xcoordinate,
         ..., yexpr +ly×α×attr as Ycoordinate,
         ..., zexpr +lz×α×attr as Zcoordinate, ...
from   ...
where   ...
```

In addition to the components used in the above example, the framework provides two more components: a JoinBox and an OverlayBox. A JoinBox accepts two input SQL queries, and defines their relational join as its output query. It allows us to specify the join condition. An OverlayBox accepts more than one query, and enables a ContainerBox to overlay the materialization of these input queries. From the query modification point of view, it outputs the union of two input queries with template specifications.

By using a ContainerBox together with an OriginBox and AxisBoxes as a template composite box, we can define a nested structure of information materialization as shown in Figure 18.25. The X coordinate is specified to represent the annual production quantity of cabbage. The displacement of the origin of each record materializing ContainerBox from the map plane indicates the annual production quantity of cabbage in the specified year in the corresponding prefecture, while each record materializing ContainerBox shows cabbage production changes during the last 20 years.

A SelectorBox is a rectangular box that you can put inside a record materializing ContainerBox with each of its three axes automatically kept parallel to the corresponding axis of the ContainerBox. A SelectorBox cuts out the materialization space with two planes perpendicular to each coordinate axis, and selects only those records materialized within the specified region. A SelectorBox performs this visual selection of records by adding the following conditions in the "where" clause of the input query to output the modified query:

$$\text{Xcoordinate BETWEEN } Xmin \text{ AND } Xmax$$
$$\wedge \text{ Ycoordinate BETWEEN } Ymin \text{ AND } Ymax$$
$$\wedge \text{ ZCoordinate BETWEEN } Zmin \text{ AND } Zmax$$

$Xmin$ and $Xmax$ are calculated from the minimum and the maximum X coordinate values of the SelectorBox in the ContainerBox. The other four values are similarly calculated.

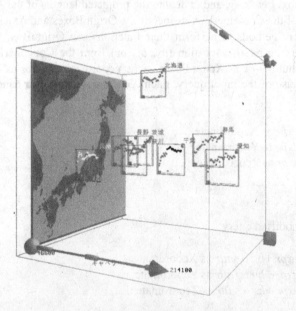

**Figure 18.25**    A nested structure of information materialization.

Figure 18.26 shows a record selection example using a SelectorBox, and its visualization overlaid with the original set of records. The three coordinate axes in the overlaid visualization on the right-hand side use another set of three attributes different from the original visualization on the left-hand side. The output query of the SelectorBox uses a bigger template to clarify the selected records in the overlaid visualization.

Our framework also allows us to store wire-frame 3D models of various shapes in a database, and to materialize some of them in a visualization space. It enables us to quantify some of these shapes by visually constructing a query. For this purpose, our framework provides a special box, ProtoShapeBox, to work as a shape template. When its #shape slot is bound with a record attribute value representing a wire-frame 3D model, a ProtoShapeBox changes its shape to the specified shape. You may join a relation storing shape records with a relation storing compositions with these shapes to retrieve information about a specific composite shape, including its component shapes and their relative locations. Our framework enables us to visually specify such a join operation and a selection operation to materialize a specified composite shape.

Figure 18.27 shows materialization of human organs in the chest area. It accesses a relation storing the shape data together with the names of organs, and joins it to another relation storing the relation between each organ and the names of the areas to which they belong, as well as the relative location of this organ inside each of these areas. This materialization allows the user to specify an area to materialize on a RecordFilterBox. This example specified the chest area. Finally, the output query is sent to a ContainerBox to materialize all the organs in the chest area.

In our framework, each materialized record is associated with a query obtained by modifying the input query of the ContainerBox with an additional condition to identify this record in the "where" clause. Our framework provides another basic component called a QueryExtractionBox to extract the associated query from a materialized record. You may take the heart out of the materialization in Figure 18.27, and put it in a QueryExtractionBox. You may join the output query of this box with a relation that works as a directory of gene expression libraries for each organ. You may connect the output of the JoinBox to a materialization tool to obtain accessible libraries about the heart. These libraries are gene expression profiles for the atrial muscle and the ventricle

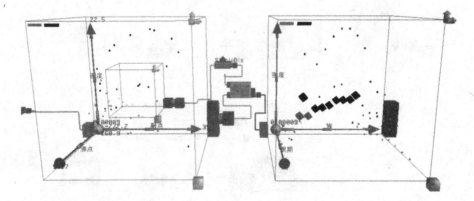

**Figure 18.26** A record selection example using a SelectorBox, and its visualization overlaid with the original set of records.

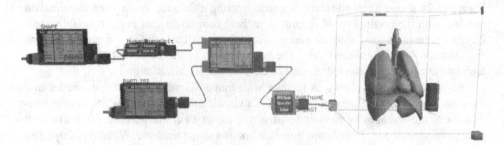

**Figure 18.27**   Materialization of human organs in the chest area using a ProtoShapeBox as the record materialization template.

muscle. You may put each materialized library in another QueryExtractionBox, and join it to another relation storing a gene expression profile of each library. You may connect this output to another materialization tool to materialize the gene expression profile of the selected library. Figure 18.28 shows these operations and the resultant materialization.

We have applied our new component-based database materialization framework to materialize the animation of the sea squirt cleavage so that it visualizes the gene expression profile of each cell. The gene expression profiles and cleavage process information, as well as cell shape data, are all stored in a database. Our new framework enabled us to dynamically construct the same functionalities provided by the previous system shown in Figure 18.22 within 15 minutes, without writing any program codes or any SQL queries.

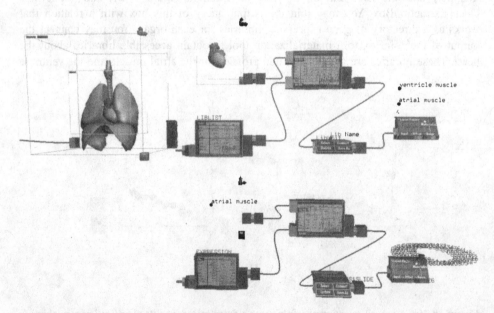

**Figure 18.28**   Use of QueryExtractionBoxes to extract the associated queries from materialized records, and further materialization with the extracted queries.

## 18.8   VIRTUAL SCIENTIFIC LABORATORY FRAMEWORK

Virtual scientific laboratories are another prospective application area of IntelligentBox. Different from conventional scientific visualization systems, virtual scientific laboratories reify scientific phenomena in virtual interactive 3D environments, and allow us not only to observe invisible phenomena, but also to directly manipulate intangible phenomena.

AVS [45], the most widely used scientific visualization tool, for example, allows us to visually construct a program by defining data flows among functional modules that can be selected from a large library of such modules. Its computation result is graphically presented as a 2D or 3D image in a separate window. Users can interact with its visual programs, but not with its visual outputs. Its visual outputs are just graphical images, not interactive objects. We may consider its program and its visual output as the genotype and the phenotype of a computation, respectively. AVS and other currently available scientific visualization tools allow us to visually and directly interact with the genotypes but not with the phenotypes. Our project focuses on the visual and direct interactivity with phenotypes and, furthermore, the unification of the genotype and the corresponding phenotype so that we can directly change various conditions of a computation by directly manipulating its phenotype.

The unification of the genotype and the corresponding phenotype is fundamental to real-time interactive simulations based on scientific computations. There are significantly increasing demands for such interactive simulations in education, advanced research, and high-tech engineering [51, 52, 53, 54, 55, 56]. However, because of the computation-intensive nature of scientific simulations, some systems allow us to interact only with the visualized genotype to change simulation conditions, whereas others use a priori computed data for different conditions, and allow us to interact with the phenotype only to change the data file used for the rendering.

Our framework aims to unify the genotype and the phenotype of scientific simulations in a generic way. To achieve this goal, our group developed a generic linkage mechanism between an IntelligentBox system and an AVS module network. An AVS module network is an AVS program defined as a network of AVS modules. Repetitively used AVS module networks constitute a library of scientific visualization software components. We may define, for each of these AVS module networks, its proxy as a primitive box of IntelligentBox. This proxy box wraps the AVS module network, and works as an interactive visual component box in an IntelligentBox environment. Our virtual scientific laboratory framework provides a generic wrapper box, AVSModuleWrapperBox, for wrapping an arbitrary AVS module network to define its proxy box.

All the parameters in such an AVS module network define the corresponding slots in the proxy box for this module network. Some proxy boxes work purely as computation components, whereas others provide 3D graphical outputs on their surface or within themselves. Some of them provide volume-rendering functions. Proxy boxes may have additional functions. Some proxy boxes, for example, may change some of their slot values, namely some parameter values of their corresponding AVS module network, when they change the relative location within their parent box.

Slot connections among these boxes define dynamical linkages among their corresponding AVS module networks. This allows us to directly construct both a scientific computation program and a visualization environment just by combining primitive boxes. The visualization result also allows us to interact through direct manipulation of the visualizing boxes.

Figure 18.29 shows how an AVS module network is wrapped by an AVSModuleWrapperBox to define a proxy box. When you wrap an AVS module network, the AVSModuleWrapperBox allows you to specify some ports in this AVS module network to work as slots of the proxy box. You may select these ports from more than one AVS module in the module network. You may arbitrarily name these slots. Each proxy box stores, for each of its slots, the information about which port of which AVS module is associated with this slot. When a "set" message sends a new value to one of these slots, the proxy box transfers this value to the corresponding port in the AVS module network. When the AVS module network outputs a new value to one of these ports that are associated with slots, the interface module explained later sends this value with the output port address to the proxy box, which then transfers this value to the corresponding slot, and issues an "update" message to each of its child boxes.

The slot connection between two proxy boxes indirectly connects the corresponding two AVS module networks through these proxy boxes and their linkage. This is functionally equivalent to the direct connection of these two AVS module networks in an AVS environment. Figure 18.30 shows the detailed mechanism of an AVSModuleWrapperBox. Our framework provides two server modules in the AVS system for the communication between an AVSModuleWrapperBox and an AVS module network. These server modules are the ib2avs server and the avs2ib server. An ib2avs server receives data from a proxy box, whereas an avs2ib server sends data to a proxy box. Our framework uses V language for AVSModuleWrapperBoxes to send commands to these two server modules to load an AVS module network and to connect type conversion modules to it. Our framework also provides another server module, ib daemon, which, when invoked by an AVSModuleWrapperBox, creates a dedicated ib2avs server module and a dedicated avs2ib server module, and asks them to perform the remaining required task.

An AVSModuleWrapperBox has the following four slots: a #avshost slot to hold the name of the host machine running an AVS system, a #avsport slot to hold the port number of the ib daemon server module, a #avsnet.directorypath to hold the absolute path name of the directory in which the wrapped AVS module network is stored, and a #avsnet.filename

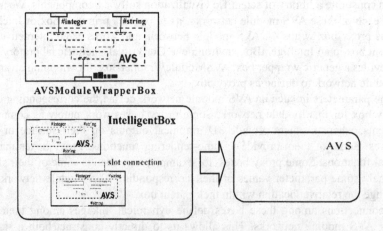

**Figure 18.29**  AVS program modules are wrapped by AVSModuleWrapperBoxes to define proxy boxes, which you may combine through slot connections to indirectly connect AVS program modules.

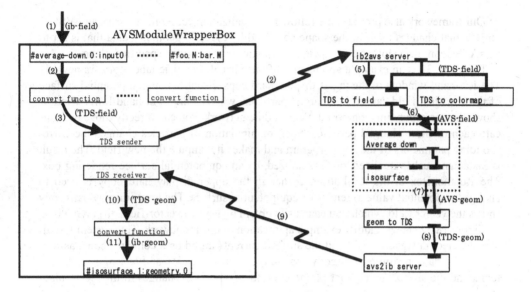

**Figure 18.30** Details of the mechanism to wrap an AVS module network with an AVSModuleWrapperBox.

to hold the name of the AVS module network to wrap. To wrap an AVS module network, you need to set the necessary values to the four slots of an AVSModuleWrapperBox. Then you need to specify some input ports together with their modules to work as new input slots of the proxy box. You also need to specify some output ports together with their modules to work as new output slots of the proxy box.

These server modules use the TDS (tagged data stream) format for their data exchange with AVSModuleWrapperBoxes and other AVS components. TDS data consist of four fields: the first field holds the size of data, the next two fields work as the data type tag and the address tag, and the last holds value data. The data type tag specifies the data type of the exchanged data, whereas the address specifies which port of the AVS program module will receive or has sent the communication data. The ib2avs server module dispatches its input data to a specified port of a specified component. The address tag is used to specify this component and the port. The avs2ib server module, on the other hand, sends its input data together with the port address to the proxy box. This port address specifies the port that has output the communication data. The proxy box transfers the received data to the slot associated with the specified port. The TDS data type is further classified into three different ones: StreamTDS, TaggedBinary, and fieldTDS data types. The StreamTDS format is for the communication between an AVSModuleWrapperBox and a wrapped AVS module, i.e., between a proxy box and AVS. The TaggedBinary format is used for the exchange of large data such as geometrical shape data or array data between boxes through the structure sharing without sending the whole data copy. The fieldTDS format is the same as the AVSfield type used for exchanging large data such as multidimensional array data between AVS components through the structure sharing without sending the whole data copy. Our framework also provides data conversion modules in AVS for the conversion between various data types and the TDS data type.

Our framework also provides the following visualization component boxes: an AVSGeomBox that changes itself to the shape specified by the AVS geometry data that is set to its #AVSGeom.data slot, and a ClipBox to cut another box with a specified plane.

Figure 18.31 is an example application of our virtual scientific laboratory framework. The left-hand window in the upper display hard copy visualizes an equipotential surface of the electrical field caused by charged particles, whereas the right-hand lower window shows the corresponding composed AVS module network. You can directly move or replicate each of these charged particles. Such manipulation of particles changes the corresponding parameters of the AVS program and makes it compute the new field. The result is instantaneously visualized, or materialized, by an equipotential surface-rendering box. The RotationBox at the left-bottom corner in the upper display hard copy is used to change the potential value to render its equipotential surface. The lower display hard copy shows the vector field, which you can easily obtain by using a vector-field displaying box.

Figure 18.32 shows another example application of our framework. This system visualizes the electromagnetic field and the surface current caused by a cellular phone, as well as its radio pattern. You may directly change the relative location and/or length of the antenna and the size of the cellular phone body to examine the changes in the electromag-

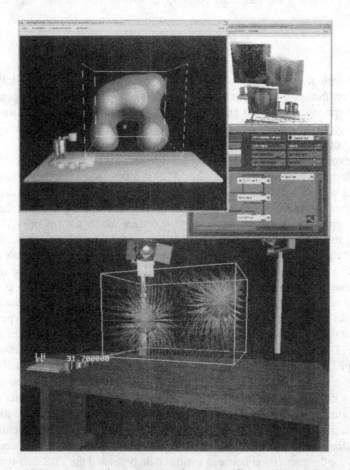

**Figure 18.31**  An example application of our scientific visualization framework.

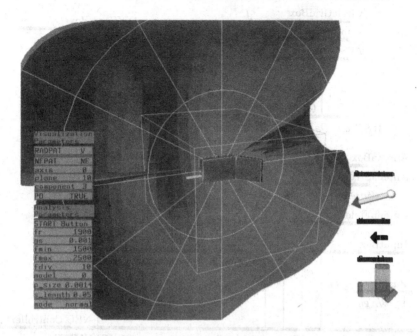

**Figure 18.32**  Another example application of our framework for the interactive simulation of the electromagnetic field and the radio pattern caused by a cellular phone.

netic field, the surface current on the phone body, and the radio pattern. Different from the previous example, this system uses a solver behind the AVS system. Since a solver is invoked by an AVS module, use of such a solver does not change the interface between an IntelligentBox system and an AVS system. Figure 18.33 shows how an AVSModuleWrapperBox wraps an AVS module network accessing a solver. The example system used a NEC2 solver developed at Lawrence Livermore Research Laboratory. The input filter and the output filter in this figure are necessary to convert data types between the AVS system and the solver. Figure 18.34 shows the whole composition structure of this system. Each horizontal line segment represent a box, whereas each vertical line segment represent a slot connection between the lower parent box and the upper child box. AMWBoxes denote AVSModuleWrapperBoxes. Each AMWBox(Read_UCD) wraps a Read .. UCD AVS

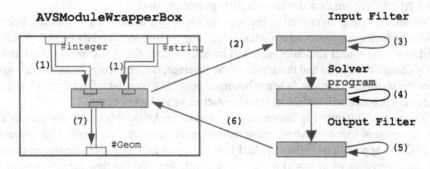

**Figure 18.33**  An AVSModuleWrapperBox may wrap an AVS module network calling up a solver.

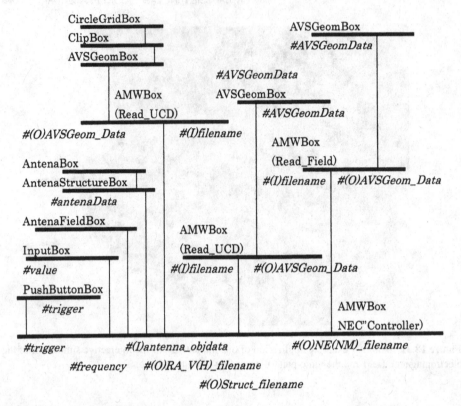

**Figure 18.34** The whole composition structure for the interactive virtual simulation of the electromagnetic field caused by a cellular phone.

module. One reads the radio pattern geometry data file, whereas the other reads the surface current geometry data file. Each has two slots. i.e., a #(I)filename slot to store the file name of the geometry data to read, and a #(O)AVSGeom.data slot to store AVS geometry data. An AMWBox(orthoslice) wraps Read.File and orthoslice modules. It is used to display a cross section of the electromagnetic field. It has the following four slots: a #(I)filename slot to store the file name of the geometry data to read, a #(I)plane.axis slot to specify which of the three planes—xy, yz, and zx—to use as the cutting plane, a #(I)plane.number slot to specify which of the three planes—xy, yz, and zx—to display, and a #(O)AVSGeom.data slot to store AVS geometry data.

We are especially interested in the application of this technology to medical science, molecular biology, genome informatics, electromagnetism, and fluid dynamics. When applied to a wind-tunnel simulator, you will be able to enter the virtual wind tunnel and directly change the shapes and the angles of the fuselage, fin, and wings of an aircraft to observe the changes in airflow. When it becomes possible to compute fluid dynamics in real time, our approach will realize such an interactive virtual wind tunnel.

We are also interested in integrating our virtual scientific laboratory framework with our component-based database materialization framework, especially for advanced CAD/CAM applications. When applied to CAD databases, our database materialization framework enables us to model not only the shapes but also the functions of our product components and their compositions, to store them in a CAD database, and to retrieve desired components and compositions as materialized interactive 3D objects. You may put these retrieved objects in a virtual science laboratory environment to evaluate them through interactive simulations.

## 18.9  3D MEME MEDIA AND A WORLDWIDE REPOSITORY OF BOXES AS A MEME POOL

In IntelligentBox, each box has its save-format representation, which also works as its exchange-format representation used for its network transportation. Boxes can be easily recombined with each other, easily replicated, and easily transported to other users for reuse. All these operations can be easily performed by end-users. Boxes work as 3D meme media.

We need a worldwide repository of boxes in which people around the world can publish, access, reuse, reedit, and redistribute various boxes. Such a repository will work as a meme pool of 3D meme media. In 1996, the IntelligentPad/IntelligentBox Project developed a special pad called an IntelligentBoxPad that works as a window for the execution of IntelligentBox. On this pad, you can execute an IntelligentBox environment and manipulate its boxes. You may open any number of IntelligentBoxPads in your single IntelligentPad system, and transport any boxes from any one of them to another. Since IntelligentBoxPads are pads, our HTMLViewerPad enables us to embed them in arbitrary Web pages and to publish them through the Internet. Figure 18.35 shows a Web page with an embedded

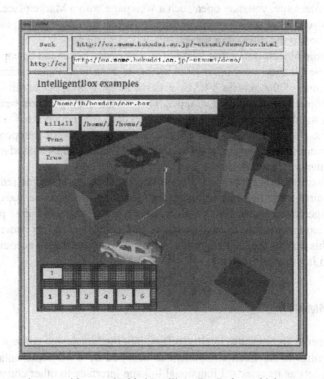

**Figure 18.35**  A web page with an embedded IntelligentBoxPad on which a composite box is published.

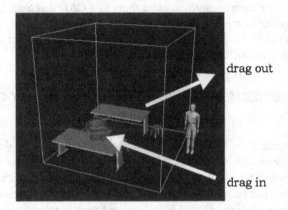

**Figure 18.36**   A MarketplaceBox works as a 3D extension of a PiazzaPad.

IntelligentBoxPad on which a composite box is published. This facility provides IntelligentBox with its worldwide repository of composite boxes, i.e., its meme pool.

Figure 18.36 shows a 3D extension of a PiazzaPad. This MarketplaceBox is associated with a server, and shows in itself all the boxes registered in this server. Using an IntelligentBoxPad embedded in a Web page, you can publish a MarketplaceBox through the Internet. At the client site, you may open such a Web page with a MarketplaceBox, drag out some box into your local environment, or drag some box into this MarketplaceBox to register this new box to the associated server.

Different from objects defined in VRML [5], embedded boxes can be copied and locally reused in combination with other local boxes, or even with those embedded in other Web pages. None of the current VRML systems adopt a wrapper architecture to wrap each VRML object with a standard wrapper, whereas the IntelligentBox wraps each of its objects with a standard wrapper that provides a standard connection interface among various VR objects. Boxes are not just 3D graphical objects or software components. Each of them is a software component wrapped by a wrapper with a standard interface, and has its own 3D graphical representation.

The superdistribution of composite boxes allowing their reediting and redistribution by end-users requires only the same technologies as those for composite pads. The embedding of IntelligentBoxPads in Web pages realizes a worldwide 3D meme pool. The embedding of a request module in each primitive box enables each box provider to charge each use of this box to the user's account, which is managed by an account module installed in each IntelligentBox kernel system.

## 18.10   SUMMARY

A 3D meme media architecture, IntelligentBox, inherited its design concept and architecture from IntelligentPad. Each component is wrapped by a 3D representation wrapper with a list of slots as its standard functional linkage interface to other components. Each component has an MVC architecture. View linkage among components defines a composite 3D object. Instead of pasting a pad on another pad, we can bind a box in the coordinate system of another box. This defines a parent–child relationship between these two components. Each component in a composition has no more than one parent component, and can access no more than one of this parent's slots. Each slot can be accessed by each of the two standard messages, "set" and "gimme." Each slot defines two different methods for these two messages. The updating of components propagates from each parent component to its children. Composite boxes work as meme media, and their worldwide repository forms a meme pool.

Different from VRML and its extension with Java, IntelligentBox provides an open set of interactive 3D components that can be directly manipulated for use and directly combined to define composite applications. Composed boxes are kept decomposable, unless otherwise specified, for their future reediting by end-users.

Instead of a FieldPad, IntelligentBox provides a RoomBox to define a shared workspace. You can make a shared copy of any box.

IntelligentBox provides application frameworks not only for interactive 3D animation but also for interactive information visualization and interactive scientific visualization. For interactive animation, it provides motion-constraint boxes, shape-deformation boxes, and camera boxes. A motion-constraint box imposes a constraint on the motion of its child box. A shape-deformation box deforms its child box. A camera box provides a real-time view taken by this camera.

For interactive information visualization and virtual materialization, IntelligentBox uses a special box that works as a proxy of an external database system. Instead of representing each record in 2D form, we use a 3D animation template to represent each record. This template is defined as a composite box. When registered as a template, some of its slots are associated with record attributes. This template has its display offset as its slot, which is also associated with some record attributes. Each record retrieved from a database is represented as a 3D animation object using this template.

Various research fields in science and technology are now accumulating large amounts of data in databases. Researchers believe that such an extensive data accumulation in databases will allow them to simulate various physical, chemical, and/or biological phenomena on computers without carrying out any time-consuming and/or expensive real experiments. Information visualization for DB-based simulation requires an information materialization framework that allows us to materialize each record as an interactive visual object in a virtual space. Furthermore, researchers in these fields develop their individual or communal mental models on their target phenomena, and often like to visualize information based on their own mental models. We need to provide these researchers with a new visualization environment in which they can easily define their own visualization schemes as well as various query conditions. Our component-based database materialization framework provides visual interactive components for (1) accessing databases, (2) specifying and modifying database queries, (3) defining an interactive 3D object as a template to materialize each record in a virtual space, and (4) defining a virtual space and its coordinate system for the information materialization. These components are represented as boxes.

For interactive scientific visualization or virtual scientific laboratories, IntelligentBox provides a generic linkage mechanism with the AVS system. This allows us to define a box as a program module of AVS so that combination of such boxes defines a composition of an AVS program, and the manipulation of such a box changes parameter values of its corresponding AVS program module. These allow us to define a virtual laboratory in which we can construct a scientific simulation world through direct manipulation of a priori given components, directly manipulate objects in this world to change situations, and interactively observe the simulation result in this world.

## REFERENCES

1. D. Sampe, B. Roehl, and J. Eagan. *Virtual Reality Creations.* Waite Group Press, Corte Madera, CA, 1993.

2. D. Shaw, M. Green, J. Liang, and Y. Sun. Decoupled situation in virtual reality with the MR toolkit. *ACM Transactions on Information Systems, 11*(3): 287–317, 1993.

3. G. Chris. XOBS: A formalism for representing the behavior of virtual objects. In *Proceedings of the 4th Annual Conference On AI Simulation and Planning in High Autonomy Systems,* 1993.

4. D. B. Anderson, J. W. Barrus, et al. Building multiuser interactive multimedia environments at MERL. In *Proceedings of IEEE Multimedia 95,* pp. 77–82, 1995.

5. NCSA. *Virtual Reality Modeling Language.* Technical Report, National Center for Super Computing Applications. See *http://www.ncsa.uiuc.edu/General/VRML/VRMLHome.html,* 1995.

6. D. B. Conner, S. S. Snibbe, K. P. Herndon, D. C. Robbins, and R. C. Zeleznik. 3D widgets. In *Proceedings of ACM SIGGRAPH'92 Symposium on Interactive 3D Graphics,* pp. 183–188, 1992.

7. P. S. Strauss, and R. Carey. An object-oriented 3D graphics toolkit. In *Proceedings of ACM SIGGRAPH'92 Symposium on Interactive 3D Graphics,* pp. 341–349, 1992.

8. Y. Okada and Y. Tanaka,. IntelligentBox: A constructive visual software development system for interactive 3D graphic applications. In *Proceedings of the Computer Animation '95 Conference,* pp. 114–125, 1995.

9. T. W. Sederburg. Free-form deformation of solid geometric models. *ACM SIGGRAPH, 20*(4): 151–160, 1986.

10. P. Bézier. General distortion of an ensemble of biparametric surfaces. *Computer Aided Design, 10*(2): 341–349, 1992.

11. Y. Okada and Y. Tanaka. Collaborative environments of IntelligentBox for distributed 3D graphic applications. In *Proceedings of the Computer Animation '97 Conference,* pp. 22–30, 1997.

12. C. Ware, and S. Osborne. Exploration and virtual camera control in virtual three dimensional environments, In *Proceedings of ACM SIGGRAPH '86,* pp. 175–183, 1986.

13. S. K. Card, J. D. Mackinlay, and B. Shneiderman. *Readings in Information Visualization—Using Vision to Think.* Morgan Kaufmann, San Francisco, 1999.

14. E. Freeman, and S. Fertig: Lifestreams. Organizing your electronic life. In *Proceedings of AAAI Fall Symposium on AI Applications in Knowledge Navigation,* 1995.

15. J. D. Mackinlay, G. G. Robertson, and S. K. Card. The perspective wall: Detail and context smoothly integrated. In *Proceedings of CHI'91,* New York, pp. 173–180, 1991.

16. S. K. Card, G. G. Robertson, and W. York. The web book and the web forager: An information workspace for the World-Wide-Web. In *Proceedings of CHI'96,* New York, pp. 111–117, 1996.

17. S. G. Eick, J. L. Steffen, and E. E. Sumner. Seesoft—A tool for visualizing line oriented software statistics. *IEEE Transaction on Software Engineering, 18*(11): 957–968, 1992.

18. C. Ahlberg and E. Wistrand. IVEE: An information visualization and exploration environment. In *Proceedings of Info-Vis'95,* New York, pp. 66–73, 1995.

19. T. Bray. Measuring the Web. *Computer Networks and ISDN Systems, 28*(7–11): 992, 1996.

20. M. C. Chuah, S. F. Roth, J. Mattis, and J. A. Kolojejchick. SDM: Malleable information graphics. In *Proceedings of InfoVis'95,* New York, pp. 36–42, 1995.

21. R. J. Hendley, N. S. Drew, A. M. Wood, and R. Beale. Narcissus: Visualising information. In *Proceedings of InfoVis'95,* New York, pp. 90–96, 1995.

22. W. Wright. Information animation applications in the capital markets. In *Proceedings of Info-Vis'95*, New York, pp. 19–25, 1995.

23. S. Feiner and C. Beshers. Worlds within worlds: Metaphors for exploring n-dimensional virtual worlds. In *Proceedings of UIST'90*, pp. 76–83, 1990.

24. D.A. Keim and H. P. Kriegel. VisDB: Database exploration using multidimensional visualization. *IEEE Computer Graphics and Applications*, Sept. 1994, 40–49.

25. G. G. Robertson, J. D. Mackinlay, and S. K. Card. Cone trees: Animated 3D visualizations of hierarchical information. In *Proceedings of CHI'91*, pp. 189–194, 1991.

26. B. Johnson and B. Shneiderman. Treemaps: A space-filling approach to the visualization of hierarchical information structures. In *Proceedings of InfoVis'91*, pp. 275–282, 1991.

27. K. M. Fairchild, S. E. Poltrock, and G. W. Furnas. SemNet: Three dimensional representations of large knowledge bases. In R. Guindon (ed.), *Cognitive Science and Its Applications for Human–Computer Interaction*, Lawrence Erlbaum, Hillsdale, NJ, pp. 201–233, 1988.

28. S. G. Eick and G. J. Wills. Navigating large networks with hierarchies. In *IEEE Proceedings of InfoVis'93*, pp. 204–210, 1993.

29. A. Inselberg. Multidimensional detective. In *Proceedings of InfoVis'97*, pp. 100–107, 1997.

30. J. Lamping and R. Rao. The hyperbolic browser: A focus+context technique for visualizing large hierarchies. *Journal of Visual Languages and Computing*, 7(1): 33–55, 1996.

31. R. Rao and S. K. Card. The table lens: Merging graphical and symbolic representations in an interactive focus+context visualization for tabular information. In *Proceedings of CHI'94*, pp. 318–322, 1994.

32. Y. K. Leung and M. D. Apperley. A review and taxonomy of distortion-oriented representation technique. *ACM Trans. on Computer–Human Interaction*, 1(2): 126–160, 1994.

33. M. S. T. Carpendale, D. J. Cowperthwaite, and F. D. Fracchia. Extending distortion viewing from 2D to 3D. *IEEE Computer Graphics and Applications*, July/Aug., 42–51, 1997.

34. G. G. Robertson and J. D. Mackinlay. The DocumentLens. In *Proceedings of UIST'93*, pp. 101–108, 1993.

35. J. Rekimot and M. Green. The information cube: Using transparency in 3D information visualization. In *Proceedings of WITS'93*, pp. 125–132, 1993.

36. U. Wiss and D. A. Carr. An empirical study of task support in 3D information visualizations. In *Proceedings of InfoVis'98*, pp. 392–399, 1999.

37. B. B. Bederson and J. D. Hollan. Pad++: A zooming graphical interface for exploring alternate interface physics. In *Proceedings of UIST'94*, pp. 17–22, 1994.

38. C. Ahlberg and B. Shneiderman. Visual information seeking: Tight coupling of dynamic query filters with Starfield displays. In *Proceedings of CHI'94*, pp. 313–317, 1994.

39. K. Fishkin and M. C. Stone. Enhanced dynamic queries via movable filters. In *Proceedings of CHI'95*, pp. 415–420, 1995.

40. C. Ahlberg and B. Shneiderman. Visual information seeking: Tight coupling of dynamic query filters with Starfield displays. In *Proceedings of ACM CHI'94*, ACM Press, New York, 1994.

41. C. Ahlberg E. Wistrand. IVEE: An information visualization and exploration environment. In *Proceedings of IEEE Symposium on Information Visualization*, Atlanta, 66–73, 1995.

42. J. MacKinlay. Automating the design of graphical presentations of relational information. *ACM Transactions on Graphics*, 5(2): 110–141, 1986.

43. S. M. Casner. A task-analytic approach to the automated design of graphic presentations. *ACM Transactions on Graphics* 10(2): 111–151, 1991.

44. S. Roth, J. Kolojejchick, and J. Goldstein. Interactive graphic design using automatic presentation knowledge. In Mark T. Maybury and Wolfgang Wahlster (eds.), *Intelligent User Interfaces*, Morgan Kaufmann, San Francisco, pp. 237–242, 1998.

45. C. Upson, T. Faulhauber, Jr., D. Kamins, D. Laidlaw, D. Schlegel, J. Vroom, R. Gurwitz, and A.

van Dam. The application visualization system: A computational environment for scientific visualization. *IEEE Computer Graphics and Applications, 9*(4): 30–42, July, 1989.

46. *Data Explorer Reference Manual.* IBM Corp., Armonk, NY, 1991.

47. C. North and B, Shneiderman. Snap-together visualization: a user interface for coordinating visualizations via relational schemata. In *Proceedings of Advanced Visual Interfaces 2000,* Palermo, Italy, pp. 128–135, 2000.

48. M. Livny, R. Ramakrishnan, K. Beyer, G. Chen, D. Donjerkovic, S. Lawande, J. Myllymaki, and K. Wenger. DEVise: Integrated querying and visual exploration of large datasets. In *Proceedings of ACM SIGMOD,* May, 1997.

49. S. A. Roth et al. Visage: A user interface environment for exploring information. In *Proceedings of Information Visualization,* 3–12, 1996.

50. A. Aiken, J. Chen, M. Stonebraker, and A. Woodruff. Tioga–2: A direct manipulation database visualization environment. In *Proceedings of the 12th International Conference on Data Engineering,* pp. 208–217, New Orleans, LA, 1996.

51. *Proceedings of the IEEE 2001 Symposium on Parallel and Large-Data Visualization and Graphics,* IEEE Press, Piscataway, NJ, 2001.

52. M. Schulz, F. Reck, W. Bartelheimer, and T. Ertl. Interactive visualization of fluid dynamics simulations in locally refined Cartesian grids (case study). In *Proceedings of the conference on Visualization '99,* San Francisco, 1999.

53. K. Vidimče, J. T. Foley, D. C. Banks, and Y. Chi. WebTOP: 3D interactive optics on the Web. In *Proceedings of the Web3D-VRML 2000 Fifth Symposium on Virtual Reality Modeling Language,* Monterey, 2000.

54. G. Leach and J. Gilbert. VRML molecular dynamics trajectories. In *Proceedings of the Fourth Symposium on Virtual Reality Modeling Language.* Paderborn, Germany, 1999.

55. S. Chakaveh, U. Zlender, D. Skaley, K. Fostiropoulos, and D. Breitschwerdt. DELTA's virtual physics laboratory (case study): A comprehensive learning platform on physics astronomy. In *Proceedings of the Conference on Visualization '99,* San Francisco, 1999.

56. K. Ma and T. W. Crockett. Parallel visualization of large-scale aerodynamics calculations: A case study on the Cray T3E. In *Proceedings of the 1999 IEEE Symposium on Parallel Visualization and Graphics,* San Francisco, 1999.

# CHAPTER 19

# ORGANIZATION AND ACCESS OF MEME MEDIA OBJECTS

The meme media and meme pool architectures that we have discussed in the preceding chapters will bring about a rapid accumulation of memes in our societies, which will require a new way of organizing and accessing them. No conventional information organization method—table-based, hierarchical, or indexed—is suitable for organizing and allowing access to a huge number of heterogeneous intellectual resources. The situation here is similar to the management and access of commodities. Commodities of the same type can be managed by a single database, but there are so many different types that consumers cannot tell which commodity belongs to which type, or which database manages which type. To solve this problem, we used to use documents or spaces to arrange information about mutually related commodities. Examples include catalogs, stores, department stores, malls, and towns. Here we propose a new framework for organizing and accessing intellectual resources. This framework uses documents to contextually and/or spatially select and arrange mutually related resources. Examples of such documents may include figures, images, movies, maps, and any combinations of them. These documents, as well as their component resources, are all represented as meme media objects. Therefore, these documents, together with related resources, may also be arranged in other documents, which forms a complex web of such documents.

## 19.1 ORGANIZATION AND ACCESS OF INTELLECTUAL RESOURCES

Pads and boxes are subject to international distribution, exchange, and reuse. Data, tools, and documents, either in pad or box form, serve as intellectual resources in our societies. The meme media and meme pool architectures that we have discussed in the preceding chapters will rapidly increase the variety of such intellectual resources, and encourage their accumulation.

In this chapter, we will consider how to manage and access a huge accumulation of intellectual resources represented as pads or boxes. Here we will consider only pads, but our conclusions are also applicable to boxes. Let us first consider if databases can manage pads. If the platform has the pad definition code and all the necessary DLLs, a composite pad only needs to store its exchange format representation; no other information needs to be stored. The exchange format representation of a composite pad includes two kinds of information. One is the form information that describes what kinds and sizes of component pads are used, how they are geometrically pasted together, and which slot is used in each connection between component pads. The other is the state information of this pad. The state information needs to be sufficient to specify the current values of all of its internal variables whose values are not specified by its form information. Composite pads with the same form information but with different states are said to share the same form. Without loss of generality, we can assume that the state information is of the record type, i.e., it can be represented as a list of attribute-value pairs for the ordered attribute set that is determined by each form.

If we need to manage a large number of pads of a few different forms, we can store the state information of pads in a database with as many relations as the different forms, and keep the form information of these forms outside the database. Such a database is called a form base. If the state information of a record type has only atomic and simple values for its attributes, we can use a relational database management system to store these pads. If some attributes allow variable-length data, stream data such as movies and sounds, or complex data such as compound documents and other relations, we can use an extended relational database management system or a structural OODB management system. In this case, we can even deal with a composite pad storing other composite pads in some of its state attributes.

Pads representing various intellectual resources accumulated in our societies, however, have a huge number of different forms. Although we may store a group of pads of the same form in a single database relation, we have to manage a huge number of different relations together with the same number of different forms.

The situation here is similar to the management and access of commodities. Different from standardized prefabricated parts that are usually managed by databases, there are a huge variety of commodities and no common attributes to describe them, which makes it difficult to manage them with databases. Commodities of the same type can be managed by a single database, but there are so many different types that consumers cannot tell which commodity belongs to which type, or which database manages which type. Types are usually defined by producers, and not always directly related to functions, uses, or appearances that consumers can identify. For the integration of a reasonable number of databases, you may introduce an ontological meta-level description to integrate the member database schemas, as well as a query translation mechanism between the meta-level schema and the member database schemas. Some systems like SIMS [1] and OBSERVER [2] enable us to provide such an integrated ontology for relational and flat databases, and perform the necessary query conversions. Some other systems like FLORID [3], ONTO-BROKER [4], and MOMIS [5] even introduced the reasoning capabilities of logic systems to integrate more than one object-oriented database. These systems, however, cannot be applied to such cases in which we cannot describe integrated ontological schemas. To solve this problem in our daily lives, we typically use documents or spaces to arrange information about mutually related commodities for ease of access. Examples of such documents are catalogs published by producers or independent publishers, advertising brochures from producers or stores, books, periodicals, and newspaper articles referring to commodities. Catalogs adopt various different criteria in the selection and arrangement of commodities. Books, periodicals, and newspapers may refer to each other. Examples of commodity-organizing spaces include shops, department stores, malls, and towns. The first three use planned selections and arrangements, whereas the selections and arrangements in towns evolve over time. Shops are nested in malls and department stores, which are nested in towns.

Let us consider one more example. "The Trinity" is one of the most popular themes of Christian paintings. Each painting with this theme includes the images of the Father, the Son, and the Holy Spirit. Suppose you have a collection of these three images extracted from a large number of paintings of the Trinity. Our question here is where to store this collection so that we or even other people can access this collection in a future. You may think that we can define a relation in a database to store this collection. This relation has three attributes, the Father, the Son, and the Holy Spirit. Each tuple is a triple of file pointers, pointing to the three images extracted from the same painting. This solution, however, does not tell where to memorize the fact that this newly created relation represents the collection of three images from a large number of paintings of the Trinity. We have to deal with a huge number of different concepts as well as relations among them. "The trinity" is only one of them. A potential solution in this example may be to store this collection in association with the article on the Trinity in some encyclopedia.

## 19.2  TOPICA FRAMEWORK

Based on the above observations, here we propose a new framework for the organization of and access to intellectual resources represented as pads. This framework uses documents to contextually and/or spatially select and arrange mutually related intellectual resources. Such documents may be texts, images, figures, movies, maps, or compound documents consisting of various multimedia components. These documents as well as these intellectual resources are all represented as pads. Therefore, these documents may be also arranged together with related resources in other documents.

We call this framework "Topica," after Aristotle's *Topica*. In the Topica framework, documents used to arrange resources are called Topica documents. Each Topica document is a pad that displays a document and stores relations among some other Topica documents and/or some pads. Such a document is represented by an XHTML text, with some slot definitions. Relations in a Topica document are called "Topica tables," and may be defined by tables, or by queries that may access local or remote databases, XHTML texts defining other Topica documents, or relations defined in other Topica documents. A Topica document has some areas through which users can store and retrieve other Topica documents, pads, or character strings; we call these areas on a Topica document "topoi." Each topos is basically associated with an attribute of the Topica tables stored in the Topica document. Each attribute within a Topica table may take as its value a character string, an exchange format representation of a pad, or a URL identifying a Topica document or a pad stored in a local or remote file.

A topos of a Topica document is either a geometrically specified area of this document or a tagged text string in the XHTML document that is viewed by this Topica document.

Figure 19.1 shows an XHTML document on "the Trinity" in Christianity, where a special kind of tag is used to specify that the three phrases—"the Father," "the Son" and "the Holy Spirit"—in this article, together with the title "Trinity, The," work as four topoi of this Topica document, which stores a relation among the images of the three depicted within each of a number of paintings of the Trinity. Instead of directly storing images, the relation stores URLs of these image files. We can use a Topica viewer pad to view the corresponding Topica document as a pad. The Topica viewer pad is basically Microsoft Internet Explorer (IE) wrapped by the pad wrapper. It has extended IE to perform topoi functions. Topica documents may also provide some slots, which can be easily defined by using special tags in their XHTML definitions. Figure 19.2 shows the Topica document of the XHTML definition in Figure 19.1, a selector popped up by double-clicking "the Father" topos, and the selection of one candidate within this selector to pop up the corresponding image. This selection automatically influences the information available through other topoi. The clicking of "the Son" topos now pops up a selector showing only one candidate. All these images also work as Topica documents. Each image of a whole Trinity painting includes three topoi covering the Father, the Son, and the Holy Spirit, respectively, and a Topica table that refers to the Topica table in the original Trinity article as shown in Figure 19.3.

Topoi are different from Xlink [6] and XPointer [7] in the following two respects. First, topoi on the same Topica document are related with each other by the Topica table stored in this Topica document. Second, you may drag and drop new Topica documents into some topoi to update the Topica table.

```
<?xml version="1.0"?>
<html xmlns="http://www.w3.org/..."    xmlns:topica="..." >
  <head>
    <title>Trinity</title>
    <topica:table>
      <tuple>
        <father>file://C:/pub/trinity/father1.jpg</father>
        <son>file://C:/pub/trinity/son1.jpg</son>
        <spirit>file://C:/pub/trinity/spirit1.jpg</spirit>
      </tuple>
      ...
    </topica:table>
  </head>
  <body>
    <h1><topica:topos name="trinity" ref="//tuple/trinity/text()">Trinity</topica:topos>, The</h1>
    <p> The central ... in Three Persons,
      <topica:topos name="father" ref="//tuple/father/text()">the Father</topica:topos>,
      <topica:topos name="son" ref="//tuple/son/text()">the Son</topica:topos>, and
      <topica:topos name="spirit" ref="//tuple/spirit/text()">the Holy Spirit</topica:topos>. ...
    </p>
```

**Figure 19.1**  An XHTML definition of a Topica document on the Trinity.

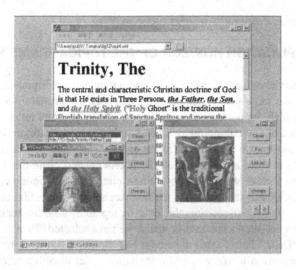

**Figure 19.2** A Topica document on the Trinity defined by the XHTML text in Figure 19.1

```
<?xml version="1.0" encoding="Shift_JIS"?>
<html xmlns="http://www.w3.org/1999/xhtml"
       xmlns:topica="http://ca.meme.hokudai.ac.jp/topica">
<head>
  <title>Trinity1</title>
  <topica:table type="xml-ql">
<![CDATA[
WHERE
  <html>
    <head>
      <topica:table>$t</>
  </></> IN "http://ca.meme.hokudai.ac.jp/trinity.xml"
CONSTRUCT
  $t
]]>
  </topica:table>
</head>
<body>
<p>
  <img height="600" src="file://C:/pub/trinity/trinity1.jpg" usemap="#map"/>
  <map name="map">
    <topica:topos name="father" ref="//tuple/father/text()"><area shape="rect" color="red" alt="father"
        coords="76,23,286,164" href="#" /></topica:topos>
    <topica:topos name="son" ref="//tuple/son/text()"><area shape="rect" color="red" alt="son"
        coords="134,250,247,483" href="#" /></topica:topos>
    <topica:topos name="spirit" ref="//tuple/spirit/text()"><area shape="rect" color="red" alt="spirit"
        coords="141,180,218,235" href="#" /></topica:topos>
  </map>
</p>

</body>
</html>
```

**Figure 19.3** A Topica document showing a painting of the Trinity shares the same Topica table as the Topica document in Figure19.1.

## 19.3 THE APPLICATION HORIZON OF THE TOPICA FRAMEWORK

Figure 19.4 shows the management of invitation letters using a Topica document. Invitation letters from the same person for the same category of purposes may share the same letter template, which the person can reuse repeatedly to generate letters by filling in the blanks. This Topica document, on the one hand, works as a template; underlined italicized strings may be rewritten to generate different letters. The same Topica document, on the other hand, works to store and manage all the letters created using this template; the underlined italicized strings work as topoi. When clicked, each topos pops up a selector showing all the candidate strings filling in this placeholder; a selection of one of them replaces the current string, and rewrites the letter by replacing all other topoi with appropriate strings. The figure shows the case in which we have selected "Prof. Y. Tanaka" for the topos just after "Dear." This Topica document has another topos to store resumés sent by invitees; an instantiation to some specific invitation letter also instantiates this topos to pop up the resumé of the selected invitee. Here the resumé of "Prof. Tanaka" is popped up. This resumé also works as a Topica document with some topoi. When you send invitation letters, you may also send the template for a resumé, and ask the invitee to fill in and send back this form. All the returned resumés can be stored in the same single Topica document.

Topoi of a Topica document may be defined in terms of the transposed image of the stored relation. Figure 19.5 shows a Topica document that stores a relation between file names and files. The transposed image of this relation has file names as its attributes; it has a single tuple specifying for each file name the URL of the corresponding file. The Topica document in this figure can switch views between the default and its transposition.

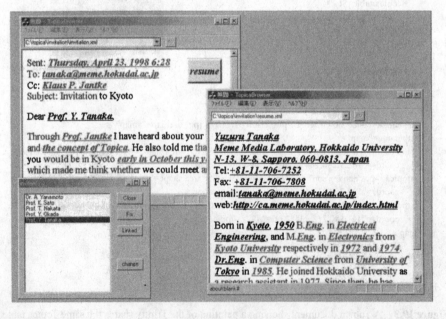

**Figure 19.4** A Topica document for the management of invitation letters together with invitees' résumes.

**Figure 19.5**   This Topica document storing a relation between file names and files can switch from one view to its transposition, and vice versa.

Its XHTML definition is generated by processing its XML content using one or the other of its two stored XSL styles. These two styles access the stored relation in different ways to define different sets of topoi. Figure 19.6(a) shows the XML definition of the contents, whereas Figure 19.6(b) shows the XSL definition of the transposed file directory view in the right-hand side of Figure 19.5.

Suppose you have presented talks at many conferences in the past. For each conference, you have files of the call-for-paper mail, the submitted paper manuscript, the letter of acceptance with reviewers' comments, the camera-ready manuscript, the conference program, and the Power Point presentation. With our conventional file directory system, you have two alternative ways to store these files. You may either define an independent folder for each conference to store all the related files, or define six different folders for six different categories of files. In the first case, you cannot scan through all the files of the same category. In the second case, you cannot jump from one file to another of a different file category of the same conference. The Topica document in Figure 19.7 solves this problem. It looks like a file directory. Each folder in this directory corresponds to one of the six file categories, and works as a topos. Double-clicking on it pops up a selector that looks like another file directory listing all the files of this category. A selection of one file in this selector determines the corresponding conference, and restricts every other topos to show only those files of the same conference.

Since the definition of a Topica document exploits XHTML, and is viewed by an extension of the IEPad (Internet Explorer pad), it is not difficult to extend an arbitrary Web page document to work as a Topica document without losing any of its functionality. For example, home pages of Holiday Inn hotels at different locations use different documentation styles, but they provide information on several common entities including hotel name, location, pictures, address, telephone number, and fax number. Each of these home pages can be easily translated to a Topica document with these entities working as topoi. These Topica documents share the same Topica table, which could be a view relation defined over, for example, the Holiday Inn headquarters database. You may also define the Holiday Inn logo in each of these Topica documents to work as another topos, which lists the home-page Topica document URLs of the selected hotels on its corresponding selector.

Each Topica document may play three different roles. First, it works as is. Second, it may work as a template in a way as shown in the invitation-letter example. Third, it works as a

```
<?xml version="1.0" encoding="Shift_JIS"?>
<topica xmlns="http://ca.meme.hokudai.ac.jp/topica">
<body>
<table>
  <file>
    <name>trinity1.jpg</name>
    <uri>file://c:/pub/topica/folder/trinity1.jpg</uri>
    <size>40KB</size>
    <type>text/plain</type>
  </file>
    ...
</table>
</body>
</topica>
```

(a)

```
<?xml version="1.0"?>
<xsl:stylesheet xmlns="..." xmlns:xsl="..." xmlns:topica="..." version="1.0">

  <xsl:output method="xml" encoding="Shift_JIS" indent="yes"/>

  <xsl:template match="/">
    <html>
     <body>
       <h1>My Directory</h1>
       <xsl:apply-templates/>
     </body>
    </html>
  </xsl:template>

  <xsl:template match="text()"/>

  <xsl:template match="topica:table">
    <p><topica:topos name="file name" ref="/ file/name/text()" show="embed">
       File name</topica:topos></p>
    <p><topica:topos name="objct" ref="//file/uri/text()" show="replace">File</topica:topos></p>
  </xsl:template>

  </xsl:stylesheet>
  </style>
```

(b)

**Figure 19.6**  The XML contents definition and the XSL definition of the transposed view in Figure 19.5. (a) XML definition of the file directory contents. (b) XSL definition of the right-hand directory view in Figure 19.5.

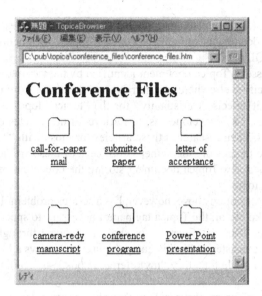

**Figure 19.7**   A Topica document that works as a file directory with six categories of files.

schema of the stored Topica table; you may use a Topica document to specify a query to the Topica table. The last role will be detailed in the following section. To distinguish these three different roles of the same Topica document, we have introduced three modes for each Topica document: the document mode, the template mode, and the schema mode. You can change the mode of a Topica document by popping up the right button menu of this document. Unless otherwise specified, each Topica document is in its document mode.

If we restrict every Topica document to store a single relation with a single tuple, then each topos works as an anchor to another Topica document. Therefore, Topica documents can include Web page documents as their special cases.

Topica documents are natural extensions of Web documents. Once they are in the Web, they become subject to search engines such as Google and Yahoo. Such search engines help you search for Topica documents including given keywords. Instead of directly searching for specific pads or boxes, you may search for a Topica document storing them or their addresses in its Topica table. If the target pads or boxes are a priori stored in an appropriate Topica document, this document may include some keywords related to these pads or boxes. You may send these keywords to some search engines to find this Topica document. Such a search performs a context search to find specific pads or boxes. Topica documents work as the contexts of pads and boxes, and search engines can use the textual information of Topica documents to index them for their search.

## 19.4   QUERIES OVER THE WEB OF TOPICA DOCUMENTS

The Topica framework provides a unified approach for organizing and accessing local and/or remote files, databases, conventional Web documents, and Topica documents over the Internet. In addition, the framework allows us to describe queries in XML-QL that, by navigating through these different types of information, quantifying properties of some documents on the navigation path, and picking up selected resources on the way, can construct the XHTML documents and relations of new Topica documents. Figure 19.8 shows an example XML-QL query.

This query accesses a Topica document identified by the variable $myReferenceBook, whose value is specified elsewhere, and retrieves all the books from its topos named "encyclopedia." Then it selects "Christianity" for the "topics" topos defined on each title page of these books, i.e., encyclopedias, to retrieve all the articles on Christianity from each of these books. Then it searches these articles for those with "Trinity" as its header, and retrieves all the images of "the Father" from each of these article Topica documents. Finally, it generates a new Topica document storing the collection of these retrieved images in its "image" topos.

The XML-QL description above, however, has a serious problem. Is it reasonable to assume that the user knows all the Topica tag names necessary to specify this query? Obviously, the answer is "No." However, he or she can navigate through Topica documents along a single path consistent with this query. Figure 19.9 shows a history of such a navigation starting from a file directory "myReferenceBook," and ending with an article on "Trinity, The."

By changing these Topica documents to the schema mode, you can specify a query as shown in Figure 19.10. This visual query specification basically exploits the QBE (query-

```
CONSTRUCT
<topicaDocument>
        <style ref="http://ca.meme.hokudai.ac.jp/ scrapbook.xsl"/>
        <contents>
        This is a collection of <topos name="father" ref="//image/text()"> the Father images</topos>
        in the paintings of Trinity.
</>
<topicaTable> {
WHERE
    <topicaTable> <tuple>
            <encyclopedia>$encyclopedia</>
            </></> IN $myReferenceBook.
    <topicaTable><tuple>
            <topics>Christianity</>
            <articles>$articles</>
            </></> IN $encyclopedia,
    <html>
            <head><title>Trinity</></>
            <body>
                    <topicaTable><tuple><father>$father</></></>
            </>
            </> IN $articles
CONSTRUCT
    <tuple><image>$father</></>
    } </>
</>
```

**Figure 19.8** An example of XHTML to create a new Topica document by navigating through existing ones.

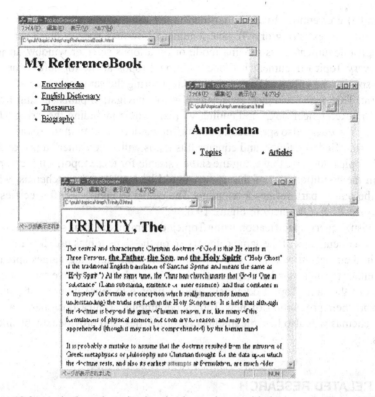

**Figure 19.9**   A single-path navigation that is consistent with the query in Figure 19.8.

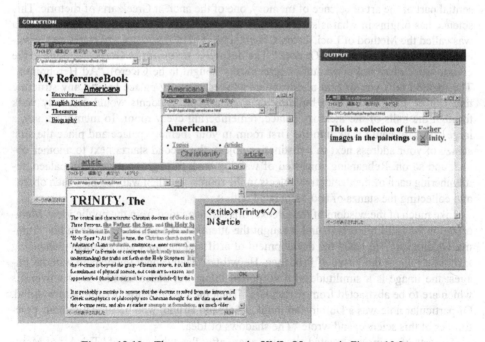

**Figure 19.10**   The same query as the XML-QL query in Figure 19.8

by-example) convention. Every underlined topos value works as a variable, which may specify either a text string or a Topica document. You may specify these variables either on a Topica document in its schema mode or on a topos selector window. In its schema mode, every Topica document has one additional topos at the top-left corner, which is used to specify the URLs of Topica documents sharing the same schema with this Topica document. This query searches for all the possible navigation paths starting from the directory "myReferenceBook," and ending with an article including the string "Trinity" in its header. The query also specifies an output Topica document with the phrase "the Father images" specified as a topos, and equates this topos with "the Father" topos of the "Trinity, The" Topica document by using the same variable for these topoi. All the Topica documents in the condition part of this query should be interpreted as schemas, whereas the one in the output part defines a template. The query in Figure 19.10 specifies the same query as the XML-QL query in Figure 19.8.

The visual query specification using Topica documents in their schema mode assumes that Topica documents of the same category or on the same topics use the same Topica tag names in their definitions. This convention of using the same tag names spreads among people either through standardization efforts, or through the extensive replication and distribution of the same Topica document among people to reuse its contents, style, and/or schema in their production of new Topica documents. Topica documents as templates and/or schemas will also become intellectual properties, and provide new business opportunities.

## 19.5 RELATED RESEARCH

The idea of using topoi, i.e., loci or places to put things you want to memorize, is the essential part of the art or science of memory, one of the ancient Greek arts of rhetoric. This science has origins in what is surely a myth about the poet Simonides of Ceos. This idea was called the Method of Loci. Later, Cicero (106–43 B.C.) wrote a few pages on the science in his classic work, "De Oratore." The definitive treatment in Greek literature is the classic work of an unknown author (previously thought to be Cicero), "Ad Herennium." The method tells you to first construct a so-called memory palace having any structure that can be imagined, i.e., a building or even a book. Students would carefully walk through the halls of the memory palace, remembering every room. To memorize, say, a large text, you could walk into the first room in your memory palace and place the first stanza of your address next to a distinctive object, the second stanza next to another object, and so on. Rehearsing consisted of walking back through your memory palace, remembering each of the distinctive objects in the rooms, and then walking past each object, and collecting the stanza of text associated with it.

Like much of the wisdom of the Greeks, this science faded from the public view. Memorization was still important, and it caught the attention of Thomas Aquinas in his "Summa Theologica." He listed the development of artificial memory and memory-enhancing techniques under the virtue of Prudence. He wrote: "Man cannot understand without images; the image is a similitude of a corporeal thing, but understanding is of universals which are to be abstracted from particulars." Then the memory arts became almost a fad. Of particular note was a Dominican monk, Giordano Bruno, who became a famous practitioner of this science, and wrote "The shadows of Idea."

The arts of memory attracted attention again after the publication of "The Art of Memory" by Frances A. Yates in 1974 [8]. Since then, the arts of memory have been attracting researchers, especially in architecture [9] and hypermedia [10]. Spatial hypertext/hypermedia studies [11, 12], though without any explicit reference to the arts of memory, share the same consciousness with Thomas Aquinas on the effective use of images, diagrams, and spatial arrangements for our better understanding.

Spatial hypertext lets users express categories and interrelationships through the visual similarity and colocation of information objects. Office workers frequently shuffle papers to make sense of them, and use the physical space around their offices as important adjuncts to their more organized file cabinets [13, 14]. People may find it difficult to express how or why content is interconnected, but they are accustomed to arranging media, either physical or electronic, in space. In noncomputational environments, people fasten documents together with paper clips, or staple them, but often interconnections are left implicit, to be resolved only if use demands it. They sometimes prefer to express relationships among objects by using geometric cues like proximity and alignment, and visual cues like graphical similarity. VIKI [15], WebSquirrel [16], D-Lite [17], WebForager [18], and Data Mountain [19], early spatial hypertext systems, emphasized the expression and manipulation of information structures implicit in the layout of their components. Users can easily change a visual property or move an object. The resulting hypertext is not meant as a publication, but as a continual work in progress for an individual or small group. Visual Knowledge Builder (VKB) [12], the successor of VIKI, added support for long-term collaboration and tasks requiring explicit links; it includes a history mechanism that records the evolution of the spatial hypertext and local, global, and historical links for explicit navigational connections between chunks of information.

Whereas spatial hypertext/hypermedia studies focus on the use of visual similarity and colocation of information objects to express relationships among objects, the Topica framework focuses on how we can associate an $n$-ary relation among $n$ topoi, or $n$ loci, defined on an ordinary and/or spatial hypermedia document, and use such documents as cues to find out appropriate relations for organizing and accessing various kinds of intellectual resources represented as pads.

Although the Topica framework also shares basic ideas with the arts of memory, it depends more on ideas in Aristotle's "Topica" than those in Cicero's "De Oratore." Aristotle's "Topica" denotes a catalog of topoi; it lists rhetorical patterns especially for debates. Each pattern is a parameterized sentence with some variables. Instantiation of these variables with some concrete entities in a current debate context will generate a sentence you can use in the debate. The same idea can be applied to any situations in which you need to express your ideas or to compile your knowledge. In the Topica framework, each Topica document may work as such a rhetorical pattern. Topoi defined on such a document may work as parameters or place holders of the pattern.

The Topica framework also shares the concept of the Semantic Web of how to make vast amounts of information resources (data, documents, programs) available. The Topica framework focuses on collaborative organization of resources. People may use some existing document, or, if necessary, define a new document to define and to store a relation among intellectual resources. Since each Topica document is also an intellectual resource, people may use a Topica document to define and to store a relation among Topica documents. In the web of Topica documents, meta-level description of semantic relationships among Topica documents uses relations defined over the set of Topica documents, and stores each of these relations in some Topica document. Each Topica document in its schema mode works as an RDF (resource description framework) schema of the Semantic

Web defining an $n$-ary relationship among Topica documents. Whereas Topica focuses on facilities for users to organize resources for ease of their future access, Semantic Web focuses on facilities for information resource providers and brokers to describe semantic relationships among resources so that their and/or requesters' programs may access these resources based on the described semantic relationships. Since Topica is a natural extension of the current Web, and exploits XML, an application of Semantic Web technologies to Topica will provide Topica with ontological semantic relationships among Topica documents. The relationships stored in Topica documents are emergent, and collaboratively organized through individuals' independent activities of publishing new Topica documents and storing new relations among Topica documents in other Topica documents. The relationships described by Semantic Web technologies, on the other hand, are based on the ontology among Web objects, and mainly defined by organizations or communities, but not intended to be defined by individuals independently. These two types of relationships among Topica documents are complementary and enrich the semantics of Topica documents and their web.

The Semantic Web originated in Tim Berners-Lee's proposal in 2001 [20] of a new form of Web content that is meaningful to computers and linked to be easily processable by machines on a global scale. This new vision is attracting great attention. Central to the vision of the Semantic Web are ontologies. Ontologies are seen as facilitating knowledge sharing and reuse between agents, be they human or artificial [21]. Better knowledge about the meaning, usage, accessibility, or quality of Web resources will considerably facilitate automated processing of available Web content and services. The Resource Description Framework (RDF) [22, 23] enables the creation and exchange of resource meta-data as any other Web data. RDF provides (1) a standard representation language for meta-data based on directed labeled graphs in which nodes are called resources (or literals) and edges are called properties; (2) a schema definition language (RDFS) [23] for creating vocabularies of labels for these graph nodes (called classes) and edges (called property types); and (3) an XML syntax for expressing meta-data and schemas. RDF allows us to superimpose several descriptions of the same Web resources in a variety of application contexts. RDF is particularly useful for real-scale Semantic Web applications such as knowledge portals and e-marketplaces. In knowledge portals such as the Open Directory Project (ODP) (www.dmoz.org), CNET (home.cnet.com), and XMLTree (www.xmltree.com), various information resources such as sites are aggregated and classified under large hierarchies of thematic categories or topics. The descriptions are exploited by push channels aiming at personalizing portal access, using a standard like the RDF Site Summary [24]. Entire catalog of portals can be also exported in RDF. White (or yellow) pages of emerging e-marketplaces also require RDF resource descriptions. Descriptions involve not only information about potential buyers and sellers, but also about provided/requested Web services. Standards like UDDI [25] and ebXML [26] are intended to support registries with service advertisements using keywords for categorization under geographical, industry, or product classification taxonomies.

Query languages for querying both RDF resource descriptions and related schemas have also recently been proposed. These include DAML-OIL [27, 28] and RQL [29]. RDF schemas have substantial differences from XML DTDs [30] or the more recent XML Schema proposals [31, 32]. Due to multiple classification, resources may have quite irregular structures modeled only through an exception mechanism in the XML proposals. These XML proposals cannot distinguish between entity labels and relationship labels. On the other hand, XML element content models cannot be expressed in RDF since properties are unordered, optional, and multivalued. Therefore, query languages proposed for semistructured or XML data, such as LOREL [33], StruQL [34], XML-QL [35], XML-GL [36], Quilt [37], or XQuery [38], fail to interpret the semantics of RDF node or edge labels.

Topic Maps [39] also aim to introduce semantic interrelations among documents. The structural information conveyed by topic maps includes the groupings of addressable information objects around topics (occurrences), and the relationships between topics (associations). A topic map defines a multidimensional topic space—a space in which the locations are topics, and in which the distances between topics are measurable in terms of the number of intervening topics that must be visited in order to get from one topic to another, and the kinds of relationships that define the path from one topic to another, if any, through the intervening topics, if any. In addition, information objects can have properties as well as values for those properties assigned to them externally. These properties are called "facet types." Several topic maps can provide topical structure information about the same information resources. The Topic Maps architecture is designed to facilitate merging topic maps without requiring the merged topic maps to be copied or modified. The base notation of topic maps is SGML. An interchangeable topic map always consists of at least one SGML document, and it may include and/or refer to other kinds of information resources. Like Semantic Web technologies, Topic Map technologies are complementary with the Topica framework.

## 19.6  SUMMARY

Meme media and meme market system architectures will significantly accelerate the evolution of memes in our societies, which will lead to a need for new ways of organizing and accessing them. This chapter has explored a new framework called "Topica" for organizing and accessing the huge accumulation of intellectual resources in our societies. Topica uses documents to contextually and/or spatially select and arrange mutually related intellectual resources. Each Topica document stores relations among some other Topica documents and/or meme media objects. Relations in a Topica document are called "Topica tables," and may be defined by tables, queries that may access local or remote databases, or relations defined in other Topica documents. A Topica document has some areas on itself through which users can store and retrieve other Topica documents, meme media objects, or character strings. We call these areas on a Topica document "topoi." Each topos is basically associated with an attribute of the Topica tables stored in the Topica document. Each attribute within a Topica table may take as its value a character string, a URL identifying a Topica document, or a meme media object stored in a local or remote file. The Topica framework provides a unified approach for organizing and accessing local and/or remote files, databases, conventional Web documents, and Topica documents over the Internet. It uses documents to contextually and/or spatially select and arrange mutually related intellectual resources distributed over the Internet.

Since Topica is a natural extension of the current Web, and exploits XML, an application of Semantic Web technologies to Topica will provide Topica with ontological semantic relationships among Topica documents. The relationships stored in Topica documents are emergent, and collaboratively organized through individuals' independent activities, whereas the relationships described by Semantic Web technologies are based on the ontology among Web objects, and mainly defined by organizations or communities. These two types of relationships among Topica documents are complementary and enrich the semantics of Topica documents and their web.

# REFERENCES

1. Y. Arens and C. Knoblock. SIMS: Retrieving and integrating information from multiple sources. *SIGMOD Records, 22*(2): 562–563, June 1993.

2. E. Mena, V. Kashyap, A. Sheth, and A. Illarramendi. OBSERVER: An approach for query processing in global information systems based on interoperation across pre-existing ontologies. *Distributed and Parallel Databases, 8*(2): 223–271, 2000.

3. R. Himmeroeder, P. Kandzia, B. Ludaescher, W. May, and G. Lausen. Search, analysis, and integration of Web documents: A case study with FLORID. In *Proceedings of the International Workshop on Deductive Databases and Logic Programming (DDLP),* pp. 47–57, UK, 1998.

4. S. Decker, M. Erdmann, D. Fensel, and R. Studer. Ontobroker: Ontology based access to distributed and semi-structured information. In *DS-8: Semantic Issues in Multimedia Systems.* Kluwer-Academic, Norwell, MA, 1999.

5. S. Bergamaschi, S. Carstano, and M. Vincini. Semantic integration of semistructured and structured data sources. *SIGMOD Record, 28*(1): 54–59, 1999.

6. S. DeRose, E. Maler, and D. Orchard. *XML Linking Language (XLink).* Version 1.0. http://www.w3.org/TR/xlink/, June, 2001.

7. S. DeRose, E. Maler, and R. D. J. (eds.). *XML Pointer Language (XPointer).* Version 1.0. http://www.w3.org/TR/xptr/, Sept. 2001.

8. F. A. Yates. *The Art of Memory.* University of Chicago Press, Chicago, 1974.

9. D. Lyndon and C. W. Moore. *Chambers for a Memory Palace.* MIT Press, Cambridge, MA, 1996.

10. J. Wong and P. Storkerson. Hypertext and the art of memory. *Visible Language, 33*(1): 126–157, 1999.

11. C. Marshall and F. M. Shipman III. Spatial hypertext: Designing for change. *CACM, 38*(8): 88–97, 1995.

12. F. M. Shipman III, H. Hsich, P. Maloor, and J. M. Moore. The visual knowledge builder: A second generation spatial hypertext. In *The 12th ACM Conference on Hypertext and Hypermedia,* pp. 113–122, 2001.

13. T. W. Marlone. How do people organize their desks? Implications for the design of office information systems. *ACM Trans. Office Information Systems, 1*(1): 99–112, 1983.

14. R. Mander, G. Salomon, and Y. Y. Wong. A "Pile" metaphor for supporting organization of information. In *Proceedings of ACM CHI'72,* Monterey, pp. 627–634, 1992.

15. C. C. Marshall, F. Shipman, and J. H. Coombs. VIKI: Spatial Hypertext Supporting Emergent Structure. In *Proceedings of the ACM European Conference on Hypermedia Technology (ECHT '94),* Edinburgh, pp. 13–23, 1994.

16. M. Bernstein. *Web Squirrel.* Eastgate Systems, Watertown, MA, 1996.

17. S. B. Cousins, A. Paepcke, T. Winograd, E. A. Bier, and K. Pier. The digital library integrated task environment (DLITE). In *Proceedings of ACM Digital Libraries '97,* pp. 142–151, 1997.

18. S. K. Card, G. G. Robertson, and W. York. The WebBook and the Web Forager: An information workspace for the World-Wide Web. In *Proceedings of ACM SIGCHI '96,* Vancouver, pp. 111–17, 1996.

19. G. G. Robertson, M. Czerwinski, K. Larson, D. Robbins, D. Thiel, and M. van Dantzich. Data mountain: Using spatial memory for document management. In *Proceedings of ACM UIST '98,* San Francisco, pp. 153–162, 1998.

20. T. Berners-Lee, J. Hendler, and O. Lassila. The Semantic Web. *Scientific American, 284*(5): 34–43, 2001.

21. D. Fennel. *Ontologies. Silver Bullet for Knowledge Management and Electronic Commerce.* Springer-Verlag, Berlin, 2001.

22. O. Lassila and R. Swick. *Resource Description Framework (RDF) Model and Syntax Specification.* W3C Recommendation, 1999.

23. D. Brickley and R. V. Guha. *Resource Description Framework (RDF) Schema Specification 1.0.* W3C Candidate Recvommendation, 2000.

24. G. Beged-Dov, D. Brickley, R. Dornfest, I. Davis, L. Dodds, J. Eisenzopf, D. Galbraith, R. V. Guha, K. MacLeod, E. Miller, A. Swartz, and E. van der Vlist. *Rich Site Summary Specification Protocol (RSS 1.0).* August 2000.

25. The UDDI Community. *Universal Description, Discovery, and Integration (uddi v2.0).* http://www.uddi.org/, October 2001.

26. The ebXML Community. *Enabling a Global Electronic Market (ebxml v. 1.4).* http://www.ebxml.org/, February 2001.

27. F. van Harmelen, P. Patel-Schneider, and I. Horrocks. *Reference Description of the DAML+OIL Ontology Markup Language.* http://www.daml.org/2001/03/reference. html, March 2001.

28. R. Fikes. DAML+OIL *Query Language Proposal.* August 2001. http://www.daml.org/listarchive/joint-committee/0572.html

29. G. Karvounarakis, S. Alexaki, V. Christophides, D. Plexousakis, and M. Scholl. RQL: A declarative query language for RDF*. In *The 11th International World Wide Web Conference (WWW2002),* Hawaii, pp. 592–603, 2002.

30. T. Bray, J. Paoli, and C. M. Sperberg-McQueen. *Extensible Markup Language (XML) 1.0.* W3C Recommendation, February 1998. http://www.w3.org/TR/REC-xml/.

31. H. S. Thompson, D. Beech, M. Maloney, and N. Mendelsohn. *XML Schema Part 1: Structures.* W3C Candidate Recommendation, October 2000. http://www.w3.org/TR/xmlschema-1/.

32. M. Maloney and A. Malhotra. *XML Schema Part 2: Datatypes.* W3C Candidate Recommendation, October 2000. http://www.w3.org/TR/xmlschema-2/.

33. S. Abiteboul, D. Quass, J. McHugh, J. Widom, and J. Wiener. The Lorel query language for semistructured data. *International Journal on Digital Libraries, 1*(1): 68–88, 1997.

34. M. F. Fernandez, D. Florescu, J. Kang, A. Y. Levy, and D. Suciu. System demonstration—Strudel: A Web-site management system. In *Proceedings of ACM SIGMOD Conference on Management of Data,* Tucson, AZ, May 1997. Exhibition Program.

35. A. Deutsch, M. F. Fernandez, D. Florescu, A. Levy, and D. Suciu. A query language for XML. In *Proceedings of the 8th International World Wide Web Conference,* Toronto, Canada, 1999.

36. S. Ceri, S. Comai, E. Damiani, P. Fraternali, S. Paraboschi, and L. Tanca. XML-GL: a graphical language for querying and restructuring XML documents. In *Proceedings of International World Wide Web Conference,* Toronto, Canada, 1999.

37. D. Florescu D. Chamberlin, and J. Robie. Quilt: An XML query language for heterogeneous data sources. In *WebDB'2000,* pp. 53–62, Dallas, May 2000.

38. D. Chamberlin, D. Florescu, J. Robie, J. Simeon, and M. Stefanescu. *XQuery: A Query Language for XML.* Working draft. World Wide Web Consortium, June 2001. http://www.w3.org/TR/xquery/.

39. M. Biezunski, M. Bryan, and S. Newcomb. *ISO/IEC FCD 13250:1999—Topic Maps.* http://www.ornl.gov/sgml/sc34/document/0058.htm, April, 1999.

# CHAPTER 20

# INTELLIGENTPAD CONSORTIUM
# AND AVAILABLE SOFTWARE

The main goal of our project is to share, with people all over the world, our concept of meme media, meme pools, and meme markets. We have developed IntelligentPad (IP), IntelligentBox, and Piazza to allow people to experience meme media and meme pools in externalizing, editing, and managing their intellectual resources, and, furthermore, in distributing, reediting, and redistributing them among people all over the world. We established the IntelligentPad Consortium in 1993 in order to provide a forum for the further promotion, research, and development of IntelligentPad. We have developed several versions of IntelligentPad systems using different implementation languages including Smalltalk, C++, and Java. This chapter will give you information about the consortium and the available software systems.

## 20.1  INTELLIGENTPAD CONSORTIUM

The IntelligentPad Consortium (IPC) is an international consortium that was started in Japan in July of 1993. It was established in order to provide a forum for the further promotion, research, and development of IntelligentPad and its related technologies. The IP Consortium is a nonprofit, privately funded organization with over 50 members including companies, institutes, and prominent individuals from Japan and worldwide. The IP Consortium is vendor neutral, open to all, and welcomes individuals and organizations from all over the world to join in its efforts to further develop and promote the IP architecture and software component integration to bring us closer to a meme media society.

The IntelligentPad Consortium is open to all individuals and organizations that would like to join. To join the IP Consortium, just visit IPC's website at http://www.pads.or.jp/english/ for a membership application. With a wide range of membership schemes, anyone from the individual who would like to work with personal-use pad development to the large transnational corporation that would like to develop a distributed enterprise-wide, pad-based system can join the IP Consortium.

Different from other Japanese initiatives of the past, for example, SIGMA, TRON, and The 5th Generation Computer Project, the IP Consortium is a nonprofit association that is entirely privately funded (i.e., no government funding) with members from industry and academia. National government bodies like the Japan Ministry of Economy, Trade and Industry (METI) are not members, and the IP Consortium recognizes the merits of remaining an independent, private, and global consortium. The history of the IP Consortium has been a truly "bottom-up" development. The concept was developed in the research circles of academia and picked up momentum with interest from industry. The IP Consortium is also primarily focused on software technology, although the impacts of IP are socially far-reaching. The Japanese members of the IP Consortium are represented by the actual key individuals involved in the day-to-day development of object-oriented, middleware, and open systems.

## 20.2   AVAILABLE SOFTWARE

We have developed several versions of IntelligentPad systems. Our laboratory at Hokkaido University developed the Smalltalk-80 version, the SmalltalkAgent version, and the X-widget version. The X-widget version provided a systematic method to develop new pads using existing X-widgets as their display objects. All these systems were mainly focused on the basic architectural research on new systems, new generic utilities, and new application frameworks. Among them, the Smalltalk-80 version is the most complicated system, with more than 600 different primitive pads. They were, however, not intended for public use. All the technologies developed in these systems have been immediately transferred to the IP Consortium and its members. The IPC developed the evaluation version using Interviews in 1994, which was downloadable from IPC's Web site. This version was used to encourage open discussions on kernel system technologies. In 1993, two of the IP Consortium members, Fujitsu and Hitachi Software developed commercial versions running on the Windows PC and Macintosh, respectively. Both of them are programmed in C++, and are cross-platform compatible with each other. Then, in 1999, Hitachi Software released a new version for the Windows PC. Fuji Xerox brushed up our lab's Smalltalk-80 version to develop a new Smalltalk version. In 1999, Fuji Xerox also developed a Java version of IntelligentPad. A research group in Fujitsu has also developed a Java Beans version, in which pads can be defined by combining Java Beans. In 2000, a newly established venture company, K-Plex Inc., in San Jose, developed a new version of the IntelligentPad system called Plexware. This version uses XML both as the save format of pads and for message exchange with servers. Plexware uses SOAP to communicate with Web services. Pads in Plexware run on an Internet Explorer browser. Plexware has wrapped Internet Explorer and provides its full function as a standard component pad. You can visit IPC's website at http://www.pads.or.jp/english/ to download the C++ versions and the Java version free for nonprofit use. We will also include Plexware in this list.

IntelligentBox now has two versions developed by our university laboratory, one for Unix workstations and the other for Windows PCs. Different from university versions of IntelligentPad, these versions were intended to be distributed free for nonprofit use from the initial stage of their development. They are written in C++ using Open GL, and easily transportable to any machines running C++ and Open GL. The system can be downloaded from our Web site at http://ca.meme.hokudai.ac.jp/.

## 20.3  CONCLUDING REMARKS

Our current research activities are focused on application frameworks, mathematical treatment of patterns and their composition/decomposition, management and retrieval of pads and boxes, superdistribution of pads and boxes, a virtual laboratory or interactive scientific visualization environment based on IntelligentBox technologies, a new type of information browser called Topica for the organization and access of intellectual assets, and meme pool/meme market infrastructures.

Meme media technologies are essentially wrapper technologies to wrap various applications and/or data with a standard media wrapper having connectors for interoperation. They can wrap existing legacy applications and data to work as meme media objects. Although the required tools for the reediting and redistribution of meme media objects over the Internet should have been also developed as pads, we had no legacy wrapping tools for making such pads before the development of Web technologies. When we established IPC in 1993, most members were interested in the application to software development, and did not focus on the reediting and redistribution of meme media objects by people over the Internet. Thanks to the development of Web technologies, we developed the required tools for the reediting and redistribution of meme objects over the Internet simply by wrapping these Web technologies. Such wrapping has enabled nonprogrammers to easily convert legacy applications, data, and/or services that are available through Web pages to meme media objects, to reedit them to compose new applications or composite services combined with complex data, and redistribute these composite media objects by attaching them to e-mails or by publishing them as new Web pages. Developers may easily add new functionalities to legacy programs when they wrap them with standard wrappers. With the current rapid development of Web technologies, meme media technologies are now increasing their potentialities, especially to enable people to reedit and coordinate Web content for new purposes, and to redistribute newly composed content through the Web.

Meme media technologies, when applied to Web content, open a new vista in the circulation and reuse of scientific knowledge and cultural heritage. In bioinformatics for example, there are already thousands of different database and analysis services on the Web. However, they are serviced by independent groups, and are difficult to interoperate with each other. Except for a few well-known typical combinations that have already become routine, there are no a priori defined ways of coordinating some of them to discover new knowledge. Such a combination itself is a target of research studies. Researchers want to combine Web content, including applications, data, and services, using a straightforward approach. Meme media technologies will allow them to do this. In addition, people can exchange such composite content as components embedded in documents, annotate any portions of such a document, extract any portions, combine them to define a new composite object, embed it in another document, and publish such a document again. Such media will be our next-generation knowledge media.

# AUTHOR INDEX

# SUBJECT INDEX

# ABOUT THE AUTHOR

**Yuzuru Tanaka** has been a professor of Computer Architecture in Electronics and Information Engineering Division of Hokkaido University, Japan since 1990. He founded the Meme Media Laboratory at the university in 1995. He also worked as a professor of Digital Library at the Graduate School of Informatics, Kyoto University between 1998 and 2000. He received his Masters degree in electronics and Ph.D. in computer science from Kyoto University and University of Tokyo, respectively. Dr. Tanaka's research areas included database design theory, database machine architecture, and component-based media architecture. His current research focuses on meme media system architectures, IntelligentPad and IntelligentBox, and their integration with Web technologies. IntelligentPad has been attracting Japanese industries and government organizations. This led to the establishment of the IntelligentPad Consortium in 1993, and later in 1995, to an alliance with CI Labs in United States. In 1994, Dr. Tanaka received the grand prize of annual technological achievement awards from Nikkei BP.